ARCHAEOLOGICAL SURVEY OF WESTERN INDIA.

REPORT
ON THE
ANTIQUITIES OF KATHIAWAD
AND
KACHH

ARCHAEOLOGICAL SURVEY OF WESTERN INDIA.

REPORT
ON THE
ANTIQUITIES OF KATHIAWAD
AND
KACHH,

BEING THE RESULT OF THE SECOND SEASON'S OPERATIONS OF THE ARCHAEOLOGICAL SURVEY OF WESTERN INDIA.

1874-75.

BY

JAMES BURGESS, F.R.G.S., M.R.A.S.,

MEMBRE DE LA SOCIETE ASIATIQUE, ETC.,
ARCHAEOLOGICAL SURVEYOR AND REPORTER TO GOVERNMENT, WESTERN INDIA.

GYAN

Published by

GYAN

Gyan Publishing House
5, Ansari Road
Daryaganj, New Delhi-110002
Phone: 011-47034999, 9811692060
E-mail: books@gyanbooks.com

Distribution Network
gyanbooks.com
India, USA, Canada, UK, Australia, France

ISBN : 978-81-212-2648-6 (HB)
First Published, 1876

2nd Impression 2021

Printed at: Gyan Press, Delhi.

Report
on the
Antiquities of Kathiawad and Kachh
Author: James Burgress

ARCHÆOLOGICAL SURVEY OF WESTERN INDIA.

REPORT

ON THE

ANTIQUITIES

OF

KÂTHIÂWÂD AND KACHH,

BEING THE RESULT OF THE SECOND SEASON'S OPERATIONS OF THE ARCHÆOLOGICAL SURVEY OF WESTERN INDIA.

1874-75.

BY

JAMES BURGESS, F.R.G.S., M.R.A.S.,

MEMBRE DE LA SOCIÉTÉ ASIATIQUE, ETC.,

ARCHÆOLOGICAL SURVEYOR AND REPORTER TO GOVERNMENT, WESTERN INDIA.

LONDON:
INDIA MUSEUM.
876.

Wm H. ALLEN AND CO., 13, WATERLOO PLACE, S.W.;
TRÜBNER AND CO., 57 & 59, LUDGATE HILL; H. S. KING AND CO., 65, CORNHILL;
EDWARD STANFORD, CHARING CROSS.
Publishers to the India Office.

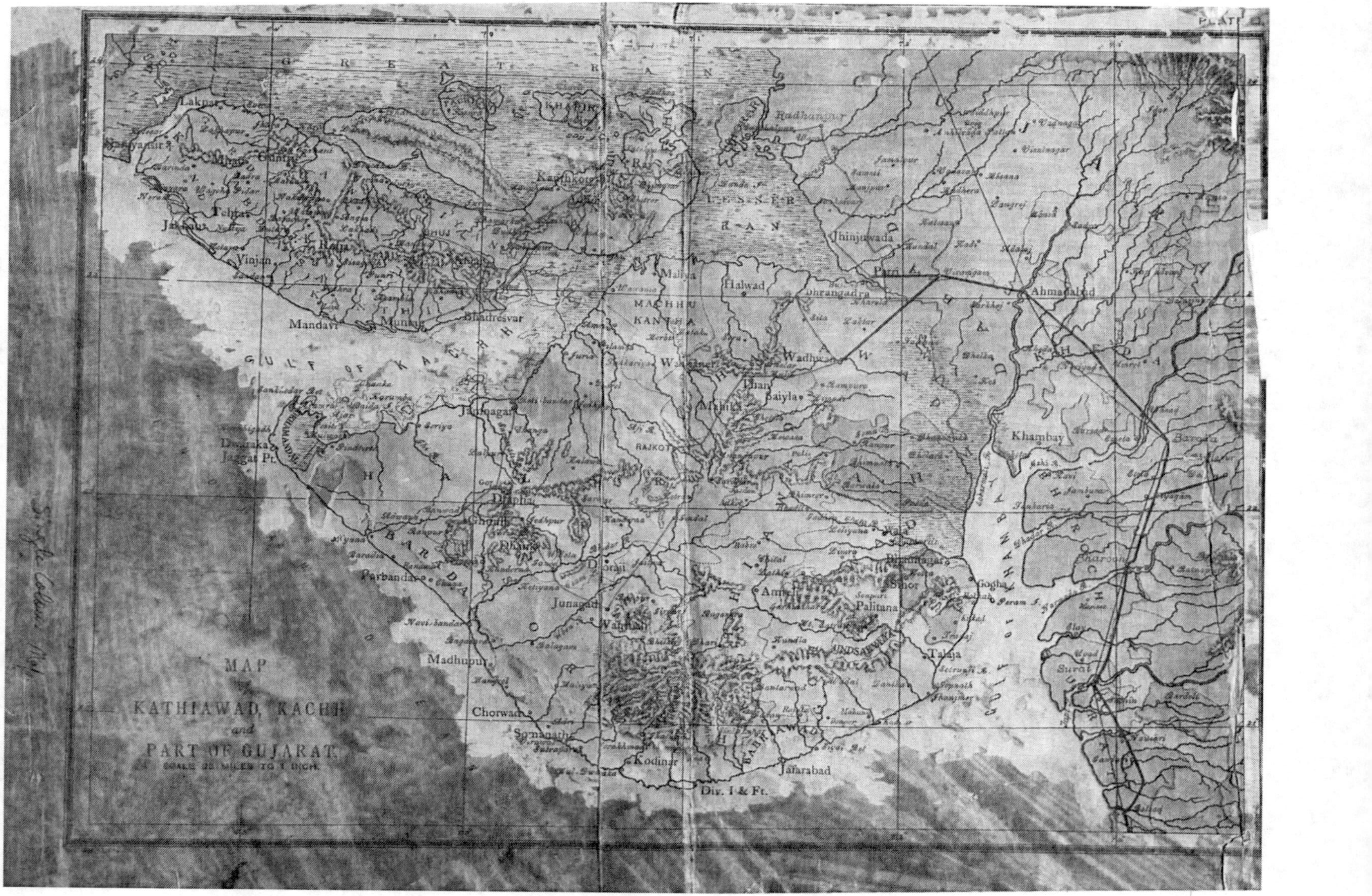
MAP
of
KATHIAWAD, KACHH
and
PART OF GUJARAT
SCALE 32 MILES TO 1 INCH
GREAT RAN
LESSER RAN
GULF OF KACHH
Lakpat
Mandavi
Bhadresvar
Vinjan
Jakhau
Radhanpur
Jhinjuwada
Patri
Ahmadabad
Halwad
Dhrangadra
Maliya
MACHHU KANTHA
Wadhwan
Saiyla
Than
RAJKOT
Jamnagar
Dwarka
Jaggat Pt.
Parbandar
Madhupur
Chorwad
Somanath
Kodinar
Junagad
Amreli
Palitana
Sihor
Gogha
Talaja
Jafarabad
Div. I & Ft.
Khambay
Surat

CONTENTS.

ILLUSTRATIONS.

PREFACE.

The present Report ought to have been issued before Christmas last, and this would have been done but for unavoidable delays. Had it been so, however, it must have been issued without much direct superintendence on my part, and the latter portion of it at least in a more abridged form. On my return from India last June, only about 80 pages had been printed off, and little more than 40 additional pages were in type; this gave me the opportunity of revising the remainder as it passed through the press, and of correcting and adding to it according to the most recent information I had obtained.

Though devoted chiefly to Kâṭhiâwâḍ and Kachh, it is not to be regarded as in any sense a complete report on the antiquities of either of these provinces. Kachh has hitherto been a *terra incognita* to the antiquarian, and, though probably not very rich in remains, it deserves a much fuller examination than I could bestow upon it in a few weeks at the commencement of the hot season of 1875. Of Kâṭhiâwâḍ we know more; but I have not been able to touch in this Report, on Śatruñjaya* with its city of temples, the ancient Valabhi, Somanâth, and many other places of interest, and it would require that I should devote at least another season to the province, in order to be able to represent these places in a manner at all adequate to their interest. The want also of anything like a sufficient staff of draughtsmen prevented a good deal being accomplished that might have been done with more effective assistance.

A complete set of impressions were taken of the great Aśoka inscription at Girnâr and of Rudra Dâmâ's, and are now lodged in the India Office Library, where they can be examined by scholars. The Sâh and early Arabic coins of Sindh have been made the basis of an able chapter in the Report, kindly contributed by Edward Thomas, Esq., F.R.S., &c., which will be read by oriental numismatologists with interest. For the

* This want, so far as Śatruñjaya is concerned, was to a certain extent supplied by the publication in 1869 of my work on *The Temples of Śatruñjaya*, containing 45 photographs with an historical and descriptive introduction; and as to Somanâth, by the work entitled *Photographs from Somanâth, Girnâr, Junâgaḍh*, &c., published in 1870, with views of Sânâ, Bhîmanâth, Somanâth, Girnâr, &c., &c. The negatives of the photographic illustrations of both these works are now in possession of the India Office; but the places above referred to require a more detailed examination than was practicable in the circumstances under which the materials were collected for these works.

rest, the Report must speak for itself. Having to prepare the letterpress and all the accompanying drawings for publication within the space of the four months I am annually in Europe, but little time is at my command for study and research, which are indispensable for the full illustration of the subject, and for the working out of the many points of history, ethnology, &c. that present themselves for investigation. I have consequently been obliged, among other things, to pass over some inscriptions quite unnoticed, but in the hope that at some future date I may be able to have them prepared for publication.

Much and valuable aid has been afforded me in the preparation of the work: in the field—by Mr. J. B. Peile, Bo.C.S., and Colonel W. Chase Parr, the Political Agents in Kâṭhiâwâḍ and Kachh respectively, who gave me every assistance while in their respective provinces, and to whom my thanks are accordingly due; and in information —by Major J. W. Watson, Dr. Georg Bühler, Professors Kern of Leiden, Eggeling of Edinburgh, and Blochmann of Calcutta,—the latter of whom translated the Arabic and Persian inscriptions from Ahmadâbâd given in the first chapter; while to the Rev. A. Milroy of Moneydie, N.B., I am indebted for the translation from the Dutch of large extracts from Dr. Kern's excellent monograph on the date of Buddha and the Aśoka edicts. For other translations from the same I am indebted to my friend the late lamented Professor R. C. Childers, Assistant Librarian at the India Office, whose services were ever readily available to all who required them, and who also revised the proofs of the sixth chapter of this report. Lastly, Mr. J. F. Fleet, of the Bombay Civil Service, a distinguished Sanskṛit and Canarese scholar, has supplied the translations of inscriptions given in the Appendix from my first season's Report; and to Edward Thomas, Esq., F.R.S., &c., is not only due the chapter on Sâh and Gupta coins, &c., but the careful superintendence of the proofs of the earlier portion of the volume.

The photographs and drawings have been produced under the care of Mr. Walter Griggs, of the Art Department at Peckham, who has spared no pains or trouble to make them as satisfactory as the materials I was able to put into his hands would enable him. The illustrations alone will, I trust, be regarded as some addition to our knowledge of Indian art.

J. BURGESS,

Archæological Surveyor and Reporter
to Government for Western India.

REPORT

OF THE

OPERATIONS OF THE ARCHÆOLOGICAL SURVEY

OF

WESTERN INDIA.

26TH OCTOBER 1874 TO 24TH APRIL 1875.

IN the present Report, it is not intended to follow strictly the order in which the places were visited; the account of the Buddhist Caves at Junar will be reserved for a subsequent report; the gates at Dabhoi near Baroda will be described along with those at Jhinjuwâḍâ, belonging to the same age and style; and with the description of the Buddhist Caves at Junâgaḍh will be combined some account of others previously visited at Talâjâ and Sânâ, and of those at Ḍhank, and near Siddhsar—on the way from Junâgaḍh to Gumli.

I. AHMADÂBÂD.

About two hundred and fifty miles north of Bombay the railway crosses the river Mahî—the *Mais*, and perhaps also the *Mophis*, of ancient Western writers, and the *Mahindrî* of the Muhammadan historians of the time of Akbar, which here divides the territory of the Gaikwâḍ of Barodâ from the British Collectorates of Kheḍâ and Ahmadâbâd, lying round the head of the Gulf of Cambay or Khâmbât. Ahmadâbâd, fifty-five miles north-west from the Mahî, is by far the largest city in this district—once the most splendid capital in India, and still the second city in the Western Presidency. It is the *Râjnagar* of the Jains, and perhaps occupies the site of the older *Karṇavati*, also called *Śrînagar*, built by Śrî Karṇa Deva, the Solanki sovereign of Gujarat (A.D. 1073–1093). Ahmadâbâd was founded on the 4th March 1411 A.D., in the first year of his reign by Ahmad Shâh I., whose full name was Nâṣiru-'d dîn Abû-'l Fatḥ Aḥmad Shâh, the grandson of Muzaffar the son of Sehâran a convert from the Tañka or Taka Rajput tribe* of Hindus, who assumed the name of Wajih-ul-Mulk. "The King," says Firishtah, "who had always expressed himself extremely partial to the air and situation of Yessawal, situated on the banks of the Sâbarmatî, in the latter end of this year† (the first of his reign) laid the foundation of a new city, which he caused to be called Ahmadâbâd." The older town of Yessawal or Aśâwal, is mentioned by Albiruni, four centuries earlier, as two days' journey from Kambaya and thirty parasangs from Bahruj or Bharoch; and Al-Idrisi, a little later, speaks of it as near Hanâwal or Janâwal,‡ another large city. But, as indicated in the following

---

* See Tod's *Rajasthan*, vol. I. pp. 103 ff. (Madras ed. p. 93); Beames's edition of Elliot's *Races of the N.W.P.*, vol. I. pp. 109, 114; Cunningham's *Archæol. Reports*, vol. II. (1863–64), pp. 8ff.

† Briggs gives 815 A.H. here; Mr. Blochmann 813, conf. his *Ain-i-Akbari*, vol. I. p. 507.

‡ Sir H. Elliot's *India*, vol. I. p. 87; and *Géographie d'Edrisi*, par M. Jaubert, tom. I. p. 176.

legend, it seems to have quite fallen into decay by the commencement of the fifteenth century. According to the legend, as told by Professor Blochmann, "the Saint Aḥmad Khattu* (so called from the town of Khaṭṭû near Nâgor) had settled in Gujarât during the reign of Sulṭân Muẓaffar, who held him in great respect. Aḥmad Shâh, too, often visited the Shaikh, and on one occasion expressed a desire to see the prophet Khizr (*Elias*). The Shaikh's prayers and certain ascetic penances performed by Aḥmad Shâh brought about the desired meeting, and when the king asked Khizr to tell him something wonderful, the prophet said that in former times a large town stood on the banks of the Sâbarmatî, where now only jungle grew. The name of the town had been Bâdânbâd. This town had suddenly disappeared. Aḥmad Shâh asked whether he might not build a new town on the spot. Khizr said that he might do so, but the foundations would not be safe unless four persons of the name of Aḥmad came together who had never in their life omitted the afternoon prayer (*'aṣr*). Aḥmad Shâh searched throughout the whole of Gujarât, but found only two Aḥmads that fulfilled the condition, viz. one Qâzî Aḥmad and one Malik Aḥmad. These two the king took to Shaikh Aḥmad Khaṭṭû, who then said, 'I am the third.' The king said, 'Then I am the fourth Aḥmad.' The town was thus founded. When the walls of the fort had been raised about a man's height, the foundations unexpectedly gave way at one place. The king and the Shaikh inspected the locality, when a man whose name was Mânik Jogî came forward, and said that the presence of the four Aḥmads at the laying of the foundation was not sufficient to secure the permanence of the undertaking: the place where the fort had been commenced was his property, and the fort would not stand without his consent. The difficulty was, however, settled when the king agreed to call a part of Ahmadâbâd after the name of Mânik Jogî."

Hence it is said the **Mânik Burj**, or south-west tower of the **Bhadr** or citadel, derived its appellation: it is also said to contain the foundation stone. The Bhadr itself, according to tradition, was an old Hindu enclosure containing a temple of Bhadra Kâlî. Be this as it may, in making certain excavations within it last year, Colonel Mellis came upon foundations, which he exposed for a considerable distance and raised the stones for building purposes. These were evidently the foundations of the first Muhammadan citadel, built by Aḥmad Shâh I., and which was perhaps enlarged to its present dimensions by **Mahmud Bîgarah**,† who in A.D. 1486 surrounded Ahmadâbâd with a wall

* Born A.H. 738, died at the age of 111 (lunar) years, on the 10th Shawwâl 849, Shaikh Aḥmad lies buried at Sark'hej, to the S.W. of Ahmadâbâd: the biographical works on Saints give many particulars regarding this personage.—Blochmann's *Ain-i-Akbari*, vol. I. p. 507.

† بیکره Prof. Blochmann (*Ain-i-Akbari*, vol. I. p. 506 n.) remarks that this word is generally pronounced بیگڑه (*bigaṛh*), and is said to mean the conqueror of two forts (*gaṛh*), because Mahmûd's armies conquered on one day the forts of Champânîr and Jûnâgaṛh. But Jihângîr in his *Memoirs* says that بیکره means *burût-i-bargashtah*, "having a turned up or twisted moûstache," which Sulṭân Mahmûd is said to have had.—(*Tuzuk-i-Jihângiri*, p. 212.) In corroboration of this, he quotes the following passage from Barthema's *Travels* (Murray's *Historical Account of Discoveries and Travels in Asia*, vol. II. p. 37): "The Guzurates are a generation who eat nothing that has blood, and kill nothing that has life. They are neither Moors nor Gentoos, but if they were baptized they would certainly be all saved on account of the many good works which they perform. This excess of goodness has rendered them the prey of Machamuth, the present king, who is of a very different disposition. The beard of this prince is so huge that his moustachios are tied over his head like a lady's hair, while the rest dependeth downwards as far as his girdle. He is continually chewing a fruit like a nut wrapt in leaves, and when he squirts the juice upon any one it is a signal that this person should be put to death, which sentence is executed in half-an-hour."—Conf. *The Travels of Ludovico di Varthema* (Hakluyt Soc. 1863), pp. 108 ff.

and bastions, inscribing the date (A.H. 892) of its completion on one face of the fortification in the chronogram *—

مَنْ دَخَلَهُ كَانَ آمِنًا

"Whoever enters it, is safe."

Many of the large blocks raised by Col. Mellis were carved stones and had evidently been taken from Hindu or Jaina temples, and one of them bears a short inscription dated Samvat 1359, *i.e.* A.D. 1303. Most of the sculptured stones have been set aside, some of them being worth preserving, and a few have been indicated as specially interesting, which might be sent to Bombay to be placed in the Asiatic Society's Museum there.

One of the earliest buildings in Aḥmad Shâh's new capital was, of course, the Mosque in the south of the Bhadr. It is hidden away from general notice, in a court-yard filled with rubbish and weeds, and has not been used for worship for at least a century, but when carefully examined, it will be found scarcely second in interest to any at Ahmadâbâd as to structural proportions and internal arrangements. It well deserves to be cleaned out and kept in such repair as to prevent its going to ruin; very little repair is needed at present, and nothing in the way of restoration.

From the time of Aḥmad Shâh, this city continued the capital of the Muhammadan kingdom for about a hundred and sixty years till the fall of the dynasty in the time of Akbar, after which it was governed by Viceroys of the Dihli emperors till taken by Dâmaji Gaikwâḍ in 1755.† Early in 1780 General Goddard took it by storm, assaulting it at the Khân Jung Gate in Mirzapur,‡ where the Masjid is pitted with shot, and considered as desecrated by the Musalmans. It was again restored to the Marâṭhâs in 1783, but reverted to the British on the fall of the Peshwa in 1818.

Under the Muhammadan kings in the fifteenth and sixteenth centuries, Ahmadâbâd attained the zenith of its splendour: it is said to have had a population of more than two millions; the circumference of its suburbs was about twenty-seven miles; the principal streets were sufficiently wide to admit of ten carriages abreast,§ it had "a thousand masjids built of stone, each having two large minarets, and many wonderful inscriptions;"‖ its palaces, fountains, tombs, caravansarais, and courts of justice were spacious; and, like Anhilawâḍâ under the Solanki kings, it was one of the greatest commercial entrepôts in the east, visited by traders and travellers from Arabia, Persia, the coast of Africa, Europe, and every province of India, and trading in brocades, satins, velvet, calico, paper, lacquered ware, indigo, cotton, opium, spices, &c.

During this period and under the viceroys who succeeded,—among whom were Shâh Jihân and Aurangzîb before they succeeded to the throne of Dihli,—the architectural style of Muhammadan buildings in Gujarât was elaborated, a style bearing evidence of the circumstances under which it took its rise, but in its zenith quite as beautiful as any other variety in the East, if not even more so. No wealth or taste was spared on the mosques and tombs of its Sulṭâns, their families, grandees, and even favourite

* Briggs's *Firishtah*, vol. IV. p. 70.

† Grant Duff's *History of the Marathas*, vol. II. p. 72.

‡ Ib., vol. II. pp. 406 ff., and H. G. Briggs's *Cities of Gujarashtra*, pp. 212, 213.

§ Briggs's *Firishtah*, vol. IV. p. 14.

‖ Gladwin's *Ayin Akbari*, vol. II. p. 63.

slaves. But the Muslim iconoclasts despoiled and ruined the cities of Anhilawâḍâ Paṭṭan and Chandravati to embellish it,* while the wonderful perseverance and æsthetic skill of Hindu workmen were employed in the construction and manipulation of details, and so impressed the style of art with a character that gives it a charm and a value peculiarly its own. In the beauty and appropriateness of form of its details, at least, it is unrivalled, "after a century's experience," says Mr. Fergusson, "they produced forms which, as architectural ornaments, will in their own class stand comparison with any employed in any age or in any part of the world."†

About eight years ago the architecture of Ahmâdâbad was illustrated by a series of 120 photographs taken by Colonel Biggs with valuable historical and architectural introductions by Mr. T. C. Hope, Bo.C.S., and J. Fergusson, D.C.L. But important and interesting as that work is, it by no means adequately represents the art and architecture of the place, and it would be well worth while, since that volume is now out of print, to devote a few months to the delineation of the more beautiful architectural details, with ground plans, sections, &c., with a view to the preparation of a volume analogous in matter to that issued by the Committee of Architectural Antiquities of Western India on Bijâpur, with the addition of a complete series of the inscriptions, both Muhammadan and Hindu.

The inscriptions at Ahmadâbâd have never, so far as I am aware, been copied, and while there I devoted a couple of days to making rubbings of such as I noticed in visiting a number of the mosques. Of these the rubbings of six Arabic and two Persian inscriptions have been reduced by photography in the accompanying plates (II.–V.), and translated by Professor Blochmann of Calcutta, so well known for his acquaintance with the Musalman inscriptions and history of India.

"These inscriptions," Professor Blochmann remarks,‡ "add somewhat to our knowledge of Gujarâtî history; but it would be desirable to have more, and also to obtain a complete set of Gujarâtî coins of the Muhammadan period."‖

I.—FROM AHMAD SHÂH'S MOSQUE.

No. I. (Plate II.) is a beautifully carved inscription in three lines on a large slab of white marble over the *Mihrâb*, in the Mosque of Aḥmad Shâh, dated A.D. 1414, and is read and translated thus :—

بنى هذا البناء الرفيع والمسجد الوسيع العبد الراجي والثاني الملتجي الي رحمة الله
المعبود في المساجد بالركوع والسجود غير مدعو احد معه ابداً لقوله تعالي وان المساجد
لله فلا تدعوا مع الله احدا الواثق بالله المستعان احمد شاه بن محمد شاه بن مظفر
السلطان وكان تاريخ بنائه من الهجرة الرابع من شوال سنة سبع عشر وثمانمائة ۞

This lofty edifice and extensive mosque was built by the slave who entreats and returns and has recourse to the mercy of God, who is worshipped in mosques with bows and prostrations, who alone

---

* Bird's *Mirat Ahmadi*, p. 164; Tod's *Travels in Western India*, p. 238.

† *History of Architecture* (ed. 1866), vol. II. p. 671.

‡ In a paper in the *Indian Antiquary*, vol. IV. (Oct. 1875), pp. 289ff., from which the following translations are taken.

‖ Mr. Thomas in his work on the Pathân kings of Dihli (London, 1871), gives a description of the coins of fifteen kings of Gujarat, ranging from Aḥmad Shâh to Mu affar Shâh, 1511 A.D.

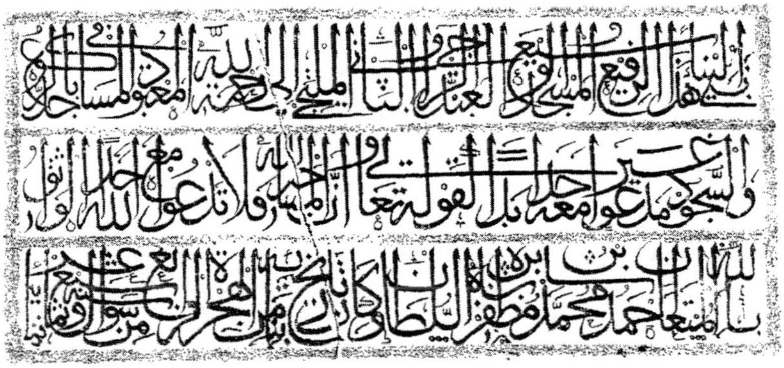

No. 1. AHMAD SHAH'S MASJID IN THE BHADR. (A.D. 1414)

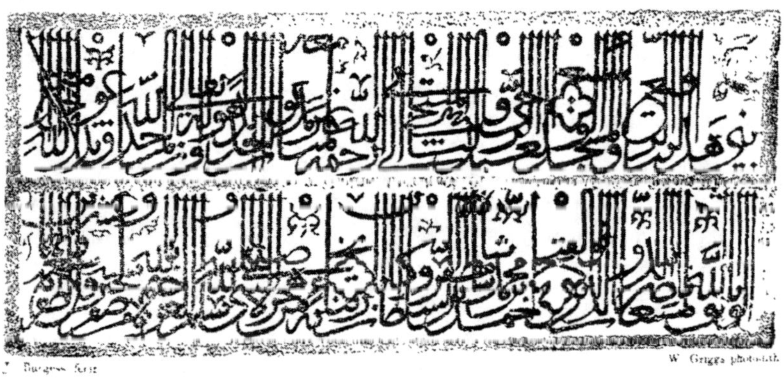

J. Burgess fecit W. Griggs photo-lith.

No. 2. AHMAD SHAH'S JAMI MASJID. (A.D. 1424).

is worshipped according to the Qorân verse "Verily, the mosques belong to God, worship no one else with him"—by the slave who trusts in the helping God, Aḥmad Shâh, son of Muḥammad Shâh, son of Muẓaffar, the King, and the date of its erection is the 4th Shawwâl, 817 A.H.* [*17th December* 1414.]

II.—FROM AHMAD SHÂH'S JÂMI' MOSQUE.

No. II. is in two lines on a marble slab in the Jâmi' Masjid of Aḥmad Shâh, built nine years later, and runs thus :—

بني هذا البناء الرفيع والمسجد الوسيع العبد الراجي والثاني الملتجي الي رحمة الله
المنّان غير مدعو احد معه ابدا لقول الله تعالي وان المساجد لله فلا تدعوا مع الله
احدا الواثق بالله المستعان ناصر الدنيا و الدين ابو الفتح احمد شاه بن محمد شاه بن
مظفر السلطان و كان تاريخ بنائه من هجرة النبي صلي الله عليه و سلم الغرة من
صفر ختمه الله بالخير والظفر سنة سبع وعشرين وثمانماية ۞

This lofty edifice and extensive mosque was built by the slave who trusts and returns and has recourse to the mercy of God who is kind, who alone is to be worshipped according to the Qorân verse, "Verily, the mosques belong to God; worship no one else with him,"—(by the slave) who trusts in the helping God, Nâṣiru-'d dunyá wa-'d dín Abú-'l Fatḥ Aḥmad Shâh, son of Muḥammad Shâh, son of Muẓaffar, the King. The date of its erection from the Flight of the Prophet (God's blessings on him!) is the first day of Ṣafar (may the month end successfully and victoriously!) in the year 827 [*4th January* 1424].

It is noticeable in these two inscriptions as remarked by Professor Blochmann, that Muzaffar's grandson does not style him "Shâh." "Like the founder of the Jaunpûr dynasty, he does not seem to have struck coins. On the other hand, Muḥammad Shâh, Aḥmad Shâh's father, though styled Shâh, has no place in history,"—for he never reigned, Aḥmad having succeeded his grandfather,—"but he is mentioned in inscriptions and on coins."

III.—FROM HAZÛRÎ SHÂH'S OR SHA'BÂN'S MOSQUE.

Inscription III. (Plate III.), in three lines on a slab in Malik Sha'bân's mosque, near the Karanj, a small building, bearing every appearance of having originally been the Manḍap of a Jaina temple. It belongs to the reign of the fourth of the Ahmadâbâd kings, usually styled Quṭb Shâh (1451–1459), but whose full name we now learn from this inscription was Quṭbu-'d dîn Abû-'l Muẓaffar Aḥmad Shâh. Professor Blochmann's transliteration and translation are as follows:

قال الله تبارك وتعالي وان المساجد لله فلا تدعوا مع الله احدا و قال النبي صلي الله عليه
وسلم من بني مسجدا لله بني الله له بيتا في الجنة بني عمارة هذا المسجد في عهد سلطان السلاطين
قطب الدنيا والدين ابو المظفر احمد شاه بن محمد شاه بن احمد شاه بن محمد شاه

---

* Sura LXXII. 18.—Quotations from the Qorân are introduced by *qâl-a'l-'lâhu ta'âla*, "God who is exalted, says;" quotations from the Hadîṣ by *qâl-an-nabi*, "the Prophet says."

بن مظفر شاه السلطان العبد المفتقر الى الله المستعان اعني شعبان ابن تحفه سلطاني المخاطب
بعماد الملك عارض ممالك ابتغاء مرضات الله و طلبا لجزيل ثوابه وكان ذلك في تاريخ
الثاني من جمادي الاول سنة ست وخمسين وثمانماية ۞

God Almighty says, "Verily, the mosques belong to God; worship no one else with Him." And the Prophet (God's blessing on him!) says,—"He who builds a mosque for God will have a house built for him by God in Paradise." The edifice of this mosque was built during the reign of the king of kings, Quṭbu-'d-dunyá wa'd-dín Abú-'l Muẓaffar Aḥmad Sháh, son of Muḥammad Sháh, son of Aḥmad Sháh, son of Muḥammad Sháh, son of Muẓaffar Sháh, the King, by the slave who has need of God the helper, I mean Sha'bán, son of Tuḥfa Sulṭání, who has the title of 'Imádu-'l Mulk, the Lord Chamberlain, from a desire to obtain the favor of God and to get his great reward. This took place on the 2nd Jumáda I, 856 [*21st May* 1452].

In point of penmanship, these first three inscriptions are better than the remaining five. "Like the Bengal and Jaunpur inscriptions of the same time," Professor Blochmann adds, "they are superior in this respect to Dihlí inscriptions." Some of them are chipped a little in places, and though carved on beautiful marble slabs, all of them have been again and again whitewashed, until it is very difficult to clean them so as to get perfect rubbings. This is the principal cause of the want of sharpness in the outlines of the letters in several of them in the plates.

IV.—FROM DASTÛR KHÂN'S MOSQUE.

Inscription IV. is from Dastûr Khân's Masjid, portions of which are photographed in the *Architecture of Ahmadabad* (plates 86, 87, and Introd. p. 57). It is one of those buildings at Ahmadâbâd which deserves a little attention to preserve it. The modern brick partitions and rubbish about it might be cleared away, and the perforated stone screen enclosing the cloisters—one of great beauty—might be better cared for. Professor Blochmann says, "Malik Ghanî Dastûru-'l Mulk (*i.e.*, Vazir of the Kingdom) was a noble of the court of Nâṣiru-'d-dîn Abû-'l Fatḥ Maḥmûd Shâh, better known under the nickname of Bîgarah * (A.D. 1459–1511)." He renders the inscription thus:

قال الله تبارك وتعالي وأن المساجد لله فلا تدعوا مع الله احدا وقال النبي صلي
الله عليه وسلم من بني مسجدا لله بني الله له بيتا مثله في الجنة بني عمارة هذا
المسجد الجامع في عهد سلطان السلاطين ناصر الدنيا والدين ابو الفتح محمود شاه بن
محمد شاه بن احمد شاه بن محمد شاه بن مظفر شاه السلطان العبد الراجي برحمة الله
المالك الملك غني خاصه زاد المخاطب من حضرة الاعلى و الملجأ المعلّي بدستور الملك
يديم الله معاليه ابتغاء لمرضات الله وطلبا لجزيل ثوابه وكان في العاشر من شهر شعبان
سنة (*illegible*) ثمانماية ۞

God who is blessed and great, has said, "Verily, the mosques belong to God; worship no one with him." And the Prophet (God's blessings on him!) has said, "He who builds a mosque for God will have a house like it built by God for him in Paradise." The edifice of this Jámi' mosque was built during the reign of the king of kings Náṣiru-'d-dunyá wa'd-dín Abú-'l Fatḥ Maḥmúd Sháh, son of Muḥammad Sháh, son of Aḥmad Sháh, son of Muḥammad Sháh, son of Muẓaffar Sháh, the

* See note † on page 2.

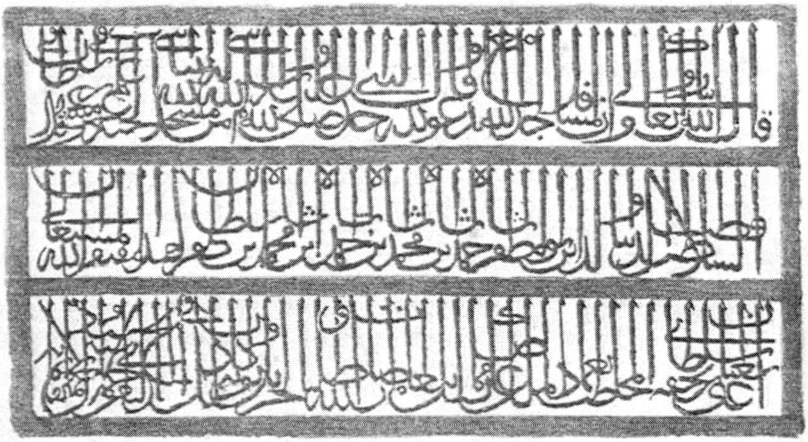

No. 3. SHA'BAN'S MOSQUE. (A.D. 1452).

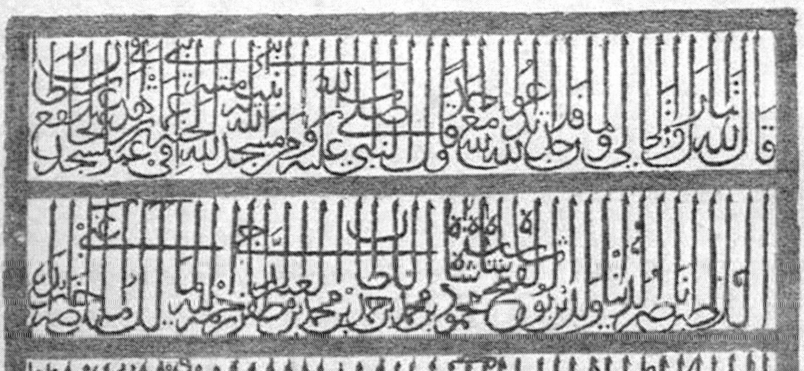

J. Burgess fecit. W. Griggs Photo-lith.

No. 4. DASTUR KHAN'S MOSQUE. (A.D. CIR. 1486).

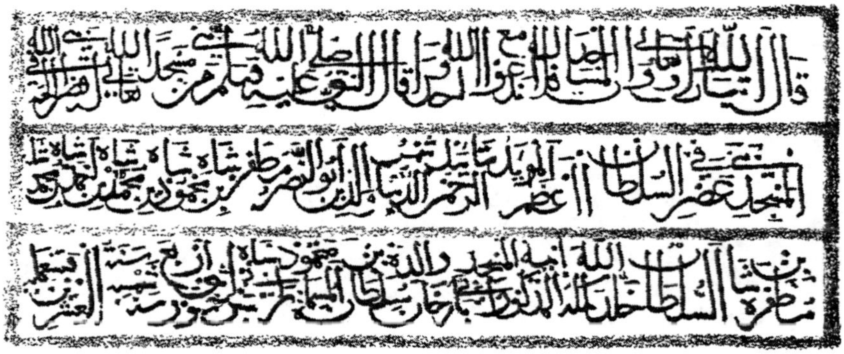

No. 5. RANI ASNI'S MOSQUE. (A.D. 1514).

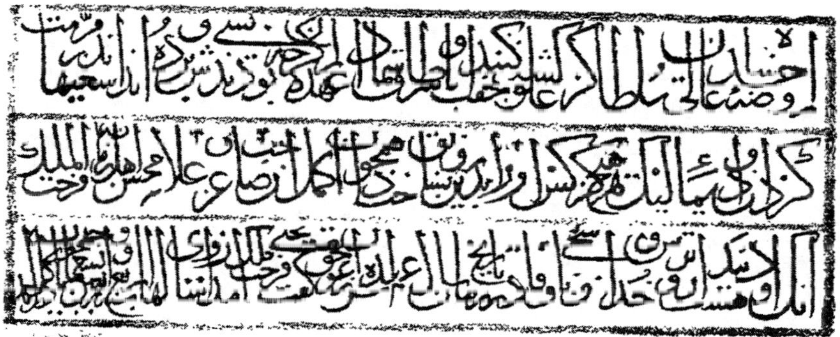

W. Griggs photo-lith

No. 6. AHMAD SHAH'S TOMB. (A.D. 1537).

*king, by the slave who hopes to obtain the mercy of God, the Mâlik Malik Ghanî Khâṣa-zâd, who has received from his august majesty and the exalted refuge (of the people) the title of Dastûru-'l Mulk—may God continue him in his exalted position! —in order to obtain the mercy of God and to secure his great reward. This was on the 10th Sha'bân of the year 8**.*

The year of this inscription is not clear, but it may be 890 or 892 A.H., which would be 1485 or 1487 A.D.

V.—FROM RÂṆÎ AṢNÎ'S MOSQUE.

Inscription V. (Plate IV.) is from the beautiful little mosque commonly known as Râṇî Sîprî's, the gem of Ahmadâbâd buildings, which has hitherto been ascribed to the wife of a son of Aḥmad Shâh I., and said to have been completed, with the neighbouring tomb, in A.H. 853 or A.D. 1431–32.* The inscription, however, supplies us with an important correction both of the name and date, and we now find that it was really built more than eighty years later, in the fourth year of the reign of Muzaffar Shâh II. (A.D. 1511–1526), by a Râṇî Aṣnî (Uṣnî or Iṣnî), the widow of Maḥmûd Shâh Bîgarah. From it we learn that the full name of the king was Shamsu-'d-dîn Abû-'l-Naṣir Muẓaffar Shâh II. "The inscription also mentions another son of Maḥmûd Shâh Bîgarah, of the name of Abû Bakr Khân. The name shows that the royal family were Sunnîs." The inscription runs thus:

قال الله تبارك و تعالي وان المساجد لله فلا تدعوا مع الله احدا وقال النبي صلى
الله عليه و سلم من بني مسجدا لله تعالي بنى الله له قصرا في الجنة بني المسجد في
عصر السلطان الاعظم المؤيد بتائيد الرحمن شمس الدنيا والدين ابو النصر مظفر شاه بن
محمود شاه بن محمد شاه بن احمد شاه بن محمد شاه بن مظفر شاه السلطان خلد الله
ملكه بانية المسجد المذكور والدة ابي بكر خان بن محمود شاه سلطان المسماة براني اثني
بين شهور سنة اربع شمسية سنة العشرين وتسعماية ۞

God who is blessed and high has said, "Verily the mosques belong to God, then invoke ye no one else with him." And the Prophet has said, "He who builds a mosque for God Almighty, will have a castle built for him by God in Paradise." This mosque was built during the reign of the great king, who is assisted by the aid of the All-merciful, Shamsu-'d-dunyâ wa'd-dîn Abû-'n-naṣir Muẓaffar Shâh, son of Maḥmûd Shâh, son of Muḥammad Shâh, son of Aḥmad Shâh, son of Muḥammad Shâh, son of Muẓaffar Shâh, the King—may God perpetuate his kingdom! The builder of this mosque is the mother of Abû Bakr Khân, son of Maḥmûd Shâh Sulṭân, who is called Râṇî Aṣnî.† During the months of fourth solar [regnal] year, in 920 [A.D. 1514].

This mosque has lately undergone extensive restoration, and the adjoining tomb is being also restored.

VI.—FROM AḤMAD SHÂH'S TOMB.

Inscription VI. is from the tomb of Aḥmad Shâh and refers to repairs made on it by Nau Khân Farḥatu-'l-Mulk (Joy of the Kingdom), son of Chîman, in A.D. 1537-38.

---

* Conf. H. G. Briggs's *Cities of Gujarâshtra*, p. 245; and Hope's Descriptive Sketch in *Architecture of Ahmadabad*, p. 45.

† It is doubtful whether the initial vowel of this name is *a*, *u*, or *i*. As an Arabic word it can hardly be pronounced otherwise than *asnâ*.

روضهٔ عالي احمد شاه سلطان کز علو
جنت گشته گنبذ او با سر طاق سما
عهده داران گرچه بودندش بسي و برده اند
سعيها اندر مرمّت کردن او دائما
ليک هرگز هيچ کس اورا بدين رونق نساخت
همچو ذات اکمل آن صاحب عز و علا
محسن اهل زمانه فرحت الملک آنک او
هست ديندار و خدا ترس و سخي و با وفا
در زمان تاريخ سال عهده اش از عون حق
گفت يحيي فرحت ملک آمد از وي سالها

سنه اربع و اربعين و تسعماية ۞ يادگار احمد چهجو

1. *(This is) the lofty mausoleum of Aḥmad Shâh, the king, the dome of which, on account of its loftiness, matches the vault of the heaven.*

2. *Though he* had many officers, and though they always exerted themselves to repair it,*

3. *No one has hitherto done so in so splendid a manner, as the perfect mind of that respected and exalted man.*

4. *The benefactor of the present generation, Farḥatu-'l-Mulk, who is pious, God-fearing, liberal, and faithful.*

5. *The chronogram of his office-tenure has been expressed, with God's help, by (the poet) Yaḥyâ, in the words "Farḥat-i-Mulk," these letters give the year.*

A.H. 944 [A.D. 1537-38]. *The memorial is executed by Aḥmad Chhajjû.*

VII.—FROM SHÂHAB SAYYID'S MOSQUE.

Inscription VII. (Plate V.) is from a mosque with two slender minarets, locally known as Shâhab Sayyid's or the lesser Jâmi' Masjid, and relates to its building by the same Nau Khân Farḥatu-'l-Mulk, mentioned in the preceding inscription.

يا الله يا الله قطعه در تاريخ بناء مسجد جامع
ملک الشرق ملک نو خان چيمن المخاطب
بفرحت الملک

مسجدے با صفا و پر انوار — آنکه نورش بآسمان برود
بيت معمور و سقف مرفوعش — گر بخواند لسان غبب سزد
هست در عز همچو بيت عتيق — خالي از عابدان بدان نبود
چاه او عين زمزم [و] چو منا — جنب او سوق با رواج بود

* Or *it* (*sc.* the mausoleum).

No. 7. SHAHUB SAYYID'S MASJID. (A.D. 1558).

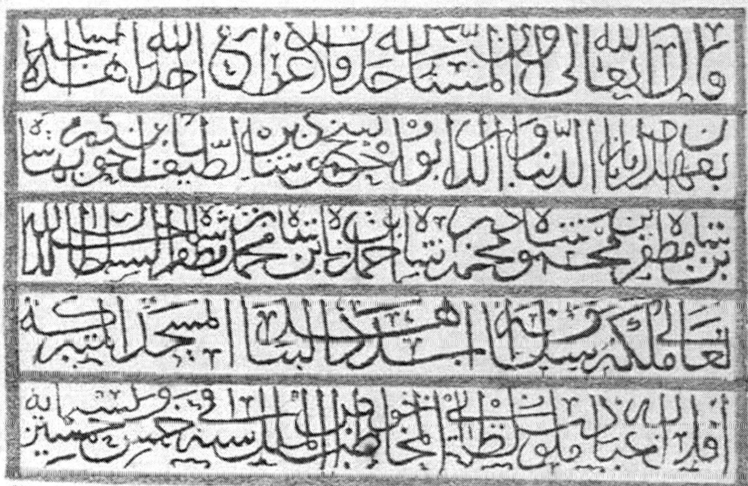

J. Burgess, fecit. W. Griggs, Photo-lith.

No. 8. HAMSA SALAT'S DHALGAWARI MASJID. (A.D. 1548).

شد بنایش بعهد آنکه شهیش   تا بکرسي هشتمین برسد
شاه محمود ابن شاه لطیف   که سلاطین را پناه دهد
بانیش نو خان ابن چمن کو   فرحت الملک شد ز لطف صمد
بنده تاریخ این بناء قبول   از سر صدق خواستم ز خرد
گفت في الحال رو بگو یحیی   قد بنا خالصًا لوجه احد
نهصد و چهل و پنج مجموع بود   گر در آري حروف وي بعدد

O God! A chronogram on the erection of the Jámi' Mosque by the Maliku-sh-Sharq [chief of the east], Nau Khán, son of Chiman, who has the title of Farḥatu-'l-Mulk.

1. *(This is) a mosque shining and beaming forth, whose rays go up to heaven.*

2. *If the tongue of the angel calls it "the raised house," and "the elevated dome," it is but proper.**

3. *For in honour it is like "the old house;" may it never be empty inside of worshippers!*

4. *Its well is like the Zamzam well; and like Miná,† at the side of it, is a well attended bâzâr.*

5. *The building was erected during the reign of him whose kingdom reaches the eighth throne,*

6. *Sháh Mahmúd, son of Sháh Laṭíf, who gives an asylum to other kings.*

7. *Its builder is Nau Khán, son of Chiman, who, through the grace of God, became Farḥatu-'l-Mulk.*

8. *I sincerely asked Genius for the chronogram of this acceptable building.*

9. *And he replied at once, "Go, Yaḥyá, and say, He built‡ it from pure motives, for the sake of God."*

10. *This gives together 945, if you count up the value of the letters.*

VIII.—FROM THE DHALGEWÂRI MASJID, OR HAMZA SALÂT'S.

Inscription VIII. is from a mosque consisting of a masonry wall with *Mehráb* niches, and a tiled roof, supported on pillars in front, and is chiefly interesting as giving the full name of Mahmûd Shâh III., the son of Laṭîf Khân (1538–1553–4), as Nâṣiru-'d-dîn Abu'l Fatḥ Maḥmûd Shâh. As Prof. Blochmann remarks—"Mr. Thomas, in his *Chronicles of the Pathan Kings of Delhi* (p. 352), gives Quṭbu-'d-dîn as the name of the king; but the coin figured by him does not give that name. We may therefore assume that this inscription gives the correct name."§

---

* *Lisân-i-ghaib*, pr. the tongue of the unseen world. This is also the well-known epithet of the poet Ḥâfiz. "The raised house" is the Ka'bah in Makka; and "The elevated dome" is the heavenly vault. "The old house," the same as the Ka'bah.

† The construction is forced: *chu-minâ* is either an adjective to *Zamzam* [the well in the Ka'bah], or the engraver has left out a *wâw*, "and," after *Zamzam*. Minâ is a sacred spot near Makka where a bâzâr is held.

‡ The engraver has wrongly spelt بنا instead of بني. The latter form is required to make up 945. The whole poem is inferior; and in the last line we have to scan *chihlŭpan*; and in the sixth distich a foot *mustaf'ilun* occurs for *mafâ'ilun*.

§ In the names of the other Gujarâti kings given by Mr. Thomas on p. 353, I find that Bahâdur Shâh (No. 11) is given with two *kunyahs*, which is unusual. The name of Muzaffar Shâh bin Mahmûd (No. 15) cannot be correct, because it is against grammar and idiom.—*H.B.*

قال اللہ تعالي وان المساجد لله فلا تدعوا مع الله احدا [بني] هذه المسجد عهد
الزمان ناصر الدنيا والدين ابو الفتح محمود شاه بن شاه لطيف خان اخو بهادر شاه بن
مظفر شاه بن محمود شاه بن محمد شاه بن احمد شاه بن محمد شاه بن مظفر شاه
السلطان خلد الله تعالى ملكه وسلطانه سدّد هذا البنا المسجد المتبركه اقل عباد الله ملّو
سلطاني المخاطب بخواص الملك في سنة خمس خمسين وتسعماية ۞

God Almighty says, "Verily the mosques belong to God, then invoke ye no one else beside him." This mosque was built during the time of the reign of Nâṣiru-'d-dunyâ wa'd-dîn Ab-'l Fatḥ Maḥmûd Shâh, son of Shâh Laṭif Khân brother of Bahâdur Shâh, son of Muẓaffar Shâh, son of Maḥmûd Shâh, son of Muḥammad Shâh, son of Aḥmad Shâh, son of Muḥammad Shâh, son of Muẓaffar Shâh, the king—may God Almighty continue his kingdom and his rule! The edifice of this blessed mosque was strengthened by the meanest of God's slaves, **Mallû-Sulṭânî,** *who has the title of Khawâṣ su-'l-Mulk, in* 955 [A.D. 1548].

Nawâb Shajâ'at Khân's masjid* has a marble floor divided by piers into five bays, with two slender minarets, not at the extremities of the building, but three bays apart. The *Mimbar* or pulpit is of three steps of yellow marble, and over the *Mihrâb* is written in ornamental style the Muslim creed—

Lá iláha illá alláh : Muhammadun rasúlu-'l-'láh. Sana 1107 (*i.e.* A.D. 1695-96).

The walls are wainscoted with marble to a height of about 6 feet, and let into the back wall is a small slab on which is carved, as a sort of monogram, the words—

Yá fattáh,
"O opener!"

The adjoining tomb is of brick, but its marble floor is much destroyed.

The Râṇîs' tombs† have suffered sadly from people being allowed to carry off the beautifully carved marble slabs. The court and corridors with the exquisitely latticed screens require to be cared for and preserved.

The perforated stone and marble work at Ahmadâbâd and throughout Gujarât and Râjputânâ, presents an almost endless variety of beautiful patterns. Plate VI. presents a few of the more common designs, taken from photographs, but materials exist for a very interesting collection.

Sarkhej is about 5 miles south-west from Ahmadâbâd, and on the right bank of the Sâbarmatî. It was here that, as already mentioned, Shaikh Ahmad Khaṭṭû Ganj Bakhsh died in 1445. Over the door of his Dargâh or tomb is the quatrain:

1 *Baḥr i kaff i Ahmadí chu dur-ríz shawad,*
2 *Dámán i umíd ganj i Parwíz shawad.*
3 *Az bahr i sujúd i dargahash níst 'ajab,*
4 *Gar rúy zamíṇ tamám sarkhíz shawad.*

"When the ocean of Ahmad's palm scatters pearls,
Hope's hem becomes the treasure of Parwîz.
No wonder if, in order to bend before his shrine,
The whole surface of the earth raises its head." ‡

There are other inscriptions here which should be copied. On the tomb of Râjabâî, the queen of Mahmûd Bîgarah, there are two.§

* See Briggs's *Cities of Gujarashtra*, pp. 222, 223.
† *Architecture of Ahmedabad*, p. 47.
‡ Transliterated and translated by Prof. Blochmann. There is a pun between *Sarkhej* and *sarkhíz*.
§ For some account of Sarkhej, see *Architecture of Ahmedabad*, pp. 44 ff.

SPECIMENS OF PERFORATED STONE & MARBLE WORK. PLATE VI.

From photographs. W. Griggs photo-lith.

Several of the buildings at Ahmadâbâd have fallen into the hands of Government, and there are perhaps few places in India where General Cunningham's suggestion to place religious buildings, *no longer in use as such*, under the local civil authority could be more easily or usefully carried out. It has already been so done in several cases where there are funds specially bequeathed for the preservation of the buildings, with the best results; and in such cases it would be well if the surplus funds were not largely expended on *restorations*, but used in part at least for the conservation of all the Musalman remains placed in charge of the civil officers.

II.—KÂṬHIÂWÂḌ.

The peninsula of Kâṭhiâwâḍ or Surâshṭra, lying between the gulfs of Kachh and Cambay or Khâmbât and surrounded on the south and west by the Arabian sea, is the holy land of Western India. It was known to the Greeks and Romans under the name of Σαυραστρηνη; the Muhammadans called it by the Prakritised name of Sorath, and to this day a large district in the south-west, a hundred miles in length, still retains that name. Another district, quite as large, to the east of the centre, however, has long been known as Kâṭhiâwâḍ, from having been overrun by the Kâṭhis who entered the peninsula from Kachh, perhaps first in predatory bands in the thirteenth or fourteenth century; in the fifteenth the whole tribe was driven out of Kachh, and in that and the following century conquered a considerable territory. The Marâṭhâs who came into contact with them in their forays and were sometimes successfully repelled by them, extended the name of Kâṭhiâwâḍ to the whole province, and from them we have come to apply it in a similar wide sense; but by Brâhmaṇs and the natives it it still spoken of as Surâshṭra.

The extreme length of the peninsula, from Goghâ in the east, to Jagat or Dwârakâ in the west, is nearly 220 miles; its greatest breadth is about 165 miles, and its area 22,000 square miles, with an estimated population of about two-and-a-half millions.

It is divided into 188 separate states large and small, of which thirteen pay no tribute; ninety-six are tributary to the British Government, seventy to that of the Gaikwâḍ as the representative of the Marâṭhâs; and nine pay tribute to both; while of the latter three classes one hundred and thirty-two pay a tax called *Zortalabi* to the Nawâb of Junâgaḍh. The states are arranged in seven classes with varying civil and criminal powers,—five of the larger belonging to the first class.

Kâṭhiâwâḍ is usually divided into ten provinces or *prânts* of very unequal size:

(1.) Jhâlâwâḍ, in the north, containing about fifty states, of which Dhrângadhrâ, Limṛî, Wadhwân, Wânkanêr, and Thân-Laktar, are among the largest; the Dhandhukâ district in it belongs to Ahmadâbâd.

(2.) Machhukântâ, comprising Morbî and Maliâ, lies to the west of Jhâlâwâḍ.

(3.) Hâlâr, in the north-west, derives its name from the Hâlâ branch of Jâḍejâs from Kachh, and embraces twenty-six states, of which Jâmnagar or Nawânagar is the largest, Râjkoṭ, Gondal-Dhoraji, Dharol, Drâphâ, &c., are smaller.

(4.) Okhâmandal, in the extreme west, belongs to Bârodâ.*

(5.) Barâdâ or Jaitwâḍ, along the south-west coast, is known also as Purbandar.

(6.) Soraṭh in the south, is occupied by the Junâgaḍh State, and the two small holdings of Bântwâ and Amrâpur; but the sea coast from Mangrol to the island of Diu or Div is also known as Nâgarwâḍ, its old name when held by the Nâgars.

(7.) Bâbriâwâḍ, so called from the Babriâ tribe of Kolis, is a hilly tract in the south-east, divided into many very small states, or village holdings, and includes many villages belonging to the Gaikwâḍ of Bârodâ.

(8.) Kâṭhiâwâḍ, near the middle, is a large district comprising Jeṭpur-Chital, Amrelî, Jasdhan, Choṭilâ, Ânandapur, and fifty other smaller estates.

(9.) Und-Sarveyâ, lying along the Śatruñji river and divided into small holdings.

(10.) Gohilwâḍ, in the east, along the shore of the gulf of Cambay, is so named from the Gohil Râjputs, who are the ruling race in it. It comprises the Goghâ district belonging to the Ahmadâbâd Collectorate,—Bhaunagar, a first class state, Pâlitâṇâ, Walâ, Lâthî, Bhojawadar, and many others.

Generally speaking, with the exception of the Tâṅgâ and Mâṇḍhav hills in the west of Jhâlâwâḍ, and some nearly isolated hills in Hâlâr, the northern portion of the country is flat; but in the south—from near Goghâ—the Gir range runs nearly parallel with the coast, and at a distance of about twenty miles from it, along the north of Bâbriâwâḍ and Sorath, turning northwards towards Girnar. Opposite this latter mountain again is the solitary Ośam hill, and then still farther west is the Baradâ group between Hâlâr and Baradâ, running about twenty miles north and south from Gumli to Râṇâwâv, near which iron ore was dug in early times.

The principal river is the Bhâdar, which rises in the Mâṇḍhav hills and flows south-west falling into the sea at Navî-Bandar in Baradâ, after a course of about a hundred and fifteen miles in a direct line, everywhere marked by the lands near its banks being in a high state of cultivation. It is a saying in the districts through which it passes that it receives ninety-nine tributary streams. From the same hills rises another Bhâdar which flows eastwards past Râṇpur and Dhandhuka into the gulf of Cambay or Khâmbât, and in its short course attains a considerable size.

The Ajî, perhaps the prettiest stream in the province, rises near Sardhâr and runs northwards past Râjkoṭ, receiving the Marî from the left, and falls into the gulf of Kachh near Bâlambâ in Hâlâr. It is noted for the excellence of its water, and the gold dust found in small quantities in its bed.

The Machhu, from near Sardhâr, flows north-west, through the district to which it gives name, past Wânkanêr and Morbî into the gulf of Kachh near Maliâ.

The Śatruñjî, from the Gir range, receives a large number of tributaries, and passes Palitâṇâ and Tâlâjâ on its way to the entrance of the gulf of Khâmbâṭ. One of its tributaries, the Rewâ, from Bâbriâwâḍ, is unparalleled in the province for wild and romantic scenery: "It pursues its course over an alternately rocky and

* The island (*bét*) of Śankhodâr belongs to Okhâmandal. It was long famous for its pirates.

gravelly bed, varying in breadth from twenty to sixty or a hundred yards, buried as it were between lofty mountains, which rise abruptly from its bed covered with wood of the most large and beautiful kind; the bed of the river also abounds in the tree known by the native name of Jambu, which here grows to a noble size, and the darkness of its leaves is finely contrasted with the lively and varied colours of the forest. A road leads in many parts along the bed of the Rewâ; and the traveller in a broad and convenient path finds the heavens excluded from his view, or very partially seen through the small spaces left by the lofty mountains and the luxuriousness of their clothing."*

Surâshṭrâ was doubtless at a very early period brought under the influence of Brahmanical civilization, and, from its position at the extreme north of the coast line of Western India, it was the most accessible to influences from the west. As early as the reign of the great Aśoka of Magadha (B.C. 265–229) we find him inscribing his famous edicts upon the huge granite boulders at the entrance of the pass that leads from Junâgaḍh to Girnâr. If the reading in Strabo† of *Saraostos* is really, as there is good reason to suppose, a corruption of some form of Surâshṭra, then it was included in the conquests of the Indo-Skythian kings, Demetrios the son of Euthydemos (B.C. cir. 190), and Menander (B.C. 144), who, he says, pushed their conquests eastwards and "got possession not only of Patalēnē, but of the kingdoms of Saraostos and Sigerdis (or Sigertis)‡ being the remainder of the coast."

Its shores were well known to the Alexandrian merchants of the first and second centuries, but there is considerable difficulty in identifying the places they mention. Dr. Vincent,§ Lassen,‖ and Col. Yule¶ have each attempted the task.

Lassen places the city of Surastra at Junâgaḍh, and this is as probable a conjecture as perhaps any other that could be formed. Yule places it at Navi-bandar, which is very doubtful. If not Junâgaḍh or Vanthali, then Virâwal and Sihor are the only two other sites that seem likely.

Bardaxima is located by Yule at Purbandar, perhaps from the resemblance of the name to Baradâ; but Śrinagar, in the same district, is a much older place, and near it is a small village named Bardiyâ which may possibly be a reminiscence of the Greek name.

Yule places the Baraké of Arrian at Jagat or Dwârkâ; Lassen also identifies it with Dwârakâ, but apparently Mûla-Dwârakâ, which he places on the coast between Purbandar and Miyânâ, near Śrinagar. Mûla-Dwârakâ—or the original site was farther east than this, but is variously placed near Mâdhupur, thirty-six miles north-west from Somanâth-Paṭṭan, or three miles south-west from Koḍinâr, and nineteen miles east of Somanâth.

* Macmurdo, *Trans. Bom. Lit. Soc.*, vol. I. p. 265.

† Οὐ μόνον δὲ τὴν Παταληνὴν κατέσχον, ἀλλὰ καὶ τῆς ἄλλης παραλίας τήν τε Σαραόστου καλουμένην καὶ τὴν Σιγέρδιδος βασιλείαν.—Strabo, lib. XI. cap. xi. 1. The copies, however, differ in the names, giving Τεσαριόστου (Ald.) Τεσσαριόστου, and Τεσαριόστου, for the first, and Σιγέρδιδος (Medic.) and Σιγέρτιδος (Kram.) for the second.

‡ Prof. H. H. Wilson (*Ariana Antiqua*, p. 212) was inclined to think that the kingdom of Sigertis might be a Greek form of *Śrigartta*, as conjectured by Lassen, and might indicate Kachh. But Prinsep, in 1837, pointed out that the reading Σαραόστου, found in some of the best copies of Strabo, by merely altering to Συραίστου, would give a form nearly approaching to the indigenous name in its Prâkrit form of Soratha.—*Journ. As. Soc. Beng.* vol. VI. p. 390; *Essays*, vol. I. p. 434.

§ *Periplus of the Erythræan Sea.*

‖ Map of Ancient India in his *Indische Alterthumskunde.*

¶ In Smith's *Ancient Atlas*, pp. 22–24, and map 31.

Astakapra or Astakampra, Yule would place at Tâlâjâ, and Lassen near by it—at Gopnâth, where Yule would have Papiké promontory.

The Horatæ are doubtless the people of Sorath, who have an inveterate propensity to sound the letter *S* as an *H*; and the Pandæ are the Pâṇḍava dwelling in the north of the peninsula in the district traditionally known as Panchâl or Deva-Panchâl, in which the chief town was Thân, possibly the same as Theophila, which Yule places doubtfully a little farther east about Talsânâ.

Peram island is probably rightly identified by Yule with the Baiones Insula of the ancients; Monoglosson he identifies with Mangrol.

Among the sacred places in the province, Prabhâsa Paṭṭan or Somanâtha in the south, and Dwârakâ in the extreme west, are famous shines of the Śaiva and Vaishṇava forms of Brahmanism,—the former, one of the twelve great Śaiva Mahâlingas of India, and the account of whose destruction by Mahmûd of Ghaznî is so familiar to every reader of history, is also the spot where tradition says the great Yâdava hero and demi-god Kṛishṇa was slain; whilst Dwârakâ is one of his most celebrated shrines, where he is fabled to have saved the sacred books. Thân, in the north, is an old site of sun worship, and in the neighbourhood are several snake shrines; and in the Gir is Tulasî-Śyâm, a noted Hindû shrine, with a hot spring.*

Among the "high places" the Jains reckon Śatruñjaya as their great *tírtha* or

* The following is Tod's account of this Tîrtha or sacred spot, though the legend he gives is scarcely a satisfactory one for the origin of the name. *Tulasi* is the sacred Basil plant, so favourite an object of worship among the Hindûs; and the shrine, I believe, is a Śaiva one rather than Vaishṇava. "Tulsiśyâma," says Tod, "is a very sanctified spot, and celebrated as the arena of combat between Śyâma (an epithet synonimous with Kṛishṇa, and denoting his black complexion) and Tula, the demon (*daitya*) of Saurâshṭra, the terror of all the sacred classes, who, having obtained the boon of invulnerability by any mortal weapon, set the gods themselves at defiance; but he was told to beware of the incarnation of Kṛishṇa, which would be fatal to him. And the legend sayeth that as he lay expiring at the feet of his conqueror, he preferred this last request, that his name might not perish with him; and hence the conjoined names of the victor and vanquished, Tuli-śyâma, to designate the scene of combat. The abode of this Titan is a wild dell, completely enclosed by hills, and may not unaptly be compared to a large bowl, having its sides covered with wood, and at its base a *Sitâ-Kuṇḍa*, or hot-well, the grand object of curiosity. A reservoir has been constructed to retain the waters, which are deemed efficacious in certain complaints. It is eighty feet in length by forty-five in breadth at top, with a flight of steps, which diminishes its base to fifty-five by twenty. I was tempted to bathe in it. The temperature of the water was 21° above that of the external air, and it was disagreeably hot. At this hour, within the tent, the thermometer was 86°, and only 89° outside. After some minutes' immersion in the *kuṇḍa*, it rose to 110°; but when taken out it fell almost instantaneously to 76°, and as rapidly recovered the external temperature of 89°.

"There is a small and rude temple, dedicated to the black deity, whose image decorates the interior, and presides over these sanitary waters. There are also shrines to the warlike divinities, Śiva and Bhairava, at the entrance of the enclosure. If we accept the local tradition for the origin of the hot spring, it would appear that it did not exist in the lifetime of the giant Tula. Śyâma, hungry and fatigued after his battle, was awaiting with some impatience the culinary operations of his favourite wife, Rukmanî, who with her own fair hands was preparing a mess of rice. But hunger getting the better of temper, he used some phrase which she resented, and overturning the boiling rice, she ran up the hill, leaving her hungry and sulky spouse to 'chew the cud of sweet and bitter fancy.' As the gods of Hind, like those of Greece, never get into 'hot water' without some consequences resulting from it, the rice-water then spilt became a perennial stream, bestowing sanctity and sanity on all who used it. In proof of the tradition they appeal to Rukmani, whose enshrined image still looks down upon the *Sitâ-Kuṇḍa*.

"It is a wild sequestered spot, but too confined for a large party, and here, within our bowl, horses, foot, and carts were crowded, creating a din most unsuited to such a solitude. An outlet from the *kuṇḍa* allows the superfluous water to drain off, and this is the origin of a small stream, bordered by date and other trees, which meanders through abrupt and broken ridges, presenting some pretensions to the picturesque."—Tod's *Western India*, pp. 320, 321.

holy place, on the isolated mountain south of Pâlitâṇâ; Tâladhvaja, commonly known as Tâlâjâ Tekrî, the isolated hill at Tâlâjâ; Ujjayanta or Raivata, the famous Mount Girnar in Soraṭh and Ḍhañka in Hâlâr. Perhaps the Lor or Lauhar hill in Bâbriâwâḍ is also intended by the Lauhitya of their sacred books.*

Of the early history of the country we have but scanty notices. It was probably governed by satraps under Aśoka and the great Maurya kings. From coins that have been found pretty abundantly in different parts, it appears that for a period of about two centuries a dynasty known as the Sâhs or Siñhas ruled,—perhaps at old Sîhor, Siñhur or Siñhapura. Of this dynasty we learn from coins the names of some twenty-four princes, many of them with dates ranging from 72 to 292; but it may be doubted if in all cases the symbols for the figures have been quite correctly made out, and it is not certain from what era they are to be reckoned. Prinsep seemed inclined to place them all before 153 B.C.; Mr. Justice Newton, assuming that they date from the Vikramâditya Samvat, to between 60 or 70 B.C. and 240 A.D.;† and the late Dr. Bhau Dâji, reckoning from the Śaka era of A.D. 78, placed them between about A.D. 140 and 380.‡ Mr. E. Thomas has given much attention to these coins and his opinion will be given in the next chapter.

Besides coins of the Sâhs, however, we have at least two inscriptions, unfortunately both somewhat defaced.

The first of these is on the famous rock between Junâgaḍh and Girnâr, recording the repair of the dam there by Râja Mahâkshatrapa Rudra Damân in the year 72 of their era. His father's name is obliterated, but that of his grandfather is given as Makâkshatrapa Chashṭana. This inscription will be dealt with further on.

The second is a short one on a pillar on the bank of the lake at Jasdhan in the north of the Kâṭhiâwâḍ division. It has been thus translated by the late Dr. Bhau Dâji:

"In the year 127 Bhâdrapada (*month*) dark half 7th (*day*) of the moon, this Satra (*tank*) of Râjâ Mahâkshatrapa Bhadramukha Swâmî Rudra Sena, the great-grandson of the son of Râjâ Mahâkshatrapa Swâmî Chashṭana; the grandson of the son of Râjâ Ksh(*atrapa*) Swâmî Jayadâmâ, the grandson of Râjâ Mahâkshatrapa . . . . . . Rudra Dâmâ, (*son of*) Râjâ Mahâkshatrapa Bhadramukha Swâmî Rudra. Of the son of Supra Nâthaka of Mânasagotra, the grandson of Khara, with brothers . . . . . ."

This short inscription yields the names, then, of five of the Sâh kings, viz.:

1. Râjâ Mahâkshatrapa Bhadramukha Swâmî Chashṭana;
2. Râjâ Kshatrapa Swâmî Jayadâmân, his son;
3. Râjâ Mahâkshatrapa . . . Rudra Dâmâ, his son;
4. Râjâ Mahâkshatrapa Bhadramukha Swâmî Rudra Siñha, his son;
5. Râjâ Mahâkshatrapa Swâmî Rudra Sena, his son, ruling in 127.

"The other individuals mentioned in the inscription were in all likelihood officers of the district." §

---

* *Satruñjaya Mâhâtmya*, I. śl. 352.

† *Journ. Bom. Br. R. As. Soc.*, vol. VII. p. 30; vol. IX. pp. 17, 18.

‡ *Ibid.*, vol. VIII. p. 238.

§ *Ibid.*, vol. VIII. pp. 234, 235.

Coins supply the remainder of our knowledge of these princes, but fortunately the first of them is mentioned in the inscriptions on some of the caves in the Bombay Presidency: thus at Kârleṅ we read :—

"Peace. By Ushabhadâta, the son of Dinaka, the son-in-law of Râjâ Kshaharâta Kshatrapa Nahapâna."

At Nasik :—

In Sanskrit :—"Peace. By Ushavadâta, the son of Dinaka, the son-in-law of Râjâ Kshaharata Kshatrapa Nahapâna."

In Magadhî :—"Peace. In the year 42, month Vaisâkha, by Ushavadâta, the son of Dinaka, the son-in-law of Râjâ Kshaharâta Kshatrapa Nahapâna."

And again, in Magadhî :—"The cell, the religious assignation of Dakshamitrâ, the daughter of Râjâ Kshaharata Kshatrapa Nahapâna."

At Junnar :—

"[Constructed by] Ayama, the minister of . . . . Mahâkshatrapa Svâmî Nahapâna."*

Mr. Justice Newton was fortunate enough to obtain a coin of this Nahapâna from Kâṭhiâwâḍ. He thus describes it: "It is of silver, and its weight is 31 grains. The obverse has a well cut bust facing to the right, with fillet and ear ornaments, and in the exergue, a legend of which sufficient remains to show that the letters were purely Greek, although in consequence of original indistinctness, wear, or corrosion, not more than a single character here and there can be made out, and these hardly justify me in hazarding a conjecture as to the filling in. Additional difficulty has been caused by the circumstance,—an ordinary one in coins of that time,—that the disc of the coin was too small to receive the whole impression of the die. On the reverse are two central emblems, one of which is a spear or an arrow, and the other possibly a double-headed dagger, with an exergue legend in which the letters Nahapânsa (the ordinary Baktrian or Pâli genitive of Nahapâna) are distinct, though nothing more can be deciphered. The characters are those of the rock inscriptions, the most ancient form from which the present Devanâgarî has been derived; and though a portion of the legend has fallen altogether outside the coin and some letters have been eaten away, a larger portion would be legible but for the artist's evident want of acquaintance with the character."†

From all this he argues that Nahapâna flourished between 80 and 50 B.C., that he was a Parthian, and that possibly some others are yet to be interposed between him and Chashṭana, whom he would place in A.D. 10 or 20.

As to the origin of the titles Kshatrapa and Mahâkshatrapa which "appear to have originated with Nahapâna, and were continued to every member of the Sâh dynasty," Mr. Newton remarks that, "Nahapâna or his predecessors may have governed in Baktria, or the neighbouring regions, as the satraps of a distant monarch, but this supposition is not a necessary one. The designation doubtless at first implied that the power exercised was delegated, but after a time, in common with other similar titles, it must have come to be looked on as indicating authority only and not

---

* *Journ. Bom. Br. R. As. Soc.*, vol. IX. p. 6 n.

† *Ibid.*, p. 7.

subordination. We may, therefore, I think, conclude that Nahapâna himself was probably an independent sovereign, and that his successors who retained the title for more than two centuries certainly recognised no superior."*

Having obtained a number of Sâh coins from Kâṭhiâwâḍ, principally through the kindness of Major J. W. Watson, I placed them in the hands of E. Thomas, Esq., F.R.S., late Bengal Civil Service, who long since made this branch of Numismatics a special study, and he has obligingly contributed the following chapter to the present Report.

---

* *Journ. Bom. Br. R. As. Soc.*, vol. IX. pp. 17–19.

III. SÂH AND GUPTA COINS, &c.

By Edward Thomas, Esq., F.R.S., Correspondant de l'Institut de France.

Introduction.

Mr. Burgess, during his late tour, succeeded in obtaining some very interesting specimens of the coins of the local Sáh kings of Suráshtra and their imperial Gupta successors which he has requested me to describe.*

I have taken advantage of the opportunity to arrange and classify in the accompanying autotype plate, contrasted examples of the various provincial currencies of the latter dynasty, and I have attempted, in a general way, to collect the extraneous data bearing on the still obscure history of a race, whose domination forms so important an epoch and hitherto undefined time-mark amid the dynastic revolutions of India within itself. This may be held to be a very bold expansion of a text based upon a handful of coins, but Numismatic studies I have always maintained, when properly and scientifically treated, open out a very large and expansive circle of investigation.

In the present instance there have unfortunately been few opportunities for systematic arrangement, or for the ordinary completion of details; but, incidentally, where coins have proved their leading title I have admitted them into the front rank, in which prominent position I can usually sustain them, when their rough edges preserve but fair traces of the marginal legends of the original die, and when the native engravers have not subsided into ignorant and mere mechanical imitators of device and superscription.

The materials available for the determination of the age and the spread of the dominions of the Guptas seem to arrange themselves in the following order:—

a. Inscriptions.

b. Written history.

c. Tradition.

d. Coins.

a.—Inscriptions.

The genealogy of the Gupta family has been singularly well-preserved, considering the limited range of their extant inscriptions and the persistent oblivion to which their successors would, perhaps designedly, have consigned them.

The earliest of these, in point of time, is the Allahábád manifesto of Samudra Gupta, the fourth in succession of an ancestry claiming little pretension to renown, and the

* A slight difference will be observed between the system of transliteration employed in the following pages and that followed by Mr. Burgess. The chief departure from his usage is in the marking the श by ṣ, in preference to the unsightly ś. My theory is, that dots *below* the line should, as far as possible, constitute the discriminating mark for consonants, and that accents *above* the line should be reserved for vowels. I prefer the acute accent ′ to the circumflex ^ as less disfiguring to the vowel letter, a disadvantage inherent in the ^, and especially detrimental in maps.

second only in the order of kings, who attained anything beyond restricted celebrity. This first heir to an imperial father took advantage of a ready prepared monolith, to supplement, in the writing current in his day an account of his own rise, in the form of a quasi palimpsest,* attached to the original contemporary palæograph in the old square *láṭ* character in which Aṣoka, in the twenty-seventh year of his reign (B.C. 232), had proclaimed, unwittingly, his undeveloped Buddhistic tendencies, and his advocacy of the more simple doctrines of mercy to animals, the preservation of animal life, and the alleviation of animal woes.†

The second record of the Gupta heritage, likewise perpetuated on stone, is to be seen in the Mathurá inscription from the Katrá mound, wherein Samudra's parentage is apparently repeated in accordance with the tenor of the earlier monument.‡ The genealogy of the family is further extended in the inscription on the Bhítari *láṭ* or monolith, in the district of Ghúzipúr and in its counterpart at Bihár,§ which carries the succession down to Skanda Gupta and an unnamed heir.‖

From these inscriptions the recognised line of kings may be restored after the following order:

The Gupta Kings.

1. *Mahárája* Ṣrí Gupta.
2. *Mahárája* Ṣrí Ghaṭotkacha.
3. *Mahárájádhirája* Ṣrí Chandra Gupta.
4. ,, Ṣrí Samudra Gupta.
5. ,, Ṣrí Chandra Gupta II.
6. ,, Ṣrí Kumára Gupta.
7. ,, Ṣrí Skanda Gupta.

The family tree, originally reconstructed by Dr. Mill,¶ is of importance, in the present inquiry, as showing the moderately advanced position of the early members of the so-called regal line:—

1 Gupta.
|
2 Ghaṭotkachá. — Lichchavi, a private Rájput, whose daughter was
|
3 Chandra Gupta — + — Kumára Deví, wife of the king. — Sanhāriká, an independent princess, whose daughter was
|
4 Samudra Gupta *Rája and Sovereign* { ——+—— (1) A Queen, name unknown, / ——+—— (2) Deví, daughter of Mahádaitya.
|
5 Chandra Gupta II.
|
6 Kumára Gupta.
|
7 Skanda Gupta.
|
8 A young prince (Mahendra Gupta?), a minor at the date of this inscription.

---

* *Journ. As. Soc. Beng.* vol. III. p. 105; vol. VI. p. 978; *Journ. Bom. Br. R. As. Soc.* (*revision by Bhau Daji*), vol. IX. p. cxcvii., Prinsep's *Essays*, vol. I. p. 233.

† My *Ancient Indian Weights*, Marsden's (International) *Numismata Orientala*, London, 1874, p. 27.

‡ General Cunningham's *Archæological Report*, vol. III. plate XVI. No. 24, p. 37.

§ *Journ. As. Soc. Beng.* 1866, p. 271; *Journ. Bom. Br. R. As. Soc.*, 1871–2. p. 59, Bhau Daji's *revised reading*: Cunningham's *Archæological Report*, vol. I. pl. XVII. p. 38, and pl. XXX. p. 94.

‖ *Journ. As. Soc. Beng.* 1836, p. 661; Prinsep's *Essays*, vol. I. p. 240.

¶ Dr. Mill, *Journ. As. Soc. Beng.* vol. III. p. 344; Prinsep's *Essays*, vol. I. pp. 235, 243, 245.

Much emphasis has been laid by some modern commentators* on the appearance of the words *Sháhán Sháh* in the Samudra Gupta inscription at Allahábád, above quoted, as tending to prove that the Guptas must have been contemporary with the Sassanian kings of Persia (226–632, A.D.). I wish to rectify any such misapprehension, as the point is of real importance as collateral evidence. I have from the first contended† that this title was in nowise exclusively the property or impress of the Sassanian family. We have the *Khsháyathiya Khsháyathiyánam* of Darius,‡ and the counterpart ΒΑΣΙΛΕΥΣ ΒΑΣΙΛΕΩΝ with the *Rajaraja* and *Adhiraja* of the Bactrian or rather Indo-Scythian coins.§ We can now further cite the existence of a *Shahíyah* dynasty in Khárizm of the race of Cyrus,‖ and point to the more immediate testimony of our Mathurá inscriptions, where Vásudeva is designated as *Sháhi*, and, in other epigraphs, by the parallel *Devaputra*, which reappears in conjunction with the *Sháhán Sháh* on the Allahábád column—combinations, which would preferentially indicate the continued rule of some members of this Scythic race in outlying portions of their old dominions.

It does not form part of the immediate object of the present résumé, to examine the entire series of the Gupta inscriptions, but the following passages have been selected as furnishing authentic dates, applicable, as other data may chance to sanction, to the general determination of the Gupta place and epochal position in Indian history.

No. 2. Inscription of Chandra Gupta.¶

The short inscription at Udayagiri contains the name of Chandra Gupta under the title of "*Parama-bhattáraka Mahárájádhirája*," and the date of *Samvat* 82 [in figures] 11th of the bright half of Ṣrávana.

*No. 3. Inscription of Chandra Gupta.***

The inscription on the eastern gate at Sanchí, near Bhilsa, commences, "To all respected Ṣramanas, the chief priests of the *ávasatha* ceremonial . . . The son of Amuka, the destroyer of his father's enemies, &c. . . . obtaining the gratification of every desire of his life through the favor of the great emperor Chandra Gupta

---

* Cunningham, *Bhilsa Topes*, p. 147; Lassen, *Ind. Alth.* vol. II. p. 752, &c.; Fergusson, *Journ. R. As. Soc.*, vol. IV. p. 108.

† On the Epoch of the Gupta Dynasty, *Journ. As. Soc. Beng.* (1855), vol. XXIV. p. 387; Prinsep's *Essays*, vol. I. pp. 272, 274. See also vol. II. pp. 109, 110, and *Journ. R. As. Soc.*, vol. XII. pp. 341–344; *Ariana Antiqua*, plates XVI.–XVII.

‡ *Journ. R. As. Soc.* vol. X. p. 195; Scythic, *Kokofuinna*, vol. XV. p. 95; Persian variant *Naqa Naqayánám*, p. 159.

§ Prinsep's *Essays*, vol. II. pp. 205 *et seq.*

‖ "Abu Rihán further speaks of the Kharizmian writing and records, which were carefully investigated by Kotaibah Ibn Moslem when he conquered the country, and strengthens the authority of these native documents, by showing that a single family, named the Shahíyah, and supposed to be derived from Cyrus, had reigned in Kharizm—with the exception of a Turkish or Scythian interregnum of ninety-two years—from the Achæmenian period down to the time of the Mahommedan invasion."—Sir H. Rawlinson, *Central Asia*, London, 1875, p. 246.

¶ Cunningham, *Bhilsa Topes*, p. 151; Prinsep's *Essays*, vol. I. p. 247.

** *Journ. As. Soc. Beng.*, vol. VI. p. 455, plate XXV., and vol. VII. p. 455; Prinsep's *Essays*, vol. I. p. 246.

. . . . . has given, &c. as an act of grace and benevolence of the great emperor Chandra Gupta, generally known among his subjects as Deva Rája (Indra). . . . .

" In the *Samvat* year 93 [in figures], Bhádrapada 10th."*

No. 4. Translation of an Inscription on the Monolith of Kuhaon, in the Gorakhpúr division, N. W. P., India, by Babu Rajendra Lála.

" The year 141 having been over (or the close of the year 141), and the month of Jaishṭhya having arrived, the empire of Skanda Gupta—the floor of whose audience chamber had been swept by gusts from the bowing of the heads of kings by hundreds; sprung from the line of the Guptas; of wide extended fame; opulent beyond all *others*; comparable with Ṣakra; lord of hundreds of monarchs."†

No. 5. Translation of an Inscription of the time of Skanda Gupta, on a copper-plate grant found at Indor, near Anupshahar on the Ganges.‡

" Amen; may he, whom Brahmans, in obedience to law, bepraise with the harmony of meditation and the entire devotion of their minds . . . be your protection!"

" In the year 146, in the month of Phálguna, the — (?) of the thriving and invincible kingdom of his most noble majesty, the supreme sovereign of great kings, the auspicious Skanda Gupta, for the promotion of prosperity in the possession of the owner Sarvanága in Antarvedi (or the Doáb of the Ganges and Yamuná)."§

No. 6. Inscription of Skanda Gupta on the Northern face of the Girnár rock. ||

"To the perfect one, Vishṇu, who snatched from Bali for the happiness of Indra," &c. "Afterwards he . . . who by his own arms obtained glory (*parákrama*), and who is the most distinguished of kings," . . . "may he, Skanda Gupta, be glorious" . . . (the text goes on to detail Skanda Gupta's difficulties in the selection of a fit ruler for Suráshtra and his ultimate choice of) Parṇadatta" . . . (who delegates his authority to his son) "Chakrapálita." . . . "Afterwards, when in the course of nature the rainy season arrived . . . the lake Sudarṣana burst (its embankments). When a century of years *plus* thirty passed, in the sixth day of Bhádrapada, at night, counting from the era of Gupta" (*Guptasya kála*).

(Seven years seem to have elapsed before its repairs were either commenced or fairly advanced when a record appears) "for the benefit of the king and of the city, in a

---

* Prinsep's *Essays*, vol. I. p. 246.

† *Journ. As. Soc. Beng.* vol. VII. p. 37; Prinsep's *Essays*, vol. I. p. 250; *Journ. As. Soc. Beng.* 1861, p. 3; 1863, p. 429; 1874, p. 364. Bháu Dájí, in the *Journ. Bom. Br. R. As. Soc.* article "Kalidasa." p. 31, and his revised translation of the inscription itself, *Journ. Bom. Br. R. As. Soc.* 1871, p. 59. General A. Cunningham in his *Archæological Report* for 1861-2, p. 92, gives a carefully corrected transcript of the original record, pl. XXX.

‡ *Journ. As. Soc. Beng.* 1874, p. 363, translation by Babu Rajendra Lála.

§ Under date 23rd April 1875, General Cunningham, in a private letter to Mr. Fergusson, reports the discovery of no less than four *new* inscriptions belonging to the Gupta period. "One of them is of Samudra Gupta, with the slokas numbered in figures at the end. . . . A rock inscription of Chandra Gupta has the lines numbered in figures at the ends. A third inscription, dated S. 106, speaks of the Guptan maya, or Gupta family; and a fourth inscription is dated in S. 191."

|| Translation of Dr. Bhau Daji, *Journ. Bom. Br. R. As. Soc.*, vol. VII. p. 121.

century of *samvatsaras* (years) *plus* thirty *plus* seven" (in the "month of *Chaitra*") . . . on the "first day of the first lunation of the (first) month of the Ghíshma season," &c.

The concluding division of the inscription proclaims the completion of the undertaking, in the construction of a temple by Chakrapálita, when, "from the era of the Guptas (*Guptánán kála*) a century of years *plus* thirty-eight (having passed)."

Up to this time, I have been somewhat disposed to question the validity of the above interpretation, in respect to the use of the term *Gupta kála*. I have now had an opportunity of comparing Messrs. Westergaard and Jacob's facsimile, published in the *Journ. Bom. Br. R. As. Soc.* with Sir Le Grand Jacob's own eye-transcript in MS., and the improved version of the original, undertaken for Dr. Bhau Daji, by Pandurang Gopála Páḍhye. I can have no hesitation in accepting the latter as the most intelligent reproduction; it brings out into perfect form letters that were merely fragmentary before, it seldom conflicts with, but constantly improves what were previously chaotic signs and symbols in the copies of Messrs. Westergaard and Jacob.*

As regards the bearing of the term *Gupta kála* upon this and other dated inscriptions, while I am fully prepared to admit the figures 130–138 into the ordinary family system of reckoning, I am not so sure that the designation of *Gupta kála* in this instance, implies identity with Albírúní's understanding of the same term. I should rather connect it with the era then recognised and employed by the Gupta's, whatever its origin and derivation, in contrast to the *local* system of annual dates, which we find on the Sáh coins, and which clearly does not accord with the Eastern scheme of proximate usage.

No. 7. Translation of an Inscription on the Pillar at Eran in Bhopál. Dr. Fitzedward Hall's version.

"Triumphant is the four-armed divinity: omnipresent; of whom the broad waters of the four seas are the couch; cause of the continuance, origin, destruction, and the like, of the universe; whose ensign is Garuḍa. In the year 165 on the twelfth *day* of the light fortnight of the month of Áshâḍha† on the day of *Brihaspati*, and when Budha Gupta —ruling, with the genius of the regents of the quarters, over the interval, chosen land of the gods, between the Kálindí and the Narmadá . . . was king . . . a Brahman saint of the illustrious Maitráyaṇíya monarchs . . . the great king Mátṛivishṇu, a

---

* This copy, made for Dr. Bhau Dâjî, is reproduced as plate XV. in this Report.

† It is necessary, in producing evidence for or against the ultimate import of these figures, to say that Professor Hall submitted the context of the passage embodying this date to Bápú Deva Ṣástrin, a Benáres mathematician, with a view to an opinion as to its concurrence with the Vikramáditya era or that of Ṣaka. The gist of the reply was, "it conforms to the era of Vikramáditya, and does not conform to that of Ṣáliváhana."—*Journ. As. Soc. Beng.* 1861, pp. 15–139. But with all respect for our Benáres calculator, we require to be told whether he has seen and met Colebrooke's objections to the effect that "the eclipses mentioned in the [later] grants do not appear reconcilable with their dates," and that "it seems difficult to account for this disagreement of the dates and eclipses in any other way than by impeaching the inscription, the authenticity of which there is not otherwise any reason to question."—(*Essays*, vol. II. p. 245.) See also (p. 357) for a possible explanation of the faulty results, in the introduction of "*Ráhu* as an eighth planet, and as the immediate cause of eclipses." Prof. Whitney, in his latest essay on "the Lunar Zodiac" (New York, 1874) ruthlessly exposes the *imperfection* of Indian astronomical knowledge and their methods of observation, which he climaxes by quoting their prediction of a *total* instead of a *partial* eclipse for February 6, 1860 (p. 368).

most devout worshipper of Bhagavat; who by the will of the Ordainer (Brahmá) acquired . . . the splendour of royalty . . and also of his younger brother Dhanyavishṇu, who does him obeisance," &c.*

We here take leave of Gupta dates and find ourselves in the presence of an inscription of Toramáṇa, who seems to have succeeded immediately to Budha Gupta's kingdom in central India. The importance of this monumental record will be better understood when we reach the numismatic sequence and obvious connexion between the two princes.

No. 8. Translation of an Inscription engraved on the neck of the Varáha image or Boar Incarnation at Eran.†

"Triumphant is the god who, in the likeness of a boar, lifted up the earth; who, by blows of his hard snout, tossed mountains aloft; the *upholding* pillar of that vast mansion, the three-fold world.

"In the first year that the auspicious Toramáṇa, sovereign of great kings, of extended fame and wide spread effulgence, is governing the earth; on the 10th day of Phálguna . . a Bráhman saint of the illustrious Maitráyaṇíya monarchs . . of the great king Mátṛivishṇu, who has departed to elysium, . . the younger brother Dhanyavishṇu, who did him due obeisance," &c.

No. 9. Inscription on the Porch of a Temple in the Fort of Gwalior.‡

"He who was celebrated as Ṣrí Toramáṇa . . full of talents innumerable, who subjugated the earth by truth, charity, conciliation, his army and the like. Unto him of the renowned race was born a son of unrivalled prowess named Pashupati, the lord of the earth, and the most distinguished of the Solar race . . in the fifteenth year of the prosperous reign of the remover of all suffering, the pre-eminent sovereign (lit. *Nṛipabṛisha*, 'the bull of kings')," &c.

Before taking leave of the subject of inscriptions, I wish to advert to a series of quasi-monumental documents for which, I think, too much value has been claimed. I mean the land and other royal grants or Ṣásanams engraved upon copper plates, and usually found in the possession of the families of the grantees.

I must confess that I have as little faith in these metallic title deeds, as the "Laws of Manu" seem to have extended to many of their earlier counterparts.§

---

* *Journ. As. Soc. Beng.* 1838, p. 634; 1861, p. 19.

† *Journ. As. Soc. Beng.* vol VII (1838), p. 633. Dr. Hall's revised rendering, above given, was published in the same Journal for 1861, p. 21.

‡ Bábu Rajendra Lála's version, *Journ. As. Soc. Beng.* 1861, p. 277.

§ Yájnavalkya, chap. II. sect. 240. "Whoever falsifies seales or a royal order."—Dr. Roer's Calcutta edition. Prof. Wilson translates "copper-plate grants by the head of the state."

I see that Mr. Burnell shares my distrust of this species of documents. He remarks: "Royal grants are by far the most important documents for historical purposes that exist in South India, such as they are; but they must be interpreted in the genealogical part with the greatest caution, especially those of the later dynasties, even if their authenticity be beyond suspicion. Unfortunately there is reason to believe that forgeries were common: for in the comparatively brief lists of crimes preserved in the Dharmaṣástra, the penalty of death is assigned for the forgeries of royal grants."—*Manu*, chap. IX. v. 232 (Haughton's translation. p. 324). *South Indian Palæography*, 1874, p. 76. See also Colebrooke's *Essays*, vol. II. pp. 236, 252–4, 264.

There is much of the air of manufacture even in those examples the genuineness of which we need not contest; but when we find formal repetition upon repetition, the same quotations of denunciatory texts recurring time after time, merging almost into the similitude of "a printed form of bequest," and we are told by impartial examiners of the present day that, in one case, the sign manual of the grantor proves to be in the writing of some centuries later than the forms of the letters of the text* to which he is asserted to have affixed his signature with his own hand (स्वहस्तो), we cannot divest ourselves of the suspicion that the dates may have been just as loosely manipulated as other portions of the documents themselves, especially when it is felt that the natural tendency, in such cases, would be to *ante-date*, with the view of giving meretricious age, authenticity and the semblance of perpetuity to the title.† It is true that this retention and continued use of the earlier form of character, for the body of the text, may merely imply the official recognition of a sort of black-letter style of writing in the local Patent Office, and that any intentional deception in the matter of the grant itself may have been foreign to the purpose of the engrossers; while, nevertheless, imposing or auspicious dates ‡ may have been *found*, or possibly old figures may have been copied mechanically with the standard phraseology from previous exemplars. I do not propose to enlarge upon the general question of the authenticity of these documents at the present moment, as they only contribute incidentally a side view to my leading subject; but it has become necessary to advert to the possible value of this species of evidence, as it has been occasionally put forward as a corrective of the true period of the Guptas, whose kingdom, in its western provinces, fell to the share of the Valabhís, who with their conterminous monarchies mainly supply the extant series of copper-plate grants, from whence these critical *test* dates are derived.

---

* This attestation or note at the end of the document is worthy of especial notice. The words are: "This is the own hand of Praṣánta-rága." . . . . "When the writing of this attestation is compared with the body of the grant, a very considerable difference is apparent. The general style of the whole, and the forms of many individual letters, present a much more modern appearance. Judging from the character of the writing alone by Prinsep's alphabets, it would seem to belong to a period at least three centuries later than the character and date of the grant itself."—Prof. J. Dowson, ***Journ. R. As. Soc.*** N. S. vol. I. p. 265.

† Prinsep had, from the first, felt a difficulty in reconciling the dates of the kings named in the Gujarát copper plates, remarking that "though there were six successions" (between the execution of the first and third Valabhí grants) "these must have been of less than the ordinary duration, for the minister who prepared the grant in Ṣrí Dharasena's reign was Skanda Bhaṭṭa; whereas the minister who prepared the present grant is named as Madana Híla, son of Skanda Bhaṭṭa. Thirty or forty years will, therefore, be the probable interval occupied by the reigns of all (these) princes." But it has been left for later decypherers to discover that the self-same Skanda Bhaṭṭa must have had a tenure of office lasting at least fifty-four years; and to confess that "our new grant shows that he held office under Guhasena also. If the second sign in the date of our grant is taken, with Prof. Bhánḍárkar, for 50, the grant is dated in 256, consequently Skanda Bhaṭṭa must have been at least seventy years in office. It seems very improbable that a man should last so long."—Dr. Bühler, ***Indian Antiquary***, June 1875, p. 174.

‡ I prefer, in this preliminary stage of the inquiry, to quote the unprejudiced and casually-pronounced opinions of others who have had to comment, directly or indirectly, on the measure of reliance that can be placed upon the "time tables" of the western copper plates. General Cunningham, without contesting the real data these documents might supply, expresses himself as follows in regard to Dr. Bhau Daji's Brief Survey of Indian Chronology (*Journ. Bom. Br. R. As. Soc.* vol. VIII. p. 236), in order "to note the curious error in what he calls a *correct* genealogical table of the Balabhi kings supported by dates from copper plates. In this genealogy I notice that Dhruvasena, who is dated in 310, is followed by ***six*** generations, all of which are made to pass away by 346, so that ***seven generations***, including Dhruvasena, or six without him, are born, marry, and die in thirty-six years, which allows exactly six years to each generation."—Cunningham's ***Arch. Report***, I. xxxiv.

In conclusion, I wish it to be distinctly understood that my objections do not extend to the good faith of royal grants or private endowments for religious purposes, when the texts, embodying the terms of the benefaction, are formally inscribed *on stone* in or near the building, cave, or other monument in whose cause the grant is made. In these cases there must have been a dedicatory formality and an abiding publicity which forbids all idea of deception, and hence this class of documents, as will be seen hereafter, may be welcomed as among the most trustworthy data within our reach.

b.—Written History.

We have now to collect the passages wherein chance mention of the Guptas is to be found in works compiled in India. Written history in its proper sense has rarely been attempted in that land, and the materials now available are confined to the pseudo-prophecies of the Puráṇas, the chance allusions to imperial changes which find a place in the local history of the valley of Kashmír, and the critical investigations of Albírúní, which are only raised above tradition by his elaborate exposition of dates and eras, which elucidate the rise and fall of so many dynastic rulers of Hind.

The Vishṇu-Puráṇa.

"In Magadha, a sovereign named Viṣwasphaṭika will establish other tribes: he will extirpate the Kshattriya (or martial) race, and elevate fishermen (Kaivarta), barbarians (Yadus and Pulindás), and Brahmans (and other castes) to power." "The nine Nágas will reign in Padmávatí, Kántipurí and Mathurá; and the Guptas of Magadha along the Ganges to Prayága." The Váyu-Puráṇa has another series analogous to that of the (Vishṇu-Puráṇa) text. "The nine Náka kings will possess the city Champávatí; and the seven Nágas (?), the pleasant city of Mathurá. Princes of the Gupta race will possess all these countries, the banks of the Ganges to Prayága, and Sáketa, and Mágadhá (the Magadhas)." Professor Wilson adds, "This account is the most explicit, and probably the most accurate of all. The Nákas were Rájas of Bhagulpúr; the Nágas of Mathurá*; and the intermediate countries along the Ganges were governed by the Guptas (or Rájas of the Vaiṣya caste).†

The Rája Tarangini.

The Rája Tarangini, which has more pretensions to systematic history than most works of its class, is a compilation from various authorities, arranged by Kalhaṇa Paṇḍit, in Ṣaka 1070=A.D. 1148.

Though taking an avowedly provincial view of the annals of Kashmír, it contributes incidentally several suggestive combinations with the larger margin of Indian

---

* *Journ. As. Soc. Beng.* 1865, pp. 116, 117. See also *Journ. As. Soc. Beng.* 1837, pp. 10, 16, 17; and Wilford, *Asiatic Researches*, vol. IX. pp. 114, 115. Wilford says, "then came a dynasty of nine kings, called the nine Nágás, or Nákás. These were an obscure tribe, called for that reason, *Gupta-vansas*: there were nine families of them, who ruled independent of each other, over various districts in Anuganjam, such as Padmávatí [Champávatí], Kántipurí, Magadha, Prayága, Saketa, and Benares."

† The Vishṇu-Puráṇa expressly says, "Gupta and Dása are best fitted for the names of Vaiṣyas and Ṣúdras." Wilson's *Vishṇu-Puráṇa*, edited by Dr. Fitzedward Hall, vol. IV. p. 218; Quarto edit., Oriental Translation Fund, book IV., cap. xxiv. p. 479.

imperial politics. It gives us, in the most complete form we are able to cite, a notice of the dominant Scythic brotherhood, which extended its sway to Mathurá on the one side, and to Bháwalpúr on the other, before the Gupta rule; regarding which, if the chronicle is wholly silent, it furnishes suggestive indications of the extinction of their power, in the accession of a Toramáṇa, should this joint king of the Kashmír Chronicle eventually prove to be identical with the monarch named in the inscriptions at Eran and Gwálior given in abstract, pp. 5–6 ante.

After enumerating the reigns of (1) Aṣoka, (2) Jaloka (s. f.), and (3) Dámodhara, the chronicle continues :—

"Dámodhara was succeeded by three princes who divided the country, and severally founded capital cities named after themselves. These princes were called Hushka, Jushka, and Kanishka,* of Turushka or Tatar extraction. . . . They are considered synchronous, but may possibly be all that are preserved of some series of Tatar princes who, it is very likely, at various periods, established themselves in Kashmír."†

"Ṣreshṭasena also called Pravarasena reigned 30 years and left his kingdom to his two sons Hiraṇya and Toramáṇa; the former holding the superior station of the *Sámrájya*, and the latter that of the *Yauvarájya*, or being respectively Emperor and Cæsar, a division of power of considerable antiquity amongst the Hindus. . . . . The latter having proceeded to strike coins (*dínárs*) in his own name, the elder brother (the *Sámrája*) took offence at the measure, and deposed the *Yuvarája* and kept him in close confinement. . . . . Toramáṇa died in captivity. The ruler of Ujain at that time was Ṣríman Harsha Vikramáditya, who after expelling the Mlechchhas and destroying the Ṣakas, had established his power and influence throughout India. In his train was a Brahman named Mátri-gupta to whom he was much attached; upon hearing of the vacant situation of the Kashmír throne, he recommended Mátṛi-gupta for election, who was accepted by the nobles as their king."

Albírúní.

A marked contrast will be detected between the vague utterances and confined purpose of the Hindu Pandit and the critical efforts at precision and comprehensive range of inquiry of the Muslim mathemetician,‡ trained in the old *nidus* of Aryanism,

---

* Abulfazl says "brothers." Gladwin's Translation, ii. 171.

General Cunningham considers that he has succeeded in identifying all the three capitals the sites of which are placed within the limits of the valley of Kashmír, *i.e.*,

"*Kanishka-pura* (Kanikhpur) hod. Kámpur, is 10 miles S. of Sirinagar, known as Kámpur Sarai.

"*Hushka-pura*, the Hu-se-kia-lo of Hiuen Thsang—the Ushkar of Albírúní—now surviving in the village of *Uskara*, 2 miles S.E. of Baráhmula.

"*Jushka-pura* is identified by the Brahmans with Zukru or Zukur, a considerable village 4 miles N. of the capital, the *Schecroh* of Troyer and Wilson."—*Ancient Geography of India*, London, 1871, p. 99.

† Prof. H. H. Wilson, "An Essay on the Hindu History of Kashmír," *Asiatic Researches*, vol. XV. p. 23. See also Troyer's Histoire des Rois du Kachmir, vol. II. p. 19. See also Hiouen-Thsang, Paris, 1858, vol. II. pp. 42, 106, &c.

‡ In the proper order of dates Albírúní precedes the author of the *Rája Tarangini*. I have placed him last in the present résumé as giving the fullest summary of dates and events, and as more directly associated with tradition, which singularly supports some of his most contested statements.

who came in the suite of the great Mahmúd of Ghazní,* not to participate in the devastating plunder of the conqueror, but to investigate the science and learning of the land, a task for which he was eminently fitted by his previous studies, and into which he entered with a philosophical earnestness altogether foreign to the rough associations around him. The result, confessedly imperfect, has been embodied in his Táríkh-i-Hind, from which the following epitome of the serial dates culminating in the Gupta era has been extracted.

" On emploie ordinairement les ères de Sri-Harcha, de Vikramáditya, de Saca, de Ballaba, et des Gouptas. . . L'ère de Vikramáditya est employée dans les provinces méridionales et occidentales de l'Inde. . . L'ère de Saca, nommée par les Indiens ' Saca-kála,' est postérieure à celle de Vikramáditya de 135 ans. Saca est le nom d'un prince qui a régné sur les contrées situées entre l'Indus et la mer. Sa résidence était placée

---

* Abú Rihán *Muhammad bin Ahmad* al Birúní *al Khwárizmí* was born about A.H. 360, A.D. 970–1. He was an astronomer, geometrician, historian, and logician, under which latter claim he obtained the sobriquet of "*Muhakkik*" or "the exact," on account of the rigorous precision of his deductions. Abú-l Fazl Baihakí, who lived about half a century after Al Bírúní, says, "*Bú Rihán* was beyond comparison superior to every man of his time in the art of composition, in scholar-like accomplishments, and in knowledge of geometry and philosophy. He had, moreover, a most rigid regard for truth;" and Rashídu-d dín, in referring to the great writer from whom he has borrowed so much, says, "The Master *Abú Rihán* al Bírúní excelled all his contemporaries in the sciences of philosophy, mathematics, and geometry. He entered the service of Mahmúd bin Subuktigín, and in the course of his service he spent a long time in Hindustan, and learned the language of the country. Several of the provinces of India were visited by him. He was on friendly terms with many of the great and noble of that country, and so acquired an intimate knowledge of their books of philosophy, religion, and belief. The best and most excellent of all their books upon the arts and sciences is one resembling the work of Shaikh Raís Abú 'Alí ibn Siná (*Avicenna*). It is called Bátakal, or in Arabic Bátajal; this book he translated into Arabic. From this work also he extracted a great deal which he made use of in his Kánún-i Mas'údi, a work upon mathematics and geometry, named after the Sultán Mas'úd. All that the sages of India have said about numbers, ages, and eras (*tawáríkh*), has been exactly given by *Abú Rihán* in his translation of the Bátakal. He was indebted to the Sultán of Khwárizm for the opportunity of visiting India, for he was appointed by him to accompany the embassies which he sent to Mahmúd of Ghazni. Al Farábí and Abú-l Khair joined one of these embassies, but the famous *Avicenna*, who was invited to accompany them, refused to go, being, as it is hinted, averse to enter into controversy with Abú Rihán, with whom he differed on many points of science, and whose logical powers he feared to encounter. On the invitation of Mahmúd, *Abú Rihán* entered into his service, an invitation which *Avicenna* declined. It was in the suite of Mahmúd and of his son Mas'úd that *Abú Rihán* travelled into India and he is reported to have staid forty years there. He died in A.H. 430, A.D. 1038–9. He wrote many works, and is said to have executed several translations from the Greek, and epitomised the Almagest of Ptolemy. His works are stated to have exceeded a camel-load, insomuch that it was supposed by devout Muhammadans that he received divine aid in his compositions. Those most spoken of are astronomical tables, a treatise on precious stones, one on Materia Medica, an introduction to astrology, a treatise on chronology, and the famous Kánúni-Mas'údí, an astronomical and geographical work frequently cited by Abú-l Fidá, especially in his tables of latitudes and longitudes." (Sir H. Elliot's Historians of India.) Sir H. Rawlinson, in a late number of the "Quarterly Review," observes: "*Abú Rihán* was the only early Arab writer who investigated the antiquities of the east in a true spirit of historical criticism," and he proceeds to give some examples of his knowledge of ancient technical chronology which are of the highest importance in establishing the early civilization of the Aryan race. Abú Ríhán declares that "the solar calendar of his native province, Khwárizm, was the most perfect scheme for measuring time with which he was acquainted, and it was maintained by the astronomers of that country, that both the solar and the lunar Zodiacs had originated with them; the divisions of the signs in their systems being far more regular than those adopted by the Greeks or Arabs. Another statement of *Abú Rihán's* asserts that the Khwárizmians dated originally from an epoch anterior by 980 years to the era of the Seleucidæ (equal to B.C. 1301), a date which agrees pretty accurately with the period assigned by our best scholars to the invention of the Jyotisha or Indian calendar." Though I am bound to add that the authenticity of the latter test is by no means unquestioned.

au centre de l'empire, dans la contrée nommée Aryavartha. Les Indiens le font naître dans une classe autre que celle des Sakya; quelques-uns prétendent qu'il était Soudra et originaire de la ville de Mansoura; il y en a même qui disent qu'il n'était pas de race indienne, et qu'il tirait son origine des régions occidentales. Les peuples eurent beaucoup à souffrir de son despotisme, jusqu'à ce qu'il leur vînt du secours de l'Orient. Vikramáditya marcha contre lui, mit son armée en déroute, et le tua sur le territoire de Korour, situé entre Moultan et le château de Louny. Cette époque devint célèbre, à cause de la joie que les peuples ressentirent de la mort de Saca, et on la choisit pour ère principalement chez les astronomes.

"Ballaba, qui a donné aussi son nom à une ère, était prince de la ville de Ballaba, au midi de Anhalouara, à environ trente *yodjanas* de distance. L'ère de Ballaba est postérieure à celle de Saca de 241 ans. Pour s'en servir, on pose l'ère de Saca, et l'on en ôte à la fois le cube de 6 (216) et le carré de 5 (25). Ce qui reste est l'ère de Ballaba. Il sera question de cette ère en son lieu. Quant au Goupta-kála (ère des Gouptas), on entend par le mot *goupta* des gens qui, dit-on, étaient méchants et puissants; et l'ère qui porte leur nom est l'époque de leur extermination. Apparemment, Ballaba suivit immédiatement les Gouptas; car l'ère des Gouptas commence aussi l'an 241 de l'ère de Saca. L'ère des astronomes commence l'an 587 de l'ère de Saca. C'est à cette ère qu'ont été rapportées les tables Kanda Khátaka, de Brahma goupta. Cet ouvrage porte chez nous le titre de *Arkand*. D'après cela, en s'en tenant à l'an 400 de l'ère de Yezderdjed, on se trouve sous l'année 1488 de l'ère de Sri-Harscha, l'an 1088 de l'ère de Vikramáditya, l'an 953 de l'ère de Saca, l'an 712 de l'ère de Ballaba et celle des Gouptas. . . .

"Déjà je me suis excusé sur l'imperfection de ce qui est dit ici, et j'ai averti que les résultats que je présente offraient quelque incertitude, vu les nombres qui excèdent celui de cent."*—*Journal Asiatique*, 4me. série, tom. iv. (1844).

M. Reinaud's translation here quoted was based upon a confessedly imperfect copy of the then unique but faulty Constantinople MS. of the Táríkh-i-Hind. It has frequently been called in question by those Indian commentators to whom its data came as a revelation from within. As I had to a certain extent accepted the value and importance of the information it conveyed, I sought the earliest opportunity of confirming or correcting its terms by the text of the new and more perfect manuscript of M. Schefer, which has been entrusted to Professor Sachau to aid his grand undertaking of a corpus of the works of Albírúní; the most important sections of which are about to be published under the joint auspices of the London Oriental Translation Fund and the German Text Society.

---

* Albírúní, in another part of his work, attributes many of the complications and obscurities imported into Indian texts, to the prevailing system of reducing everything into verse, for the sake of the obvious facility of learning by heart, so often to the entire detriment of the sense of the original; he adds, "J'ai reconnu, à mes dépens, l'inconvénient de cet usage."—Reinaud Mem. sur l'Inde, p. 334. Perhaps one of the most instructive expositions of the gradations of the process, under which the Indian art of memory was forced and matured, is to be found in Professor Haug's paper, presented to the Oriental Congress of London in 1874, from which I take the following extracts :—

"The *Veda* is the only sacred code that has been handed down to posterity solely by oral tradition, which has remained, even up to the present day, the only legitimate way of transmitting the ancient divine

M. Sachau has kindly sent me the subjoined list of variants from M. Reinaud's printed Arabic text,* but naturally prefers to await a final revision of the whole work, a larger acquaintance with Albírúní's style, and a consideration of the combined difficulty of this portion of the text, with the intricacies of Indian mathematical calculations before committing himself to any revised translation, such as I desired to have substituted for the French version now quoted."

c.—Tradition.

There remains, under this section of our inquiry, the single avowed dole of *tradition* the odd corners of the land have preserved intact, to support much that was previously

---

knowledge to the future generations of Brahmans. The wonderful state of correctness in which the ancient Vedic texts have reached our time may well excite our admiration, principally, if we bear in mind, that this is exclusively owing to oral teaching, and not to the use of MSS. Although the Brahmans are at present in the possession of MSS. of their sacred books, they are never used for instruction. The Brahman boy has to acquire all knowledge of sacred texts from the mouth of a competent and properly qualified teacher, but never from a MS. For according to Brahmanical notions, which are still current, that *Veda* only which is in the mouth of the Brahmans is the true *Veda ;* all knowledge of it that has been acquired from MSS. is no longer regarded as *Veda.* The use of them is only permitted in the way of assisting the memory, after the oral instruction has been completed. In former times the aid afforded by MSS. could be more readily dispensed with, since oral instruction took about thirty years, whereas it is now reduced to about half the time. In order to prevent tho e who had learnt the *Veda* from the mouth of the teacher from ever forgetting what they had committed to memory, it was made incumbent on them to communicate before their death their sacred knowledge to qualified persons. By such means it has been really brought about that the Vedic texts, that is, the *Mantras, Bráhmaṇas, Upanishads,* and *Vedáṅgas,* rest so firmly in the heads of the professional Vedics, the so-called *Bhaṭṭas,* that if all the MSS. should be collected and destroyed, they could be restored in the very words, even to each single letter and accent, from memory, as I was often assured by trustworthy Brahmans during my six years' stay in the *Mahratta* country. Hence one might justly attribute to texts obtained from a body of renowned Vedics, both in the *Saṅhitá* and *Pada* forms, at least the same degree of accuracy and authority which is ascribed to an edition prepared from a number of the best MSS. ; for all really good MSS. have not been copied by the *Bhaṭṭas* from others, but written from memory ; errors which may be detected in MSS. are generally not corrected by consulting other copies, but on the authority of the living tradition, viz., one of the *Bhaṭṭas,* since any Vedic text which is written is never looked upon with the same degree of confidence that is attached to oral tradition. * * * I once had occasion to converse with a large number of *Bhaṭṭas,* who are the legitimate preservers of Vedic texts : they told me, to my surprise, that the understanding of the texts they were in the habit of reciting was regarded as perfectly useless, and was consequently wholly disregarded. They learn the *Vedas* by heart for practical purposes, only to recite them at the sacrifices, or before private individuals of the Brahman caste who may wish to hear them for their welfare.

"Although this opinion seems to have prevailed with the professional reciters among the Brahmans, it was fortunately not shared by the more intelligent and inquisitive members of their caste, who looked upon the *Bhaṭṭas* as a kind of beasts of burden, carrying loads without knowing their nature.

*	Reinaud's text.	Schefer (MS. fol. 108–9).		Reinaud's text.	Schefer (MS. fol. 108–9).
p. 128, l. 5.	حمن	. . . . جمن	p. 129, l. 14.	والامتداد	. . . . والامتداد
p. 128, l. 6.	حمن	. . . . جمن	p. 129, l. 14.	زمن	. . . . زمر
p. 128, l. 11.	السابقة	. . . . السابعة	p. 130, l. 1.	فكان	. . . . فكانوا
p. 128, l. 16.	محله	. . . . بجلة	p. 130, l. 2.	وكان بلب	. . . . وبلب
p. 128, l. 20.	بنددريته	. . . . بندريں or بسر	p. 130, l. 8.	پنج	. . . . سح
p. 129, l. 2.	محزبا	. . . . محزبا	p. 130, l. 8.	٩٢٤	. . . . ٥٢٤
p. 129, l. 8.	شودد	. . . . شودرا	p. 130, l. 9.	١٩	. . . . ٢٥

irreconcileable in the statements of Albírúní. The tradition may be imperfect* as such old-world tales are liable to become, but there is an instructive confirmation of one obscure portion of the earlier history given by the Muhammadan inquirer, and a clear explanation of the causes of the local transfer of power, combined with an important reference to the conventional Imperial delegation of authority to a son, as well as an indication of the length of the reigns of two kings, to be found nowhere else; and to complete the tale, we trace in its details a fully reasonable accord with the more precise data furnished independently by inscriptions and coins.

"The bards relate that Váḷá Rájá, son of Váḷá Warsingji, reigned in Junágaḍh and Vanthalí. . . . Ráma Rájá was of the Váḷá race. It is said in Sauráshṭra that, previous to the rise of the kingdom of Junágaḍh-Vanthalí, Valabhinagar was the capital of Gujarát. The rise of Valabhi is thus told by the bards. 'The Gupta kings reigned between the Ganges and Jamná rivers. One of these kings sent his son Kumára-pál Gupta to conquer Sauráshṭra, and placed his viceroy Chakrapáni, son of Prándat, one of his Amírs, to reign as provincial governor in the city of Wámanasthalí (the modern Wanthali). Kumára-pál now returned to his father's kingdom. His father reigned twenty-three years after the conquest of Sauráshṭra and then died, and Kumára-pála ascended the throne. Kumára-pál Gupta reigned twenty years and then died, and was succeeded by Skanda Gupta, but this king was of weak intellect. His *senápati*, Bhaṭṭaraka, who was of the Gehlotí race, taking a strong army, came into Sauráshṭra, and made his rule firm there. Two years after this Skanda Gupta died. The *senápati* now assumed the title of King of Sauráshṭra, and, having placed a governor at Wámanasthalí, founded the city of Valabhinagar. At this time the Gupta race were dethroned by foreign invaders."†

---

* Professor Bháṇḍarkar has criticised certain items of this tradition in the following terms :—

"But the tradition itself, though interesting as giving the truth generally, cannot be considered to be true in the particulars. For, in the first place, it makes Chakrapáṇi the son of Prándat, who is certainly the Chakrapáḷita son of Parṇadatta of the Junágaḍh inscription (*Journ. Bom. Br. R. As. Soc.* vol. VII. pp. 122, 123, *supra* p. 4), viceroy of the father of Kumára Gupta, and grandfather of Skanda Gupta, while the inscription represents Parṇadatta as Skanda Gupta's viceroy, and Chakrapálita as governor of a certain town, appointed to that place by his own father. Again, Skanda Gupta is represented as a weak king in the tradition; while his inscriptions, magniloquent though they are, do show that he must have been a powerful monarch. Lastly, Bhaṭárka is mentioned as having assumed the title of King, while the Valabhí copper plates speak of him as Senápati, and represent Droṇa Sinha, his second son, to have first assumed that title. (*Journ. As. Soc. Bengal*, vol. IV., Mr. Wathen and an unpublished grant of Guhasena). The tradition, therefore, is not entitled to any reliance as regards the particulars. It simply gives us what was known before, that the Valabhís succeeded the Guptas."—*Indian Antiquary*, vol. III. (1874), p. 303.

† Major J. W. Watson, Legends of Junágaḍh, *Indian Antiquary*, (Nov. 1873,) vol. II., p. 312.

d.—Coins.

As fitly introductory to the Gupta gold coinage, I prefix a specimen prototype in the rare and little known coins of the Indo-Scythian king *Vásudeva*, whose name or title figures so prominently in the Mathurá inscriptions.

As the general range of the dates and localities of the Indo-Scythian inscriptions are calculated to throw important light upon the history of the period, and have a special bearing upon the distribution of the contemporary Bactrian and Indian Páli alphabets, I annex a résumé of these documents lately prepared for my publication on "Ancient Indian Weights."*

Indo-Scythian Inscriptions (in the Indo-Páli Alphabet).

At Mathurá.—Kanishka. *Mahárája Kanishka. Samvat* 9.

Huvishka. *Mahárája* Devaputra *Huvishka.* Hemanta, *S.* 39.
Mahárája Rájatirája Devaputra *Huvishka.* Grishma, *S.* 47.
Mahárája Huvishka. Hemanta, *S.* 48.

Vásudeva. *Mahárája Rájátirája* Devaputra *Vásu(deva).* Varsha, *S.* 44.
Mahárája Vásudeva. Grishma, *S.* 83.
Mahárája Rájatirája, Sháhi, *Vásudeva.* Hemanta, *S.* 87.
Rája Vásudeva. Varsha, *S.* 98.

Indo-Scythian Inscriptions (in the Bactrian-Páli Alphabet).

In other localities.—Bháwalpúr. *Maharaja Rajadiraja* Devaputra *Kanishka.* Samvat 11, on the 28th of the (Greek) month of Dæsius.†

Manikyála Tope. *Maharaja Kaneshka,* Gushana *vaṣa samvardhaka.* "Increaser of the dominion of the Gushans" (Kushans). *Samvat* 18.

Wardak Vase. *Maharaja rajatiraja Huveshka. Samvat* 51, 15th of Artemisius.

In addition to these Bactrian-Páli inscriptions, we have a record in the same alphabet, of a king called Moga (Moa?), on a copper plate from Taxila, wherein the *Satrap Liako Kusuluko* (Kozola?) speaks of the 78th year of the "great king, the great *Moga,*" on the 5th of the month of Panæmus; and an inscription from Takht-i-Bahi of King Gondophares, dated in his 26th year, with a corresponding entry of the month of Vaiṣákh, Samvat 103.‡

---

* "Ancient Indian Weights." The introductory chapter of Marsden's *Numismata Orientalia,* Trübner, 1874.

† The opening line of the Zeda inscription of Samvat 11, with the Indian month *of Ashádha,* can only be doubtfully associated with the two lines of small writing below it, in which the name of Kanishka is found. Cunningham's *Arch. Rep.* vol. V. p. 57.

‡ *Journ. R. As. Soc.* vol. VII. N. S. p. 377; Cunningham, *Arch. Rep.* vol. V. p. 59.

It would contribute very material aid towards the reconstruction of the general chronology of India if we could determine the era to which these inscription dates refer; it is clear that many of them are mere regnal dates, but as some of them run up as high as 98, this alone puts them beyond any such confined system of reckoning, and even outside the probable duration of the combined reigns of the three brothers, "Hushka, Jushka and Kaniskka" of the Kashmír chronicles.

The next point we have to consider is the nature of the inscriptions themselves, as a rule they are not royal manifestoes, but records of the piety, in gifts or endowments, of private individuals, and as such would primarily refer to some well established and generally recognised era. What was that era? Vikramáditya (57 B.C.) would place the documents too early; Ṣaka (79 A.D.*) too late. I have recently suggested the claims of the Seleucidan era (1st September, B.C. 312), allowing for the omission of the current figure for *hundreds*, which is now discovered to have been the practice adopted by the Baktrian Greeks.

As the simplest way of stating my views, under the latter aspect, I quote in its integrity a letter I lately addressed to "*The Academy*," which has already attracted much attention among Numismatists.†

"*Baktrian Coins and Indian Dates.*

"December 16, 1874.

"Those of your readers who concern themselves with the vexed question of Indian dates may be interested to learn that evidence of some importance, in that direction, has recently been obtained from the coins of the Baktrian Greeks. Since Bayer's premature attempt to interpret a Mint-monogram on a piece of Eukratides as 108,‡ Numismatists have not lost sight of the possible discrimination of dates as opposed to Mint-marks on the surfaces of these issues.§

"In 1858 I published, in my edition of Prinsep's *Essays on Indian Antiquities*, a notice of the detached letters **OΓ** as occurring on a coin of Eukratides (No. 3, p. 184, vol. II.) and **ΠΓ** as found on the money of Heliokles (No. 1, p. 182), which letters would severally represent the figures 73 and 83; but these numbers were apparently too low to afford any satisfactory elucidation in their application as dynastic dates.

"On a chance visit to the British Museum, a short time ago, Mr. Percy Gardner was so obliging as to show me all the latest acquisitions of Baktrian coins, and among them a specimen of Heliokles with the full triliteral date, after the manner of the Syrian mints, of **PΠΓ** or 183,‖ which, when tested by the Seleucidan era (311–183), brings his reign under the convenient date of B.C. 128, and authorises us to use the abbreviated figures, under the same terms, as **OΓ**=73 for 173 Sel.=138 B.C. for Eukratides, and

* Monday, 14th March, A.D. 78, Julian style.

† *Num. Chron.* 1875, p. 5; Agra Archæological Society, Annual Meeting, 1875.

‡ *Hist. Reg. Graecorum Baetriani.* St. Petersburg, 1738, p. 44.

§ H. H. Wilson, *Ariana Antiqua*, pp. 235, 238. General A. Cunningham, *Numismatic Chronicle*, vol. IX. N. S. p. 230.

‖ The *unique* coin of Plato lately purchased by the British Museum, which is closely associated in its obverse device with the money of Eukratides, is also dated, apparently, **PMZ** = 147 Sel., or 164 B.C. A full description, with an illustrative woodcut of this coin, has since been published by Mr. Vaux in the *Numismatic Chronicle* for 1875, p. 6.

the repeated ΠΓ=83 for 183 Sel.=128 for Heliokles, a date which is further supported by the appearance of the exceptionally combined *open* monogram ͞Α (ΠΑ), or 81 for 181=130 B.C. on his other pieces.

"In addition to the value of these data as fixing definitively, though within fairly anticipated limits, the epochs of these prominent Bactrian kings, the conventional use of the abbreviated definition introduces us at once to local customs, to which the Greeks so readily lent themselves, in their adoption of the method of reckoning by the Indian *Loka Kála*,* which simplified the expression of dates, as we do now, in the civilised year of our Lord, when we write 74 for 1874.

"The domestication of the Seleucidan era and its incorporation of Indian methods of calculation, leads on to the consideration of how long this exotic system of computation maintained its ground in Upper India, and how much influence it exerted upon the chronological records of succeeding dynasties. I have long been under the impression that this influence was more widespread and abiding than my fellow antiquarians have been ready to admit,† but I am now prepared to carry my inferences into newer channels, and to suggest, as a commencement, that the Indo-Scythian 'Kanishka' kings continued to use the Seleucidan era, even as they retained the minor sub-divisions of the Greek months which formed an essential part of its system; and under this view to propose that we should treat the entire range of dates of the 'Hushka, Jushka, and Kanishka' *family* of the Rája Tarangini,‡ which their inscriptions expand from ix. to xcviii.§, as pertaining to the fourth century of the Seleucidan era, an arrangement which will bring them into concert with our reckoning from 2 B.C. to 87 A.D. A scheme which would moreover provide for their full possession of power up to the *crucial* 'Ṣaka' date of 78–79 A.D., and allow for the continuance of certain local reigns as claimed by their subordinate public epigraphs.

"The Ṣaka era, with its Indian months as recorded in the Gupta inscriptions,‖ belongs to a new order of things, but this much may be added in conclusion, that the earliest epigraph of Chandra Gupta, the fifth of that race, dated in 82 Ṣaka, or 161 A.D., leaves a satisfactory margin for the heroic efforts and successful conquests of the second Vikramáditya (of Albírúní's legends) and his immediate successors."

I have no wish to press these suggestions for more than they are worth, or to precipitate a decision in their favour; but in addition to the incorporation of the Macedonian months in the Baktrian-Páli inscriptions, which clearly, in their higher numbers, follow an identical era with the Mathurá dedicatory epigraphs couched in the Indian Páli alphabet, there are many other evidences of the spread and continued use

* Albírúní, writing in India in 1031 A.D., tells us, "Le vulgaire, dans l'Inde, compte par siècles, et les siècles se placent l'un après l'autre. On appelle cela le Samvatsara du cent. Quand un cent est écoulé, on le laisse et l'on en commence un autre. On appelle cela Loka-kála, c'est-à-dire comput du peuple."—(Reinaud's Translation, *Fragments Arabes*, Paris, 1845.)

† *Journ. R. As. Soc.* vol. XII. p. 41; *Journ. As. Soc. Beng.* 1855, p. 565, and 1872, p. 175; Prinsep's *Essays*, vol. II. p. 86, *Journal Asiatique*, 1863, p. 388.

‡ P. 9, *supra*.

§ *Journ. R. As. Soc.* vol. V. N.S. p. 122. "Ancient Indian Weights," 1874, p. 46. General Cunningham's *Arch. Rep.* vol. III. p. 29. (Reproduced above p. 31.)

‖ Prinsep's *Essays*, vol. I. p. 231 *et seq.*

of the Seleucidan system of dating,* which would have tended to commend it to the less enlightened occupying Scythians who succeeded to outlying sections of the dominions of the Baktrian Greeks in India.

The Indo-Scythian inscriptions extant at Mathurá are not dated in *months*, but in the old triple seasons, *Gríshma*, *Varsha*, and *Hemanta*, like so many of the ancient writings in the caves of Western India,† and it is a suggestive fact, as bearing upon the omission or non-specification of the *hundreds*, that none of the Indo-Scythian inscriptions at Mathurá run into three figures: they approach closely but do not touch the *100*. And the first inscription, *in situ*, of *later* date, or 135 of some undefined *Samvat*, presents us with the earliest specimen among these records of a fully developed *Hindu* month (*Pushya*).‡

Since the publication of my letter of the 15th December 1874 Albírúní's account of the method of dating, in the *Lokakála*, by the omission of the *even* hundreds, has been opportunely confirmed by the discovery that the inhabitants of Kashmír follow this system of computation in all its integrity to the present day.§

I am well aware that Menander had so far departed from the traditional Indo-Greek abbreviated dates, as to confine himself on his coins to *regnal* years, inasmuch as I am able to cite from his extant money the dates Α 1, Β 2, Γ 3, Δ 4, Ε 5, Η 8; but this no more proves the general surrender of the consecutive eral system of dating than the Mathurá regnal dates establish the rule in the mixed instances above adverted to.

I can also quote a newly discovered Parthian era, commencing in 248 B.C.‖ which viewing its now ascertained employment in the Cuneiform documents of the

---

* Since proposing the above identifications, I have examined all the Bactrian coins within reach to seek for new examples of these abbreviated dates, but without success. I am able, however, to revert to two very curious contributions in the same line from the coins of Apollodotus, in the letters Ξ = 60 and ΞΕ = 65, published by me some years ago in Prinsep's *Essays*, vol. II. p. 188, and in the *Numismatic Chronicle*, vol. XIX. p. 22 (*Monograms*, p. 66). Under the system of the omission of the hundreds, these dates would correspond with B.C. 151 and 146—a period which would not be at all inappropriate for this king, who has been variously placed by Lassen at 160 B.C., by Wilson at 110 B.C., and by Cunningham at 165 B.C. One coincidence in connexion with these two Greek *letter*-dates is that they are in both cases either preceded or succeeded by the letters ΝΟ in a similar position at the foot of the device on the reverse, which may possibly stand for the *initial* letters of νόμος "usage, custom," &c., or some of its derivative forms, though this is avowedly a mere conjecture open to further investigation.

† Cunningham's *Arch. Report*, vol. p. III. 36; *Journ. R. As. Soc.* vol. V. p. 190, and the Cave Inscriptions, in the *Journ. Bom. Br. R. As. Soc.* See also *Hiuen Thsang*, vol II. p. 63; and Elliot's *Glossary*, vol. II. p. 47.

‡ This can by no possibility be made into a Vikramáditya date; it is more than a question if it can even refer to Ṣaka. Similarly, in regard to these dates, I am altogether undisturbed by the *Hindu* month in the Gondophares inscription, p. 30 *ante*; in short, whenever we pass *the hundred* we lose Seleucidan *months*, though it would be unwise to propound any absolute law on the subject with our present scanty materials.

§ This second inscription ends with the words *Ṣaka Kála* gatávdah 726—that is, "Ṣáka Kál years elapsed 726," equivalent to A.D. 804, which is therefore the date of the temple. This date also corresponds with the year 80 of the local cycle, which is the *Lok-kál* of Kashmír or cycle of 2,700 years, counted by centuries named after the 27 *nakshatras*, or lunar mansions. The reckoning, therefore, never goes beyond 100 years, and as each century begins in the 25th year of the Christian century, the 80th year of the local cycle is equivalent to the 4th year of the Christian century. General Cunningham, *Arch. Rep.* 1875, vol. V. p. 181. See also Dr. Bühler's *Report*, quoted in the *Athenæum* of the 20th Nov. 1875.

‖ *Assyrian Discoveries*, by George Smith. London, 1875, p. 389. From the time of the Parthian conquest it appears that the tablets were dated according to the Parthian style. There has always been a doubt as to the date of this revolt, and consequently of the Parthian monarchy, as the classical authorities have left no evidence as to the exact date of the rise of the Parthian power. I, however, obtained three Parthian tablets from Babylon; two of them contained double dates, one of which, being found perfect, supplied the required evidence, as it was

period, and obvious official preference may have secured a larger range of acceptance than could otherwise have been conjectured, and may thus, in its associate extension with the power of the race, arrogate some claim to rule and regulate our obscure Indo-Scythian dates. Testing the Mathurá figures by this system with its third century commencing in 48 B.C., we have another possible approximation towards the solution of this great enigma.

The comparative estimates by the four methods of computation, stand roughly as follows :—

Vikramáditya - - - -	B.C. 48 to A.D. 41.
Ṣaka - - - - -	A.D. 88 to A.D. 177.
Seleucidan - - - -	B.C. 2 to A.D. 87.
Parthian - - - -	B.C. 39 to A.D. 50.

Vásudeva.

No. I*.* Gold.

Trésor de Numismatique, Pl. LXXX. figs. 10, 11.†

Obverse.—Scythian figure, standing to the front, casting incense into the recognised small Mithraic altar. To the right a trident with pennons; to the left a standard with bosses and streamers.

Legend, around the device, portions of the full titles of PAO NANO PAO KOPANO.

Below the left arm वसु *Vasu*, in the exact form of character to be seen in his Mathurá inscriptions.‡ To the left, on the side of the altar, the letter घ.

Reverse.—The Indian Goddess Párvatí seated on an open chair or Greek throne, extending in right hand the classic regal fillet; Mithraic monogram to the left.

Legend, APΔOXPO,§ "half Ṣiva," *i.e.* Párvatí.

---

dated according to the Seleucidan era, and according also to the Parthian era, the 144th year of the Parthians being equal to the 208th year of the Seleucidæ, thus making the Parthian era to have commenced B.C. 248. This date is written : "Month . . . . 23rd day 144th year, which is called the 208th year, Arsaces, King of kings."

* The Roman numbers, further defined by a star (*), are used to denote such coins as do *not* find a place in the exclusively continuous *Gupta* series embodied in the Autotype Plate.

† Those who wish to see nearly exact counterparts of these types may consult the coins figured in plate XIV., *Ariana Antiqua*, figs. 19, 20. The latter seems even to have an imperfect rendering of the व *va* on the obverse, with सु *su* (formed like *pu*) on the reverse. For corresponding types see also *Journ. As. Soc. Beng.* vol. V. pl. 36, and Prinsep's *Essays*, pl. 4. General Cunningham, *Numismatic Chronicle*, vol. VI. O. S. pl. I. fig. 2.

‡ Plate XV. figs. 8, 16, 20. The *u* is not curved, but formed by a mere elongation of the down stroke of the स *s*, which constitutes the vowel, as in the case of the *u* on *Samudra Gupta's* coin No. 2 of the accompanying autotype plate VII. The omission of the *Deva* on the coins is of no more importance than the parallel rejection of the *Gupta*, where the king's name is written *downwards* in the confined space below the arm. Facsimiles of these inscriptions may also be consulted in Professor Dowson's paper on the Mathurá Inscriptions, *Journ. R. As. Soc.* vol. V. N.S. pl. IV. figs. 15, vi., &c. See also General Cunningham's remarks on Vásudeva, *ibid.* p. 195. General Cunningham proposes to amend Professor Wilson's tentative reading of *Baraono* on the two gold coins, *Ariana Antiqua*, pl. XIV. figs. 14, 18 (p. 378), into PAO NANO PAO BAZOΔHO KOPANO. The engraving of No. 14 certainly suggests an initial B in the name, and the AZ and O are sufficiently clear. We have only to angularise the succeeding O into Δ to complete the identification. These coins have a reverse of Ṣiva and the Bull.—*Arch. Rep.* vol. III. p. 42. Dr. Kern does not seem to have been aware of these identifications when he proposed, in 1873 (*Révue Critique*, 1874, p. 291), to associate the Mathurá Vásudeva with the Indo-Sassanian Pahlvi coin figured in Prinsep. pl. VII. fig. 6. *Journ. R. As. Soc.* vol. XII. pl. 3; *Ariana Antiqua*, pl. XVII. fig. 9.

§ APΔOXPO, Ard-Ugra. The latter is the name of Ṣiva. The preceding Khadphises Indo-Scythians had, for

GHAṬOT KACHA.

No. 1. Plate VII. Gold, weight 116 gr. Very rare. B. M.

[*The numbers prefixed to these coins correspond, without break or interruption, with the serial order of the numbers entered in the accompanying Autotype Plate. The extra or casual specimens are marked by Roman figures, with a further discriminating* ⁎.]

Obverse.—The King standing to the front, clothed very much after the manner of his Indo-Scythian predecessors.* The right hand casts incense into the conventional diminutive Mithraic altar, while the left holds the typical standard of the rayed Sun.

Marginal legend imperfect.

Under the arm का *ká.*
च *cha.*

Reverse.—*Párvatí* holding a lotus flower in the right hand, with a cornucopia of western design on the left arm. In the field, the Indo-Scythian monogram.†

Legend.—सर्वराजोच्छेत्त *Sarvarájochchhetta.* "The exterminator of all Rájas."

SAMUDRA GUPTA.

No. 2. Gold. B. M.

Obverse.—The king arrayed after the Indian fashion with a *dhotí* tightly bound round his loins, elaborate native head-dress, very large ear-rings, necklace, and armlets of chosen jewels, &c., in the act of shooting a tiger who faces him to the full front.

Legend, restored.—व्याघ्रपराक्रम *Vyághra parákrama.* "The tiger hero."

Reverse.—Párvatí with lotus flower and *Garuḍa* standard, standing upon a Dragon or some oriental type of marine monster.‡

Legend.—राजासमुद्रगुप्तः *Rájá Samudra Guptah.*

---

their reverse device, a figure leaning on a Bull (*Nandi*), regarding which Professor Wilson remarks: "The figure leaning on the Bull appears, by the breasts and protuberant hips, to be female; but it is not invariably so, and is sometimes, what it probably always should be, of an androgynous outline, the figure being that of Ṣiva and his spouse in their composite character of *Arrdha náriṣwara*, Ṣiva half-feminine."—*Ariana Antiqua*, p. 351.

* A very suggestive note on this question is to be found in Huen Thsang: "Après la mort du roi *Kia-ni-se-kia* (Kanishka), la race des *Ki-li-to* (Kritíyas) s'arrogea encore la royauté, chassa les religieux et abolit la loi du *Bouddha*," ii. 178. These kings are subsequently spoken of, in the text, as "cette race ignoble," p. 179. The commentator adds at p. 454, vol. iii. "*Kritíyas* en Chinois *Maï-te* (hommes) achetés." (See also, i. 248.) Hiouen-Thsang, Paris edit. Cf. *dúsa*, *kríta*, and *gupta* under the sense of "protected," in connexion with note †, p. 25 *ante*; and also Elliot's *Glossary*, vol. II. p. 281.

† This monogram has a curious similitude to the old Egyptian symbol for the Bee which, as M. Oppert has shown, was the sign royal in the Hieratic, the prototype of *ṣarru*, שׂר of the inscription of Nebuchadnezzar at Borsippa. *Journal Asiatique*, 1857, p. 143. See also *Journ. R. As. Soc.* vol. I. N.S. pp. 224, 482.

‡ A similar aquatic monster may be seen below the feet of an ancient statue at Nongarh (6 miles S.S.E. of Jayanagar). "The statue is made of the red-spotted sandstone of the Sikri quarries near Mathurá."—Cunningham, *Arch. Report*, vol. III. p. 161.

GUPTA AND SURASHTRAN COINS. PLATE VII.

No. 3. Gold. B. M.

Reverse.—King appareled in close-fitting native costume, with the Indian *dhotí*, armlets, bangles, &c., reserving unexhausted arrows for a retreating lion.

Legend.—म हराजाधिराज श्री

Ma há rájádhirája Sri.

Reverse.—The Goddess *Párvatí* seated on a lion, with fillet, lotus flower, and the usual Scythian monogram.

Legend.—श्री सिङ्हविक्रम *Srí Siñha Vikrama.* "The Lion-hero."

No. 4. Gold. B. M.

Obverse.—A horse decked for the Asvamedha sacrifice.

Legend (restored).—नवजमधः राजधिराज पृथिवी जियत्य

Navajamadhah Rájadhirája Prithiví jiyatya.

Below the horse से *se.*

Reverse.—A rayed female figure (*Párvatí* ?) holding a *chaurí* or Yák's tail, ordinarily used as a fly-whisk in the train of royalty.

Legend.—अश्वमेध पराक्रमः *Asvamedha parákramah.* "The hero of the Asvamedha."

A recent contributor to the *Journal Asiatique*, has taken me to task for discovering any traces of Scythism in the Indian *Asvamedha* rite, and after other curious criticisms, intrenches himself in the direct assertion that "le cheval des sculptures est le cheval des légendes et du culte bráhmanique."*

To my apprehension the Indian Aryans have put on record, in their own Vedas, a much more mundane account of their notions of the Asvamedha sacrifice, which seems to have been little more to them than a religious feast, with all the sensual accessories of fat horse flesh, baked meats, aromas of cooking, with essays on the merits of skilful carving: descending at last into gross questions of skewers, and the stray remnants that adhere to the hands of the operators.†

Far different is the impression conveyed by what we can gather from the local conceptions of the *Asvamedha*; here the ideal seems to have been eminently Scythic, both in its inception and application; it was in effect a martial challenge which consisted in letting the *victim*, who was to crown the imperial triumph at the year's end, go free

---

* *Journ. Asiatique*, 1875, p. 126. Essai sur la légende du Buddha, par M. E. Senart. The passage to which the author takes exception is to be found in my article in the *Journ. As. Soc. Beng.* 1865, p. 57; it has been reproduced in my *Indian Weights*, p. 62.

† *Rig Veda*, ii. iii. *súktas*, vi. vii., Wilson's *Translation*, vol. II. p. 112, and note *a*, p. 121, also Preface, p. xii.—xv.; Colebrooke's *Essays*, Prof. Cowell's edit., vol. I. pp. 50, 55, 56; *Asiatic Researches*, vol. III. p. 429; Max Müller's *Anc. Sanskrit Literature*, pp. 37, 46, 357, 533.

to wander at will over the face of the earth, its sponsor being bound to follow its hoofs, and to conquer or conciliate the occupiers of all "fresh fields and pastures new" his equine pioneer chose to fancy.* Surely such a prototype shadows forth more of the conditions of the life of desert communities of the horseman class, than of the surroundings of Aryan cattle-drivers, entangled in the narrow passes of the Himálaya, or dubiously skirting the southern base of the outer range towards the plains of India in straggling companies. The original germ and development of the contrasted heroic aspect almost declares itself in associations belonging to Nomadic tribes, among whom a steed captured in hostile forays, had so frequently to be traced from camp to camp and surrendered or fought for at last.

Of course the ultimate decision of this and many other international questions, must depend upon how much of the Turánian element we are to recognize as having existed amid the occupying prehistoric races of India; a subject far too large to be discussed with advantage in this place.

Kumára Gupta.

No. 5. Gold. B. M.

Obverse.—King standing to the left, the right hand is extended as if casting incense into the small Mithraic altar, of which traces can still be recognised. The king is girt the *Khaṇḍá* or Indian straight broad-sword. To the right the *Garuḍa* standard, to the with left the initial letters of the name of Kumára, कु *Ku.*

Legend.—गमवजित्य सुचरत कुमर

Reverse.—*Párvatí* seated on a raised throne, below which are expanded the leaves of the lotus. In the right hand, the Grecian fillet, with the recognized Scythian monogram above the shoulder.

Legend.—श्री कुमार गुप्त
Ṣrí Kumára Gupta.

Mahendra Gupta.

No. II*. Gold, weight 125·5 grains. Marsden,† No. MLIX. B. M.

Obverse.—King on horseback, to the right, with nimbus, seemingly bare-headed, with long flowing curls.

Legend.—महेन्द्र गुप्त
Mahendra Gupta.

---

* Wheeler's *Mahábhárata*, vol. I. p. 377. Prof. Goldstücker has pointed out (in the *Westminster Review* for April 1868) that the passages here quoted belong to the more recent "Jaiminiya Aṣvamedha." See also Wheeler's *Rámáyaṇa*, pp. 10, &c.

† See also Prinsep's *Essays*, pl. XXIII. fig. 30, vol. I. p. 387. See also variants, pl. XXX. figs. 3, 4, 5, *ibid.* and *Ariana Antiqua*, pl. XVIII. figs. 16, 17. No. 16, has देवजमत after the *Gupta.*

Reverse.—*Párvatí*, seated on an Indian *Moṛhá*, feeding a peacock.

Legend.—अजित महेन्द्र *Ajita Mahendra.* "The unconquered king."

No. III*. Gold, weight 119 grains. B.M. (?)

This is another coin of some interest, which I doubtfully attribute to Mahendra Gupta. It may be described as follows:

Obverse.—Standing figure with spear and flowing pennons, trident, and small Mithraic altar. Outside the spear the letters म *Ma.* हे *he* On the inside प *p.*

Reverse.—Párvatí seated, with traces of the Greek ΑΡΔΟΧΡΟ.

Nára Gupta.

No. IV*. Gold. *Ariana Antiqua*, Pl. XVIII. fig. 22.*

Obverse.—King standing to the front, with Garuḍa standard on the right, and bow in the left hand. Device similar to the designs of Samudra and Chandra Gupta's coins (*Ariana Antiqua*, XVIII. 7, 8, 9, 4, Marsden, No. ML. and MLVII.), but materially deteriorated in the artistic execution.

Legend, below the left arm.—ना *Ná.*

र *ra.*

At the foot गु *Gu.* Marginal legend?

Reverse.—The usual type of Párvatí seated on lotus leaves to the front (disclosing greatly debased art.)

Legend, restored from other specimens.†—बालादित्य *Báláditya.*

THE SÁH KINGS OF SURÁSHTRA.

The history of the Sáh kings of Suráshtra is so interwoven with the progress and final supremacy of the Guptas, that we must devote full space to the consideration of their independent rise and advance to power—as well in regard to the monumental palæographic records, in which the western coast is so rich, as in respect to the Numismatic remains of the dynasty which equally preserve marked local characteristics, and disclose instructive indications of a source and derivation other than Indian.

The inscriptions claim priority in the order of arrangement. These commence with a group of representative mural tablets which repeat the name of the presumed founder of the Sáh family, *Nahapána.* I have transcribed the first of these records in full, as furnishing a specimen of the ordinary style and motive of this class of dedicatory

---

* I formerly had doubts about the due attribution of these coins; but now that I have examined several specimens, I concur in General Cunningham's assignment.—*Bhilsa Topes*, p. 145. The marginal legend is there quoted as *Para-madhi Raja.*

† There are three specimens in the British Museum.

epigraphs, reducing the subsequent quotations to the bare enumeration of royal names or other material data. For the preliminary materials I am indebted to a paper by Professor Bandarkar, which was presented to the London Oriental Congress of 1874, and which is now in course of correction for the volume embodying their Proceedings.

I.—*Inscription of Nahapána in the Násik Caves.*

(No. 17 of Mr. West's facsimiles.*)

"To the Perfect One! This cave and these small tanks were caused to be constructed on the mounts Triraşmi in Govardhana, by the benevolent Ushavadáta, the son-in-law of King Kshaharáta Satrap Nahapáṇa,† son of Dínika, who gave three hundred thousand cows, presented gold, and constructed flights of steps on the river Bárnásáyá, gave sixteen villages to gods and Brahmans, fed a hundred thousand Brahmans every year, provided (the means of marrying) eight wives for Brahmans at Prabhásu ‡ the holy place, constructed quadrangles, houses, and halting-places at Bharukachchha, Daşapura, Govardhana and Şorparaga; made gardens, tanks, and wells; charitably enabled men to cross Ibá, Parádá, Damaná, Tapí, Karabená, and Dáhunuká by placing boats on them; constructed Dharmaşálas, and endowed places for the distribution of water, and gave capital worth a thousand for thirty-two *Náḍhigeras* for the Charanas and Parishads in Pínditakávaḍa, Govardhana, Suvarṇamukha, Şorparaga, Rámatirtha, and in the village of Nánagola. By the command of the Lord I went in the rainy season to Málaya to release Hirudha the Uttamabhadra. The Málayas fled away at the sound (of our war music), and were all made subjects of the Khatriyas the Uttamabhadras. Thence I went to Poksharaṇi, and there performed ablutions, and gave three thousand cows and a village."

Remarks.

"The first part of this inscription is in Sanskrit. The latter part contains a mixture of Sanskrit and Prákrit."

II.—*Translation of Inscription No.* 16 *of Mr. West's facsimiles, Lines* 1, 1.

"To the Perfect One! This apartment is the benefaction of Dakhamitrá, the daughter of King Kshaharáta Satrap Nahapána and wife of Ushavadáta, son of Dínika."

Continuation of Translation of No. 16, *Lines* 3–6.

"To the Perfect One! In the year 42, in the month of Vaişákha, the son of Dínika, and son-in-law of King Kshaharáta Satrap Nahapána, gave three thousand 3,000 to the priesthood from the four quarters residing in this cave, as capital for [providing] garments and kuşana. Out of this sum on 1,000 the interest is three-quarters of a

---

* *Journ. Bom. Br. R. As. Soc.* vol. VII. p. 42.

† "I think upon the whole this way of interpreting the expression is more in consonance with known facts than making Nahapáṇa satrap of a king named Kshaharáta."

‡ "Prabhásu, as Dr. Stevenson says, is a place near Pattan Somnath. Bharukachchha is now known to be Broach. Daşapura must be some place in Gujarát or in the Maraṭhí country bordering on Gujarát. It occurs in Inscription No. 1 of Mr. West's series. Şorparaga is Supara near Bassein. The Damaná and Dáhanuká must be rivers flowing into the sea at those places in the Tanna District. Tapi is well known. The others I am not able to identify. Rámatírtha is, I am told, a small place near Supara. Ushavadáta's charities do not seem to have gone further to the north than Gujarát, or further to the south than the northern district of the Puṇa zillah. The expedition to the south described in the inscription was occasional, the object being to assist a friendly race of Kshatriyas." (Conf. *Ind. Ant.* vol. III. pp. 100, 214, 322; vol. IV. p. 282; Yule's *Marco Polo*, vol. II. p. 353. —Damanâ is doubtless the Damaná Gánga, and Dáhanuká the river of Dehnu to the south of it.—J. B.)

hundred [*i.e.* 75] Kárshápaṇas. These Kárshápaṇas bearing interest are not to be repaid. Out of this [sum] two thousand, which is the capital bearing an interest of one hundred Kárshápaṇas is for garments. A capital of 8,000 Náḍigeras was given in Kapuráhára and the village of Chikhalapádra."

Remarks.

"From this and No. 18 of the same series it appears clear that Ushavadáta left three thousand Kárshápaṇas; two deposited with one body of weavers, bearing an interest of 100 Paḍikas or Kárshápaṇas, from which chívarikas or garments were to be provided, and one with another body of weavers, bearing an interest of 75 Paḍikas, out of which kuṣana was to be given. Lines 4 and 5 of this and 3 of No. 18 are thus consistent with each other.

We see from the above that the cave was dedicated to the use of mendicants in the year 42, and from No. 28 that Ushavadáta bestowed other charities in the years 41 and 40. What era these are to be referred to will be considered in the remarks."

III.—*Translation of No.* 14 *of Mr. West's series.*

1. Son-in-law of Satrap Nahapána ——— t.
2. Usual deeds of Ushavadáta the Ṣaka.*
3. In Chechika, city of Dáhanuká, Kekápura.
4. In each village, in Ujjayini,† Sikhá . . [eleven lines more].

---

* "This has been usually taken to be Ṣaka, as if there were no doubt about it, but it is not quite safe to do so in the mutilated state of the inscription.

† "This is not without doubt."

I quote Prof. Bandarkar's final summing up and the resulting conclusions, with a view of showing the difficulties which still environ the question of the Sáh dates. "In the first place we have the inscriptions of Ushavadáta, which mention a king of the name of Kshaharáta Nahapáṇa, who is also called Kshatrapa or Satrap. Kshaharáta looks very much like Khagárata, and the characters in these inscriptions occupy a middling position between those of No. 6 and No. 26. Kshaharáta Nahapáṇa therefore may well have been the founder of the dynasty that displaced the Ṣátaváhanas some time after Kṛishnarája. And coins of a race of kings calling themselves *Kings* and *Kshatrapas* or *Satraps* have been found in Gujarát and elsewhere, and amongst them one of Nahapáṇa himself. There are two inscriptions also in Gujarát, which mention some of these kings. Very likely therefore it was this dynasty that Gautamíputra displaced."

"These inferences would be rendered highly probable if what is known or believed with regard to the dates of these kings were made to harmonize with the similar information we have with regard to the dates of Kṛishnarája and Gautamíputra. The coins of the Satrap or Sáh dynasty bear dates, but it is not known to what era they are to be referred. For the dates of the Ṣátaváhana kings the only authorities are the Puráṇas. Though there is no very satisfactory agreement amongst them as to the names and number of the individuals composing the dynasty, the period of its total duration, given by all, nearly corresponds. Starting from the date of Chandragupta Maurya, which is generally believed to be 315 B.C., and deducting 294, the number (Wilson's *Vishṇu Puráṇa*, chap. XXIV. book IV.) of years for which the intervening dynasties reigned, we have 21 B.C. as the date of the foundation of the Ândhrabhṛitya dynasty; and going on further in the same way we have 2 A.D. for Kṛishnarája's accession; and 319 A.D. for that of Gautamíputra. Now if we take Nahapáṇa to be the founder of the Ṣaka era, and refer all the Sáh dates to that era, the information got from the caves and the inferences based on it are perfectly consistent with these dates. Nahapáṇa's career of conquest must have ended in A.D. 78, when the era began; and this agrees with what we have stated above that the Ṣátaváhanas were deprived of the province of Násik some time after Kṛishnarája. In the same manner, if the statement that Gautamíputra exterminated the race of Khagárata is true, the last of the Sáh dates must come up near enough to 340 A.D., that being the date of Gautamíputra's death, or, the end of his reign. This last date, if the era is Ṣaka, is, according to Mr. Fergusson (*Journ. R. As. Soc.*, vol. IV., N.S.), 376, in which case it would not agree with the other; but there is a mistake here. Mr. Justice Newton, whom he follows, assigns 235

Other inscriptions of Nahapáṇa at Kárlen and Junir :—

At Kárlen—
"Peace! By Ushabhadáta, the son of Dínika, the son-in-law of Rája Kshaháráta Kshatrapa Nahapáṇa."

At Junir—
"[Constructed by] Ayama, the minister of ——— Mahákshatrapa Svámí Nahapána."

The next palæographic reference to the Sáh kings is an elaborate but imperfectly-preserved recapitulation of the consecutive repairs of the dam or bridge which retained the waters of the Paleṣani river. This document Mr. Burgess will give in full both in text and translation hereafter. I have merely to anticipate it by a brief quotation, with a view to secure the continuity of my serial evidence: which in this instance, however, is only important as confirmatory of a foregone date, already suggested by the coins. The greatest interest, to us Europeans, in this long detail of the fate and fortunes of the embankment, consists in the reference to its previous restoration by the agents of Chandra Gupta *Máurya*, our classical Sandrokoptos, whose name appears on this single occasion in the whole range of Indian epigraphy. This public

---

A.D. (*Journ. Bom. Br. R. As. Soc.*, vol. IX. p. 18) to Svámi Rudra Sáh, the 25th in his list, on the supposition that the era is Vikrama's, whence it appears that he reads the figure on the coin of that monarch as 291. But if we turn to the copies of the figures given by him at page 28, vol. VII. *Journ. Bom. Br. R. As. Soc.*, we shall find that there must be some mistake as to the right-hand stroke on the mark for a hundred in the last of the three dates given under Svámi Rudra Sáh. For the first of these is 224, the middle figure being the mark for 20, since the circle has one diameter (see the numerals in the Násik Cave Inscriptions, and my paper, p. 67, vol. X., *Journ. Bom. Br. R. As. Soc.*); the second 192, the mark for a hundred having no side stroke. It is impossible then that the king, whose date is 192, should be reigning in 291. It is extremely probable that this king, No. 18 in Mr. Newton's first list (*Journ. Bom. Br. R. As. Soc.* vol. VII.), or No. 25 in his second (vol. IX.), whose date appears thus to have been misread, is the same person as No. 12 in the former or No. 19 in the latter. For the name of the individual and that of the father is the same in both cases. There is only the prefix *svámi*, "lord," in the former, which makes no difference, and the date 192 in the one case and 197 in the other. The final date of the Sáhs, therefore, is that of No. 17 (p. 28, vol. VII. *Bom. Br. R. As. Soc.*), which is 250, for the figure resembling the letter स *sa* stands really for 50, as I have shown in my paper (p. 72, vol. X. *Bom. Br. R. As. Soc.*) on the Valabhí dates. This date in the era of the Ṣaka kings is 328. About that time then, *i.e.* about nine years after his accession, the Sáhs must have been conquered by Gautamíputra. If, on the contrary, we should take the era to be Vikrama's, Nahapáṇa's date would be about 60 B.C., *i.e.* he reigned 62 years before Kṛishnarája; which, it will be seen, does not agree with the evidence of the caves, the Ṣátaváhana dynasty having been in possession of Násik in A.D. 2. In the same manner, the final date, which, according to Mr. Newton and Mr. Fergusson, is 235 A.D. on the hypothesis that the era is Vikrama's but which really should be 196 A.D. in conformity with my reading of the dates, is so remote from Gautamíputra's, 319 A.D., that he can in no sense be said to have exterminated the "race of Khagáráta." The Vikrama era will, therefore, not do. The objection brought by Mr. Fergusson against the Ṣaka is that if the dates were referred to it, the Sáhs would overlap the Guptas by a considerable period. But this period has now been reduced to about ten years, the Guptas being supposed to have come into power in 319 A.D. And a difference of ten years in the uncertain condition of our chronology is almost nothing. Besides, there is nothing to show that the Guptas obtained possession of the countries over which the Sáhs ruled in 319, or immediately after. Thus the date 319–340 A.D. for Gautamíputra, and the Ṣaka era for the Sáh dates, alone appear to be consistent with what we find in the cave inscriptions about that monarch and the Ṣátaváhana dynasty. The dates in Ushavadáta's inscriptions, therefore, viz., 42, 41, and 40, would be 120, 119, and 118 A.D. respectively."

recognition of his dominion amid the memorial records of the western coast is a new testimony to his influence in those quarters, of which we had already external evidence in his traditional treaties with Seleucus.* So also is there an importance in the distinct mention of his grandson Aṣoka, whose *proper name* is elsewhere subdued under the *title* of *Devanampiya Piyadasi* throughout the entire series of religious manifestoes he set up in so many chance places over the broad continent of India: one transcript of which appears on the eastern face of this very rock, which, as has been seen, Nature had constituted as the ready-prepared proclamation stone of successive generations.

The Sáh or Rudra Dáma Inscription, Junágaṛ.

"To the Perfect one! This Sudarṣana lake, being from Garanagar (Girinagara) . . to the foot . . constructed in its length, breadth, and height of unbroken masonry," &c.

"This work gave way in the 72nd year . . of *Rája Mahákshatrapa* Rudra Dáma, whose name is oft repeated by the great, the grandson of *Mahákshatrapa* Chastana of well accepted (propitious) name. Afterwards (?) by the Maurya Rájá Chandragupta . . his (governor ?) Ṣyena Pushpagupta of Suráshṭra (?) (*rástiriya* only visible) caused to be made . . and by the celebrated Yavana Rájá of Aṣoka Maurya named Tushaspa having been repaired."

[The text then goes on to proclaim the glories of the king, the enemies he overcame, &c., and continues] "who himself acquired the title of Mahákshatrapa, who won, &c., . . . by this Mahákshatrapa Rudra Dáma," and concludes with his own account of his special work in the ultimate repair of the dam.†

The last inscription in this list, which I have to notice, is the brief record on the Jasdan pillar, which proves to be purely genealogical—and would be otherwise immaterial were it not for its mention of the ancestral "Chashtana," whose name figures in such prominence in the initial order of the coin series.

Inscription at Jasdan in the North of Káṭhiáwáṛ piánt.

"In the year 127 Bhádrapada (*month*) dark-half, 7th (*day*) of the moon, this Satra (*tank*) of Rájá Mahákshatrapa Bhadramukha Swámí Rudra Sena, the great-grandson of the son of Rájá Mahákshatrapa Swámí Chashṭana; the grandson of the son of Rájá Ksh(*atrapa*) Swámí Jayadáman, the grandson of Rájá Mahákshatrapa . . . . . . Rudra Dámá, (*son of*) Rájá Mahákshatrapa Bhadra-Mukha Swámí Rudra. Of the son of Supra Náthaka of Mánasagotra, the grandson of Khara, with brothers . . . . . ."‡

---

* Justin, book XV. cap. 4; Diodorus, book XIX. cap. 24, book XX. cap. 12; Strabo, book II. c. 1, § 9, and book XV. cap. 1, §§ 10, 36, 53, cap. 2, § 9; Pliny, vi. 17; Arrian, Ind., cap. v. Plutarch in Demetrius.

† Dr. Bhau Dáji, *Journ. Bom. Br. R. As. Soc.* vol. VII. p. 120.

‡ *Ibid.* vol. VIII. p. 235.

COINS OF THE SÁH KINGS.

Thus much for the inscription data, we must now fill in the canvas with the more expanded revelations of the coins. As I have not been able in the brief period which has chanced to intervene between the commencement of the present chapter and its call for the press, to re-examine the conflicting bearings of the evidence affecting the domination of the Sáhs, I content myself with reproducing the latest inferences of Mr. Newton, who from the first has exclusively devoted himself to the study of the Numismatic remains of this group of kings, and achieved a veritable specialité in this department. Though in making these quotations I must guard myself by saying that I by no means invariably concur in the interpretations or deductions of the author.

Mr. Newton, in one of his latest papers, has had to review, and in some cases to revise my own early contributions to this subject,* I am the more anxious therefore that he should be heard in his own words. He says in all frankness, "The arrangement (of the dates) having been thus discussed and fixed, there remains the determination of the era to which the dates on the Sáh coinage are to be referred. Professor Wilson, in his *Ariana Antiqua*, was able only to state the priority of the Sáhs to the Guptas, but he could not restrict the rule of the latter within smaller limits than 'from the second or third to the seventh century of our era.' Mr. Thomas in his article published in 1848, in the XII. vol. of the *Journ. R. As. Soc.* (to which I have been, in many respects, much indebted), being compelled by the supposition, then entertained, that the first numerals on all the Sáh coins represented 300, was led to reject eras, which would otherwise doubtless have appeared preferable, and to select that of Ṣrí Harsha, dating 457 B.C., made known to us by Albírúní, as the one which seemed best to meet the apparent requirements of the case. . . . . Mr. Thomas thus placed the Sáh dynasty between about 170 and 50 B.C., and Mr. Prinsep placed the last member of the series in 153 B.C. The initial numerals being now read as 100 and 200, the era of Vikramáditya at once suggests itself as the one to be preferred."†

Proceeding upon these principles Mr. Newton subsequently framed the subjoined list of the Sáh kings, in which he was able to insert the names of six newly identified monarchs.

1. Nahapána, B.C. 60 or 70.
2. The unknown King whose coin is given as figure 10 of the plate (p. 4, *Journ. Bom. Br. R. As. Soc.* vol. IX.)
3. (Syamo?) tika.
4. Chashṭana, son of Syamotika, B.C. 10 or 20.
5. Jaya Dámá, son of Chastana.
6. Jiva Dámá, son of (Dámá ?) Ṣri, A.D. 38.
7. Rudra Dámá, son of Jaya Dámá.
8. Rudra Sinha, son of Rudra Dámá, A.D. 45–47.
9. Rudra Sáh, son of Rudra Sinha.

---

* *Journ. R. As. Soc.* vol. XII., 1848, p. 32.
† *Journ. Bom. Br. R. As. Soc.* 1862, p. 30.

10. Ṣri Sáh, son of Rudra Sáh.
11. Sangha Dámá, son of Rudra Sáh.
12. Dámá Sáh, son of Rudra Sinha.
13. Yaṣa Dámá, son of Dámá Sáh.
14. Damajata Ṣri, son of Rudra Sáh, A.D. 97.
15. Vira Dámá, son of Dámá Sáh.
16. Iṣvara Datta.
17. Vijaya Sáh, son of Dámá Sáh, A.D. 115.
18. Dámajata Ṣrí, son of Dámá Sáh.
19. Rudra Sáh, son of Rudra Dámá, A.D. 131, 141.
20. Viṣva Sinha, son of Rudra Sáh, A.D. 143.
21. Atrí Dámá, son of Rudra Sáh, A.D. 153, 157.
22. Viṣva Sáh, son of Atrí Dámá, A.D. 160, 168.
23. Rudra Sinha, son of Svámí Jiva Dámá, A.D. 173 or 213.
24. Yaṣá Dámá, son of Rudra Sáh.
25. Svámí Rudra Sáh, son of Svámí Rudra Dámá, A.D. 223, 235.
26. Svámí Rudra Sáh, son of Svámí Satya Sáh.*

I shall reserve any comments or observations upon the still vexed subject of the era to which these coin-dates belong, till I come to compare the entire range of recorded time-marks supplied by the more recent archæological discoveries; but I may remark, parenthetically, that the A.D. 235 of the twenty-fifth king in the above list, comes into conflict with the age I am disposed to assign to the Guptas under the Ṣaka test.

As to the correction in regard to the increase of the values of the sign for hundreds by the addition of side strokes, I long ago arrived at a similar conclusion, having, indeed, myself first suggested the probability of such a method of augmentation which the materials available in 1848 did not suffice definitively to establish.†

* "The inscriptions do not tell us that Nahapána had a son, and I have not inserted the name of his son-in-law as he is not shown to have succeeded to the sovereignty. For the same reason I have omitted the name of Chashtana's father. It is given on the coin, but we do not know that he reigned. Though no coin intermediate between Nahapána and Chastana has yet been found, I am sure that several years intervened between them. The difference of type and execution observable between their coins is certainly greater than that which exists between that of the former and the coins of the Indo-Bactrians. I have, therefore, adopted a longer interval, and hope that coins of at least two or three kings between Nahapána and Chastana may yet be found. It does not appear that Nahapána's or Chastana's coin bore a date, and it is almost certain that none was marked on the copper coin of Jaya Dámá. If the interval which I have placed between Nahapána and Chastana and the reigns which I have assigned to Chastana and Jaya Dámá be considered too long, I should be led to shorten these rather by assigning to them and all the subsequent sovereigns of the Sáh series earlier dates than by bringing down Nahapána to a time further removed from the Indo-Bactrians.

"I see no reason to modify in any respect the results arrived at in my paper of 1862 as to the succession of the Guptas to the Sáhs, the Valabhi kings to the Guptas, and the Indo-Sassanians to the Valabhí line.

"The limits of the Gujarát sovereignty in Nahapána's time mustnow be extended beyond the territories which I was enabled in the paper above referred to to assign to the dominion of the Sáhs. The extent, however, of the districts held in subjection probably varied from reign to reign."

† *Journ. R. As. Soc.* vol. XII. p. 37. See also *Journ. As. Soc. Beng.* 1855, p. 569, and the Paris *Journal Asiatique*, 1863, p. 383.

THE SAH KINGS OF SURASHTRA.

Nahapana.

No. 6. Silver; weight 31 gr. *Unique*, trilingual. Mr. Newton.*

Obverse.—King's head to the right, with rough hair bound with a fillet. Very coarsely executed.

Legend, imperfect Greek.—*τυ*PANN

Reverse.—A crude spear, with an axe on the side,† and an Indian definition of a thunderbolt ?

Legend, in Bactrian-Páli characters, reading from the right, commencing below the point of the spear, נהפנש NAHAPANASA, following which, reading from the inside, but in the reverse direction, in Indian-Páli letters, **नहपनस** *Nahapanasa.*

The engraver or designer of this die was evidently more conversant with the outlines of the Bactrian alphabet than he was with the forms of the character of the concurrent system of writing of Indian origin.‡ The repetition of the letters of the name of the King in the latter alphabet, retain so much of the appearance of Bactrian writing, that at first, I imagined the line of the legend followed uniformly on to the left of the Semitic version of the leading name; whereas there is an obvious break in the continuity of the legend, and a complete reversal of the run of the alphabetical signs, a system

---

* Mr. Newton's description of this coin is to be found in Mr. Burgess's text, p. 16 *ante*.

† The custom of placing the axe half way down the staff was common with the Indo-Scythians, see Kadphises series, *Ariana Antiqua*, pl. X. figs. 12–21., and pl. XXI. fig. 19. Prinsep's *Essays*, pl. VIII., &c.

‡ Mr. Burnell, in his elaborate review of "South-Indian Palæography" (Mangalore, 1874), has naturally had to refer to the earlier types of the alphabets of Northern India, regarding which our views to some extent differ. The author has quoted certain passages from a foot-note of mine, published in the Vth volume of the Journal of the Royal Asiatic Society, N.S., p. 420. This is not the place to enlarge upon subordinate transitions of alphabets extending over some centuries, but I wish to explain, in reply to Mr. Burnell's queries, that my inference regarding the Turánian or quasi-Dravidian origin of the *lâṭ* character of Aṣoka's inscriptions does not imply a copying or imitation of any given Tamil *alphabet*, and far less so of the modern form now current; my object in giving the series of the *romanized* letters of that alphabet was merely to show what letters were required, and what were not required, to express *one* group of Dravidian languages. I estimate Mr. Burnell's services to the cause of Indian archæology so highly that I trust he will do me the honour to read what I have elsewhere written upon these subjects, when he may discover how little we really disagree on most points, though I certainly should object to the evidence of Aṣoka's monuments, as found in two separate sets of characters of 250 B.C., being tried by the test of the *Vaṭṭeḷuttu*, in which the author detects "most points of resemblance to the Sassanian of the Inscriptions" [of A.D. 226–384] (p. 41).

As I write a curious item of testimony as to the guiding and abiding influence of the old Aṣoka letters comes to us from Ceylon in the letter on Dr. Goldschmidt's report on the "North Central Inscriptions" of that island, published in the *Academy* of 20th November 1875, in which he says, "by finding the links between the old Indian [*i.e.* Aṣoka Lât] alphabet and the modern Simhalese, I was enabled, after a short time, to decipher inscriptions of all ages."

of definition equally maintained in the coin of Chashtana (No. 7), where, on the other hand, the Bactrian characters were subordinated and evidently left to the mercies of Indian die-cutters trained in the conventional schools of their own land.

It is interesting to observe the conjoint employment of the two *local* alphabets, in concurrence with the fading lines of the Greek, and the retention on both these coins, in a subsiding degree, of the Bactrian system of writing which marks its erratic spread into Suráshtra, following probably the line of the Indus downwards from Bháwalpur,* hitherto the lowest point to which its presence could be traced with any degree of certainty.

CHASHTANA.

No. 7. Silver; weight 23 gr. *Unique.*—Legends, in *three* different characters.
MR. NEWTON.

OBVERSE.—King's head to the left, with flat cap and well executed profile.

Legend, imperfect Greek.—τυρΑΝΝ.

REVERSE.—A *chaitya*, composed of superimposed arches, with a demilune capital. Wavy line below; above a well-defined sun to the right and moon to the left.

Legend,† in INDIAN-Pâli.—रञ्ञ महक्षत्रपस . . . जतिक पुत्रस चष्टनस גְשַׁתַנשׁ

Rajno mahakshatrapasa . . . jatika putrasa Chashṭanasa—CHASTAṆASA.‡

Any attempt at the decipherment of the Greek legends on these two coins has hitherto, perhaps wisely, been avoided. But I have so often found myself indebted to numismatic hints, extending even to the right appreciation of single letters, that I feel bound to put on record even my own short-comings in this instance. The materials it will be seen, are not very promising, but I may mention that the accompanying Autotype Plate only represents copies of copies§; short of the coins themselves, I have before me first reproductions in electrotype, and photographs taken direct from the originals in the possession of Mr. Newton, so that my decipherments may possibly appear in advance of my ostensible illustrative proofs.

---

* See inscription of Kanishka, *ante*.

† Mr. Newton's reading of this legend, in July 1868, was "Rajno Mahakshatrápasa (Syamo?)tika putrasa Chastanasa (ḍala?) ramua." He did not detect the repetition of the name in the Bactrian character. General Cunningham subsequently improved Mr. Newton's decipherments, remarking, "I notice that the native legends of the coins of Nahapana and Chashtana have only been partially read . . . It seems to me from the engravings that the names of both rulers are repeated in Aryan-Páli. Thus the legend on Nahapana's coin appears to me to be *Chatrapa Nahapanasa*, perhaps *Chatrapa putrasa*; and on Chashtana's coin I read *Chashtanasa* in Aryan-Páli. The Indian and Aryan names are brought together."—*Journ. Bom. Br. R. As. Soc.*, vol. IX. p. cix.

‡ Repeated in Bactrian-Páli. The Hebrew type will only imperfectly render the adapted Aryan letters of their common Semitic prototype. I have *pointed* the consonants after the system of Michaeli.

§ *i.e.* the plaster casts here photographed have themselves been taken from electrotype reproductions of the original coins, which I was favoured with by Mr. Newton some years ago.

The only letters which strike the eye, at the first glance, are ANN above the king's head in No. 7, and in the same position in No. 6, we can trace in coarser outlines the forms of PANN and a possible Υ before the P. Reverting again to No. 7, as exhibiting the best cut characters though they depart more obviously from normal Greek forms, we have a suggestive O after the second N, but the concluding letter or letters are only vaguely preserved in either specimen. The next point to determine is whether the legend should be assumed to run round the central device in one uniform line, as is the exceptional case in some of the Bactrian coins,* or whether we should look for a break in the continuity, consequent on the insertion of the King's name at the foot of the bust, which is the more constant rule in the Greco-Bactrian currencies.

The balance of evidence—apart from the reverse coincident testimony—would preferentially lead to the latter conclusion. The opening N in the name of *Nahapana* is sufficiently pronounced in its top lines under such conditions; but what then is to be said of the prefix to the possible τυραννου representing in space 6 or 7 letters, and what is to be understood to follow that title to the right in the circular legend? These are, perhaps, questions that had better be left for future solution under the auspices of better numismatic specimens, but thus much may be indicated from the struggling letters which seem to complete the list of titles that they may possibly represent in a degraded form ΣΡΑΤΙΧΙΟΥ for στρἄτηγός, or, assuming a still greater failing in the local definition of the Greek alphabet, a more directly imperfect rendering of the title of ΒΑΣΙΛΕΩΣ which commends itself under a closer examination of the prominent letter X which may easily be reduced to an MS. Greek λ.

An important branch of the general inquiry here presents itself as to the course and survival of the Greek alphabet in India, which followed the conquering progress of the Bactrian Hellenes, as the affiliated alphabet of Semitic origin attended the more complete domestication of the Ayran races. The accessory incidents differed, however, in this respect, that the Greek language was reserved more exclusively for the ruling classes during their ephemeral sway, though its literal system was preserved in a degraded form, obviously beyond the duration of the currency of the Semito-Aryan character. Its geographical extension may be defined as nearly parallel to that of the Aryan writing towards the Gangetic provinces, while it penetrated in a comparatively independent identity to the Western coast. It is singular that there is no trace of any solitary inscription in the Greek language in India, which might, however, easily be accounted for; but, in its numismatic form it remained the leading vehicle of official record, with a subsidiary vernacular translation, during more than two centuries under Greek and Scythian auspices. It was similarly employed in conjunction with Aryan legends by the Kadphises Indo-Scythians (*Ariana Antiqua*, pl. X. figs. 5, *et seq.*), while the Kanerki Horde used it solely and exclusively in the definition of their barbarous titles (*Ariana Antiqua*, pls. XII., XIII., and XIV.) The gold coins of the latter merge into those of our Guptas, but the degraded Greek, as we have seen, gives place to a cultivated type of Indian-Páli letters.

Alexander's (Greek) colonies settled in India must have been both numerous and important, if as Arrian (Justin, xiii. iv.) and Orosius (iii. c.) declare they were erected

* Antimachus. *Ariana Antiqua*, plate II. fig. 15; Menander, do., plate IV. fig. 1; Apollodotus, do., plate IV. fig. 15; Prinsep's *Essays*, plates XIV. fig. 1; XV. fig.

into an independent charge under Python the son of Agenor, on the distribution of the provinces after the death of the conqueror. Later on, we have evidence of the retention of this political organization in the Indo-Greek contingent, under Eudamus, which joined Seleucus with horse, foot, and 120 elephants (Diod. Sic. xix. 1.)

The mention of Antiochus and the four Greek kings by name,* in the edicts of Aṣoka, would also imply an intercourse more or less free, between the East and the classic West, coupled with the incidental use of the Greek language in states within or adjoining Indian boundaries. And the settlement of the Bactrian kings must largely have encouraged the domiciliation of Greek adventurers and with it the renewed continuity of the use of their language.

Our coins have long since testified to the occupation of the districts around Mathurá by the Bactro-Greeks, and Sanskrit texts have recently established the extension of their conquests to Sáketa (Oude) and Palibothra (Patna).†

Incidentally we learn from the Indian Embassy to Augustus (22–20 B.C.) that the credentials of the emissaries were written on parchment (διφθερα) in the name of Porus and in Greek (*Journ. R. As. Soc.* XVII. p. 309), the very mention of the employment of skins indicating a custom opposed to Indian predilections.

---

* General Cunningham has lately published an admirable fac-simile of a portion of the Indian-Páli Inscription at Khalsi (*Archæological Report*, vol. I. p. 247), and an improved eye-copy of the XIII. tablet of the Semitic Aṣoka edict at Kapur-di-giri (vol. V. p. 20). These revised texts are valuable in the geographical sense as suggesting new identifications; and the clear mention of *Andra* is of considerable importance in fixing the epoch of a race of kings about whose period there has been much discussion. I have, therefore, tentatively transliterated the joint texts and added the parallel fragmentary version from Girnár.

TRANSLITERATIONS OF THE AṢOKA INSCRIPTIONS OF KAPUR-DI-GIRI, KHALSI, AND GIRNÁR.

1. *Kapur-di-Giri.* Antiyoka namá Yona raja paran cha tenan Antiyokena chatura IIII rajano Traramaye
2. *Khalsi.* Antiyoga náma Yona . . lan chá tena Antiyo . ná chatali + lajane Tulamaye
3. *Girnár.* . . . . . Yona raja paran cha tena . . . chapṭena [*sic*] rajano Turamáyo

1. *K.* namá Antikina namá Máka namá Alikasandaro namá nicham Choḍa, Panḍa,
2. *Kh.* náma Antekina . . náma . . Máká . . náma Alikyasadale náma nicham Choḍa, Panḍiya,
3. *G.* cha Antakana . . cha . . . Magá . . cha . . . .

1. *K.* Avam Tambupanniya hevammevamhena raja Vishatidi Yonam Kamboyeshu Nibha Ka
2. *Kh.* Avam Tambapaniyá hevamevâhevamevá . . . . lájá Vishmavasi Yona Kambojasu Nábha Ku
3. *G.* . . . .

1. *K.* nabhatina Bhojam Piti Nikeshu, Andrapulideshu savatam . .
2. *Kh.* nábha Pantisa Bhoja Piti Nikesa Adhapiladesa savatá . .
3. *G.* . . . . . ndhepirandesu savata . .

Under the Elephant *at Khalsi*, Gajatemre? *at the foot of the XIII. tablet at Girnár:* Sveto ha-ti savaloka sukháharo námam.

† "Then the viciously valiant Greeks, after reducing Sáketa (Ayodhya, *Oude*), Panchála-country and Mathurá, will reach (or take) Kusamadhvaja (Palibothra): Pushpapura (Palibothra) being reached (or taken) all provinces will be in disorder, undoubtedly." . . "The fiercely-fighting Greeks will not stay in Madhyadeṣa: there will be a cruel, dreadful war in their own kingdom." . . . "It appears that for a time after the Greeks, a rapacious Ṣaka, or Scythian king, was most powerful." Dr. Kern, from the Yugapuráṇa of the Gárgi-Sanhitá pp. 35, 38, 39; his Preface to the *Brihat Sanhitá* (Calcutta, *Bibliotheca Indica*, 1865). The Yugapuráṇa is assigned by Dr. Kern to B.C. 50. "We thus see that Patanjali lived in the reign of Pushpamitra" . . . and "we thus see that when this portion of the *Bháshya* was written, a *Yavana* king (Menander?) had laid siege to Sáketa or *Ayodhyá*, and Pushpamitra was reigning at Páṭaliputra." Professor Bhandarkar. *Indian Antiquary*, i., p. 299. See also ii. 59, 70, 96, and likewise Professor Weber, in *Indian Antiquary*, i. 173, 179 *note*, 239; ii. 58, 143; Goldstucker *Páṇini*, 230; Bábu Rajendralála, *Journ. As. Soc. Beng.*, 1874, p. 263.

Could we rely upon the statements of Apollonius of Tyana, they would carry us still further towards the proof of the extended currency and survival of the Greek language in India up to A.D. 50. We are supposed to discover Phraotes, king of Taxila, conversing fluently in that tongue, and Iarchus, chief of the Sophoi, is said to welcome his visitor "in Greek;" in like manner certain villagers are reported conventionally, and without effort, *or* pretence, to have used that form of speech. (*Journ. R. As. Soc.* vol. XVII., pp. 78, 81, 90). This might perchance explain the unusual occurrence of so many numismatic examples of legends couched in current-hand Greek letters as opposed to the ordinary or what we term uncial capitals of monumental Greek, which gradually fell out of use about this period (*Ariana Antiqua*, Pl. XIV., figs. 12, 13), and finally merged into the unintelligible jumble of other Scythic examples discovered on Nos. 16 and 17 of the same plate.

If the decipherment of the four most prominent letters "PANN" of the Greek legends in the allied coins of Nahapana and Chashtana proves correct, it may open out several new lines of inquiry as to the status and position of Chashtana and his contemporaries; and in the enlarged numismatic associations, establish connecting links, both epochal and geographical, that we have hitherto scarcely dared to speculate upon.

A short time ago Mr. Percy Gardner, of the B.M., published a representative coin of a Ṣaka king named "Heraüs," of which the following wood-cut is a fac-simile, with his appended description, originally printed in the *Numismatic Chronicle*.

HERAÜS, ṢAKA KING.

No. IV.* Silver. B.M.

OBVERSE.—"Bust of a king, right, diademed and draped; border of reels and beads

REVERSE.—ΤΥΙΑΝΝΟΥΝΤΟΣ ΗΙΑΟΥ
ΣΑΚΑ
ΚΟΙΙΑΝΟΥ.

(Τυραννοῦντος Ἡράου Σάκα κοιράνου.)

A king, right, on horseback; behind, NIKE, crowning him."*

The assignment of this piece to Heraüs has been objected to by General Cunningham, who claims its attribution to the well-known king "Mauas," whose coins cover a large range both in number and variety of types.† It is quite true that the

* *Numismatic Chronicle* (1874), XIV., N. S. p. 161.

† General Cunningham reads the name as ΜΙΑΙΟΥ ΚΟΙΡΑΝΟΥ. See also *Numismatic Chronicle*, p. 109. Colonel Pearse, R.A., possesses a small *silver* coin, displaying the obverse head in identical form with the outline in the wood-cut. The reverse type discloses an ill-defined, erect figure, to the left, with two parallel legends in obscure Greek, the leading line, *with the title*, is altogether unintelligible, but its central letters range × ▭ ΙΑΙΙΝ or × ▭ ΙΑΙΙΚ×. The second line gives a nearer approach to "Moas" in a possible initial M, followed by the letters ◖▭ ΙΙΔΗΣ=μουδης, μοπρης, μουαης, &c.

imperfectly defined designation might be read as *Mauas*, though the additional second letter in the name is against such a rendering.*

But the difference in the style of the legends and the typical details of the piece seem to separate it from all other published examples of Mauas' money, and to connect it, in a marked manner, with the Parthian rather than the Partho-Bactrian section of the occupying conquerors of India.

To commence with the indications furnished by the legends, the unusual form of the kingly title ΒΑΣΙΛΕΥΟΝΤΟΣ ΒΑΣΙΛΕΩΝ which we now understand to imply direct administrative exercise of power, under the confessed authority of an imperial superior,† appears for the first and only time in the Parthian mintages on a coin of Arsaces XII. Phrahates III., B.C. 70–60, which may, as General Cunningham suggests, indicate his position as joint or sub-king under his father, in charge of a province of the empire, in contrast to the ΒΑΣΙΛΕΩΣ ΒΑΣΙΛΕΩΝ,‡ which he, subsequently, insisted on so emphatically in his correspondence with Pompey.§

The first example of the use of the term ΒΑΣΙΛΕΥΟΝΤΟΣ among the Indo-Parthian currencies occurs on a coin of Gondophares similar to No. 5, (Prinsep, vol. II. p. 215),‖ which is repeated on the money of Arsaces (Prinsep, vol. II. p. 217, and *Journ. As. Soc. Bengal*, vol. XI. p. 135). The coins of Mauas, on the other hand, appear to confine themselves to the ordinary legends of ΒΑΣΙΛΕΩΣ, ΒΑΣΙΛΕΩΣ ΒΑΣΙΛΕΩΝ, and ΒΑΣΙΛΕΩΣ ΒΑΣΙΛΕΩΝ ΜΕΓΑΛΟΥ ΜΑΥΟΥ.¶

Moreover on no occasion do they display the title of ΚΟΙΡΑΝΟΣ, still less that of the *unique* definition of the all-important ΣΑΚΑ of the coin of Heraüs.

The practical question then presents itself, as to whether this departure from ordinary routine, in the case of Gondophares and Arsaces, does not imply a recognition of the Imperial power held by the *nominal* head of the family in Persia, and co-relatively whether the employment of the nearly parallel form of ΤΥΡΑΝΝΟΥΝΤΟΣ does not in like manner, indicate merely executive administration and allegiance to a distant suzerain? The ΚΟΙΡΑΝΟΣ the dictionaries tell us, is simply a synonym of ΤΥΡΑΝΝΟΣ,** and we know that the Parthians were eccentric in their selection of Greek titles, the force of which they, perhaps, did not always comprehend, so that we must not criticise, too closely, any titles *a Ṣaka*, whose still more vague ideas of Greek filtered through such dubious channels, may have chosen to adopt.

---

* The Bactrian-Páli rendering of the name on the coins is invariably *Moasa*, which has been assumed to correspond with the Inscription definition of *Mogasa* : see *ante*, p. 17.

† *Journ. R. As. Soc.* vol. XX. p. 126 ; *Numismatic Chronicle*, (My article,) vol. II. N. S. p. 186 ; and General Cunningham's article, vol. IX. N. S. p. 29.

‡ Mr. Lindsay remarks, "the title of ΒΑΣΙΛΕΩΣ ΒΑΣΙΛΕΩΝ appears on the coins of Arsaces XII. for the first time since (its disuse after) the reign of Arsaces VI."—*Coins of the Parthians*, Cork, 1852, p. 21.

§ Plutarch in Pompey. § 38 ; Dio Cass. cap. XXXVII. § 6 ; Lindsay, p. 21 ; Rawlinson, p. 145.

‖ This example is as yet unpublished. The coin belongs to Sir H. Dryden.

¶ Prinsep's *Essays*, vol. II. p. 200 ; *Ariana Antiqua*, p. 314.

** "Τύραννος strictly Dor. for κοίρανος, from κῦρος, κύριος, a *lord*, *master*." The editors add, "the term rather regards the way in which the power was *gained* than how it was *exercised*, being applied to the mild Pisistratus, but not to the despotic kings of Persia."—Liddell and Scott. The ancient Persians must have been fully conversant with the use and meaning of the term, in the Ἑλλησποντίων μὲν τύραννοι of Darius, referred to by Herodotus IV. cap. 137, who elsewhere seems to admit that its interchange with βασιλεὺς was optional and unimportant.

It is in regard to the typical details, however, that the contrast between the pieces of Mauas and Heraüs is most apparent. Mauas has no coins with his own bust among the infinite variety of his mint devices; nor has Azas, who imitates so many of his emblems. But, in the Gondophares group, we meet again with busts and uncovered heads, the hair being simply bound by a fillet, in which arrangement of the head-dress Pakores, with his bushy curls, follows suit. But the crucial typical test is furnished by the small figure of victory crowning the horseman on the reverse, which is so special a characteristic of the Parthian die illustration.

We have frequent examples of Angels or types of victory extending regal fillets in the Bactrian series, but these figures constitute as a rule the main device of the reverse, and are not subordinated into a corner, as in the Parthian system. The first appearance of the fillet in direct connexion with the king's head in the Imperial series, occurs on the coins of Arsaces XIV., *Orodes*,* (B.C. 54–37), where the crown is borne by an eagle,† but on the reverses of the copper coinage, this duty is already confided to the winged figure of Victory.‡ Arsaces XV., Phrahates IV. (37 B.C.–4 A.D.), continues the eagles for a time, but progresses into single§ and finally into double figures of Victory eager to crown him,‖ as indicating his successes against Antony and the annexation of the kingdom of Media.¶

Henceforth these winged adjuncts are discontinued, so that, if we are to seek for the prototype of the Heraüs coin amid Imperial Arsacidan models, we are closely limited in point of antiquity, though the possibly deferred adoption may be less susceptible of proof.

Supposing this adoption, however, to have been contemporaneous, the dates B.C. 37 to A.D. 4 will mark the age of Heraüs, whereas Moas is speculatively assigned to a much earlier period.** But we must await the authoritative determination of many international complications in the annals of Western Asia before we can venture to draw definite inferences from the typical devices of the border-land of India.

I feel that no apology is needed for still further breaking the continuity of the leading subject of this paper by the introduction of a rare and important class of coins, which appear, in a measure, to be connected with the unique piece of Heraüs, while their Parthian peculiarities are associated with seemingly Indian forms of costume, which our friends in the Western Presidency may perchance identify, and further secure new numismatic specimens to aid a final decipherment. Though Russia has hitherto contributed the best of our examples,†† several have been traced to the lines of the Lower

* I see that the French numismatists quote the coins of Pacorus I. (joint king under his father Orodes I.), which follow western models. These coins exhibit the figure of Victory.

† Lindsay, *History of the Parthians*, Cork, 1852, pl. III. fig. 2, pp. 146–170; *Trésor de Numismatique*, pl. LXVIII. fig. 17.

‡ *Ibid.*, pl. V. fig. 2, p. 181.

§ *Ibid.*, pl. III. fig. 60; V. fig. 4, pp. 148, 170; *Trésor de Numismatique*, pl. LXVIII. fig. 18; pl. LXIX. fig. 5.

‖ *Ibid.*, pl. III. figs. 61–63.

¶ Lindsay, p. 37; Rawlinson, *The Sixth Monarchy*, p. 182.

** Wilson, 100 B.C.; Lassen, 120 B.C.; Cunningham, after 126 before 105 B.C.; Prinsep's *Essays*, vol. II. p. 173.

†† "Il y a quelques semaines qu'en Russie (au gouvernement de Perm) a été découvert un petit vase en bronze renfermant quatre monnaies en argent, dont j'ai l'honneur de vous envoyer les empreintes ci-jointes.

"A juger d'après le type de ces monnaies je serais tenté de les attribuer à quelque roi indo-scythe, mais cette supposition me semble être revoquée en doute par une autre trouvaille (faite en 1851 dans la même contrée) qui outre une monnaie du même genre contenait quelques monnaies sassanides (du VIe siècle) et des monnaies

Indus, localities which, as far as may be gathered, cannot be far removed, from the site of issue of the coins themselves.

These coins, whatever grade in Eastern history may be finally assigned to them, are of considerable typical importance in opening out an entirely fresh field of numismatic research. I must admit, however, that hitherto my success in their decipherment has not been commensurate with the bold outlines and apparent clearness of their legends. Nevertheless, I have not hesitated to put on record what little I have been able to unravel, and to follow out more largely the associations involved in the die-devices, with the aim of drawing attention to this promising subject of investigation, and in advocating a renewed search for similar specimens in public and private cabinets:* as it is well known that a single letter, on many a defaced piece, will often give the clue to a legend, comparatively complete in itself, but still wanting in the touch of legible vitality. While in the preliminary stage, I must frankly premise, that, though, in this case, almost every typical coincidence points to a near association with the Parthians in Bactria, or, preferentially, with their spread in more directly southern and western localities, the leading geographical evidence tending to a similar conclusion; yet the authoritative reduction of the ornamental scroll over the horse's loins (in No. V.) into the Kufic word نصر, would fatally reduce the epoch in point of time. The unknown letters on the margin, at the foot of coins Nos. VI., VII., VIII., have, moreover, a suspiciously current or cursive appearance, and, certainly, do not accord with the stiff and formal outlines of the freely legible *Malka*, in the opening letters of the variety of Syriac here employed. We have too many striking instances, in the series of Indian and quasi-Indian coinages, of the indigenous faculty of imitation, and aptitude in the reproduction of fixed and accepted designs, at times persevered in, mechanically, till all trace of the original fades before the eye and vanishes into thin air; so that typical resemblances and even close and seemingly immediate copies can hardly be held to prove what they would establish under other and less exceptional circumstances. Hence we may yet have to surrender the choicest of our specimens, in this limited list, to stand as a subdued monument of Bahrám Gor's visit to India, or as a still more modern sign and

---

byzantines d'Héraclius et de son fils Constantin. Puis les lettres qu'on voit sur ces monnaies diffèrent de celles qui se trouvent sur les monnaies indo-scythes."

* Since these illustrative wood-cuts first reached me, a coin similar in general characteristics to Nos. V., VI., VII., has been found in the collection of General Abbott, acquired in the Hazára districts of the Panjáb, which has recently been added to the Numismatic Treasures of the India Office. The piece in question, though it contributes nothing to our knowledge in the matter of types or legends, gives very significant hints in the direction of identities of metal which, in the greasy alloy, opens out mineral and geological connexions with Arachotian and other Nickel-using nationalities. See Apollonius of Tyana, quoted in *Journ. R. As. Soc.*, vol. XVII. pp. 72, 77; Strabo, bk. XV. cap. ii. § 10, bk. XV. cap. iii. § 11, and bk. XV. cap. i. § 69; Pliny, *Nat. Hist.*, bk. XXXIV. cap. ii. (§ 2, Aurichalcum, "fine copper," Oricalcum, Caiducium?), and bk. XXXVII. cap. xlii.; Marco Polo, cap. XIV., XX.; and in these days Kenrick's *Phœnicia*, p. 206; General A. Cunningham, *Numismatic Chronicle*, N. S. vol. VIII. p. 279, etc.; with Dr. W. Flight, *ibid.*, p. 305; and My *Indian Weights*, p. 43.

I have lately been favoured with two new examples of this class of coin—the one from the Royal cabinet of Copenhagen, and a new piece from Russia. They must both be placed, typically, before No. VI., as the horseman is more on the move, and the general execution of the dies approaches nearer to the style of No. V. Both coins show very elaborate horse-trappings, with the quiver full of arrows behind the right thigh of the rider. The legends in front of the profile, on the obverse, seem to follow Pehlví tracings, but they are no more definitively legible than the scroll on No. V.; and the reverse legends fail to add anything to our previous knowledge.

symbol of Muhammad bin Kásim's first Arabian settlement on the banks of the Lower Indus.

No. V.* Silver. Musée Asiatique, St. Petersbourg.

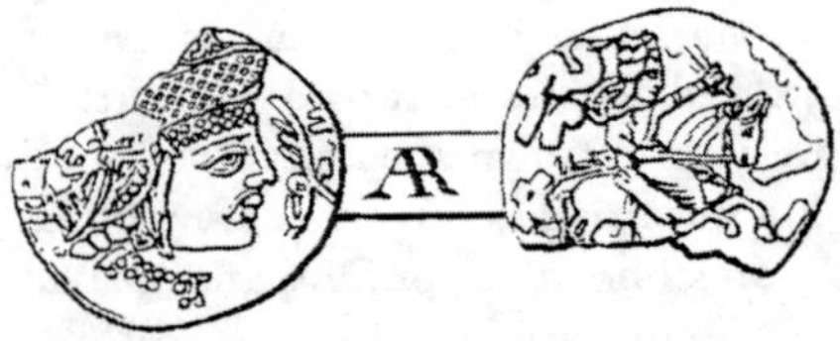

There is little or no trace of pure Parthianism in these devices, except in the peculiar tooling of the neck ornament.* The obverse head would almost seem to represent a young Indian-born Greek, who was so far reconciled to local customs as to cultivate with shaven cheeks a small moustache, and to recognise the manifest advantage of a turband. The eccentric eagle crowning the rider on the reverse may, possibly, imply a newly erected kingdom, or a more moderate extension of ancient boundaries.

The free action of the horse recalls the attitude of the front charger of the classic *Dioscuri* of Eucratides, or the single light horseman of the Baktrian Philoxenes ;† but, here, the huntsman supplants the warrior, and the seat and saddle, and even the horse itself, if truly designed, are Indian, in ideal and execution, rather than imitations of Greek designs. The dog (if such it be)‡ is, also, an innovation upon any hitherto recognised medallic device. The use of the distinctive adjunct of the eagle placing a chaplet on the king's brow, as we have seen, was derived, in the first instance, by the Parthians from Roman teachings ; it appears on the coins of Phraates IV. and Tiridates II. (B.C. 37),§ but soon gives way to the more natural winged figure of victory. The legend on the obverse I am as yet unable to decipher, but I must add, that I have neither seen this particular coin, nor even obtained rubbings or impressions of it. The curious ornamental scroll over the crupper of the horse has been read by my friends in St. Petersburg, who have sent me this wood-block, as the Arabic term فضل "excellence, wisdom ;" but, though such an interpretation might be put upon the letters as they appear in the wood-cut, I should not at present be disposed to concur in any such rendering, though I must confess that the word in front of the king's profile looks more like cursive and comparatively modern Sassanian Pehlvi than any other style of writing of which I have knowledge.

---

* The letters on the Parthian coins are what we should call nail-headed (not arrow-headed), *i.e.*, the characters, instead of being cut out and sunk on the die, in continuous lines, are produced by a series of holes drilled in consecutive order upon the general outline of the letter, and connected more or less clearly by minor attaching links. On the coin itself these studs stand up like the nail-heads on a well-made mediæval chair. A similar system of dotting the leading outlines of the letters was in favour among the Indo-Scythians in India. An authoritative ink-tracing could by this means be followed, mechanically, with great exactness, where a free line engraving might, under the circumstances, have simply proved difficult and delusive.

† *Journal des Savants*, 1836, pl. II. fig. 5 ; *Ariana Antiqua*, pl. II. fig. 17 ; Prinsep's *Essays*, vol. II. p. 187, pl. XV. fig. 1.

‡ It may possibly be the foal following the mare.

§ Longpérier, pl. IX. figs. 8, 9 ; pl. X. figs. 5, 6, 7 ; Lindsay, pl. III. figs. 55, 56, 57.

This coin and the two succeeding specimens present us with more distinct Parthian identities. The head-dress on the obverse would, at first sight, appear to have nothing

No. VI.* Silver. CABINET OF COMTE STROGANOFF.

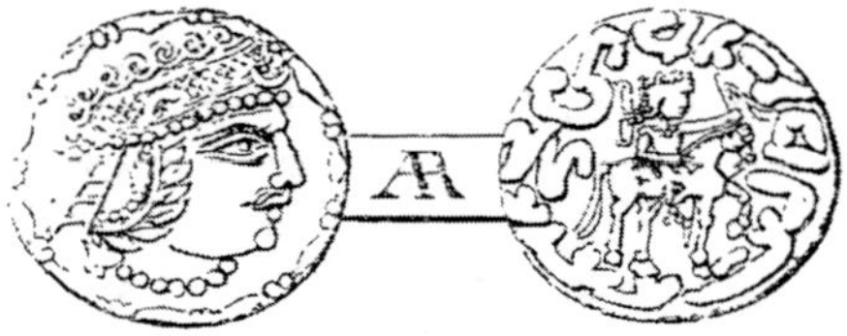

in common with the ordinary upright Tiara helmet of the Imperial dynasty; but, though the local turband is retained in a somewhat reduced and modified shape, the scroll-like ornament at the top, so seemingly exceptional, can be readily traced to an association with the crest pattern first introduced by Phraates II. (B.C. 136–126) and maintained in occasional use by Sanatrœces* (B.C. 77–70), finding favour among the local kings of Edessa,† and appearing, in a less formal design, on the Eastern Parthian coins of Sanabares‡ (A.D. 2). The horseman, on the reverse, is a close copy (even to the details of the double-thonged whip and occasional hooked-*ankus*, or subdued elephant-goad,) of the charger, which continued to furnish the standard device of so many monarchs of the Parthian race in Scytho-Bactria, typified in the devices of Gondophares, Abdagazes, Arsaces, &c., whose dates are roughly assumed at from about B.C. 26 to 44 A.D.; and, singular to say, we have an example of a nearly similarly outlined horse in the Parthian Imperial series *proper*, on the money of Artabanus III. (on a coin *dated* in A.D. 13), where the unkempt hair around the front face of the monarch, typical, perhaps, of the rude fashion prevailing amid the camps and tents of the Dahæ, nearly fills one surface of the coin, while his charger on the reverse, either in bone or limb, may fairly claim kindred with the stud-bred representatives of the Baktrian stables.§

The physiognomy of the king on the obverse of Nos. VI., VII., VIII., bears no analogy to the conventional Parthian portraiture, but is clearly derived from Indian ideals of the human face. The almond eye, the slight moustache, and the smooth-shaved rounded jowl, all associate themselves with Eastern models, ranging from the Kodes coins of Sistán‖ on the one side, to the Suráshtran pieces of the Sáh kings,¶ and the types special to the Guptas.** Hence, in admitting local influence in the composition of the profile, we must infer, either an entire surrender of Parthian predilections, a facile concession to indigenous art, or a confession of fealty by the established dynasty, and their recognition, as local rulers, by a Parthian Suzerain. Among the minor indications may be noticed the germ, or possibly, according to the age eventually to be assigned to the coins themselves, the later development, of the Sassanian broad floating fillet, together with the

---

* Longpérier, pl. V. figs. 7, 8, 9; pl. VII. figs. 4, 5.

† Bayer, *Historia Osrhoena*. Abgar's tiara, p. 130.

‡ Longpérier, pl. XII. fig. 4; My Sassanian Inscriptions, p. 121; Prinsep's *Essays*, vol. II. p. 215, note.

§ Visconti, *Icon. Greque*, pl. L. No. 2; Longpérier, pl. XII. fig. 9.

‖ Prinsep's *Essays*, vol. I. p. 337; vol. II. p. 203, pl. XIII. figs. 11, 12; *Ariana Antiqua*, pl. IX. figs. 1–5; *Numismatic Chronicle*, vol. IV. N.S. p. 210.

¶ Prinsep's *Essays*, vol. II. p. 94; *Journ. R. As. Soc.*, 1850, vol. XII. pls. I. II. p. 72.

** *Journ. As. Soc. Beng.*, and Prinsep's *Essays*, vol. II. pl. XXXVII. Nos. 16, 17, &c., *supra*.

crescent in front of the head-dress, which, though essentially Sassanian, was not exclusively so, as the Guptas alike affected the symbol.*

One of the grounds for preferring the later date for these coins consists in the fact, that the similitudes of the wave of the curl and general arrangement of the crest are undoubtedly closer, and more marked between the comparatively subsequent Parthian issues of Pacorus II.† and Vologeses IV. (A.D. 148–190),‡ than those of the primary patterns employed by Phraates II. and Sanatrœces; and the elegant leaf-scroll, pendant from the Indian turband of Nos. VI. and VII., finds a curious and almost exact counterpart in the ornamental fall at the back of the Parthian tiara introduced by the same Vologeses IV.,§ and revived or retained in use by Vologeses VI.,‖ and Artavasdes,¶ with whom the Arsacidan dynasty became finally extinct. But, here again, we must be cautious how we pronounce in favour of any definite period for these fashions, or pretend to determine priority of usage, which may have been dependent upon so many contrasted motives—old institutions, recent conquests, or pervading provincial designs, which would necessarily repeat themselves in the outlying portions of conterminous territories.

Nos. VII. VIII.* Silver. Cabinet of Comte Stroganoff.

The monogram, at the back of the horseman on the reverse, offers another instance of the strange modifications ancient devices were liable to be subjected to, in the hands of artists who, probably, did not comprehend the intent and meaning of the prototype. I have felt some diffidence in identifying the odd jumble of lines on No. V. as a reproduction of the Parthian eagle; but, in truth, the original designs on the Imperial mintages, did not contribute any very exact delineation of the form of the sacred bird, and the Indian copyist may have been even less instructed in ornithology and less conversant with the flight of eagles than the Western designers; while his own local imitators may well have failed to detect a likeness he himself was incompetent to give effect to. Be this as it may, the symbol or device on Nos. VI., VII., and VIII. has clearly arrived at the monogrammatic stage, though quaint traces of the bird's head are still to be detected on Nos. VI. and VII. The monogram, in its advanced form, is assimilated to several designs in established favour with neighbouring dynasties; in its lower limbs it singularly accords with the special symbols or crypto-monograms employed by Kadphises, Kanerki and

* *Journ. R. As. Soc.* vol. XII. pl. II. figs. 39, 49; *Ariana Antiqua*, pl. XV. figs. 17, 18; Prinsep's *Essays*, pl. XXVII.

† Longpérier, pl. XV. fig. 6.

‡ *Ibid.*, pl. XVI. fig. 11.

§ Longpérier, pl. XVI. fig. 11; pl. XVII. fig. 7; *Trésor de Numismatique*, pl. XXI. figs. 13, 14, 17. Lindsay, pl. VI. fig. 28.

‖ Longpérier, pl. XVIII. fig. 6; Lindsay, pl. VI. fig. 31.

¶ Longpérier, pl. XVIII. fig. 11; My *Sassanian Inscriptions*, London, 1868, p. 127.

Ooerki (Kanishka and Hovishka)*; while, in its central, upper portion it approaches nearer to the Indo-Sassanian typical design, which occupies the entire coin reverse, as depicted in pl. XVII. fig. 20 of Wilson's *Ariana Antiqua*,† and otherwise, in general characteristics, it has much identity with the ordinary mystic diagrams of the Sassanian seals ‡; but both these latter may merely represent continuous imitations or developments of an abiding ideal, furnishing a fixed point of departure, which, varied in its minor details, according to the ruling conceptions or acquired tendencies of the nation, under the religious teaching dominant at the moment.

No. IX.✳ Copper. Musée Asiatique, St. Pétersbourg.

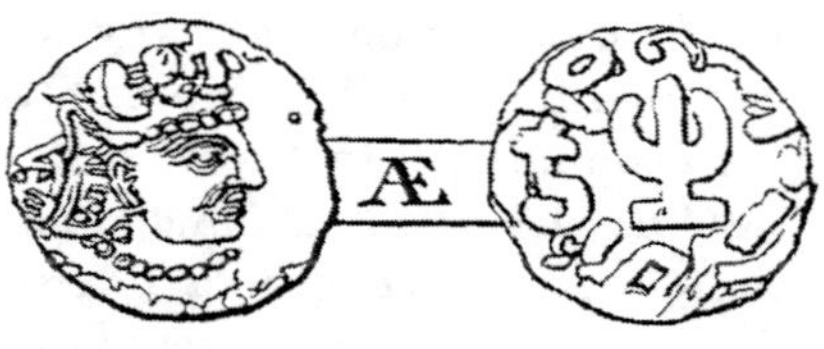

The obverse head, in this instance shows a considerable amount of degradation, even from the imperfect models, which it clearly follows. The variation in the reverse device is of moment, not only as removing the mintage from any very close connexion with its predecessors, but as shadowing forth a possible change in locality. The symbol which occupies the field belongs to one of the many forms of the Indian *Triṣula*, or trident, of *Ṣiva*,§ which crops up upon so many occasions amid the emblems of the East and the West, and which acquires an importance in the present inquiry, on account of the prominence similar devices will be seen to hold in collateral issues.‖

Having completed the incidental references to the Numismatic devices, I have to encounter the more difficult task of explaining the purport of legends.

Those illiterate savages, the Parthians, finding themselves, amid the chances of conquest, so often domesticated as alien rulers; in the absence of any alphabet of their own, very wisely accepted the casual varieties of writing current in the localities in which they held sway. Among the leading and more important systems thus adopted the following may be enumerated:—

1. *Greek*, which was taken over as part and parcel of the Court and Official language, prevailing in the dominions of the Seleucidæ, about 255 B.C.

2. *Bactrian*, or the special adaptation of a normal Semitic alphabet for the

---

* *Ariana Antiqua*, pl. X. fig. 5; pl. XI. fig. 16; pl. XIV. fig. 1; and pl. XXII. No. 155, *et seq.*, *ante*, p. 17.

† See also pl. XVII. fig. 21.

‡ *Journ. R. As. Soc.* vol. XIII. p. 425, *et seq.*; *Mordtmann Zeitschrift*, 1864, Nos. 63, 101, 124, 140; Lajard, *Culte de Mithra*, pl. X., numerous examples, but especially No. 13. Also plates XLV. figs. 1, 2, 4, 5, 8, 15, and plate LIV. figs. c, 6, 7, 8, 9–16, 19, 20, 21.

§ See coins of Kadphises (105 B.C.); *Ariana Antiqua*, pl. X. figs. 5, 12, &c.; and of Kanerki, pl. XII. fig. 4; Ooerki, pl. XIV. fig. 14.

‖ See coins No. XI.,✳ &c., and note, p. 62, *infra*.

definition of an Aryan tongue, which was largely developed in India about B.C. 250, but which first appears upon Parthian coins, only in 110 B.C.

3. Various forms and modifications of Phœnician and Aramæan, employed on coins of an imitative type of the Tetradrachms of Euthydemus of Bactria (now assigned to Characene) of uncertain date; and other survivals of an old type of Syriac, such as that found on the coins of Edessa, and in allied branches of coinage of indeterminate locality.

4. The double alphabets of the ancient Pehlvi, discriminated as Chaldæan and Sassanian, which intrude among the Greek legends of the Imperial series so early as A.D. 2, and which finally supersede the Greek itself in the official records of Western Asia about the third century, A.D.

I release my Indian readers from the dry details of any attempted identification of the hybrid letters of which the coin legends V.–VIII. are composed, and simply say that I can only decipher with any pretence to certainty, the word מרכא *Marka*, for *Malka*, which commences in front of the head of the horseman, and is to be read from the *outside* of the piece. The succeeding letters seem to belong to a different alphabet, and the utmost I venture to guess at is something approaching the sounds of *Shahach* or *Shemach*,* on fig. V., which interpretation, however, is seriously shaken by the almost modern Arabic style of the letters on VI., VII., and VIII., which might be taken for لعب or لعبس

I now revert to the largely interrupted serial succession of the local Sáh kings of Suráshtra, of whose coins, however, I propose to give merely typical examples.

ÍṢWARADATTA.

No. 8. Silver. B.M.

OBVERSE.—The typical and "numismatically" *constant* Sáh head, in profile.

Legend, imperfect, with vague outlines of the Greek characters.—A C C I Υ

REVERSE.—The conventional *Chaitya*.

Legend.—राज्ञो महा चत्रपस ईश्वर दत्तम वर्ष प्रथमे.

Rájno mahá kshatrapasa Īṣwara dattasa, varsha prathame.

(*Varsha prathame*, in "the first year" of his reign?)

It still continues an unexplained mystery, why the coins of the XVI. king in Mr. Newton's serial list, p. 44, should depart from the established custom of inserting a date at the commencement of the Greek legend, and supplant it by a new form of regnal date at the conclusion of the monarch's titles and designations in the *local* character on the *reverse*.

---

* *Chach?* سیهرش صقمد جاجاج. Reinaud, *l'Inde*, pp. 126, 147, 176; *Mas'oudi*, vol. I. p. 342; A'ín-i-Akbari, vol. II. p. 146; Elliot's *Historians*, p. 138 *et seq.*; *Journ. R. As. Soc.* vol. XII. p. 341.

VIJAYA SÁH.

No. 9. Silver. ROYAL ASIATIC SOCIETY. (Dates, according to local custom, 140 to 154.)

OBVERSE.—Sáh head as usual.

Greek legend, imperfect.—. . . IIVIIOIICVA

Date behind the head, expressed in ancient Indian *numeral figures*, following the initial I, 154. Confirmatory dates, 142 (Mr. Freeling's coin),* and 153 (B.M. coin).

REVERSE.—*Chaitya*, half-moon and a cluster of nine stars.

Legend.—राज्ञो महा चत्रपस विजय साहस रांज्ञो महा चत्रपस दामा साहस पुत्रस

Rájno mahá Kshatrapasa Vijaya Sáhasa, Rájno mahá Kshatrapasa Dámá Sáhasa putrasa.

DAMA JATA ṢRIYAH.

No. 10. Silver. ROYAL ASIATIC SOCIETY.

OBVERSE.—The usual Sáh head.

Legend, illegible. Date, in ancient ciphers, 1*7.†

REVERSE.—*Chaitya*, half-moon and cluster of four stars.

Legend visible on this coin.— . . . . श्रीय राज्ञो मह चत्रपस दम

Full legend restored.—*Rájno mahá Kshatrapasa Dámá jata Ṣríyah, Rájno mahá Kshatrapasa Dámá Sáha-putrasa.*

KUMÁRA GUPTA.

Sauráshtran Series.

No. 11. Silver. MR. BURGESS.

OBVERSE.—The standard Sáh head, but much corrupted in the die execution.

REVERSE.—The goddess *Párvatí*, apparently imitated from the Eastern type of that deity, found on Kumára's gold coin, No. 5. Proving, in effect, the purport, hitherto unsuspected, of the original design, which is so strangely distorted in all other cotemporary issues. Cluster of six stars, as in the Sáh coins, but located in a new position in the lower portion of the field.

Legend.—परम भगवत महराजधिराज श्री कुमर गुप्त महेन्द्रदित्य

Parama Bhagavata Mahárájadhirája Ṣrí Kumara Gupta Mahendraditya.

---

* Mr. Newton gives independent fac-similes of the dates 140 and 154, *Journ. Bom. Br. R. As. Soc.* vol. VII. p. 28.

† There is another doubtful date, of 1*4, on Dr. Stephenson's coin.

No. 12. Silver. Mr. Burgess.

Obverse.—The usual imitation of the typical Sáh profile.

Reverse.—*Párvatí*, one degree less recognisable than in No. 11. Cluster of six stars, in the old position, above and to the right of the central figure.

Legend as in No. 11. Legible portion.—*Parama Bhagavata Maha . . . . hendraditya.*

No. 13. Silver. Mr. Burgess.

Obverse.—A totally new style of treatment of the typical Sáh head, shown in the sensual air, thick-necked profile, short curled moustache, and altered form of ear-ring.

Legend in barbarous Greek.—O NONO O, constituting a corrupt rendering of fragments of the standard Scythic legend of PAO NANO PAO. Our *Ráo* of modern days, combined with the NANO, which is referred to the masculine moon, the associate of the Babylonian NANA, NANAIA. This may possibly suggest identities, more or less remote, with the Indian *Chandra Vanṣas* ?*

Reverse.—*Párvatí*, further degraded from the original type, but still freely identifiable. Cluster of eight stars.

Legend as in No. 11. Portion legible.— . . . . *rama Bhagavata Maharájadhirája Ṣrí Kumara Gupta* . . .

No. 14. Silver. Mr. Burgess.

Obverse.—The original Sáh head, but slightly modified in its details, and more closely adhering to the local prototype than the preceding examples.

Legend.—Traces of badly-formed Greek letters. The style of writing follows the unintelligible mechanical Sáh model more closely than the independently debased and free-hand Greek legend on No. 13.

Reverse.—*Párvatí*, degraded type; with cluster of six stars.

Legend, expressed in bolder Nágarí letters than in the previous specimens. Portion of superscription visible.— . . . . *maha rájadhirája Ṣrí Kumára Gupta.*

No. 15. Silver. Mr. Burgess.

Obverse.—The Sáh head, debased in execution.

Legend, degraded Greek.—ONOυ.

Reverse.—*Párvatí*, still less recognizable, but clearly following, *longo intervallo*, the established model. The cluster of stars is driven up, in the want of surface space, into the run of letters of the legend.

Legend, visible on the coin.—*Maharájadhirá . . Ṣrí Kumara Gupta.*

---

* *Journ. R. As. Soc.*, vol. XII. p. 15; *Journal Asiatique*, 1839, p. 7; *Ariana Antiqua*, pp. 358, 364; My *Ancient Indian Weights* (Marsden), p. 45. Certain gold coins were called, after the Greek name of NANO, in Sanskrit नाणक, *Náṇaka's*, described as coins with the mark of Ṣiva.

No. 16. Silver. Mr. Burgess.

Obverse.—Sáh head, further debased.

Legend.—UHOU (NANO).

Reverse.—*Párvati* further disintegrated. The Sáh stars continue to find a refuge amid the ordinary course of letters of the superscription.

Legend, expressed in coarse ill-defined characters: visible on the coin.— . . . *jadhirája Ṣrí Kumara Gupta.*

No. 17. Silver. Royal Asiatic Society. (Presented by the late Ráo of Kutch.)

Obverse.—The Sáh head, finely rendered, with an air and suggestion of Greek art.

Legend.—ONO (NANO).

Reverse.—*Párvati,* scarcely recognizable, though the execution of the die is otherwise sharp and unhesitating.

Legend, in bold, well-cut square characters.—

परम भगवत राजधिरा . श्री कुमर गुप्त . . न्द्रदित्य

Parama Bhagavata Rájadhirá(ja) Ṣrí Kumara Gupta (Mahe)ndraditya.

This piece represents a class of money of which we have absolutely multitudes of specimens,* it has been entered in the plate, to illustrate a well understood distinction from Nos. 11–16, indicated by the absence or omission of the quasi-superlative *Mahá* before the "*Rájadhirája.*"

The intention of this titular discrimination, as I understand it, was to mark the relative grades of Kumára's dignity; I suppose the class of coins of which No. 17 is the representative to have constituted the currencies of the Prince while acting as Viceroy on the part of his father in the Kingdom of Guzarát. He was then a "King over Kings," but not a "*Great* King over Kings" as he became in later days on succeeding to his father's imperial throne and the position of Lord-paramount of India.†

---

* *Journ. R. As. Soc.,* vol. XII. p. 65.

† Objection might be taken to this conclusion on the ground that the typical degradation of the central figure on the reverse in No. 17 is greater, and evidences a more distinct departure from the prototype than the device on the coin bearing the *imperial* prefix to Kumára's name. But the character of work of the No. 17 class is better as a rule, while more local in adhering to the Sáh model, than that of the coins with the improved definition of the figure of *Párvati,* which perhaps may have been entrusted to artists sent from the capital on the accession of the new Emperor, and who would have understood the intent and meaning of the device they had to execute better than the provincial die-cutters, who perhaps worked mechanically from their own anterior models. It will be noticed that the heads on the obverses of Nos. 11 and 13 follow different ideals, and are less finished than those on Nos. 10 and 17; and the style of the Greek character further marks a different school.

No. X.* Silver. Mr. Newton.

Obverse.— 

Reverse device similar to No. 18, Autotype Plate, and Bakra Gupta's coin, No. XI.*

One of the most suggestive coins in the entire series emanating from the Western mints is the piece here reproduced, *on wood*, from Mr. Newton's original design given in his Plate, p. 3, *Journ. Bom. Br. R. As. Soc.* vol. VII.

The coin bears the conventional imitation of the Sáh profile, with the still clearly marked system of local dating so far as the position is concerned, commencing from the base of the skull on the left, and retaining the ordinary initial prefix of the *iota* (I), whose purport is as yet unfathomed ; after this symbol, if originals and copies are not at fault, we encounter the distinct and universally accepted sign for 90 (⊕) ; following this, in the ordinary line of reading of the Greek legend, some vague outlines of a unit may be traced, which would still keep the date within the reasonable limits of Kumára's succession, *i.e.* within the full *hundred*, or up to seven indeterminate years subsequent to the inscription date of 93 of his father Chandra Gupta II.

The given 90 or any number up to 99 may be tested by three different systems of interpretation; first, under the theory of the omission of *hundreds* seen in Bactrian and other examples, but alien to the ordinary course of Suráshtran definitions ; second, under the supposition of a casual default in the expression of the sign for *hundreds*, and the implication of an immediate succession by Kumára to Swámí Rudra Sáh, who concludes the series of Sáh coin dates, in the numbers 280–292, expressed in the ciphers of their own system, which would, in so far, account for the consecutive appearance of the 90 *odd* on Kumára's coin ;* or, third, under the more satisfactory and conclusive inference that the number 90 had reference to the family system of dating already in use in the home dominions of the Guptas, which would curiously confirm many independent verifications of their epoch. It is, therefore, under this last head that I propose to class the formulated date in question. Thus, taking it in consecutive order with the 93 of Chandra Gupta II., Kumára must have succeeded to the throne some time before 100 of his dynastic system of reckoning and assuming this to have followed the era of Ṣaka, about A.D. 179.

No. XI.* Silver. Mr. Newton. (*Journ. Bom. Br. R. As. Soc.*) 1862, p. 3, Plate (un-numbered) Fig. 11.

Obverse.—A very straggling and chaotic outline of the Sáh profile, its defects are apparently less attributable to the ineffectual efforts of the modern native copyist than to the faulty dies of the ancient mints.

Reverse.—The device shown in the accompanying wood-cut, which has been copied implicitly by Mr. Adeney from the original in the Bombay lithograph. 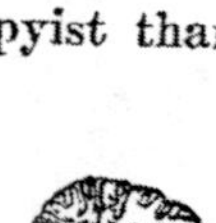

* Mr. Newton apparently advocated this view of the question (*Journ. Bom. Br. R. As. Soc.*, vol. VIII. p. 10), though he was quite clear about the absence of any cipher before the 90, and recognized the I, or, as he calls it, the "figure which appears to be a mint mark, commonly found on the Sáh coins."

Legend.—Mr. Newton, who had the original piece before him, confidently transcribed the characters as *Parama bhagavata (rájádhirájá) Ṣrí Kumára Gupta Mahendrasya.* The Kumára Gupta is clear in the wood-cut, but the device separates the piece from the ordinary issues of that King.

BAKRA GUPTA.*

No. XII.* Silver. MR. NEWTON.

OBVERSE.—Sáh head but slightly varied, and still retaining the conventional ornamental collar.

Legend.—Traces of NANO.

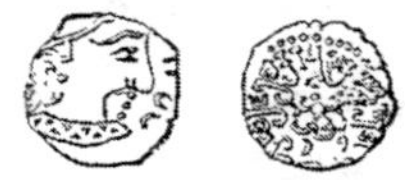

REVERSE.—Párvatí, not far removed from the type shown in No. 15 of the accompanying Autotype Plate. Cluster of seven stars.

Legend.—परम . . . . राजधिराज श्री बक्र गुप्त विक्रमादित्य

Parama . . . . rájadhirája Ṣrí Bakra Gupta Vikramáditya.

SKANDA GUPTA.

Surásthran Series.

No. 18. Silver. ROYAL ASIATIC SOCIETY.†

OBVERSE.—The typical Sáh head, greatly debased.

REVERSE.—Párvatí reduced to fragmentary lines and dots.

Legend, in full, restored from better specimens—

परम भगवत श्री स्कन्द गुप्त क्रमदत्य

Parama Bhagavata Ṣrí Skanda Gupta kramaditya.

Visible on this coin, *Parama . . . Ṣrí Skanda Gupta kramaditya.*

No. 19. Silver; *double struck.* ROYAL ASIATIC SOCIETY.‡

OBVERSE.—The Sáh head, obscured by the second impression of the die.

Legend.—Traces of NANO.

REVERSE.—Figure of Ṣiva's Bull, *Nandí,* recumbent.

Legend, restored.—परम भगवत श्री स्कन्द गुप्त क्रमादित्य

Parama Bhagavata Ṣrí Skanda Gupta kramáditya.

Legible of the first die impression, *Bhagavata Ṣrí Skanda Gupta kramáditya.* Traces of the second or superstruck die, . . *ya par* . . .

---

* Published by Mr. Newton, *Journ. Bom. Br. R. As. Soc.,* 1862, p. 11. The coin is stated to have been found in company with a collection of pieces of Kumára Gupta.

† Engraved as No. 20, pl. XV., *Ariana Antiqua.* So unintelligible was the device, that Párvatí was placed both by the author and the engraver, upside down.

‡ See also engravings of this coin in *Journ. R. As. Soc.,* vol. XII. pl. II. fig. 45, p. 66; and *Ariana Antiqua,* pl. XV. fig. 16.

No. 20. Silver. B. M.

Coin similar to the last.

Legible, on reverse of the original piece.—*Parama Bhagavata Ṣrí Skanda Gupta.*

The recumbent Bull, *Nandi*, which figures on the reverses of these coins was adopted intact as the emblem of the succeeding dynasty of the Valabhís; hence we find it on the seals of the copper-plate grants of Ṣrí Dhara Sena* and Dhruva Sena,† which are further attested with the regal stamp of श्रीभटार्कः *Ṣrí Bhaṭárkah*, below the Bull.

No. 21. Silver. B. M.

Obverse.—The typical Sáh head, much debased.

Legend.—NAN . . . *vavo.*

Reverse.—A small Altar, which may be intended either for the Mithraic altar, figured on Nos. 1 and 5 ante, or for the conventional shrine of the sacred Túlsí tree of the Hindús.

Legend restored.—परम भगवत श्री स्कन्द गुप्त क्रमादित्य
Parama Bhagavata Ṣrí Skanda Gupta kramáditya.

Legible on this specimen, *Parama Bhagava . Skanda Gupta kramáditya.*

It is worthy of remark that this altar symbol, like the Bull of Skanda Gupta's other type of money (Nos. 19, 20), which passed on as the heritage of the Valabhís, is adopted by his Gurjjara successors as their distinctive emblem. It may be followed in its course on the copper-plate grants of Prasánta-rága, a monarch "devoted to the worship of the Sun," under the dates of 380 and 385 Ṣaka.‡ The interpretation of the parallel dates by the Ṣaka-era test seems to be almost necessitated by the discovery of a later grant of 417, to which date the words *Ṣaka Nṛipa* are subjoined.§

Ṣrí Gupta.

No. XIII*. Silver. Weight, 31 grains. Mrs. Freeling. *Unique.*||

Obverse.—The original device of the Sáh head, closely approximating to the normal outline.

Legend, in imperfect Greek.— . . ACIOIO . .

Reverse.—The standard *Párvati* device, deteriorated to the extent shown in the accompanying fac-simile, with the Sáh cluster of stars and associate half moon. 

Legend.—Tentative reading.—श्री न्दगुप्तवक्रमद्रस्य श्रीगुप्त

* *Journ. As. Soc. Beng.*, vol. IV. pl. XL. p. 486.

† *Ibid.*, vol. VII. p. 978; Prinsep's *Essays*, vol. I. pp. 257, 262.

‡ *Journ. R. As. Soc.*, N. S., vol. I. pp. 262, &c.

§ Inscription of Dadda, whose capital seems to have been Broach. *Journ. Bom. Br. R. As. Soc.* 1871, p. 19.

|| Prinsep's *Essays*, vol. II. p. 94.

I am afraid that we must reduce the pretensions of the *Srí Gupta*, whose name appears on this unique coin, from the possible position of father of the family, down to a very minor and incidental succession to the later glories of his falling race. Whatever speculations may have been encouraged by the mere discovery of the name of *Srí Gupta* must now give way to the stern determination of numismatic facts. Tried by such tests the *reverse* of our specimen sinks it into comparative obscurity and carries down, with its own typical degradation, the claims of the king who issued it.

Kumára Gupta.

Peacock types.

Nos. 22, 23. Silver. My Cabinet.

Obverse.—A localized and greatly debased imitation of the Sáh head, especially disfigured by the Oriental rendering of the almond eye.

Legend.—In this class of coins all pretence of copying or attempting to reproduce the imitative Greek legends is fairly abandoned.

But in lieu thereof we are presented with the far more definite record of the three-figured date transposed from the ordinary position behind the Sáh head, to the less contracted space in the field, in front of the profile. In these cases the use of the indigenous ciphers, each of which expressed its own *full* number, arranged in the same perpendicular order as the initials of the royal names on the gold coins (Nos. 5, &c.), has this advantage over any system of dating in figures dependent on relative position, that in broken sequences, so inevitable in hand-struck pieces, we can pick out the *hundreds*, *tens*, and *units*, with absolute certainty, and combine the general result from independent specimens, without being tied down to the proof of a continuous entry on any single coin.

Reverse.—An admirably executed figure of a Peacock with full front expanse of plumage. To the right, at the foot, a reduced cluster of three stars.

Legend.—देवं जयति विजितावनिरवनिपति कुमार गुप्तो

Dev(o) jayati vijitávanir avanipati(h) Kumára Gupto.

"His Majesty, Kumára Gupta, who has subdued the earth, rules." *

---

* When once fairly deciphered, these obscure legends will be seen to present but few difficulties. The lapidary inscriptions have already proved that the Gupta artists indulged in faulty Sanskrit orthography as well as in grammatical errors, so I need not detain my readers by any comments upon minor imperfections, while the general sense of the legend remains sufficiently clear. I must mention that, in my Devanágari transcripts, I have adhered servilely to the original legends impressed upon the coins; the version in the Roman type has been corrected up to Sanskrit requirements, by Dr. Fitzedward Hall.

There is a superfluous य *y* (or possibly an म *m*) after the गुप्त on Skanda Gupta's coins, the use of which is not apparent, but which clearly takes the place of the final *o* in Kumára's legends

I may note that Kumára Gupta's coins display both the old form of म *m* and the more specially Gupta outline of that character. (*Journ. As. Soc. Beng.* vol. IV. pl. XLIX., figs. 10 and 12.) The य *y* is also seen in its transition state from the triple-lined letter of early days to the almost modern form; while at times it appears, on Skanda's money, as a character not easily distinguishable from the later Kumára म *m* just adverted to. This extensive modification of the य *y* in the numismatic alphabet, is the more curious, as the corresponding lapidary character retains all the essentials of its ancient outline throughout the Gupta inscriptions, from the Allahábád pillar to Budha Gupta's record at Eran; and even on to Toramána's inscription at the same place.

The range of dates on this class of Kumára coins is more complete in the units than in the tens. We have but a single example of the latter which, however, recurs frequently and constitutes unmistakeably the *θ*, or casual likeness of that character, which stands for 20. The units for the numbers 1, 4, 8,* 9 and entered below the *θ* are equally positive.

SKANDA GUPTA.

Nos. 24 and 25. My Cabinet.

OBVERSE.—Head as above. Traces of a date in front of the profile. The figure for 100 is quite plain and distinct on the original of No. 24.

REVERSE.—Peacock as above. The stars are omitted.

Legend.—विजितावनिरवनिपति जयति देव स्कन्द गुप्त य

Vijitáranir avanipati(h) jayati deva(h) Skanda Gupta-y.

BUDHA GUPTA.

No. 26. Silver.

OBVERSE.—Head as above. Date in front of the profile, 155.†

REVERSE.—Peacock as in No. 25.

Legend.—देव जयति विजितावनिरवनिपति श्री बुध गुप्तो

Dev(o) jayati vijitávanir avanipati(h) Ṣrí Budha Gupto.

TORAMÁṆA.

Nos. 27 and 28. Silver. B. M.

a. Colonel BUSH's coin; *b.* Miss BARING's late donation to the B. M.

OBVERSE.—Gupta head, facing to the *left*, thus marking an *intentional* modification of the conventional Gupta dies.

Legend, in front of the profile, reading downwards, from the outside. 82 or rather 182, the figure for 100 is obliterated.

REVERSE.—Peacock as in the proper Gupta series, greatly debased in form and design.

Legend restored.—देव जनित विजितावनिरवनिपति श्री तोरमण

Deva janita vijitávanir avanipati Ṣrí Toramaṇa.

---

* The 8 has not hitherto been quoted. It may be seen on one of the coins of Kumára, in the Stacey Collection in the Museum of the Asiatic Society of Bengal. The same collection contributes the *unique* figure of 9.

† The unit on the British Museum coin figured in my plate II. *Journ. R. As. Soc.*, vol. XII. No. 56, would seem to carry us on to 157.

Bhaṭṭaraka Kings.

Nos. 29, 30, 31. Debased silver. Mr. Burgess.

Obverse.—The Sáh head, but little modified.

Reverse.—Fragmentary traces of the design exhibited in coin XI.* and in the wood-cut of the copper coin, No. XIV.*

Legend, partially restored.—राज्ञो मह चत्रपरस . . . कस महस . . भट्टरकस
Rajno Maha Kshatraparasa . . . . *Mahasa* . . *Bhuṭṭarakasa.*

Nos. 32, 33. Copper.

Obverse.—Sáh head.

Reverse.—The combined form of the bow and trident, greatly obscured.

Legend. As in No. 29.

No. XIV.* Copper. Weight, 12 grains.

Obverse.—Humped Bull to the left, with a dotted circle.

Reverse.—Strung and drawn bow, with arrow projecting into a curved trident, of which it forms the central prong.

This little mite of copper proves to be worth far more than its weight in gold, for the light it throws upon the primary design of the hitherto incomprehensible device on the class of Suráshtran coins Nos. 29–33. But far beyond the mere mechanical identification of an obscure symbol is its value, in the historical sense, in the link it establishes between the Guptas, or their immediate successors, and the proximately contemporary dynasty of the nine Nágas, adverted to the quotation from the *Vishnu-Purána* (p. 11 *ante*).

The reverse devices of the Gupta Suráshtran coins have already exercised our conjectures: the Párvatí solution, in the one case, was as unexpected as the discovery of the prototype of the device of No. 29 in the simple bow and arrow combination with Ṣiva's trident, disclosed in the wood-cut.

Many and various have been the guesses as to the purport of this combination of lines on these coins. My latest impressions were in favour of a crude copy of the figure of "Minerva Promachos" of the currencies of Apollodotus and Menander, which entered so largely into the circulating media of Western India, the degraded types of which would almost have justified any shortcomings on the part of native imitators. Looking at the autotype reproductions of Nos. 30, 31, 32, 33, from the top of the page, the flowing garments and the extended shield readily suggest themselves; but now we discover, under the teaching of the independent home device, that the trisula or special emblem of Ṣiva, whose worship is so distinctly to be traced by independent testimony, constituted the banner of the Bhaṭṭarakas, and Minerva's shield subsides into the light battle-axe of the Scythians, which is preserved in its form and relative position on the staff of so many village weapons of Northern India to this day.*

The Numismatic identifications of the currencies of the Nágas have been followed out in detail, in General Cunningham's later Archæological Reports; it will be sufficient for my present purpose, to append his remarks in a foot note.† Merely premising that the connection between the Nágas and the Western successors of the Guptas is indicated in the identity of the outline of the Bull on coins Nos. XIV.✳, XV.✳, and that the

* The presence of the triṣula or trident is an indication of the adoption of the worship of Siva; and the trident, it may be remarked, is combined with an axe on one side of the staff like the tridents at Barahat and Gopeswara.—*Journ. As. Soc. Beng.*, 1836, p. 485; H. H. Wilson, *Ariana Antiqua*, p. 350, pl. X. figs. 12–21, pl. XXI. fig. 19, and Chandra Gupta coin, pl. XVIII. fig. 10.

Varieties of the *triṣúl, balá*, or trident, continued to be emblematic on the coins of the first *third* of this century in Mathurá, Jalaor, Ságar, Ṣrínagar, Kálpí, &c.

Prinsep's *Essays*, "Useful Tables," p. 67, pl. XLVI. figs. 42–46; *Journ. As. Soc. Beng.*, 1834, pl. III., "Useful Tables," p. 55.

† "If I am right in the identification of Narwar with the Padmávati of the Puráṇas, we obtain one of the most interesting and important facts in ancient Indian history in fixing the actual locality of the kingdom of the nine Nágas. The identification is strongly corroborated by the numerous coins of various Nága kings which have been found at Narwar, Gwalior, and Mathurá, all of which have been described by me in the Journal of the Asiatic Society [*loc. cit.*]. It is further supported by a passage in the 18th line of the Allahábád pillar inscription of Samudra Gupta, in which the king boasts of the extent of his dominions, and enumerates the different princes and countries which had become subject to this power. Amongst the former he mentions *Ganapati-Nága* as one of the tributary princes of Aryavartta. Now, *Ganapati* or *Ganendra* is the name of the Nága Raja, whose coins are the most common and the most widely diffused of all these Narwar kings: and as the legends of his coins are in the very same characters as those of the Gupta coins and inscriptions, it is certain that he must have been a contemporary of one of the princes of that dynasty. I think, therefore, that there is every probability in favour of the identity of the Ganapati-Nága of the Narwar coins with the Ganapati-Nága of Samudra's inscription. My discovery of an inscription of Samudra Gupta in Mathurá itself is sufficient to show that the Nágas must have lost their dominion over that city at least as early as the reign of Samudra."

"The period to which the nine Nágas must be assigned depends solely on the date of their contemporaries the Guptas, whose power became extinct in A.D. 319. If, therefore, we refer the rise of the Gupta dynasty to the Saka era, the date of Samudra Gupta will fall in the first half of the second century of the Christian era. But as in his reign the power of the Nágas had already begun to decline, I think that the establishment of the Nága dynasty may be fixed with some certainty about the beginning of the Christian era. According to this view, the rule of the nine Nágas would have extended over the whole of the first and second centuries, or from A.D. 0 to 225. In the following list I have arranged the names of these Nága Kings according to the devices of their coins, beginning with those types which seem to me to be the earliest on account of the more ancient appearance of their accompanying inscriptions. It is worthy of note, as corroborative of the date which I have assigned to the Nágas, that the whole of the devices of their coins are to be found also on the silver coins of the Guptas themselves, or on those of their acknowledged contemporaries:—"

No.	A.D.	Names on Coins.	Devices.
I.	0	Bhima Nága	Peacock to the left.
II.	25	Kha* Nága (? *Kharjjura*, or *Kharpara*)	Ditto to the right.
III.	50	Va* Nága (? *Varma*, or *Vatsa*)	Ditto ditto.
IV.	75	Skanda Nága	Ditto ditto.
		Ditto	Bull recumbent to the right.
V.	100	Bribaspati Nága	Ditto ditto.
VI.	125	Ganapati, or Ganendra	Bull as in coin No.
		Ditto	A wheel.
VII.	150	Vyághra Nága	Ditto.
VIII.	175	Vasu Nága	Ditto.
IX.	200	Deva Nága	Ditto.
		Ditto	Bull recumbent to right.
	225	Ditto	Triṣula.
		Close of the dynasty.	

association of the Nágas with the central Indian Guptas is more distinctly shown in the annexation by the latter of the typical Peacock of the first-named dynasty, who, singular to say, latterly abstained from its use, and adopted the new device of the Bull under Skanda Nága.*

GANAPATI NAGA.

No. XV.✳ Copper. Weights (in full currency order) average 36·4, 18·2, 9·1 grains.† Prinsep's *Essays*, pl. VIII. fig. 9, pl. XXXIV. fig 31, *Journ. As. Soc. Beng.*, 1834, pl. XXVI. fig. 9, 1865, pl. XVIII. figs. 7, 8, 9.

OBVERSE.—Bull, as in the coin above figured, (No. XIV.✳) with a margin of dotted lines of identical design.

REVERSE.—No devices. The field is filled in with the circular legend.

Legend restored.—श्रीगणपत्य
Sri Gaṇapatya.

PAṢUPATI.

No. XVI.✳ *a.* Copper. Weight, 92 grains. Fig. 15, pl. XVIII., *Journ. As. Soc. Beng.* 1865, p. 115; and Prinsep's *Essays*, pl. XXVIII., fig. 23.

OBVERSE.—Figure of the King seated cross-legged in the Indian fashion, his right hand holding a flower, and his left resting on his hip; the whole surrounded by a circle of large dots.

REVERSE.—A vase surmounted by a crescent and star, or perhaps a flower, and enclosed in a circle of large dots.

Legend, in Gupta *Nágarí* characters.—पशुपति
Paṣupati.

No. XVII.✳ *b.* Copper. Weight, 92 grains. Fig 17, *ibid.*

OBVERSE.—A short trident or *trisul*, on a stand surrounded by a circle of small dots.

Legend in two lines.— प शु *Pa ṣu*
प ति *pa ti*

REVERSE.—The sun, with prominent rays surrounded by a dotted circle.

Legend as in Obverse.

"As the Nágas would appear to have been tributary to the Guptas in the time of Samudra, I think it most probable that the kingdom or district of Narwar must have remained subject to them, until near the close of their dynasty, about A.D. 275, when their sovereignty to the south of the Jumna fell to Toramáṇa."

"Of Toramáṇa's dynasty we have two inscriptions, one of himself at Eran to the south of Narwar, and the other of his son Pasupati at Gwalior to the north of Narwar. From the relative positions of these inscriptions we may fairly infer that the intermediate country must also have belonged to the Toramáṇa dynasty. The date of Toramáṇa himself is fixed by Mr. Thomas on the authority of a silver coin to the year 180" [*proved* by the second example in the plate from, No. 28] "odd of the Gupta era, which referred to the initial year of Ṣaka would place him in A.D. 260. If, then, we allow twenty-five years to each generation, the reign of Toramaṇa will range from 260 to 285 A.D., and that of his son, Pasupati, from 285 to 310 A.D."

* *Journ. As. Soc. Beng.*, 1865, pl. XVIII. p. 120.

† These coins are common and abundant in the extreme. Colonel Stacy's collection alone contained no less than 3479 specimens; and General Cunningham mentions that he has acquired, at various times, many more than 3000."

Résumé.

The description of the Gupta coinage, with its provincial ramifications, in unstinted array, has now been extended, far beyond my original design, in the previous pages.

The critical observer of my text will notice an apparent absence of method, leading me to expand on the one part and contract on the other the general scope of my annotations. These anomalies have been chiefly due to the uncertain demands of a printing office in England, and the irregular reception of editorial sanction from the Archæological Surveyor of the Western Presidency, who is once again at his post, occupied with the duties of a new season's operations. Thus, as chance would have it, I have had ample opportunity of completing progressively certain minor details, but find myself limited in point of time, at the last moment; so that I have had to withdraw, perhaps, the most interesting chapter of the whole series, consisting of a comprehensive essay on the source, progress, and development of the ancient Indian numerals, as well as to defer a more complete review of Indian dates as rectified or confirmed by the numismatic evidence above submitted; so that I have had to reduce my recapitulation of the Gupta and other international dates to the abstract form embodied in the subjoined table, which however effectively combines most of the existing data available for the scrutiny and ultimate adjustment of independent commentators.

Abstract of the Recorded *Gupta Dates.*

Names of Kings.	Inscriptions.	Coins.	Tradition.	Result, A.D., derived from the Saka Era.	Remarks.
1. Gupta - -					
2. Ghaṭot Kacha -					
3. Chandra Gupta I. -					The first Mahárájádhirája.
4. Samudra Gupta -					
5. Chandra Gupta II. -	82 93		Reigned 23 years after the conquest of Suráshtra.	161 172	
6. Kumára Gupta -		90 odd 121 129		? 200 208	Coin of Kumára, No. X.*
7. Skanda Gupta -	130 138 141 146		Reigned 20 years. Senápati Bhattaraka, two years before Skanda's death.	209 217 220 225	
8. Budha Gupta -	165	155		234 244	
Toramáṇa - -		182		261	
Other local *unrecorded* Gupta Kings.					
Vallabhís - -				319	The first even nominal *Mahárája* in the irregular dynastic lists is the third *Senápati.* The VIIth ruler, in the same order, seems to have been the earliest Monarch of any real pretensions.

COINS OF THE ARABS IN SIND.

Some of the less prominent examples among Mr. Burgess's recent acquisitions may possibly prove of more direct and immediate interest to Antiquarians in Western India, than the numismatic remains of unrecorded history with which we have hitherto been concerned.

The conquest of Sind by the Arabs, in A.H. 93 (A.D. 712), constitutes a marked epoch in the annals of the land, and is associated with many instructive coincidences—in its inception, in the domestication of the conquerors on an alien soil, and their abrupt disappearance into comparative obscurity.

The daring and chivalric advance of Muhammad bin Ḳásim, was freely backed by the encouragement and support of the celebrated Hijáj bin Yúsaf, who so completely reversed the Khalif 'Umar's policy of non-extension of the Muslim boundaries to the eastward.

It is curious to note the readiness with which the conquerors settled themselves as residents and the facile refuge this extreme corner of the Muhammadan world afforded to persecuted or heretical members of the new faith, while they retained among themselves so many of their ancient tribal divisions and jealousies; and it is instructive to follow the untold tale of ethnic subsidence and final absorption into the Indian native element, when the true Arab blood came to be exhausted by foreign admixture, as in other cases wherever the standard of the Prophet carried with it, the loose teachings of polygamy, beyond the nomadic tents of the desert.

The sole preface to such obscure investigations as the present must be gleaned from the casual contributions of Arabian writers to the annals of an outlying province, with which they were seldom brought in contact.

In the subjoined table of the Arab rulers of Sind, I have taken, as my leading authority, a writer, who seems to have had extensive and exceptional knowledge of his subject. This list was originally compiled from Reinaud's text and translation of *Belázarí* for my edition of Prinsep's Essays, being further collated with Sir H. M. Elliott's excellent work on the Arabs in Sind, which has since been incorporated in his *Historians of India*, vol. I. p. 113.

A.D.	A.H.		
711–712	93	1.	Muḥammad bin Ḳásim.
		2.	Yazíd bin Abú Kabshah *as-Saksakí.*
714–715	96	3.	Ḥabíb bin Muhallab.
		4.	'Amrú bin Muslim *Al-Baháli.*
		5.	Junaid bin 'Abd al raḥman *Al-Marrí* (under Hishám).
725–726	107	6.	Tamím bin Zaid *Al-'Utbi.*
		7.	Al ḥakim bin 'Awánah *Al-Kalbi.*
			('Amrú bin Muḥammad.)
			(Sulaimán bin Hishám and Abú Al-Khattáb)† under the 'Abbásides.

---

* Abu J'afir Aḥmad bin Yahya ibn Jábir al Balázarí, ob. inter 256 and 279 A.H., Ibn Khaldun, p. 438. Reinaud *Fragments Arabes et Persans inédits, relatifs à l'Inde*, pp. xviii., 182.

† Appendix to the *Arabs in Sind*: Cape Town, 1853. Elliot quoting "Tohfat ul Kirám," *Historians of India*, I., 443.

A.D.	A.H.		
		8.	’Abd al rahman bin Muslin *’Al-Abdi* defeated by
		9.	Manṣúr bin Jamhúr *Al-Kalbi* the local Governor under the Ummaih Khalifs.
		10.	Músa bin K’aab, *Al-Tamimí*; overpowers Manṣúr. (The Tohfat ul Kirám attributes this victory to Dáúd bin ’Ali.)
757–8	140	11.	Hishám bin ’Amrú *Al-Taghlabi.*
		12.	’Amar bin Ḥafṣ bin ’Usmán, Hazármard.*
770–1	154	13.	Rúḥ bin Ḥátim.†
800	184	14.	Dáúd bin Yazíd bin Ḥátim.
		15.	Bashir bin Dáûd (about 200 A.H., Reinaud).
828	213‡	16.	Ghassán bin ’Abád.
		17.	Músa bin Yaḥia bin Khálid, *Al Barmaki* (dies in 221 A.H., 836 A.D.)
		18.	’Amrán bin Músa.§
		19.	Fazl bin Máhán.
		20.	Muḥammad bin Fazl, his brother Máhán rebels, and eventually The Native races regain possession of the soil.

In addition to the kingdoms of Manṣúrah and Multán there were other quasi independent governments at Bánia, where ’Umar the son of ’Abdal ’Azíz *Habbári* seems to have held sway,‖ and at Ḳasdár where the governor, in Ibn Haukal’s time (A.D. 943) was Mu’ín bin Aḥmad.¶ But in all these cases, as indeed at Manṣúrah and Multán, the *Khutbah*, or public prayers, were read in the name of the Khalif.

I have one remark to make with reference to the peculiarly local characteristics of the numismatic remains discovered by Mr. Bellasis near the old site of Brahmanabad and the identification of the new town of Manṣúrah, as tested by the produce of the inhumed habitations hitherto penetrated, in the fact of the very limited number of Hindú coins found among the multitudes of medieval Muhammadan pieces, and that the former, as a rule, seem to have been casual contributions from other provinces, of no individual uniformity or appearance of age such as should connect them with the ancient Hindú capital.**

---

* Transferred from Sind to Africa in A.H. 151. Reinaud, p. 213.

† A.H. 160 to 161. Reinaud, p. 213.

‡ Gildemeister quoting Abulfida, II. 150.

§ Killed by عمر بن عبد العزيز الهبادي Belázari, p. 215.

‖ Ibn Haukal, p. 231 text وبانية مدينة صغيرة ومنها عمر بن عبد العزيز الهباري القرشي

¶ Text معين بن احمد Gildemeister *De rebus Indicis*, Bonn., 1838, p. 171; Col. Anderson *Journ. As. Soc. Beng.*, 1852, p. 54; Elliot’s *Historians*, vol. I. pp. 37, 38.

** The note which I compiled in 1858 to aid my first fragmentary description of the coins discovered by Mr. Bellasis at Brahmanábád, contains so many references that may prove useful to Antiquarians in Western India, that I have thought it advisable to correct and enlarge it, as far as possible, up to the requirements of the present day.

“Amrou, fils de Mohammed fils de Cassem . . . . . . fonda, en deçà du lac, une ville qu’il nomma Almansoura. C’est la ville où résident maintenant les gouverneurs.”—p. 120. In a previous passage, Balázari tells us “Ensuite Mohammed fils de Cassem, se porta devant la vieille Bahmanábád, qui se trouvait à deux parasanges de Mansoura. Du reste Mansoura n’existait pas encore, et son emplacement actuel était alors un bois . . . . . Mohammed plaça un lieutenant à Bahmanábád; mais aujourd’hui la ville est ruinée.”—“Balázari,” Reinaud, *Fragments Arabes et Persans relatifs à l’Inde*, Paris, 1845, pp. 198, 211. The Arabian author from whom these traditions are derived, احمد بن يحيي البلاذري died in 279 A.H. (892 A.D.). See also Reinaud quoting Albírúní’s “Tárikh-i-Hind,” *Fragments*, p. 113. Ibn Khurdádbah (A.H. 260) المسالك وممالك text and translation by M. B. de Meynard, *Journal Asiatique*, 1865, pp. 277–8, 289, 292, &c. Sir H. Elliot’s MS. of Albírúní’s *Kánún* has the following:—قال فاتحها لان منصورة و سميت الكبري و هي منه بهمنوا نصرت Jaubert, in his translation of Edrisi, on the authority of original MSS., states that the local native

The first coin introduced into the following list is not supposed to belong to the province of Sind. It has been inserted here, with a view to trace the apparent prototype, upon which the arrangement of the reverse devices of the local coinage was based.

'Abd al Raḥman bin Muslim.

No. XVIII.* Copper. A.H. 133, 4, 5, 6. (A.D. 750–753, 4.)

Obverse	Reverse
لا اله ا لا الله وحده بسم الله مما امربه الامير عبد الرحمن بن مسلم سنة اربع وثلثين ومية	محمد ⋘ ⋙ رسول الله قل لا اسلكم .·. عليه اجرا .·. الا المودة .·. في القربي
"*Nomine Dei. Est ex iis, quos (cudi) jussit Emirus 'Abd al Raḥman bin Muslim* (A.H.) 134."	"*Dic: non peto a vobis ullam hujus facti mercedem, nisi amorem in propinquos.*" (Ḳurán, 42. 22.)*

---

name of the place was ميرمان (variants, تاميرامان, تامبران, and ماموه'). Masúdi tell us, "I visited Multán after 300 A.H. when ابو الدلهات المنبه بن اسد القرشي السامي was king there." "At the same time I visited el Manṣúrah, the king of that country was then ابو المنذر عمر بن عبدالله' [of the family of Habbár bin el Aswad]."—p. 385, Sprenger's Translation; M. Barbier de Meynard's edition, text and translation, Paris, 1861, vol. I. pp. 151, 372, 377, &c. With regard to the extent and importance of the kingdom we are informed that "All the estates and villages under the dependency of el-Manṣúrah amounted to 300,000; the whole country is well cultivated, and covered with trees and fields."—p. 386, *ibid.* Further references to the geographical and the other questions involved occur as follows:—Ḳodámah (ob. 337 A.H.), *Journal Asiatique*, 1862, p. 168; Vincent's *Commerce of the Ancients*, London, 1807, vol. I. p. 145; Gladwin's *Ayín-i-Akbari*, vol. II. p. 137, *et seq.*; *Marásid-al-Ittila'*, vol. II. p. 161. "Istakhrí" (A.H. 300 to 309) "and Sind is the same as Manṣúrah . . . . Manṣúrah which they call Sindhi."—pp. 12 and 147; M. Goeje's new edition of the text, 1870, p. 171, *et seq.*; Ouseley's *Oriental Geography*, London, 1800. Ibn Haukal (A.H. 331 to 366).—M. Goeje's new edition of the text (Lugd. Bat., 1873), p. 226, *et seq.*; Gildemeister *de Rebus Indicis*. Bonn, 1838, p. 166; Col. Anderson's translation *Journ. As. Soc. Beng.*, vol. XXI. p. 42; *Liber Climatum*. Arabic text, J. H. Mœller, Gothæ, 1829; Sprenger's *Post- und Reiserouten des Orients*, Leipzig, 1864, pl. XIV. "Karte von Indien nach Byrúny"; Reinaud's *Géographie d'Aboulfeda*, vol. I. p. 386, &c.; *Tabari*, Paris ed., vol. III. p. 518; Reinaud's *Mémoire sur l'Inde*, pp. 169, 192, 235, &c.; *Ancient Accounts of India and China*, London, 1733; ditto, Reinaud's French edition, Paris, p. 212; Elliot's *Historians of India*, Calcutta, 1849; Elliot's *Appendix to the Arabs in Sind*, Cape Town, 1853. Most of the available information up to date has latterly been incorporated in vol. I. of Prof. Dowson's excellent edition of Elliot's *History of India, as told by its own Historians*, London, Trübner, 1867. *Ariana Antiqua*, p. 414; *Journ. As. Soc. Beng.*, vol. VII. pp. 93, 279; vol. X. p. 183; vol. XIV. p. 75; McMurdo, *Journ. R. As. Soc.*, vol. I. p. 23. *et seq.*; Burnes' *Bokhára*, vol. III. p. 31; Dr. Bird, *Journ. R. As. Soc.*, vol. I. p. 199; Postan's *Observations on Sindh*, p. 143; Pottinger's *Beloochistan and Sinde*, London, 1816, p. 381; Wood's *Oxus*, London, 1841, p. 20; Mohammed Ma'súm's *History of Sind*, A.D. 710 to 1590; *Bombay Government Selections*, New Series, No. XIII., 1855; Mr. A. F. Bellasis, *The Ruined City of Brahmanábád, in Sind*, Bombay, 1856; Col. Sykes in the *Illustrated London News*, Feb. 21 and Feb. 28, 1857, p. 187. With numerous illustrations of Brahmanábád and engravings of coins of Manṣúr bin Jamhur [No. XIX. of *this* series] and of Muhammad [No. XXII.]

* In Fræhn's Recensio (1826, p. 18) a second similar piece is given of the year 135 A.H., a new specimen of the same date is quoted by Stikel (Jena collection, 1845, p. 5). Tornberg cites a coin of 130 A.H. in his *Symbolæ ad Rem numariam Muhammedanorum* (Upsaliæ, 1856), p. 8; and finally M. Tiesenhausen produces a specimen bearing the date of A.H. 133, *Monnaies des Khalifes Orientaux* (St. Pétersbourg, 1873), pp. 65, 66.

MANṢÚR THE SON OF JAMHUR, *Al Kalbí.*

No. XIX. Copper. Weight, 33 grains. Size, 6 of Mionnet's scale. MR. BELLASIS.
Manṣurah, A.H. ?

OBVERSE.
Area.

لا الـــه الا
الله وحده
لاشريك له

Margin.—Illegible.

REVERSE.
Area.

محمـــد

رسول الله

Margin بسم الله ضرب [هذا الفلـ]س بالمنصورة مما امربه منصو . .

"In the name of God, this copper coin was struck, at Manṣúrah, under the orders of Manṣú(r).

No. XX. Copper. Size, 4. MR. BELLASIS. Manṣúrah, A.H. ?

OBVERSE.

Device.
Altogether effaced and obliterated.

REVERSE.
Area.

محمـــد

رسول الله

Margin بسم [الله] ضرب ه بالمنصورة مما امربه منصو . . .

'ABD UL-RAḤMAN.

No. XXI. Copper. Size, 5. Weight, 44 grains.

OBVERSE.—Central device, a *star*, reduced to four points, on the sides of which are disposed, in the form of a square, the words محمد رسول الله عبد الرحمن The outer margin of the piece displays a line of dots enclosed within two plain circles, with four small dotted semicircles to fill in the space left vacant by the angular central legend.

REVERSE.—A scalloped square, surrounded by dots, within which, arranged in three lines, are the words, بالله عبد الرحمن لسلعار ; the concluding word I am unable to decipher, it is possibly the name of 'Abdulraḥman's tribe.

When the English government originated a "Star of India," they were perhaps not aware that Sind had a star of its own; a very special and discriminative symbol, which attained such permanent recognition in and around the province itself, that the device here discovered on 'Abdulraḥman's coins, continued to constitute, in a slightly modified form, the typical emblem of the state, down to the time of Táj-ud-dín Ilduz, the lieutenant of Muhammad bin Sám, eventually independent *Sultán* of Sind, and likewise that of his opponent and successor Kubáchah, another general of the *Ghorí* conquerors of India, who established himself in Sind about 600 A.H. (1203–4 A.D.) to fall at last before the troops of the chivalric Jalál-ud-dín *Khárizmí*, who, in his turn had to swim the Indus for his life, before the hordes of Changís Khán.*

MUḤAMMAD.

No. XXII. Copper. Size, 3.

A unique coin of apparently similar type, (though the obverse is, in this case, absolutely blank,) replaces the name of 'Abd-ul-raḥman on the reverse by that of محمد Muḥammad. The concluding tribal term seems to be identical with the designation embodied in the Ḳufic scroll at the foot of the reverse of No. XXI.

'ABDALLAH.

No. XXIII. Copper.

OBVERSE.—Device as in No. XXI. ('Abd-ul-raḥman).

Legend : محمد [رسول الله] عبدالله

REVERSE.—Blank.

No. XXIV. Copper. Size, 3½. Weight, 18 grains.

OBVERSE.—Central device the conventional four-pointed star, as in No. XXI., around which, in a circular scroll, may be partially read the formula لا اله الا الله وحده لاشريك له.

REVERSE.—Central device composed of the name of عبدالله *Abd-allah*; the two portions عبد and الله being crossed at right angles, so as to form a *tughra* or monogrammic imitation of the outline of the star with four points of the obverse device.

The marginal legend is arranged in the form of a square, and consists of the words محمد رسول الله [الا]مير

No. XXV. Silver. Size, 2. Weight, 8·4 grains.†

Palm branches, roses, stars, and all other mundane devices are rejected and replaced by simple Ḳufic legends, so cherished by severe Muhammadans, to the following effect :

OBVERSE.— لا اله الا الله وحده لاشريك له

REVERSE.— محمد رسول الله الامير عبدالله

No. XXV A. Copper, bearing similar legends. Other specimens vary in the division of the words, and omit the title of *Al-Amír*.

---

* Ilduz's special symbol was a "star" beneath the conventional figure of the Rájpút horseman. See coin No. 24, p. 31, of My *Pathán Kings of Delhi*, Trübner, 1871. Kubáchah follows in the occasional use of the Star, No. 87, p. 101, *ibid.*; so also Muhammad bin Sám's *own* coin, No. 7. (Prinsep's *Essays*, pl. XXVI. fig. 45,) and Altamsh's coin, No. 48, continue to display the local device. The coins of Uzbeg Pái, the Indian General of Jalálud dín, Khárizmi struck at Multán, reproduce the identical cluster of the seven stars of the Sáh Kings, and the Guptas (plate VII. figs. 9–13 *ante*),—which discriminating mark survived, till lately, on the native currencies of Údipúr and Ujjain. *Pathán Kings of Delhi*, No. 85, p. 99; Prinsep's *Essays*, Useful Tables, No. 18, p. 67.

† Among the silver coins exhumed from the so-called Bráhmanábád, some are so minute as to weigh only 1·2 gr.

BANÚ-DÁÚD. (Dáúd-putra's ?)*

No. XXVI. Silver. Weight, 5·6 grains. My CABINET. Unpublished.

محمد	بالله بنو
رسول	د ا و د
الله	و ا ص

The archaic form of Ḳufic stamped on these coins, would, under ordinary circumstances have placed them in a far earlier position, in point of time, than their apparent associates in size and style, whose almost identical legends are couched in less monumental letters; but I prefer to attribute any divergence in this respect to local rather than epochal influences, regarding which we have had so many instructive lessons in the parallel Nágarí alphabets of India.†

BANÚ-'UMAR.‡

No. XXVII. Silver. Size, 1½. Weight, 9 grains. *Five specimens.* Mr. BELLASIS.

OBVERSE.—Legends arranged in five lines.

بالله محمد رسول الله عمر

Marginal lines, plain or dotted, complete the piece.

REVERSE.—Ḳufic legends in three lines.

‡بالله بنو عمرويه منذر

No. XXVIII. Copper. Size, 4. Weight, 35 grains. Common.

Legends as in the silver coins, with the exception that the بنو is placed, for economy of space, in the opening between the two ل's of بالله.

No. XXIX. Copper. Size, 3½. Weight, 21 grains. *Unique.* Mr. BELLASIS.
Manṣúrah, A.H. . . 4.

OBVERSE.—Blank. REVERSE.—
Centre: بنو . . . . عمروية منذر
Margin: . . . . س بالمنصورة سنة اربع . . . . ?

---

* Dáúd-putras, *Journ. R. As. Soc.*, vol. VII. p. 27.

† The patronymic, in its local application, may have been derived from *the* Dáúd bin 'Ali bin 'Abbás No. 10 in the above list (p. 72), who was so prominently associated with the overthrow of the 'Ummaih Khalifs. (Tabari IV. pp. 289, 326, 342.) As uncle of the new Khalif he was all powerful, and as governor of Kufah (in A.H. 132), of which Sind was a dependency, *his troops* would naturally have effected the final transfer of dominion in that province. Mas'audi VI. pp. 88, 91, 98; price II. pp. 2, 4.

‡ I am inclined to identify this ruler with the *Abúl Manżar* 'Umar bin Abdallah, indicated in the general note p. 73 *ante*, as the reigning sovereign of Manṣúrah, in A.H. 300– , at the period of the geographer M'asúdí's visit to the valley of the Indus, and of whom he speaks further in the following terms:—"There is some relationship between the royal family of el-Manṣúrah and the family of esh-Shawárib, the Kadi, ل ابي الشوارب القاضي or the kings of el-Manṣúrah are of the family of Habbár ben el-Aswad, هبار بن الاسود and have the name of Beni 'Amr ben 'Abd el-Azíz el-Karshí, بني عمر بن عبد العزيز القرشي who is to be distinguished from 'Amr ben 'Abd el-Azíz ben Merwán, the Omaïyide (Khalif)".—Sprenger's *Meadow of Gold*, p. 385. The Arabic is from M. B de Meynard's edition, p. 377. See also Gildemeister, quoting *Ibn Haukal*, p. 166; and Elliot, citing the same author (*Historians of India*), p. 63; and Professor Dowson's edition, vol. I. pp. 21.

BANÚ 'UMAR.

No. XXX. Copper. Size, 4½. Weight, 36 grains. Unique. Sir BARTLE FRERE.

OBVERSE.—Central device, four lines crossing each other at a common centre, so as to form a species of star of eight points; four of these are, however, rounded off by dots.

Legend, arranged as a square:

محمد رسول الله سر

with single dots at the corner angles, and two small circles filling in the vacant spaces outside of each word.

Margin.—Two plain circular lines, with an outer circle of dots.

REVERSE.—Central legends in three lines within a triple circle composed of dots, circlets, and an inner plain line. I transcribe the legend, with due reservation, as:

بالله بنو عمروبه منذر

AHMAD.

No. XXXI. Silver. Mr. BURGESS. Unpublished.

OBVERSE.

لا اله الا
الله وحده
لاشريك له

REVERSE.

محمد
رسول
الله الامير
احمد

'ABD-ALLAH (*Wali* and *Malik.*)

No. XXXII. Silver. New varieties. Mr. BURGESS. Unpublished.

OBVERSE.

محمد
رسول
الله
عبدالله

REVERSE.

بالله ولي
عبدالله
ومل

In terminating this brief Muhammadan section, I ought to advert, momentarily, to the information obtained from the early Arabian travellers in India, respecting the mixed currencies of Sind and the adjoining provinces.

The Merchant Sulaimán, A.H. 237 (A.D. 851), is the first who affords us any insight into the condition of the *circulating media* of the land; he tells us that, among other pieces used in commerce in the dominions of the *Balhará*, *Ṭâtariya* dirhams took a prominent place, and that these were reckoned in value as equal to 1½ of the ordinary coins of the King.*

---

* Abú Zaid, circâ 303 A.H. who follows Sulaimán, incidentally mentions: "Autrefois, l'on portait dans l'Inde les dinárs du Sind (وكان يحمل الي الهند في القديم الدنانير السندية) dont chacun équivalait à trois dinárs ordinaires et davantage,"—(وما زاد) p. 153, Reinaud's translation.

So, later in point of time, the Egyptian author of the Masálik-al-Abṣár refers to the "*Tankah* d'or" as equal to 3 *Mithkals.* This was the modern representative of the normal ancient weight of 100 Ratis, (*Ṣataraktika,*) or, as nearly as possible, 175 grains. See My *Pathan Kings*, pp. 217 *et seq.*, and My *Ancient Indian Weights*, pp. 12, 36, 70.

The identification of this term *Ṭáṭariya*, has formed the subject of much vague speculation; M. Reinaud's latest conjecture pointed at a derivation from the Greek *στατήρ*, *Stater*.*

I myself have, for long past, persistently held that the true term was to be found in *Ṭáhiriya*, the name of a dynasty dominant above all others in Eastern Asia at the period of the Merchant's visit to India.†

This conclusion has gradually been strengthened by the discovery of the exact generic *word* in the unique Oxford MS. text of Ibn Khurdádbah,‡ and in the more critical version of Mas'audi,§ lately completed in Paris.

To these evidences, I am now able to add the definite legend of a coin of Ṭalḥah bin Ṭáhir, struck at Bust, on the Helmund, in A.H. 209 (A.D. 824).

Ṭalḥah bin Ṭáhir, A.H. 209.

Copper: size, 5½; weights, 30, 31, and 22·5 grains. Bust. A.H. 209 (A.D. 824). Two specimens, Cunningham collection, B.M. A third coin, recently acquired, by the B. M., contributes the legible name of the Mint.‖

OBVERSE.—

Centre:— لا اله الا الله وحده لاشريك له

Margin:— بسم الله ضرب هذا الفلس ببست سنة تسع و ماتين

REVERSE.—Central device, a reduced Sassanian head, to the right, with the usual flowing back-hair, and traces of the conventional wings above the cap; the border of the robe is bossed or beaded.

In front of the profile the name of الطلحة is inserted.

Margin:— محمد رسول الله مما امربه الامير طلحة علي يدي عبدالله

This coin has further claims upon our attention, in its testimony to the survival of old types and the continuity of the recognition of Sassanian devices in Seistán, extending, in its local influences, even to the confessed followers of Islám, up to so late a period as 209 years after the Hijerah of Muhammad.

---

* "La monnaie qui circule dans ses États consiste en pièces d'argent, qu'on nomme *thatherya* الطاطرية. Chacune de ces pièces équivaut à un dirhem et demi, monnaie du souverain." *Relation des Voyages*, Paris, 1845, I. p. 25; Reinaud, *L'Inde*, 1849, p. 235; Gildemeister, *de Rebus Indicis*, Bonn, 1838, p. 166; Tod's *Rajasthan*, quoted in Prinsep's Essays, I. 86. Dr. Sprenger, in his edition of Mas'audi, proposes the interpretation of *Ṭalatawiya*.

† The Arabic text of Y'aḳúbí, edited by Juynboll (Lugd. Bat., 1861), gives the dates of this family as follows:—

Ṭáhir bin Al Ḥusain - - -	A.H. 205	A.D. 820–1
Ṭalḥah bin Ṭáhir - - -	A.H. 207	A.D. 822–3
'Abdallah bin Ṭáhir - - -	A.H. 215	A.D. 830
Ṭáhir bin 'Abdallah - - -	A.H. 230	A.D. 844–5
Muḥammad bin Ṭáhir - - -	A.H. 248	A.D. 862–3
Y'aḳúb bin Laiś - - - -	A.H. 259	A.D. 872–3

See also Prinsep's *Essays*, U. T., p. 304; *Hamza Isfaháni* (Gottwaldt), pp. 177, 228, &c., &c.

‡ *Journ. Asiatique*, 1865, p. 289. M. B. de Meynard, I find, adhered to the *Tatherides*, in defiance of Professor Cowell's testimony to *Ṭaheriya*. Elliot's *Historians*, vol. I. p. 4.

§ Text, vol. I. p. 382.

‖ Mr. S. L. Poole discovered the correct reading of this mint from a later coin of *Laiś bin 'Ali*, A.H. 298. N.C. vol. XIII. p. 169.

Considered under this aspect of fixity of national designs, it may instruct us in the classification of some of the devices previously noticed,* about which our knowledge is at present indeterminate in the extreme. We know from the later developments of the Indo-Muhammadan coinages of the immediate successors of Mahmúd of Ghazní,† that the Eastern *Turkí* Muslims were less strict in their denunciations of emblems and figures, than their presumedly more orthodox co-religionists of the West, and that in these cases the Northern invaders of India freely accepted the national types of the conquered kingdoms, which in this sense may furnish data for tracing back and discriminating the earlier examples of parallel assimilations.

To return to the material estimates of the *Sindí* currencies, we are in a position to cite the consecutive testimony of Iṣtakhrí and Ibn Ḥaukal, whose verbatim texts in their latest exhaustive form are reproduced in the foot-note.† These restored versions authorize us to infer that there were, among other impinging or still extant national methods of weighing and estimating metallic values *inter se*, certain market rates, or prices current, for international exchanges, which were quoted in fractions at that time, as our half-crowns still count, in defiance of decimals, in the London stock lists.

From these returns we gather that there were coins termed "Victorious" equivalent to five ordinary dirhams in the local exchange, and that, concurrently the *Bázár* or open market recognized a totally different scale, based upon a coinage only *plus* ⅛th or ⅓rd above the home issues.

With the very imperfect numismatic materials extant, it would be presumptuous to pretend to fix, even approximately, the coin weights and measures obtaining in such a vague international crossway as Manṣúrah; but I could quote within narrow geographical or epochal limits, such extreme variations of weights of dinárs, dirhams and copper coins a discretion, that, if I wished it, I might prove almost any given sum to momentary demonstration, an exercise which, as a collector of positive facts, I specially desire to avoid.

---

* p. 40 *ante.*

† Prinsep's *Essays*, vol. I. p. 333; *Pathán Kings of Delhi*, p. 58; *Journ. R. As. Soc.*, vol. XVII. pp. 171, 177.

ونقودهم التاهريات كل درهم نحو خمسة دراهم ولهم درهم يقال له الطاطري في الدرهم—*Iṣtakhrí*,

ونقودهم القندهاريات كل درهم منها خمسة دراهم ولهم درهم يقال له الطاطري في الدرهم—*Ibn Ḥaukal.*

وزن درهم وثلثين

درهم وثمن

The conversion of the *Ḳahcriya* into *Ḳandahâriya* seems to have been a purely arbitrary correction, and one not justified by the tenor of the associate text.

Kandahár is not mentioned elsewhere in Ibn Ḥaukal's geographical lists. The town at this period does not appear to have attained any degree of importance. See Goeje's text, p. 297. The name, however, occurs in Ibn Khordádbah. IV., p. 278.

IV.—THE VALABHI DYNASTY.

After the Sâhs come the Guptas of Kanauj* who introduced an era of their own, commencing in A.D. 319. These apparently governed by Senâpatis or Viceroys, and it is not necessary, as seems to have been supposed, that the Sâh dynasty should have terminated before the rise of the Guptas.† The latter doubtless arose to considerable power before they added Kâṭhiâwâḍ to their dominion. Indeed it is said in Surâshṭra that the conquest of the country was only effected by Kumârapâla Gupta early in the reign of his father, and that he left a Senâpati, or provincial governor, who ruled at Wâmanasthalî, the modern Wanthali near Junâgaḍh. This, I incline to think, was probably between 400 and 405 A.D.; for Chandragupta is said to have reigned for twenty-three years afterwards, and to have been succeeded by Kumârapâla Gupta, who ruled for twenty years (cir. 107 to 127 of the Gupta Kâl). He was succeeded by Skanda Gupta, one of whose Viceroys at Wâmanasthalî was Parṇadatta, "but this king," says the legend, "was of a weak intellect. His Senâpati Bhaṭârka, who was of the Gehlotî race, taking a strong army, came into Surâshṭra and made his rule firm there. Two years after this, Skanda Gupta died." The Senâpatis afterwards assumed the title of kings of Surâshṭra, and having placed a governor at Wâmanasthalî, founded the city of Valabhînagar.‡

Valabhî, identified with the buried city at Walâ, in the east of the peninsula, eighteen miles north-west of Bhaunagar, now became the capital of the new dynasty; and when "the Gupta race were dethroned by foreign invaders," the Valabhî kings extended their sway "over Kachh, Laṭ-deśa,§ and Mâlwâ."

Bhaṭârka must have established himself at Valabhî about A.D. 480; and of the dynasty he founded we have numerous copper plates, discovered at Walâ and elsewhere in the peninsula, which, in recording grants to Brâhmaṇs and Bauddha ascetics, give also the genealogy of the family and important dates in their reigns. From such of these as have been translated‖ we gather that:

I. Bhaṭârka Senâpati was followed by four of his sons in succession.

II. Dharasena Senâpati, eldest son of Bhaṭârka.

III. Droṇasiñha Mahârâja, a second son of Bhaṭârka, "whose royal splendour was sanctified by the great gift, his solemn coronation performed in person by the Supreme Lord, the Lord Paramount of the whole earth."¶

---

* For the history of the Guptas, see preceding chapter and conf. Lassen, *Indische Alterthumskunde*, (2nd ed.) vol. II. pp. 957 ff., 983 ff., 994, 1228, who places the dynasty terminating with Nârâyaṇa Gupta, between A.D. 140 and 295; *Journ. As. Soc. Beng.*, vol. III. pp. 118 ff., 257 ff. 339 ff.; vol. IV. pp. 551 ff., 639; vol. V. pp. 646 ff., 657; vol. VI. pp. 1 ff., 672, 963 ff.; vol. VII. pp. 37, 347, 634; vol. XXIV. p. 375; Prinsep's *Essays*, by Thomas, vol. I. pp. 231 ff., 240–252, 265, 268, 270, 276, 285–288, 338, 365, 377, 389; vol. II. pp. 69, 83, 90; and *Useful Tables*, pp. 166, 250; *Journ. R. As. Soc.*, vol. XII. pp. 76, 77, and plates; vol. XIII. p. 108 ff.; *Journ. Bom. Br. R. As. Soc.*, vol. VII. pp. 11, 121; vol. IX. p. 152; vol. X. p. 59; Wilson's *Ariana Antiqua*, p. 426, and pl. xviii., &c.

† See note,* p. 30.

‡ Major J. W. Watson, *Ind. Antiquary*, vol. II. p. 372, already quoted by Mr. Thomas on p. 29.

§ The collectorates of Surat, Bharoch, Khêḍâ, and parts of Baroda territory.

‖ *Ind. Antiq.*, vol. I. pp. 14, 18, 45, 60; vol. III. pp. 235, 303; vol. IV. pp. 104 and 174; *Journ. As. Soc., Beng.* vol. IV. pp. 401, 475 ff.; vol. VII. pp. 349, 966 ff.; *Journ. Bom. Br. R. As. Soc.*, vol. III. pt. ii. pp. 213 ff.; vol. VII. p. 116; vol. VIII. pp. 230, 245; vol. X. p. 66 ff.

¶ Copper plates, *Ind. Ant.*, vol. I. p. 61; vol. IV. p. 106; *Journ. As. Soc. Beng.*, vol. IV. p. 481.

IV. Dhruvasena I., a third brother, whose sister's daughter Duḍḍâ was a Bauddha devotee, and founded a monastery. The plate mentioning this is dated Samvat 216 (evidently of the Gupta era), or A.D. 534; other two bear dates 207 and 210.

V. Dharapaṭṭa, the youngest son of Bhaṭârka, who was succeeded by—

VI. Guhasena his son, of whom there are three copper plates known, dated respectively 250,* 256 (or 266),* and 258,* *i.e.* A.D. 568, 574 (or 584), and 576. The second only has been translated, and grants four villages to "the community of the reverend Śâkya monks belonging to the eighteen schools† [of the Hînayâna], who have come from various directions to the great convent of Duḍḍâ, built by the venerable Duḍḍâ."

VII. Śrî Dharasena II., the son of Guhasena, of whom we have also two grants, dated 272 and 277,‡ or A.D. 590 and 595.

VIII. Śîlâditya (Dharmâditya) I., son of Dharasena, also made a grant to a Bauddha community dated G. 286 or A.D. 604.§

IX. Kharagraha, his brother (cir. A.D. 610–617).

X. Śrî Dharasena III., son of Kharagraha (cir. 617–630).

XI. Dhruvasena II., younger son of Kharagraha (cir. 630–642).

XII. Śrî Dharasena (Balâditya) IV., second son of Dhruvasena, of whom there are two grants both dated G. 326, or A.D. 644,—one to priests of the Mahâyâna school, belonging to a monastery erected by Divirapati Skandabhaṭṭa; and the other to Brahmans of Siñhapura,‖—the modern Sihor. A third grant is dated S. 329.

XIII. Dhruvasena III., the son of Derâbhaṭa and grandson of Śîlâditya I. (cir. A.D. 650–660).

XIV. Kharagraha II., the brother of Dhruvasena III. (cir. 660–666).

XV. Śîlâditya II., son of Śîlâditya, the brother of Dhruvasena III. and Kharagraha II.

XVI. Śîlâditya III., his son, of whom there are two grants dated 356, and one unpublished dated 358.¶

XVII. Śîlâditya IV., son of Śîlâditya III., of whom a plate has been found dated S. 403, *i.e.* A.D. 722.

---

* *Ind. Ant.*, vol. III. p. 304; vol. IV. p. 174. In these dates the second figure is read by Bhagvanlâl Indraji and Cunningham as 40, by Râmkrishna G. Bhandarkar as 50, and by Dr. Bühler as 60.

† Conf. Stan. Julien's *Mémoires sur les Cont. Occid.*, tom. I. p. 204; Vassilief, *Le Bouddhisme*, p. 78.

‡ In these dates, the second sign is read by Bhagvanlâl as 60, by Dr. Bühler and Bhandarkar as 70.

§ *Ind. Ant.*, vol. I. p. 45.

‖ Ibid., pp. 14, 45.

¶ *Journ. As. Soc. Ben.*, vol. VII. p. 966; *Journ. Bom. Br. R. As. Soc.*, vol. III. pt. ii. p. 210. In the date 348, the second sign would be read by Bhagvanlâl as 50, since he takes to be 40, but Dr. Bühler, who has read the plate for me, says he feels at present "utterly uncertain as to the import of , and waits for more plates." He adds that he "has discovered new points that go in favour of the epoch of 319 A.D. for the era." As in the case of Guhasena's plates, he reads the second symbol of the plates of Śîlâditya III., as 60 (see note * above).

The following will illustrate the genealogy of the dynasty:—

1. Bhaṭârka.

2. Dharasena I. *Senâpati.* 3. Droṇasiñha. *Mahârâjâ.* 4. Dhruvasena I. (207, 210, 216). 5. Dharapaṭṭa.

6. Guhasena (260, 266, 268).

7. Śrî Dharasena II. (272, 277).

8. Śîlâditya (Dharmâditya) I. (286). 9. Kharagraha I.

Derabhaṭa. 10. Śrî Dharasena III. 11. Dhruvasena (Balâditya) II.

12. Śrî Dharasena IV. (326, 329).

Śîlâditya. 13. Dhruvasena II. 14. Kharagraha (Dharmâditya) II.

15. Śîlâditya II.

16. Śîlâditya III. (348, 356).

17. Śîlâditya IV. (403).*

There are many other plates of this dynasty not yet translated, and every year considerable numbers are turned up in the ruins of their ancient capital, now used as a quarry for the neighbouring district. If these plates could only be secured as they are found and translated, they would doubtless yield many fresh and interesting results.

It was during the reign of Dhruvasena II. (cir. A.D. 632–640) that the Chinese Bauddha pilgrim Hiwan-Thsang visited Western India, and apparently Valabhî itself. His account† runs thus:—"The kingdom of *Fa-la-pi* is about 6,000 *li* (1200 miles) in circuit, the capital has a circumference of 30 *li* (6 miles). As to the products of the soil, nature of the climate, the manners and character of the people, they are like those of *Ma-la-p'o* (Malwa). The population is very numerous, and all the families live in wealth. There are a hundred whose wealth amounts to a million. The rarest merchandise from distant countries is found here in abundance. There are a hundred convents where nearly 6,000 devotees live, who, for the most part study the doctrines of the *Ching-liang-pu* (school or nikâya of the Sammatîyas) which adheres to the 'lesser translation' (*Hînayâna*).‡ We count several hundred temples of the gods; and the heretics of various sects are exceedingly numerous.

"When the Tathâgata (*Buddha*) lived in the world, he travelled often in this region. Wherefore in all the places where the Buddha rested King Aśoka raised pillars in honour of him or constructed *stûpas.* We observe at intervals the monuments that

* As noticed in the preceding notes I am indebted to Dr. Bühler for several of the dates given here.

† Stanislas Julien's *Mémoires sur les Contrées Occidentales*, tom. II. pp. 162 ff.; *Histoire de la Vie de Hiouen-Thsang*, pp. 369–71, 358, 447.

‡ In Chinese, *Siao-ching;* Sans. *Hînayâna.*

mark the places where the three past Buddhas had sat, performed deeds, or preached the law.

"The kings of the present age are of *Tsa-ti-li* (Kshatriya) race; all are nephews of King *Shi-lo-'o-t'ie-to*, (Śîlâditya) of Malwâ. At present, (about A.D. 636) the son of King Śîlâditya of *Kie-jo-ka-she* (Kanyakubja), has a son-in-law called *T'u-lu-p'o-po-tu*,* (Dhruvapaṭu).† He is of a quick and passionate nature, and his intellect is weak and narrow: still he believes sincerely in 'the three precious things.'‡ For seven days every year he holds a great assembly at which he distributes to the multitude of recluses, choice dishes, the three garments, medicine, the seven precious things, and rare objects of great value. After giving all these in alms, he buys them back at double price. He esteems virtue and honours the sages, he reverences religion and values science. The most eminent holy men of distant countries are always objects of respect with him.

"At a little distance from the city there is a great convent, built long ago by the care of the Arhat *'Oche-lo* (Âchâra). It was there that the Bodhisattvas *Te-hoeï* (Guṇamatî), and *Kien-hoeï* (Sthîramatî) fixed their abode and composed several books which are all published with praise."

"On leaving this country he went about 700 *li* (140 miles) to the north-west, and arrived at the kingdom of *'O-nan-t'o-pu-lo*. The kingdom of (*'O-nan-t'o-pu-lo*) Ânandapura has a circuit of about 2,000 *li* (400 miles); the circumference of the capital is a score of *li* (5 miles). The population is very numerous, and all the families live in wealth. There is no (*native*) prince. The country is dependent on *Ma-la-p'o* (Malwâ) which it resembles in the products of its soil, nature of the climate, written character, and laws. There are a dozen convents counting somewhat under a thousand devotees who study the doctrine of the *Ching-liang-pu* (nikâya or school of the Sammatîyas) belonging to the 'lesser translation' (*Hînayâna*). There are many dozen temples of the gods; heretics of different sects live intermixed."

" From the kingdom of Valabhî he went about 500 *li* (100 miles) to the west, and reached the kingdom of *Su-la-ch'a* (Surâshṭra). This realm is nearly 4,000 *li* (800 miles) in circuit. The capital, whose circumference is 30 *li* (6 miles) upon the west side, touches the river *Mo-hi* (Mahi). Its inhabitants are very numerous, and all the families are wealthy. The country is subject to the kingdom of *Fa-la-pi* (Valabhî). The soil is impregnated with salt; and its flowers and fruits are few. Though heat and cold are equally distributed over the year, storms of wind never cease. Indifference and coldness characterise the manners; the people are superficial, and do not care to cultivate learning. Some follow the true doctrine, and others are given to heresy. There are some fifty convents, where they count about three thousand recluses, who study the doctrines of the *Shang-tso-pu* school (the school of the Sthaviras), which holds by the greater translation (*Mahâyâna*). There are a hundred temples of the gods (*Devâlayas*); and the heretics of different sects live together. As this realm is on the way to the

* En Chinois *Ch'ang-juï*, "constamment intelligent."

† Or Dhruvabhaṭṭa. *Journ. Roy. As. Soc.*, vol. VI. p. 329.

‡ Sans., *Triratna*.

Western Sea, all the inhabitants profit by the advantages the sea affords, and give themselves to trade and barter.

"At a short distance from the (*capital*) city rises Mount *Yeu-shen-ta* (Ujjanta*) upon the top of which a monastery is established. The chambers and galleries have been mostly hollowed out in the face of a scarped peak. The mountain is covered with thick forests, and streams from the springs surround it on all sides.† There holy men and sages walk and fix their abode, and thither resort crowds of Rishis endowed with divine faculties."

Such is the account of the Chinese pilgrim. The convent of *'Oche-lo*, which he mentions as being in the vicinity of Valabhî, Dr. Bühler has found mentioned in a grant of Dharasena II., as founded by Âṭharya,‡ not "Âchâra," as Julien had transliterated the Chinese name.

The Ânandapura here mentioned is probably the same as that referred to in the *Kalpa Sûtra* of the Jainas, as one of their early centres of learning, and where that work was composed by Śrî Bhadra Bâhu Svâmî, in the year 980 of their era § during the reign of Dhruvasena II. (cir. A.D. 640), who had just then been deeply afflicted by the loss of his beloved son Senâgaja. M. Vivien de Saint-Martin, following Stevenson, places it outside the peninsula—at Baḍnagar, or Vaḍanagar in northern Gujarât, about twenty miles east-south-east from Siddhpur.‖ From the connexion in which it occurs, however, we might expect it rather to be within the peninsula; and though the distance does not agree with Hiwan-Thsang's, there is still a place called Ânandapur fifty miles (250 *li*) north-west from Valabhî, which was very probably in early times the capital of a province, including parts of the modern Jhâlawâḍ, Kâṭhiâwâḍ, and Hâlâr. This gains support from the mention of Dhruvasena of Valabhî, who must have been closely connected with Ânandapura, to lead the writer of the *Kalpa Sûtra* to refer to his family afflictions; and the accuracy of the latter is corroborated by Dr. Burns's copper plate, stating that Śrî Dharasena IV. was Dhruvasena's *second* son.¶

The *Śatruñjaya Mâhâtmya* a legendary Jaina work composed to celebrate the mountain of Śatruñjaya, beside Pâlitâṇâ, is a still older work than the *Kalpa Sûtra*, and was written, according to statements contained in it (i. 13–15, xiv., 283–286, 342) at Valabhî, by a Jaina teacher Dhaneśvara, who describes himself as "a guru endowed with wisdom, endued with the qualities of all the *devas*, the moon of the sea of the Chandragachha, who instructed Śîlâditya, the lord of Valabhî in the purifying Jaina religion, and caused him to expel from the country the Saugatas (*Buddhists*), to settle the tîrthas in peace, and to build many Chaityas or temples."

---

* Ujjayanta, one of the names of Raivata or Girnar.

† Or—"and one hears the murmur of gushing fountains."—*Vie de Hiouen-Thsang, Documents Géographiques*, p. 448.

‡ *Ind. Antiquary*, vol. IV. p. 174.

§ If this date could be depended on, it would place the death of Vîra, the last Tîrthaṅkara, about 340–350 B.C. The Jains themselves place it in 526 B.C., or seventeen years after the Siṅhalese date of Buddha's Nirvâṇa, and this latter event probably took place between 370 and 380 B.C. Kern, *Over de Jaartelling der Zuidelijke Buddhisten*, pp. 28–31; *Ind. Ant.*, vol. III. p. 79.

‖ *Kalpa-Sûtra*, pp. 2, 15; Julien's *Mém. sur les Cont. Occid.*, tom. II. p. 406; and conf. Weber, *Ueber das Çatrunjaya Mâhâtmyam*, p. 7.

¶ *Journ. As. Soc. Beng.*, vol. VII. p. 976.

" When 477 years had passed since Vikrama," he adds, "Śîlâditya, who brings the law to a new bloom, arose the frontal jewel of the Yaduvaṅśa."

Weber has noticed these dates,* and argued from the knowledge we had of the Valabhi plates, nearly twenty years ago, that Śîlâditya must have reigned from about A.D. 552 to 602, and that the *Mahâtmya* was written in 598, and the *Kalpa Sûtra* in 632. We now know that Śîlâditya did not ascend the throne till after A.D. 590, that he was still living in 604, and that Dhruvasena II. must have ruled about A.D. 640, so that the dates assigned by him for the composition of these two works need scarcely be disturbed. The date in the Vikramâditya era, like certain other portions of the work, may be a later interpolation, probably by a Jaina writer, and this perhaps accounts for its being so incorrect, for by no arrangement could Śîlâditya be relegated to S. 477 or A.D. 421. If we might read S. 677, *i.e.* A.D. 621, Śîlâditya might still have been living then, but the date of the *Kalpa Sûtra*—33 years later—would not then fall within the reign of Dhruvasena, which must have terminated before A.D. 644.†

How the Valabhî dynasty ended we do not exactly know. We see that late in the seventh century it still held Soraṭh, and tradition is almost unanimous in asserting that Śilâditya was overthrown and slain by a foreign invader. Merutunga, the Jaina chronicler, gives a legendary account of its destruction.‡ A Mârwâḍi, he says, from Palli had settled at Valabhi and attained to great wealth. Śilâditya forcibly took the jewelled comb of this man's daughter to give to his own daughter, which so offended the Mârwâḍi that, to be revenged, he went to 'the Mlechha country' and offered the king an immense reward to destroy Valabhi. The Jaina priests had warning and took to flight, carrying their favourite idols with them, and by this Mlechha lord Valabhi was utterly destroyed in Samvat 375.§ As Śilâditya IV. was alive in S. 403 this date cannot be correct, whatever be the epoch from which it is reckoned. Moreover Śilâditya IV. may not have been the last of the dynasty, so that if Valabhi was destroyed by a foreign, it was probably by a Muhammadan, invader from or through Sindh—not earlier than 720 A.D., and possibly 50 or 60 years later.‖ In an inscription from Baroda¶ of Râja Karka II., dated Śaka 734, or A.D. 812, it is said that, under Karka I. Surâshṭra

---

* *Über das Çatruñjaya, Mâhâtmyam*, pp. 11, 12. The *Bhaṭṭikâvya* was likewise composed at Valabhî (*Bhaṭṭik.* xxii. 35) during the reign of one of the Śrî Dharasenas: conf. Weber, *ut sup.* p. 14.

† Is it possible that the equation of the Śaka Samvat date could have been applied to the Gupta era, thus 282 + 135 = 417 (૪૧૭) and this have again been written by mistake ૪૭૭ = 477?

‡ *Prabandha Chintamani*, bk. V. conf. *Asiat. Res.* vol. IX. p. 128; *Jour. As. S. Ben.* vol. V. pp. 157, 521, 685.

§ It may be observed, however, that 375 is just the equation of the Vikramâditya and Valabhi eras, and 'Samvat 375'=A.D. 318, is the initial date of the Gupta era used by the Valabhi dynasty, not of the *fall* of the capital. Conf. Tod's *Râjasthan*, vol. I. p. 801; *Western India*, pp. 51–53, 220, 238, 506.

‖ Tod's date of Gupta Samvat 205, or A.D. 524, is evidently 300 years in error—the date G. S. 305, A.D. 624, which he mentions but to reject, shows that his authorities differed. A.D. 724 would be nearer the probable date.—*Rajasthan*, vol. I. pp. 217, 230, or Mad. ed. pp. 180, 191. General Cunningham, taking Tod's *converted* date, Sam. 580, argues (*Ancient Geography*, p. 318) by a false process for *Saka* 580, or A.D. 658, as the date of the fall of Valabhî.

¶ *Journ. As. Soc. Beng.*, vol. VIII. p. 300; conf. *Ind. Ant.* vol. V. p. 144. Karka I. probably reigned about 700-720 A.D.

had "lost its appellation of Saurâjya from the ruin that had fallen upon it." This destruction of the country may refer to forays by the same invaders in the first half of the eighth century, perhaps during the time of Śîlâditya IV., and half a century before the time when Vana Râja founded the Chàvaḍâ kingdom of Aṇhilvâḍa in northern Gujarât.*

Tradition says that, on the fall of Valabhî, the Vâlâ governor of Wâmanasthalî became independent. Râja Râma had no son, but his sister was married to the Râja of Nagar Ṭhaṭhâ in Sindh, who was of the Sammâ tribe. This sister's son was named Râ Gârio, and Râma Râja bequeathed the kingdom of Junâgaḍh-Wanthalî to this nephew, who was the first of the Chuḍâsamâ Râs of Junâgaḍh. This Râ Gârio, the grandson of Rai Chuḍa, is said to have extended his dominions into upper India, conquering Kanauj, Gwalior, and Dohad in Malwa.†

There were petty kingdoms, however, established in various parts of the peninsula, as at Ḍhank, Deva Paṭṭan, &c. of the history of which we know but little. The Châvaḍâs and Solankis of Añhilvâḍa Paṭṭan made frequent inroads against these chiefs, but do not seem to have ever permanently subjugated the western portions of the country where the Jeṭhvâs and Chuḍâsamâs held sway, the latter till the fifteenth century, when they were reduced by Mahmûd Bigarah in 1469–70.

Wilford, in his *Essay on Vikramâditya*, says that in the fourth century mention is made of the island of Diu, on the south coast, "under the denomination of Dibu or Divu,‡—its inhabitants were called Divæi, Dibeni, and Diveni; and it appears that this denomination extended to the whole peninsula." § The references are to Philostorgius and Ammianus Marcellinus, the former of whom says that Constantius (cir. A.D. 356) sent an embassy to the Homeritæ, and "at the head of this embassy was placed Theophilus the Indian, who had been sent when very young as a hostage from the Dibæans to the Romans, when Constantine was at the head of the empire. The island called Dibu is a portion of their territory, and the inhabitants of it are called Indians. . . . Theophilus having arranged everything with the Homeritæ crossed over to the island of Dibu (Δίβου or Δίβους), which, as we above showed, was his native country. Thence he made his way to the other districts of India, and corrected many disorders among their inhabitants," &c.‖ Nicephorus, however, says it was to Adiabene that Theophilus went—"A large and well-known Indian country";¶—and what Ammianus Marcellinus, speaking of the Emperor Julian (A.D. 362), says is simply this: "And as the fear of his approach pervaded both neighbouring and distant countries, embassies hastened to him with unusual speed from all quarters; at one time the people beyond the Tigris and the Armenians sued for peace; at another the Indian tribes vied with each other, sending nobles loaded with gifts even from Dib and

---

* In Prinsep's *Useful Tables* (Ed. Thomas), p. 158, the date of the foundation of Anhillawâḍâ, S. 802, or A.D. 746, is given as that of the destruction of Valabhi.

† *Indian Antiquary*, vol. II. pp. 312 ff.

‡ Diu is called Dib in the *Ayin Akbari*, Gladwin's translation, vol. II. p. 94.

§ *Asiatic Researches*, vol. IX. p. 224.

‖ Philostorg., *Epit.* lib. III. c. 4, 5, ed. Gothofred (1642), pp. 26, 28; Walford's translation (ed. Böhn), pp. 444, 445; Conf. V. Valesii ad loc. cit. annotat.; Agatharcides *de Mare Eryth.* § 95; Priaulx's *Apollonius of Tyana, &c.*, p. 188.

¶ "Adiabene verò regia est Indica, ampla et celebris."—Niceph. Call. *Eccl. Hist.* lib. IX. c. 18.

Serendib."* This latter is so vague that one is almost inclined not to question the accuracy of the translators who have rendered it by "Maldive Islands and Ceylon;"† and even the former passage is scarcely conclusive as to Diu being meant.

V.—THÂN.

The railway now extends to Wadhwân in Jhâlâwâḍ, from which I made a hurried trip to Dhrângadhrâ, and then moved westwards to Mulî, where is a fine large temple belonging to the followers of Svâmî Nârâyaṇa, much like others of the same sect throughout Kâṭhiâwâḍ and Gujarât.

Thân is a village to the north of the main road from Wadhwân to Râjkoṭ, twelve or fourteen miles north-west from Mulî. This place is interesting for its traditions rather than for the few remains now existing; and at my request Major J. W. Watson has favoured me with some account of the place, which is as follows:

"Thân is one of the most ancient places in India and the whole of the neighbourhood is holy ground. Thân itself derives its name from the Sanskrit *sthân*, 'a place,' as though it were *the* place, hallowed above all others by the residence of devout sages, by the excellence of its city, and by its propinquity to famous shrines, such as that of Trinetreśvara, now called Tarnetar, the famous temple of the Sun at Kaṇḍola, and those of the Snake-brethren Vâsukî and Banduk, now known as Wâsangji and Bàndiâ Beli respectively.

"Thân is situated in that part of the province of Surâshṭra called the Deva Panchâl—so called, it is said, from having been the native country of Draupadî the wife of the five Pâṇḍava brethren, from which circumstance she was called Panchâlî, and from her this division of the province is called the Panchâl; and because it is peculiarly sacred it is called the Deva Panchâl. Nor is Thân famous in local tradition only; one of the chapters of the *Skanda Purâṇa* is devoted to Trinetreśvara and the neighbourhood, and this chapter is vulgarly called the *Thân Purâṇa* or *Tarnetar Mâhâtmya*. Here we learn that the first temple to the Sun was built by Râja Mândhâtâ in the Satya Yuga. The city is said then to have covered many miles, and to have contained a population of 36,000 Brâhmaṇs, 52,000 Vâṇiâs, 72,000 Kshatriyas, and 90,000 Śûdrâs—in all, 250,000 souls. Thân was visited also by Kṛishṇa and his consort Lakshmî, who bathed in the two tanks near the town, whence one has been called Pṛitam a contraction from *Pṛiyatam*, 'the beloved,' after Kṛishṇa,—so called as being the beloved of the Gopîs; and the other Kamala, after Lakshmî, who from her beauty was supposed to resemble the *Kamala* or lotus-blossom. The central fortress was called Kaṇḍola, and here was the celebrated temple of the Sun. Immediately opposite to Kaṇḍola is another hill, with a fort called in more recent times Songaḍh, and another large suburb was

* *Amm. Marcell.* lib. XXII. c. 7. § 10: "Proinde timore ejus adventus per finitimos longeque distantes latius explicato legationes undique solito ocius concurrebant: hinc Transtigritanis pacem obsecrantibus et Armeniis, inde nationibus Indicis certatim cum donis optimates mittentibus ante tempus abusque Divis et Serendivis."

† Yonge's *Amm. Marcell.* pp. 285, 286.

named Mâṇḍvâ. Within a few miles was the shrine of the three-eyed god Trinetreśvara, one of the appellations of Śiva, and close to this, the celebrated *kuṇḍ*, by bathing in which all one's sins were washed away. This *kuṇḍ* was called, therefore, the Pâpnâśnu or sin-expelling, as the forest in which it was situated was called the Pâpapnod-nu-vana or the Forest of the Sin-destroyer. Close to Thân are the Mândhav hills, distinguished by this name from the rest of the Tângâ range, of which they form a part; and the remains of Mândhavgaḍh, such as they are, may be seen close to the shrine of Bândiâ Beli, the modern name of Banduk, one of the famed snake-brethren. But Thân is sadly fallen from its former state, when it could be said—

चोटीलो दे सुंदरी त्रतीए माता होल।
विसो नताल वखांणीये दाद चत्वारो पोळ ॥

" *(One gate is at) Choṭila, a second at Suṅdari, the third at Mâtâ Hol :*
Let us praise the fourth gate at Viso Natâl."

" The shrine of Hol Mâtâ is in the lands of Mahikâ, under Wânkâner; Suṅdarî is a Dhrângadhrâ village; while Viso Natâl is the shrine of a Mâtâ not far from Mulî.

" Modern tradition only carries us back as far as the Bâbriâs, who ruled here until driven out by the Parmârs, who were expelled by the Kâṭhîs, who, in their turn, were dispersed by the Shujâ'at Khân, Subâhdâr of Gujarât, and were succeeded by the Jhâlâs. Their rule still survives in the well-known couplet :—

दुहो॥ थान कंडोला मांडवा नवसे बाव कुवा
राणा पेला राजीया थान बाबरीया ऊवा ॥

" *(At) Thân Kaṇḍolâ and Mâṇḍvâ there are 900 wâvs and wells :*
Before the rule of the Râṇâs the Bâbriâs reigned at Thân."

" The Râṇâs alluded to in the couplet are the Jhâlâs, whose title is Râṇâ. The Bâbriâs were expelled by the Parmârs, who were driven out by Wâloji Kâṭhî when himself fleeing from Pâwargaḍh, in Kachh, pursued by Jâm Abḍâ. Jâm Abḍâ, it is said, followed Wâloji to Thân and laid siege to the place, and Wâloji contemplated flight when the Sun appeared to him in a dream and assured him of his aid. Wâloji risked a battle, and Jâm Abḍâ was defeated and forced to return to Kachh. Wâloji and his Kâṭhîs now established themselves at Thân, and Wâloji, in gratitude to the Sun, repaired the temple of that luminary on the Kaṇḍolâ hill. This temple, as before stated, is said to have been founded by Râja Mândhâta in the *Satya Yuga*, and there is no doubt that it is really a most ancient fane. It was, it is said, repaired by the celebrated Lâkhâ Phulânî, who for a short time appears to have ruled here, but at what date does not appear, though the neighbourhood abounds in traces of this celebrated chieftain : a neighbouring village is named after him Lâkhâmâṅchi or Lâkhâ's stool.

" This temple has undergone so many repairs and re-buildings that the original structure has entirely disappeared and its present appearance is by no means imposing. Wâloji had a daughter named Sonabâi, whom he made a priestess in this temple, he married her to one Wâlerâ Jâlu and gave her twelve villages as her marriage portion, and named after her the fort rebuilt on the hill opposite to Kaṇḍolâ, Songaḍh. The village of Songaḍh is a few hundred yards from the old fort of Songaḍh, and the present descendants of Wâlerâ Jalu to this day enjoy land at the place. As Sonabâi was a ministrant in the temple of the Sun, her offspring were called Bhagats (worshippers), and from her sprang that *shâkâ* or sub-tribe of Kâṭhîs called Bhagats.

"The Parmârs are said to have entered Jhâlâwâḍ early in the thirteenth century Samvat, and to have received the chovisis of Thân-Kaṇḍola and Choṭagaḍh (now Choṭilâ) as a reward for the extermination of Aso Bhill, from Visaldeva the then Wâghela sovereign of Wadhwân, at that time the chief city of Jhâlâwâḍ. The grant was accompanied, however, with the condition that the Bâbriâs should be expelled, a condition which Visaldeva considered it impossible to effect. The Parmârs, however, succeeded in ousting the Bâbriâs, who fled thence to Dhândhalpur. The Parmârs did not hold Thân long, as they were ousted by the Kâṭhîs under Wâloji who, as mentioned above, was himself fleeing with his Kâṭhîs from Jâm Abrâ.

"When Kârtalab Khân (who had been honoured with the title of Shujâ'at Khân) was Subâhdâr of Gujarât, the Kâṭhîs extended their marauding expeditions to the *Khâlsî* districts, harassing especially the parganâs of Dhandhuka, Viramgâm and Dholka; their excesses at length became so serious that Shujâ'at Khân, when on his usual *mulkgiri* circuit in Jhâlâwâḍ, marched from thence, in about A.D. 1690, for Thân, which fort he stormed, after a great slaughter of its defenders, dispersing the Kâṭhîs and destroying the temple of the Sun. Since this the Kâṭhîs never returned to Thân, which was occupied by the Jhâlâs shortly afterwards. On this great dispersion of the Kâṭhîs, the Khâchar tribe made Choṭilâ their head-quarters, which they had wrested from Jagsio Parmâr previously, while the Khawads who had acquired Sayilâ, in about A.D. 1769, remained here. The Wâlâs' head-quarters were at Jeṭpur-Chitâl and the Khumâns' at Mitiâlâ, and afterwards Sâbâr Kundla, at the time of Shujâ'at Khân's storm of Thân, it was principally occupied by Dhândhals, who have now been dispersed far and wide; and though still to be found as Mulgirâsiâs in Kâṭhiâwâḍ, their chief possessions lie in the Dhandhuka parganâ, and to this day they retain—in memory of the Snake-worship at the shrines of Wâsukî and Bândiâ Beli which they had adopted—a great reverence for the Cobra."*

Close to the village is a small rock-cut apartment, apparently never quite finished. It has two pillars supporting the roof, and at the back a small shrine advancing into the cave, with a stone bench in it, as if for an image; but beyond this, and the probability that, like the majority of other caves in this province, it may be Bauddha, there is nothing further to indicate the sect that excavated it, nor the age in which it was made.

About 600 yards south-west from the village, in a rock or low rocky hill, is another similar cave somewhat smaller and very rudely formed: the roof is also supported by two pillars much worn, and two others at the back not quite detached from the rock. It is low and the sides unfinished. There have also been other excavations in the rock close by, but the stone is easily weather-worn, and little of them remains.

---

* *Indian Antiquary*, vol. IV. p. 193-4.

Outside the village, on a long raised platform, are seven small structural shrines in line, each with a small open porch, and containing the *charaṇa* of the Bhaktas of the Kâṭhîs,—except one in which a linga is placed. In another, a little advanced from the line, is a small brass image of Kânya or Lâlji. On each side of him is what they call "Niklanga"—a man on horseback—representing the tenth avatar of Vishṇu, and in front of the altar are the *paglaṇ* of Jâdra Bhakta—apparently a recently deceased *Sádhu*.

Throughout the country and in Kachh, the custom long prevailed of erecting a stone called a Pâliyâ to the memory of those who died a violent death, but in more recent times it seems to have become common also to those who died from natural causes. Like grave-stones in other countries they are of very varied workmanship, from the plain stone with a rude symbol above and the name, date, and mode of death, engraven in rough ill-shapen characters and mis-spelt words, to the moulded stone surmounted by a figure of the deceased mounted on a horse or camel, or on foot, with shield and sword or spear, indicating how the deceased fell. They are also to be seen in carts, and, in the case of fishermen or pirates, on board ship.* These *pâliyâs* are sometimes erected on raised platforms, and in rarer cases they are covered by a pavilion or *chattri*. They are also raised to the memory of *satîs*, and then have a woman's arm engraven upon them. Usually they are flat upright stones; but in some cases they are square or octagonal below, with a wider cubical block above, surmounted by a moulded pyramidal top, the cube bearing the inscription on one side, the figure of the deceased on another, and other symbols on the remaining two. These monuments are usually erected outside the gate of a village or town, and not unfrequently on the embankment of a tank. As in the old lawless times villagers frequently fell in defence of their homes and families, the number of *pâliyâs* a village could show would be an indication of the warlike disposition of its people, and a standing exhortation to those whose ancestors had fallen in defence of their homes and kin to be foremost on all occasions of danger.

Almost any village in Kâṭhiawâḍ would supply abundant illustrations of *pâliyâs* and at some are to be found very picturesque groups, of various pretensions as to size and elaboration. The accompanying Plate VIII., representing a *chattri* at Thân and a portion of the group of *pâliyâs* round it, will show the ordinary character of these stones.

Snake-worship still lingers among the Kâṭhîs about Thân. On the west side of a tank near the village is a small temple devoted to it. The Devatâ is Wâsukhî (vulgarly pronounced "Vâsañji") one of the snake brethren; another being Bândiâ Beli, who has also a shrine at a place about three miles from Thân, where is a slightly warm spring, close to the ruins of Mânḍâvgaḍh (in the Mânḍav hills). Wâsukhî is deified as Śesha Nârâyaṇa, and represented in the temple, on a slab, by a triple-headed snake with the tail coiled up spirally, and two smaller monocephalous ones, one on each side. On their right (the spectator's left) is a figure of Nârâyaṇa or Vishṇu. Both images are smeared red all over, and before them are laid *śáligrâmas* and *śañkhas*.

* A neat one of this sort is to be seen at Mundrâ in Kachh.

The pûjârî is a *sannyásî* from near Banâras, and wears a brick-red cloth, and uses a Rudrâksha Mâlâ, or rosary, of nineteen beads. Shading the temple is a large *Ráyana* * tree,—the close foliage of small dark green oval leaves, which makes its shade so grateful, apparently having had to do with its being consecrated as a sacred tree in Western India, where it is specially dedicated by the Jains to their first Tîrthankara, Ṛishabhanâtha,—the patron saint of Śatruñjaya, no shrine to him being complete without a *Ráyana* tree overshadowing his *charaṇa* or footprints.

In the court of this temple are many slabs of pottery, with images in alto-rilievo of the three snakes, similar to that in the shrine: they are apparently votive offerings. Doubtless much curious information respecting snake-worship and the worship of the sun could be obtained in this neighbourhood by anyone who had the time and tact to elicit it.

The legendary history of the two snake shrines at Thân is thus given by Major Watson :—

"Brahmâ had a son named Marîchi, whose son was Kaśyapa. Kaśyapa had a hundred sons by a nâga-kanyâ, the chief of whom were Śeshjî, Vasukhî (corrupted into Wasañgji), Bânduk (corrupted into Bandia Beli), Dhumrâksha, Pratik, Paṇḍarik, Takshak, Airâvat, Dhṛitarâshṭra, &c., &c.

"Five ṛishis† named Karnâv, Gâlav, Aṅgira, Antath, and Bṛihaspati (all sons of Brahmâ) during the *Treta Yuga*, set out on a pilgrimage round the world, and in the course of their wandering came to Deva Panchâla land, and encamping in the forest of Pâpânod, near Thân, determined to perform here religious austerities. They accordingly commenced their ceremonies by performing the *Brahmayajna* or adoration of Brahmâ by means of the sacrificial fire. Information of their intention having reached Bhîmâsura, who reigned at Bhîmapuri, the modern Bhimora, he determined to throw obstacles in their way, and with this view commenced to annoy them, and owing to his persecution the Ṛishis were obliged to remove their residence to the bank of Pânchkuṇḍi tank, close to Thân, and there commence their penance. Their austerities were so severe that Brahmâ was pleased with them,‡ and appeared before them in person. On this the Ṛishis implored him to destroy Bhîmâsura Daitya. Brahmâ replied that Bhîmâsura was destined to die at the hands of Śeshajî, Vâsukhi, and others of the snake family, and that, therefore, they should address their prayers to them. So saying Brahmâ became invisible, and the Ṛishis besought the snake deities to aid them, and the whole snake family appeared to answer to their entreaties. The Ṛishis requesting them to destroy Bhîmâsura, Śeshajî at once started for Bhîmapuri, and there by the force of his poison slew Bhîmâsura, and returning, informed the Ṛishis of his death. They overwhelmed him with thanks, and begged him to reside constantly in Thân for their protection. As Śeshajî was king of Pâtâl, he was unable to comply with their request; he however ordered his brothers Vâsukhi

* The *Rájádani* of Sanskrit writers (conf. *Śatruñjaya Máhâtm* I. p. 270), the *Mimusops Kauki*, or *Butea frondosa* according to Wilson.

† The great ṛishis who aided Brahmâ in the work of creation are *seven*; they are identified with the seven stars of Ursa Major. See my *Elephanta*, § 42 and note 68.

‡ By penance and austerity it is supposed that unbounded power—even over the gods—may be attained.

(Wasaṅgji) and Banduk (or Bandiâ Beli) to remain at Thân and Mândhavgaḍh, and accordingly these two snake brethren took up their residence at Thân and Mândhavgaḍh respectively, where their shrines are to this day. Śeshajî then became invisible. To the present day no one is allowed to cut a tree in the grove that surrounds Bandiâ Beli's shrine, and it is said that should anyone ignorantly cut a stick in this grove, the snake appears to such person in his dreams and orders him to return the stick, and should he fail therein, some great calamity shortly befalls him, and in fact in or near this grove may be seen many such logs or sticks accidentally cut and subsequently returned.

"Some of the more famous snake brethren are, (1) Śeshjî, lord of Pâtâl; (2) Vásukhî; (3) Banduk, all mentioned above; (4) Kâlî Nâga, this brother was a snake of renown; he first resided in the Kâlandrio pool of the Jamnâ river near Gokal in Hindustân proper. From thence he was ousted by Krishṇa, and is now supposed to reside in the island of Ramnad near the shrine of Setubandh Râmeśvara. (5) Bhujâṅga, who is worshipped at Bhuj. It is said that in ancient times the inhabitants of Kachh were harassed by Daityas and Râkshasas, and petitioned Śrî Wâsukhî, who ordered his brother Bhujâṅga to go to their assistance. Bhujâṅga went, and effecting their liberation, at their entreaties took up his residence in Bhuj, so named after him. He is popularly called the Bhujio. (6) Another famous brother is Dhumrâksha, worshipped as the Khâmbhḍiâ Nâga, in the village of Khambhḍâ, under Dhrâṅgadhra. (7) Another Nâga shrine in Kâṭhiâwâḍ, is that of Pratik at Talsânâ in Jhâlâwâḍ; and another (8) is that of Devânik Charmâlio, in the village of Chokḍi, under Chudâ. The shrine of another brother (9) Pandarîka, is said so be at Pandarpura in the Dekhan. (10) Takshâk resides in Kurukshetra; (11) Airâvat in Hastinâpur; and (12) Dhṛitarâshṭra in the Dekhan, &c., &c.

"It will be seen from the above legend how intimately the old tree and snake worship are connected. The Nâgas seem to have been an aboriginal race in Gujarât, and to have worshipped the elephant, cobra, tiger, monkey, and trees; and the earlier Hindu immigrants have probably derived from them the cult of Gaṇeśa, Hanumân, Wâgheśvarî, Mâtâs, &c., &c. In the lapse of time the descendants of these Hindu immigrants began to confound these Nâgas with whom they had intermarried with the cobras (*nâgas*), and eventually the legends of Nâga-kanyâs, &c., sprang up."*

Four miles south from Thân is the ruin of an old *bănd* or dam known as the Sândâsar bănd, built originally of massive stones, but burst by the force of the retained water, and the stones are now found scattered down the stream for several miles. Just above the east end of it, on a rocky rising ground, stands a small deserted temple called Muni Bâwâ's. When entire it must have been a very pretty shrine—prettily situated where it commands an extensive view, much more beautiful doubtless when the Sândâsar dam formed an extensive reservoir, almost in front of it. There is no inscription on it except on the jamb of the shrine door, where we read—

मंवत १५५७ वर्षे

"The Samvat year 1557," or A.D. 1501,—but this seems to have been cut by some

* *Ind. Ant.*, vol. IV., p. 196-7.

visitor, for the temple must belong to about the same age as that of Sûrya Nârâyaṇa at Somanâth Paṭṭan, and is probably the older of the two—possibly dating from the tenth or eleventh century. The plan is the usual one for a small temple—a broken square of twelve columns, with two outside on each face, forming bays to the side windows, a vestibule to the shrine, and an inner porch; each area measuring 6 feet 3 inches by 3 feet 4 inches. The square inside measures 15 feet 2 inches between opposite columns. The pillars are square below, and built partly into the high screen wall that surrounds the maṇḍap; above the screen they are octagonal, with round capitals supporting brackets. Each bracket has a four-armed figure carved upon it—each figure different from the others or in a different position; one is a Gaṇapati, another has a dog's face on his stomach, and holds the mouth of it open with his fingers, one has his head turned downwards and his back outwards, and supports the upper member of the bracket with his feet; some gape; and most of them are comical or whimsical.

One pillar of the maṇḍap and much of the sculpture on the Śikhar or spire has fallen. The shrine door is neatly carved with a running flower pattern on the jambs, human figures below at each side, and three bands of small ones on the architrave, outside the jambs. Gaṇapati is carved on the lintel, indicating a Śaiva shrine, and the frieze above is divided into seven compartments by colonnettes; the central one is occupied by a sitting figure, and the others by standing ones.

The roof is domed on eight pillars—the central pair on each face of the square—and has been neatly carved, as have also the roofs of the porch and shrine.

Outside, round the *vimana* or shrine, are carved a number of mythological figures; one of them, on the back or west end, is a three-faced figure or *trimûrti*—possibly intended for Brahmâ. In all the receding compartments are figures of a curious nondescript animal, a sort of griffon—*grâsḍâ*—which again occurs in a much less prominent form at Gumli, but figures in Indian sculpture from the age of the Bauddha caves downwards; perhaps it is intended for a *siñha* or lion, but sometimes it is carved with a long snout like a tapir's, or an elephant's trunk, and sometimes with very long horns like an antelope's. Here it is repeated again and again as a principal figure, assailed by men with bows, spears, &c.

At Songaḍh the old temple of the Sun has been pulled down, and a modern shrine raised on the site.

VI. THE AŚOKA INSCRIPTION AT JUNÂGAḌH.

Junâgaḍh, "The Old Fort,"—not, as Lassen supposes, the *Yavanagaḍa* or "Grecian Fort,"*—is probably one of the most ancient cities of India, and, with its Uparkoṭ or citadal, now overgrown with custard apple, notwithstanding four centuries of Muhammadan Vandalism, is probably a rich mine of buried antiquities. Here lived the lieutenants of the great Maurya kings, Chandragupta, Vimbisâra, Aśoka, and their

* Mirza Muhammad Sâdik Isfahâni is quite correct when he says in his *Tahkik al Îrab*,—"Júnahgadh spelt with the Indian *D*), a fortress Gujarat (گجرات) in India; it is also called Karnál (كرنال) the name Júnagadh (جونگڈہ) signifies 'an ancient castle.'" Jiran Kot has a similar meaning.

successors, of the Sâhs, and of the Guptas; and here the later Chuḍâsamâs kept their court, though Vanthali, the ancient Wâmanasthalî, was often also the royal residence.

The modern city walls enclose a very extensive area of an irregular form. The Uparkoṭ, an inner fort or citadel, on a raised platform of rock, occupies a portion of the east side; but the greater part of it and of the northern end of the enclosure of the city walls are covered with jungle, hiding innumerable Muhammadan graves. The population may, perhaps, amount to 25,000 or 30,000, and occupies the area to the south-west of the Uparkoṭ. The streets are narrow. The palace is a large square nondescript pile, enclosing a small open square, and overtopping the houses, but in a narrow street. A spacious addition in the Italian style, however, has recently been added, and a square formed in front of it, which is a vast improvement on what was six years ago.

The temple of Swâmî Nârâyaṇa is a somewhat imposing modern structure, and beside it is a sort of monastery of very considerable extent, built and kept in repair by its inmates, who number among themselves members of all trades, such as carpenters, bricklayers, smiths, &c. The details of the economy of such a fraternity would form a curious, if not instructive, chapter in the history of modern Hindu religious habits.

But to begin with the Buddhist remains:—The Rock-Inscription of Junâgaḍh or Girnar is without exception the most interesting antiquity in the province. It is nearly a mile to the west of the city, and at the entry of the dell or gorge which leads into the valley that girdles the mighty and sacred Girnâr. It was first noticed by Major James Tod on his visit to Girnâr in December 1822, and his account* may be worth quoting almost *in extenso*. It runs thus:—

"The magnificent vanity of Sundarji, the horse-merchant, has commenced and proceeded far in his work, which will immortalize his name, while it secures the benedictions of the pilgrims, for making easy the road to the great object of adoration. From the walls of the city he has cut a noble avenue through the forest, planted on either side with mango, jamun, and other trees, which in due time will afford both shade and food to the weary votary. At the point where the avenue meets the Sonarekha is an extensive paved causeway, running parallel with it, and terminating where the river runs directly across the gorge of the pass with a bridge of three arches of great strength and in excellent taste, having an open casemated parapet. While it adds greatly to the picturesque effect of the scene, the utility of the work enhances its beauty; for not only does it give bread to a great body of poor people, but, when finished, it will entirely remove all danger from the devotees formerly apt to be swept off by the sudden rise of the river. It is already carried over the most difficult part; and although Sundarji is dead, it does not languish under his son and successor, who, with religious zeal, is executing his father's commands to continue the causeway to the second ford of the stream, beyond which it would be more ornamental than useful. The views from the bridge are sublime: in front, seen through the range called the portal of Durgâ, is the mighty cone of Girnâr, towering in majesty, while behind, the 'ancient castle' lowers 'in proud decay,' seeming as if erected as an outwork to defend the pass leading to the holy hill.

* *Travels in Western India*, p. 369 ff.

"Leaving the bridge, let me describe what to the antiquary will appear the noblest monument of Saurâshtra, a monument speaking in an unknown tongue of other times, and calling to the Frank *vedyavân*, or *savant*, to remove the spell of ignorance in which it has been enveloped for ages. Again, thanks to Sundarji, but for whose liberality it would still have remained embosomed in the pathless forest, covered with its tangled veil of the impervious babool. . . .

"The memorial in question, and evidently of some great conqueror, is a huge hemispherical mass of dark granite, which, like a wart upon the body, has protruded through the crust of mother earth, without fissure or inequality, and which, by the aid of the 'iron pen,' has been converted into a book. The measurement of its area is nearly 90 feet; its surface is divided into compartments or parallelograms, within which are inscriptions in the usual antique character. Two of these *cartouches* I had copied, by my old Guru, with the most scrupulous fidelity, and a portion of a third, where the character varied. The affinity of the former to the inscriptions on the triumphal pillars at Dihli, on the 'column of victory' in the centre of the lake in Mewar, and in various of the most ancient cave-temples in India, is apparent. Each letter is about two inches long, most symmetrically formed, and in perfect preservation. The examples of a more modern character are, from the vertex and the west side of the mass, similar to those on the Indo-Gothic medals I engraved for the *Transactions of the Royal Asiatic Society*,* and of which I found several specimens in the ruins of Kalikoṭ and other ancient cities on the opposite side of the gulf. . . I may well call it a book; for the rock is covered with these characters, so uniform in execution that we may safely pronounce all those of the most ancient class, which I designate the 'Pandu character,' to be the work of one man. But who was this man? They are of an age so evidently anterior to Menander and Apollodotus, the conqueror of the Suroi, that despite the curious admixture of characters decidedly Grecian, we cannot suppose this to have been a landmark of their visitations amongst the Râjputs or of their victory over Tessarioustos,† or Teja Râja, in all probability the Yadu prince of Junâgaḍh."

The large granite block or boulder is just at the entrance of the causeway on its right or east side, and besides fourteen tablets or edicts of Aśoka, which cover nearly the whole of the north-east face, it bears on the top a long Sáh inscription of Rudra Dâmân, and on the west face a third of Skandagupta. The first of these was probably almost perfect when Tod saw it in 1822, but most unfortunately Sundarjî's people when making the causeway seem to have broken a large piece from the stone, carrying away part of the fifth and a large portion of the thirteenth tablet. The rock, however, even after the interest of its inscriptions was discovered, was left quite uncared for; and in 1869, when I first visited it, a house had been built beside it, and was occupied by a lazy, sanctimonious, naked devotee, whose firewood lay against the sides of the stone, whilst fragments of broken earthenware covered the top of it, where the Rudra Dâmân inscription had begun to peel off. Removing these, the photograph which forms Plate IX. was taken from the wall of the causeway. A representation was also made to the

* Vol. I. pp. 313 ff.

† Tod is here misled by the corrupt reading in Strabo.

Government of Bombay, which resulted in the erection by the Junâgaḍh darbâr, of a roof over the stone to protect it from the sun and rain.

The first transcript of the whole of the Aśoka inscription was obtained by the Rev. Dr. John Wilson of Bombay, who forwarded a copy of it to Mr. James Prinsep of Calcutta, early in 1837. By a fortunate coincidence Lieut. Kittoe had discovered a long inscription at Dhaulî in Katak which proved to be identical, or nearly so, with that of Junâgaḍh, but with the omission of the last three tablets.* Prinsep, who had recently discovered the key to the character of these inscriptions, was not long in bringing their contents to notice.

In March 1838 Lieut. W. Postans was deputed by the Bombay Government to visit Junâgaḍh and copy the inscriptions; this he did in company with Capt. Lang, and the copies were sent to the Royal Asiatic Society. In 1842 Capt. (now General Sir G.) Le Grand Jacob and Professor Westergaard of Copenhagen, made a very careful copy of the whole inscription, which has proved the most faithful transcript of any of the inscriptions yet published.

Again, M. Court in the service of Ranjît Singh, in a memoir on Taxila and Peukelaotes, a notice of which appeared in the *Journal of the Asiatic Society of Bengal* for August 1836, first communicated to the world the fact of the existence of a Baktro-Pali inscription on a rock, quite close to the village of Shâh-bâz-garhî about thirty-six miles north-east from Peshâwar. In the spring of 1838 Capt. Burnes sent an agent to look after the inscription, who returned with a paper impression, which made obvious the importance of having a more perfect representation of it. In the end of the year Mr. C. Masson sent another agent, who brought back copies of a portion of it with information that led Masson himself to visit it in October 1838, when he discovered that both sides of the stone were inscribed, and brought away impressions on calico of the whole.† These were successfully decyphered by the late Mr. E. Norris and Mr. Dowson in 1845, and found to be essentially the same as those of Girnar and Dhaulî.‡ The three texts were afterwards compared, using Westergaard and Jacob's excellent transcript for that of Girnar, and a revised translation published by the late Professor H. H. Wilson§ in 1849: they were also briefly discussed by Lassen.‖ Certain of the edicts were further examined, and improved translations of them given by the late lamented E. Burnouf, which were published¶ after his death in 1852. Several of them have again been re-examined by Professor H. Kern of Leyden in an admirable memoir published at Amsterdam in 1873: his translations, so far as they go,** we shall reproduce in the following pages as the best that have yet appeared.

A fourth Aśoka inscription was discovered by Mr. Forrest in 1860 at Khâlsî, on the banks of the Jamunâ, in a very perfect state of preservation, and, like those at Girnar and Dhauli, in the Pali character; and a fifth has been found at Jogada

* *Journ. As. Soc. Beng.*, vol. VII. pp. 157, 219; Prinsep's *Essays*, vol. II. pp. 13, 18, 20.

† *Journ. R. As. Soc.*, vol. VIII. p. 293.

‡ Ibid., p. 303.

§ Ibid., vol. XII. pp. 153–251.

‖ *Indische Alterthumskunde*, (2nd edition) vol. II. pp. 224 ff.

¶ *Lotus de la Bonne Loi*, pp. 710–774.

** *Over de Jaartelling der Zuidelijke Buddhisten en de Gedenstukken van Açoka den Buddhist*, pp. 43 ff.

Naugam in the Ganjam district,* near the coast of the bay of Bengal; but no satisfactory copies of these two have yet been published.

The Aśoka inscription at Girnar covers considerably over a hundred square feet of the uneven surface of a huge rounded and somewhat conical granite boulder, rising 12 feet above the surface of the ground, and about 75 feet in circumference at the base. It occupies the greater portion of the north-east face, and, as is well known, is divided down the centre by a vertical line; on the left, or east side, of which are the first five edicts or tablets, divided from one another by horizontal lines; on the right are the next seven, similarly divided; the thirteenth has been placed below the fifth and twelfth, and is unfortunately damaged; and the fourteenth is placed to the right of the thirteenth.

Though better copies had been made of this inscription than of any of the others, there were still some doubtful readings, and it was therefore desirable, as had recently been pointed out by Professor Weber in the *Centralblatt*, to have a perfect facsimile of it. These remaining doubts, I trust, the *estampages* taken will now settle.

The taking of facsimiles was a work of considerable time and difficulty; and as I had no trained hand, I had to do it myself with the aid of my assistant, who, however, soon became quite expert in the manipulatory process. We wrought steadily from eight to nine hours a day at it, and after the first trials, which were disappointing owing to some of the paper containing size or other adhesive substance, I tried using a thicker and firmer paper brought from Ahmadâbâd for the first layer, and the thinner, softer paper from Junar for the second, and, as far as my stock of it would allow, for a third layer. This wrought very well. Unfortunately the paper ordered by me at the India Office had not come to hand at Bombay, and I could not get a further supply similar to the Junar sort at Junâgadh. This prevented my taking some of the edicts in duplicate, and for some time I could only use two layers of paper. The originals are deposited at the India Office Library, and represent with great fidelity the surface of the stone; from them the accompanying collotype plates (X.–XIII.) have been derived, by piecing the different estampages in groups, as on the stone, and photographing them.†

The principal new readings have been pointed out for me by Professor Kern, and will be noticed in connexion with each tablet or edict. The latest translation available is also given of each in order; but all are subject to revision. Professor Wilson's were offered as "subject to correction in every page;" and in his paper he bears this high testimony to Prinsep's earlier work: "With regard," he says, "to the translations which we owe to the learning and ingenuity of the late James Prinsep, we must remember that they were the first attempts to convey a knowledge of the purport of documents in a new character and unknown language; and that copies of the Lât inscriptions had been published for many years, but had baffled the most eminent scholars, and remained undeciphered, until James Prinsep discovered their real nature and rendered them readable by his successors, without which they would probably have continued to the present day as unintelligible as ever. Whatever may be objected to particular

---

* *Indian Antiquary*, vol. I. pp. 219–222.

† The third edict, having been taken with a yellowish paper, appears much darker than the others. Under a low magnifying power these plates will represent pretty well the state of the surface of the rock; only the photograph having been taken from the *under* side of the estampage, the depressions of surface appear as elevations. The letters are sunk—in intaglio, not in cameo.

passages, the substance of the inscriptions is no doubt correctly translated. Its incorrectness, even if established, will not invalidate his claims to our acknowledgment and admiration for what he has accomplished with unequalled labour, incomparable ingenuity, and unrivalled success."* Not less graceful is M. Burnouf's manner of speaking of his corrections. "Si je viens à mon tour, après de si savans hommes, proposer mon interprétation, c'est que comme personne ne peut se flatter d'arriver du premier coup à l'intelligence définitive de ces monumens difficiles, il n'y a personne non plus qui ne puisse se flatter d'aider à leur intreprétation."†

Tablet or Edict I.

The first edict of the series, at the head of the left-hand column (see Plate X.), consists of twelve lines, and reads thus :—

1 Iyaṁ dhammalipî Devânaṁ piyena
2 Piyadasinâ Râñâ ḷekhâpitâ. Idha na kiṁ-
3 chi jîvaṁ ârabhiṭṭâ paju hitavyaṁ
4 nacha samâjo katavyo bahukaṁ hi dosam
5 samâjamhi pasati Devânaṁ pîyo Piyadasi Râja
6 asti pitu ekachâ samâja sâdhumatâ Devânaṁ-
7 piyasa Piyadasino râño purâ mahânase mamâ
8 Devânaṁ piyasa Piyadasino râño anudivasaṁ ba-
9 húni pâṇa satasahasâni ârabhisu sûpâthâya
10 sa aja yadâ ayaṁ dhaṁmalipi likhitâtî eva pâ-
11 ṇa ârabhire sûpâthâya dvamerâ eko mato so pi-
12 magona dhuvo ête pâtî pâṇâ pachhâ na ârabhisaṅde.

The corrections in the estampage here are few, viz. :—

At the end of line 2 -	-	*kiṁ* for *kaṁ*
In line 4 - -	-	*samâjo* for *samaje*
At the end of line 7 -	-	*mamâ* for *jamâ*
And in line 8 -	-	*anudivasaṁ* for *anuṁdivasaṁ*.

The translation of this edict has not been revised by either Burnouf or Kern, and in place of a better we must be content with the following which is Wilson's version :—

"This is the edict of the beloved of the gods, the Râjâ Priyadasi. The putting to death of animals is to be entirely discontinued, and no convivial meeting is to be held, for the beloved of the gods, Râjâ Priyadasi remarks many faults in such assemblies. There is but one assembly indeed which is approved of by the Râjâ Priyadasi the beloved of the gods, which is that of the great kitchen of Râjâ Priyadasi; every day hundreds of thousands of animals have been slaughtered for virtuous purposes, but now although this pious edict is proclaimed that animals may be killed for good purposes, and such is the practice; yet as the practice is not determined, these presents are proclaimed that hereafter they shall not be killed."‡

* *Journ. R. As. Soc.*, vol. XII. p. 251.
† *Lotus de la Bonne Loi*, p. 738.
‡ Wilson, *Journ. R. As. Soc.* vol. XII. p. 164.

I

II

III

J. Burgess fecit. Collotype by W. Griggs.

Tablet II.

The second is in eight lines somewhat longer than those of the first, and is fully commented on by Professor Kern.

It reads thus :—

1 Savata vijitamhi Devânaṁpiyasa Piyadasino raño,
2 evamapi pâ chaṁtesu yathâ Choḍâ Pâḍâ Satiyaputo Ketalaputo â Taṁba-
3 paṁṇî, Aṁtiyako Yonarâjâ, yevâpi tasa Aṁtiyakasa sâmîpaṁ
4 râjâno, savatâ Devânaṁpiyasa Piyadasino râño dve chikîchhâ katâ,
5 manusachikîchhâ pasuchikîchhâcha ; osuḍhânicha yâni manusopagânicha
6 pasopagâni cha yata-yata nâsti, savatâ hârâpitânicha ropâpitânicha
7 mûlânicha phalânicha yata-yata nâsti, savata hârâpitânicha ropâpitânicha ;
8 paṁthesû kûpacha khanâpitâ, vachhâcha ropâpitâ paribhogâya pasumanusânaṁ

The only corrections supplied here are :

In lines 2 and 3 - - - - *â Taṁbapaṁṇi* for *a Tambapaṇi*
In line 3 - - - - - *râjâ* for *râja*
And in line 4 - - - - - *râjâno* for *râjano.*

Dr. Kern translates this literally into Sanskrit as,—

1 Sarvatra râshṭre Devânâmpriyasya Priyadarśino râjnas,
2 tathaivo prâtyanteshu, yaṭhâ Choḍâḥ, Pâṇḍyâḥ, Satyaputraḥ, Keralaputra â Tâmra-
3 parṇîm, Antiyoko Yavanarâjo, yechâpi tasya sâmantâ,
4 râjânaḥ, sarvatra Devânâmpriyasya Priyadarśino râjno dvayî chikitsâ kritâ,
5 manushyachikitsâ paśuchikitsâcha ; aushadhânicha yâni manushyopagânicha
6 paśûpagânicha yatra-yatra na santi, sarvatrâhâritânicha tadropaṇañcha kâritaṁ,
7 mûlânicha phalânicha yatra-yatra na santi, sarvatrâhâritânicha tadropaṇañcha kâritaṁ,
8 kûpâścha pathishu khânitâ, rikshâṇâṇâñcha ropaṇaṁ kâritaṁ paribhogâya* paśumanushyâṇâṁ.

Translation.†

"In the whole dominion of King Devânâmpriya Priyadarśin as also in the adjacent countries, as Chola, Paṇḍya, Satyaputra, Keralaputra, as far as Tâmraparṇî, the kingdom of Antiochus the Grecian King, and of his neighbour kings,‡ the system of caring for the sick both of men and cattle, followed by King Devânâmpriya Priyadarśin has been everywhere brought into practice; and at all places where useful healing herbs for men and cattle were wanting he has caused them to be brought and planted; and at all places where roots and fruits were wanting he has caused them to be brought and planted; also he has caused wells to be dug and trees to be planted, on the roads for the benefit of men and cattle."

"Choḍa," Lassen remarks, "is to be regarded as another spelling of Chora (as Gauḍa is pronounced *Gaura*), and an older form than Chola ; the ancients called the

* Dhouli—*pratibhogâya.*

† Kern, *u. s.* p. 91. These translations have been very kindly made for me by the Rev. Adam Milroy, of Moneydie.

‡ In the first place Baktria.

people of these parts Sola.* As the word is in the plural it is to be taken as the name of a people. The inscription has Pâḍâ, which, however, has arisen from an injury to the stone in the course of time. Pîḍâ was situated to the north of Chola in the vicinity of Arkat, and was called Pira-deśa.† Pîdâ-Satiyaputa is to be considered a compound, 'the Satyaputra of Pîḍa'; it was probably a Buddhist title 'the son of truth,' like the Dharma-râja in Butan. Through carelessness, the engraver has carved Ketala for Kerala (the Malabar coast).‡ It is said 'as far as Tambapañnî' (Ceylon), which is thereby indicated as the most southerly and distant country in that direction."§

Tablet III.

This is in six lines, still longer than those of Tablet II., and reads :—

1 Devânaṁ piyo Piyadasi râja evaṁ âha dvâdasa vâsâbhisitena mayâ idaṁ âûpitaṁ
2 savata vijite mama yutâcha râjûkecha pâdesike cha pañchasu panchasu vâsesu anusaṁ
3 yânaṁ niyâta êtâyeva athâya imâya dhaṁmânusastiya yathâ añâ
4 ya pi kaṁmâya sadhu mâtaricha pitari sustâna mitâ saṁstuta ñâtinaṁ bahmaṇa
5 samaṇânaṁ sâdhu dânaṁ pâṇânaṁ sâdhu anâraṁbho apavyayatâ apabhâṁḍatâ sâdhu
6 parisâpi yut*e* âñapayisati gaṇanayaṁ hetu to chavyañjane to cha.

Here the corrections on Westergaard and Jacob's copy are :—

At the end of line 2 -	- *anusaṁ* for *anusâṁ*.
At the beginning of line 3	- *yânaṁ* for *yinu* ;
At the end of line 3 -	- *yathâ añâ* for *yatha aña*.
In line 4 - - -	- *pi kaṁmâya* for *si kaṁmâya* ; and *saṁstuta* for *samstata*.
In line 5 - - -	- *apabhâṁḍatâ* for *apabhiṁḍatâ*.
In line 6 - - -	- *yute* (doubtful) for *yuto* ; and *âñapayisati* for *añapayisati*.

Translation.

Wilson's translation of this tablet, proposed "subject to considerable doubt," is as follows :—

"King Priyadasî‖ says: This was ordained by me when I had been twelve years inaugurated in the conquered country; that among those united in the law, whether strangers or my own subjects, quinquennial expiation shall be held for the enforcement of moral obligations, as—duty to parents, friends, children, relations, Brahmans, and Sramans. Liberality is good; non-injury of living creatures is good; and abstinence from prodigality and slander is good. The Assembly itself will instruct the faithful in the virtues here enumerated, both by explanation and by example."¶

M. Burnouf observes that this last sentence is more literally, "'D'après la cause et "d'après la lettre'; à peu près comme quand on dit, *au fond et dans la forme.*" **

* *Ind. Alth.* (2nd ed.), vol. I. p. 162, note 2.
† *Journ. As. Soc. Beng.* vol. VII. p. 406.
‡ *Ind. Alt.* vol. I. p. 188, note 1.
§ *Ind. Alt.* (2nd ed.) vol. II. p. 252, note 4.
‖ In the inscriptions at Kapur di Giri, in the Panjáb, Professor Wilson observes that this name has "the more correct Sanskrit form of *Priya*, instead of Pali *Piyadasi*." The spelling is consequently different in the different tablets.
¶ Mrs. Spiers's *Ancient India*, p. 234; Wilson, *Journ. R. As. Soc.* vol. XII. p. 173.
** *Le Lotus de la Bonne Loi*, p. 738.

Tablet IV.

This is in twelve lines, still longer than any of the preceding (see Plate XI.), and is transliterated thus :—

1 Atikâtaṁ aṅtaraṁ bahûni vâsasatâni vaḍhito êva pâṇâraṁbho vihiṁsâcha bhûtânaṁ, ñâtîsu

2 asaṁpatipatî bamhaṇasamaṇânaṁ asaṁpatîpatî ta aja Dêvânaṁpiyasa Payadasino râño

3 dhaṁmacharaṇena bherîghoso aho dhaṁmaghoso vimânadasaṇâcha hastidasaṇâcha

4 agikhaṅdhânicha aññânicha divyâni rûpâṇi dasayipta janaṁ. Yârise bahûhi vâsasatêhi

5 na bhûtapuvê târise aja vaḍhite Devânaṁpiyasa Piyadaṁsino râño dhaṁmânusa-sṭiyâ anaram-

6 bho pâṇânaṁ avihiṁsâ bhûtânaṁ ñâtînaṁ saṁpaṭipatî bamhaṇasamaṇânaṁ saṁpaṭi-patî mâtaripitari

7 susûsâ thaira susûsâ esa añecha bahuvidhe dhaṁmacharaṇe vaḍhate vaḍhayisaticheva Devânaṁpiyo

8 Piyadasi râjâ dhaṁmacharaṇaṁ idaṁ putâcha potâcha papotâcha Devânaṁpiyasa Piyadasino râño

9 vadhayisaṁti idaṁ dhaṁmacharaṇaṁ âva savaṭakapâ dhaṁmamhi sîlamhi tisṭaṁto dhaṁmaṁ anusâsisaṁti

10 esahi sesṭe kaṁme ya dhaṁmânusâsanaṁ dhaṁmacharaṇêpi na bhavati asîlasa hu ta imaṁhi athaṁhi

11 (*va*)dhîcha ahînîcha sâdhu etâya athâya ida lekhâpitaṁ imasa atha(*sa*) vadhîyu-jaṁtu hîni châ

12 lochetavyâ dvâdasavâsâbhisitena Devânaṁpiyena Piyadasinâ râñâ idaṁ lekhâpitaṁ.

The new readings here supplied by the estampage are :—

In line 1 - - *vaḍhito* for *vaḍhitâ ;* and *ñâtisu* for *ñatisu.*
 „ 3 - - *bherighoso,* the *bh* was only partially shown in Westergaard and Jacob's copy.
 „ 4 - - *yârise* for *yârisa ;* and *vâsa* for *vasa.*
 „ 10 - - *esa hi* for *sahi ;* and *ta imamhi* for *? imamhi* doubtfully read *-va imamhi.*
 „ 11 - - *idaṁ* for *ida ;* and *hîni cha,* for *hîni mu.*

Of this tablet Burnouf * has given the following version :

"Dans le temps passé, pendant de nombreuses centaines d'années, on vit prospérer uniquement le meurtre des êtres vivants et la méchanceté à l'égard des créatures, le manque de respect pour les parents, le manque de respect pour les Bàmhaṇas et les Samaṇas (les Brâhmanes et les Çramaṇas). Aussi, en ce jour, parce que Piyadasi, le roi chéri des Dêvas, pratique la loi, le son du tambour [a retenti] ; oui, la voix de la loi [s'est fait entendre], après que des promenades de chars de parade, des promenades d'éléphants, des feux d'artifice, ainsi que d'autres représentations divines ont été montrées aux regards du peuple. Ce que depuis bien des centaines d'années on n'avait pas vu auparavant, on l'a vu prospérer aujourd'hui, par suite de l'ordre que donne Piyadasi, le roi chéri des Dêvas, de pratiquer la loi. La cessation du meurtre des êtres vivants et des actes de méchanceté à l'égard des créatures, le respect pour les parents, l'obéissance aux père et mère, l'obéissance aux anciens (*Thêra*), voilà les vertus, ainsi que d'autres pratiques de la loi de diverses espèces, qui se sont accrues. Et Piyadasi, le roi chéri des Dêvas, fera croître encore cette observation de la loi ; et les fils, et les petits-fils, et les arrière-petits-fils de Piyadasi, le roi chéri des Dêvas, feront croître cette observation de la loi jusqu'au *kalpa* de la destruction. Fermes dans la loi, dans la morale,

* *Lotus de la Bonne Loi,* p. 731.

ils ordonneront l'observation de la loi; car c'est la meilleure des actions que d'enjoindre l'observation de la loi. Cette observation même de la loi n'existe pas pour celui qui n'a pas de morale. Il est bon que cet object prospère et ne dépérisse pas; c'est pour cela qu'on a fait écrire cet édit. Si cet object s'accroît, on n'en devra jamais voir le dépérissement. Piyadasi, le roi chéri des Dêvas, a fait écrire cet édit, la douzième année depuis son sacre."

In Professor Kern's analysis, he takes this edict first, and prefaces his reading and translation by the following remarks, which, as they may not be generally known to my English and Indian readers, I give here in extenso:

'Let us,' he says, 'in the first place examine the state of the Girnar text as it has come down to us. Thus much we can see, that while there are no gross errors, there is much carelessness and irregularity in the spelling. The system of sounds of a dialect cannot be too carefully considered, if firm ground is to be obtained for the settlement, and thereby for the interpretation, of the text. The pronunciation *vâsa*, Sanskrit *varsha*, is as good as *vassa* (spelt *vasa*), since it is, in Prâkrit, a matter of indifference whether a syllable is long by position or by the natural length of the vowel. Consequently the developed Prâkrit does not admit a vowel long by nature in a syllable which is long by position. The spelling *bâmhaṇa* in line 2 trangresses this rule, while *bamhaṇa* in line 6 is correct. The same inconsistency is seen elsewhere—now *a*, then *â*. In the second line *patî* (= *pati*) with the dental *t* occurs twice, in line 6 it is twice written with the lingual. These forms are both quite correct, but they should not have been interchanged in the same document. From the Sanskrit *prati* there is produced on the one hand, by the dropping of the *r*, *pati;* on the other, first, the form *pṛiti* (*pĕrti*); an *r*, as well as an *s*, serving to effect the transition to an immediately following *t* in the class of dentals. In the oldest Indian of all, this sometimes takes place, in the Sanskrit still more frequently, while in the Prâkrits it is the rule. Thus the Sanskrit *kṛita* becomes pretty generally in the Prâkrits *kata; pĕrti, pati,* and thence later *paḍi, paḷi,* and *pari.* We find the same inconsistency in *vaḍh* along with *vadh.* The distinction between the dental and lingual *n* has not yet died out, but the author or transcriber continually confuses them; thus *dasaṇâ* should have the dental; *rûpâni*, on the contrary, the lingual *n*. A carelessness of frequent occurrence in the majority of Indian MSS., even the most recent, is the use of the *ṭ* after *s*, instead of the aspirated *ṭh*, as in *tisṭaṁto, sesṭe.* This is not the only point which shows clearly that the habits of the Indian transcribers all existed at that time;—the custom of indicating every nasal sound with which a syllable closes by a spurious anusvâra, simply to save trouble, is another example. In general, those documents of 258–257 B.C. present exactly the same kind of errors that we are accustomed to find in Indian MSS. The *s* before *ṭ*, though as a sign the same as the dental *s*, cannot, for a simple physiological reason, possibly have been the dental. Before a lingual, and above all an Indian lingual, no man can bring out anything but a lingual. The reason why the *sh* was not used to indicate the required lingual, must have been, that while the *sh* is indeed a lingual, it possesses, besides that, a characteristic of its own, so that it comes near to the lingual sound of a liquid *s*.

'Two forms occur which I see no chance of explaining from the dialect of Girnar, viz., *âva* and the neuters in *e*, as *charaṇe, kaṁme,* &c. That *âva savatakapâ* corresponds to a Sanskrit *yâvat saṁvartakalpât* has been correctly perceived by Burnouf, and admits

IV

V

J. Burgess fecit.

Collotype by W. Griggs

of no doubt; but *áva* for Sanskrit *yávat* is regular Magadhî, not Girnârî. Let it serve for proof of this assertion that the Magadhî *ádise*, Sanskrit *yádṛiśam*, is in our document, line 4, *yárisa*. The termination also of the neuter in *e*, in *seṣṭe*, *kaṁme*, is Magadhî; so also is *tárise* as respects the termination; in like manner *bahuvidhe dhaṁma-charaṇe* in line 7. It would be presumptuous to assert positively that an *e* = Sansk. *aṁ* and neuter *a*, was absolutely unknown to the Girnârî; but we have doubts on the point, and that because in Magadhî the *a* stems in general, whether masculine or neuter, have *e* in the nominative and so forth. Thus Mag. *piye* is as much equal to the Sansk. *priyaḥ* as to *priyam*; but in the western dialect the masculine has always *o*. There is no explanation whatever to be given of *áva* instead of *yáva*. Briefly, however hazardous it may appear, we will not refrain from expressing the conjecture that the text had been written originally in the language of the king himself, the Magadhî, that the other redactions are translations thereof, more or less successful, and that Magadhî forms have crept into the versions. We cannot, however, regard the word *thaira*, Sansk. *sthavira*, as a Magadhîsm, for *st* becomes *th* at the beginning of a word in the Girnârî as well. This much is certain, that the Magadhî text of Dhaulî, which alas! has suffered most, and has been the most hastily transcribed, is throughout the most consistent with itself in spelling and word-formation, is the best written, and excels the two other redactions in the correct use of the connecting particles.

'It is also of importance to inquire in how far any irregularities may admit of being explained from the condition of an original text, because all those three redactions agree in the reading of a very suspicious word, viz. *hini* (and *ahini*) in line 11. Sans. *hâni* means clearly enough "diminution," and *ahâni* "non-diminution." Now if it even should be supposed that the form of the participle *hîna* had exercised some influence on that of the monster *hini*, yet in no single Prâkrit, including the Pâli, has such a *hini* been found, but on the contrary *hâni*. The fact that the three redactions agree, tends in this particular case not to establish but to weaken the reading. Because the existence of such a monstrosity as *hini* might be in some slight degree conceivable as a sporadic instance in a single dialect, but that such a thing should appear in three widely diverging dialects or languages would be altogether too singular. If, however, all the redactions are from one source, then it might be possible that there was at first an error in that source.* It is fortunate that the meaning is not obscured in the redactions by the manner of writing.

'I shall now give the text of Girnar with the slight modifications which appear to be justified by comparison with the Kapur-di-giri version:—

1 Atikâtaṁ aṁtaraṁ bahûni vasasatâni vaḍhito êva pâṇârambho, vihiṁsâcha bhûtânaṁ, ñâtisu
2 asaṁpatipati, bamhaṇasamaṇânaṁ asaṁpatipati; ta aja Dêvânaṁpiyasa Piyadasino râño
3 dhaṁmacharaṇêna bhêrighoso aho dhaṁmaghoso, vimânadasaṇâcha hastidasanâcha
4 agikhaṁdhânicha aññânicha divyâni rûpâṇi dasayiptâ janaṁ. Yârisaṁ bahûhi vasasatêhi
5 na bhûtapuvaṁ, târisaṁ aja vaḍhito Dêvânaṁpiyasa Piyadasino râño dhaṁmânusastiyâ anâram-
6 bho pâṇânaṁ, avihiṁsâ bhûtânaṁ, ñâtinaṁ saṁpaṭipati, bamhaṇasamaṇânaṁ saṁpaṭipati, mâtaripitari
7 susûsâ, thaire susûsâ; êsa aññacha bahuvidhaṁ dhaṁmacharaṇaṁ vaḍhitaṁ, vaḍhayisaticheva Devânaṁpiyo
8 Piyadasi râjâ dhaṁmacharaṇaṁ idaṁ, putâcha potâcha papotâcha Devânaṁpiyasa Piyadasino râño
9 vadhayisaṁti idaṁ dhaṁmacharaṇam; (y)âva savaṭakapâ dhaṁmamhi sîlamhi tisṭaṁto dhaṁmaṁ anusâsisaṁti;
10 sahi sesṭaṁ kaṁmaṁ ya dhaṁmânusâsanaṁ dhaṁmacharaṇaṁpi na bhavati asîlasa. Seimamhi athamhi
11 vadhîcha ahânîcha sâdhu; etâya athâya idaṁ lekhâpitaṁ; imasa atha(*sa*) vadhi(*ṁ*) yu(*ṁ*)jaṁtu, hânicha
12 (*ná*)lochitavyâ. Dvâdasavasâbhisitena Devânaṁpiyena Piyadasinâ râñâ idaṁ lekhâpitaṁ.

* The difference between *â*, *î*, and *i*, is so slight in writing that it may after all be a question whether *hini* really stands in all places where the transcripts have it.

This may be put back into Sanskrit, with the exception of what is positively at variance with the rules of Sanskrit Syntax, thus:—

1 Antikrâṇte 'ntare, bahûni varshaśatâni, vardhita eva prâṇâlambho vihiṁsâcha bhûtânâṁ, jnâtishv
2 asampratipattir, brâhmaṇaśramaṇânâm asampratipattiḥ. Tad adya Devânâmpriyasya Priyadarśino râjno
3 dharmacharaṇena bherîghosho 'bhavad dharmaghosho, vimânadarśane cha hastidarśanecha
4 agniskandheshuchânyeshucha divyeshu rûpeshu darśitavatsu janaṁ. Yâdṛiśam bahubhir varshaśatair
5 na bhûtapûrvaṁ, tâdṛiśam adya vardhito Devânâmpriyasya Priyadarśino râjno dharmânuśâstyânalam-
6 bhaḥ prâṇânâm, avihiṁsâ bhûtânâṁ, jnâtishu sampratipattir, brâhmaṇaśramaṇeshu sampratipattir, mâtâpitroś
7 śuśrûshâ, sthavire śuśrûshâ. Etad anyachcha bahuvidhaṁ dharmacharaṇaṁ vardhitaṁ, vardhayishyati chaiva Devânâmpriyaḥ
8 Priyadarśi râjâ dharmacharaṇam idaṁ, putrâścha pautrâścha prapautrâścha Devânâmpriyasya Priyadarśino râjno
9 vardhayishyantidaṁ dharmacharaṇaṁ, yâvat saṁvartakalpâd dharme śile tishṭhanto dharmam anuśâsishyanti;*
10 etaddhi śreshṭhaṁ karma yad dharmânuśâsanaṁ, dharmacharaṇam api na bhavaty aśîlasya. Tad asminn arthe
11 vṛiddhiśchâhâniścha sâdhuḥ; etasmây arthâyedam lekhitam;† asyârthasya vṛiddhiṁ yuñjantu, hâniścha
12 nâlochayitavyâ.‡ Dvâdaśavarshâbhishiktena Devânâmpriyeṇa Priyadarśinâ râjnedaṁ lekhitam.§

Translation.

"In past times, during many centuries, attacking animal life and inflicting suffering on the creatures, want of respect for Brâhmans and Śramaṇas have only grown greater. But now, when King Devânâmpriya Priyadarśin practises righteousness, his kettle-drum has become a summons to righteousness ‖ while apparitions of chariots of the gods, and apparitions of celestial elephants, and fiery balls, and other signs in the heavens showed themselves to the people. In such a manner as has not been the case in many centuries previously, now through the exhortation of King Devânâmpriya Priyadarśin to cultivate righteousness, has the sparing of animal life, the gentle treatment of creatures, respect for relatives, respect for Brâhmans and monks, obedience to father and mother, obedience to an elder,¶ grown greater. This and many other kinds of virtuous practices have grown greater, and King Devânâmpriya Priyadarśin shall cause this practice of virtue to increase still more, and the sons, grandsons, and great-grandsons of King Devânâmpriya Priyadarśin shall also** cause this culture of virtue to increase; standing steadfast in righteousness and morality until the destruction of the world,†† they shall exhort to righteousness; ‡‡ to exhort to righteousness is surely a very excellent work, while from him who is immoral no practice of righteousness is to be expected. Increase, therefore, in these things, and no diminution, is good; for this end has this been written; §§ may they attend heartily to the increase hereof, and not aim at the diminution of it! King Devânâmpriya Priyadarśin has caused this to be written twelve years after his inauguration."

'In comparing this translation with that of Burnouf, it will be seen that they differ in a marked degree only in two places. Burnouf, as well as Lassen and Prinsep before him, had perceived that the clause beginning at *vimánadaśaṇácha* and ending at *janam*,

* Dhauli,—*bhavishyantaḥ śasishyanti.*

† Dh.,—*likhitam.*

‡ Dh.,—*hâniñcha mâlulochan.*

§ Dh.,—*dvâdaśa varshâṇy abhishiktasya Devânâmpriyasya Priyadarśino râjna etal likhitam.*

‖ The meaning is, "and not to war, as is usually the case."

¶ It is not quite clear what is to be understood by "a senior." No. VIII. one text has the same word, while another has *vṛiddha.*

** "Also" is wanting in Girnar, but is found duly expressed in Dhaulî.

†† Dhaulî,—"as long as the world (*seculum*) lasts."

‡‡ Dhaulî,—"they shall rule."

§§ Girnar,—"has this been caused to be written."

exhibits an altogether irregular combination of words, and they translate as if there stood in the Sanskrit, *vimânadarśane*, &c.,—*darśiteshu*. In this they are right, I think; but the meanings which they have assigned to most of the terms are unknown in the language. *Vimâna* is a so-called "chariot of the gods;" what aerial phenomenon is to be understood by it matters little for our present purpose. Between a certain aerial phenomenon or chariot of the gods, and "char de parade," as Burnouf translates it, there is hardly any connexion to be seen. The rendering of *agniskandha* (=*agnipiṇḍa*) by "feux d'artifices," is purely arbitrary. The expression *divyâni rûpâṇi* might in itself be sufficient to convince us that celestial phenomena are meant, for the term is, in Latin phrase, "solemnis." *Darśayati* is not only "shows" but also "shows itself." The only other expression which remains to be explained is *hastidarśanam*. I have never met with *hastin* itself in the sense of an aerial phenomenon, but it is a synonym of Airâvata, which is used especially to denote Indra's elephant, and *airâvata* is an aerial phenomenon which is frequently mentioned. There is, therefore, but little doubt that *hastidarśanam* is another expression for *airâvatadarśanam*. This is confirmed by *hathîni* being neuter in Dhaulî; for *airâvata*, in the sense of an aerial phenomenon, is sometimes masculine, sometimes neuter; therefore, also, *hastin*, when it is used in the signification here assigned to it. What Aśoka says is almost as follows: 'The joyful circumstance which consisted in the fact that the sound of the war-drum would henceforth be a symbol of peace, was announced, and, as it were, received with acclaim, by the heavenly powers.' Every one who is in any degree acquainted with Sanskrit literature, knows how frequently the above-named phenomena are mentioned, and no one who knows aught of human nature will be surprised that the king, on beholding celestial phenomena which, though indeed not of daily occurrence, yet were far from being very uncommon, connected them with an event which, in his eyes, was so important.

'The words *vadhiṁ yuṁjaṁtu* and *hâniṁ mâlochayisu* are clear, when it is considered that as *vriddhi* and *ahâni* are synonyms, the predicates also must be in the same position Consequently, *yunakti* is to be taken in that sense in which it expresses almost the same thing as *âlochayati*; that is, in the meaning of *anuchintayati*, for which see *Petersb. Dict.* For the sake of distinctness I have written *vaḍhiṁ yuṁjuṁtu*, without, on that account, overlooking the fact that *vaḍhiy yu-*, with Anunâsika rejected or not expressed, agrees with *say(y)ama*, &c. The cases, however are not altogether parallel, for the phonetic alterations in a word apply in Prâkrits only exceptionally in the period.—A syllable has fallen out on the stone before *lochetavyâ*, which can have been nothing but *na* or *nâ*, because there does not appear to be room enough for *no â-*, which would signify the same thing.

'In the inscription now discussed there is nothing which could give offence to any class of the people. It is true, indeed, that the term *dharma* might be understood by some as an allusion to the Dharma, the Religion of the Buddhists, but none of that generation could fail to see, even for a moment, both on account of the connexion and the combination *dharmacharaṇam*, that the word here signified "righteousness," "virtue." Apart from the style, there is so little exclusively Buddhistic in this document that we might equally well conclude from it that the king, satiated with war, had become the president of a peace society, and of an association for the protection of the lower animals, as that he had embraced the doctrine of Śâkyamuni. More plainly, but at the same time most modestly, Aśoka mentions his conversion in No. VIII. of Girnar.'

Tablet V.

The fifth tablet consisted of nine lines and a half, of which only four are now entire, the rest being all broken away at the beginning; there is also a crack in the stone that has destroyed several of the letters in the portion left otherwise entire. Fortunately the sense at least of this can be restored from the other copies. What remains reads thus:

1 Devânaṁ piyo Piyadasi râja evaṁ âha kalâṇaṁ *du*karaṅye akalâṅe saso dukaraṁ karoti

2 ta mayâ bahu kalâṇaṁ kata to mama putâcha potâcha paraṅcha tenaya me apachaṁ âva saṁvaṅṭa kapâ anuvatisare tathâ

3 so sukatam kâsati yo tu êta desaṁ pihâpesati so *d*ukatam kâsati sukaraṁhi pâpam atikâtaṁ aṅtaraṁ

4 na bhûta puvaṁ dhaṁma mahâmâtâ nâma ta mayâ to dasa vâsâbhisit*ena* dhâmma mahâmâtâ katâ te sava pâsaṅḍesu vyâpatâ dhâṁma dhisṭânâya *

5 . . . dhaṁmayutasacha Yoṇa Kambo*cha* Gaṅdhârânaṁ Rîsṭika Peteṇikânaṁ ye vâpi aṅñe âparâ tâ bhatamayesu va †

6 . . . s*u* khây*a* dhaṁmayutânam aparâ go dhâya vyâpati te baṅdhana badhasa paṭividhânâya ‡

7 . . . . ja katâ bhîkâresu vâ thairesu vâ vyâpatâ te Pâṭaliputecha bâhir*e*sucha §

8 . . . . *n*e vâpi m*a* añe ñâtikâ savatâ vyâpatâ te yo ayaṁ dhaṁmanisṭito tîva ||

9 . . . . . dhaṁmamahâmâtâ êtâya athâya ayaṁ dhaṁma lipî likhitâ ¶

. . . .

The corrections made are:

In line 1 - - - - *kalâṇaṁ* for *kalaṇa.*
In line 2 - - - - *to mama* for *ta mama.*
In line 4 - - - - *mayâ* for *meyâ;* and *dhâma* for *dhaṁma.*
In line 5 - - - - *Gandharânaṁ Risṭika* for *Gandhârâ marisṭika,* as Wilson read it.

---

* The Dhauli copy reads:—
dhammâdhithânâye dhammavâḍhiye hita sukhâye cha dhammasutâ sanyâna *Kambocha,* &c.
The Kapur-di-giri—
dhamadhiṭhayo cha dhamavaḍhiya hita sukhaya cha dhamayatha saya *Kamb-.*

† Dhauli has after this—
babhanî anathesu ma . . . lokesucha hota bhisâsu *sukhâye,* &c.
Kapur-di-giri—
bramani bhishu anaṭeshu vaṭashu hita *sukhaye,* &c.

‡ Dhauli reads in this lacuna:—
-ye apalibodhaye mokhaye cha-iya anubandha pajâṭi . . . *ta bhikala,* &c.
And Kapur-di-giri—
paṭividhanaye apanarodhaye mocha vana va . . . pajati *kiṭa bhikati,* &c.

§ Dhaulî gives here:—
cha nagalesu savesu olodhanesu evâhi bhâtanam me . . . bhaghininam, *va-,* &c.
Kapur-di-giri—
cha nagareshu saveshu orodhaneshu bhratunacha me kusunacha ye *vapi,* &c.

|| Dhaulî:—
tivam dhammâdhithine tâva dânasayute va sava paṭhaviyam dhammayutasi viyapatâ ime *dhamma,* &c.
Kapur-di-giri—
tivara dhamadhiṭane diva danasayutra va . . . asti stanati mata dhamayatasavaṇa viyapatra *edhama* . .

¶ Dhaulî:—
dhammalipali sansa chilaṭhitî kaṭa tasacha me pa . . anavetatu.
Kapur-di-giri—
dhamalipi lipi . . thiti va ṭinika bhota panja anuvatantu.—*Journ. R. As. Soc.* vol. XII. pp. 183–185.

This has not been revised by Dr. Kern. The following is Professor Wilson's version, slightly modified by later commentators :

Translation.

" The beloved of the gods King Priyadasi thus proclaims: Vice is difficult of performance, therefore much good is to be done by me, and my sons and grandsons, and other—my posterity—(will) conform to it for every age. So they who shall imitate them shall enjoy happiness, and those who cause the path to be abandoned shall suffer misfortune. Vice is easily committed, therefore, Dharma Mahâmatra (*or* great officers of morals) are appointed by me, in the thirteenth year of my inauguration, for the purpose of presiding over morals among persons of all the religions, for the sake of the increase of virtue; and for the happiness of the virtuous among the people of Kamboja, Gandhara, Rashṭrika, and Pitenika. They shall also be spread among the warriors, the Brahmans, the mendicants, the destitute, and others, without any obstruction, for the happiness of the well-disposed, in order to loosen the bonds of those who are bound, and liberate those who are confined, through the means of holy wisdom disseminated by pious teachers; and they will proceed to the outer cities and fortresses of my brother and sister, and wherever are any other of my kindred; and the ministers of morals, those who are appointed as superintendents of morals, shall, wherever the moral law is established, give encouragement to the charitable and those addicted to virtue. With this intent this edict is written, and let my people obey it."*

In this edict Aśoka "names the extreme limits of his kingdom as Yona-Kamboja-Gaṅdhârâṇaṁ Ristika-Peteṇikânaṁ, and in the corresponding portion of the Dhaulî redaction, as 'Yâna-Kambocha-Gaṅdhâlesu Laṭhika-Piteṇikesu.' Except the last name this can easily be restored in Girnar—'Yona-Kamboja-Gaṅdhârâṇaṁ Râsṭika-Peteṇikânaṁ.'" † These names have been explained by Lassen,‡ with, perhaps, the exception of the last. "Who the Petenikas were," he remarks, "cannot as yet be certainly determined; the most probable opinion is (Prinsep's) that they are the inhabitants of the upper districts on the Godâvarî, whose capital Pratishṭhâna is mentioned by the ancients in the form Paithana."§

TABLET VI.

This begins the second column of the edicts (Plate XII.), and is in fourteen lines of moderate length: the first only, on the vertex of the rock, has lost a few letters. It reads thus :—

1 Devâ . . . pi . . . si râjâ evaṁ âha atikâtaṁ aṁtaraṁ
2 nâ bhûtapuva sava . . la aṭhakaṁme va paṭivedanâ vâ ta mayâ evaṁ kataṁ
3 save kâle bhuṁjamânasa me orodhanamhi gabhâgâramhi vachamhi va
4 vinîtamhi-cha uyânesucha savata paṭivedakâ sṭitâ athe me janasa
5 paṭivedetha iti savatacha janasa athe karomi. Yacha kiṁchi mukhatâ
6 âñapayâmi svayaṁ dâpakaṁ vâ sâvâpakaṁ vâ yavâ puna mahâmâtesu

* Wilson, *Journ. R. As. Soc.* vol. XII. pp. 188, 189.
† Kern, *u. s.* p. 107. Râsṭika is, of course, Râshṭrika, on the coast of Gujarat.
‡ *Indische Alterthumskunde* (2nd ed.), vol. I. p. 137.
§ *Ind. Alt.*, vol. I. p. 216, and vol. II. p. 239 ; and conf. *Journ. As. Soc. Beng.* vol. VII. p. 267.

7 âchâyika aropitam bhavati tâya athâya vivâdo ni *kat*î va*san*̇to parisâyam̀
8 ânaṅtaram̀ paṭivedetayam̀ me savatâ save kâle evam̀ mayâ âñapitam̀ nâsti hi me to sâ
9 ustânamhi atha sam̀tîraṇâya va katavya matehi me savâ loka hitam̀
10 tasacha puna esa mûle ustânam̀cha atha sam̀tîraṇâcha nâsti hi kam̀mataraiǹ
11 sava loka hitattâyacha kim̀chi parâkamâmi aham̀ kim̀ti bhûtânam̀ anaṇ̇amgachheyam̀
12 idhacha nâni sukhâpayâmi paratâcha svagam̀ ârâdhayam̀tu ta etâya athâya
13 ayam̀ dham̀malipî lekhâpitâ kim̀ti chiram̀ tisṭeya iti tathâcha me putâ potâcha papotâcha
14 anuvataram̀ savaloka hitâya dukaram̀tu idam̀ añata agena parâkamena.

The corrections here are :—

In line 1 - - - - -	*si râjâ* for *pi râjâ*
In line 6 - - - - -	*mahâmâtesu* for *mahâthatesu* (?)
In line 10 - - - - -	*tasacha* for *tasecha.*

Professor Kern corrects the first five lines as follows :—

1 Devânam̀piyo Piyadasi râjâ evam̀ âha : atikâtam̀ am̀taram̀
2 nâ bhutâpubam̀ savam̀ kâlam̀ athakam̀mam̀ vâ paṭivedanâ vâ ; ta mayâ evam̀katam̀ :
3 savam̀ kâlam bhum̀jamânasa me orodhanamhi gabhâgâramhi vachamhi
4 vinîtamhicha uyânesucha savata paṭivedakâ sṭitâ 'athamme janasa
5 patividetha' iti, savatacha janasa atham karomi.

'However clear,' he remarks, 'the general meaning of this document may be, some terms occur, which are not found elsewhere, and others which, though their meaning may be easily guessed, yet deserve a few observations of a grammatical nature.

'The word *paṭivedanâ* signifies, in virtue of its form, "care, inspection," and that is the meaning here, as well as "communicating, informing, reporting." We do not need to inquire at all of such forms as *vedanâ, bodhanâ*, &c., whether or not they are used in a causative signification. *Vedanâ* is "notion, feeling, painful feeling;" but is also causative, "communicating, making known." As little is the distinction to be observed in such a form as *vedaka*, and such like; it is only the connexion which shows the meaning. Thus *sam̀vedana* signifies "feeling, knowledge;" but it signifies also "to bring to knowledge, to acquaint." Moreover verbs of the 10th class also admit of a double conception; *e.g.*, *vedayate* in *Muṇḍ. Upan.* p. 279, is "to know, to think." *Prativedayati* is generally a causative with the signification of "making known, informing;" but *pratisam̀vedayati* occurs also as a denominative, "to obtain knowledge of, to be aware of, to observe." See, for instance, *Lalitav.* 147. 11: *sukhañcha kâyena pratisam̀vedayati sma.* I select this passage from among many others just because we are able to refer to the parallel passage in the Pâlî redaction quoted by Childers, *Pâlî Dict.* sub voce *jhânam̀.* The whole text given there by Childers agrees almost literally with *Lalitav.* 147 and 139, and since the Pâlî also has *sukhañcha kâyena paṭisamvedeti*, the signification of the denominative is determined not merely for the Sanskrit but for the Pâlî as well. It follows now, as a matter of course, that the *paṭivedeti* of our inscription signifies "to have care of, to observe, to inspect," as well as "to communicate, to inform." The *prativedakas*, therefore, were not spies, as others have made them out to be in spite of the plain words of the king, but inspectors, and at the same time, as would be felt in the Indian language, reporters.

'*Orodhana*, Sans. *avarodhana*, is entirely the same in meaning as *antaḥpura*, signifying therefore "women's chamber." That *antaḥpura* is the Sanskrit word for what we

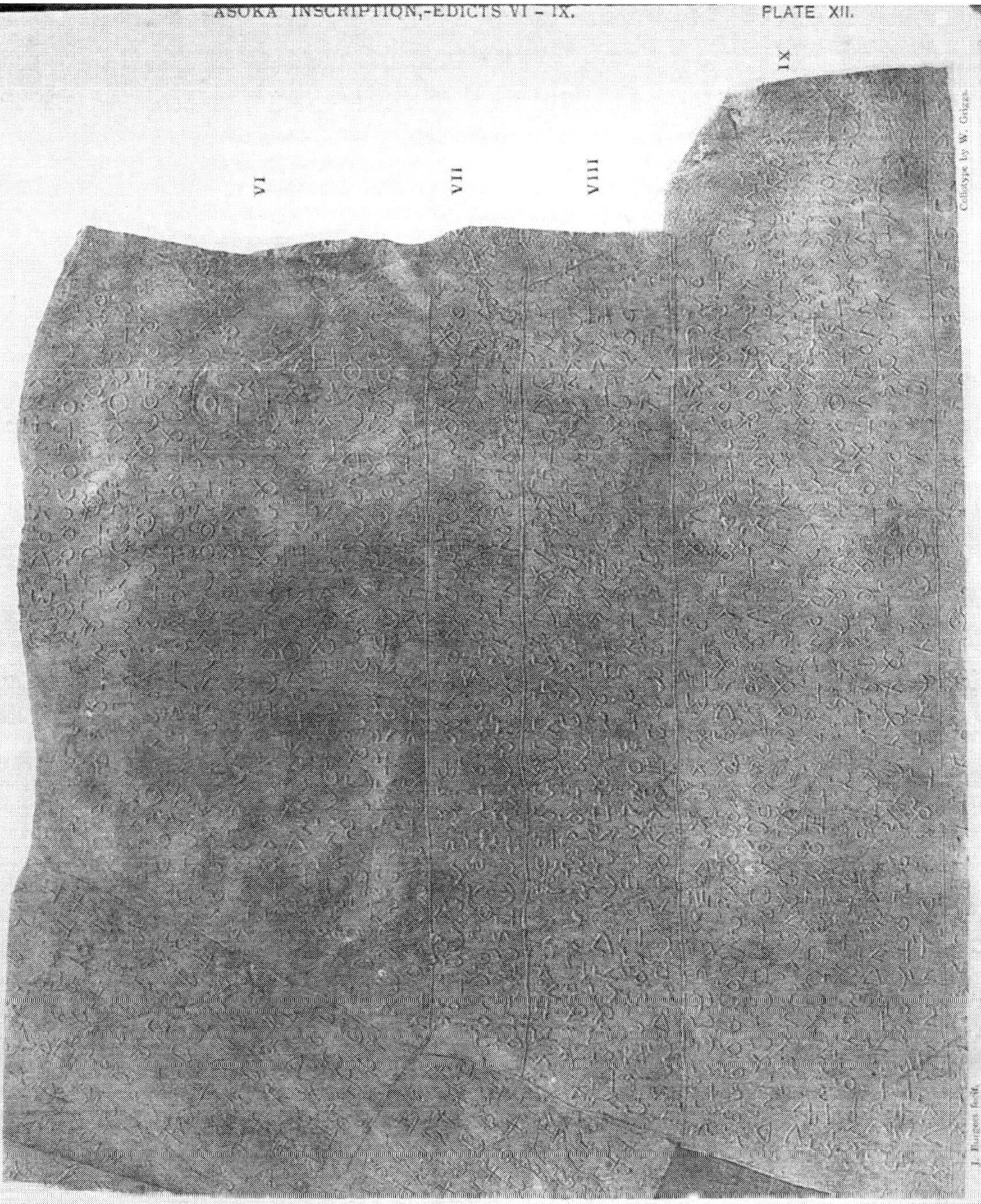

J. Burgess fecit.

Collotype by W. Griggs.

are accustomed to call "the sex," is unknown to the dictionaries; but is otherwise well enough known from Sanskrit literature. Any one may convince himself of this by reading Varâha-Mihira's *Bṛihatsaṅhîta*, chaps. 74–78, which together constitute the *Antaḥpurachinta, i.e.* "observations upon the sex."* The text of Dhaulî has *aṁte-olodhana*, which answers to a Sans. *antovarodhana*.†

'The conjecture has been made with regard to *vacha* that it is = Sans. *vrâtya*. *Vrâtya* is "wanderer, anyone without a fixed residence," and is accurately rendered by the Latin *peregrinus*, for it, too, just as the Latin word, took the signification of "pilgrim, roaming spiritual brother";‡ a guest also is sometimes addressed as *vrâtya*. The singular *vachamhi* can be here taken in a plural signification just as well as the immediately preceding *gabhâgâramhi*, "over sanctuaries, *in sacella*," and in the text of Kapur-di-Giri, *uyânisi* also "over the public gardens." The variant of *vacha* in the Dhaulî redaction is unfortunately only partially legible: *saṁ* at the beginning is recognisable, and *si* at the end; *pi* seems to stand before the termination *si*, but this might easily be a wrongly written or read *ha*. One letter unrecognisable in the facsimile remains still to be filled in, *ga* as I suppose. From the Sanskrit literature with which I am acquainted I cannot quote any instance of *saṅgraha* in the sense of lodgings, still it must have been a word in daily use, for it occurs in this sense frequently in the old Javanese.§

'It is still more troublesome to determine the sense of *vinîta*, as Girnar and Kapur-di-Giri read; and especially because Dhaulî has *ninîta*. Both are either masculine or neuter. It is a general rule that the neuter of the so-called part. perf. of all intransitive verbs in Sanskrit expresses the same thing as collectives in Dutch with or without the prefix *ge*: Thus *hasitam* is "gelach," *ruditam*, "geween," &c., the same form also serves as infinitive aorist; thus *avalokitam* is τὸ κατιδεῖν, &c. *Vinîta* is "transported," therefore *vinîtam* is "transport, traffic." Even the masculine *vinîtaḥ* is, according to the Indian lexicographers, "trader." Beyond all doubt, therefore, *vinîta* is a synonym of *nigama*; for this also is both "traffic" and "trader," and "market." However, since *vinîtam* may signify "correction," and *vinîta* "corrected," &c., we have still to inquire whether the variant *ninîta* strengthens or weakens our supposition. Unfortunately it does neither the one nor the other. If it be = Sans. *ninîtam*, it may then mean "importation," but if it originates from *nirnîtam*, it would then be the "decision, sentence." Though it were granted even that "inspectors over arbitration" may be thought of, which I doubt, still in that case, *vinîta*, which occurs in two redactions, could not agree with it. On that ground I think I may postulate it as probable that by *vinîta* is meant "trade," or "market," or "trader," according as we regard it as neuter or masculine. As regards *ninîta*, it has to be remarked that *nî*, "to lead," is nothing else than the causative of *gam*

---

* Compare the English translation, *Journ. R. As. Soc.* N. S. vol. IV. 1870, p. 439.

† A Magadhî *antepula* has been by mistake Palicised by the regulators of the Pâli into *antepura*; it ought to have been *antopura*, which indeed is also once met with.

‡ The great Vratya whose wanderings are described in mystic language in *Atharva Veda*. XV., is the Wind (Rudra); he is the counterpart of the Gangleri (*i.e.* the wanderer) of the Edda, or as Sono calls him, the *Viator indefessus*, a surname of Odhin (Rudra). Compare *Praçnop.* p. 184.

§ For instance, in the *Arjuna-Wiwâha*, v. 278, it is "reception (of a guest);" *griha saṅgraha*, v. 291, is "apartment for lodging."

"to go;"* and since *nigama* signifies "trade," *ninîtam* may signify it just as well. Superintendence of trade is one of the first duties of a well-ordered state, in order to prevent the use of false weights and measures and other evil practices.'

He then renders the first five lines into Sanskrit as follows:—

'Devânâmpriyaḥ Priyadarśi râjaivam âha : atikrânte 'ntare
na bhûtapûrvaṁ sarvaṁ kâlam arthakarma vâ prativedanâ vâ ; tan mayaivaṁ kṛitam ;
sarvaṁ kâlam bhuñjânasya me 'varodhane garbhâgâreshu vrâtyeshucha
vinîte† chodyâneshucha, sarvatra prativedakâs sthitâḥ : artham majjanasya
prativedayeteti, sarvatracha janasyârthaṁ karomi.'

Professor Kern's translation covers only the first half of this inscription, but it is complemented by Lassen's version:—

Translation.

"King Devânâmpriya Priyadarśin saith: 'In past times there has never yet existed care for the (civil) interests, nor official superintendence; therefore have I instituted the same; all the time that I have been reigning there have been everywhere inspectors over the women, sanctuaries, travelling pilgrims, (?) traders (or trade, markets), and parks for walking, in order to attend to the interests of my people,‡ and in all respects I further the interests of my people;§ and whatever I declare or whatever the Mahâmatra shall declare, shall be referred to the Council for decision. Thus shall reports be made to me. This have I everywhere, and in every place commanded, for to me there is not satisfaction in the pursuit of worldly affairs; the most worthy pursuit is the prosperity of the whole world. My whole endeavour is to be blameless towards all creatures, to make them happy here below, and enable them hereafter to attain *Swarga*. With this view this moral edict has been written: may it long endure; and may my sons grandsons and great-grandsons after me also labour for the universal good; but this is difficult without extreme exertion."||

'As the sheriffs were appointed by Aśoka, not at the beginning of his reign, but in the eleventh year after his accession to the throne, as we learn from edict V., so they do not belong to the magistrates mentioned here.'

TABLET VII.

This is the shortest of all the edicts being contained in three lines which read thus:—

1 Devanaṁpiyo Piyadasi râjâ savata ichhati save pâsaṁḍâ vaseyu savâ te sayamaṁcha

2 bhâvasudhiṁcha ichhati jano ta uchâvachachhaṁdo uchâvachârâyo te savaṁva kâsaṁti ekadesaṁva kâsaṁti

3 vipûle tupi dâne yasa nâsti sayame bhavasudhitâva kataṁñatâva daḍhabhatitacha nichâ bâdhaṁ

* *Nî (nayati)* must also be a causative of *i (eti, ayati)*, although the causative force of the *n* is no longer to be discovered in the state of the language as it is now known to us.

† Or *viniteshu*, and in the Dhauli version *ninite*.

‡ The Dhauli redaction reads: "All the time that I have been reigning, the inspectors over, &c., have had to communicate to me the interests of the people."

§ Thus far Kern, *ut sup.* pp. 75, 76.

|| Lassen, *Ind. Alt.* II. p. 268, note 1; and Mrs. Spiers's *Life in Anc. India*, p. 236. Burnouf (*Lotus de la Bonne Loi*, p. 654) translates the last sentence, "mais cela est difficile à faire si ce n'est par un héroisme supérieur."

*Translation.**

"**Priyadasi**, the king dear to the gods, desires that everywhere the ascetics of all persuasions should remain [*in peace*]; they all desire the regulation that they exercise upon themselves and purity of the soul; but people have different opinions and different likings, [and] the ascetics obtain, whether the whole, or whether a part only [of what they ask]. Nevertheless, for himself, to whom there reaches not a large alms, the empire over himself, purity of mind, knowledge, and firm devotion which lasts for ever, this is good."

This edict has been discussed by H. H. Wilson at considerable length,† and still further by Burnouf.‡

Tablet VIII.

The eighth edict is in five lines, and has been discussed by H. H. Wilson,§ Burnouf,|| and Kern.¶ It reads thus:—

1 Atikâtaṁ aṁtaraṁ râjâno vihârayâtâṁ ñayâsu etamagavya aññânicha etârisâni
2 abhîramakâni ahuṁsu; so Devânaṁpiyo Piyadasi râjâ dasavasâbhîsito saṁtoayâya saṁbodhiṁ
3 tena sâ dhamayâtâ etâ yaṁ hoti bâmhaṇasamaṇânaṁ dasaṇecha dâṇecha, thairâṇaṁcha dasâṇecha
4 hiraṇapaṭividhânecha janapadasacha janasa dasanaṁ dhaṁmânusasṭîcha dhamaparipuchhâcha
5 tadopayâ esâ bhûya rati bhavati Devânaṁpiyasa Piyadasino râño bhâge aṁñe.

And was rendered by Burnouf as follows:—

"Dans le temps passé, les rois connurent la promenade du plaisir; alors la chasse et d'autres divertissements de ce genre avaient lieu. [*Mais*] Piyadasi, le roi chéri des Dêvas, parvenu à la dixième année depuis son sacré, obtient la science parfaite que donne la Buddha. C'est pourquoi la promenade de la loi est cette qu'il faut faire: ce sont la visite et l'aumône faites aux Brahmanes et aux Samaṇas, distribution de l'or [*en leur faveur*], l'inspection du peuple et du pays, l'injonction d'exécuter la loi, les interrogatoires sur la loi; ce sont là les moyens qui causent un extrême plaisir à Piyadasi, le roi chéri des Dêvas, dans cette période de temps, différente [*de celle que l'a precédée*]."

Professor Kern thus revises and translates it:—

1 Atikâtaṁ aṁtaraṁ râjâno vihârayâtaṁ ñayâsu, etamagavyaṁ aññânicha etârisâni
2 abhiramakâni ahuṁsu; so Devânaṁpiyo Piyadasi râjâ dasavasâbhisito saṁto ayâya saṁbodhiṁ;
3 tena sâ dhaṁmayâtâ etâ, yaṁ hoti: bamhaṇasamaṇânaṁ dasanaṁcha dânaṁcha, thairâṇaṁ dasanaṁcha
4 hiranapativîdhânaṁcha jânapadasacha janasa dasanaṁ, dhaṁmânusasṭîcha dhaṁmaparipuchhâcha.
5 Tadopayâ esâ bhûya rati bhavati Devânaṁpiyasa Piyadasino râño bhâge aṁñe.

---

* Burnouf, *Lotus*, p. 755.
† *Journ. R. As. Soc.* vol. VIII. pp. 309–314: vol. XII. pp. 198, 199.
‡ *Lotus de la Bonne Loi*, pp. 668, 754 ff.
§ *Journ. R. As. Soc.* vol. XII. p. 199.
|| *Lotus de la Bonne Loi*. p. 757 ff.; and conf. Lassen, *Ind. Alt.* vol. II. p. 233, and note 2.
¶ *Ut sup.* pp. 55 ff.

In Sanskrit—

1 Atikrânte 'ntare râjâno vihârayâtrâṁ nirayâsishuḥ ; etamṛigavyam anyânichaitâdṛiśâny
2 abhirâmâṇy abhûvan. Tad Devânâmpriyaḥ Priyadarśî râjâ daśavarshâbhishiktas sann iyâya sambodhim ;
3 tena sâ dharmayâtraitâ, yad bhavati : brâhmaṇaśramaṇânâṁ darśanañcha dânañcha, sthavirâṇâṁ darśanañcha
4 hiraṇyapratividhânañcha, jâuapadasya-cha janasya darśanaṁ, dharmânuśâstiścha dharmaparipṛichchhâcha.
5 Tadauparishṭâd eshâ bhûyo ratir bhavati Devânâmpriyasya Priyadarśino râjno 'parabhâge.

Translation.

"In past times the kings went out on journeys of pleasure;* stag-hunting† and other such like recreations were in vogue.‡ But King Devânâmpriya Priyadarśin, ten years after his inauguration, came to the true insight. Therefore he began a walk of righteousness§ which consists in this, that he sees at his house, and bestows gifts upon Brahmans and monks,—he sees at his house, and presents elders with gold,—he receives subjects of town and country,—exhorts to righteousness and seeks righteousness. Since then, this is the greatest pleasure of King Devânâmpriya Priyadarśin in the period after his conversion."

'In this little piece,' adds Professor Kern, 'there is only one expression which presents any difficulty in interpreting, *tadopayâ* in Girnar and *tadâ-peyâle* in Dhaulî, though the meaning may readily be conjectured. There must be something which is generally expressed in Sanskrit by *tadâprabhṛiti; tadârabhya* and such like *upâdâya*, which the Buddhistic style, both Sanskrit and Pâlî so often employs, is not to be thought of. *Tadupâdâya*, or also *tadopadâya=tadâprabhṛiti*, signifying "thenceforth," "since that;" and if *tadopayâ* was found only in Girnar it might perhaps be attributed to an error, but Kapur-di-Giri also has *tadopayaṁ*, which deviates from *tadopayâ* sufficiently to convince us that the readings support each other, and are therefore genuine. To what Sanskrit form, then, can the Prâkrit correspond? In my opinion, to an ablative *auparyât* on the one hand, and to an adverbial accusative *auparyam* on the other. *Auparya* is derived regularly from *upari*, "after, later." Now since *auparya* becomes *opaya* in Prâkrit, just as *kârya* becomes *kayya*, &c. *tadopayâ* corresponds to a Sanskrit *tadauparyât=*"since that;"—or if a form known otherwise be preferred, *tadauparishṭât*. In the Dhaulî text there is an entirely different word, a synonym of the foregoing—*peyâle*, which, after the example of the *Lalitavistâra*, I have rendered in Sanskrit by *preyâlam*. It will be in vain sought for in the dictionaries, though its existence had not escaped the notice of Burnouf in his widely extended investigations. He seems, however, not to have found it otherwise than in the Prâkrit form *preyâla*. After having remarked, in *Lotus de la Bonne Loi*, p. 388, that he had met with this *peyâla* in a number of the writings of the northern Buddhists, he proceeds to say:—

"Dans le textes pâlis, la formule abréviative *comme ci-dessus* est exprimée par le monosyllable *pé* qui est le commencement de *péyyâlam;* car c'est ainsi qu'est orthographié ce mot en pâli. J'en trouve un example dans l'*Atânâṭiya sutta*, qui est ainsi

---

* Dhaulî has—"the kings went out on so-called journeys of pleasure."

† The expression in Dhaulî is more general, for *mṛiga* signifies not merely "stag, gazelle," but wild beast in general.

‡ Dhaulî—"There existed for them stag-hunting," &c.

§ The play on the words *vihârayatâ* and *dhammayata* is lost in the translation.

conçu : *sôyêva purimapêyyâlêna vitthârêtabhô,* 'il doit être dêveloppé avec le précédent *pêyyâla.*'* Je n'ai jusqu'à présent trouvé d'autre manière d'expliquer ce mot que de supposer qu'il dérive de *pê,* abbreviation de *pûrvê,* 'précédemment,' réuni à *alam,* 'assez,' de façon à exprimer cette idée, 'la chose a été dite précédemment d'une manière suffisante.' Je ne donne cependant encore cette explication que comme une conjecture."

'We can pay no better tribute to the memory of the greatest Indologue of France, who shortly after writing the above words was snatched away from science, than to take up the inquiry at the point where he dropped it. Let it be observed, in the first place, that the brief clause quoted above is not quite clear, and may mean "with what precedes and what follows" equally well as "with repetition of the preceding." In no case can it mean what Burnouf imagines. Fortunately the expression occurs often enough in the *Lalitavistâra* to enable us to determine its signification. In *Lalitav.* 320, 18, we see that the words *peyâlaṁ yâvat* are equivalent to the expression *pûrvavadyâvat,* which occurs four lines previously, that is, "as before on to." Hence it follows not that *peyâlam* signifies properly the same as *pûrvavat;* for if it be once supposed that the word signified "repetition," it would then be a matter of indifference whether we said "repetition" (*da capo*) on to," or "as before on to," without implying thereby that the ideas "as before" and "repetition" were in themselves allied. To confirm this further, I refer to p. 445, where *peyâlam* has, as a synonym or substitute, *vistareṇa yâvat, i.e.* "copious (to complete) on to." To determine the sense completely, we must avail ourselves of the word *preyâla,* which also occurs more than once in the *Lalita-Vistâra,* and which plainly is nothing else than the Sanskrit or Sanskriticised form of *peyâla.* The circumstance that wherever the Prâkrit *peyâla* stood as a technical, almost algebraic term, the compilers of the said book have neglected to translate it into Sanskrit, is an additional proof for the view that Sanskrit is of comparatively late date in the writings of the northern Buddhists. Where *preyâlam* is found fully written, it is not a technical term, but has a meaning which can easily be felt. This *preyâlam* admits of being represented by another Sanskrit word, viz. *bhûyas,* in the various applications in which the latter can be used. Thus we read, immediately after a song addressed by the good sons of Mâra the Wicked to their father, *Lalita-Vist.* 397, 7 :

"Preyâlam evaṁ te sarve Màraputrâḥ—Màram pâpiyasam prithakprithag gâthâbhir adhyabhâshanta," *i.e.* "Thus spoke again (Sans. *bhûyas*) all those sons of Mâra to Mâra the Wicked, alternately in songs."

'The meaning of *preyâlam* comes out less clearly p. 369, 11 ; because the verse is corrupt, or has been spoiled by the editor.

'When we compare the particulars now adduced, with each other, when we remember the opposition so common between *pûrvam* and *bhûyas,* and keep in view that *bhûyas* signifies "more, ample," as much as "later, subsequent," then there can remain no doubt that *preyâlam,* Prâkrit *peyâlam,* is = *bhûyas.* The Pâlî form *peyyâlaṁ* might, where it appears as a substantive, correspond to a *praiyâlyam* or to *bhûyastvam;* but that makes no difference in the main idea of the word. The double *yy* in the Pâlî is one of the many instances which show clearly that the regulators of that artificial and literary language have been frequently very unfortunate in rendering Magadhî words, which they misunderstood on account of the old spelling, which did not usually express

* *Dighanikaya,* f. 177 *a.*

the doubling of consonants.* That we may be convinced of this we shall investigate the etymology of the word. There is, in Sanskrit, a comparative of *puru* (from *pĕru*), viz. *prâyas,* which is used exclusively in the neuter, though the full form masculine *frâyan,* neut. *frâyo* is still preserved in Baktrian. This *prâyas* is (apparently) regular, inasmuch as it has Vṛiddhi instead of Guṇa,† but the form is perfectly regular in other Indo-Germanic languages; thus Greek πλεῖον (mas. πλειων), Latin *plus,* from *plois* (*plais*), Norse *fleir.* The superlative is lost in Sanskrit, it must have been *preshṭha;* but as there is an entirely different *preshṭha* from *priya,* it is probable that the form was avoided, and then fell into desuetude. On the contrary the Baktrian still possesses *fraeshta,* Gr. πλεῖστος, Norse *flestr* (for *fleestr, fleistr,* by the shortening of the vowel on account of the two consonants following). In making acquaintance with the Sanskrit *preyâlam,* Magadhî *peyâle,* we learn at the same time the remarkable circumstance that along with *prâyas,* there must also have existed in Sanskrit a form *preyas,* the use of which was also avoided, as being a homonym of the comparative of *priya.* The suffix *ala* joined to *preyas* or rather to *preya* = Sans. *prâya,* "multitude," has, on the one hand, an extensive or augmentative force, and, on the other hand, an iterative, and therefore a diminutive force. In *preyâla,* to judge by the common signification, *ala* is rather augmentative, and, as augmentative and comparative ideas coincide, *preyâla* is to be compared with the Dutch double comparatives *meerder, eerder;* in nature and form, though not in meaning, *preyâla* agrees with the Lat. *plusculus.* Having thus considered these particulars as briefly as it was possible, I return to the inscription. The Mag. *tadâ peyâle,* in meaning = *tadopayâ* of Girnar, Sanskrit *tadâ* (or *tato*) *bhûyaḥ,* is, therefore, "after that, since then." ' . . . .

'This short inscription,' he adds, 'is distinguished by a certain simplicity and sentiment of tone, which makes it touch a chord in the human breast. There is a tenderness in it, so vividly different from the insensibility of the later monkish literature of Buddhism, of which Th. Pavie somewhere observes with so much justice, "Tout reste donc glacé dans ce monde bouddhique!" '

'This simple tone of the passage is well calculated to awaken in us the conviction that the atrocities attributed by the later Buddhists to their benefactor, rest upon a misunderstanding. The stories of both the Northern and Southern Buddhists, to which it is usual to give the species name of traditions,‡ differ among themselves to such an extent as to be suspicious on that ground alone. The ninety-nine fold fratricide

---

* We meet with the same error in the double *y* in *moneyya,* and the absurd double *s* in *assa.* It is perfectly evident to every one who is willing to see it, that the manufacturers of the Pâli knew nothing of the pronunciation.

† This is certainly the reason why so acute a philologist as Pâṇini did not recognise the word as the comparative of *puru.* For the same reason he failed to see that *bhûyas* is a comparative of *bhûri.* Properly, *prâyas* is not irregular; it has originated from an old Indo-Germ. *pĕraias,* which must have been another form of *praias,* (compare Lat. *trans* with Sans. *tiras,* Indo-Germ. *tĕras*). The form *puru* is not identical with Gr. πολυ, and as little is *guru* identical with βαρύς, or Prâkrit *garu.* Whoever asserts that *guru* is a corrupt form from *garu* (instead of from *gĕru*) must also show that *kshipra* is a corrupt form from *kshepiyan, dûru* from *dariyan,* &c. One of the many counterfeits of *prâyas,* from *perulus,* is Lat. *gravis,* from *geravis.* It is now high time that the superficial assertion of Bopp, that *ĕ* and *r* (*rĕ, ĕr*) were not old Indo-Germ., should no longer be regarded.

‡ Tradition, in the true sense of the term, is of great value, but stories of which the time and place of origination are unknown have no title to the name of tradition. Every so-called tradition, the authenticity of which cannot be established, ceases to be a tradition, and falls under the category of rumour.

committed, as is stated, by Aśoka, is related with such circumstantiality that its untruth is palpable. The story of the Northern Buddhists is different, but, if possible, still more inept. According to them, Aśoka, at the beginning of his reign, caused a place of torture to be built in order to torment poor creatures, and so forth.* Now the king himself states, in the first tablet, that at the beginning of his reign he permitted the death of innocent creatures, that is, their slaughter for food. Is it not in the highest degree probable that the hell for the torture of poor animals is a misrepresentation, intentional or otherwise, of the slaughter-house. The contrast between the hell built by the prince before his conversion, and the monasteries built by him after that event, was too striking for so splendid an opportunity for a display of bigotry to be allowed to pass; in the midst of the conflicting variations which have sprung up under the clumsy hands of monks without humour or imagination, without feeling or love of truth, we can yet distinguish a unform theme which may thus be expressed: 'In his youth Aśoka gave himself up to depraved passions, to *vyasanâni* (to which the chase belongs): he had shown no mercy to innocent creatures (*i.e.*, deer, &c.) was cruel, a Chanda-Aśoka. But after his conversion he bade farewell to his sinful life, gave himself up exclusively to righteousness, and became a Dharma-Aśoka.' The only thing we are justified in believing after comparison of the different accounts, is the change that took place in the king's mind, in the way in which *he* has himself represented it. He acknowledges his depravities, and although we cannot from his silence regarding particular misdeeds conclude that he was wholly free from them, we are not so credulous as to believe a single one of them merely on the authority of people whose gross ignorance and tendency to distort and exaggerate shows itself in everything. Still vaguer is the information given by the non-Buddhist, the Brahman Kahlaṇa Paṇḍita. In the few lines which he devotes to Aśoka the historian tells us very little, which is exactly a proof that he says no more than he thought he was able to answer for, since the scantiness of his communications is not the result of contempt for, or a want of appreciation of, the great ruler. The *Râjatarangiṇî* I., 101 ff., we read:

Prapautraḥ Śakunes tasya bhûpateḥ prapitṛivyajaḥ |
âthâvabad Aśokâkhyaḥ satyasandho vasundharâm ||
yaḥ śântavṛijino râjâ prapanno Jinaśâsanan |
Śushkakshetraṁ Vitastâdrau tastâra stûpamaṇḍalaiḥ ||

i.e., 'The son of the great uncle of this prince (Śachînara) and great grandson of Śakuni, the upright Aśoka ruled over the land, &c.'

'With the exception of the mention of the merit which Aśoka acquired by the construction of various edifices, we find nothing further about him in the next five verses of the *Râjatarangiṇî*.†

Tablet IX.

The ninth is in nine long lines, and reads as follows:—

[1] Devânaṁpiyo Piyadasi râja eva âha asti jano uchâvachaṁ maṁgalaṁ karote âbâdhesu vâ

[2] avâhavivâhesu vâ putalâbhesu vâ pavâsaṁmhi vâ etamhicha añamhicha jano uchâvachaṁ maṁgalaṁ karote

* *Mém. de Hiouen Thsang*, I., 414 ff. Burnouf, *Introduction*, p. 358 ff.

† *See* note *, p. 119.

3 eta tu mahâḍâyo bahukaṁcha bahuvidhaṁcha chhudaṁcha nirathaṁcha maṁgalaṁ karote ta katavyameva tu maṁgalaṁ apaphalaṁ tu kho
4 etârisaṁ maṁgalaṁ ayaṁ tu mahâphale maṅgale ya dhaṁmamaṁgale tata dâsabhatakamhi samyapatipatî gurûnaṁ apachiti sâdhu
5 pânesu sayame sâdhu bamhaṇasamaṇânaṁ sâdhudânaṁ etacha añecha etârisaṁ dhaṁmamaṁgalaṁ nâma ta vatavyaṁ pitâ va
6 putena vâ bhâtâ vâ svâmikena vâ idaṁ sâdhu idaṁ katavya maṁgalaṁ âva tasa athasa nistânâya asticha pâvutaṁ
7 sâdhudânaṁ iti na tu etârisaṁ asti dânaṁ vâ anagaho vâ yârisaṁ dhaṁmadânaṁ va dhaṁmanugaho va ta tu kho mitena va suhadayena
8 ñatikena va sahâyana va ovâditavyaṁ tamhi-tamhi pakarâṇe idaṁ kachaṁ idaṁ sâdha imini saka . . .
9 svagaṁ ârâdhetu iti kâcha imini katavyatarâṁ yathâ svagârâdhî.

The new readings here are :—

Line 2	- -	*virâhesu* for *virâhesu;* and *etamhi* for *etamhi.*
Line 3	- -	*chhudaṁcha* for *chhudaṁva.*
Line 4	- -	*tata* for *tateta.* There is a trace of a  or perhaps rather 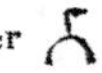; but it appears as if the sculptor had himself erased it.
Line 4	- -	*gurûnaṁ* for *gujunaṁ.*
Line 6	- -	*svâmikena* for *svamikenu.*

Professor Kern's amended text and translations are as follows :—

1 Devânaṁpiyo Piyadasi râjâ evaṁ âha : asti jano uchâvachaṁ maṁgalaṁ karote âbâdhesu vâ
2 âvâhavivâhesu vâ putalâbhesu vâ pavâsamhi vâ ; etamhicha añamhicha jano uchâvachaṁ maṁgalaṁ karote.
3 Eta tu mahâḍâyo bahukaṁcha bahuvidaṁcha chhudaṁcha nirathaṁcha maṁgalaṁ karote. Ta katavyameva tu maṁgalaṁ apaphalaṁ tu kho
4 etârisaṁ maṅgalaṁ; ayaṁ tu mahâphalaṁ ya dhaṁmamaṁgalaṁ ; tateta : dâsabhatakamhi samyapatipatî, gurûṇaṁ apachiti sâdhu,
5 paṇesu sayamo sâdhu, bamhaṇasamaṇânaṁ sâdhudânaṁ. Etacha añachadha ṁmamaṁgalaṁ nâma ; ta vatavyaṁ pitâ vâ
6 putena vâ bhâtâ vâ svâmikena vâ ; idaṁ sâdhu ; idaṁ katavyaṁ maṅgalaṁ (y)âva tasa athasa nistânâya. Asticha pâvutaṁ
7 sâdhudânaṁ iti ; na tu etârisaṁ asti dânaṁ vâ anugaho vâ yârisaṁ dhaṁmadânaṁ va dhammânugaho vâ. Ta tu kho mitena vâ suhadayena,
8 ñatikena vâ, sahâyena vâ ovaditavyaṁ tamhi-tamhi pakaraṇe : idaṁ kachaṁ, idaṁ sâdhu iti. Imâni saka-(*lâni karoṁto*)
9 svagaṁ ârâdhetu iti kachâni (?) imâni katavyatarâṁ yathâ svagârâdhî.

In Sanskrit :—

1 Devânâmpriyaḥ Priyadarśî râjaivam âha : asti jana uchchâvacham maṅgalaṁ kuruta âbâdheshu
2 vâvâhavivâheshu vâ putralâbheshu vâ pravâse vâ. Etasmiṁśchânyasmiṁścha jana uchchâvacham maṅgalaṁ kurute.
3 Etat tu mahâmûḍho bahukañcha bahuvidhañcha kshudrañcha nirarthañcha maṅgalaṁ kurute. Tat kartavyam eva tu maṅgalaṁ ; alpaphalan tu khalv
4 etâdṛiśam maṅgalaṁ, idan tu mahâphalam maṅgalaṁ yad dharmamaṅgalaṁ ; tatraitat : dâsabhṛitakeshu samyakpratipattir, gurûṇâm apachitis sâdhur,
5 jîveshu saṁyamas sâdhur, brâhmaṇaśramaṇebhyas sâdhudânam. Etachchânyachchaitâdṛiśaṁ dharmamaṅgalaṁ nâma ; tad vaktavyam pitrâ vâ
6 putreṇa vâ bhrâtrâ vâ svâminâ vâ : idaṁ sâdhu, idaṁ kartavyam maṅgalaṁ yâvat tasyârthasya nishṭhâyâḥ. Asticha prâguktaṁ
7 "sâdhudânam" iti ; na tv etâdṛiśam asti dânaṁ vânugraho vâ, yâdṛiśaṁ dharmadânaṁ vâ dharmânugraho vâ. Tat tu khalu mitreṇa vâ suhṛidayena,
8 jñâtinâ vâ, sahâyena vâvavaditavyaṁ tasmiṁstasmin prakaraṇe ; idaṁ kartavyam, idaṁ sâdhv iti. Imâni sakalâni kurvant
9 svargam ârâdhayeteti kṛityânîmâni kuryâttarâṁ yathâ svargârâdhi.

Translation.

"King Devânâmpriya Priyadarśin speaks thus: It is a fact, that men do all kinds of things which are thought to assure luck, as well in sicknesses as at betrothals and marriages, at the getting of children, or at going from home. On these and other occasions men do all kinds of things which are thought to bring prosperity. But he is a great fool who does all those manifold, multifarious, vain, and useless things. This, however, does not indeed remove the necessity of a man's doing something which will bring prosperity,* but such a kind as has been named is of little use, while of great use is true piety. To that belongs proper treatment of servants and subordinates, sincere reverence for elders and masters, sincere self-restraint towards living beings, sincere charity to brâhmans and monks. These and other such like actions,—that is called true piety. Every man must hold that forth to others, whether he is a father or a son, a brother, a lord; this is noble; this must a man do as something that assures luck, until his aim has been fully attained. Mention was made just now of "sincere charity," now there is no charity, no affection to be compared to charity or affection springing from true piety. It is just this which a well-meaning friend, relative or companion, must at every occurring opportunity impress on another, that this is duty, this is proper. By doing all this, a man can merit heaven; therefore let him who wishes to gain heaven for himself fulfil, above all things, these his duties."

Tablet X.

This is in four long lines, and is very clearly engraved (see Plate XIII.), about a fourth along the first line 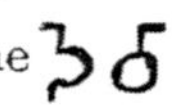 has been erased by the engraver;—these letters, however, can be distinctly traced, the first after the *si* of *Piyadasi*, and the second between the *rá* and *já* of *rájá*. It reads thus:—

[1] Devânampiyo Piyadasi râjâ yaso va kîti va na mahâthâvahâ mañate añata tadâptano dîghâyacha me jano

[2] dhaṁmasusûṁsâ susûsatâṁ dhaṁmavutaṁcha anuvidhîyatâṁ etakâya Devânaṁpiyo Piyadasi râjâ yaso va kîti va ichhati

[3] ya tu kichi parâkamate Devânaṁ Piyadasi râjâ ta savaṁ pâratikâya kiṁti sakale apaparisâve asa esa tu parisave ya apuṁñaṁ

[4] dúkaraṁ tu kho etaṁ chhudakena vâ janena usaṭena vâ añata agena parâkamena savaṁ parichajiptâ eta tu kho usaṭena dûkaraṁ.

The only new readings are—

In line 1 - - - - - - *jano* for *janâ*.
In line 4 - - - - - - *tu kho* for *ta kho*.

Prof. Kern's revised text and translations are:—

[1] Devânaṁpiyo Piyadasi râjâ yaso vâ kitiṁ vâ na mahâthâvahâ mañata añata tadâptane dighâyacha me jano

[2] dhaṁmasusûsâṁ susûsatâṁ dhaṁmavutaṁcha anuvidhîyatâṁ. Etakâya Devânaṁpiyo Piyadasi râjâ yaso vâ kitiṁ vâ ichhati.

[3] Ya tu kichi parâkamate Devânaṁpiyo Piyadasi râjâ ta savaṁ pâratikâya; kiṁti? sakalo apaparisavo asa; esa tu parisavo ya apuṁñaṁ.

[4] Dûkaraṁ tu kho etaṁ chhudakena vâ janena, usaṭena vâ, añata agena parâkamena savaṁ parichajiptâ. Eta tu kho usaṭena dûkaraṁ.

---

* If the reading of Kapur-di-Giri—*kataro amaṁgala* is not a mistake, caused by carelessness, for *añamaṁgalo*, the writer of Kapur-di-Giri has not understood the meaning. Dhauli is unintelligible.

In Sanskrit :—

1 Devânâmpriyaḥ Priyadarśî râjâ yaśo vâ kîrtiṁ vâ na mahârthâvaham, amaṁsyata, yadi na tadâtve dîrghâyacha tajjano dharmaśuśrûshâṁ śuśrûsheta

2 dharmoktañchânuvidhiyeta. Etâvata eva Devânâmpriyaḥ Priyadarśî râjâ yaśo vâ kîrtiṁ vechchhati.

3 Yat tu kiñchit parâkramate Devânâmpriyaḥ Priyadarśî râjâ, tat sarvam pâratrikâya ; kimiti ? sakalo 'pâsravas syât. Esha tv âsravo yad apuṇyam.

4 Dushkaran tu khalv etat kshudrakeṇa vâ janenonnatena vânyatrâgryeṇa parâkrameṇa sarvam parityajya. Etat tu khalûnnatena dushkaram.

Translation.

" King Devânâmpriya Priyadarśin does not deem that renown and great name bring advantage greatly, if, at the same time, his people, for the present and afterwards, were not practising right obedience, and following exhortation to virtue. In so far only King Devânâmpriya Priyadarśin desires renown and great name. All therefore that King Devânâmpriya Priyadarśin strenuously strives after, is for the life hereafter, so that he may be wholly and altogether free * from blemish. Now blemish is the same as sinfulness. But such a thing is, indeed, difficult for anyone whatever, be he a person of low degree or of high station, unless with the utmost exertion of power, by sacrificing everything.† But this is, indeed, most difficult for a person of high station."

TABLET XI.

The eleventh edict is also in four long lines, and reads thus :—

1 Devânampiyo Piyadasî râjâ evaṁ âha nâsti etârisaṁ dânaṁ yârisaṁ dhaṁmadânaṁ dhaṁmasaṁstavo vâ dhaṁmasaṁvibhâgo vâ dhaṁmasambadho va

2 tata idaṁ bhavati dâsabhatakamhi samyapatipatî mâtari pitari sâdhusususâ mitasaṁstutañâtikânaṁ bâmhaṇasamaṇânaṁ sâdhudânaṁ

3 pâṇânaṁ anâraṁbho sâdhu eta vatavyaṁ pitâ va putena va bhâtâ va mitasaṁstutañâtikena va âvapaṭivesiyehi ida sâdhu ida katavya

4 so tâthâ karu ilokachasa ârâdho hoti paratacha aṁnaṁtaṁ puṁñaṁ bhavati tena dhaṁmadânenaṁ.

Here the new readings are—

In line 2 - - *bhatakamhi* for *bhatakami* ; *saṁstuta* for *sastuta* ; and *samaṇânaṁ* for *samaṇâna*.
In line 3 - - *anâraṁbho* for *anârabho* ; and *saṁstuta* for *sastuta*.
In line 4 - - *so tâthâ karu* (or *karû*) for *so tâthâ kata*.

As revised by Dr. Kern, this reads :—

1 Devânaṁpiyo Piyadasi râjâ evâṁ âha : nâsti etârisaṁ dânaṁ yârisaṁ dhaṁmadânaṁ, dhaṁmasaṁstavo vâ dhaṁmasaṁvibhâgo vâ dhaṁmasambaṁdho vâ ;

2 tata idaṁ bhavati : dâsabhatakamhi samyapatipatî, mâtari pitari sâdhusususâ, mitasaṁstutañâtikânaṁ bâmhaṇasamaṇânaṁ sâdhudânaṁ,

3 pâṇânaṁ anâraṁbho. Sâdhu eta vatavyaṁ pitâ vâ putena vâ bhâtâ vâ mitasaṁstutañâtikena vâ, (y)âvapaṭîvesiyehi ; idaṁ sâdhu idaṁ katavyaṁ.

4 So tâthâ katâ ilokasa-cha ârâdho hoti, paratacha anaṁtaṁ puṁñaṁ bhavati tena dhaṁmadânena.

In Sanskrit :—

1 Devânâmpriyaḥ Priyadarśi râjaivam âha : nâsty etâdṛiśaṁ dânaṁ yâdṛiśaṁ dharmadânaṁ, dharmasaṁstavo vâ dharmasaṁvibhâgo vâ dharmasambandho vâ ;

2 tatredam bhavati : dâsabhṛitakeshu samyakpratipattir, mâtâpitros sâdhuśuśrûshâ mitrasaṁstutânâm brâhmaṇaśramaṇânâṁ sâdhudânaṁ,

3 jîvânâm anârambhaḥ. Sâdhu etad vaktavyam pitrâ vâ putreṇa vâ bhrâtrâ vâ mitrasaṁstutajñâtibhir vâ, yâvatprativeśyaiḥ ; idaṁ sâdhu ; idaṁ kartavyaṁ.

4 Sa tathâkartehalokasyachârâdhi bhavati, paratrachânantam puṇyam bhavati tena dharmadânena.

---

* Kapur-di-Giri has " without blemish."

† That is, by self-sacrifice and self-denial in all respects.

ASOKA INSCRIPTION,-EDICTS X-XIV.

PLATE XIII.

Translation.

"King Devânâmpriya Priyadarśin speaks thus:—There is no charity which equals right charity, or right conversation, or right liberality, or right relation. Under that is comprehended proper treatment of servants and subordinates, sincere obedience to father and mother, sincere charity towards friends and acquaintances, Brahmaṇs and monks, the sparing of animal life. This is to be commended as good, whether by father or by sons, by brothers, by friends, acquaintances and relatives, nay even by neighbours; thus it is *good;* thus must men act. He who acts thus makes this world a friend to him, and hereafter a man obtains for himself an imperishable reward through all that true charity."

Tablet XII.

The twelfth edict* is in nine long lines, and reads thus:—

1 Devṁânapiyo Piyadasi râjâ savapâsaṁḍânicha pavajitânicha ghârastânicha pûjayati, dânenacha vividhâyacha pûjâya pûjayati ne

2 na tu tathâ dânaṁ vâ pûje va Devânaṁpiyo maṁñate yathâ kitisâravadhî asa savapâsaṁḍânaṁ sâravaḍhî tu bahuvidhâ;

3 tasa-tasa tu idaṁ mûlaṁ ya vachigutî kiṁti âptapâsaṁḍapûjâ va parâpâsaṁḍagarahâ va no bhave, apakaraṇamhi lahukâ va asa

4 tamhi-tamhi pakaraṇe pûjeta yâ tu eva parapâsaṁḍâ tena-tena pakaraṇena evaṁkataṁ, âptapâsaṁdacha vaḍhayati parapâsaṁḍasacha upakaroti

5 tadaṁñathâ karoto âptapâsaḍaṁcha chhaṇati parapâsaṁḍasachapi apakaroti yohi kâchi âptapâsaṁḍaṁ pûjayati parapâsaṁdaṁ va garahati,

6 savaṁ âptapâsaṁḍabhatiyâ kimti âptapâsaṁḍaṁ dîpayema iti socha puna tatha karoto âptapasaṁḍaṁ bâḍhataraṁ upahanâti ta samavâyo eva sâdhâ

7 kiṁti mañamaṁñasa dhaṁmaṁ sunâjucha susaṁserâcha evaṁhi Devânaṁpiyasa ichhâ kiṁti savapâsaṁḍâcha bahusutâcha asu kalâṇâgamâcha asu;

8 yecha tatâ-tata pasaṁam tehi vatavyâ: Devânaṁpiyo no tathâ dânaṁ va pûjâ vâ maṁñate yathâ kiṁtisâravadhi asa savapâsaṁḍânaṁ bahakâ va etâya

9 athâ vyâpatâ dhaṁmamahâmâtâcha ithâjhakhamahâmâtâcha vachabhûmikâcha añecha nikâyâ ayaṁcha etasa phala ya âptapâsaṁḍavaḍhîcha hoti, dhaṁmasacha dîpanâ.

The new readings in the estampage are:—

In line 3 - - - - -	*lahukâ* for *lahakâ.*
In line 6 - - - - -	*savaṁ* for *sava.*
In line 7 - - - - -	*kalâṇâgamâ* for *kalâṇâgama.*
In line 8 - - - - -	*vatavyaṁ* for *vatavya.*

Professor Kern revises this as follows:—

1 Devṁânapiyo Piyadasi raja savapâsaṁḍânicha pavajitânicha ghârastânicha pûjayati, dânenacha vividhâyacha pûjâya pûjayati ne.

2 Na tu tathâ dânaṁ vâ pûjaṁ vâ Devânaṁpiyo maṁñate, yathâ kitisâravadhì asa savapâsaṁḍânaṁ. Sâravaḍhî tu bahuvidhâ:

3 tasa-tasa tu idaṁ mûlaṁ ya vachiguti; kiṁti? âptapâsaṁdapûjâ và parapâsaṁḍagarhâ và no bhave, apakaraṇamhi lahakâ vâ asa:

4 tamhi-tamhi pakaraṇe pûjeta. Ya tu eva parapâsaṁda(sa) tena-tena pakaraṇena evaṁkataṁ, âptapâsaṁdaṁcha vaḍhayati parapâsaṁḍasacha upakaroti;

5 tadaṁñathâ karoṁto âptapâsaṁḍaṁcha chhaṇati parapâsaṁḍasachapi apakaroti. Yopi kachi âptapâsaṁḍaṁ pûjayati parapâsaṁdaṁ vâ garahati

* 'The tolerant spirit of Aśoka, which the narrow intellect of Mahânâma was incapable of comprehending, manifests itself conspicuously in No. XII. of Girnar, which has no parallel either in the Dhauli or Kapurdigiri series.'—Kern, *u. s.* p. 65.

6 savaṁ âptapâsaṁḍabhatiyâ ; kimti ? âptapâsaṁḍaṁ dîpayema iti. Socha puna tathâ karoṁto âptapâsaṁḍaṁ bâḍhataraṁ upahanati. Ta samavâyo eva sâdhu ;
7 kiṁti ? maṁñamaṁñasa dhaṁmaṁ sunejucha pasamseramcha ; evaṁ hi Devânaṁpiyasa ichhâ ; kiṁti ? savapâsaṁḍâcha bahusutâcha asu, kalâṇâgamâcha asu ;
8 yecha tata-tata pasaṁñâ tehi vatavyâ ; Devânaṁpiyo no tathâ dânaṁ vâ pûjam vâ maṁñate, yathâ kîtisâravadhi asa savapâsaṁḍânaṁ bahakâ vâ. Etâya
9 athâya vyâpatâ dhaṁmamahâmâtâcha ithâjhakhamahâmâtâcha vachabhûmikâcha aṁñecha nikâyâ. Ayaṁcha etasa phalaṁ, ya âptapâsaṁḍavaḍhîcha hoti, dhaṁmasacha dipanâ.

'Before giving the translation of this we will consider some expressions in it: The meaning of the neuter *pâsaṁdaṁ*, and of the masc. *pâsaṁḍo*, comes out more clearly in this document. The first is "sect," the second "member of a sect." They are both introduced into the Sanskrit, but in the modified signification of "heretical sect" and "heretic." The word "sect" shows the same change of meaning also in English, where it is used to signify "another sect than the dominant one," and "sectarian," "any one of another sect than the recognised and common one." The Greek *haeresis* and *haereticus* have had the same history. When we have now found from the Girnar document what the older meaning of *pâshaṇḍa* is, the origin of the word becomes at the same time clear. It has arisen from a Sans. *pârshadya*, *pârshada*, with the understanding that there must have been a western form, viz., *pârshanda*, *pârshandya*. The root *sad* has no longer a nasal sound in the Sanskrit, but in kindred languages, the Sclavic among others, the form *sand* is very common; and in the Sanskrit itself there is at least one word in which the nasal sound has been preserved, viz., *âsandî*, "arm-chair, throne."* *Asa* is the Vedic *asat; asu* corrupted from *asan* by a false analogy. This conjunctive has also been adopted into the Pâli; but, as has been already observed, those who made the Pâli books no longer understood the form, and made of it *assa*, *assu*, as if *assa* were formally = *siyâ*, — a proof that they no longer knew anything of the pronunciation of the old Prâkrit. *Kiṁti*, Sansk. *kimiti*, "with what intention a thing is thought, or spoken, or done," refers to the intention or aim of what goes before. Instead of the *oratio directa*, which is such a favourite in all the older and more modern Indian languages, our idiom requires a dependent sentence. *Kiṁti* with the subsequent independent sentence becomes "in order that," and sometimes "so that," followed by a dependent clause. This syntactic peculiarity of the Indian languages is sufficiently well known, and would not have been noticed here if previous expositors had not altogether misunderstood the little word. The spelling *âpta* is incorrect, just as is that of *bâmhaṇa ;* the word ought to have been spelled *apta* (*i.e.*, *atta*) according to the vocal laws of the Prâkrit; on the other hand, *âta* (= *atta*) is permissible; and it is by no means improbable that *âpta* used to be pronounced as *âta*, and therefore no inconvenience was found in the long *â*. *Pûjita* is 3rd sing. opt. middle. The middle is here employed, probably, because the word is intransitive; *pûjayati aṁnaṁ* is "he honours another;" *pûjayrte*, "he shows his reverence, his esteem." The word *bahukâ*, "mean estimation," is not known beyond Sanskrit literature; which, how-

* The spelling *pâkhaṇḍa*, which occurs in Sans. along with the spelling with *sh*, represents a western pronunciation, which is now widely spread in all Northern India, and was also prevalent, though in a less degree, in very ancient times. *Kh* for *sh* has frequently crept into the prevailing dialect—the classical Sanskrit ; *e.g.* such a form as *drekshi*, from *drish*, could not have originated unless *sh* had been pronounced as *ch*. So also *rikh*, *likh*, with their derivatives, are only a western pronunciation of *rish*, *lish*, "to tear, to scratch ;" so also *ukhâ mayûkha*.

ever, is not saying much. A scholiast on Pâṇini 7. 3. 44, does indeed mention *bahukâ* without saying whether he regards it as a substantive or an adjective. If the former it can mean nothing else than *bahukâ* of Girnar, for the adjective *bahukâ* is "placed at a high price, dear." *Alaghukâ* has not come down to us, but must have been in use as much as *bahukâ*. In order to proceed with certainty, I shall, in the Sanskrit paraphrase, use *lâghavam* (taking therefore *laghutâ, laghutvam*) and *bahumânam*. Our resources do not enable us to decide whether the reading should not be *bahukâ* and *lahukâ*. None of the terms discussed presents the slightest difficulty, so far as the sense is concerned. It is somewhat more troublesome to determine the sense of *vachabhûmika*. The only attempt at explanation which deserves the name is that of Burnouf.* He resolves the combination into *vacha* (Sansk. *varchas*, "ordure") and *bhûmika*, derived from *bhûmi*, "ground," from which it would follow that the word means "inspectors of the privies." He had neglected to say that the Sansk. form would then, with Vṛiddhi, have been *vârchobhûmika*, but since the Sans. *vârch* would give in the Prâkrit *vachch* (spelled *vach*) as well as *vâch*, there is no other remark to be made so far as the doctrine of sounds is concerned than that *vachcha* can scarcely come from *vârcho*. The same scholar does not fail to refer to No. VI. of Girnar, where *vacha* also occurs, and certainly in the same meaning as here, though it does not appear more clearly what that meaning is. But No. VI. has been subjected to such treatment that we could not be satisfied with quoting a couple of terms from it, and a proper discussion of the part where mention is made of the appointment of overseers of *vacha*, &c., would occupy more space than we can afford. We shall, therefore, merely assume here, provisionally, without proof, that *vachabhûmika* answers to a Sans. *vrâtyabhûmika*, derived with Vṛiddhi, from *vrâtyabhûmi*, "a place for wandering comrades," *i.e.* a hospice. The usual name of the royal magistrates or overseers is *mahâmâta*, Sansk. *mahâmâtra*.† . . . .'

In Sanskrit :—

1 Devânâmpriyaḥ Priyadarśî râjâ sarvapârishadânicha pravrajitânicha gârhasthyânicha pûjayati, dânenacha vividhayâcha pûjayâ pûjayaty enâni.

2 Na tu tathâ dânaṁ vâ pûjâṁ vâ Devânâmpriyo manyate, yathâ yena kîrtisâravṛiddhis syât sarvapârishadânâm. Sâravṛiddhis tu bahuvidhâ ;

3 tasya-tasya tv idam mûlaṁ yad vâgguptiḥ ; kimiti ? âtmîyapârishadapûjâ vâ parapârishadagarhâ vâ no bhaved aprakaraṇe laghutâ vâ syât ;

4 tasmiṁstasmin prakaraṇe pûjeta. Yat tveva parapârishade tena-tena prakaraṇenaivaṁ kṛitam, âtmîyapârishadañcha vardhayati parapârishadasyachopakaroti ;

5 tadanyathâ kurvann âtmîyapârishadañcha kshaṇoti parapârishadasyachâpy apakaroti. Yo' pi kaśchid âtmîyapârishadam pûjayati,

6 sarvaṁ svapârishadabhakteḥ (kuryât) ; kimiti ? svapârishadaṁ dîpayemeti. Sa punas tathâ kurvant svapârishadam bâḍhataram upahanti. Tat samavâya eva sâdhuḥ (= śreshṭham) ;

7 kimiti ? anonyasya dharmaṁ śṛiṇuyuścha śuśrûsheraṁścha. Evaṁhi Devânâmpriyasyechchhâ ; kimiti ? sarvapârishadâ bahuśrutâścha syuḥ kalyâṇâgamâścha syuḥ ;

8 yecha tatra tatra prasannâs te hi vaktavyâḥ । Devânâmpriyo na tathâ dânaṁ vâ pûjâṁ vâ manyate, yathâ yena kîrtisâravṛiddhis syât sarvapârishadânâm bahumânaṁ vâ. Etasmây

9 arthâya vyâpṛitâ dharmamahâmâtrâścha stryâdhyakshyamahâmâtrâścha vrâtyabhûmikâśchânyecha nikâyâḥ. Idañchaitasya phalaṁ yad âtmîyapârishadavṛiddhiścha bhavati, dharmasyacha dîpanâ.

Translation.

"King Devânâmpriya Priyadarśin honours all sects, and orders of monks, and conditions of heads of families,‡ and honours them with love-gifts and with marks of

* *Lotus de la Bonne Loi*, p. 773.

† In Anglo-Saxon the steward or overseer of an estate is called *gerêfa* ; the *dhamamahâmâtra* is, therefore, the *sciregerêfa*, the English *sheriff*. "Sheriff," therefore, would be the best English translation.

‡ That is, "kinds of laics."

honour of all kinds. To be sure Devânâmpriya does not attribute so much value to love-gifts or marks of honour, as to this, that the good name and intrinsic worth of all sects may increase. Now intrinsic worth can grow greater in many ways, but the foundation thereof, in all its compass, is discretion in* speaking, so that no man may praise his own sect, or contemn another sect, or despise it on unsuitable occasions; on all manner of occasions let respect be shown. Whatever of good, indeed, a man, from any motive, confers on any one of a different persuasion, tends to the advantage of his own sect and to the benefit of a different persuasion; by acting in an opposite manner, a man injures his own sect and offends a different sect. Though everyone who praises his own persuasion may, perhaps, do all that from attachment to his own sect, for the purpose of glorifying it; nevertheless he shall, by so doing, greatly injure his own persuasion. Therefore concord is best, so that all may know and willingly listen to each other's religion. Because it is the wish of Devânâmpriya that the members of all persuasions may be well instructed, and shall adhere to a doctrine of benevolence. And to them who are inclined to all that let the assurance be given that Devânâmpriya does not attach so much value to love-gifts or show of reverence as to this, that all sects may increase in good name and intrinsic worth, and be reverenced. For this end sheriffs over legal proceedings, magistrates entrusted with the superintendence of the women, hospice masters (?), and other bodies have been appointed. And the result of this is, that Devânâmpriya's persuasion has increased in prosperity, and that he causes the Righteousness to come forth in full splendour."†

"The mention in this place of the sheriffs," adds Dr. Kern, "is certainly intended to remind the people that it has always been the earnest desire of the king to insure the impartial administration of justice, without respect to religious belief. He refers to his official acts in order to show that, though he is himself now a sincere Buddhist, yet in nothing does he favour his co-religionists above others. The jurisdiction of the magistrates charged with the superintendence of the women was certainly not limited merely to the public women. For though the hetairai played as great a part in Indian society, as their sisters in ancient Greece, and though it was necessary that such an element of society should be under state control, yet in this place something else must be meant. The mention here of certain magistrates has a specific reason; what that reason is cannot be a matter of doubt, if the beginning of the inscription be compared with the conclusion. As the appointment of high officials is a guarantee for *savvapâsaṁḍâni*, and that of *itthâjhakkha-mahâmâtâ* has been made in the interest of all *ghârastâni*, they serve to watch over the purity of morals and of domestic life. The magistrates referred to must therefore have been a kind of *censores morum*, whose duty was to restrain the luxury and other excesses of the matrons.

Tablet XIII.

We come now to the thirteenth edict, awanting in the Dhaulî redaction, and so unfortunately damaged here by the breaking of the stone. It stands below the fifth and twelfth on the stone, and reads thus:—

1 . . de patasa pasamâtaṁ etâhataṁ baha tâvata kaṁmata tatâ pachhâ adhunâ ladhesu kaliṅgesu tivo dhaṁmavâyo

2 . . . . vadho va maraṇaṁ va apavâho va janasata bâḍhaṁ vedana matacha ganamatacha Devâ

* That is, "to curb the tongue."

† *Dharmasya dipanâ* is an ambiguous expression; perhaps selected purposely, as it also signifies "to glorify, to adorn the Faith (*i.e.* religion)."

3 . . . . sâ mâtâ pitari susumsâ guru sumsumsâ mitasamstata sahâya sa dâsa

4 . . . . ya ñâtika vyasanam pâpuṇoti vata sopi tesam upaghâto patipaṭi bhago vâsâ sava . . .

5 . . . . mi(?) yato nâsti manusânam ekataramhi pâsamḍamhi na nâma pâsâde yâvakâto jana tada

6 . . . . na yasaka va mitaveyâ vapi aṭaviyo Devânampiyasa pijite pâti

7 . . . . sava bhûtânam achhatim cha sayamamcha samam(?) . . . . cheram cha mâdava cha

8 . . . . . . Yona râjâ paramcha tena chattâro râjâno Turamâyo cha Aṁtakâna cha Magâ cha

9 . . . . . . idhe pârimde savata Devânampiyasa dhammânusasṭim anuvatareyata piduti

10 . . . . . . vâjayo savathâ puna vijayo pîti raso sâ ladhâ sâ pîtî hoti dhamma vîjayammhi

11 . . . . . . yam vijayammâ vijatavyam mam ñâsarasake eva vijayechhâti cha

12 . . . . . . ilokika cha pâralokikâ cha

New readings:—

In line 4 - - - - - *tesam* (?) for *tesa*.
In line 6 - - - - - *pâti* for *sâti*.
In line 7 - - - - - *achhatim* for *achhâtim*.
In line 8 - - - - - *Aṁtakâna* for *Aṅgakana*.
In line 9 - - - - - *pârimde savata* for *vârimdesu savata*.
In line 10 - - - - - *vijayammhi* for *vijajami*.

This has not been discussed by either Burnouf or Kern, so we fall back on Professor Wilson's discussion of it, from which we extract the following remarks:—

"The division of the Girnar inscriptions numbered by Mr. Prinsep as XIII., finds a counterpart at Kapur-di-Giri; but unfortunately it is not of a nature to supply the defects and imperfections of the Girnar tablet. The rock at Girnar is, at this part, so much mutilated, that it is difficult to put together the context of the entire tablet. The rock at Kapur-di-Giri has not apparently suffered much mutilation, and the inscription is consequently more complete, supplying the words effaced from that at Girnar; but it is not only in this respect that it exceeds in length the Girnar inscription. There are evidently additional passages which the latter does not contain, and which intervene between what are apparently intended for the same passages in both places; on the other hand there are several obliterations or deficiencies in the Kapur-di-Giri inscription where that at Girnar is entire. In collating the two, therefore, wide gaps occur without a parallel, owing partly to these respective mutilations, partly to the additional matter at Kapur-di-Giri. From place to place, however, concurrent passages do occur, which leave no doubt of the general identity of the inscriptions.

"It happens, however, still unfortunately, that neither the additional nor those which are evidently identical passages in the Kapur-di-Giri inscription are, for the major part, to be satisfactorily deciphered. The circumstances under which the characters were transcribed sufficiently account for the disappointment.

"Mr. Prinsep has ventured to propose a continuous translation of the thirteenth tablet, although he admits that insulated phrases alone are intelligible. Such is the case in the Kapur-di-Giri inscription; and it were very unsafe to propose anything like a connected rendering even of what is perfect, although a few words and phrases are decipherable, and may be compared with similar words and phrases in the Girnar tablet. In most of these passages, however, the reading of the original itself is conjectural only.

"Deficiencies at the end of the seventh and beginning of line eight, at Girnar, are rather more than adequately filled up at Kapur-di-Giri, and some of the additional matter is important. The name and designation *Añtiyoka nama Yona Râja* are given distinctly; why he is introduced does not very well appear, but we might venture to connect it with what precedes, and to interpret and fill up the passages thus: 'He who had obtained the alliance of men—he has been received as the friend of (me) Devânâmpriya. We have for this conjectural rendering, *Devanam priyasa*, then some unreadable letters, *sampapi* (for *samaprâpi*) *yo janasa* (*su*) *sanyatam*. At Girnar we have only *Yona Raja*, but no name, no Antiochus, nor any circumstance relating to him. Both inscriptions next read *parancha*, 'and afterwards'; the Girnar has then *tena*, 'by him,' which, as no name was specified, Mr. Prinsep necessarily interpreted 'by whom,' (rather, 'by him'), the Greek king, in the Kapur-di-Giri tablet, *tena* refers of course to Antiochus, but not to leave any doubt on this score, the inscription repeats the name, and gives us *tena Antiyokena*, 'by that Antiochus;' thus furnishing a very important illustration of the Girnar tablet. What then was done by him? by that Antiochus? This is not to be made out very distinctly, but connected with what follows, it may be conjectured to imply that four other Greek princes were brought under subjection by him. There can be no doubt that the numeral which Mr. Prinsep read, *chaptaro*, is properly, *chattâro*. There is no *p* in the Kapur-di-Giri inscription, it is clearly *chataro*, with the usual disregard of correct orthography and identification of long and short vowels. In the Girnar inscription the form is like *pt*, no doubt, but this combination is so utterly repugnant to the most characteristic feature of Pali that it cannot be allowed; and, in this case, if the original word intended be the Sanskrit numeral *chatwâra*, the *p* would be gratuitously inserted. The only admissible reading is *chattâro*, the regular Pali form of the Sanskrit *chatwâra*. We then have the several names of the four princes remarkably distinct, and it luckily happens that M. Court's copy is also very legible in this passage, and entirely confirms Mr. Masson's readings. The passage runs thus: *Turamara nama, Antikona nama, Mako nama, Alikasunari nama*. At Girnar the last name is wanting, there being some letters obliterated. We have also some variation in the reading, but not material, the names being there, *Turamâyocha, Antakonacha, Magâcha*. The two inscriptions give us, no doubt, the names of four Greek princes.

"We have the order, 'by that Antiochus four Yavana kings were'; what? neither inscription enables us to answer, the Girnar inscription being in fact here mutilated. Mr. Prinsep in his introductory remarks, supplying the connexion conjecturally, fills up the blank by reading, "And the Greek king besides, by whom the four kings have been induced to permit," but there is nothing to warrant such a translation; and in the actual rendering of the passage the latter clause is omitted; we have there, "and the Greek king, besides, by whom the kings of Egypt, Ptolemaios, Antigonos (?), and Magas," &c. and then follows a blank.

"The translation of Mr. Prinsep is subjoined for the sake of reference, but I cannot venture to propose any connected version.

Mr. Prinsep's Translation.

" . . . . . Whose equality and exertion towards that object, exceeding activity, judicious conduct . . . afterwards in the Kalinga provinces not to be obtained by wealth . . . the decline of religion, murder, and death, and unrestrained license of mankind; when flourished the (precious maxims) of Devânampiyo comprising the essence of learning and of science: dutiful service to mother and father; dutiful service to spiritual teachers; the love of friend and child (charity) to kinsfolk, to servants, (to Brâhmaṇs and Śramaṇas, &c., which) cleanse away the calamities of generation; further also in these things unceasing perseverance is fame. There is not in either class of the heretics of men, not, so to say, a procedure marked by such grace, ... nor so glorious nor friendly, nor even so extremely liberal as Devânampiyo's injunction for the non-injury, and content of living creatures . . . . . and the Greek king besides, by whom the kings of Egypt, Ptolemaios and Antigonos, and Magas, ... both here and in foreign (countries), everywhere the religious ordinances of Devânampiyo effect conversion wherever they go; . . . . . conquest is of every description: but further the conquest which bringeth joy springing from pleasant emotions, becometh joy itself; the victory of virtue is happiness; the victory of happiness is not to be overcome, that which essentially possesses a pledge of happiness, such victory is desired in things of this world and things of the next world!" *

TABLET XIV.

The last of the edicts is engraved to the right of the thirteenth, and is in five and a half lines. It reads thus:—

[1] Ayaṁ dhaṁmalipî Devânaṁpiyena Piyadasinâ râñâ lekhâpitâ asti eva
[2] saṁkhitena asti majhamena asti vistatana nâcha savaṁ savata ghaṭitaṁ
[3] mahâlakepi vijitaṁ bahucha likhitaṁ likhâpayisaṁchema astica etakaṁ
[4] punapunavutaṁ tasa-tasa athasa mâdhûritâya kiṁti jano tatha paṭîpajetha
[5] tata ekadâ asamâtaṁ likhitaṁ asaṁdesaṁ va sachhâyakâraṇaṁ va
[6] alocheptâ lipikarâparâdhena va.

The new readings here are—

In line 2	- - - - -	*savata* for *pavta.*
In line 4	- - - - -	*kiṁti* for *kiti.*
In line 5	- - - - -	*asaṁdesaṁ* for *asadesam.*

Professor Kern's revised reading of the text is as follows:—†

[1] Ayṁ dhaṁmalipî Devânaṁpiyena Piyadasinâ râñâ lekhâpitâ; asti eva
[2] saṁkhitena, asti majhamena, asti vistatena, nocha savaṁ savata ghaṭitaṁ;
[3] mahâlakaṁhi vijitaṁ, bahucha likhitaṁ likhâpayisaṁ. Asticha etakaṁ
[4] punapunavutaṁ, tasa-tasa athasa mâdhûriyâ (*or* madhûratâya); kiṁti? jano tathâ paṭipajetha.
[5] Tata ekadâ asamâtaṁ likhitaṁ asadisaṁ vâ, sachhâyakâraṇaṁ vâ
[6] alocheptâ lipikarâparâdhena vâ.

In Sanskrit:

[1] Iyaṁ dharmalipir Devânâmpriyeṇa Priyadarśinâ râjnâ lekhitâ; asty eva
[2] saṅkshepato 'sti madhyamam asti vistâreṇa, nacha sarvaṁ sarvatra ghaṭitam;
[3] mahad dhi râshṭram bahucha likhitam alilikham. Asticha, tâvat,
[4] punaḥpunaruktaṁ, tasya-tasyârthasya mâdhuryât; kimiti? janas tathâ pratipadyeteti
[5] Tattad ekadâsamâptaṁ likhitam asadṛiśaṁ vâ,
[6] sachchhâyopekshayâ vâ lipikarâparâdhena vâ.

Translation.

"King Devânâmpriya Priyadarśin has caused this righteousness-edict to be written, here, concisely, there in moderate compass, in a third place again at full length, so that it is not found altogether everywhere worked out; for the kingdom is great,

* *Journ. R. A. Soc.* vol. XII. pp. 227–233.

† *Ut sup.* p. 106.

and what I have caused to be written, much. Repetitions occur also, in a certain measure on account of the agreeableness of various points, in order that the people should in that way (the more willingly) receive it. If sometimes the one or other is written incompletely or not in order, it is because care has not been taken to make a good transcript,* or by the fault of the copyist (*i.e.*, the stone engraver)."

The Signature.

"The reason why the name of Buddha does not occur in these inscriptions," says Professor Kern,† "is easily seen: they were intended for the whole empire, for all without distinction of creed, and it would have been unbecoming of the prince, in his admonitions, had he appealed to a Master who was not known as such to the majority of his subjects. Besides which Aśoka speaks as the administrator of the realm, and not as a religious preacher. In one place only, namely, the signature of the Girnar ‡ inscription, is Buddha referred to. Of this signature there remains—

. . . va sveto hasti savaloka sukhâharo nâmaṁ.

What has to be supplied at the beginning I leave to the ingenuity of others to determine, but what is left means—

"The white elephant whose name is the bringer of happiness to the whole world."

"That by this term Śâkya is implied there can be no doubt, since the legend says that the Bodhisattva, the future Buddha, left heaven to bring happiness to men, and entered his mother's womb as a white elephant. Thus we read in the *Lalitavistâra*, chap. 63 :—

"*Pushyanakshatrayoge Bodhisattvas Tushitavarabhavanâch chyutvâ smṛitaḥ samprajânan* pâṇḍuragajarûpo *bhûtvâ, jananyâ dakshiṇâyâṁ kukshâv avâkrâmata.*"

"With regard to *sarvalokasukhâhara*, we may compare the *gâthâ* in *Lalitavistâra*, 111, in which allusion is made to the happiness which the birth of Buddha was to bring into the world :—

apâyâścha yathâ śântâḥ sukhi sarvaṁ yathâ jagat |
dhruvaṁ Sukhâvaho jâtaḥ sukhe sthâpayitâ jagat ||

"Even if the signature is not to be attributed to the scribe, the custom evidently even then prevalent, and still in use at the present day, of naming at the end of the inscription the divinity worshipped by the writer or scribe can offer no serious difficulty. In the short inscription, No. XIV., which is neither more nor less than a postscript addressed to the reader, we find apologies which occur word for word in the postscript of modern manuscripts and even printed books. When we read at the end of the Bombay edition of the *Mahâbhârata*,—*asmin parvaṇi ślokavaishamyaṁ* lipikarapramâdâdinâ *bodyam*, we can almost fancy we have before us Aśoka's warning against the negligence of his scribes,—against *lipikaropamâdo*,—as his own words express it. So tenacious is Indian

* Skr. *châyâ*, "transcript, copy," is wanting in the dictionaries, the word is well known to the Pandits, and occurs also in the Bombay editions of Sanskrit dramas.

† *Ut sup.* p. 43. Translated by the late R. C. Childers, Esq.

‡ *Journ. As. Soc. Beng.* vol. VII. p. 241. Compare facsimile. Prinsep has wrongly assigned the signature to No. XIII. of the Girnar inscription. It is true that it stands directly under it, but this is because No. XIII. is in the middle column. One has but to look at the facsimile to see how the matter stands. Wilson's transcript is inaccurate.

tradition! The ascription to the white elephant—that is, to Buddha—corresponds to the *Śrî-Râmârpaṇam astu*, and similar expressions of Indian MSS. of the present day.

"Though the king's edicts, or rather written addresses to his subjects, contain nothing which could give offence to the adherents of other forms of belief, they are nevertheless more or less Buddhistic in their style. They are composed in a preaching tone, full of repetitions. Just as Buddhaghosha commends the sacred writings for their prolixity, so Aśoka informs us that he has intentionally repeated some things on account of their sweetness, and in order to cause them to find all the more favour with the people."

These edicts, as Professor Kern remarks,* "give an idea of what the king did for his subjects in his wide empire, which extended from Behâr to Gândhâra, from the Himâlaya to the coast of Coromandel and Pâṇḍya.† They are not unimportant for the criticism of the Buddhistic traditions, though they give us exceedingly little concerning the condition of the doctrine and its adherents. The prince went over to Buddhism in the eleventh year of his reign. He was a zealous Buddhist who concerned himself with the spiritual interest, and even with the catechism, of his co-religionists. At fitting time and place he makes mention, in a modest and becoming manner, of the doctrine which he had embraced; but nothing of a Buddhist spirit can be discovered in his state policy. From the very beginning of his reign he was a good prince. His ordinances concerning the sparing of animal life agree much more closely with the ideas of the heretical Jainas than with those of the Buddhists.

"Although, then, the inscriptions of Aśoka the Humane may be only in part of direct interest for the history of Buddhism, yet the trouble bestowed upon the reading has not been lost. The Aśoka with whom we become acquainted from his own words forms a striking contrast to the caricature which is exhibited to us in the works of Buddhists and others as the image of the noble king."

---

* *Ut. sup.* p. 107,—translated by the Rev. A. Milroy.

† *See* No. V., p. 107, and conf. Lassen, *Ind. Alt.* (2nd ed.) I. 137 ff., II. 251.

VII. THE SÂH OR RUDRA DÂMÂ INSCRIPTION.

We come next to the inscription on the top of the rock (Plate XIV.), and which is read from the south side.* Like the Aśoka inscription, it was first deciphered and translated by Prinsep.† The first portion of it was revised by Professor H. H. Wilson, from the transcript of Westergaard and Jacob,‡ and the whole by the late Dr. Bhau Dâji of Bombay,§ from a fresh copy made by his own pandits. The following transcription and translation have been kindly revised from the latter and from the estampage by Professor Eggeling:—

1 Siddham idaṁ taṭâkaṁ sudarśanaṁ Garanagarâd âpâdarama . . . . ttikopalavistârâ-
yâmochchhrayaniḥsandhibaddhadṛiḍhasarvvapâḍikṛitvotparvvatapâ-
2 dappratisparddhisuślishṭaba[ddhaṁ] . . ta[rka]ma . . . .
vajâtenâkṛitrimeṇa setubandhenopapannaṁ suppratividhitappranâḍîparivâha-
3 mîḍhavidhânaṁ cha triskanda . . . .
. . nâdibhir anugrahair mahaty upachaye varttate tad idaṁ râjño Mahâkshatrapasya sugṛihî-
4 tanâmnaḥ Svâmi-Chashṭanasya pautra . . . . ḥ
putrasya râjño mahâkshatrapasya gurubhir abhyastakâmno Rudra-Dâmno varshe dvisaptatitame 4
5 Mârggaśîrshabahulapa . . . . [ra]sṛishṭavṛishṭinâ
parjjanyena ekârṇavabhûtâyâm iva pṛithivyâṁ kṛitâyâṁ Girer-Ûrjayataḥ Suvarṇasikatâ-
6 Palâśinîprabhṛitînâṁ nadînâṁ atimâtrodvṛittair vvegaiḥ setum a . . . . yamâṇânurû-
papratikâram api giriśikharatarutaṭâṭṭâlakopatalpadvâraśaraṇochchhrayavidhvaṁsinâ yuganidhanasadṛi-
7 śaparamaghoravegena vâyunâ pramathitasalilavikshiptajarjjarîkṛitâva . . . .
pprâśmavṛikshagulmalatâpratânaṁ ânadîtalâd ity udghâṭitam âsît chatvâri hastaśatâni viṅśaduttarâṇy âyatena
etâvaṁty eva vistîrṇena
8 pañchasaptati hastân avagâḍhena bhedena nissṛitasarvvatoyaṁ marudhanvakalpam atibhṛiśadû*na*(?) . . . .
. . . . syârthe Mauryasya râjñaḥ Chandragu‖ . . râshṭriyeṇa Śyenapushyaguptena kâritaṁ Âśokasya
Mauryasya te Yavanarâjena Tushaspenâdhishṭhâya
9 pranâḍîbhir alaṅkṛitaṁ tatkâritayâ cha râjânurûpakṛitavidhânayâ tasmin bhede dṛishṭayâ pranâḍyâ vistṛi-
tase*tu* (?) . . . . no âgarbhâtprabhṛittyavihatasamuda(ya ?) râjalakshmî[śara ?]ṇâguṇatas
sarvvavarṇair abhigamya rakshaṇârthaṁ patitve vṛitena âprâṇochchhvâsât purushavadhanivṛittikṛita-
10 satyapratijñena anyatra saṁgrâmeshv abhimukhâgatasadṛiśaśatruprahaaraṇavitaraṇatvaviguṇari . . . . .
. . . . . takâruṇyena svayamabhigatajanapadapraṇipatti . . paśaraṇadena dasyuvyâḍamṛigarogâdi-
bhir anupasṛishṭapûrvvanagaranigama*ne* (?)
11 janapadânâṁ svavîryyajitânâm anuraktasarvvaprakṛitînâṁ pûrvvâparâkarâvanty Anûpanîvṛid-Ânartta-Surâsh-
ṭraśva . [kava ?] ruka . . chha-Sauvîra-Kukurâparânta-Nishâdâdînâṁ samagrâṇâṁ tatprabhâvâd ya . . .
. . . . kâmavishayâṇâṁ vishayâṇâṁ patinâ sarvvakshatrâvishkṛita-
12 vîraśabdajâtotsekâvidheyânâṁ Yaudheyânâṁ prasahyotsâdakena Dakshiṇâpathapates-Sâtakarṇer dvir api ni-
rvyâjam avajityâvajitya saṁbandhâvadûrayâ anutsâdanât prâptayaśasâm â . . . . . . (pra)vijayena
bhrashṭarâjyapratishṭhâpanena yathârtthahaste-
13 chchhavârjitârjitadharmânurâgeṇa śabdârtthagândharvvanyâyâdyânâṁ vidyânâṁ mahatînâṁ pâraṇadhâraṇa-
vijñânaprayogâvâptavipulakîrttinâ turagagajarathacharyyâsicharmaniyuddhâdyâ . . . .
parabalalâghavasaushṭhavakriyeṇa ahar ahar dânamânâna-
14 vamânaśîlena sthûlalakshena yathâvatprâptair baliśulkabhâgaiḥ kanakarajatavajravaidûryaratnopachayavi-
shyandamânakośena sphuṭalaghumadhurachitrakântaśabdasamayodârâlaṅkṛitagadyapadya . . . .
. . . napramâṇamânonmânasvaragativarṇnasârasatvâdibhiḥ
15 paramalakshaṇâvyaṁjanair upetakântamûrttinâ . . . . narendrakanyâsvayaṁv-
arânekamâlyaprâptadâmnâ mahâkshatrapeṇa R . . . . ma . . . .
. . . . rtthadharmmakîrttivṛiddhyarthaṁ cha api dayitâkaravishṭiṁ
16 praṇayakriyâbhiḥ paurajânapadaṁ janaṁ svasmât kośân mahatâ dhanaughena anatimahatâ cha kâlena tri-
guṇadṛiḍhataravistârâyâmaṁ setuṁ vidhâya . . nvitaga . . . . pra-
darśanataraṁ kâritam iti yasminn artthe
17 mahâkshatrapasya matisachivakarmasachivair amâtyaguṇasamudyuktair apy atimahatvâd bhedasyânutsâ-
havimukhamatibhiḥ pratyâkhyâtâraṁbhaṁ
18 punaḥ setubandhanairâśyâd hâhâbhûtâsu prajâsu ihâdhishṭhâne paurajânapadajanânugrahârthaṁ pârthivena
kṛitsnânâm Ânartta-Surâshṭrâṇâṁ pâlanârtthan niyuktena
19 Pahlavena Kulaipaputreṇâmâtyena Suviśâkhena yathâvad arthadharmavyavahâradarśanair anurâgama-
bhivarddhayatâ śaktena dântenâchapalenâvismitenâryyeṇâhâryyeṇa
20 svadhitishṭhatâ dharmakîrttiyaśâṁsi bhartur abhivarddhayatânushṭhitam iti.

---

* This inscription has already been referred to, *ante*, pp. 42, 43.

† *Journ. As. Soc. Beng.* vol. VII. p. 334; and *Essays*, vol. II. p. 57 ff.

‡ Prinsep's *Essays*, vol. II. p. 68; *Journ. Bom. Br. R. As. Soc.* vol. I. p. 148.

§ *Journ. Bom. Br. R. As. Soc.* vol. VII. pp. 118, 125.

‖ Two syllables broken off, probably *-ptasya*.

INSCRIPTION OF RUDRA DAMA ON THE ASOKA ROCK NEAR JUNAGADH. PLATE XIV.

J. Burgess fecit.

Collotype by W. Griggs.

Translation.

1 "To the Perfect One.—This Sudarśana lake, being from Girinagara . . . to the foot . . . . having been supplied with an embankment all round strongly lined with masonry continuously in its length, breadth, and height, so as to rival the hill region itself . . . .

2 and being possessed of a natural causeway formed by . . . . . . it has been completed with appliances against inundations in the matter of well-constructed canals,

3-5 and by means of three banks (?) . . . . and other advantages is in excellent condition. This work gave way on the 4th day of the dark fortnight of the month Mârgaśirsha of the 72nd year, of Râjâ Mahâkshatrapa Rudra Dâman, whose name is oft repeated by the great, the grandson of Mahâkshatrapa Chashṭaṇa of well accepted (propitious) name* . . . . the son of . . . . in consequence of the rain having poured down heavy showers everywhere, converting the surface of the earth as it were into one ocean.

6 and by the excessive swelling of the currents of the gold-sand river Palâśinî† and other rivers of the Urjayata hill, the embankment . . . . was carried away . . . . in spite of suitable devices employed to . . . . the water, agitated by a hurricane, destroying the hill-top, trees, walls, towers, collections of houses with stories and doors,

7 and whose terrible force was fierce as the deluge, washed down, fallen and dismantled . . . . . . stones, shrubs, networks of creepers . . . . (gave way) down to the bottom of the river. Through a broken passage of four hundred and twenty cubits length, and of the same breadth,

8 and seventy-five cubits deep, the whole of the water escaped and converted (the lake) as it were into the (arid) country of Marwar. Afterwards (?) . . . . for the sake of . . . . it was ordered to be repaired by Ṣyena Pushyagupta, brother-in-law (*râshṭriya?*) of the Maurya Râja Chandragupta;

9 and was embellished with embankments under the governor(*ship*) (*adhishṭhâya*—under the supervision?) of Tushaspa, the (celebrated)‡ Yavana Râja of Aśoka Maurya. By the parapet seen in this break, which he (*Tushaspa*) has had constructed, and which has been executed in a manner worthy of the king, . . . the extensive (?) bridge . . . . who—on account of his virtues, the abode of royal fortune, which manifested itself in uninterrupted prosperity from his childbirth,—was wooed by all classes approaching for protection as his subjects;

10 who, except in war, had taken the true vow never in his life to kill a human being . . . . the killing of an equal and opposing enemy and liberality . . . . who has compassionate to . . . . who afforded protection . . . . in lieu of the submission of the people he encountered . . . . city never afflicted by thieves, serpents, wild animals, and diseases . . . .

11 The lord of the countries of eastern and western Âkarâvati (*or* Âkara and Avantî), Anûpadeśa, Ânartta, Surâshṭra, Aśva-kachha (*or* Bharukachha ?), Sauvîra, Kukura, Aparânta, Nishâda, &c., conquered by his own might, and the people of which are well affected; who rooted out the Yaudheyas,

12 who would not subject themselves from their pride of their title of hero, acknowledged by the Kshatriya tribe; who, without treachery, after twice thoroughly

---

* The inscription has *hâmno*, but *nâmno* was evidently intended.

† The stream flowing out of the valley round the foot of Girnâr, also known as the Svarnarekhâ.

‡ *Te* (*na*), supplied by Dr. Bhau Dâji.

conquering Śâtakarṇi, lord of Dakshiṇâpatha, did not completely destroy him, on account of their near connexion, and thus obtained glory . . . . of great exploits by the re-establishment of deposed kings, by properly raising his hand (*i.e.* by gifts)

13 has repeatedly earned the love of Dharma; who has secured great renown by his complete study of the theory and practice of the great sciences of grammar, polity, singing, philosophy, &c.; who was skilled in the sciences of (managing) the horse, the elephant, the chariot, the sword, the shield, close fight, &c.; whose attacks on his enemies' army are impetuous and effective; who is always of a charitable, courteous, and

14–15 obliging disposition; who is munificent; whose treasury overflows with abundance of gold, silver, diamonds, lapis-lazuli (*vaiḍûrya*), and jewels, acquired by just and proper taxes and duties and tribute; whose speech is graced by clear, simple, sweet, admirable, and beautiful sentences in prose and poetry; whose beautiful form has the best mark and qualifications in gait, height, voice, walk, colour, vigour, strength, &c.; who himself acquired the title of Mahâkshatrapa (protector of warriors), who won numerous garlands of flowers in the Swayamvara ceremony of the daughters of kings; by this Mahâkshatrapa Rudra Dâman, for cows and Brahmans . . . . and for the increase of his merit and fame

16 by gentle means exacted taxes, and forced labour from the people of the city and country, and by a liberal amount of money from his own treasury, in no great length of time constructed the bridge of three times the length and breadth . . . . caused the most delightful lake (*sudarśanataram*) to be made.

17 On account of the largeness of the gap, the undertaking was forbidden by the king's advisers and executive officers, although possessed of all the qualifications of ministers, and not disinclined to encourage enterprise.

18 The people, losing all hopes of the rebuilding of the bridge, raised woeful cries, when the work was executed by the

19 Pahlava minister Suviśâkha, the son of Kulaipa, appointed by the king to look after the welfare of the people of towns and districts, and for the protection of the whole of Ânartta and Surâshṭra . . . . who (*Suviśâkha*) by the proper dispensation of justice in temporal and spiritual matters secured the love of the people; who was powerful, patient, unshaken, free from pride, honourable, unconquerable,

20 the establisher of religious fame, and the increaser of the glories of his master."

This inscription, if the conquests of Rudra Dâma are not an idle boast, shows that the power of the Sâhs was of very considerable extent, reaching from the Tâpi over a large part of Mâlwa to the borders of Sindh,—for Avantî is the country round Ujjain.* Anûpadeśa Professor Bhandarkar supposes to have been on the Narmadâ about Nimâr, with Mâhishmatî as its capital; this, however, is not sufficiently supported. Anûpa is mentioned in the *Harivanśa* as having been given by King Prithu to the bard Sûta, and again as annexed by Haryasva to his kingdom of Ânartta which, as we shall see below, was also included in the peninsula we now call Kâṭhiâwâḍ. Anûpa or Arûpa is again spoken of as "dependant on the king of Sindh," which might be regarded as pointing to Kachh, if it was not, as seems more probable, Okhâmaṇḍal.†

* *Bṛihat Sanhitâ*, v. 39, 73 ; ix. 18, 21, in *Jour. R. A. Soc.* (N.S.), vol. IV. pp. 462, 467 ; vol. V. p. 58.

† *Harivanśa*, caps. 5, 33, 93, 94, 112, and 114 ; *Raghuvanśa* vi. 37–43 ; *Ind. Ant.*, vol. I. p. 234 *Trans. Orient. Cong.* 1874, p. 313.

Ânartta is mentioned in the *Râmâyaṇa* as a western region towards the sea-coast of Gujarât;* and is referred to in the *Harivanśa* as having been settled by King Reva, the grandson of Saryâti, with Kuśasthali as its capital, situated between the ocean and Anûpa, and the name of which was afterwards changed, when it became the Yâdava capital, into Dvâravati or Dvâraka, on an island of Ânartta. Further Ânartta is spoken of as part at least of Surâshṭra, 'bounded on one side by the sea and on the other by Anûpa, with Girivara (Girnâr I suppose) for its fortress.' To this Haryasva annexed Anûpa, and 'extended his sway over the whole of Ânartta.'†

Aśvakachha—if the reading can be trusted—I would identify as Kachh; Sauvîra is frequently mentioned as in Sindh or its vicinity;‡ Kukura, as Prof. R. G. Bhandarkar suggests, may be the equivalent of Hiwan Thsang's *Kiu-che-lo*, of which the capital was *Pi-lo-mi-lo*, identified by Vivien de Saint Martin with Bâlmer in Râjputâna;§ Aparânta must be the western coast below the Ghâṭs or Sahyâdri range, as indicated by Prof. R. G. Bhandarkar, from a passage in the *Raghuvanśa* where Raghu is represented as crossing the Sahya mountains to conquer the country which he fills to the sea-shore with his army:‖ This is confirmed by the *Harivanśa* from which we gather that the city of Sûrpâraka belonged to it, and which I have identified with Sûpâra in the Konkan near Bassein.¶ Nishâda, the kingdom of Nala, must belong to the south of Malwa, among the Vindhya hills, or perhaps, as Lassen has placed it, along the Sâtpura hills to the north-west of Berar.**

Who the "Śâtakarṇi lord of the Dakshiṇâpatha" was, is not quite certain. Among the kings known by the various names of the Andhra, Śâtavâhana, Vrispala, Andhrajâtiya, and Andhrabhṛitya dynasty, which according to different *Purâṇas* ruled for 435½, 456, or 460 years, there are several of the name of Śâtakarṇi. Though the *Vâyu* and *Bhâgavata Purâṇas* state that there were thirty kings, the former gives the names of only seventeen, and the latter with the *Vishṇu Purâṇa* give twenty-four, while the *Matsya* gives twenty-nine.†† And as the Maurya, Sunga, and Kâṇwa dynasties are said to have lasted in all 294 or 296 years, and that Sipraka killed Suśarman, the last of the Kâṇwas, and founded the Andhra dynasty, if we assume that

---

* *Râmâyaṇa*, iv. 43; *Bṛihat Sanhitâ*, v. 80 in *J.R.A.S.* (N.S.) vol. IV. p. 468.

† Ânartta was the son of Saryâti, and Ânartta's son was Reva who ruled the country of Ânartta. Raivata Kakudmin was the eldest of the hundred children of Reva, and succeeded him on the throne of Kuśasthali. This prince went one day, accompanied by his daughter Revatî, to the abode of Brahmâ, where for a little while (of the gods)—but really many human ages, he assisted at a concert of Gandharvas. On returning he found his capital occupied by the Yâdavas and named Dvâravatî. Raivata thereon gave his daughter to Balarâma and retired as a devotee to Mount Meru.—*Harivanśa*, caps. 10, 93, 111, 112, and 155. As Raivata is the proper name of Girnâr, this reads as if intended to be understood as an allegory.

‡ The *Târâ-tantra* calls Sauvira the worst of countries and places it east of Sûrasena. Conf. Lassen, *Alterthums.* (2nd ed.) I. 804; *Râmâyaṇa*, iii. 53, 56 Gorr.; *Mahâbh.* iii. 16,040, vii. 44; *Bṛihat Sanhitâ*, v. 79; ix. 19; x. 6, in *Jour. R. A. S.* (N.S.) vol. IV. p. 468; and vol. V. pp. 58, 64; *Harivanśa*, c. 31 and 90; *Ind. Ant.*, vol. II. p. 145; *Schol. on Pâṇini* IV. ii. 76, 123; *Trans. Orient. Cong.* 1874, p. 345, and *Satruñjaya Mâhâtmya*, sarg. x. 391, quoted below p. 158, note.

§ Stanislas Julien, *Mem. sur les Cont. Orient.* t. II. pp. 166, 406–408; *Bṛihat Sanhitâ* v. 71 in *Jour. R. As. Soc.* (N.S.) vol. IV. p. 467; *Trans. Orient. Cong.* 1874, p. 312–13.

‖ *Raghuvanśa* iv. 52, 53, 58; *Trans. Orient. Cong.* 1874, p. 313, and Conf. *Ind. Ant.* vol. IV. p. 104.

¶ *Harivanśa*, cap. 95; *Ind. Ant.* vol. I. p. 321; Reinaud, *Frag. Arab. et. Pers*, p. 321.

** *Harivanśa*, caps. 5 and 94; *Manu* x. 8, and 48; *Raghuvanśa* xiii. 59 xiv. 52, xviii. 1; Lassen, *Ind. Alt.* I. 119.

†† Wilson's *Vishṇu Purâṇa* (Hall's Ed.), vol. IV. pp. 194–203.

Chandragupta the Maurya began to reign in 317 B.C., the Andrabhṛityas must have arisen about 22 B.C. And taking this as an initial date, we may represent the chronology of the dynasty as follows :—

Andrabhṛitya Kings.	Vâyu.	Matsya.	Brahmaṇḍa.	Probable Date of Accession.
Śipraka, Sindhuka, or Śiśuka	23	23	23	22 B.C.
Krishṇarâja, his brother	10	18	18	1 A.D.
Śâtakarṇi I., *Śrîmallakarṇi* or Śantakarṇa	56	10 (or 18)	18 (or 10)	19 „
Pûrṇotsanga or Paurṇamâsa	wanting	18	18	29 „
Skandhastambhi, *or Śrivasvâmî*	„	18	—	47 „
Śâtakarṇi II.	„	56	56	65 „
Lambodara	„	18	18	121 „
Ivîlaka, Apîlaka or *Apîtaka*	12	12	12	139 „
Sangha, *or* Meghasvâti	wanting	18	18	151 „
Śâtakarṇi III. or *Svâti*	—	18	12	169 „
Skandasvâti	—	7	7	187 „
Mṛigendra, *or* Mahendra Śâtakarṇi	—	3	3*	194 „
Kuntala or *Svâtikarṇa*	—	8	8	197 „
Svâtikarṇa	—	1	1	205 „
Paṭumat, Paṭumâvi or *Pulomâvi*	24	(36 ?)	34	206 „
Arishṭakarṇi, Gaurakṛishṇa, or *Gorakshâsvaśrî*	25	25	25	240 „
Hâla or Haleya	1	5	5	265 „
Pattalaka or *Maṇḍalaka*	(5 ?)	5	5	270 „
Pravilasena or *Purîndrasena*	21	5	12	275 „
Sundara Śâtakarṇi	1	1	1	287 „
Chakora Śatakarṇi or *Rajâdasvâti*	½	½	6	288 „
Śivasvâti	28	28	28	289 „
Gautamîputra Śâtakarṇi	21	21	21	317 „
Pulimat, Pulomâvit, or Puḍumâyi Śatakarṇi	wanting	28	29	338 „
Śivaśrî Śatakarṇi, or Avi	„	7	4	367 „
Śivaskanda Śatakarṇi, or *Skandhasvâti*	„	7 (9)	8	374 „
Yajnaśrî, or Yajna Śâtakarṇî Gautamîputra	29 ?	9 (20)	19	382 „
Vijaya	6	6	6	401 „
Chandraśrî Śatakarṇi, *Vadaśrî* or Chandravijna	3	10	3	407 „
Pulomârchis or Pulomâvi	7	7	7	410 to 417

The statement of Pliny (cir A.D. 75) that the 'Andaræ have many villages, thirty cities protected by walls and towers, and which support a force of 100,000 infantry, 1,000,000 (?) cavalry, and a thousand elephants,'† is a proof that the early kings of this dynasty were very powerful in the first century of the Christian era.

But from external sources we have little or nothing to check the above chronology. Wilson suggested that the embassy mentioned by De Guignes as sent to China in A.D. 408, from a Buddhist king, Yue-gnai or Yueï-'aï of Kia-pi-li, in India,‡ might have been from Yajnaśrî; but as it arrived in the time of the emperor Wen-ti of the Song dynasty, who reigned from 424 to 453, and the date intended was A.D. 428,—it was long after the death of Yajnaśrî. As the name Yueï-'aï, or 'beloved of the moon,' in Chinese is equivalent to Chandrapriya (in Sanskrit) or Chandragupta, Lassen

* In the *Brahmâṇḍa Purâṇa* Mahendra Śâtakarṇi, Kuntala Śâtakarṇi, and Svatishena (1 yr.) follow after Chakora Śâtakarṇi.

† *Hist. Nat.* lib. VI. c. 22 § 4 :—" Validior deinde gens Andaræ, plurimis vicis, XXX oppidis, quæ, muris turribasque muniuntur, regi præbet peditum C.M., equitum M.M., elephantos M." The "M.M." must surely be a corruption of the text. To the Prasii, who are stated to be by far the most powerful, are assigned only 30,000 cavalry.

‡ *Histoire General des Huns.* t. I. p. 45 ; conf. *Journ. Asiat.* IVme Ser. t. X. p. 99.

naturally supposes he was one of the Gupta kings;* if Yueï-'ai, then, were neither Yajnaśrî nor Chandraśrî, the date of the embassy does not aid in fixing the chronology of the Andhrabhṛityas. Still less, as Lassen remarks, can we identify Hulomein of the Chinese, who, according to De Guignes,† was also a king of middle India, with Puloman, because this king must have reigned at an earlier date.

Ptolemy (cir. A.D. 150) mentions a Siri Polemios of Paithana, and this might have referred to a Pulomâvit, but, unless our lists are useless, or Puḍumavi was as common a name as Śâtakarṇi, the first of that name flourished long after the death of Ptolemy.

On the testimony of the above inscription, however, Rudra Dâma was contemporary with a Dekhan king named Śâtakarṇi. Now if, as I suppose with Mr. Fergusson‡ and Professor Bhandarkar, the Sâhs dated from the Śaka era, the date of this inscription is 150 A.D.—possibly 30, and almost certainly more than 20 years, after the death of Śâtakarṇi II.§ and 18 years before the accession of Śâtakarṇi III. of the lists; but as Śâtakarṇi seems to have been a surname of the Śâtavâhana race it was probably applied to Ivîlaka and Sangha also, who were the contemporaries of Rudra Dâma, and the first of whom may be the Śâtakarṇi whom he "twice overthrew."

The Nâsik and other cave inscriptions show that the Sâhs were influential in the Dekhan in the second century. While one speaks of Nâsik as if it were Kṛishṇarâja's capital, others state that some of the caves were executed by Ushavadâta, the son-in-law of Kshaharâta Nahapâna in 40, 41, and 42 of the Sâh era, or A.D. 118-120—that is, during the reign of Śâtakarṇi II. But we hear no more of the Śâtavâhanas after Kṛishṇarâja till Śâtakarṇi Gautamiputra, "the lord of Dhanakaṭaka (A.D. 317–338), who claims to have "quelled the boast and pride of the Kshatriyas," to be "the destroyer of the Śakas, Yavanas, and Palhavas," to have extirpated "the race of Khagârâta," to have "established the glory of the family of Śâtavâhana," and to be sovereign of "Asika, Aśmaka, Muḍhaka, Surâshṭra, Kukura, Aparânta, Anûpa ,Vidarbha, Akara, and Avantî." If, as Professor R. G. Bhandârkar and Mr. Fergusson suppose, the Khagârâtas were the same as the Sâhs,—and the last date on the Sâh coins seems to be 250 or A.D. 329, which tends to confirm this,‖ then the Sâhs may really have held many of the provinces here claimed by Gautamîputra during the interval from A.D. 150 or even 110 down to his time. And it will be remarked that the provinces he conquered include nearly all those over which Rudra Dâma had ruled a hundred and eighty years earlier.

---

* *Alterthumskunde*, 2nd ed., vol. II., pp. 785, 1211; a suggestion, by the bye, tending to support the Gupta chronology as dated from A.D. 318, for this embassy reached China in the Gupta year 109, and so might have been sent by Chandragupta II., and the second embassy in A.D. 502 or 183 Gupta Samvat, from a Gupta (Chinese *Kio-to*,) may have been sent either by Budha Gupta or Toramâṇa:—Stanislas Julien in *Journ. Asiatique* IVme Ser. t. X. pp. 91, 100; and conf. *ante*, p. 70; Cunningham, *Bhilsa Topes*, pp. 140 ff.; Fergusson, *Journ. R. As. Soc.* (N.S.) vol. IV. p. 125.

† *Hist. des Huns*, tom. I. pp. 56, 621. *Alterthumskunde* (2nd ed.), vol. II. p. 121.

‡ *History of Indian and Eastern Architecture*, p. 721.

§ Cunningham, *Bhilsa Topes*, pp. 264, 272.

‖ *Trans. Orient. Congress*, 1874, pp. 311, 317, 324, 327, 333, 335, 337, 350–353.

VIII. SKANDAGUPTA'S INSCRIPTION.

The third and last long inscription on the Junâgaḍh stone is that already referred to (p. 21) as on the north-west side, facing the causeway. Of this the time and means at disposal did not admit of a copy being taken; and indeed it is very doubtful if a satisfactory copy could now be taken without the aid of very skilful paṇḍits. The surface is weather-worn and the letters, originally small and but rudely cut in a later style than the Sâh inscription, are mostly very indistinct.* The copy on the accompanying Plate XV. is from that made by Bhagwanlâl Indraji for the late Dr. Bhau Daji in 1861,† whose transliteration and translation are as follows:

Transcript.

१ सिद्धम् श्रियमभिमतभोग्यां नैककालापनीतां त्रिदशपतिसुखार्त्थं यो बलेराजहार कमलनिलयनायाः शाश्वतं धाम लक्ष्म्याः

२ स जयति विजितार्त्तिर्विष्णुरत्यन्तजिष्णुः तदनु जयति शश्वत् श्रीपरिक्षिप्तवक्षाः स्वभुजजनितवीर्यो राजराजाधिराजः नरपति

३ भुजगानां मानदर्पोत्फणानां प्रतिकृतिगरुडाज्ञा निर्विषिस्त्रावकर्ता नृपतिगुणनिकेतः स्कन्दगुप्तः पृथुश्रीः चतुरुदधिजलान्तां स्फीतपर्यन्तदेशाम्

४ अवनिमवनतारि र्यश्चकारात्मसंस्थां पितरि सुरसखित्वं प्राप्तवत्यात्मशक्त्या अपि च जितमिव तेन प्रथयति यशसि यस्य रिपवोपि आमूलभग्नदर्पानिव वदने म्लेच्छदेशेषु

५ क्रमेण बुध्वा निपुणं प्रधार्य ध्यात्वा च कृत्स्नान्गुणदोषहेतून् व्यपेत्य सर्वान्मनुजेन्द्रपुत्रांल्लक्ष्मीः स्वयं यं वरयांचकार तस्मिन्नृपे शासति नैव कश्चिद्धर्मादपेतो मनुजः प्रजासु

६ आर्तो दरिद्रो व्यसनी कदर्यो दण्ड्यो न वा यो भृशपीडितः स्यात् एवं स जित्वा पृथिवीं समग्रां भग्नाग्रदर्पान्द्विषतश्च कृत्वा सर्वेषु देशेषु विधाय गोप्तॄन् संचिन्तयामास बहुप्रकारम् स्यात्कोनुरूपो

७ मतिमान्विनीतो मेधास्मृतिभ्यामनपेतभावः सत्यार्जवौदार्यनयोपपन्नमाधुर्यदाक्षिण्ययशोन्वितश्च भक्तोनुरक्तो नृविशेषयुक्तः सर्वोपधाभिश्च विशुद्धबुद्धिः आनृण्यभावोपगतान्तरात्मा सर्वस्य लोकस्य हिते प्रवृत्तः

८ न्यायार्जनेर्थस्य च कः समर्थः स्यादर्जितस्याप्यथ रक्षणे च गोपायितस्यापि च वृद्धिहेतो र्वृद्धस्य पात्रप्रतिपादनाय सर्वेषु भृत्येष्वपि संहतेषु यो मे प्रशिष्यान्निखिलान्सुराष्ट्रान् आज्ञातमेकः खलु पर्णदत्तो भरस्य तस्योद्वहने समर्थः

९ एवं विनिश्चित्य नृपाधिपेन नैकानहोरात्रगणान्स्वमत्या यः संनियुक्तोर्थनया कथंचित् सम्यक्सुराष्ट्रावनिपालनाय नियुज्य देवा वरुणं प्रतीच्यां स्वस्था यथावन्मनसो बभूवुः पूर्वेतरस्यां दिशि पर्णदत्तं नियुज्य राजा धृतिमांस्तथाभूत्.

१० तस्यात्मजो ह्यात्मजभावयुक्तो द्विधेव चात्मात्मवशेन नीतः सर्वात्मनात्मेव च रक्षणीयो नित्यात्मवानात्मजकान्तरूपः रूपानुरूपैर्ललितैर्विचित्रै र्नित्यप्रमो(दा)न्वितसर्वभावः प्रबुद्धपद्माकरपद्मवक्त्रो नृणां शरण्यः शरणागतानाम्.

---

* See *Journ. As. Soc. Beng.* vol. VII. pp. 347, 348, 873.

† *Journ. Bom. Br. R. As. Soc.* vol. VII. pp. 114, 121, 128. A transcript was also taken by Westergaard and Jacob, *Journ. Bom. Br. R. As. Soc.* vol. I. p. 148.

PLATE XV

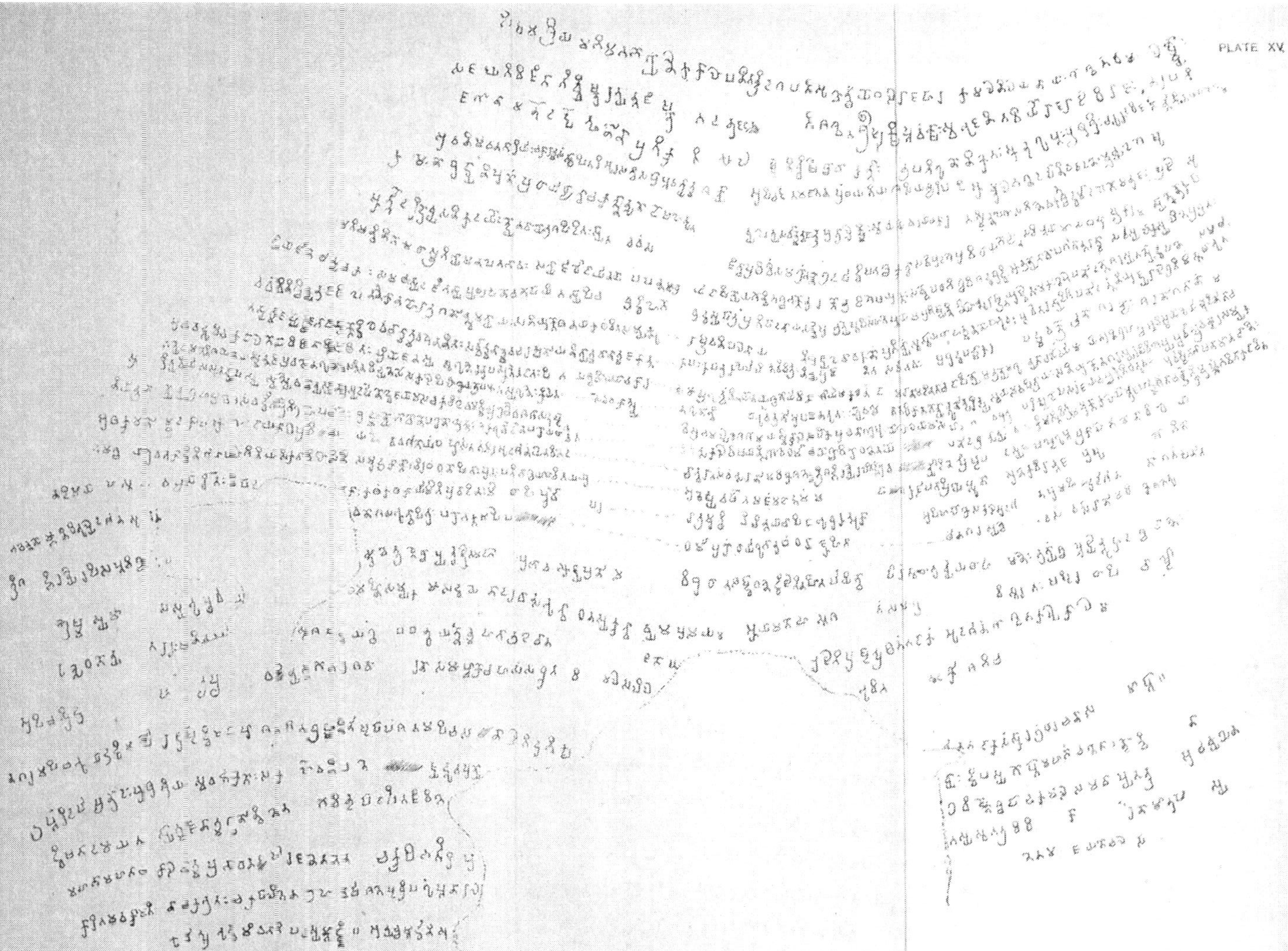

W. Griggs photo-lith. from a copy by Bhagwanlal Indraji.

THE SKANDAGUPTA INSCRIPTION NEAR JUNÂGAḌH IN SURÂSHTRA.

SCALE 1-15th.

११ अभवद्भुवि चक्रपालितोसाविति नाम्ना प्रथितः प्रियो जनस्य स्वगुणैरनुपस्कृतैरुदात्तः पि(त)रं यश्च विशेषयांचकार चमा प्रभुत्वं विनयो नयश्च शौर्यं विनाशौर्यमक? नं च . . . . मादानमदीनता च दाचिण्यमानृण्यमशून्यता च सौंदर्यमार्येतरनिग्रहश्च अविस्मयो धैर्यमुदीर्णता च

१२ इत्येवमेते तिशयेन यस्मिन्नविप्रवासेन गुणा वसन्ति न विद्यते सो सकलेपि लोके यत्रोपमातस्य गुणैः क्रियेत स एव कार्त्स्न्येन गुणान्वितत्वात् बभूव नृणामुपमानभूतः इत्येवमेतानधिकानतोन्यान्गुणान्परीच्य स्वयमेव पित्रा यस्सन्नियुक्तो नगरस्य रचां विशेष्यपूर्वान् चकार सम्यक्

१३ आश्रित्य वीर्यं स्वभुजद्वयस्य स्वस्यैव नान्यस्य नरस्य दर्पं नोद्वेजयामास च कंचिदेवमस्मिन्पुरे चैव शशास दुष्टा(न्) विस्रंभमल्पन्न शशास यस्मिन् काले स लोकस्य च नागरेषु यो लालयामास . . पौरवर्गान् . . पुत्रान्स परीच्य दोषान् संरंजयां च प्रकृती र्बभूव पूर्वं स्मिता भाषणमानदानैः

१४ निर्यंत्रणान्योन्यगृहप्रवेशैः संवर्द्धितप्रीतिगृहोपचारैः ब्रह्मण्यभावेन परेण युक्तः शक्तः शुचिर्दानपरो यथावत् प्राप्यान्सकाले विषयान्सिषेवे धर्मार्थयोश्चाप्यविरोधनेन (जवननोतेवक्त)पर्णदत्तात्सन्यायवानत्र किमस्ति चित्रम् मुक्ता कलापाम्बुजपद्मशीताच्चंद्रात्किमुष्णं भविता कदाचित्

१५ अथ क्रमेणाम्बुदकाल आगते निदाघकालं प्रविपटा(तोयदे)ववर्ष तोयं बहु संतत चिरं सुदर्शनं येन विभेदचात्वरात् संवत्सराणामधिके शते तु त्रिंशद्भिरन्यैरपि तद्भि(षड्भि)रेव रात्रौ दिने प्रोष्ठपदस्य षष्ठे गुप्तस्य कालागणनां विधाय

१६ इमाश्च या रैवतकाद्विनिर्गता पलाशिनीयं सिकताविलासिनी समुद्रकान्ताः चिरबन्धनोषिता द्रवुः पतिं ताश्च यथोचितं ययुः अवेच्य वर्षान्तमजं मदोद्रमं महोदधेरुर्जयता प्रियेप्सुना अनेकवीरान्तजपुष्पशोभितो

१७ नदीमयो हस्त इव प्रसारितः विषीद(मानाः खलु सर्वलो)काः कथंकथंकार्यमिति प्रवादिनः मियोहि पूर्वापररात्रमुत्थिता विचिन्तया चापि बभूवुरुत्सुकाः अपीहलोके सकले सुदर्शनं पुमांहि दुर्दर्शनतां गतं चणात्

१८ भवेन्न साम्भो निधितुल्यदर्शनं सुदर्शनं . . . वणगसभूत्वा पितुः परो भक्तिमपि प्रदर्श्य धर्मं पुरोधाय शुभानुबंधं राज्ञो हितार्थं नगरस्य चैव संवत्सराणामधिके शतेतु

१९ त्रिंशद्भिरन्यैरपि सप्तभिश्च प्र . . . . स्वचैत्र . . . आ(स्या)प्यनुज्ञातमहाप्रभावः आज्यप्रणामैर्विबुधानथेष्ट्वा धनैर्द्विजातीनपि तर्पयित्वा पौरांस्तथाभ्यर्च्ययथार्हमानैः भृत्यांश्च पूज्यान् सुहृदश्च दानैः

२० ग्रैष्मस्य मासस्य तु पूर्वप . . . . . प्रथमेह्नि सम्यक् मासद्वयेनादरवान्स भूत्वा धनस्य कृत्वा व्ययमप्रमेयम् आयामतो हस्तशतं समग्रं विस्तारतः षष्टिरथापि चाष्टौ

२१ उत्सेधतोन्यत्पुरुषाणि स . . . हस्तशतद्वयस्य बबंध यत्नान्महता(नृदेवान्)सुसम्यग्घटितोपलेन . . . सुजातिदुष्टात्प्रथितं तटाकं सुदर्शनं शाश्वतकल्पकालम्.

२२ अपि च सुदृढसेतुप्रान्तविन्यस्तशोभं रथचरणसमाह्वक्रौंचहंसं स भूतं विमलसलिल भुवित . . . . वदर्कः शशिप्र

२३ नगरमपि च भूयाद्वृद्धिमत्पौरजुष्टं द्विजबहुशतगीतब्रह्मनिर्नष्टपापं शतमपि च समानामीतिदुर्भिच . . . . दर्शनतटाकसंस्कारग्रंथारचना समाप्ता.

२४ दृप्तारिदर्पप्रणुदः पृथुश्रियः स्ववंशकेतोः सकलावनोपतेः . . . . ज्यद्भुतपुण्य . . . . . . द्वीपस्य गोप्ता महतां च नेता दण्डान्विना

२५ द्विषतां दमायत्तस्यात्मजेनात्मगुणान्वितेन गोविन्दपादार्पितजीविते . . . . नविष्णोश्च पादकमले समवाप्य तत्र अर्थव्ययेन

२६ महता महता च कालेनात्मप्रभावनतपौरजनेन तेन चक्रं बिभर्ति रिपु . . . . विश्रे . . . . तस्य स्वतंत्रविधिकारणमानुषस्य

२७ कारितमवक्रामति चक्रभृतः चक्रपालितेन गृहं वर्षशतेष्टत्रिंशे गुप्ता नां काल(तोव्यतोते) . . . . र्थे . . त्यितनवोजयंताचलस्य

२८ कुर्वन्प्रभुत्वमिव भाति परस्य मूर्ध्निद . . . . अन्यच्च मूर्द्धनि अ . .

*Translation.**

[1] " To the Perfect One ! Vishṇu, who snatched from Bali, for the happiness of Indra, that wealth (*Srî*) which is worthy of enjoyment by his beloved (*devotees*), and which was carried off for a long time, who conquered misery, and who is the constant asylum (or light) of that Lakshmî whose residence is the lotus,

[2] and who is ever victorious :—may he be glorious ! Next to him, may he (*Skandagupta*) be victorious, whose breast is encircled with splendour (*Śrî*), who obtained the fame of a hero (*virya*) by his own arm, the supreme king of kings, who, acting by the command of Garuḍa, as his substitute, destroyed the poison of the royal snakes (*snake-like kings*)

[3] with their hoods expanded in pride and conceit. The asylum of kingly qualities, he, the far-famed Skandagupta, of great wealth, who, on his father's attaining the friendship of Devas (*i.e., on his father's death*), humbled his enemies by his might, and possessed himself of the earth, which contains the gems of the four oceans, and which is skirted by rich countries ;

[4] by whose ever-increasing success his enemies in Mlechchha countries, whose pride has been destroyed from the root, were, as it were, conquered, and were ashamed to show their faces.

[5] Lakshmî, in her wisdom, having carefully reflected and considered all the causes of good and bad qualities, rejected, one after another, the sons of kings, and at last married him herself. Whilst this king was governing the earth no one amongst his subjects departed from the path of duty (*dharma*),

[6] or suffered, or was poor, vicious, miserly, deserving of punishment, or suffered from extreme misery. Having conquered all the world and humbled the pride of his enemies, and having established protecting officers in all the countries, he began to think intently. What person is there who is at once competent

[7] and far-seeing, modest, and with faith, full of wisdom and memory ; who is endowed with truth, straightforwardness, generosity, moral worth, sweetness, talent, and glory ; who is devoted and attached, manly, whose mind is devoid of every kind of deceit ; whose heart is ever intent on the discharge of his obligations, who is devoted to the good of mankind ;

[8] and who by righteous means is able to earn wealth, to preserve and increase it, and to spend it on proper objects ? Who is there qualified best to govern all the districts of Surâshṭra amongst all my servants ? Yes, I know surely, only Parṇadatta is competent to bear the burden.

[9] In this way this king of kings meditated for successive days and nights, and with firm resolve and earnest entreaty appointed (*him*) for the good government of the country of Surâshṭra. The Devas obtained rest after appointing Varuṇa to the west ; so the king by appointing Parṇadatta to the west felt secure.

---

* Revised by Professor Eggeling, who remarks that "the Inscription is composed for the most part in the *Indravajrâ* and *Upendravajrâ* metres, intermixed with *Vaṁśasthavila* couplets ; the two opening couplets being in the *Mâlinî* metre."

10 His (*Parṇadatta's*) son, full of filial duty, was, as it were, the victorious Parṇadatta, divided into a second self-same spirit, who was brought up as his own (*dear*) self, whose mind* was serene, whose form was beautiful as that of Cupid, ... in keeping with the form, beautiful and variegated* . . . . whose acts were ever truthful . . . . and whose face resembled an expanded lotus; who afforded protection to those who sought his protection.

11 He who was renowned in the world by the name of Chakrapâlita; was beloved by the people and made his father greater by his (*good*) qualities; in whom ever dwelt power tempered by mercy, humility, morality, bravery that boasts not, charity, cheerfulness, talent, freedom from debt, restless energy, beauty, contempt of the mean, freedom from pride, courage, and generosity.

12 These various qualities in an eminent degree resided in him without interruption. There is no one in this world to be compared to him in (*good*) qualities. He being endowed with all (*good*) qualities became worthy of example to mankind. The father (*Parṇadatta*), having recognized these and other greater qualities, himself appointed him (*Chakrapâlita*). He then protected the city better than his predecessors.

13 He availed himself of the bravery of his two arms, did not depend on others, nor did he cause distress to any from pride, but punished the wicked in the town. The people placed implicit confidence, and studying the character of the people he pleases them as if they were his children, with cheerfulness, sweet conversation,

14 civility, liberality, by the familiarity of social intercourse, by respect for their family usages, by devotion to Brahmanism, powerful, pure, charitable according to the rules, he enjoyed such pleasures as he could without transgressing wisdom, religion, and prosperity; what wonder that he (who was descended) from Parṇadatta should be virtuous? Is warmth ever caused from the moon, which is cool as a collection of pearls and aquatic lotuses?

15 Afterwards, when in the course of nature the rainy season arrived after the hot season, it rained copiously and continuously for a long time, whereby the Sudarśana burst (*its embankments* ?)—When a century of years *plus* thirty-(six ?) passed, on the sixth day of Bhâdrapada, at night, counting from the era of Gupta (*Guptasya kâla*)

16 . . . . and the rivers of the sea (*waves*), arising from the Raivata (*mountain*), and pent up for a long time, and also the Palâśinî, shining with its (*golden*) sands, again as usual proceeded (*rolled*) towards their lord (*the sea*), the friendly Urjayat, observing the flow of love on the part of the ocean,

17 and spread, as it were, his river-hands. All the people, frightened and crying to one another what to do and how to do, were all night (*or morning and evening*) thrown into still greater consternation. The Sudarśana (*good-looking*) lake in this world instantly became ill-looking (*was destroyed*).

18 Would the Sudarśana be ever filled with water and assume an appearance like that of the sea? . . . . (*letters lost*) . . . . he being greatly devoted to his father . . . . having put forward Dharma, ever of beneficial sequence to its observers . . . . for the benefit of the king and of the city, in a century of Samvatsaras

19 (*years*) *plus* thirty *plus* seven (*having passed*). . . . . Chaitra (*month*) . . . . . . and whose might is known. . . . . . . Having pleased the gods by ghee and obeisances, and the twice-born by gold, and similarly the people of the city by entertaining them with proper civility, and also servants and respectable friends by gifts. . . . . On the first day of the first demi-lunation of the (*first*) month

20 of the Grishma season (*latter half of summer*), in two months, in the best manner, he with great courtesy, and by expending immense wealth, constructed with great effort . . . . whose total length is 100 cubits, and breadth 68 cubits,

---

* The poet plays upon the word *âtman*, which is repeatedly introduced.

21 height (7 ?) persons (*men's height*) . . . . (200 *cubits* ?) . . . . with well-set stones . . . . the Sudarśana lake (*destined* ?) to last till the deluge,

22 and also . . . and whose bănd (*setú*) is ornamented . . . and in the chakraváka (*heron*) and the geese . . . . beautiful water . . . . as long as the sun and moon. . . . .

23 May the city be prosperous and populous ! May its sins be removed by hundreds of Brahmans singing the Vedas . . . . century of years, also (*may they be saved from*) all kinds of evils, and from famine . . . . the arrangement of the description of the construction of the Sudarśana lake is finished.

24 The destroyer of the pride of haughty enemies of great fortune, a banner of his race, the lord of the whole earth . . . . (*ten syllables lost*) . . . . (*four syllables not made out*) . . . . (*fourteen syllables lost*) . . . . the protector of the Dwîpa . . . . the lord of the great . . . . (*four syllables not made out*) . . . .

25 for the suppression of enemies . . . . his son endowed with his own qualities, who (*son*) has offered his soul to the feet of Govinda (*Vishṇu*), by him . . . . (*about fourteen syllables lost*) . . . and having been to the lotus-feet of Vishṇu . . . . whom the people of the city have submitted on account of his exploits, by him,

26 with a great expenditure of money and time, who by his prowess has had in submission the people of the city . . . . the holder of the discus . . . . enemy . . . . who is independent, and who for the sake of Brahmadeva became a man (?)

27 to this discus-holding Vishṇu, a temple was constructed by Chakrapâlita . . . and . . . . From the (*kála*) era of the Guptas . . . a century of years *plus* thirty-eight (*having passed*) . . . . (*about twelve syllables lost*) . . . . . (*seven doubtful syllables*) . . . . on the top of the Jayanta mountain,

28 appears as if ruling . . . . and secondly on the top . . . ."

This inscription has already been referred to (page 22), and the legend that has survived in support of it (pp. 30 and 80), preserving, though in corrupted forms, the names of Chakrapâlita and his son Parṇadatta, their relation to the Gupta sovereign, and the subversion of the Gupta power in Surâshṭra by the Valabhis. And this confirms what could scarcely otherwise be doubted—that the Valabhis immediately succeeded the Guptas. Thus, whatever meaning we may attach to *Guptánáṅ kâla* in this inscription, the Valabhi plates must be dated in the *same* era; and as the earliest of these is one of Dhruvasena I. dated 216, Bhaṭârka must have ruled as Senâpati not earlier than 160, nor much later than 180, when the Gupta power was broken up by Toramâṇa, and when the opportunity would be the most tempting to throw off the yoke of his masters (*ante*, pp. 68–70). Now proofs are accumulating that the Valabhi's used Albiruni's Gupta era, and rose to power at the end of the fifth century, A.D., hence Skanda Gupta must have ruled about the middle of that century—say 450 to 470 A.D.; and the dates 136, 137, and 138 in this inscription must be those of the same Gupta era, and fall to the years A.D. 455, 456, and 457.

On a smaller stone to the south-east of the large one is carved in large letters—

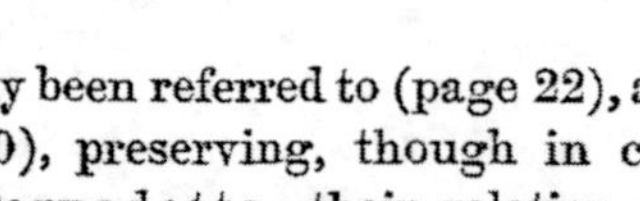

read by Prinsep as—*Śrí Tiratha Svámí*—the circle denoting the final *í* passing over the edge of the stone.

PLAN OF THE CAVE AT BÂWÂ PYÂRÂS MAṬH JUNÂGAḌH. PLATE XVII.

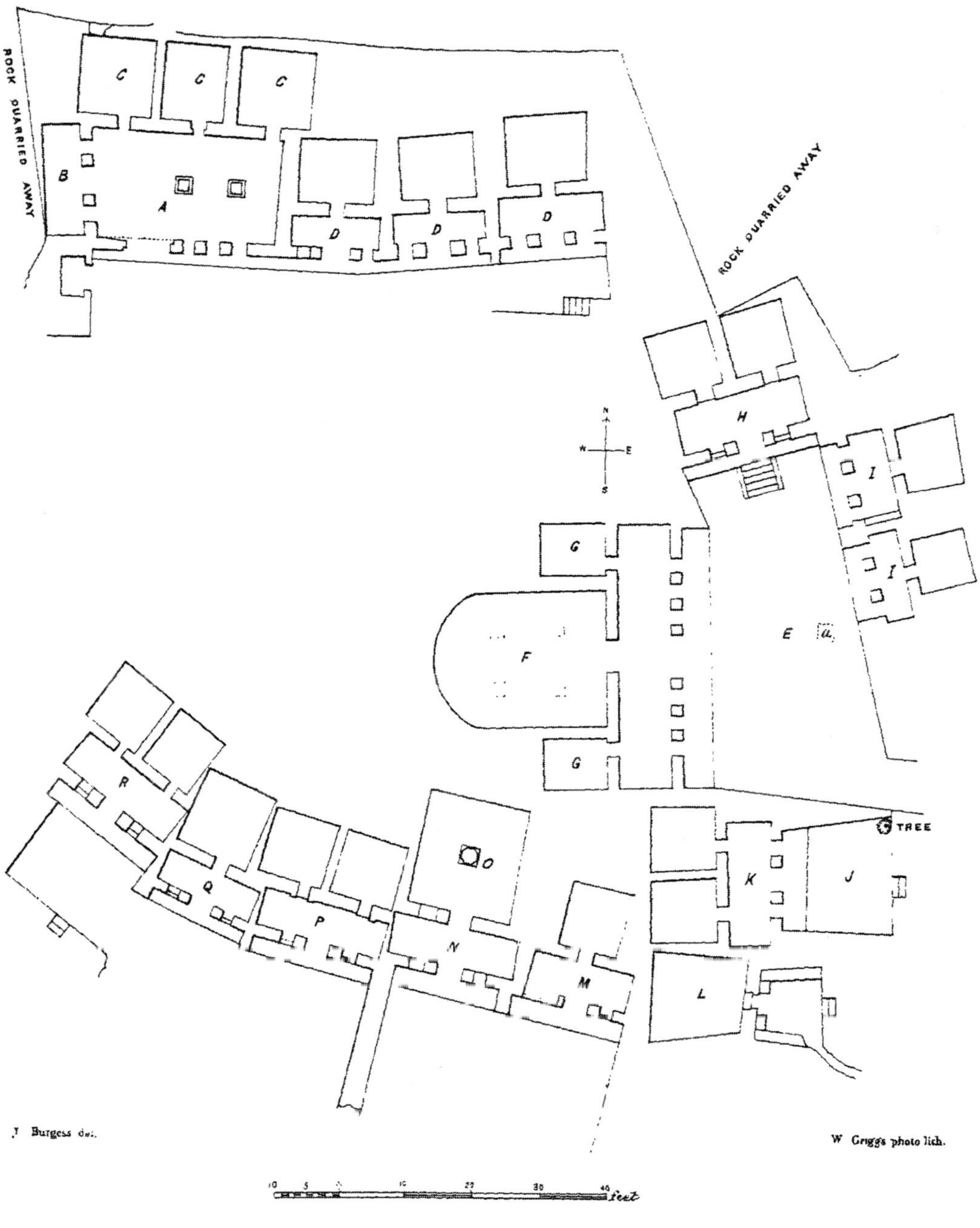

J Burgess del.

W Griggs photo lith.

IX.—CAVES AT JUNÂGAḌH, TALÂJÂ, SÂNÂ, ḌHÂNK, &c.

a. Caves in Junâgaḍh.

We now come to the Buddhist caves, which at one time must have been very numerous about Junâgaḍh. Hiwan-Thsang, the Chinese pilgrim of the seventh century, as already quoted (p. 83) states that there were in his time about fifty convents, with about three thousand recluses, of the *Sthavira* sect, belonging to the *Mahâyâna* or "greater translation."

Of these Buddhist convents there are still remains, though four hundred years of Muslim dominion and strife have obliterated every trace of most of them. In the east of Junâgaḍh, between the inhabited part and the walls, and beside the modern monastery or Maṭh known as Bâwâ Pyârâ's, are a number of monastic caves. A quarry has been opened behind them, and if it has not cut away some of them entirely, it has already been wrought up so close as to go under and into those on the north-west and into one on the east of the series.

These caves are arranged in three lines (see plates XVI. and XVII.): the first, on the north, faces southwards, and consists of one larger cave at the west end (A, plate XVII. and photograph, plate XVI.), about 28 feet by 16, having two pillars (perhaps originally three in line) supporting the roof, with three cells (C, C, C) at the back and a chamber (B) at the west end screened off by two plain square pillars and their corresponding pilasters. The front is partly destroyed, but has still three square pillars with octagonal necks, and on the façade over the central opening is the only fragment of carving—a semicircular arch slightly raised on the surface with a cross bar or diameter—in fact a very early form of the chaitya-window ornament, that, in later times, became so fashionable as an architectural ornament (see plate XVI.). East of this are three smaller caves (D, D, D), each consisting of a verandah with two square pillars and a cell about 11¼ feet by 9½ feet.

The second line runs south from the east end of the last (plates XVII and XIX.). It has an open court (E) about 18 yards long, on the west side of which is the principal cave of the group (F) apparently a very primitive chaitya, flat-roofed, originally with four pillars supporting it, but they are all gone. The back has a nearly semicircular apse; and the cave measures 20 feet wide, by fully 26 feet deep, with a door nearly 5 feet wide. It is much filled up with earth, which the Darbâr began to clean out, but did not complete so far as to show whether there had been a Dahgoba inside or not: I suspect, however, if there was such an object in it, it must have been structural. In front of this apartment is a verandah 39 feet long by 7 feet 10 inches deep, from which two cells (G, G) are entered, one on each side the principal hall, and measuring about 7¾ feet wide by 9½ feet deep. The verandah has six square pillars, with *siñha* or lion brackets to the roof, which projects about 4 feet 2 inches. The façade of the verandah is also carved with very rude chaitya-window ornaments (see photograph, plate XIX.). At each end of the verandah a winged *siñha* is carved in low relief on the wall.

At the north end of the court and at a higher level, approached by steps, is a cave (H) having a verandah 6 feet 10 inches by 19 feet 7 inches, with a door and two windows. At the back of the verandah are two cells each about 9 feet 8 inches square. Into the back of these cells the quarry has already entered.

On the east side of the court are other cells, entirely choked up on my arrival, but which the Darbâr obligingly cleaned out partially. Two of them (I, I) consist of a small verandah with a cell at the back: the third was not excavated.

The base of a square pillar was found in the court (at *a*), but it was not fully excavated down to the rock.

Outside this court, to the south, is a cave (K) with a small sunk court (J) in front. The cave consists of a verandah and two cells, each about 9 feet 8 inches square. On the doors are some roughly executed carvings (plate XVIII. figs. 2 and 3), and over one of them is the *swastika* and other Bauddha symbols.

Next to this is another cave (L) with a bench round the small outer court. The door has a sort of arch traced over it (plate XVIII. fig. 1), and the cell inside, though partially filled up with earth, is considerably lower in the floor than outside. It is about 14 feet deep, by 11 feet wide in front, and 13 feet 4 inches at the back.

The third line of caves begins at the back of this and runs W.N.W. The first (M) consists of a small verandah with a door and two windows, and inside a cell 9 feet 3 inches by 9 feet 9 inches. The second (N) has a verandah 19 feet long by 5 feet 9 inches wide, and a hall 15 feet 5 inches by 17 feet 3 inches, with a single octagon pillar (O) in the centre supporting the roof. This is sketched in plate XVIII. fig. 4. The base of it is too much damaged to allow us to determine its shape, but the capital consisted of an abacus of three thin members, with the inverted water-jar form under it, as in the oldest caves at Nâsik and Junar.

The remaining three caves (P, Q, R) are quite plain, consisting of verandahs with door and two windows separated by square pillars, and two cells each inside, except the middle one, which has only one cell.

The rock in which these caves are cut, slopes down considerably to the south, so that the roofs of the last line are considerably beneath the floors of the first.

In front of the cells I, I (plate XVII.), which enter from the level of the court in front of them, was found, during the excavation, a square stone slab about 2 feet each way and 8 inches thick, with part of a Sâh inscription on one edge of it, in characters closely resembling those of the Rudra Dâmân inscription (see plate XX. fig. 1). Unfortunately the stone is soft calcareous sandstone, and many of the letters are indistinct; the workmen damaged one end of it, but, to add to the misfortune, some one carried it off to the Palace in the city, and in doing so seriously injured it at one corner. When I went to photograph it, I had a difficulty in tracing it; at length, however, it was found lying in a verandah in the circle in front of the palace. Dr. Bühler has kindly supplied me with the following transcript and notes on it:—

TRANSCRIPT OF THE SÂHA INSCRIPTION FROM A CAVE IN JUNÂGAḌH.

. . . . त्रृ . रग . . . चत्रप १
[स्वामि]चष्टनस्य प्र[पौ]त्रस्य राज्ञः चत्रपस्य स्वामिजयदामपौत्रस्य राज्ञो महाच २
[चै]त्रशुक्लपचस्य दिवसे पञ्चमे ५[५] इह गिरिनगरे देवासुरनागयचराचसेन्द्रि ३
. . प्रक(?)मिव प . . . केवलिज्ञानसंप्राप्तानां जितजरामरणानं(?) ४

" The slab on which the above inscription is written appears to have lost more than half of its original length. For as the inscription belongs to the time of a

1

2

3

4

Dinkar Moreshwar del.

W. Griggs lith.

PLATE XX.

I. SAH INSCRIPTION - FROM JUNÂGADH CAVES.

ROCK EXCAVATION AT MAHI GADECHI.

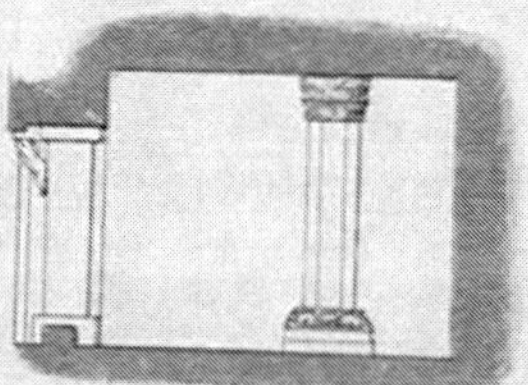

2. SECTION.

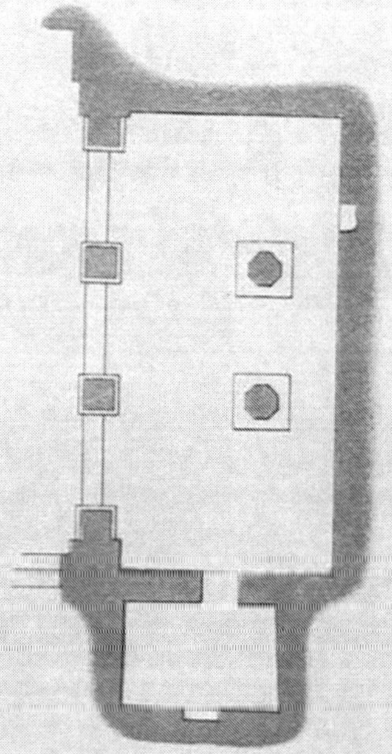

3. PLAN.

grandson of Svâmi Jayadâman, probably to Rudrasiṁha, son of Rudradâman,* the lost portion must have contained at least चपस्य रुद्रदामपुत्रस्य राज्ञः चत्रपस्य रुद्रसिंहस्य It is also probable that after the name of the king the year followed, both in words and figures, since line 4 gives the day of the month.

" The inscription gives no new information about the so-called Sâha kings. The most interesting point about it is the word *kevalijñânasamprâptânâm* ' of those who have obtained the knowledge of Kevalins.' *Kevalin* occurs most frequently in the Jaina scriptures, and denotes 'a person who is possessed of the *kevalajñâna* or true knowledge which produces final emancipation.' It would, therefore, seem that the inscription is Jaina."

From this it would appear that these caves were probably excavated for the Jainas by the Sâh kings of Surâshṭra about the end of the second century of the Christian era. They may, however, be much older, and the inscription may merely commemorate their being devoted to the Jainas by the Sâh king, possibly after they had ceased to be used by the Bauddhas: or, the inscription may have been brought from some other caves now entirely destroyed.

South-west by south from these caves, in a portion of rock left in the middle of a quarry, is a cave with two pillars in the front of the verandah. In plan these pillars are broken squares—so permanent in all Hindu works; and the capitals have drooping ears. Large numbers of caves most probably have been quarried away around this.

In the jungle within the north wall of Junâgaḍh, at Mâî-Gaḍechi, under an old Hindu or Jaina temple converted into a mosque, is a cave 26 feet 8 inches wide by 13 feet deep: the roof supported by two octagonal columns 9 feet 10½ inches high, with sculptured capitals (see plan and section, plate XX. figs. 2 and 3)—the sculpture, however, defaced and plastered over by its Muhammadan appropriators. The two square pillars which divide the front of the cave, have had *siñha* brackets on the outer face, and are 7 feet 10 inches high. At the west end is a small cell 8 feet 11 inches by 6 feet 2 inches.

It is by no means clear that this was a monastic abode: it seems quite as likely that it was a sort of garden retreat with a bath in front, similar to the one described below on the Uparkoṭ, and connected with the palace at Khâparâ Khodi. In the sunk area or court in front now stands the small cell or shrine of a *pîr* or *avliá*, about whom the attendant and others tell stories of the most grovelling and silly ignorance, of marvels equally absurd as they are purposeless.

b. The Uparkoṭ.

The Uparkoṭ or upper fort of Junâgaḍh, is probably a rich mine of antiquities. It seems to have been the citadel of the old city, where the lieutenants of the great Aśoka, and still later, of the Gupta kings, lived. Of the rise of the Chuḍâsamâ kings of Junâgaḍh we as yet know nothing. They held their court here, though they seem to have also lived occasionally at Wâmanasthali—the modern Vanthali or Banthali, where ruled Wâmanrâja, and later the Grâharipu†—probably a Chuḍâsamâ king—defeated and slain by Mularâja of Paṭṭan in the end of the tenth century (cir. A.D. 980).

* See the Jasdan pillar, *Journ. Bom. Br. As. Soc.* vol. VIII. pp. 234, 235; and *ante*, p. 15.

† Grâharipu is only a title or a nickname; he is described as an Ahir, a title which would apply to Naughan the foster son of Devât the Ahir: for the story as related in the *Dvyâśraya*, see *Ind. Antiq.* vol. IV. p. 72–77.

The whole enclosure of the Uparkoṭ is now covered with custard-apple trees, which are said to yield a rent of Rs. 1000 a year; but the débris on which they grow, and which is scattered unevenly in heaps, is suggestive of masses of buildings, of which these heaps cover the remains, and possibly of rock chambers below, with much sculpture.

The Uparkoṭ still contains some wells such as the Adî Chaḍî and Naughan wâvs, cut to a great depth in the soft rock. The Adî-Chaḍî wâv is descended by a long flight of steps, and has also a shaft just over the well. The sides of the descent show the most remarkable overlappings and changes of lie in the strata—for which alone it is worth a visit by anyone with geological tastes.

The Naughan wâv has a rock-cut passage, at least 10 feet wide, winding round its ample square area down to the bottom—perhaps 120 feet, with apertures into the shaft for light. On one side is a balcony, where tradition says the *kusumbâ* draught was brewed in a built cistern, still shown, when the Court came down to hold a drinking bout. This—like the story of the celestial horse that fell into the well, and only extricated himself at the instigation of a faqîr—is probably without a shadow of foundation: the cistern was used perhaps for ablution.

About the time I first visited Junâgaḍh in 1869, some rock-cut apartments were discovered at the bottom of a descent on the north of the Jâmi' Masjid. They are of considerable interest, for, though much defaced, they manifest a high style of art. Few bases, for example, could be found anywhere to excel in beauty of design and richness of carving those of the six pillars in the lower hall. (See plates XXI. and XXIV.)

Quite close to these excavations on their south side the ground sounds hollow, and there is a line of wall cropping up, exactly similar to those round the tops of the two openings which led to the discovery of those excavated.

The excavations opened up consist of a deep tank or bath (E, plate XXII.) about 11 feet square, with a covered verandah round three sides of it: that on the west side is occupied with a built seat (F)—like the *âsana* for an idol,—probably for laying the garments upon while bathing; and the pipes for the water come down the wall (H) from the surface, pass the front of this seat, and enter a small cistern (G) near the entrance at the south-west corner. The water must have been raised from some well in the neighbourhood and conveyed to the supply pipe; and the small cistern may have been formed to assist in filtering the water pure into the bath.

The corridor (D) on the south side is supported by two columns (B) with spiral ridges round them, making half a revolution in 4 feet 2 inches of height (fig. 5, plate XXIII.). They have octagonal plinth bases and capitals with floral ornamentations —the capitals probably carved with animal figures. The shafts of two corresponding attached pilasters (C, and fig. 6) on the north wall are divided into three sections each, having the grooves or ridges running in opposite spirals.

Over the bath (E) the roof is open, and round the opening a wall has been built, and still stands a foot or so above the ground level. (See section, fig. 3, plate XXIII.)

In the north wall is a large aperture or window (K) into the next chamber. This apartment (L) is entered from a door in the north-east corner of the bathroom leading to another in the south-east of this second room, which is a large chamber, 35 feet 10 inches long by 27 feet 10 inches wide, with six columns supporting the roof: the area between the first four of these—like that over the bath—is open to the air

ROCK EXCAVATION IN THE UPARKOṬ, JUNÂGAḌH. PLATE XXII.

1. UPPER FLOOR.

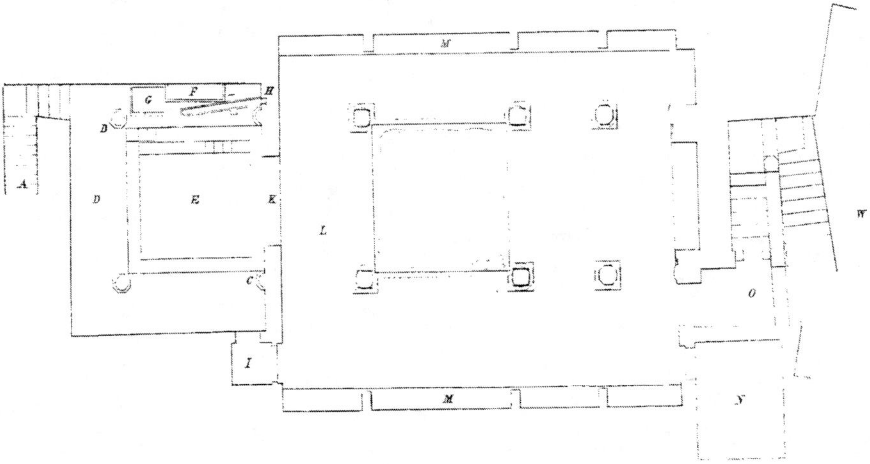

2. LOWER FLOOR.

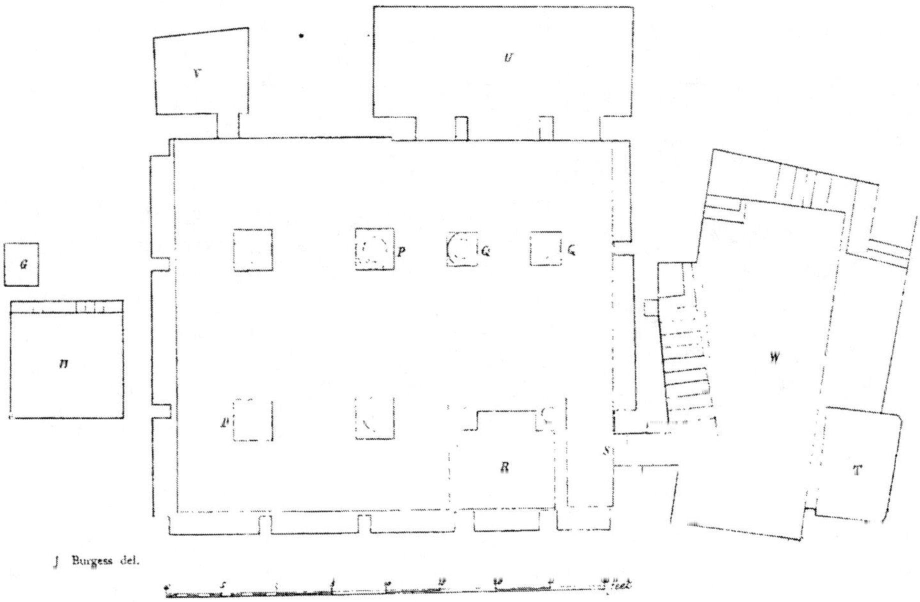

J Burgess del.

3. SECTION.

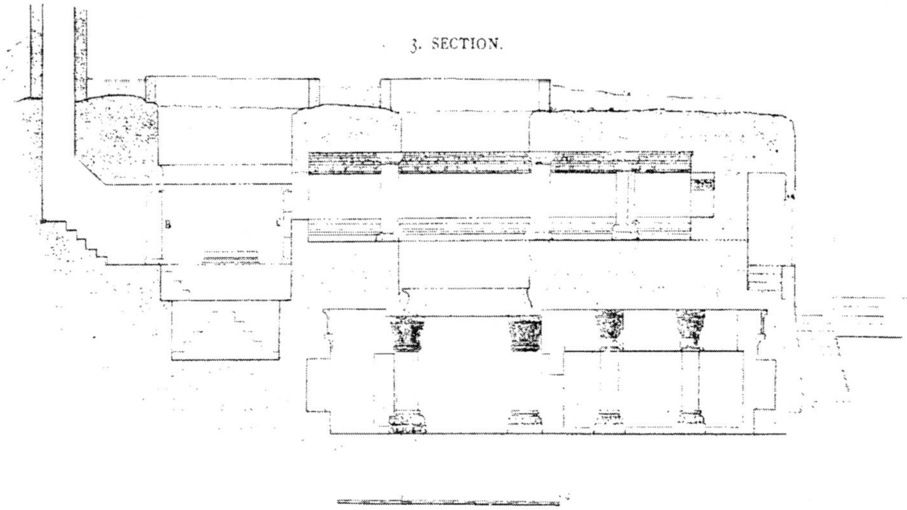

4. FRONT OF THE CELL (D) ON THE PLAN

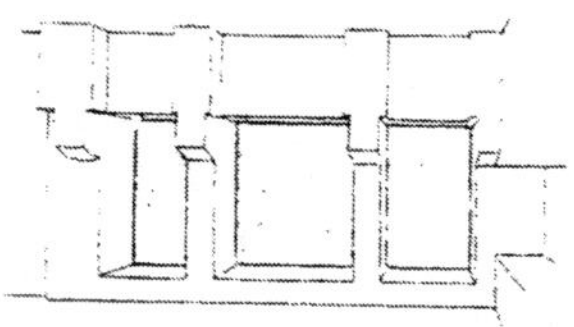

J. Burgess del.

7. ORNAMENTS FROM THE FRIEZE.

5. THE PILASTER (C) ON THE PLAN.

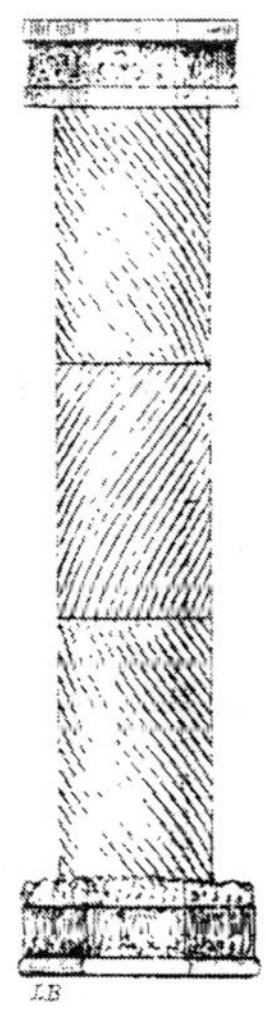

6. SKETCH OF THE PILLAR B.

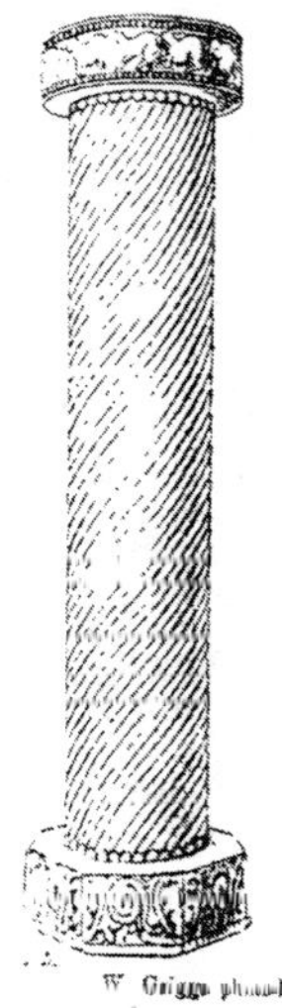

W. Griggs photolith.

COLUMNS IN THE ROCK-CUT HALL IN THE UPARKOṬ, JUNÂGAḌH PLATE. XXIV.

J. Burgess
Dinkar Moreshwar } delt.

W. Griggs lith

Scale of feet.

above, with a surrounding wall on the surface of the rock. It is also open to a hall below; and the four columns at the corners of it have been connected by a thin low parapet wall, about 20 inches high and 6 inches thick, now entirely destroyed. The rest of the area is occupied by the corridor on three sides, and by the space on the north where the remaining two pillars stand. In the walls on the north, east, and west sides are stone bench-recesses (M, M) divided into long compartments, with a base moulded in architectural courses below, and a frieze above, ornamented with *chaitya*-window and chequer carvings. The four pillars round the open area are square, the other two are sixteen-sided, and have been carved with animal figures on the abaci; but the bases and capitals of all six have been so destroyed that it is impossible to restore them.

In the north-east corner a door leads into a small apartment (N), which has a hole in the roof blackened with smoke, and which may have been used as an occasional cookroom, to prepare warm drinks, &c., for those who had been enjoying the bath. By the side of this apartment a door leads to a stair (O) descending to the entrance of the hall below.

This lower room measures 39 feet 6 inches by 31 feet and had evidently been filled up long before the one above it, and is consequently in a better state of preservation. It has been elaborately and very tastefully carved, as will be shown by the photograph (plate XXI.). On entering it we come on a platform (R, plate XXII., fig. 2) slightly raised and nearly square, with two short pillars on its west side, supporting a frame above descending from the roof. What this was meant for is hard to say, unless the depression within was intended to be filled with cotton or other soft substance to form a dais or a bed.

Except on the west side, the remainder of the walls is surrounded by a bench recess, divided at regular intervals, as in the apartment above. Over this recess the frieze is ornamented with *chaitya* windows having the Buddhist rail in the lower part of the opening, and two figures looking out of each: in many cases two females with something like "ears" on their head-dresses—but too indistinct to be distinguished what they represent (fig. 7, plate XXIII.).

The four columns (P, P) in the south end of this hall are larger than the two (Q, Q) in front of the supposed dais or bed, but the bases of all are alike, and the bodies of the capitals are similar. The rich bases have been already alluded to, and the drawings, (plate XXIV.) where the original pattern has been truthfully restored from the different fragments still left entire,—will give a better idea of them than any description could.

The abaci are carved with lions couchant at the corners; and in the middle of each is a figure, intended for a lion, facing outwards, with a human figure on each side of it. The body of the capital consists of eight divisions round, indicated by the breaks in the ledge at the bottom, on which the human figures of the different groups stand. Most of the figures, if not all, are females, apparently nude, or nearly so, and some standing under foliage. They have been cut with considerable spirit, and in high—almost entire—relief: unfortunately many of them have been seriously damaged. In the two smaller columns the principal member below the body of the capital is carved with the heads of animals—mostly goats or rams. On the larger columns the corresponding member is not so deep, and is a serrated torus (plate XXIV.).

At the back or west side of this hall are two small rooms; that on the south (V) with a single door, the other (U) with three entrances between jambs slightly advanced, and with a projecting frieze. The front of this is represented in Fig. 4, plate XXIII.

On the south wall are some scratchings, at first supposed to be an inscription: they are quite illegible, but were probably very much like those in Khâparâ Khodi or Khangâr's Mehal, referred to below, and probably the work of some visitor after the place had become neglected.

On the north side of this is an irregular excavation (W), in a corner of which there seems to be a shaft of a well (T) choked up; but the whole excavation here is more like the work of Maḥmûd Bigarah's quarrymen than any portion of the original work,—though it is quite probable that other chambers have been quarried away.

These rooms could have been no part of a monastic establishment, and the example of the old Mehal just to the north of this, suggests that they may have been either a sort of garden house belonging to the palace, or possibly the bath and pleasure house of another palace now interred under the débris that covers the whole of the Uparkoṭ.

The masjid is a very large structure, 136 feet 9 inches by 103 feet 6 inches inside,—but outside it looks clumsy and ugly to a degree, with horse-shoe kângrâs all round the walls and four plain solid tapering granite pillars at the corners. The inside is much better,—the columns, a hundred and forty in number, being slender and lofty, with demi-columns above, in all 15 feet 1 inch high. The third rows from the front and back, and the fifth and tenth rows across are rather stronger than the others, and in many cases arches have been thrown in between them, forming a sort of screen, which, if uniformly carried out, would have divided the whole into three great central areas and three of about half the size each along both back and front. The masjid was begun by Mahmûd Bigarah, but was probably never finished. The columns of the three principal octagonal areas in the centre are of granite, with truncated conical bases and thick toruses dividing the shaft into three equal portions, with a 10-inch bracket capital. These four columns in each area, 27 feet 3 inches high, rise above the roof, and on those of the south octagon lie wooden beams as if for a temporary roof. The columns in the other areas were perhaps never all set up. (See plan on plate XXV.)

The *mimbar* or pulpit is high, supported on arches with eleven steps up to the platform. The *mehrabs* are of white marble and exquisitely carved, but have lately been besmeared with whitewash.

Nearly opposite the Masjid is a large brass gun, 16 feet 11 inches long, 2 feet diameter at the breach, and about 19 inches at the muzzle, with a 9-inch bore. From the muzzle to the touch-hole is 16 feet 3 inches. Over the mouth, and on the middle of the barrel, are two inscriptions, recording that it was 'ordered to be made by Sulṭân Suliman bin Sulîm Khân in A.H. 937 (A.D 1530–31) on purpose that it should be employed in the destruction of the infidels in Hind. Maker of the gun Muhammad bin Hamzal of Misr (*or* Egypt).' With another about 13½ feet long, now on one of the bastions, it was brought here from Diu.

The inner gate of the fort is a genuine fragment of the old Râjput citadel, but it would be difficult to say precisely of what age; it is probably older than the time of Manḍalika V., who repaired the fort in A.D. 1450, but it does not seem older than A.D. 1200,—to about which date it may be assigned.

On the ramparts above is an inscription of Manḍalika V., dated Samvat 1507 (A.D. 1450), but much defaced by the Muhammadans.

PLAN OF THE GREAT MOSQUE ON THE UPARKOṬ AT JUNÂGAḌH. PLATE XXV.

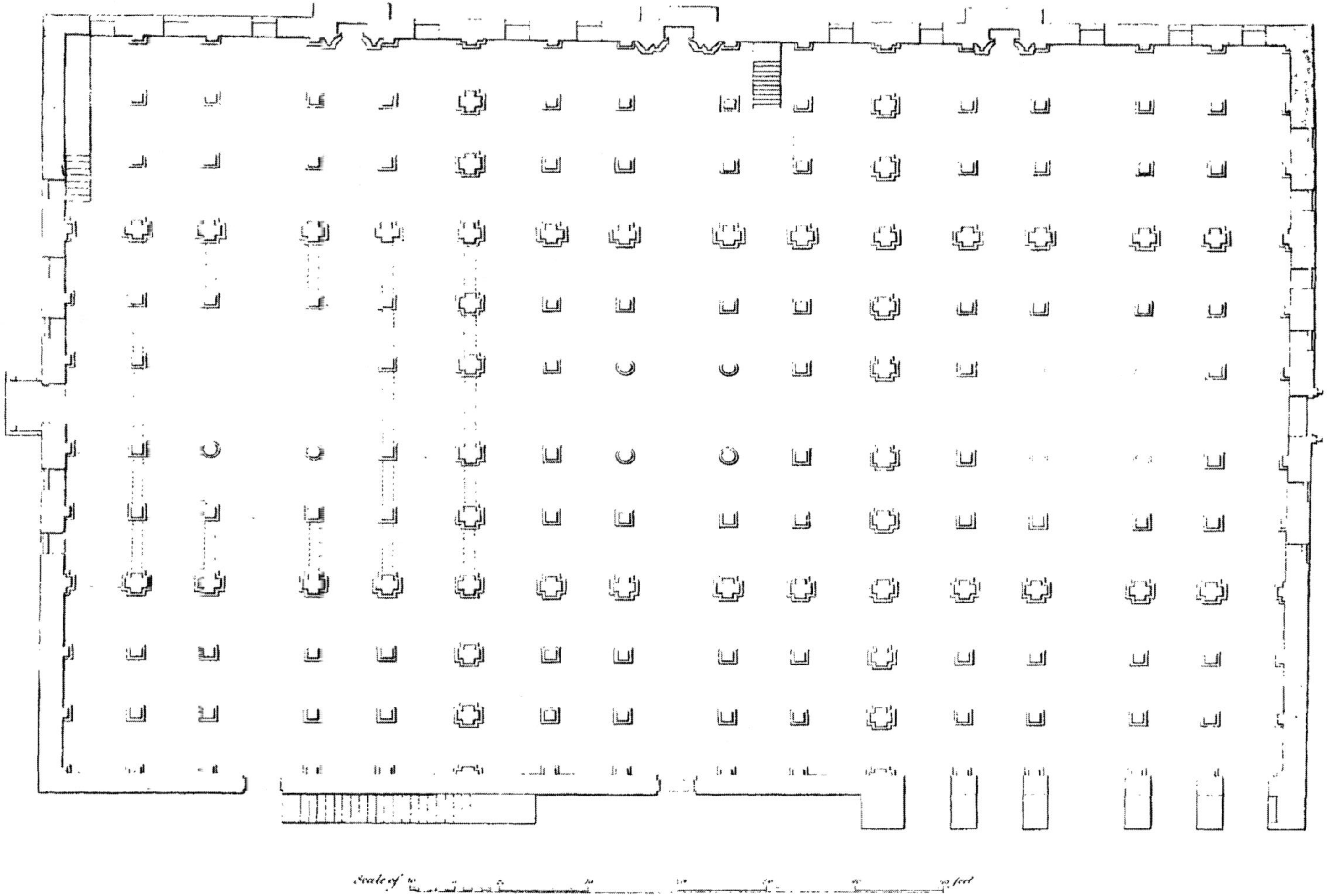

J. Burgess Surv.

Gangadi Purshotam del.

c. KHÂPARÂ KODI OR KHANGÂR'S MEHAL.

To the west of the cave at Mai Gaḍechî is the rock of Kâparâ Khodi, now rapidly disappearing before the Nawâb's quarrymen,—but in which is still to be seen a *portion* of an ancient rock-hewn dwelling, originally of great extent, and still locally known as Khangâr's Mehal or palace. (See plates XXVI. and XXVII.) What still remains of it extends fully 250 feet in length, through the rock, and has a width at one part of about 80 feet; but as the rock has been quarried entirely away, up to these limits, on three sides, it is impossible to tell what was its original extent or plan. "It was too old," said a man I spoke to, "to be of any use, and so the Darbâr gave it up to be quarried." This, I believe, represents the genuine local view on the point. Would that we had had a plan and a few descriptive notes of its original extent and details with copies of its inscriptions, before the quarrymen touched it!

Beginning at the west end (see plate XXVII.), we find on the top of the rock two stairs descending, the one (A) from the south, and the other (B) from the north; by the former of these we enter the south side of a hall (C) about 38 feet 8 inches square, with four heavy pillars in the floor enclosing an area about 15 feet square, which is open to the air above. In the south-west corner the wall has been broken through from the quarry (at D). On the west side is a small unfinished recess (E); and at the north-west corner is a somewhat larger one (F) with two pillars in front, and open into the quarry on its west side. At the south-east corner a door leads to the foot of the other stair already mentioned, and opposite to it is a door entering a much larger hall (G), 61 feet by 60, with sixteen pillars on the floor (one of them destroyed) arranged in fours round four areas, each about 15 feet square, and open above, leaving between them two aisles crossing at right angles in the centre. All the pillars are quite devoid of carving, and have a re-entrant angle at the corner of the open square. They are not exactly of the same dimensions, nor perfectly symmetrically arranged, nor are the sides of the rooms quite straight. Round the walls has been a bench. On the north wall is the following inscription: but the wall is rough and full of small holes, so that the points are read doubtfully:—

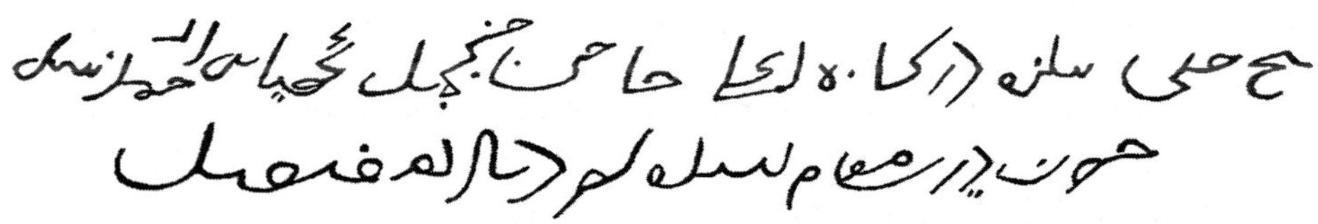

This is defective, probably from some word or words wanting or hewn away at the beginning. After the first few letters, Professor Blochmann reads *bandah i dargâh i a'la Hâjî Muhammad* . . . . "the slave of the highest throne Haji Muhammad" . . . the rest of the line being unintelligible. The second line reads,—*Hazrat derî-maqâm bandah bimurd sâl haftsad,* "Hazrat (*God*?) is everlasting. The slave died, year 700." The style is very bad; but if a genuine record, it would seem to indicate that Muhammadans were settled in Junâgaḍh in the end of the thirteenth century.

On the east side, near the north end, a door leads into what must have been a spacious apartment. The back or north corridor (H) is 111 feet in length by 10½ feet wide, and has returned along the east and west sides. The west side is entirely ruined by the quarry, but on the east it extends about 90 feet, by 8 feet 10 inches wide inside the pillars. In front of this has been a passage (I) about 9 feet wide and open above, and within this again a second covered corridor (J) about 10 feet wide, including the columns: on the east side, however, there is a wall affording support to a stair (K) ascending from the open passage to the roof or top of the rock. Within this the whole is quarried away. Under the centre of this apartment there is a passage, but whether for sewage or as a sècret entrance, can scarcely be determined: it is quite choked up with earth and rubbish.

Leaving this by a door on the north side, we enter a hall (L) extending east and west, 67 feet 4 inches by about 16 feet 10 inches wide, which has recently been used to burn lime in. Two pillars still support the roof, but others have been destroyed, as has the whole of the front up to and under which the quarry has recently been extended. At each end is a chamber measuring 17 feet by 8 feet 9 inches with two pillars in front —one gone in each case.

At the north-east corner of this a fragment of an apartment (M) is left, showing that, in this direction at least, the excavations extended further. And just behind this is the side of a shaft (N) which descended from the top of the rock into the subterranean passage already mentioned. The rest has been recently quarried away.

Returning into the long corridor we find another door further east, which, by a short passage (O) running to the north-east, leads into a long deep passage (P) running ESE, about 30 yards, till stopped by a wall: in the other direction it passes a recess (Q) 11 feet 4 inches by 9 feet 9 inches, and is then lost in the quarry. This passage is open up to the top of the rock, and, in parts at least, is much filled up with rubbish.

On the back wall of the recess (Q) just mentioned is a short inscription cut in very large characters, thus:

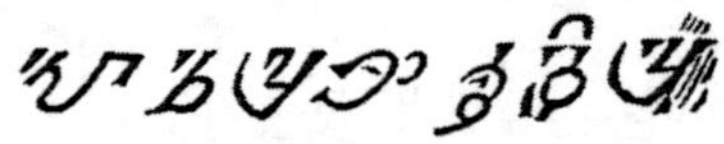

There are many scribblings on the pillars and walls of the other apartments, but the stone is so rough and worn that without a thorough knowledge of the alphabet or alphabets (for there are more than one) it would be almost impossible to transcribe a single line with perfect accuracy. The following three may be taken as specimens:

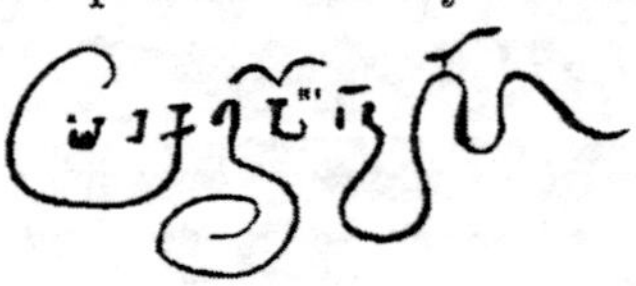

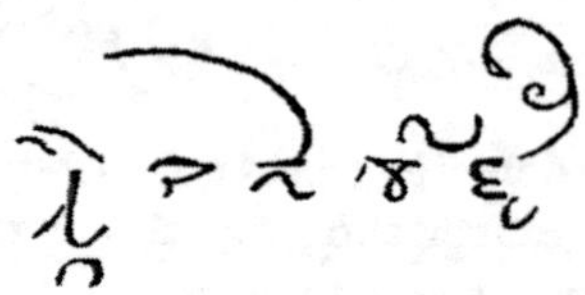

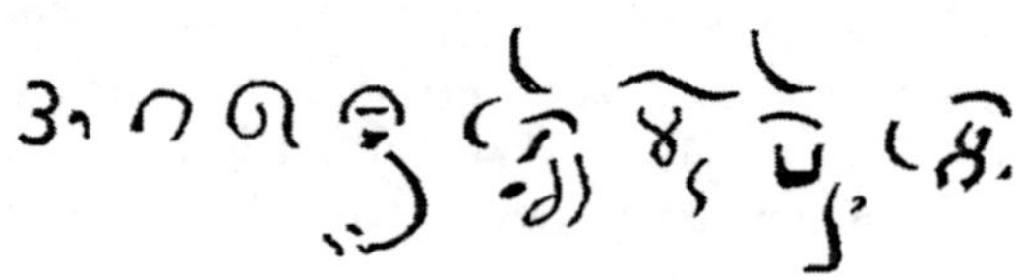

But, so far as my memory serves me, there were inscriptions, only six years ago, in the old Pâli character; Colonel Tod also distinctly states so. But now they have entirely disappeared with the chambers in which they were: the forms of the letters alone would have helped us to assign an age to these works; but, unless copies are to be found among

ROCK-CUT APARTMENTS AT JUNÂGADH. PLATE XXVII.

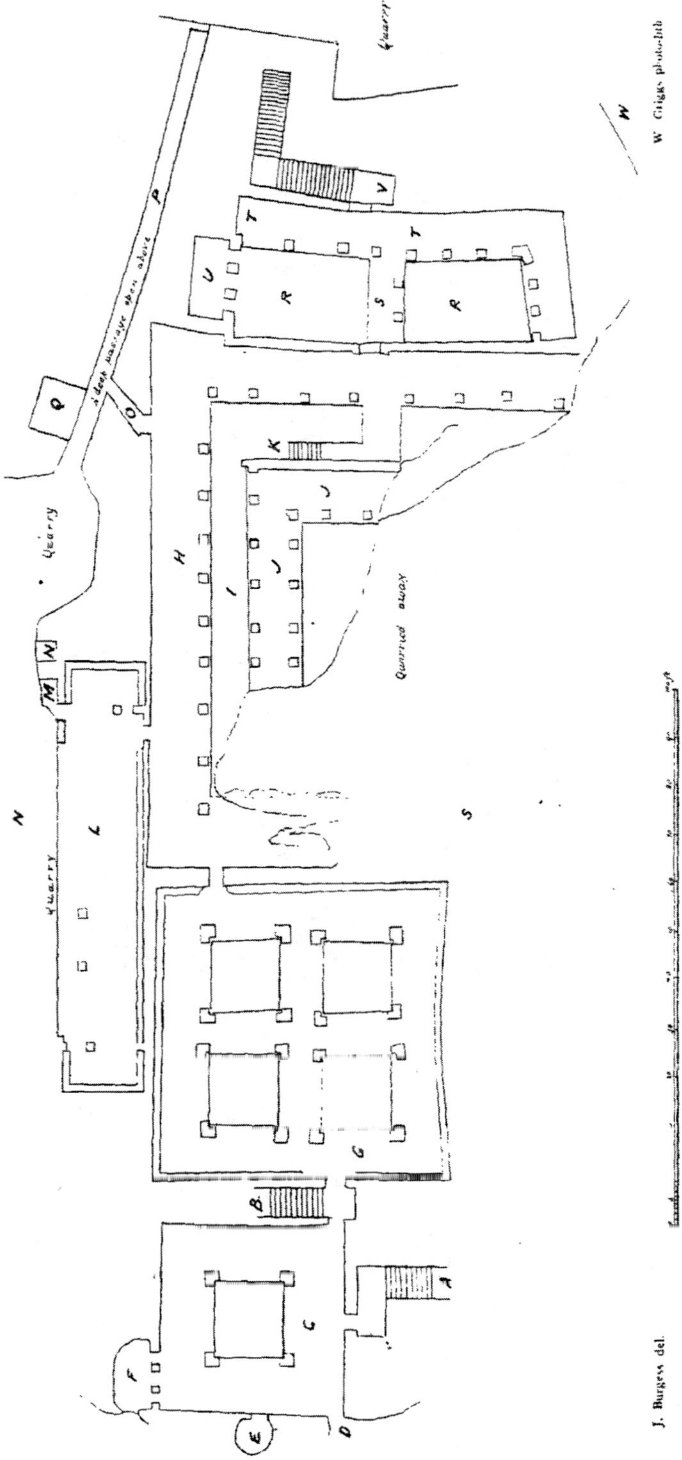

J. Burgess del.

W. Griggs photo-lith

Dr. Bhau Dâji's papers, there is probably no record left of these inscriptions. Let us hope there are, and that they will be given to the world in time to be of some use!

Returning again to the large corridor, and leaving it by a door in the east side, we enter the last apartment, more irregular in shape than any of the rest, and consisting of two open areas (R, R), divided by a covered passage (S), and having a corridor (T, T) round the east and south sides, and at the north end a room (U), 7 feet 5 inches deep by 17 feet long, with two pillars in front. The two areas with the covered passage measure together about 62 feet by 17.

Opposite to the entrance door another leads out to the foot of a stair (V), which ascends to the north, turning round to the east and landing within a few feet of the end of the deep open passage referred to, and over the brink of the quarry on this side.

A little to the south of this (at W) are a few small detached rooms, quite choked up.

The roofs over these chambers are 10, 12, or more feet in thickness; and along the edges of the open areas are fragments of pillars and indications of sockets, &c. (see plate XXVI.), showing that, while excavated to give air and light, these areas were protected by roofs to keep out the glare of the noon-day summer sun and the rains of the monsoon. There are some traces also of what I take to have been channels to carry off the water. The indications, however, do not tend to show that any considerable portion of the structure was above the rock, from which to infer that these retreats were only the substructures of a palace intended for coolness during the heat of the day.

Besides the Mai-Gaḍechi excavations there are other fragments left, well to the south of these last, and just under the scarp of the Uparkoṭ and also at Naudurgâ. These also have quite recently suffered from the quarrymen; but no doubt many others were quarried away in the time of Mahmûd Bigarah (A.D. 1470–82) when he built the present city and renamed it MUSTAFÂBÂD.

d. TALÂJÂ AND SÂNÂ CAVES.

In the south-east of the peninsula, at Talâjâ, called in Sanskrit Tâlugiri, and in modern vernacular parlance the *Tékri* of Talâjâ, near the mouth of the Śatruñjî river, is an almost conical, isolated rock, probably of volcanic origin and about 320 feet high, crowned by two modern Jaina temples, one on the vertex, the other on a sort of shoulder on the west face. The town lies on the north and west slopes, having the Talâjî—a feeder of the Śatruñjî river, to the north of it.

At the confluence are three images of Mahâdeva or Śiva, called by the joint name of Panchanâtha, "the five lords," regarding which, tradition says, that Râmachandra, on his way to the south, set up five images here, whence the name of Panchanâtha: the fourth is in the town in the temple of Talâjâ Bhavânî Mâtâ, and the fifth at the village of Śobhâwad, a mile from it.

The view from the top of the hill is one of surprising beauty; the almost perfectly level, rich plain stretching away to the east, west, and south, the Śatruñjî river winding across the foreground until it debouches into the Gulf of Khâmbhât to the south-east, whilst away to the north-west are low hills, behind which rises the famed Śatruñjaya Mount.

The Talâjâ hill is remarkable for the Buddhist caves on its north-west face, of which there are fully thirty, with fifteen to twenty tanks or cisterns for water. They have once been more numerous; but many of them have been destroyed probably to make room for, and a passage up to the Jaina temples or their predecessors on the top. One of the largest of them, and the only one that now presents any remains of ornamentation, is at a height of fully a hundred feet. It is locally known as the Ebhal Maṇḍapa, and measures 75 feet by 67½, and is 17½ feet high. This large hall, without any cells entered from within, had four octagonal pillars in front, but none inside, to support the roof; nor has it the wall that at Ajaṇṭâ and elsewhere usually divides such excavations into an outer verandah and an inner hall. Outside the entrance, however, there are wells or tanks on both sides, and several cells. There are fragments of a modified—perhaps a very primitive—form of the horse-shoe or chaitya-window ornament, and of the Buddhist rail pattern on the façade of the cave (see photograph, plate XXVIII.); but this is the only remains of sculpture now traceable among these caves. It takes its modern local designation from one of the Wâlâ Râjput chiefs, of whom Ebhal, the founder of the race, is said to have come from Mewâḍ, perhaps about 1000 A.D., and another Ebhal, the sixth in descent from him, took Talâjâ from the Kolîs about the beginning of the twelfth century. The tradition runs, that this Ebhal performed the marriage ceremonies (*kanyâdana*) of his daughter here; and for the preparation of the accompanying feasts so much clarified butter (*ghî*) was necessary, that two Vânias—Ranka and Vanka, who contracted to supply it—conveyed it by a drain into the tank on the west side of the entrance to the cave, since called the Ghî well (*Ghî no kuo*).

A somewhat difficult path past the Ebhal Maṇḍapa leads up to the caves known as Mor-Medi, from the peafowl (*mor*) making them a roosting place. To the west of them are the Chambeli (or Jasmine) caves, below which is a tank, and through one of them we pass into an inner dark cell. A little to the east is the cave of Kodiyâr—a local Mâtâ or demon goddess, and by the path to it is a tank of excellent water which lasts throughout the year. In a cell near by is a liṅga attended by an Atît Bâwâ, supported by an allowance from the Bhaunagar Darbâr.

Higher up the hill is a small cave called the shop of Ranka and Vanka, and still higher one called the school of Narsingh Mehta—the famous Śaiva mystic poet of Surâshṭra. It is now used as a shrine of the monkey demigod Hanumân. A little above this, on the right hand, is a pretty large cave with some seven or eight cells in it, and a tank at each side of it. In an enclosure above this are eight tanks said to contain water all the year round, and close by is a ruined Chaitya cave, containing a *dahgoba* or stone cylinder with hemispherical top—of a very simple type—the base only entire, and the remains of the *torana* or capital still attached to the flat roof of the cave. It is now called the "storehouse of wealth" (*dravya*), and is believed by the people to contain hidden treasure. The *dahgoba* and general arrangements of these caves are sufficient indications of their being Buddhist works; and though we have no very definite means of determining their antiquity, yet from the simplicity of their arrangements, and—except that already mentioned on the façade of the Ebhal Maṇḍap—from the entire absence of sculpture, such as is common in all the later Buddhist caves, we may relegate them to a very early age, probably before the Christian era, and possibly even to the age of Aśoka or soon after.

The rock is of very different qualities in different parts of the hill, but where the existing caves are executed it is full of quartz veins, ramified among nodules of varying degrees of hardness, and the disintegration of these, under the effects of atmospheric

1. CHAITYA CAVE

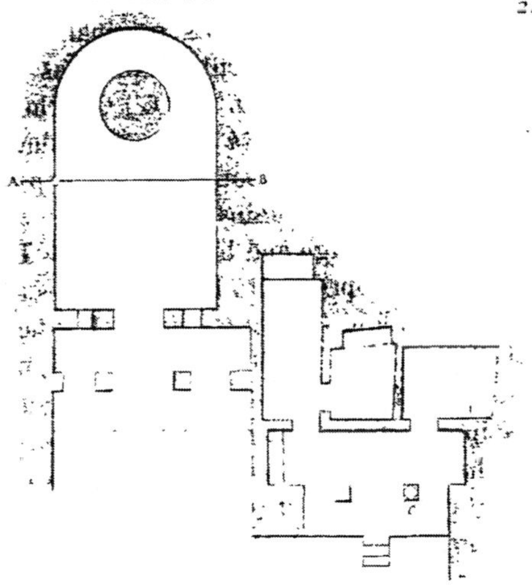

2. SECTION ON A.B.

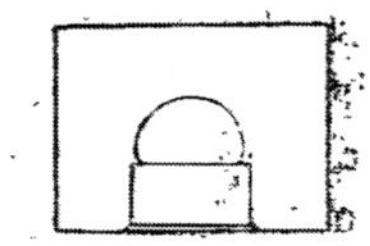

3. PILLAR C

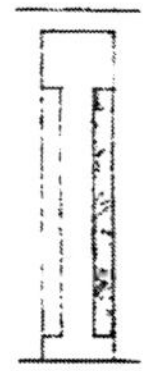

4. BHIMA CHAWADI VIHARA.

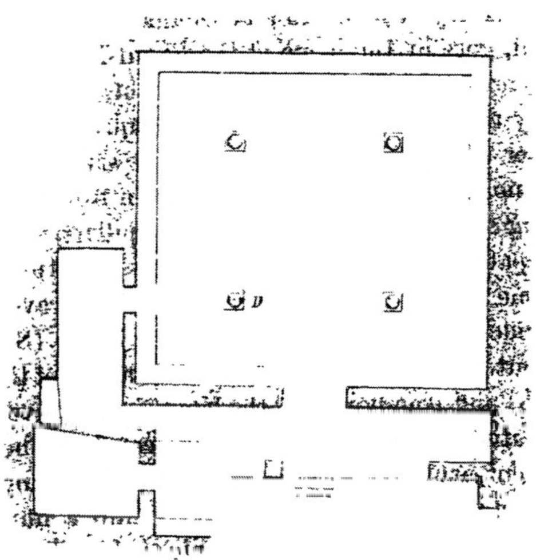

5. PILLAR D

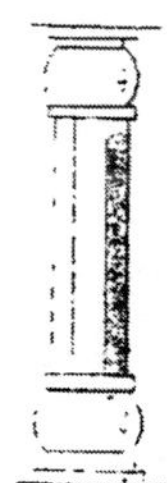

J. Burgess del. W. Griggs photolith

Scale to the Plans

influences, has so destroyed the original surface that if any inscriptions ever existed they must have disappeared long ago.

The court round the small Jaina temple on the shoulder of the hill is paved with slabs, and the temple itself has a pretty marble floor. The image of the Tîrthankara it contains was discovered in an underground cellar when digging the foundations of a house about sixty-five years ago, and bears a short inscription of its original dedication in Samvat 1437 (A.D. 1380) by two Vaiśya brothers. The present temple was built to enshrine it by a Śeth or Jaina of Râdhanpur and completed in 1814. On the top of the *tekrî* or hill is another temple with a four-faced or *chaumukh* image of Ṛishabnâtha, the first of the twenty-four Tîrthankaras, erected in 1820 by another Râdhanpur Śeth and his wife, of the Śrîmâli *gachha* or caste-division of the Jainas.

A march to the south-west from Râjulâ is the village and hill of Lor or Lauhar in Bâbriâwâḍ, in which are some natural caves appropriated to local divinities and one small and perfectly plain excavation probably a Buddhist ascetic's cell. Farther west, and not far from the village of Vânkiâ is the Sânâ hill,—a wild, desolate place, with not a human habitation in sight. Close to the foot of the hill is a perennial stream which aids to redeem the view, and doubtless helped to tempt the first ascetics to hew out their dwellings in the adjoining rock. The hill consists of several spurs from a central ridge, on the top of which are some brick foundations. The bricks are of that very large size never made, so far as we know, in mediæval times or modern, and only found in the most ancient class of buildings in the province.

The hill is honeycombed by about sixty-two caves, some of them much ruined, but all of them of the same plain types as those at Talâjâ, Junâgaḍh and Ḍhânk. Here too, one of the largest, near the bottom of the hill, goes by the name of the Ebhal Maṇḍapa. It is 68½ feet by 61, and about 16½ feet high, originally with six pillars in front, but none inside. A modern stone erection—apparently the den of some outlaw—occupies a large portion of the interior. About 120 feet higher up the hill, on the face of the same spur, is a cave called the Bhima Chauri, facing the north-east;* it has a verandah in front, and measures about 38 by 40½ feet, the roof being supported by four octagonal pillars, with capitals and bases of the Lotâ, or water-pot, pattern so frequent in the Nâsik and Junar caves. Round the sides also runs a raised stone bench—a common feature in such caves. Close by is a Chaitya or chapel cave, 18 feet wide by 31 feet deep and 13½ feet high. (See plan, plate XXIX. fig. I.) The roof is flat, but the inner end or back of the cave is of the semi-circular form already noticed at Junâgaḍh, and common in all the later Chaitya caves. It wants the side aisles usual in such excavations, and the *dahgoba*, 7 feet 10 inches in diameter, is very plain and without ornament, while its *torana* or capital is wanting, having probably been broken off by later Hindus in order to convert it into a huge *linga* or emblem of Śiva, which it is now worshipped as such by the people of the villages in the neighbourhood. (See plate XXIX. fig 2.) Some of the excavations consist merely of verandahs with cells opening from them, as at Junâgaḍh, and having recesses in the walls, as at Junar and Nâsik, as if for sleeping places; others are halls like the Ebhal Maṇḍapa, with cells arranged near the entrance, while there are two other small Chaityas besides that mentioned above. High up the face of the hill there is at least one large cistern of excellent water; and large portions of the stairs, hewn out in the rock and leading from one group of caves to another, are still pretty entire.

* See Plate XXIX., fig. 4.

The caves here, as at Talâjâ, must be attributed to a very early age, and may be regarded as among the oldest in Western India.

e. Caves at Ḍhânk.

Ḍhânk is about 30 miles W.N.W. from Junâgaḍh, and is the old Tilatila Paṭṭan, Prehpaṭṭan, or Rehewâs Paṭṭan,* a place formerly of considerable extent, though but little now remains of the ancient city but dust and débris. To the west of the present town is a rocky hill with a small temple a-top; this hill is covered with the ruins of an old fort. One of the old wells or *wâvs* is called the Wâv of Manjuśrî (a name familiar to the northern Buddhists) or Manjêsarî—for the villagers pronounce the word in more ways than one. In one of the *gokhlês*, or niches, is an old loose image, so like a Buddhist figure of a Nâga-protected worshipper as to suggest this as its origin. The Chaitya window ornament over the niches, in the well and the lintel of the doorway into the enclosure where it is—which lintel is the *siñhâsana* of a Buddha, with lions at the ends, two folds of the cloth depending in front, and the wheel set edgewise in the centre —both indicate that Buddhism must have prevailed here. The old temple of Manjesarî or Manjuśrî was pulled down some time ago, and a Śaiva or *liṅga* shrine now stands on its base. The chambers that remain in the old fort are also associated in local tradition with this Manjuśrî.

In a small ravine to the west of the hill are some Buddhist caves. The sides of this ravine,—of the same soft calcareous sandstone as at Junâgaḍh,—have been quarried or cut out; the bottom is now filled up with soil. The first cave faces north-west, and is entered by a door scarcely 4 feet high, inside which there is a descent of about 2 feet to the floor. The cell measures 7 feet 9 inches deep by 8 feet 4 inches long, with a small niche about 22 inches square in each end. At the back, on each side of the shrine door, and now much decayed, has been the figure of a Buddha in the usual attitude, with the soles of the feet turned up and his hands over them. Over his head is the triple *chattri* or umbrella, a *chauri*-bearer at each side, and small flying figures above. The sill of the shrine door is about 20 inches from the floor, and the door about 3 feet high by 2½ feet wide. The shrine is only a large niche about 2 feet deep, with a Buddha squatted on a *siñhâsana* at the back of it: on the *siñhâsana*, the lions, drapery, and central wheel are all distinctly traceable; at each side stands a *chauri*-bearer with a high head-dress or *mukuṭa* now much rotted away.

A little to the north of this, up the ravine, the face of the wall has been sculptured with a number of figures in low relief, and without much evidence of art. The largest figure is only about 30 inches high, including the snake hood over his head. They are:—

1. A woman with a child on her left knee, her right elbow resting on her right knee, and her hand pointing up. She has heavy earrings, and apparently a frontal ornament in the parting of her hair, which is wavy and clustering.

2. Close to her is a standing figure exactly like a Pârśvanâtha in the IVth cave at Bâdâmî (figured in my *Report on Belgâm and Kaladgi*, plate XXXVI. fig. 3), standing on a triple pillow, with a snake rising behind him, and its seven hoods just over his head. There are five bends of the snake on each side. The image has elongated ears, and short curly hair, and is about 27 inches high.

---

* *Ind. Ant.* vol. II. p. 315.

3. At his right hand is a small sitting figure about 8 inches high.

4. Buddha with a broad face, poorly cut, on a *siñhâsana* or lion-throne, having the wheel and deer or antelopes in the centre, folds of the drapery of the seat hanging down, and lions at the ends. His hair is represented, as usual, with a knob or tuft on the crown :—or, perhaps, this is meant to represent the staff of the triple umbrella over his head. Standing on the ends of the throne are the usual *chauri*-bearers.

5. A standing Buddha 26 inches high, with elongated ears, and what look like ringlets over each shoulder, as in the figure of a Jina in Cave IV. at Bâdâmi, and repeated in Cave I. at Aihoḷe, with long arms, as at Cave XIX. at Ajaṇṭâ, and two *chauri*-bearers 10 to 12 inches high,—one apparently with the head of an animal,—but they are so decayed that it is doubtful to say with certainty what it is. Below the one on Buddha's right is a compartment 16 inches high by 12 inches wide, out of which the figure has been entirely obliterated.

6. A squatting Buddha, 18 inches high, on a pillow placed upon the *siñhâsana*, with bearers as in No. 4.

7. A similar figure, but the seat is worn away.

8. Another, of which the head is gone. The throne is higher; and over this figure and the last, the triple umbrella is rudely carved, with something like foliage at each side over the *chauri*-bearers, who are 15 inches high with disproportionately big heads.

9. A third, similar to the last two; the *chattris* are better represented and pendant foliage or tassels hang over the head of the *chauri*-bearers. The *âsana* has three lions in front, as at Bâdâmi and Aihoḷe, and the wheel is carved on the rock below the central lion. At the four corners of this sculpture are holes in the rock as if to fasten on some screen or covering :—the same thing was remarked of a similar Bauddha figure in one of the caves of the Mânmoḍi Hill at Junar.

10. A deep recess in which there has been sculpture, but it has entirely disappeared, except a small flying figure at one corner.

These figures seem pretty well to have exhausted the pantheon of the Preh Paṭṭan Buddhists,—who were perhaps a poor and but little patronized community,—for we find but few traces of sculpture elsewhere.

At the north side of the recess, the rock is cut away for some distance back, leaving a sort of court open to the ravine on the WNW. side. There is a considerable accumulation of rubbish in it, so that the floors of the cells entered from it are all under the outside level. At the south end is the upper part of a door, through which, with difficulty, one can squeeze himself, feet foremost, into a cell, in which it is said there was a sort of well of considerable depth, if not a cave below it; but the whole was filled up a few years ago by the political officers to keep outlaws from making a den of it.

On the east wall of the court are two horizontal grooves: the upper and smaller one running along the north and south ends also: the lower, at least, has been for the bearings of a roof which doubtless originally covered this court; and the squared stones lying about, may be those of the front wall of it.

In the east side is a recess from which the image has entirely disappeared; but over the front of it is left the triple *chattri*, and remains of flying figures or Buddhist cherubs on each side. A little to the south of this is a door leading into a cell, much filled up, measuring 8 feet 9 inches by 12 feet 2 inches. It has a small recess at the back.

On the north side of the court is another cell with two entrances,—nearly filled up; and over the front of this is a groove in the rock, slanting up from each side—gable-end fashion. At the corner, where the scarp turns to the north again, are two niches (*gokhlés*) in the rock, with holes above as if for wooden fastenings or bearings.

f. Siddhsar Caves.

Some miles west from Ḍhank, towards Siddhsar, in a ravine called Jhinjuri-jhar, are some caves cut in calcareous sandstone. Probably there have been others further up the ravine, but, if so, the decay of the rock has destroyed all trace of them. The furthest to the south has been a verandah facing east, with two cells, measuring 8 by $9\frac{1}{2}$ feet and $7\frac{3}{4}$ by $9\frac{1}{2}$ feet respectively. It probably never had any pillars in front, and the drip line is not straight, but follows the edge of the rock.

The next cave has two cells, one $9\frac{1}{2}$ by 8 feet communicating with the second, on its north side measuring $7\frac{3}{4}$ by $9\frac{1}{2}$ feet, which has two octagonal pillars in front with square bases and capitals. The pillars are connected below with the pilasters by a low screen carved in front with the Buddhist rail of a large pattern—each division being 5 inches wide. This is the only trace of ornament about these caves.

The next and last to the north is a much larger one, and has had six square pillars in front of a narrow verandah; of these the three pillars to the south of the door and one at the north end still remain. The front wall is pierced only for a door, and this had been built up some years ago to keep out the Wâgher outlaws. On pulling down so much of it as to gain entrance I found that, like the excavations in Khâparâ Khodi at Junâgaḍh, it had an open area in the centre measuring about 13 feet by 20; this had been quite filled in from above, which rendered it impossible to examine the entire arrangements and secure a plan; but it appeared to consist of apartments round this open court, divided by walls and with pillars in front.

On a stone a little to the west of this, I observed the first three letters of what appeared to be an inscription, but on clearing it of earth I could make little out except the following:—

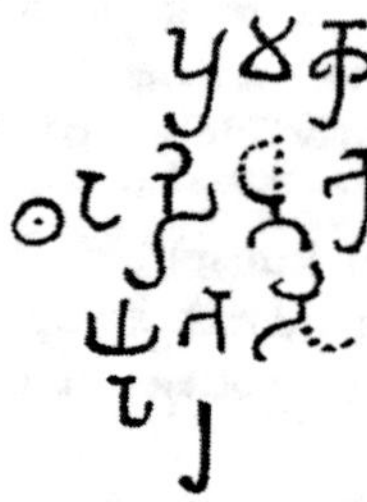

There were similar letters also on other stones close by.

In another ravine to the west of this, and running into it a little to the north-west, are other caves. The first reached is a verandah $18\frac{1}{2}$ feet long and fully 5 feet wide, with two windows, and a door about 4 feet wide, separated by square pillars, as at Junâgaḍh, and in the second cave in Jhinjuri-jhar. The drip is an irregular line accommodated to the face of the rock. From the north end of the verandah a cell is entered by a door and two narrower openings each about 14 inches wide. This chamber measures

$6\frac{1}{2}$ by $8\frac{3}{4}$ feet, and has a door in the right-hand wall, near the back, into a second room $8\frac{3}{4}$ by $7\frac{1}{4}$ feet.

A little higher up the ravine, to the south-west, is a second cave having a verandah with two square pillars in front, and two cells, one of them much decayed.

On the way back to Ḍhank I struck the road to Siddhsar near a large old well or *wâv*, repaired, like others around, in comparatively modern times, with arches thrown across where the old lintels had given way. This *wâv* belongs to the ancient city, said to have been overthrown by the curse of an ascetic, and which, if covering anything like the area pointed out, must have been a very large place. One of the *gokhlês* has a rough sketch of a chaitya window over it filled with a *kirtimukh* or large grinning face. At the turning of the descent, near the top, are four niches, the sill of which is carved with the Greek-like pattern, found at Bâdâmî, and also at many places in Kâṭhiâwâḍ, of leaves and dentils: the old base below is much decayed.

Turning off to the west from the village of Hariêsana on the way from Ḍhank to Bhânwâḍ, into a gorge on the west side of the Gaḍhkâ hill, I visited the Kâprâ Kodiâ caves between Pâṭṭan and Siddhsar. Like most others all over Kâṭhiâwâḍ, they are perfectly plain with square pillars in the verandahs, and without any trace of shrines or images.

Of the most southerly, furthest up the ravine, and facing east, the front has fallen away, and the two cells only remain.

The second is a single cell, of which the front of the verandah also has dropped down.

The third is a verandah returning forwards on the left, with five square pillars roughly blocked out, and a cell at the back on the extreme right.

The fourth has a verandah $23\frac{1}{2}$ feet long by 6 feet wide, with two massive square pillars in front, and two cells behind—one 8 feet by $10\frac{1}{4}$, and the other $11\frac{1}{4}$ feet by $9\frac{1}{4}$ feet.

The fifth has been a large cave, but the roof has fallen in, and the apartment at the back, with a wide door, is quite choked up. If there has been any chaitya or shrine in the series it must have been in this cave.

The sixth is a simple cell.

The seventh has two octagonal pillars in front, and is $12\frac{1}{2}$ feet deep by $15\frac{1}{4}$ feet long, with two large cells—one at the back and the other on the left side.

Close to it is the eighth, the pillars of the front of which are gone. It is $9\frac{3}{4}$ feet deep by 33 feet in length, with two cells at the back very clumsily cut.

Next to this we come to the remains of a stair up to the top of the rock, and beyond it to the ninth and last cave, which is only a roughly hewn-out verandah, with one cell at the north end, and the entrance to another begun.

X. MOUNT GIRNAR.

The present bridge at the inscribed rock, as stated before, is a modern erection, and leads into a picturesque glen, well wooded, and with frequent Hindu shrines on the bank of the river that winds through the bottom. Soon we come to the great temple of Dâmodar, with its noisy priests gabbling at the top of their voices as they wash in the pool in front of their temple. And here we begin to remark the number of naked ascetics that prevail in these parts. They are of all ages and most diverse fashions, some besmeared all over with ochre, others with ashes, others decently clean, some with short glossy hair, some having it stained with lime, others winding it round the head like ropes, but all without decent clothing, in which their asceticism seems principally to consist, for—almost without exception—they were plump, able-bodied fellows, who live well on the superstition of their more industrious countrymen. The defile opens out again into a valley, round the foot of the lofty central mountain, and in crossing it we come upon some magnificent Banian trees. Near a cluster of them is an old shrine called Bhavanâtha, with a few dilapidated temples, on a slab in the doorway of one of which I read the name of *Bhoja Râja*. There are many wells, &c. about this place, indicative, perhaps, of a renown it no longer enjoys, though a fair is still kept up at it.

From Bhavanâtha, a short walk leads to the foot of Girnar—the ancient Raivata or Ujjayanta—sacred among the Śrâvaks or Jaina sect to Neminâtha the twenty-second in their list of Tîrthaṅkaras,—and doubtless a place of pilgrimage even before the days of Aśoka. In his time it probably became a Bauddha tîrtha or sacred place where monasteries were early formed, and cells cut in its granitic scarps for the devotees. The Brâhmaṇs, ever ready to consecrate with legend and pretended sanctity, what may conduce to their own profit, have not forgotten Girnar, for about thirty chapters of the *Prabhâsa Khaṇḍa* of the *Skanda Purâṇa* is devoted to the account of the sanctity of Girnar and the surrounding neighbourhood: this forms the *Girnâra Mâhâtmya*, consisting chiefly of stories fabricated or copied from other Paurâṇic legends, by the Girnâra Brâhmaṇs, and placed in the mouth of Śiva, their favourite divinity, as being related by him to Pârvatî.

According to the *Girnâra Mâhâtmya*, Prabhâsa Kshetra or Somanâtha Paṭṭan and its vicinity on the sea shore on the south coast of Soraṭh, is the holiest of all places of Hindu sanctity, but Girnâr or Vastrâpatha, as it is called, is holier still by some almost infinitesimal amount. Many of the chief Hindu gods and heroes have their names connected with the numerous places of sanctity in Vastrâpatha. The gods have consented to reside here permanently, and the heroes have performed pilgrimages to Girnâr.

The priests who are to officiate in the ceremonies of pilgrimages are the Girnâra Brâhmaṇs.* Their ministry is strictly enjoined on the pilgrim. The number of this

* The Girnâra Brahmans reckon themselves among the Pancha-Gauḍas. They are principally of the *White Yajur Veda*, but are said to profess all the others also except the *Sâma*. Besides those of Junagâḍh, there are two other castes of them,—the Chorvâḍa Girnâras of the coast town of Chorvâḍ, and the Âjakiyas of the village of Âjak; the three divisions eat together but do not intermarry.

class of Brâhmaṇs in Kâṭhiâwâḍ is considerable, and a peculiar sanctity attaches to them; though it appears from the *Prabhâsa Khaṇḍa* that they were not originally natives of Kâṭhiâwâḍ, but came from the foot of the Himâlayas.

The general name for the holy places about Girnâr is Vastrâpatha. It is not now in general use, but the following story from the *Mâhâtmya* relates how it came to have this name:—

" One day Śiva and Pârvatî were sitting together in Kailâsa, when the latter inquired of Śiva, 'My lord, will you kindly tell me by what kind of devotion, by what kind of charity, by what charms, what adventures and what works you are propitiated by men?' Śiva said, 'I am pleased with those who are kind to all creatures, who always tell the truth, never commit adultery, and always stand in the front in the field of battle.' The discourse had arrived at this stage when Brahma and other gods came to Kailâsa; Vishṇu was also among them. Vishṇu said to Śiva, 'You always give boons to Daityas, which greatly interferes with the proper performance of my duty of protecting. By the boons granted by you the Daityas are enabled to harass mankind. Moreover you are propitiated with a trifling service. Such being the case, who will undertake to perform my duties?' Śiva said in reply, 'It is my natural habit to be pleased at once, and it shall never be abandoned. However, if you do not like it, I walk away.' So saying, Śiva left Kailâsa and instantly disappeared. Pârvatî said she could not live without Śiva: thereupon all the gods, together with Pârvatî, set out in search of him. Śiva having arrived at the Vastrâpatha Kshetra cast off his garments, and divesting himself of his bodily form became invisible and dwelt there. The gods and Pârvatî also arrived soon after at the Vastrâpatha, pursuing their search after Śiva. Vishṇu sent away his vehicle (Garuḍa) and took a seat on the mountain of Raivata. Pârvatî took a seat on the top of the Ujjayanta (Girnâr). The king of serpents also came thither by a subterranean path. The Gaṅgâ and other rivers also came by the same way. The gods, choosing different spots, seated themselves there. Pârvatî then, from the top of Girnâr began to sing the praises of Śiva, who was therewith greatly delighted, and graciously showed his form to Pârvatî and the gods. Pleased at seeing Śiva, all the gods requested Mahâdeva to return to Kailâsa, and he consented to do so on condition that Pârvatî, the gods, and the Gaṅgâ and other rivers agreed to remain in Vastrâpatha. They all agreed, whereupon Mahâdeva, leaving a part of his essence there, went to Kailâsa. Pârvatî also did the same. Vishṇu from that time has continued to reside on the Raivataka mountain, and Pârvatî or Ambâ has dwelt on the top of the Ujjayanta."

This extract shows how the Kshetra received the name of Vastrâpatha from the circumstance of Śiva's casting off his *vastra* or garments when he repaired thither, incensed at the offence given by Vishṇu.

The following extract relates to the sanctity of the Vastrâpatha Kshetra:—

" There ruled formerly in a certain country a king whose name was Gaja. In the decline of life he entrusted the government of his kingdom to his son, and repaired to the banks of the Gaṅgâ with his wife, and dwelt there. After some time there came to the banks of the river a sage named Bhadra, accompanied by a large number of other sages. The sage, having bathed in the waters of the Gaṅgâ, sat down on the bank for meditation and devotion. The Râja happened to see him, and was tempted to go near him. The Râja was rejoiced to see him, and requested the sage to honour his house by a visit. The sage consented, and went to the Râja's abode. The Râja and his wife worshipped him, and, seating themselves before him with joined palms, they entreated Bhadra with great humility to show them the way to salvation. They said: 'O sage, mankind are wandering in a maze of life and death, being deceived by the temptations of the world. Will your holiness oblige the world by pointing out a way by which eternal bliss may be secured?' The sage replied: 'The world abounds with many sacred rivers, such as the Gañgâ, and abodes of Vishṇu and Śiva. But they bestow eternal bliss when people bathe in the rivers, and visit the places at particular seasons. But the Vastrâpatha Kshetra grants to the pilgrim everlasting happiness in heaven at whatever time he chooses to go there. I was once on a tour to the sacred places and I happened to see Vishṇu. He told me I need not bother myself with visiting all the sacred places,—that I should only pay a visit to Dâmodar and bathe in the waters of the Dâmodar Kuṇḍa, and that when I had done that, there would be nothing left for me to do. I have accordingly visited that sacred place.' When the Râja heard this he said, 'Reverend sire, it is my desire to know in what country the Vastrâpatha Kshetra is situated, and what rivers, what mountains, and what forests there are in it.' The sage replied: 'The land which contains the Kshetra is surrounded by the sea. It contains many large towns. There is a mountain named Ujjayanta near Bhavanâtha, and to the west of it the mountain of Raivataka, from whose golden top rises a river which is called Svarṇarekhâ. The summits of the mountain look like huge elephants. Birds of various kinds amuse the pilgrim with their sweet melody. Many persons are engaged in digging in the mines for metals. Nala, Nṛiga, Nahusha, Yayâti, Dhuṅdumâra, Bharata, and Bhagiratha have, by the performance of sacrifices there, attained everlasting celestial happiness. The river Svarṇarekhâ has its origin in Pâtâla. The king of serpents also came from Pâtâla, through the channel of the river, to visit the god Dâmodar. Sâṁba, Pradyumna, and other Yâdavas dwell in the Kshetra, with their wives and children and protect it with their countless forces. Their wives bestow large charities on Brâhmaṇs. There is a tank or kuṇḍ near Dâmodar, constructed by Revati which goes by the name of Raivataka. There is also another holy tank called Brâhma Kuṇḍ, where the god Dâmodar comes to bathe at noon every day. Anyone who erects a temple of five stones in this kshetra can thereby obtain the happiness of heaven for five thousand years. The period of happiness varies according to the size of the temple built. Around the Raivataka is a plain four miles in extent which is called Antargraha Kshetra. It is of the highest sanctity. Its water possesses the property of dissolving the bones of dead bodies, and on that account it is termed Viliyaka. There dwell also many ascetics, who by practising austerities procure salvation. The sage then left the place. The Râja and his wife, attended by some followers, went to the Vastrâpatha Kshetra, reaching there about the full-moon in the month of Kârtik. After bathing there, the Râja was proceeding to visit Bhavanâtha and Dâmodar, when cars from heaven arrived and waited for him. The Râja, with his wife and followers, got into the cars and ascended to heaven."

In reply to Pârvatî's questions asking for the boundaries of the Antargraha Kshetra, Śiva says, "The Kshetra extends from the river Svarṇarekhâ which lies to the east of the town of Karṇakubja (Junâgaḍh) to the mountain of Ujjayanta. It contains the following sacred spots: Dâmodar, Bhavanâtha, Dâmodar Vishṇu, the Svarṇarekhâ, Brahmâ Kuṇḍa, Brahmeśvara, Gañgeśvara, Kalmegha, Indreśvara, Raivataka mountain, Ujjayanta mountain, Revati Kuṇḍa, Kubhiśvara, Bhîma Kuṇḍa and Bhîmeśvara. These are the celebrated sacred places in the Antargraha Kshetra."

Śiva gives the following directions for the guidance of pilgrims visiting the Vastrâpatha:—

"In the west of the Vastrâpatha lies the holy mountain of Unnavishka (now called Ośam), which receives its name from the circumstance of Bhîma having killed the giant Unnaka there. In that mountain there is a cavity which goes down as far as Pâtâla. There are many *liṅgas* or emblems of Śiva there, and sixteen seats of saints, and many gold mines. When the pilgrim has finished his work here he should bathe in the waters called Gaṅgâ Strota, which lie to the west of the mountain of Maṅgal, and then bow down to Gaṅgeśvara Mahâdeva, situated near it, and perform a *śrâddha*. He should then go to Siddheśvara Mahâdeva and Chakra Tîrtha, now known as Trivenî, then to Lokeśvara, and then to Indreśvara, which lies to the west of Siddheśvara. Then he should pay his respects to the goddess Yaksheśvarî, which is in the Yakshvan (now called Lâkhâvan) wood, also lying to the west of the mountain of Maṅgal. He should then direct his steps towards the mountain of Raivataka, and having there bathed in the Revati Kuṇḍ and Bhîma Kuṇḍ and seen the image of Dâmodar, he should come to Bhavanâtha. There also bathing in the Mṛigi and other kuṇḍs, he should ascend the mountain of Ujjayanta. The pilgrim should perform the rites which are to be performed in a pilgrimage at the holy spots in the mountain, such as Ambâ-Devî, Hâthîpaglaṅ, or the elephant's foot, the Rasakupikâ or mercurial well, the Sâtkuṇḍa or seven tanks, Gaumukha, Gaṅgâ, and the shrines of Pradyumna and other Yâdavas who have become Buddhas in the Kâli age."

The Jainas or Śrâwaks have also their *Raivatâchala Mâhâtmya* of the hill, forming the tenth, eleventh, twelfth, and thirteenth sargas or chapters of the *Śatruñjaya Mâhâtmya*. It is principally occupied, however, with the history of the Paṇḍavas in its main features as connected with that of Kṛishṇa, who is the cousin of Neminâtha the twenty-second Jaina Tîrthaṅkar, the special subject of their reverence on this mount, where he is said to have attained *Nirvâṇa*.*

---

* In the introduction Indra is represented as asking Mahâvîra to give some account of the fifth of the twenty-one famous summits of the Siddhâdri or sacred mountains. Mahâvîra 'the lord of the triune world' accordingly began by stating that this fifth summit is the great mountain Raivata which gives the *fifth* knowledge (*pañchamajñân*), *i.e.* salvation. Gifts and offerings made here from the heart are productive of benefits in this and the next world. The merit acquired here causes to dissolve the mass of sins accumulated during several transmigrations. Here sages who have ceased to eat and who pass their days in devotion, as well as gods, worship Nemi; here Apsarasas and numerous heavenly beings—Gandharvas, Siddhas, Vidyâdharas, &c.—always worship the Jina Nemi. Animals naturally hostile, as cats and mice, lions and elephants, serpents and peacocks, live in harmony on this mountain. All the planets, pretending to rise and set daily, move round Nemi to worship him. All the seasons are perennially present here; the tanks, among which Gajendrapada is the chief, are filled with nectar by the gods. This Raivata, when remembered, gives happiness; when seen, removes misery; and when touched, grants what is desired. Of such a mountain, O Indra! listen to the story.

As an argument for its expiating power, Mahâvîra then relates the history of Bhîmasena the spoilt son of Vajrasena king of Śrâvastî (śl. 50–232, of which Weber has translated the outline,—*über das Çatruñjaya Mâhâtmyam*, pp. 31–34). Then as the Jina Nemi, worshipped on Raivata—which was first made a *Tîrtha* by Bharata in the *Avasarpiṇi* age—was of Harivaṅśa race, the history of this race is added. In Champâpuri was born a king Somayaśas, the son of Bâhubali, and grandson of the *prathamasvâmin* Vṛishabha—the first Jina; and the princes descending from him are called the Somavaṅśya or Lunar race. His son Śreyânsa first pointed out the duty of liberality by presenting sugar-cane juice (*ikshu*) to the Yugâdhiśa (or presiding

The ascent commences on an outlying spur, and may be made either on foot or in a *doli* or square seat slung from one or two poles borne by Koli porters. In less than half an hour the Chodia-paraba, the first rest house, is reached, about 480 feet above the level of the plain below; the second halting-place, named Dholi-Deri, is on the

---

god) of the Avasarpiṇî age, whence he and his descendants were called Aikshvâka. The last king of this line was Chandrakîrti, who dying without heirs, Hari succeeded him, who was consecrated in the temple of Śîtalasvâmin—the tenth Jina. From him descended the Harivanśa race, in which line Suvrataswâmin, the twentieth Jina, was born (*Ind. Ant.* vol. II. pp. 136, 138), whose history is next introduced (śl. 320–385). Then follow the ancestors and relatives of Nemi and Kṛishṇa. After many kings of the Harivanśa race had passed away King Vasu ruled at Mathurâ, and was succeeded by his son Bṛihaddhvaja and others until Yadu, the progenitor of the Yâdavas. Sûra, the son of Yadu, had two sons,—1. Śauri, who surrendered Mathurâ to his younger brother, and went to the Kuśâvarta country, where he founded Śauryapura as his capital, and was succeeded by his son Andhakavṛishṇi; and 2. Suvîra, who gave up Mathurâ to his eldest son Bhojavṛishni, and went to Sindh, where he founded the city Sauvîra (*puram Sindhushu Sauvîram*, see above, *p.* 131). Bhojavṛishṇi's son was Ugrasena, the father of Kanśa; and Andhakavṛishṇi of Śauryapura had ten sons called the Daśârhâs, among whom the eldest was Samudravijaya, the father of Nemi or Arishṭanemi, and the tenth, Vasudeva, the father of Kṛishṇa by Devaki, daughter of Devakanṛipa and of Bala Râma by Rohiṇî. He had also two younger daughters, Kuntî and Madrî, the wives of Paṇḍu. The descent of the Pâṇḍavas is likewise traced from a son of Vṛishabhasvâmin named Kuru, who gave name to Kurukshetra. A long story is then introduced respecting Śântanu and his sons Gâṇgeya Bhîshma and Vichitravîrya,—the father of Dhṛitarâshṭra (Weber, *ut sup.* pp. 35, 36). After relating the story of the birth of Kṛishṇa much in the usual way, that of Nemi is introduced (śl. 703 ff.):—'At dawn on the 12th of Kârtikavadya in Śauryapura, Śivâ, the wife of Samudravijaya, dreamed the fourteen great dreams, and at the Chitrâ Nakshatra, a great sage, Aparâjita, descended from a chariot and entered her womb. Then at midnight of 5th Śrâvana suddha, at the Chitrâ Nakshatra she gave birth to a child of dark colour marked with a *śankha* or conch-shell, when on the top of Mount Meru fifty-six *dikkumâris* (or maidens of the points of direction) and sixty-four Indras celebrated the birth of the Jina.' Samudravijaya called his child Arishṭanemi. It was nursed by crowd of Apsarasas, and waited upon by Devas, who, by order of Indra, had become of the same age.

The story then turns to the Pâṇḍavas, Kṛishṇa, and the death of Kanśa, when Ugrasena again becomes king of Mathurâ, and gives his daughter Satybhâmâ to Kṛishṇa. On being consulted as to the result of the enmity of Jarâsandha of Râjagṛiha, who was enraged with Kṛishṇa and the Yâdavas on account of the death of Kansa, his son-in-law, Kroshṭuki, an astrologer, advises that they should go to the shores of the Western Sea, and settle where Satyabhâmâ should be delivered of twin sons. Accordingly Samudravijaya and the Yâdavas set forth through the Vindhya mountains, where their protecting goddesses persuaded Kâla, the son of Jarâsandha, that they had destroyed themselves (śl. 704–818). No further molested, the Yâdavas went to Surâshṭra, and encamped to the north-west of Girnar, where Satyabhâmâ gave birth to Bhânu and Bhâmara. 'Then the Daśarhas worshipped Jina on the Girinâra mountain, and thus purified themselves.' Kṛishṇa on a propitious day bathed, worshipped the Ocean-god, and performed the eighth *tapa*, and on the third night the god of the Ocean presented Kṛishṇa with the conch *Panchajanya*, and Balarâma with the *Sugosha*. Kubera then built them Dvârakâ for a capital with palaces, temples of Arhant, wells, tanks, &c., and gave Kṛishṇa a suit of yellow clothes, the precious *kaustubha* gem, the *Sâruga* bow, the sword *Nandana*, the club *Kaumodakî*, the chariot *Garuḍadvhaja*, &c.; to Balarâma black clothes, the chariot *tâladhvaja*, the *tulasa*, a bow, &c.; to Arishṭanemi, a suit of white clothes, the *Chandrasûrya* earrings, &c.; to Samudravijaya, the sword *chandrahâsa*, a chariot, &c., &c. Then they crowned Kṛishṇa and Balarâma to govern the new state (śl. 819–847).

The inhabitants of Suradhârâpura (which I suppose must be Sardhâr) at the foot of Raivata, harassed the Yâdavas. Anâdhṛishṇi, the eldest son of Vasudeva, gave them battle, but was taken prisoner. Kṛishṇa and Balarâma were next carried off. Nemi then, urged by the wives of Kṛishṇa, attacked and defeated the inhabitants of Suradhârâpur, took it, and delivered Anâdhṛishṇi and the others. Kṛishṇa then went to Vidarbha, and carried off Rukmiṇî, the sister of prince Rukmi. He also married six other wives, viz., Jâmbavatî, Lakshmaṇâ, Susîmâ, Gaurî, Padmâvatî, and Gândhârî.

The next *sarga* (XI.) describes the game at dice, the forest life, &c. of the Pâṇḍavas, agreeing on the whole with the *Mahâbhârata*; and the third (XII.) describes the war of the Pâṇḍavas, &c. The thirteenth *sarga* of the *Satruñjaya Mâhâtmya* gives the life of Nemi. After long resistance he agreed to marry, and Kṛishṇa selected for him Râjîmatî, the daughter of Ugrasena of Girnar; after a year, Nemi went on pilgrimage to the Uttarakurus, became an ascetic at the age of three hundred, and spent seven hundred years as such, attaining *Nirvâṇa* on Girnar. But for more details consult the *Mâhâtmya* or its *tika*; and see *Ind. Ant.* vol. II. pp. 138, 139.

INSCRIPTION AT THE GATE OF THE JAINA TEMPLES, MOUNT GIRNAR.

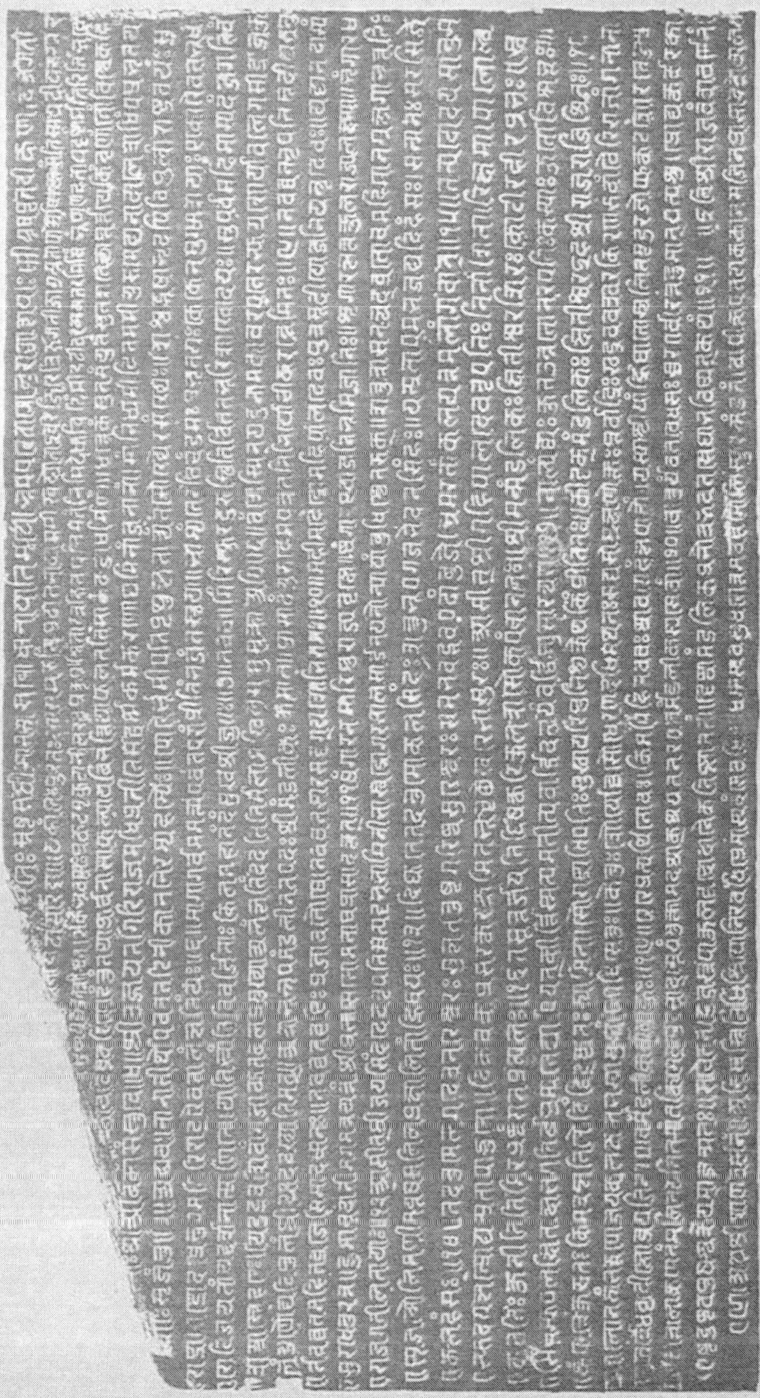

ridge of the spur, fully 1,000 feet above the valley and but little below the foot of the great scarp. The ascent now becomes more difficult as the path winds on under the face of the cliff to the third rest-house 1,400 feet up. Stairs of sandstone then commence, and taking advantage of every ledge on the almost vertical scarp, wind up the face of it,—the *doli* frequently grating against the rock on one side of the narrow path whilst its occupant looks down into an abyss on the other. The present steps, worn as they are, are of no great age; and the expense of the first third of the ascent is said to have been 12,000 rupees. The rest-houses or *visamas* on the way, having fallen into ruin, were repaired in 1841 by Harakuvar Shethani. At an altitude between 2,000 and 2,100 feet there is an inscription of the date of either 1,258 or 1,158 A.D., and under a large stone on the outer side of the descent are some letters of an old type. A few hundred feet below the gate there are some natural caverns in the rock, and taking advantage of these, it is believed, some Wâghars, about eight years ago, succeeded in scrambling up the scarp at night and entering one of the temples in the Devakoṭa, they robbed the idol of its gold ornaments and jewels. At length the gate is reached,—the Aneroid barometer indicating 2,250 above Bhavanâtha, 2,370 above Junâgaḍh, and 2,700 from zero.

The Buddhist "chambers and galleries mostly hollowed out in the face of a scarped peak" of which Hiwan-Thsang speaks, probably occupied pretty nearly the site of the present temples and of the Bhîma-kuṇḍa to the north of them. There is a fragment of a cave to the south of the temples on the now inaccessible verge of the cliff, which may have belonged to them, and the sunken cell of Amijherâ, on the south of the court of Neminâtha's temple, may have been one of the cells attached to some of the caves cleared away by the Jainas to make room for their temples.

On entering the gate, the large enclosure of the temples is on the left, while a little to the right from the path is the temple of Mân Singh Bhoja Râja, and further on the much larger one of Vastupâla standing on a platform. The door into the Devakoṭa or sacred fort, is evidently part of an old building, which still goes by the name of Râh Khangâr's Mehal or palace; and probably it is the lower floor of some such structure, built perhaps both as a summer palace and a stronghold, now modified to form a barrack for the guard and dwellings for the pujâris and temple servants. Built into the wall, on the left of the entrance, is an inscription, imperfect at the upper left corner, but which Dr. Bühler has kindly transliterated and translated as follows (see facsimile plate XXX.) :—

Transcript.

1 ॥* . . . . मते: श्रेष्ठं सधीमानसोमबोधानाया·
तिमयाभूपपरित्राणानुरागाश्च: ॥ पीयूषपूतवीचणादिजगतो
2 ॥ . . . . तायदामारज्ञ ॥ १ ॥ यत्कांति: पुरत: ममसम-
रुचिप्रद्योतनाद्या अमी खद्योता इव रेजिरे त्रिजगती जाग्रत्प्रतापा अपि ॥ दासंति स्म यदीयसस्मर
3 ॥ . . . . हखयकं हतश्रीश्वत ॥ २ ॥ किं भूवध्या: प्रकटमृकुटा नील-
रत्नप्रसूतसिंतारत्नजितपणिपतंनिमिरेषांबिविं गोवटीबरगगतरमिणिं भृंगेणरतापट्टष्टां गतिरितिभवे

* The mutilation and indistinctness of most of the letters render a restoration of this line impossible—for me at least.—G.B.

The numerals affixed to the following notes refer to the lines :—

2. Read यत्कांते: समं सम°; कांचंति uncertain.

3. Nineteen letters have been lost at the beginning of line 3.

4 ॥ . . . .[1] तो च विघ्नकरिणो हंतुं तथा प्रार्थनासाफल्याय बिभर्त्ति
या फलततिं माकंदजां धर्मिणां । धत्तेकं सुतसंयुतं सुतशतेच्छापूर्त्तये किं नृणांतोंविश्वेकहि
5 ॥ . . . . : श्रीअंबिकां संस्तुवे ॥ ४ ॥ श्री उज्जयतगिरिराजमधिप्रतीते सद्धर्मकर्मकरणो-
द्यमिनां जनानां । सांनिध्यमोहितममी गुरुमेघनादा लेशधिंपप्रभृतय
6 ॥ . . शाः सृजंतु ॥ ५ ॥ अद्य च ॥ नानातीर्थोपवनतटिनीकानने रम्यहर्म्यैः ॥ पौरैर्भूमीपतिपृथुकृता-
त्यंतसौख्यैरसंख्यैः ॥ शश्वद्भूषाश्वदपि विपुलां राष्ट्रवर्यः सु-
7 ॥ राष्ट्र ॥ राष्ट्रो दधेनुपमगिरिराट् रैवतालंकृतिं यः ॥ ६ ॥ मा गा गर्वममर्त्यपर्वत परां प्रीतिं
भजंतस्त्वया भ्राम्यंते रविचंद्रमःप्रभृतयः के के न मुग्धाशयाः ॥ एको रैवतभूध-
8 ॥ रो विजयतां यद्दर्शनात् प्राणिनो । यांति भ्रांतिविवर्जिताः किल महानंदं सुखश्रीजुषः ॥ ७ ॥
तत्र च ॥ गिरिस्फुरदुरुस्थितिर्विततभूरिशाखोदयः॥ सुपर्वमहिमास्पदं जगति वं-
9 ॥ श आस्ते हरेः॥ यदुद्भवशिवांगजाच्युतबलप्रमुख्या अलंकृतिं ददति निर्मलामखिलसत्सु मुक्ता अपि
॥ ८ ॥ वंशेस्मिन् यदुनासकावरपतेरभ्युग्रशौर्यावलेरासीद्राजकु-
10 ॥ लं गुणौघविपुलं श्रीयादवख्यातिमत् ॥ अत्राभून्नृपमंडलीनतपदः श्रीमंडलीकः क्रमात् ।
प्रासादं गुरुहेमपत्रततिभिर्योचीकरन्नेमिनः ॥ ८ ॥ नवघननृपतिस्तदीयसूनु-
11 ॥ र्नवघनमहितव्रजेसिमादधानः ॥ नवघनवृष्टिः प्रजावतौघे नवघनसारसदृग्यशोभिरामः ॥ १० ॥
महिमहेंद्रो महिपालदेवः पुत्रस्तदीयो जनि यन्नृदेवः यद्दानदास्यं
12 ॥ सुरधेनुरत्न ॥ द्रुमास्तदानीमगमन्नयत्नं ॥ श्रीप्रभासे सोमनाथप्रासादकृत् ॥ ११ ॥ षंगारनामा
रिपुराज्यवृत्ते- ॥ ष्वंगार एवाजनि भूमिजानिः ॥ शृंगारकृत्तत्कुलराज्यलक्ष्म्या ॥ भ्रंगारध-
13 ॥ रा जगतीलतायाः ॥ १२ ॥ आसीत् श्रीजयसिंहदेवनृपतिस्तत्पट्टभूभामिनीभाग्यश्रीगरसाल-
सार्द्रनयनोन्यायांवुधिश्वेतरुक् ॥ शत्रुत्रासनकृद्व्रतोचमहिमानम्रचमाभृत्तति:
14 ॥ स्फूर्जन्मौलिमणीमयूषसलिलप्रचालितांह्रिद्वयः ॥ १३ ॥ दियुते तदनु मोकलसिंहः शत्रुभूपगजभे-
दनसिंहः ॥ यत्प्रतापमभजद्यदि हंसः। सन्मनःसरसिजे
15 ॥ कलहंसः ॥ १४ ॥ तदनु मेलगदेवनरेश्वरः सुकृततुष्टगरिष्ठसुरेश्वरः समभवद्भव × × पदांबुजे। भ्र-
मरतां कलयन्नमलांगवान् ॥ १५ ॥ तत्पदोदयसानुम-
16 ॥ भ्युदयकृत्प्रोद्यत्प्रतापाद्भुतो ॥ दिक्चक्रप्रसरत्करक्रमितभूभृच्छेखरे भासुरः। आसीत् श्रीमहिपालदे-
वनृपतिः निर्नाशितारिचमापालोल्व-
17 ॥ कततिः कुनोतितिमिरप्रध्वंसनप्रत्यलः ॥ १६ ॥ तत्सूनुर्जयति द्विपत्करिकुलत्रासौकपंचाननः ॥
श्रीमन्मंडलिकः चितीश्वरशिरःकोटीरहीरप्रभः ॥ स्वः-

---

4. Seven syllables have been lost at the beginning of line 4.

5. Five syllables have been lost at the beginning of line 5; perhaps लोकाधिप° for लेशधिंप, and शा is uncertain.

6. Two syllables lost at the beginning; read पौरैर्भू°. 7. Read रैवतोलंकृतिं. 8. Read यांति-.

9. Read श्रीयादवं. 12. Read खंगार for षंगार°; भ्रंगारधारा.

13. Read तत्पादोदय°; व्रतोच्चमहिमा; चमाभृत्तति.

15. Read °गरिष्ठ सुरेश्वरः; the third pâda is two syllables short.

16. Perhaps भव्य is to be inserted after *bhava*; चमापालोलूकततिः

17. Read तत्सूनु°; °त्रासैकपंचाननः; स्वःसिन्धू° कोटि: सत्यं°.

18 ॥ सिंधुर्म्युंपलचिताचतगतिर्बभ्रम्यते द्यापि यत्कीर्तिस्त्यमतीत्य वार्द्धिवलयं वर्द्धिष्णुसारत्वरा ॥ १७ ॥
नाल्पंध्यः कुत उन्नतो नरपतिः कस्याः कुतो विश्वभूः ॥ . .
19 ॥ स्वं पात्रे कुरुतः किमत्र क्रतिनौ किं दिट्क्रतः स्वामिना । सौराष्ट्राधिपतिः । सुखायरिपु भिस्सक्रे ध
किं प्रीतितः॥ कीदृक् मंडलिकः चितीश्वर इह श्रीराजराजिश्रितः ॥ १८ ॥
20 ॥ आलोनस्तंभरूपो जयकलकलभस्यासुखांभोधिसेतुः ॥ केतुः शौर्यौघसौधे रणदधिमथनः
मयमोम्रचणोत्कः पूर्वाद्रिः खड्गुवपत्खरकिरणरुचां वैरिराजांगनाना-
21 ॥ मुवेवैंधव्यदीचो जयति नरपतेर्मंडलीकस्य बाहुः ॥ १६ ॥ रे रे प्रत्यर्थिनो वः । किमपि हितवचः
श्रावये हं क्रपातों ॥ यस्याश्वीयांह्रिघातोस्खलितमृदुरजो प्युत्कटग्गोरतेजः।
22 ॥ हत्वा भूलोकमेनं मलिनयतितमां तत् किमेतत्पुरस्ताद् । यूयं मुक्तामद श्राक् श्रयत नरपतेर्मंडली-
कस्य सेवां ॥ २० ॥ चातुर्यं वत वेधसः सुरगवीरत्नद्रुमान्यत्पशु । प्रोद्यत्कर्करका-
23 ॥ ठदुष्टवपुषस्चक्रे यमा जन्मतः ॥ सचैतन्ययुजस्तपाकुलहृदो दानैकनिष्णाततां ॥ दृष्ट्वा मंडलीक
प्रभो चभवतस्ते द्याभविष्यत्कथं ॥ २१ ॥ ॥ इति श्रीराजवंशवर्णनं
24 ॥ ॐ अथश्रीग्राणवर्णनं ॥ अस्ति स्वस्ति निधिश्रियो निरवधिप्रेमास्पदं सेवधिश्रीधर्मस्य वसुंधरोत्त-
मवधूमौलिस्फुरन्मंडनं । वापीकूपतटाककाननजिनप्रासादशैवालय

Translation.

V. 1–3. [No translation is possible, as not more than one or two pâdas of each verse are without mutilation or in good order. But the three verses contain the so-called *mangalâcharana*. Verse 1 appears to be addressed to Sâradâ or Sarasvatî, the goddess of poetry.]

4. I praise Śrí Ambikâ* who . . . . to destroy the obstacles (formidable) like elephants, and to fulfil the prayers of those endowed with spiritual merit, carries numerous mango-fruits, and places her son in her lap to fulfil the desire for a hundred sons. . . . .

5. May the lord of the world and the rest whose voices sound deep like thunder, give their desired presence at the well-known (spot) on the glorious king of mountains Ujjayanta for the sake of men who are devoted to the performance of works of pure merit.†

6. And now the incomparable king of mountains, Raivata, the best in the kingdom, that is situated in the kingdom Surâshtra, though bearing all kinds of ornaments, has been greatly adorned by numerous tîrthas, pleasure groves, rivers, woods, beautiful

---

18. Read नोत्तंध्यः —

19. Read आलानस्तंभ ; शौर्यौघ° ; मथनो प्रचणाकः ; खड्गपयस° is nonsense, and offends against the metre just as does मुववैंधव्य, where a particle is required before वैधव्य.

20. Read प्युत्कटं सौरतेजः ; यूयं मुक्ता मदं द्राक् श्रयत ; dele stop after वः

* Ambikâ is one of the guardian deities of Girnâr, where her temple now occupies a prominent position. The mango-fruits which the goddess is said to carry, acquire a particular significance thereby, that the mango-fruit is the *amritaphalam*.

† The translation is merely tentative, the lacuna and the incorrect reading *les'adhimpa* prevent me from coming to a certain interpretation.

palaces fit for towns, made large by kings, giving exquisite pleasure, and countless in number.*

7. Do not become vain, O mountain of the immortals; the sun, moon, and the other heavenly bodies, who bear thee the greatest affection, are caused by thee to err (inasmuch as thou makest them turn round thyself); (*but*) who is not befooled? Glory to Mount Raivata alone, by the sight of which the creatures, free from error and enjoying pleasure and prosperity, gain highest bliss.†

8. And there dwells the race of Hari occupying a broad seat glittering with mountains endowed with many spreading branches, a dwelling-place in the world of those who are great like gods, whose scions (*Nemi*) the son Śivâ, Achyuta, and Bala are (*its*) spotless ornaments, though . . . .‡

9. In that race rose a famed and illustrious royal house distinguished by numerous virtues called Yâdava after Yadu, a king of later times. In course of time the illustrious Maṇḍalika was born in this (*family*), at whose feet numerous princes bowed, and who built with many gold-plates a temple of Nemi.

10. His son was king Navaghana, who took up his new, strong (*navaghana*) sword against a multitude of enemies, who (*gladdened*) his subjects as the rain from newly-risen clouds (*navaghana*) gladdens the forest, and who was resplendent with a fame brilliant like (*a lump of*) camphor (*navaghana*).§

11. His son was the lord of the earth, Mahîpâladeva. When that king was born, the cow of the gods, the (*philosopher's*) gem, and the (*heavenly*) trees (*which fulfil desires*) became easily the slaves of his liberality. At Śrî Prabhâsa he built a temple of Somanâtha.

12. (*To him*) was born king Shangâra (*Khangâr*), a brand (*angâra*) in the dominions of his foes that were (*destructible like*) trees, who enjoyed the favours of the guardian goddess of his race, and resembled the stream from a watering pot, (*to refresh*) the world (*likened to*) a creeper.‖

13. The illustrious king Jayasiṁhadeva showed fatigue and swimming eyes on account of the brilliant pleasures which he enjoyed with that (*Khangâr's*) first queen, the earth.¶ He was a moon of the ocean of justice; high rose his power because he made his enemies tremble; his feet were washed by streams of light proceeding from the jewels in the glittering diadems of a multitude of prostrated kings.

---

* The *yaḥ* at the end of the verse has not been translated, and I am unable to find its antecedent *sa* either in the preceding or the following verses. The translation is merely tentative.

† The verse is intended to show the superiority of the Girnâr over Mount Meru. In the first half of the stanza the latter is addressed and warned not to feel too proud on account of his superiority. For, though Meru makes (according to the Paurânic astronomy) the heavenly bodies turn round himself, and is thus the centre of the world, it commits thereby a fault, since he causes their *bhramana, i.e.*, wandering or erring. Mount Raivata is incomparably greater, as a visit to this sacred place of pilgrimage takes away all *bhranti*, "error," and gives *mukti* or salvation. The whole point is a wretched pun on the verb *bhram*, which means both "to turn" and "to err," &c. See the *Mâhâtmya* quoted, p. 157, note *.

‡ According to the Jainas, the Tîrthaṅkara Neminâtha is a Yâdava.

§ Camphor, on account of its white colour, is one of the substances to which fame is frequently compared.

‖ The world may be likened to a creeper, because it is of the feminine gender, because it occupies the place of a wife to the kings, or because it clings to the king for protection.

¶ This is merely a polite way of saying Siddhârâja Jayasiṁha that of Anhilvâḍa (1093–1142 A.D.) conquered and annexed Râ Khengâr's dominions. See Forbes, *Râs Mâlâ*, vol. I. pp. 156–170, 328; but compare the remarks further on.

14. Afterwards shone Mokaḷasiṁha, a lion to destroy the elephants of hostile kings. If a weak king (*Haṁsa*) obtained his prowess, he became in (*the estimation of*) the lotus-like minds of good men an excellent king (*Kalahaṁsa*).*

15. Then came king Melagadeva, endowed with spotless limbs, who acted the part of a blue bee near the lotus feet of Śiva,† and pleased the supreme lord by his pious deeds.

16. At his feet, that resembled the mountain of the east, rose the illustrious king Mahîpâladeva, wonderful on account of his high rising lustre, resplendent at the head of kings who were subjected by his hands extended over the universe.‡ He scared away the multitude of owl-like kings, and was able to drive away the darkness of injustice.

17. Hail to his son, the illustrious Maṇḍalika, the unique lion to frighten the elephants of his enemies, who derives lustre from the diamonds in the diadems of princes, whose fame, marked but not obstructed by the waves of the stream of heaven, wanders forsooth everywhere beyond the sea . . . .

18. He cannot be passed by. Why? He is exalted. Of what land is he the lord? He rules everywhere . . . .§ What is Maṇḍalika like? A king in this world served by numerous illustrious princes.

19. Glory to the arm of king Maṇḍalika, that is a tying post for the noisy elephant calf (*called*) victory, that is a bridge (*to cross*) the ocean of misfortune, a banner on the palace of valour, a churning stick to churn the battle-milk, who is anointed with the ointment, fame, who is the mountain of the east on which appear the rays of the sun, ... and who consecrates to widowhood the wives of his enemies.

20. Ho ye enemies, out of compassion I will give you a word of good advice. The hoofs of king Maṇḍalika's squadrons raise the fine dust that, obscuring even the bright light of the sun, makes this earth excessively murky. What! do you stand up against him? Lay aside your pride and quickly become his servants.

21. Alas for the cleverness of the Creator who gave, from their birth, to the cow of the gods, to the philosopher's gem, to the (*heavenly*) tree, the blemished forms of a beast, of a stone, and of wood! O prince Maṇḍalika, how could they exist to-day, if, being endowed with sense, they had seen, their hearts oppressed by shame, the unique expertness of your Majesty in bestowing gifts.

Thus ends the description of the race of kings . . . .

The names of the kings here given are those of the Chuḍâsamâs of Girnar, descended from the first Naughana, who gained the throne by the assistance of the Ahirs in the tenth century. The first Maṇḍalika in this inscription probably reigned in the

* The meaning of the second half of the verse is that Mokalasiṁha was as much superior to other kings as the Kalahaṁsa or Râjahaṁsa is to common Haṁsas.

† Acted the part of a blue bee near the lotus of Śiva's feet, *i.e.*, was Śiva's worshipper.

‡ Instead of "at the head of kings who were subjected by his hands," we may also read, "at the head of kings subjected to his taxes, which extended over the universe." *Bhâsura* may also be taken to mean the sun, and the two first epithets may also be so turned as to agree with that explanation. In that case *bhûbhṛit* means "mountains," *kara* "rays," and *pâda* "the minor neighbouring hills." *Pratyala* is a hyperkoristicon formed out of *parti* and *alam*. It occurs also in the Valabhî grants.

§ I regret that the second and third pâdas of these stanzas are not intelligible to me. The translation of *kasyâḥ kuto* by "of what land is he?" may be defended by this,—that *ku* means "the earth," and the affix *taḥ* (*tasil*) stands for all cases. "He cannot be passed by," *i.e.*, "his commands must be obeyed."

latter part of the twelfth century; Khangâr is perhaps the son of Râ Kavât. Unfortunately no date is given.*

A local history of Sorath, written in Persian by Amarji Ranchodji, a Diwân of Junâgaḍh about the beginning of the present century, gives a list of the Chuḍâsamâs —who claimed to belong to the Chandravañśa or Lunar race—from Navaghana I. The few manuscripts I have seen of the work are not always in perfect agreement as to the dates of accession and lengths of the reigns, and in one instance the names of two kings are transposed. The reigns of the first four kings beginning with Navaghana I., however, extend over 151 years, and then a blank occurs of 22 years between Navaghana II. and his successor Maṇḍalika I. Otherwise the list is pretty consistent, and gains support from this inscription. I give it corrected by the inscription for what it is worth, inserting such additions from other sources and conjectural corrections in the dates as seem required.†

MS. dates. Samvat.	Probable date, A.D.	
„	*904 ?*	Râ Dyâs or Dyâchh, the third in descent from Râ Gâriyo, the grandson of Râ Chuḍâchand, and first of the Chuḍâsamâs of Junagaḍh. Râ Dyâs was defeated and slain by the king of Paṭṭan S. 874 (*? 917 A.D.*).‡
894	*937 ?*	Navaghana or Naughan his son, reared by Devait Bodar, the Ahir; during a severe famine he invaded Sindh and defeated "Hamir," the Sumarâ prince.
916	*959 ?*	Khangâr, his son, killed at Bagasarâ by the Anhilvâḍâ Râja (possibly by Mularâja, who ruled from A.D. 942 or 961 to 996, and defeated "Graharipu the Ahir" of Vanthali).
952	*968 ?*	Mularâja, "son of Khangâr" (perhaps of Anhilvâḍa).
1009	*992 ?*	Navaghana II., his son, "ruled for 38 (18 ?) years."
1047	*1011 ?*	Maṇḍalika, son of Navaghana, joined Bhima Deva of Gujarât in pursuit of Maḥmûd of Gazni, S. 1080, A.H. 414.
1095	1038	Hamir Deva, son of Maṇḍalika, 13 years.
1108	1051	Vijayapâla, son of Hamiradeva.
1162	*1085 ?*	Navaghana III., subdued the Râja of Umetâ.
—	*1107 ?*	Khangâra II., slain by Siddharâja Jayasiñha of Anhilvâḍa §; (omitted by Amarji).
1184	1127	Maṇḍalika II., 11 years.
1195	1138	Âlansiñha, 14 years.

* Conf *Râs Mâlâ*, vol. I. p. 309. In a note at the foot of Jacob's transcript of this inscription (*Jour. Bom. B. R. A. S.* vol. I. p. 94), it is said that, "That the date of this inscription is S. 1115, Chaitra Śudh 7, which Capt. Jacob supposes a mistake for S. 1215, &c." Whence this date is derived we are not told; the inscription doubtless belongs to about the date S. 1435 or 1440. Tod has given an outline of the sense of the historical portion of this inscription (*Travels*, p: 511), and Mr. Wathen has added (*ibid*, p. 516) a fuller version, but he omits altogether the names of Naughan, Mokal and Melag, while to the end of it is added part of *another* inscription, dated S. 1277, relating to Tejahpâla and Vastupâla.

† These corrections are applied only to the dates when converted into A.D., and where doubtful are marked with a (?).

‡ *Ante*, p. 86, and *Ind. Antiq.* vol. II. pp. 312 ff. Some copies give S. 874 as the date of Naughan's accession, and allow 42 years for his reign. Tod, counting Chuḍachand as the fortieth prince before his own time, and the eighth before Jam Unaḍ, whom he places in S. 1110, assumes that Chuḍachand must have lived about S. 960. Very little dependence, however, can be placed on such a computation. He says he was contemporary with Râm Kamâr, the fourteenth prince of Ghumli. *Travels*, p. 469.

§ *Râs Mâlâ*, vol. I. pp. 154 ff.

MS. dates. Samvat.	Probable date, A.D.	
1209	1152	Gaṇeśa, 5 years.
1214	1157	Navaghana or Naughan IV., 9 years.
1224	1167	Khangâra III., 46 years.
1270	1213	Maṇḍalika III., son of Khangâra III. (mentioned in the inscription l. 9), 22 years.
—	*1235 ?*	Navaghana or Naughana V.*
1302	1245	Mahîpâladeva (Râ Kavât), 34 years, built a temple at Somanâth Paṭṭan.
1336	1279	Khangâra IV., his son, repaired the temple of Somanâtha, conquered Diu, &c. Shams Khân took Junâgaḍh.
1390	1333	Jayasiñha deva, son of Khangâra IV., 11¾ years.†
1402	1345	Mugatsiñha or Mokalasiñha, 14 years.
1416	1359	Melagadeva or Megaladeva.
1421	*1371*	Mahîpâladeva II. or Madhupat.
1439	*1376*‡	Maṇḍalika IV. (son of Mahîpaladeva).
1450	1393	Jayasiñhadeva II. (apparently "the Ray of Jehrend" or "Jiran" mentioned by Firishtah§ as defeated by Muzaffar Khân of Gujarât in A.D. 1411).
1469	1412	Khangâra V.; war with Ahmad Shâh.‖
1489	1432	Maṇḍalika V. restored the Uparkoṭ in S. 1507; subdued by Mahmûd Bîgarah in A.D. 1469–70.¶

After their subjugation to the Ahmadâbâd kings the dynasty seems to have been preserved as tributary Jaghirdars for another century; the list of these princes stands thus :—

A.D. 1472, Bhâpat, cousin of Mandalika V., 32 years.
" 1503, Khangâra VI., son of Bhâpat, 22 years.
" 1524, Naughana VI., son of Khangâra, 25 years.
" 1551, Śrî Siñha, 35 years; Gujarat subdued by Akbar.
" 1585, Khangâra VII., till about 1609.

Then follows a list of Governors or *Motassadîs* on the part of the Dihli emperors, —about thirty of them in 106 years,—who, the author says, "spent their time dishonourably, like owls in a wilderness, and did nothing worthy of record."**

* Amarji omits Naughana after Mandalika, to whom he assigns a reign of 22 years 3¾ months beginning in S. 1270, and then makes Mahipâla's reign begin in S. 1302, leaving 10 years unaccounted for, or about the same time as Navaghan IV. reigned.

† This Jayasiñhadeva is mentioned in the above inscription in such a way as to suggest to Dr. Bühler and Kinloch Forbes that Siddharâja Jayasiñha of Gujarat, who slew Râ Khangâra the son of Naughan, in the early part of the twelfth century, is meant. If this be the case Amarji's chronology is useless ;—an interval of 200 years would occur between Siddharâja Jayasiñha (d. 1142 A.D.) and his successor Mokalasiñha or Mugatsiñha 1345 A.D.

‡ Amarji gives the three successors of Mugatsiñha in the order—Madhupat, 5 years (S. 1416–1421); Maṇḍalika, 17½ years (S. 1421–1439); and Megaladeva, his illegitimate brother, 12 years (S. 1439–1450). I have allowed the dates S. 1421 and 1439 to stand, but have no doubt they should be altered to 1428 and 1433.

§ Briggs's *Translation of Firishtah*, vol. IV. pp. 5, 6; conf. Forbes, *Râs Mâlâ*, vol. I. p. 328.

‖ Briggs, *ibid.* pp. 17, 20.

¶ *Ibid.* pp. 52—56; the inscription over the gate of the Uparkoṭ is dated S. 1507; but has been badly used by the Muhammadans.

** Were the *Mirat Ahmadi* translated, as it ought to be, it would probably furnish many details of the history of Kâṭhiâwâḍ from the beginning of the fifteenth century. Information might perhaps also be collected about Junâgaḍh, especially as to the sources from which Amarji derived the materials for his early history of the place.

In the hot season many families go up from Junâgaḍh and live in the apartments within this gate, making a sort of sanitarium of the enclosure. But as there are no such sanitary arrangements here as at Śatruñjaya—which is remarkable for its perfect cleanliness—Girnâr, in the vicinity of the Jaina temples, during the hot season, is filthy in the extreme.

The Jaina temples here form a sort of fort, perched on the ledge at the top of the great cliff, but still 600 feet below the summit; and they are disappointingly few—about sixteen in all,—and neither larger nor finer than many among the numerous collection on Śatruñjaya,—whilst the few *pujaris*, or officiating priests, that attend them are most ignorant.

The largest temple is that of Neminâtha (plates XXXI. and XXXII.), standing in a quadrangular court about 190 feet by 130, and bears an inscription on one of the pillars of the *maṇḍapa* stating that it was repaired in A.D. 1278. It consists of two halls, and the shrine (G)—which contains a large image in black stone of Neminâtha the twenty-second *Tîrthaṅkara*, bedecked with massive gold ornaments and jewels. The principal manḍapa (B) in front of this measures across from door to door inside 41 feet 7 inches by 44 feet 7 inches from the shrine door to that leading out at the west end. The roof is supported by twenty-two square columns of granite coated with perfectly white lime, while the floor is of beautifully tesselated marble. Between two of the pillars on the left of the approach to the shrine is an octagonal slab or low seat (*bajurt*, Q) about fourteen inches high, on which to grind the saffron, &c., with which the images are marked every morning after washing them. Round the shrine is a passage (H, H), corresponding to the *pradakshina* or circumambulatory passage round the sacellum in Hindu temples, containing many images in white marble, with the glaring eyes covered with lenticular pieces of rock-crystal so usual among the Jains. Among these are Gaṇeśa, a Chovisvata or slab of the twenty-four Tîrthaṅkaras, &c. Between the outer and inner Manḍaps are two small shrines. The outer hall measures 38 feet by 21 feet 3 inches, and has two raised platforms (E and F) the slabs on which are of a close-grained yellowish stone, known in Gujarât as *pîlu patra*, covered with representations of feet in pairs: they are intended to represent the 2452 feet of the *gaṇadhara* * or first disciples of the Jina or Tîrthaṅkara, but are in fact scarcely more than a third of this number of pairs. On the west of this is a closed entrance, with a porch almost overhanging the nearly perpendicular scarp of the hill.

This temple is of very considerable age,† but the columns and walls inside and out are carefully coated with lime and kept in such a state of repair that it looks quite a modern erection. The enclosure in which it stands is nearly surrounded inside, by some seventy little cells each enshrining a marble image on a bench; with a closed passage (J, J, J) running round in front of them and lighted by a perforated stone screen. The principal entrance has been originally on the east side of the court (at K), but it is now closed, and that used is from the court in Khangâr's Mehal (at A).

* The 2452 feet of the *gaṇadhara* are frequently represented in Jaina temples. In the Bauddha *Sûtras* likewise, mention is often made of the 1250 disciples of Gautama, composed of the followers of his five great disciples Sariputra, his brother Maudgalyayana, Mahâkaśyapa, and his two brothers, who each brought him 250 followers.

† It bears on two of the pillars of the Manḍap, inscriptions dated 1275, 1281, and 1278, relating to donations of wealthy Srâvaks for the daily worship of the Jina.

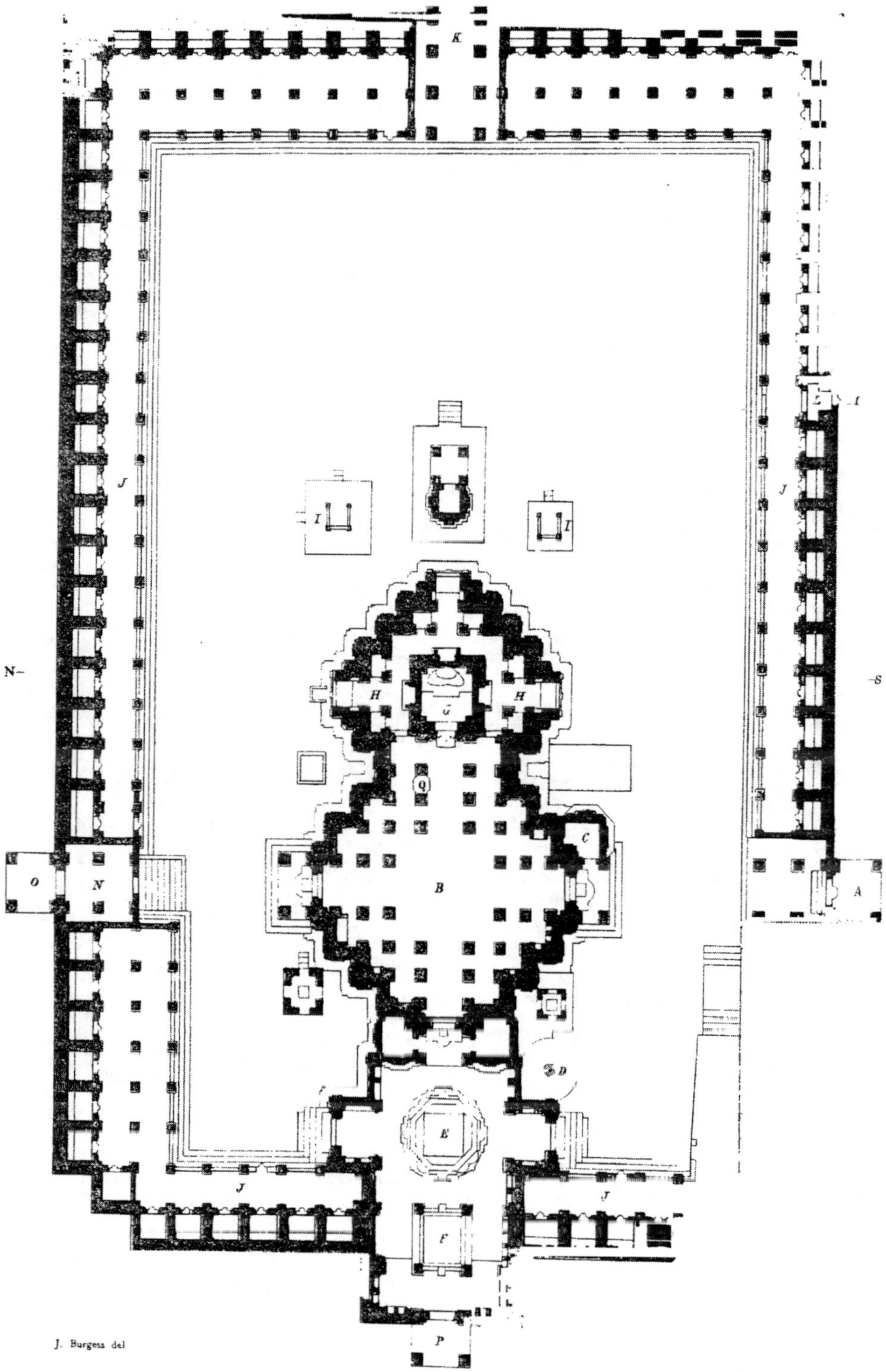

J. Burgess del

On the south side there is a passage (L) leading through between two of these shrines into a low dark temple (at M) with granite pillars placed in lines at regular intervals. Opposite the entrance is a recess containing two large black images remarkably like the old Buddhist type: that in the back of the recess has a lion rampant and over it a *makara* or allegorised crocodile in bas-relief, on the slab behind each arm of the figure; and at Nâsik and elsewhere, we find the same figures on Bauddha images, but scarcely anywhere else on a veritable Jaina one.* A small door admits into an apartment behind these figures, whence a descent leads down into a sunken story or cave in which is a large white marble image—held in the most superstitious veneration by the sect—and to conceal which the *pujâris* will tell any number of lies, each in succession contradicting the preceding. It has a slight hollow in the shoulder *said* to have been caused by water that used to drop from the ear,—whence it obtained the name of Amijhera—"nectar drop." In the right end of the same cell is also an old black image somewhat like that seen in the room above.

On the right hand of the south entrance door of the temple is a small shrine (C) of Ambikâ Mâtâ the Śâsanadevi or tutelary goddess of Neminâtha; and (at D) by the side of the door of the outer maṇḍapa is an Amba or Mango tree, the "Bo-tree" peculiar to the same Jina. In the court are some small shrines (I, I) over the *pâduka* or footprints of deceased *Gorjîs* or high priests.

As we descend from the court of Neminâtha's temple by the northern door, we find some old inscriptions in the porch (N), partly destroyed, however, by the exfoliation of the granite. So far as can be made out, the two longest run as follows:—

५° संवत् १२१५ वर्षे चैत्र सुदि ८ रवौ अद्येह श्रीमदूर्ज्जयंततीर्थे जगत्यां समस्त
देवकुलिकासकक्काजाकुवालिसंविरणसर्वेठ°सालवाहणप्रतिपत्या
सू° जसहडठ° सावदेवेन परिपूर्णकृता तथा ठ° रूरचसुत ठ° परि
सालिवाहणेनवागहरिसिरायापरितः कारितश्रीचंच्चारिदिवांक्षत
कंडकमंतिरंतदविधाचीश्रीअंबिकादेवितिमादेवकुलिका च निष्पादिता ॥

This states that 'in Sam. 1215 the Ṭhâkuras Sâvadeva and Jasahada completed, out of regard for Ṭhâkura Sâlavâhana, shrines for all the divinities in the holy Ujjayanta. . . . . And in the same year Ṭhâkura Pari . . . the son of Ṭhâkura Ruraksha . . . . and built a small temple of Śrî Ambikâ who presides over the actions of men.'

५° ॥ श्रीमत्सूरिधनेश्वरः समभवच्छ्रीशीलभद्र . . .
शिष्यस्तत्पादपंकजे मधुकरः कीडाकचोपो . .
शिषाः सोभितच्चनेमिसदनेश्रीभद्रसूरि . . त . .
श्रीमद्रैवतकेचकारयभदेकापप्रति [घादिका]
श्रीसज्जातमहामात्यपृष्ठार्थविहितोत्तरः भिं ° [अदत]
⌣ वश्रादेव चंडादिजननान्वितः [२सं°१(२७६)]

* In the cave temples at Dhârâsinva in the Haidarâbâd territory, however, the original images are almost identical with those in the Ajaṇṭâ caves, while there are also nude standing ones of the Digambara Jainas.

Translation.

Śrîmat Sûri Dhaneśvara flourished; his disciple (?) Śrî Śîlabhadra, like a bee, (*sported*) on his lotus-like feet . . . His disciple (?) again, Śrî Bhadrasûri, on the splendid and awful mountain Raivataka on which there is a temple of Nemi with a splendid pavilion. . . . .

A third and shorter inscription is unintelligible.

Turning to the left, there are three temples;—that on the south side contains a colossal image of Ṛishabha Deva, the first Tîrthaṅkara, called Âdi-Buddhanâtha—similar in every respect to that vulgarly known at Śatruñjaya as "Bhîm-Pâdam," only that this one—locally known as Garhigatuk—has been carefully coated with the whitest chunam and has a *kausagiya*, or standing meditative figure, over each shoulder. In Mârwâḍ, the Śrâvaks make large images like this—perfectly nude—at the Holi festival, when they are worshipped especially by their women. On the throne of this gigantic image is an old slab of yellow stone carved in A.D. 1442, with figures of the twenty-four Tîrthaṅkaras. On the north side, opposite this temple is another—Panchabai's,—said by the pujâri to have been built about fifty years ago, by the Śrâvak panchâyat, and containing five *śikhars* or spires, each enshrining quadruple images, such as we find in the Nandiśwara Dwîpa at Pâlitâṇâ,—that is, a sort of square pyramid or pillar with an image on each side of the upper portion of it. To the west of these two temples is a much larger one called Malakavisi, dedicated to Pârśwanâtha, and having an open portico. Its ceilings have been very fine, but are now much damaged. In the *bhâmti*, or cloisters surrounding the court, there are also some remarkable designs in carved ceilings.

Coming out of this and proceeding to the north we enter the enclosure of the temple of Pârśwanâtha, rebuilt, it is said, by Singharâma Soni in the latter part of the sixteenth century, and repaired by Premabhâi Hemâbhâi about 1843. It contains a large white marble figure of Pârśwanâtha bearing the date 1803 A.D. with the polycephalous cobra over him, whence he is styled *Śeshphaṇi*. This temple is peculiar in having a sort of gallery; and, like the previous one of the same Tîrthaṅkara, it faces the east whilst the others mostly face the west.

The next and last temple to the north is Kumârapâla's. It has a long open portico on the west supported by twenty-four columns. The temple proper or *maṇḍapa* and shrine are small, and the ceilings and architraves bear marks of iconoclastic violence. Indeed, towards the end of last century, there was little of this temple standing, except the *maṇḍapa* with its beautiful pendentive and the pillars and lintels of the portico; and when the Śrâvaks began to repair it, they were suddenly and unexpectedly stopped: a wealthy and influential *sharâf* or banker, devoted to the worship of Śiva, resolved to instal his favourite idol there. The Śrâvaks, it is said, threatened to perform the desperate ceremony of *dhàrṇâ*—sitting at the door of the temple fasting until the desired boon was granted, or till the suitor perished, when the sin of his death and its consequences would fall upon the occupants. Both parties were thus brought to a stand for a while. In 1824, however, Śeth Śrî Pancha Hansrâja Jeṭha appears, from an inscription, to have been able to proceed with the restoration. The shrine contains three images—in the middle Abhinandanâtha, the fourth Tîrthaṅkara, dedicated in 1838, and on either side Adinâtha and Śambhava—dated in 1791.

PLAN

J. Burgess del.

These temples are along the western face of the hill and are all enclosed. Outside the enclosure, to the north is the Bhîma-Kuṇḍa—a large tank, about 70 feet by 50, frequented chiefly by Hindus for bathing. Below it, and on the verge of the cliff is a smaller tank of good water, and near it a small canopy supported by three roughly hewn pillars and a piece of rock, containing a short octagonal stone called Hathi-paglâ,—"the elephant's foot," a stratum on the top of which is of light granite and the rest of dark; the lower part is immersed in water most of the year, and of course it has its connexion with the supernatural.

Between the wall of the Devakoṭa, or large enclosed group of temples just described, and the verge of the cliff there are also two or three fragments of very old temples,—a pillar or two and some lintels of granite,—the last vestiges of works whose plan and style the archæologist wishes most to know about. It was very disappointing therefore to find no more remaining of these older buildings, and that they had been pulled down in order to use the materials in the repairs of more modern structures. This species of Vandalism is no new thing here, however, for Tod read in one inscription,

"By order of Śrî Paṇḍita Devasena Sangha in S. 1215* (A.D. 1158) Chaitra Śuddha 8th, Sunday, the old temples of the *devatâs* were removed and new ones erected."

And in another—

"In S. 1339 (A.D. 1283), Jyeshṭha Śuddha 10th, Thursday, the old ruined temples being removed from their sites on the mountain of Revatâchala, new ones were erected."

And this process may be seen in active operation even at present. The walls of every inclosure reveal scores of carved stones built into them.

To the east of the Devakoṭa, there are several temples, the principal being the temple of Mân Singha Bhoja Râja of Kachh—an old granite temple near the entrance gate, which Tod calls a Digambara temple of Neminâtha, but which seems to have been recently repaired by the Śrâvak community, and is now dedicated to Śambhavanâtha, the third *jina;* next is Vastupâla and Tejaḥpâla's, which is a triple temple (plates XXXIII. and XXXIV.): the central fane, measuring 53 feet by 29½, has two domes (A and C) finely carved but much mutilated, and the shrine (D), which is 13 feet square, with a large niche or *gokhlê* on the left side, contains an image of Mallinâtha the nineteenth Jina, bearing beneath it the inscription:

महामात्यश्रीवस्तुपालमहंश्रीललितादेवीमूर्ति ।
महामात्यश्रीवस्तुपालमहंश्रीसोखुमूर्तिं ।

thus translated :—

'The wife of the great minister Vastupâla—Śrî Lalitâdevî's image.'

'The wife of the great minister Vastupâla—Śrî Sokhu's image.'

On a lintel on the left side of the first dome of the Maṇḍap is also carved the line—

महामात्यश्रीवस्तुपालमहं:श्रीसोखुमूर्त्तिः

'Śrî Sokhu's image, wife of the great minister Vastupâla;'

And on the opposite side—

महामत्यश्रीवस्तुपालमहंश्रीलालतादेविमूर्त्ति

'Śrî Lâlatâ devî's image, the wife of the great minister Vastupala.'

---

* This is dated on the same day as the first inscription given on p. 167.

On either side this central temple is a large hall (E, F), about 38 feet 6 inches from door to door, containing a remarkable solid pile of masonry called a samosan,—that on the north side named Sumeru,* having a square base, and the other, Sameta Sikharat† with a nearly circular one. Each rises in four tiers of diminishing width, almost to the roof, and is surmounted by a small square canopy (G, H) over images. The upper tiers are reached by steps arranged for the purpose. On the outside of the shrine tower are three small niches (I, I, I) in which images have been placed, and there are stone ladders up to the niches to enable the pujârîs to reach them. There are inscriptions over the doors of this temple, from which it appears to have been built in A.D. 1231. On plate XXXV. are given photo-lithographs of three of these, of which the following is a transliteration of the first:—‡

1 ॥ ॐ नमः श्रीसर्वज्ञाय ॥ पायान्नेमिजिनः स यस्य [कथितः स्वागो]§ कृतागस्थितावघ्रे [रूप] दिदृक्षया
[स्थितवति] प्रीते सुराणां प्रभौ ॥ कायेभागवते[वनेवक द्विपोलाविनेशंसंतामिदृशां मपि]- वनाजव
॥ १ ॥ स्वस्ति श्रीविक्रमसंवत् १२८८ वर्षे फागुण [शुदि १० बुधे श्रीमदणहिल]-
2 ॥ [पुर] वास्तव्यप्राग्वाटान्वयप्रसूत ठ° श्रीचंडपात्मज ठ° श्रीचंडप्रसादांगज ठ° श्रीसोमतनुज ठ° श्री-
आशाराजनंदनस्य ठ° श्रीकुमारदेवीकुक्षिसंभूतस्य ठ° श्रीलुणिग महं° श्रीमालदेवयोरनुजस्य
महं श्रीतेजःपालाग्रजन्मनो महामात्यश्रीवस्तुपालस्यात्मजे महं श्रीललितादेवीकुक्षिसरो-
3 ॥ वरराजहंसायमाने महं° श्रीजयतसिंहे सं ७९ वर्षपूर्वं स्तंभतीर्थमुद्राव्यापारान् व्यापृण्वति सति सं ७७
वर्षे श्रीशत्रुंजयोज्जयंतप्रभृतिमहातीर्थयात्रोत्सवप्रभावाविर्भूतश्रीमद्देवाधिदेवप्रसादासादितसंघाधिपत्येन
चौलुक्यकुलनभस्तलप्रकाशनैकमार्त्तंडमहाराजाधिराजश्रीलवणप्रसाददेवसु-
4 ॥ तमहाराजश्रीवीरधवलदेवप्रीतिप्रतिपन्नराज्यसर्वैश्वर्येण श्रीशारदाप्रतिपन्नापत्येन महामात्यश्रीवस्तु-
पालेन तथा अनुजेन सं ७६ वर्षपूर्वं गूर्ज्जरमंडले धवलक्ककप्रमुखनगरेषु मुद्राव्यापारान् व्यापृण्वता
महं° श्रीतेजःपालेन च श्रीशत्रुंजयार्बुदाचलप्रभृतिमहातीर्थेषु श्रीमदणहिल [पुरभृगुपु]-
5 ॥ रस्तंभनकपुरस्तंभतीर्थदर्भवतीधवलक्ककप्रमुखनगरेषु तथा अन्यसमस्तस्थानेष्वपि कोटिशोऽभिनवधर्म-
स्थानानि प्रभूतजीर्णोद्धाराश्च कारिताः ॥ तथा सचिवेश्वरश्रीवस्तुपालेन इह स्वयंनिर्मापितश्रीशत्रुं-
जयमहातीर्थावतारश्रीमदादितीर्थंकरश्रीऋषभदेवस्तंभनकपुरावतारश्रीपार्श्वनाथदेवसत्यपु-
6 ॥ रावतारश्रीमहावीरदेवप्रशस्तिसहितकश्मीरावतारश्रीसरस्वतीमूर्त्तिदेवकुलिकाचतुष्टयजिनयुगल
अम्बावलोकनाशाम्बप्रद्युम्नशिखरेषु श्रीनेमिनाथदेवालंकृतदेवकुलिकाचतुष्टयतुरगाधिरूढस्वपितामह
ठ° श्रीसोमनिजपितृ ठ° श्रीआशाराजमूर्त्तिद्वितयचारुतोरणत्रयश्रीनेमिनाथ-
7 ॥ देव आत्मीयपूर्वजाग्रजानुजपुत्रादिमूर्त्तिसमन्वितसुखोद्घाटनकस्तंभश्रीअष्टापदमहातीर्थप्रभृति अने-
ककीर्त्तनपरंपराधिराजिते श्रीनेमिनाथदेवाधिदेवविभूषितश्रीमदुज्जयंतमहातीर्थे आत्मनस्तथा स्वसध-
र्मचारिण्याः प्राग्वाटज्ञातीय ठ° कान्हडपुत्र्याः ठ° राणुकुक्षिसंभूताया महं° श्रीललितादेव्याः
8 ॥ पुण्याभिवृद्धये श्रीनागेंद्रगच्छे भट्टारकश्रीमहेंद्रसूरिसंताने शिष्यश्रीशांतिसूरिशिष्यश्रीआणंदसूरि-
श्रीअमरसूरिपदे भट्टारकश्रीहरिभद्रसूरिपट्टालंकरणप्रभुश्रीविजयसेनसूरिप्रतिष्ठितश्रीअजितनाथदे-
वादिविंशतितीर्थंकरालंकृतोयमभिनवः समंडपः श्रीसम्मेतमहातीर्थावतारप्रासादः कारितः ॥ छ ॥

* A fabled mountain of the Buddhists and Jainas.

† Mount Pârśwanâtha, or *Parisnath*, in Bengal.

‡ Text revised by Dr. Bühler.

§ The letters enclosed within brackets [ ] are not legible in the lithograph. They have been simply taken over from the transcript done by Wâman Âcharya, Pandit, who had access to the originals.—G. B.

INSCRIPTIONS FROM THE TEMPLE OF VASTUPÂLA TEJAPÂLA.

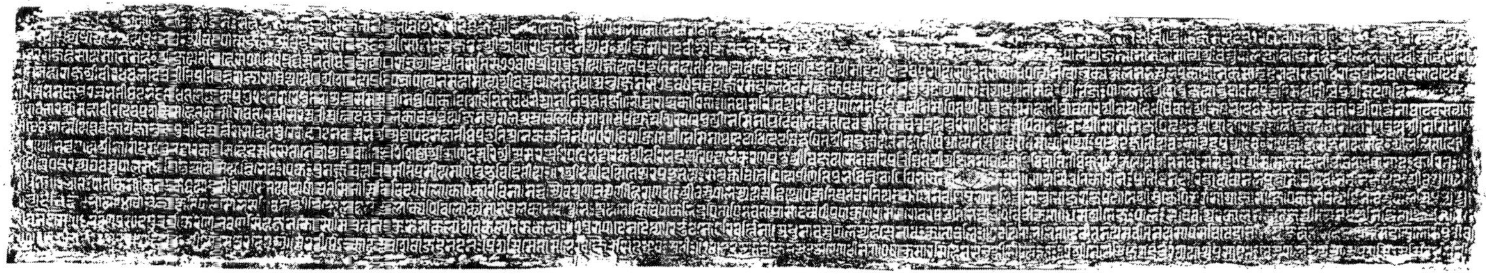

OVER THE SOUTH DOOR ON THE WEST FRONT

OVER THE NORTH DOOR ON THE WEST FRONT

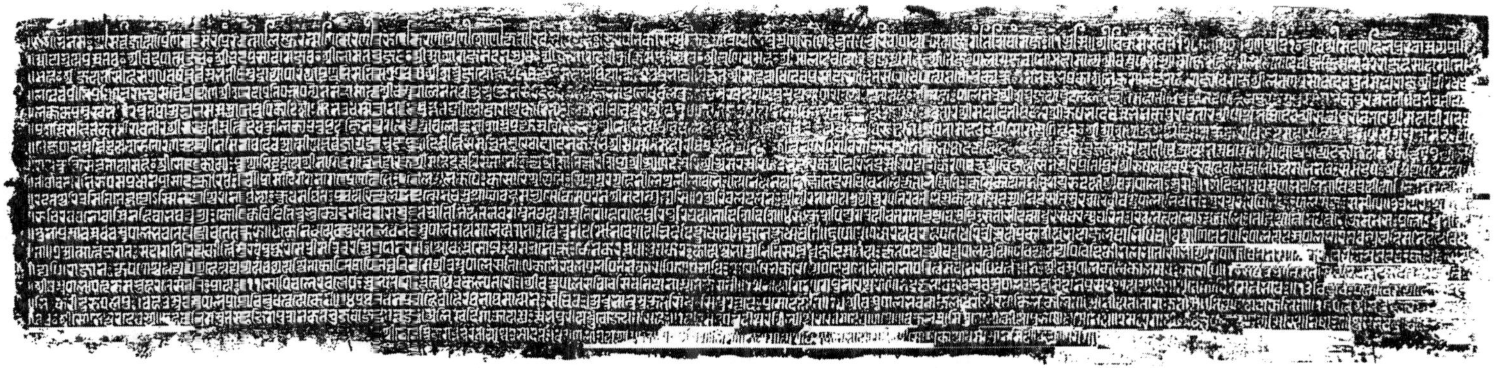

J. Burgess fecit.

OVER THE NORTH END DOOR

9 ॥ पीयूषपूरस्य च वस्तुपालमंत्रीशितुस्त्रायमियान्विभेदः॥ एकः पुनर्ज्जीवयति प्रमीतं प्रमीयमाणं तु भुवि
द्वितयिः ॥१॥ श्रीदश्रीदयितेश्वरप्रभृतयः संतु क्वचित्तेपि ये प्रीणंति प्रभविष्णवोपि विभवै [र्नाकिंचनं]
कंचन। सोयं सिंचति कांचनैः प्रतिदिनं दारिद्र्यदावानलप्रम्लानां पृथिवीं नवीनजलदः श्रीवस्तुपालः
10 ॥ पुनः ॥२॥ भ्रातः पातकिनां किमत्र कथया दुर्मंत्रिणामेतया येषां चेतसि नास्ति किंचिदपरं
लोकोपकारं विना। नन्वस्यैव गुणान् गृणीहि गणशः श्रीवस्तुपालस्य यस्तद्दिश्योपकृतिव्रतं चरति
यत्कर्णेन चीर्णं पुरा ॥३॥ भित्त्वा भानुं भोजराजे प्रयाते श्रीमुंजेपि स्वर्गसाम्राज्यभाजि॥ एकः
संप्रत्यर्थिनां वस्तुपालस्तिष्ठत्यश्रु
11 ॥ स्यंदनिष्कंदनाय ॥४॥ चौलुक्यक्षितिपालमौलसचिव त्वत्कीर्तिकोलाहलस्त्रैलोक्येपि विलोक्यमानपु-
लकानंदाश्रुभिः श्रूयते। किंचैषा कलिदूषितापि भवता प्रासादवापीप्रपाकूपारामसरोवरप्रभृति-
भिर्द्धात्री पवित्रीकृता ॥५॥ स श्रीतेजःपालः सचिवश्चिरकालमस्तु तेजस्वी ॥ येन वयं
निश्चिंताश्चिंतामणिने-
12 ॥ व नंदामः ॥६॥ लवणप्रसादपुत्रश्रीकरणे लवणसिंहजनकोसौ। मंत्रित्वमत्र कुरुतां कल्पशतं
कल्पतरुकल्पः ॥७॥ पुरा पादेन दैत्यारेर्भुवनोपरिवर्तिना। अधुना वस्तुपालस्य हस्तेनाधःकृतो
बलिः ॥८॥ दयिता ललितादेवी तनयमवीतनयमाप सचिवेंद्रात्॥ नाम्ना जयंतसिंहं
जयंतमिन्द्रात्पुलोमपुत्रीव
13 ॥ — — श्रीगुर्जरेश्वरपुरोहित ठ° श्रीसोमेश्वरदेवस्य॥ स्तंभतीर्थेऽत्र कायस्थवंशे ; वाजडनंदनः॥
प्रशस्तिमेतामलिखज्जैत्रसिंहभुवः सुधीः ॥१॥ वाहडस्य तनूजेन सूत्रधारेण धीमता॥ एषा
कुमारसिंहेन समुत्कीर्णा प्रयत्नतः ॥२॥ श्रीनेमेस्त्रिजगद्भर्तुरंबायाश्च प्रसादतः ॥ वस्तुपा
लान्वयस्यास्तु प्रशस्तिः स्वस्तिशालिनी ॥३॥

Translation.

[1] Adoration to the omniscient one! May the Nemi Jina, with whom the lord of gods was pleased, while he was standing before him, to see the form of the latter protect [all (?)].* May it be well! In the Samvat year 1288, in the month of Phâlguna, bright fortnight, 10th day, Wednesday,

[2-4] while the prosperous Jayantasiñha, who graced the womb of his mother Lalitâ Devî, as the swan does the lotus-pond, and who was the son of the great and prosperous minister Vastupâla,—who was the elder brother of the prosperous Tejaḥpâla, and he younger brother of the Ṭhâkura Luniga, and the respected and prosperous Mâladeva; who was the son of the prosperous Kumâra Devî, and the great Ṭhâkura Âsârâjâ, who was the son of the prosperous Thâkura Soma, who was the son of the Tâkura Chandaprasâda, who was the son of the Ṭhâkura Chandapa, who was born in the family of Prâgvâta, residents of the city of Aṇahila;—while that Jayantasiñha, in the Samvat year 78, [*i.e.* 1278], was trading in shroffage in Stambha-Tîrtha,† many crumbling temples were repaired and thousands of new religious houses were built in the great holy places like Satruñjaya, Mount Abu, &c., in the known towns of Aṇahila, Bhrigu, Stambhanaka, Stambha-Tîrtha, Darbhavatî, Dhavalakkaka,‡ &c., and in all other places, by the great and prosperous minister Vastupâla, who became the leader of all the merchants

---

* The latter half of this stanza is unconnected and unintelligible.

† Khâmbât or Cambay.

‡ Bhrigu is Bhrigukachha or Bharuch; Dharbhavatî is Dabhoi; and Dhavalakka is Dholakâ.

through the grace of the lord of the gods, bestowed upon him in consideration of his power acquired by making pilgrimages to the great holy places like Śatrunjaya, Ujjayanta, &c., and who gained the glories of royalty through the love of the great king Vîradhavaladeva,—who was the son of the king of kings Lavanaprasâda, the sun that illumines the sky of the family of Châlukyâs—and who was endowed with children through the grace of the goddess Śâradâ, in the Samvat year 77 [*i.e.* 1277], and by his worthy younger brother Tejahpâla, who was trading in shroffage in the known towns of Dhavalakkaka, &c., belonging to the Gujarâtha district in the Samvat year 76 [*i.e.* 1276].

[5-6] Moreover, this great minister Vastupâla built himself the four small temples, viz.: of the holy First Tîrthaṅkara Ṛishabha Deva in the great holy place of Śatrunjaya; of the prosperous and divine Pârśvanâtha Deva in the city of Stambhanaka; of the great Vîradeva in the city of Satyapura; and of the goddess Sarasvatî, with panegyrics on it in Kaśmîra. He built the two temples of Jina and the four temples of Neminâtha Deva on the small hills named Ambâ, Avalokanâ, Śamba, and Pradyumna. He adorned the temple of Neminâtha with the image of his grandfather seated on a horse, with a pair of images of his father, the great Thâkura Aśârâjâ, and three high-arched gates.

[7-8] The holy place Ujjayanta* ornamented with the temple of Neminâtha, the lord of gods, was adorned by him with many works of fame, like the great holy place Ashtâpada, in which there are pillars . . . . † with the images of his ancestors, of his elder and younger brothers, and of his sons, engraved on them. He also built a new splendid palace in the great holy place [Ashtâpada], which was adorned with the images of twenty Tîrthaṅkaras, such as the prosperous Ajitanâtha deva, &c., which were ceremoniously *fixed*‡ there by the prosperous Nagendragachha Bhaṭṭâraka, Mahendrasûrisantâna Śishya, Śântigûri Śishya, Ânanda Sûri, Amara Sûripada Bhaṭṭâraka, Haribhadra Sûri Pattâlankaraṇa, and the prosperous and powerful Vijayasena Sûri, for the increase of his own merit and for that of his wife, the respected and prosperous Lalitâ Devî born from the womb of Râṇu, and daughter of the Thâkura Kânhada born in the family of Prâgvâta.§

[9] There is this much difference between a large quantity of nectar and Vastupâla, the lord of ministers: the former calls to life a [*thoroughly*] dead being, while the latter revives what is dying. (1) There may be men like the donor Dayiteśvara; also there may be such as, even if they are able, do not please a penniless person by their riches; but this Vastupâla, like a new cloud here, always sprinkles with gold this earth which is burnt down by the wild fire of poverty. (2)

[10] Brother, it is needless to tell a long story of those bad and sinful ministers in whose minds no other idea but that of injuring the public revolves. Sing, indeed, the numberless merits of this Vastupâla, who observes the vow of benefiting the people, in hearing of which vow we have been old enough (?) (3) King Bhoja having gone up, penetrating the world of the sun, and the king Munja having got the brilliant possession of heavens, here lives Vastupâla alone to wipe off the dropping tears of beggars. (4)

[11] O great minister of Châlukya kings! The dint of your reputation is heard with tears, and the hair standing on end through joy even in the three worlds, if well observed; and this earth, even though polluted by Kâlî, is made holy and pure by you with palaces, wells, water-places on the way, ponds, gardens, lakes, &c., [*built by you*]. (5) May that

---

* Mount Girnâr.

† Two words unintelligible.

‡ For प्रतिष्ठित प्रतिष्ठापित is probably meant here.

§ The Porwâla division of Vaniâs.

prosperous and illustrious minister Tejaḥpâla live for a long time! by whom, as by Chintâmaṇi* made free from anxiety we rejoice. (6)

[12] Here is Śrikarana (?) the son of Lavaṇaprasâda and the father of Lavaṇasiñha. May you [*Tejaḥpala,*] who are like a wish-fulfilling plant, be his minister for hundreds of ages. (7) Formerly Bali was sent down by the enemy of giants [*Vishṇu*] with his foot resting on the surface of the earth, while now by the hand of Vastupâla. (8) From the best of ministers [*Vastupâla*] the loved Lalitâ Devî obtained a son named Jayantasiñha, as the daughter of Puloma got Jayanta from Indrâ. (9)

[13] Jaitrasiñha, Dhruva, the talented son of Vâjada, born in the family of Kâyasthas, wrote this panegyric in Stambhâ-Tîrtha [*where is a temple?*] of Someśvara Deva, the preceptor of Gurjareśvara (?) (1) This was engraved with great efforts by the talented artizan (?) Kumârsiñha, the son of Vâhada. (2) May this panegyric of the family of Vastupâla remain safe through the grace of Ambâ and of the prosperous Nemi, the lord of three worlds. (3)

The other inscriptions are much to the same effect, being fulsome praises of Vastupâla son of Âśârâja the wealthy Śrîmâli Vâniâ who was Kârbhâri or prime minister to Vîradhavala Vâghela king of Gujarât (A.D. 1214–1243), and of his brother Tejaḥpâla, and others of their families.

On a stone behind the temple is the following inscription, briefly descriptive of Vastupâla's temple, which seems to have been hitherto almost unnoticed :—

वस्तुपालविहारेण हारेणेवोज्वलश्रिया ॥ उपकंठस्थितेनायं शैलराजो विराजते
श्रीविक्रमसंवत १२८८ वर्षेअश्विनवदी १५ सोमे महामात्यश्रीवस्तुपालेनआत्मश्रेयोर्थं
पश्चाद्भागे श्रीकपर्दियक्षप्रासादसमलंकृतः श्रीशत्रुंजयावतारश्रीआदिनाथप्रासादस्तदग्रतोवायपक्षे
स्वीयसद्धर्मचारिणीमहंश्रीललितादेवीश्रेयोर्थंविंशतिजिनालंकृतः श्रीसमेताशिखरप्रा-
सादस्तथा दक्षिणपक्षेदि° भार्यामहंश्रीसोखुश्रेयोर्थं चतुर्विंशतिजिनोपशोभितः श्रीअष्टा-
पदप्रासादः ;' अपूर्वघाटरनारुचिरतरमभिनवप्रासादचतुष्टयं निजद्रव्येण कारयांचक्रे ॥

Translation.

"This lord of mountains looks graceful, with the monastery of Vastupâla standing on its neck like a necklace of dazzling lustre.

"In the Vikrama Samvat year 1288 (A.D. 1231) in the month of Aśvina, dark fortnight, 15th day, Monday, the great minister Vastupâla built, for his own good, a temple of Âdinâtha [*vanpi* unintelligible] of Śatruñjaya adorned with another temple of the prosperous Kapardi Yaksha at the back. In front of this, to the north-west, he built, for the good of his dutiful and illustrious wife Lalitâ Devî, a beautiful temple Sikharaprasâda adorned with [*images of*] twenty Jinâs. So also to the south [*of this*] he constructed, for the good of another illustrious wife Sokhu, a beautiful Ashṭaprasâda. gold temple adorned with [*images of*] twenty-four Jinâs. He also built with his own money four new temples, looking splendid by the singular construction of the steps."

Still farther north is the temple of Samprati Râja, called on Tod's plate "the Palace of Khengar." It is partly a very old temple and partly a modern erection, built against the side of a cliff, and is ascended to by a stair. Inside the entrance there is another very steep flight of steps in the porch leading up to a large *maṇḍapa*, to the east

* Gaṇeśa, the remover of obstacles.

of which is added a second *maṇḍapa* and a *gaṁbhara* or shrine, containing a black image of Neminâtha dedicated by Karṇarâma Jayarâja in 1461. The temple is probably one of the oldest now standing on the hill, and an inscription in it dates from A.D. 1158; but Samprati, whom the Jainas represent as one of their greatest patrons, is said to have ruled at Ujjayini about the end of the third century B.C. and to have been the son of Kuṇâla, Aśoka's third son,* who, they say, became ruler of the Panjâb. The Buddhists represent him as succeeding his grandfather Aśoka at Pataliputra.

To the east of these, and on the face of the hill above, are other temples,—among them an old one going by the name of Dharmaśâ of Mângrol, built of grey granite—the image being also of granite. Near it is another ruined shrine, in which delicate granite columns rise from the corners of the *siṅhâsana*, or throne, carved with many squatting figures, reminding one very forcibly of Bauddha, rather than Jaina carving. Near this is the only shrine on this mount to Mahâvîra Swâmi—the twenty-fourth Tîrthaṅkara.

On the verge of the hill, at some distance to the north of the Jaina temples, and above them, stands a huge isolated rock, the Bhairava-jap,† or "Leap of Death," otherwise styled the *Raja-melavana-pathar*—the "desire-realizing rock,"—whence poor wretches have often been tempted by demoniac superstition to throw themselves away in the sadly deceitful hope of a happy future. Laying a cocoa-nut on the dizzy verge of this rock, the deluded victim attempts to poise himself upon it, and in another instant he is beyond humanity's reach, and his body a prey to the vultures that soar under the lofty cliff. Such suicide has been for long forbidden, but only ten or eleven years ago three Kuṅbis, keeping secret their intentions, ascended and made the fatal leap; some Rabâris had also determined to do the same, but were restrained.

Not far from the Bhairava-jap is a substantial dwelling, occupied by one Śivadâs, a *yogi* who has acquired great influence over the ignorant by his sanctimonious austerities and his charities—bestowed, of course, out of the offerings of his worshippers. South from this, and about 200 feet above the Jaina temples, is a Hindu shrine, called Gaumukha, beside a plentiful spring of water. From it the ascent is by a long steep stair to the crest of the mount, 400 feet higher, or about 3330 feet above the sea-level. There we find a pretty large temple, of great age, which once had a large open portico (plate XXXVI.); but the outer line of columns has been bricked up and a *śikhar* or spire added or renewed, containing an unsightly stone, the image of Ambâ Mâtâ—a goddess of ancient times, one of the many forms of Umâ or Pârvatî, whom Tod dignifies with the titles of "Universal Mother," and "Mother of the Gods." And though here she is now exclusively appropriated by Hindus, she has a shrine at the door of Neminâtha's temple; an image of her is mentioned also among the works of Vastupâla on Girnar; and an inscription thus celebrates her praise:—

"The destroyer of doubts and fears, the accomplisher of all human desires and wishes, who causes to be completed the designs of the devout—such a goddess is Śrî Mâtâ Ambikâ, the sole power whereby the prayers of mankind are fulfilled. To her be praise and glory!"

* He appears to have been officially styled Dharma-Vivardhana. He is mentioned by Fa-Hian, c. 10, and his history is told by Hiwan-Thsang, and in the *Divya Avadana*, where his son is called Sampadi. See S. Julien, *Mém. sur les Cont. Occ.* tom. i. p. 154; and Burnouf, *Int. Buddh.* pp. 404 and 427, 430.

† *Jap* is the muttering of *mantras*, charms, or the names of a god; hence this name means a place where are repeated the names of Bhairava,—a devil or destructive manifestation of Śiva.

The Jaina temples are all beautifully clean inside; this of Ambâ is filthy with smoke, and seems scarcely ever to have been swept since the Buddhists or Jainas had to leave it.

This summit is of but small extent, and at a short distance eastward there is a still higher rocky spire; beyond it is another almost as high, but still steeper and without a blade of vegetation on its granite sides; and at a still greater distance is a third but lower summit: these are the Gorakhanâtha, the Dattâtraya or Neminâtha, and the Kâlikâ peaks. From the Ambâ Mâtâ we descend about 70 feet, and then climb up by steep stairs about thrice that height to a level of about 3470 feet above the sea—passing at the foot of the ascent a bush covered with rags;—for every pilgrim, as he turns in safety from these wild rocky summits, tears a shred off his cloth, and leaves it on this bush. On this second and highest summit there is a very small shrine, perhaps three feet square, to Gorakhanâtha, the *śishya*, or disciple of Matsyendranâtha—a famous Bauddha *guru*, and—according to tradition—a less virtuous man than his pupil. From this peak we descend full four hundred feet, to about the level of the Kamandala-kuṇḍa—a reservoir of water on the face of the hill, and again climb a steep ascent, that tries the muscles of the traveller's legs, towards the Guru Dattâtraya peak. On the way we pass immense numbers of small stones, collected in little groups upon the rocks at the sides of the path, as if every visitor made a virtue of forming his own little pile. By and bye the ascent becomes so steep that the hands come easily to the help of more wearied limbs, and at length the summit is gained. It has a small open shrine or pavilion over the footmarks or *pâduka* of Neminâtha cut in the rock, and was being ministered to by a naked ascetic. Beside it hung a heavy bell.

This Neminâtha or Arishtanemi, who gives his name to this summit, and to whom the Jainas consider the whole mount as sacred, is the twenty-second of their deified saints,—men who, through their successful austerities, they imagine, have entered *nirvâṇa*, and have done with the evils of existence. This one is the favourite object of worship with the Digambara, or naked Jainas. His complexion, they say, was black, and most, if not all of his images here, are of that colour; like all the other Tîrthaṇkaras, he was of royal descent, being the son of Samudravijaya, King of Śauryanagara or Soriyapuri, in the country of Kuśavarta, and of the Harivaṅśa race—his paternal uncle being Vasudeva, the father of the famous Kṛishṇa.* At the age of three hundred he renounced the world, and leaving Dwârakâ went to Girnâr to spend the remaining seven hundred years of his long life in asceticism; he received his "Bodhi," or highest knowledge whilst meditating at Śeshavana, to the east of the Bhairava-jap, where footprints (*pâylâṅ*) are also carved—some say Neminâtha's, others Râmânanda's. His first convert was a king Dattâtri, to whom he became *guru*, after which he gradually rose to the exalted rank of a Tîrthankara, and finally attained *nirvâṇa* on this lonely pinnacle of rock which retains his name. He had as tutelary goddess, or familiar *devi*—Ambikâ Mâtâ, the same to whom the old temple on the first summit is dedicated. The Mango tree is also appropriated to him by the Śrâvaks as his "Bo-tree," whilst the *śankha* or conch shell is his cognizance. He is in fact, the Kṛishṇa of the Jainas. But it is not to them alone he is sacred here; the pilgrims met on the ascent and the naked ascetic at the shrine are not Śrâvaks. The Vaishṇavas

---

* *Ante*, p. 158, note.

who come from the pilgrimage to Dwârakâ consider they only reap the fruit of their toils when they have paid their respects here to Guru Dattâtraya. May he not have some connexion also with Kâla-Nemi, the Râkshasa ascetic of the Gandha-madana mountain, in the *Râmâyaṇa?*

Outside this very small enclosure was a most astonishing collection of pilgrims' staves. Every one leaves his support here; some doubtless have been carried many a weary mile, till the hand had worn the end smooth; but here they had been laid down at last. Is it the burden of sin, or rather the ambitious desire of merit, that leads men to pilgrimages, penances, and sacrifices? And why is this *merit* so desired? If there were a position attainable by human effort where man might confront his Creator on equal terms, and by his merit make demands on Him, how surely would it be crowded by men of every nationality and of every age! "Ye shall be as gods" is still, as at the first, the most seductive of all temptations to the wilful human mind.

Dattâtraya is about 3450 feet high, or within 20 feet of the height of Gorakhanâtha; between them is a lower rocky peak called Oghad's tuk; and eastward from the first is another similar one—the Rénuka Śikhara; whilst beyond this is Kâlkâ or Kâlikâ's, the last summit on the ridge of Girnâr, but much lower than the first three. It has a small shrine of the goddess Kâlikâ, and is the traditional haunt of the dreaded Aghoras—Śaiva devotees feeding on carrion and even on human flesh* but now extinct. From any of the three higher points the view is well worth the toil of the ascent. Girnâr is engirdled by a line of lower hills, the highest being Dâtar on the south, and over these hills the eye wanders across the plains of Kâṭhiâwâḍ, stretching away to the sea on the south and past the hills about Ḍhank to the west, towards Dwârakâ; to the south-east are the Gir Hills, and to the north and east the vast plains of the centre of this beautiful peninsula. The valleys between the central mount and the surrounding hills are thickly wooded and said to abound in game.

XI. THE ROYAL TOMBS AT JUNÂGAḌH.

Before leaving Junâgaḍh we may notice the latest, and perhaps the last, purely indigenous specimens of architecture: for Public Works officers and Italian workmen are doing their best to kill native art, and in the larger and wealthier towns of Gujarat with fatal effect, by erecting palaces for the chiefs, in a foreign style, badly imitated and unsuited to the climate or the age: and this example is rapidly being copied in less prominent places by native workmen.

About eighteen years ago the mother of the present Nawâb of Junâgaḍh began to erect her own tomb, and entrusted the design to a native *Salât.* (Plates XXXVII. and

* See Tod's *Travels in Western India*, p. 384.

MAQBÂRÂ AT JUNÂGAḌH. PLATE XXXVIII.

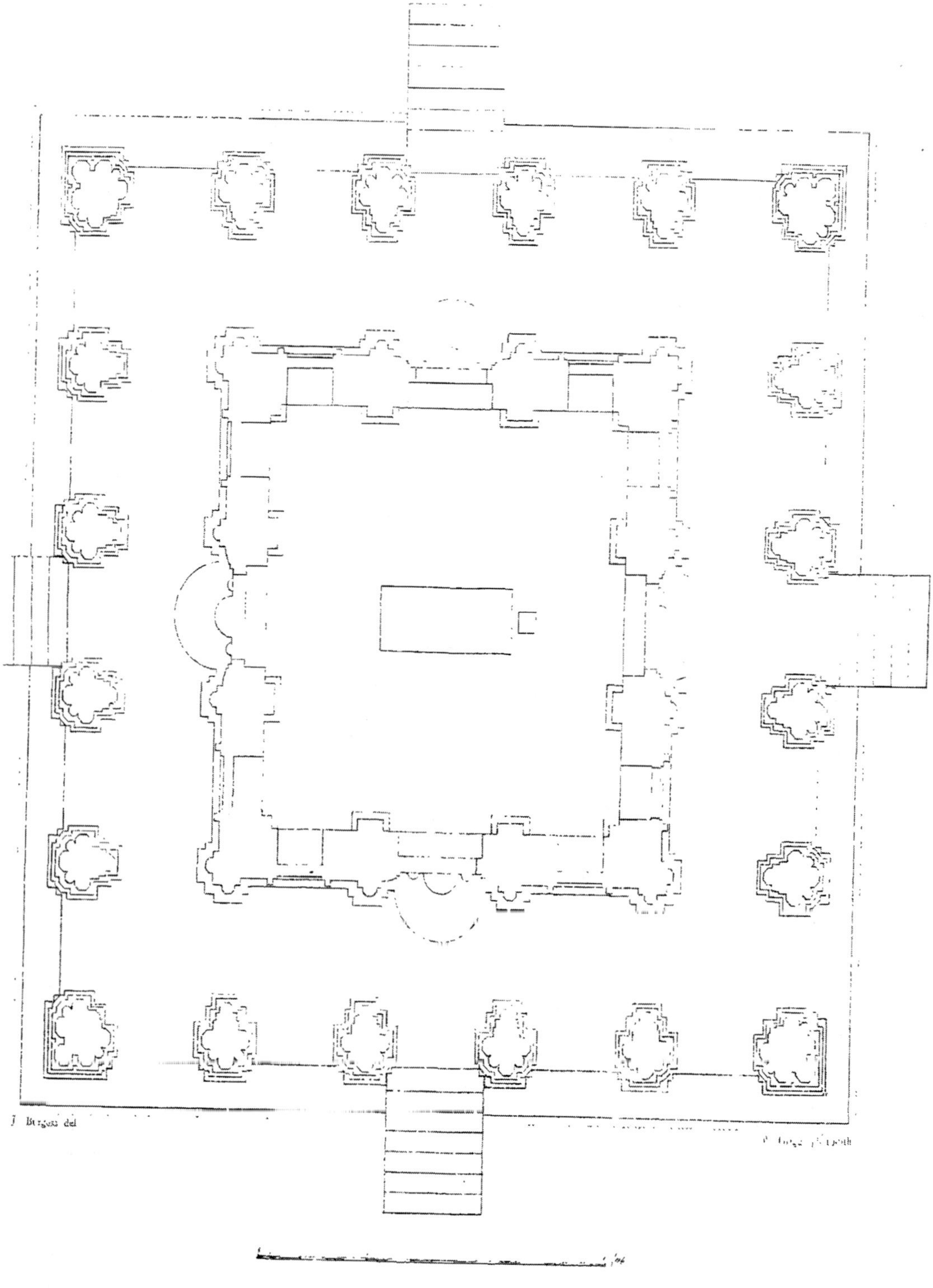

J. Burgess del.

XXXVIII.) In style it differs but little, if at all from the tombs of the late Nawâbs in the north-west of the city, but standing by itself in a walled enclosure near the tombs of the *Bára Sayyid* or twelve saints, the architect had more space and better opportunities to display his taste. On a low basement 38 feet square, stands a second platform 34 feet 5 inches square, from the edges of which rise the twenty columns supporting the colonnade or verandah surrounding the *Maqbárá* or tomb. These columns peculiarly rich and elegant, being supposed to represent a shaft oblong in section, to are each face of which a slender octagonal pillar 8½ inches in diameter is applied, while are two outer corners are covered by two others 6½ inches in diameter: the shafts the fluted and taper upwards exposing slightly the shaft they are supposed to cluster round. At three-fifths their height there is a cincture round each, and the bases are cut and ornamented in a style of elegance of detail we seldom see elsewhere, even in wood. Between the pillars are scolloped arches, sculptured round in an elaborate florid pattern. The three front colonnettes, however, of each pillar support the baluster-shaped shafts of the supports of brackets under the projecting eaves; these supports turning over like a foliated shoot under the bracket and descending in beautiful buds. Over the eaves the line of the column is carried up and terminates above the upper frieze and crenellations of the wall in slender pinnacles.

The corridors are flat-roofed, only broken by the arches at each corner of the walls which connect them with the outer columns. The building itself is about 21 feet 5 inches square outside, and 16 feet 4 inches inside; each wall being pierced by a door and two windows. The doors have scolloped arches and elaborately carved architraves, with slender half-octagon pilasters and florid pediments (see plate XXXIX.). The windows are of perforated stone and of different tracery patterns on each face, while the pair on one side, though generally alike, differ in minute details: several of them are of exquisite beauty.

Inside are two pilasters against each wall from which arches are thrown to support the roof. Outside, the roof has not a very pleasing effect: the round masses on each corner and on the summit serve no constructive purpose, nor are they in very good taste as mere ornaments. As Mr. Fergusson has recently remarked:—"All the carving is executed with precision and appropriateness, but it is all wooden, or in other words, every detail would be more appropriate for a sideboard or a bedstead, or any article of upholstery, than for a building in stone. The domes especially can hardly be traced back to their grand and solemn form as used by the Pathân architects. The pinnacles are fanciful, and the brackets designed more for ornament than work. It is a style, in fact, broken loose from the true principles of constructive design, and when this is the case no amount of ornament, however elegant it may be, will redeem the want of propriety it inevitably exhibits."*

Until the death of the Maiji Sàhiba it was of dull reddish standstone colour, but since then it has been bedaubed and disfigured by a thick coating of whitewash.

* *History of Indian and Eastern Architecture*, pp. 606, 607.

XII. GHUMLÎ OR BHUMLI.

In the south of the Navânagar territory and about forty miles west from Ḍhânk is Ghumlî, an old deserted capital of the Jaiṭwâs—now of Purbandar. It lies about four miles south of Bhanwâr, in the last valley facing the north, in the north-eastern end of the Baraḍâ hills, and concealed from the north by a low ridge, which bends round in front of the opening to the valley or dell, shutting up the town in a sort of *cul de sac*, open only through the narrow valley to the north-west, by which it is approached from the modern village of Mukhânâ. Up both sides of the dell its ruined walls wind in various directions along the shelving ridges, which overlook it, up to the summit of the mountain, where was a fortified citadel still containing the walls of many of the houses in a tolerable state of preservation, but entirely deserted except by wild beasts. The very vertex is occupied by a small temple of Mâtâ Âsâpurî—a favourite object of superstitious reverence with the Jaiṭwâ Râjputs.

According to the traditions of the province, the earliest seat of the Jaiṭwâs was at Śrînagar, a few miles from their present one of Purbandar. Soon afterwards it was at Bhimor or Mordwajpuri, now a ruined site opposite to Morvî, and six generations later —probably early in the tenth century, Ghumlî or Bhumli was made the capital, and adorned with imposing buildings by Râja Sâl Kumâra, but in Samvat 1369 (A.D. 1313), it fell, after a desperate siege, by an army from Sindh. From Ghumlî the Jaiṭwâ chief then removed to Chaya, near Purbandar,—the latter being its port, which has since supplanted Chaya.

This ruined and deserted capital was visited by the indefatigable Colonel Tod in 1822, and described by him in his *Travels** in his usual glowing and exaggerated style. In 1837 Captain (now General Sir G.) Le Grand Jacob gave an account of a visit to it with much more accuracy and detail.†

"All is now jungle," says the latter, "where once multitudes of human beings resided; within and without the ruined ramparts so thick is it, as to make it difficult to trace them even from a height. The ground plan of Gumlî resembles a wide spread fan, the two sides of which are formed by the gorge of the valley, leading up to the peak on which the fort is built, the circular portion being represented by the ramparts."

"The extreme breadth from the eastern to the western wall," he adds, "is about three quarters of a mile; its length from the north wall to the narrow of the gorge, less than half a mile; there are two flanks of about two hundred and fifty yards length, joining the northern face to the natural flanks offered by the hills; the eastern one with its semi-arched battlements, reaching half way up the scoop of the hill, is in a tolerable state of preservation, but the remainder is in ruins, the bastions have fallen in, and are only faintly to be traced through the jungle. A ditch, of the usual Hindu dimensions, surrounds the wall; the masonry I was surprised to find for the major part of well chiselled stone, with dove-tailed grooves for clamps; the iron or lead which may have been used for this purpose, has doubtless been long since pilfered. There were originally

* Tod's *Travels in Western India*, pp. 404 ff.

† *Jour. R. A. Soc.*, vol. V. pp. 73 ff.

two gateways to the north and west." The last only was still standing till within a few years ago, and bears the name of Râmapoḷa, but only a fragment of it now remains.

"The area contained within the limits I have above described, is now tenanted only by wild beasts, and other jungle inhabitants; mounds or lines of rubbish faintly pourtray the line of streets, though I am disposed to consider the houses were chiefly of frail materials; nothing remains as witness of its former state, save an insignificant temple near the eastern wall, two small flat-roofed ones of the earlier age of Brahmanism, a splendid well, itself worthy of description, and the ark or royal citadel, the contents of which peculiarly merit notice; wells of good masonry are sunk here and there, which the traveller should take heed not to stumble into. This ark occupies the centre of the area, and contains, originally guarded by a wall all round, the palace* and its adjuncts; a large bathing reservoir, surrounded with small apartments as if for dressing rooms to the Zenana, if not the Zenana itself, is separated from the palace by a court."

The temple known as Navalâkhâ stands in the middle of the other ruins, on a raised platform 153½ feet long by 102 feet broad. The enclosing wall or screen on the top of this, however, has entirely disappeared; and of the entrance only the steps and the bases of the two massive pillars above them remain. (Plates XL. to XLIV.)

The temple itself measures 51 feet 5 inches from the threshold of the *Maṇḍap* to that of the shrine, and 67 feet 8 inches to the back of the *pradakshina* or passage round the shrine inside. The width from the north to the south doors of the Maṇḍap is 55 feet 7 inches. The level of the temple is considerably raised above that of the court, and is approached by a flight of steps at each of the three doors. The Maṇḍap is of two storeys, with twenty-two columns on the floor, each 9 feet 7 inches high, and thirty shorter ones on the low screen walls that enclose it. It is of a pretty common cruciform shape, the central area being 29 feet square; to each side of this an aisle is added, 19 feet long, except on the west side, where in front of the shrine it is only 15 feet 7 inches long; outside these, on the three outer sides, is further added a portico about 8¼ feet square.

The shrine is 9 feet 1 inch square inside, and is roofed by a neat dome with *chakwás*† or sacred birds on the lintels of the octagon. The linga that once occupied it was carried off to Purbandar long ago, and is now to be seen there in the temple of Kedarnâth.

Round the shrine is a *pradakshina*, about 3 feet wide, but opening to over 5 feet opposite the three windows that throw light into it on the different sides.

The walls of this temple are built of slabs of moderate size of the calcareous sandstone so common over Western Kâṭhiâwâḍ, and are set on edge and clamped together. This mode of construction has hastened the ruin of this stately pile, for the walls being thin, when once a tree or plant has got its roots in between the slabs it has split the wall.

The central octagon of the *Maṇḍap* supports a frieze with a low parapet wall above, in front of the gallery or upper floor, to which there does not appear to have been any regular means of access, unless it may have been by some wooden ladder. The dome rests on the columns of the second storey, but the pendentive in the centre and

* Captain Jacob has, curiously enough, mistaken the two-storeyed Maṇḍap of the Navalâkha temple for a palace: the palace probably stood close by this temple, but to the north-east of it, and is now represented only by a heap of stones.

† Cuculus melanoleucus?

some of the upper courses of stone have fallen in, and it is now open in the middle. The east or front entrance is more dilapidated than either of the other two; the upper storey of the porch on this side has fallen, much of the débris lying in front; and the lintel of the entrance is broken and supported in the middle by a rough pillar built of blocks of the stones which lie about. (See plate XLII.)

The brackets of the columns, both in the upper and lower floors, are sculptured, each with a different device (see plate XLIII.), consisting of *Kirtimukhs* (fig. 1), the *gatachuk*, or four armed figure (fig. 2), a bird trimming its feathers (fig. 7), an elephant or an elephant's head (figs. 3, 5, 16), a large human face (4), a monkey, two with one head (10), a bird with a flower in its beak (6), a horse with a man before and another behind, a pair of bullocks butting, an elephant and horse, a cock and sheep, a swordsman and elephant, a pair of birds (15), a couple of fishes (9 and 17), three monkeys, &c.

The columns of the octagon (plate XLIV. fig. 2) and four in front of the shrine have bases of the broken-square plan, with a figure of a goddess or devî, having the left foot raised on the right knee, placed in a small compartment, enclosed by colonnettes and a canopy. Over this are horizontal mouldings to a height of 2 feet 3 inches. The next division is 1 foot 8 inches high, and has a standing figure of a *devata*, Gaṇapati, Śiva, Pârvatî, &c., &c., on each face, the small pilasters at the sides have the *grasḍá* or griffon attached as a bracket to the outward sides. Over this is more ornamentation, and the column changes to an octagon, on the sides of which are carved eight *devís*, as on the base, only somewhat smaller. At 5 feet 11 inches from the floor, the pillars become circular and are girt, first by a collar of sixteen leaves and buds then by a string of *Chakwás*, or birds, hanging by eight short bands from a cincture of lozenge-shaped carvings, over which is a belt, about 8 inches deep, of eight Kirtimukhs. The capital is 9 inches deep, and the bracket 13½ inches. The other ten columns (fig. 1) are much plainer: they are broken-squares to a height of about 4 feet from the floor, then change into octagons, which at 5 feet 11 inches terminate in leaf points, and the shaft becomes circular up to 7 feet 1½ inches where the capital begins and is exactly the same as in the other columns.

The carving on the outside walls is what has chiefly attracted attention to this temple. On each face of the base of the shrine or *Vimána*, under the windows, are two elephants, and a *makara* or *grasḍá* with their trunks intertwined. On the upper members of the base are—1. A line of *Kirtimukhs*. 2. Elephants holding a band or rope in their trunks, their ears just touching, and at the outer angles a human figure struggling as if to keep the rope off from him; and, 3. A line of figures, mostly human, dancing, kneeling, playing music, fighting, &c., &c., intermixed with elephants, horses, a linga altar, a pair of intertwined snakes, birds, figures sitting on chairs, &c. Above this the first belt of the walls is occupied with figures of Devî or Lakshmî, four-armed, with the left foot raised as on the pillars of the Maṇḍap. Over this is a torus and some mouldings; then the principal belt, as at Amarnâth and elsewhere, filled with larger figures, principally gods and goddesses of the Śaiva mythology—some of the figures tolerably well executed, and the females without much of the usual exaggerations. The brackets supporting these have each a flower carved on the under side, with two leaves. Each compartment is enclosed by a pair of colonnettes with brackets of the goat-shaped or griffon figure (*śardula*), with long legs and horns. The figures in the receding portions

BRACKETS FROM THE PILLARS IN NAULÂKHA TEMPLE, GUMLI.

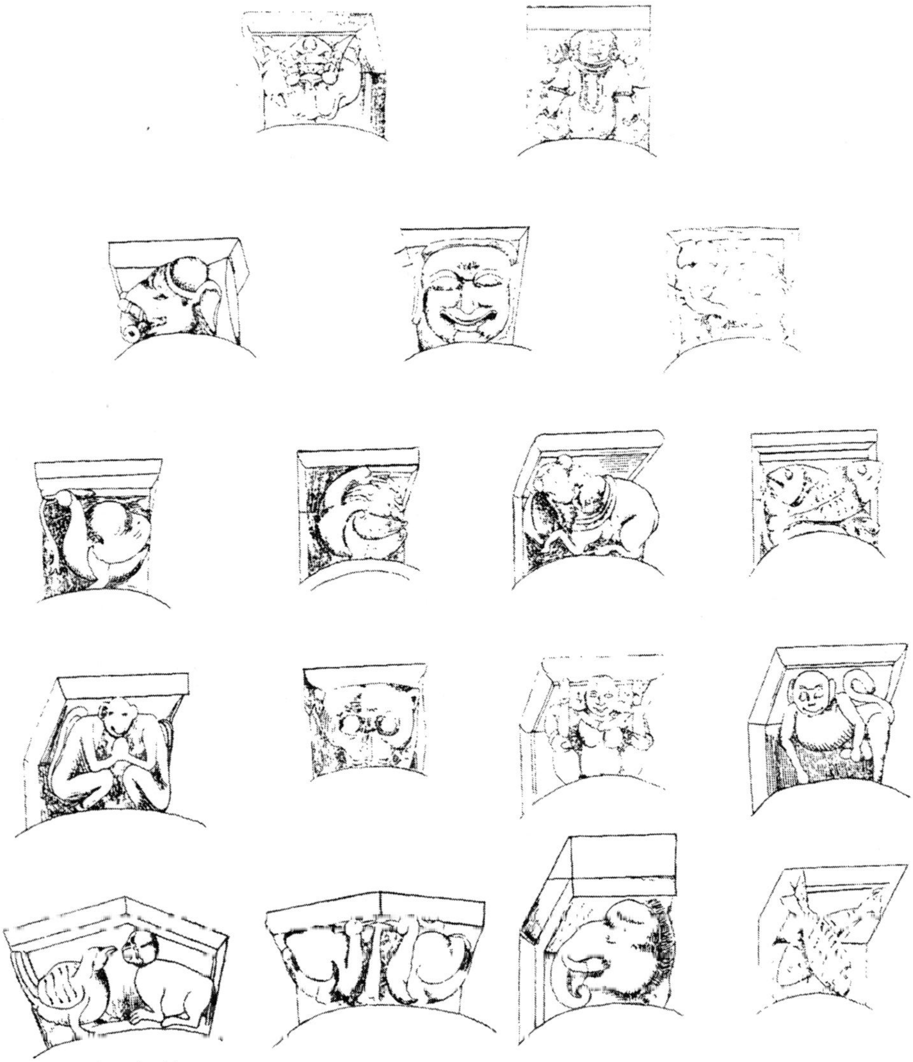

W. Griggs photo-lit

PILLARS FROM THE GREAT TEMPLE AT GHUMLI, &c.

1.

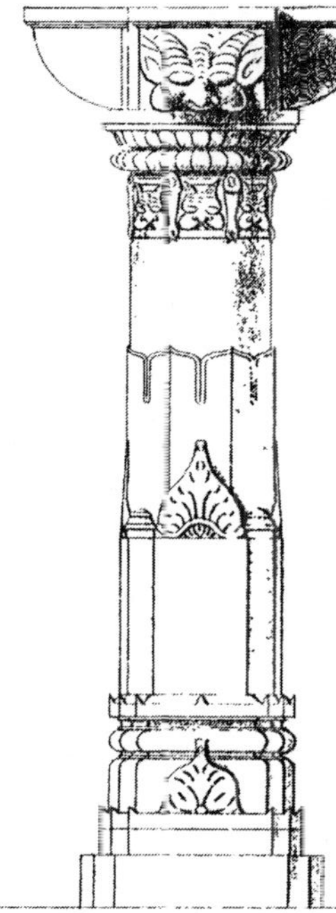

2.

3. SIKHAR
IN A JAINA CHATTRI
AT MUNRA

Scale of 1 0 1 2 3 4 5 6 7 8 9 feet

J. Burgess surv.

H. Cousens del.

and re-entrant angles are all males, or nearly so, and have beards of the formal cut so common on Râjput sculptures, and on the figures Mr. Sherring has styled 'Bhar';* some have also moustaches and occasionally a turban badly set on. Indeed until within a century ago or so, turbans are not usual on Hindu sculpture, and such as do exist are represented rather *over* the head than *on* it. Close above these last are two very small figures on a sort of shelf. Above this belt is a cornice, of which monkeys crown all the projecting corners. Among the minor sculptures in this temple are some obscene figures, but not many, and in obscure corners. On a Vaishṇava temple they would, probably, have been a characteristic feature.

Under the shrine window on the south side, and just over the two elephants, is a figure of Brahma and Saravatî; in the corresponding position on the west is Śiva and Pârvatî; on the north the figures are completely destroyed; they were probably Vishṇu and his consort Śrî or Lakshmî.

The porches have been roofed with slabs, carved with human and animal figures, but they have nearly all fallen. The other compartments of the roofs have lotuses or other circular flowers carved upon them.

Heaps of stones lie about, many of them elaborately sculptured. But no inscription or date helps us to form any estimate of the age of this temple. It hardly seems to belong in style to the tenth or early half of the eleventh century, but may have been erected in the latter half of the eleventh or in the twelfth century, A.D.

In many of the stones there are small natural cavities, which when exposed have been occupied by plants that at first sight seem to grow out of the solid stone.†

To the south-west of this temple, and only a few yards from the outer enclosure of it, is the *Śikhar* or spire of what Tod calls "the Temple of Wisdom," or of Gaṇapati, and Jacob that of "Hanuman": it is now so utterly ruined that no one can say to whom it was dedicated (plate XLV.). Nothing remains of it but the *Vimana* or tower, bereft of the jambs and lintel of the door, and three or four pillars of the Maṇḍap. But the style of this tower is of an old type; it measures 7 feet 9 inches square inside, and the walls are 2 feet 3 inches thick, but unlike those of the Navalâkha, the stones are smaller, very carefully jointed, and laid on their beds. The mode of closing the spire, too, is the same as that of the Son or Suvân Kâṅsârî temples on the hill above, to be described presently, and must belong to the same age, probably not later than the eighth or ninth century, A.D.

A little to the east of this is the Vaniâvasî—the ruin of an old Jaina temple, of which only a few pillars of the Mandap and three of the small cells that surrounded it now remain—scarcely sufficient, without turning over a large portion of the fallen stones, to determine the plan and dimensions.

The pillars are plain, but the bracket capitals have the same whimsical variety of sculpture as those of the Navalâkha temple. The doors of the little shrines of the *Bâmtî* or Court have been elaborately carved in sandstone, but are mostly ruined.

---

* *Journ. R. As. Soc.* (N.S.) vol. V., pp. 376 ff., and figs. 7, 8, and 10.

† "I observed," says Jacob, "a small tree growing out of the side of one of the stones which from the absence of any artificial fissure, and its smoothly-wrought surface, I could only account for by supposing the seed to have been incrusted within it, on its original formation in the quarry, which the rain of so many centuries had at length succeeded in fructifying. If this surmise be correct, it affords a striking instance of the vitality of the vegetative principle. The stone was a compact conglomerate."

Among the stones I found an image of Pârśvanâtha, carved in a hard yellowish stone of great specific gravity; it is about 4 feet high and but little damaged (see plate XLVI. fig. 1).

East of this again is the Jethânî wâv, which must orignally have been a large and noble public well with steps down to the bottom of it, and galleries above, as in the Adâlaj wâv near Ahmadâbâd; but half of it has entirely disappeared, and the stones have been carried off. At the bottom of the descent on each side is a *gokhle* or niche, very neatly carved. On a slab on the right side, near the entrance at the east end, under a cow and calf eating balls of food, is an inscription, of which only small fragments here and there are legible. It began :—

१° ॥ संवत १३८३

probably Samvat 1383=A.D. 1326–7; fourteen years after the traditional date of the destruction of the city, a circumstance which throws doubt on even Jacob's date for that event. This great well was doubtless a royal work, and as the Jaiṭwâ chiefs never attempted to rebuild the city after its sack, we must suppose that this event did not occur till some time, but not long, after Samvat 1383.

Scattered about all over the site of Ghumli are fragments of temples and other buildings, but so far as I could discover by visiting all I could catch a glimpse of over the jungle or hear of from the villagers at Mukhânâ, there are no others worth special notice either for size or carving. They appear to have been mostly small shrines of the 12th and 13th centuries, and now quite ruined.

Ascending the gorge above Ghumli, however, to the south-west, under some magnificent old mango trees, and commanding a splendid view of the Navalâkhâ and all the valley round it, are three old temples. Of the first—perhaps a Vaishṇava temple —the shrine remains, 5 feet 1 inch square inside, with walls 18 inches thick, and a *pradakshina* 2 feet 5 inches wide round it. On the lintel of the shrine door is Gaṇeśa, and on the frieze above is Vishṇu seated with Garuḍa below his *ásana* or throne, a nimbus behind his head, and female figures at each side; to the left of Vishṇu, in another compartment, is Brahmâ, three-faced, seated cross-legged on two *haṅsas* or sacred geese, with two female attendants; and to the right is Śiva, three-faced, with the bull Nandi below, and two females. All three have four arms each, and are about 15 inches high. In front of the shrine door two pillars of the *Maṇḍap* still remain, divided into three nearly equal lengths of four, eight, and sixteen sides, with bracket capitals of the usual cruciform shape.

The second temple, on the south side of the last, has had a Maṇḍap with low screen wall 1 foot 9 inches thick. The shrine is 6 feet 4 inches square inside, with walls 2 feet 2½ inches thick, surrounded by a *pradakshina* 3¼ feet wide, the outer wall of the temple forming an oblong 17 feet 4 inches by 29 feet inside and 21 by 32½ feet outside, with four pillars in front of the shrine 2 feet 2 inches square below, octagon above, and having square bases. They have round capitals and brackets of grinning Kirtimukhas and four-faced figures. The walls are of plain ashlar, the stones neatly dressed and jointed. There has also been a porch, but it has fallen.

The Śikhar is much ruined, but has been carved with a sort of Chaitya-window pattern, not deeply cut, and other mouldings usual in temples from the eighth century, or earlier, to the 10th or 11th, and crowned with a large flat *amlaśila*.

SCULPTURES FROM GUMLI.

1
JAIN IMAGE
FROM THE VANIAVASI TEMPLE.

2
VISHNU
FROM SUVAN KAṄSARI TALAO.

W. Griggs lith.

On the south side of this are three small cells, occupied by an ascetic Kâki Bâwâ, and beyond them is a large old well, built of well-dressed stone.

On the very summit of the hill is a small plain square shrine of Âsâpurâ Mâtâ,* and near it the walls of many of the houses of the long-deserted fort surrounded by a massive wall of which the crenellations only have fallen.

Of the Râmapoḷa or west gate,—which was standing only a few years ago, and might have then been saved by a few props, and cutting down the vegetation over it,—only two of the brackets now remain, hanging over the ruin (plate XLVII.). "It is narrow," says Jacob, "but of considerable depth, containing five arches and apparently spaces for a double portcullis. The sculpture is worthy of observation; it consists of figures in parallel compartments, elephants, lions, tigers' heads, warriors, musicians, and dancing women, well and boldly executed; a catalogue of ancient musical instruments could be compiled from these walls." The gate, however, notwithstanding the praises it has received from visitors, was never probably equal to those at Dabhoi. It belonged to the same style and was of about the same dimensions, the walls being 13 feet apart, and the clear roadway between the pilasters 11 feet 6 inches.

Outside this gate are a few pâliyâs still standing, and many more trampled into the earth by the cattle, while others have been carried off for building purposes. They were formerly much more numerous. Jacob says—"I counted nearly a hundred of these testimonies to Jaiṭwâ valour; in the centre, that of some grandee is sheltered by a small mausoleum; most of these warriors, whether on horse or foot, have immense shields, and are boldly sculptured; under one bearing a striking resemblance to the Grecian satyr, I distinctly traced the date of Samvat 1118, corresponding to A.D. 1062. Time had been too busy with the other inscriptions to enable me to decipher them." The figures carved on them are mostly represented on horseback—the horses covered with what may equally pourtray a thick quilt or chain armour.

Just outside is the Derânî Wâv, a much smaller and plainer structure than the Jethânî Wâv, and also much decayed. Between the Râmapoḷa and Mukhânâ, in the valley to the east of the old city, are the remains of several other wells.

Outside the Râmapoḷa, and to the south-west of the Derânî Wâv, are the remains of a pretty large artificial lake, the Salêsar Talâo, formed by an embankment thrown across the mouth of a valley. At the east end of it is a small Śaiva temple, now a complete ruin, the maṇḍap entirely fallen, and the shrine only remaining, much dilapidated about the Śikhar. There is nothing, however, remarkable about it.

About 350 or 400 feet above this is another large talâo, the Son or Suvân Kâṅsârî, with some eighteen or twenty temples at the west end of it, and two or three at the east, none of them very large, but all apparently of an earlier date than those below, and perhaps dating from the eighth to the tenth century (see plate XLVIII.). The larger ones consist of a square shrine built near one end of an oblong court or maṇḍap, and the smaller ones of an outer room or porch and a cell. The maṇḍaps

* Âsâ is the goddess of Hope, mentioned in the *Harivaṅśa* (c. 135) along with Hrî, Śrî, Dhriti, Kîrtti Medhâ, Prîti, Mati, Khyâti, and Sannati, the goddesses of Chastity, Riches, Firmness, Glory, Devotion Pleasure, Wisdom, Fame, and Modesty respectively.

have fallen, except that of one of the three larger ones, shown in the background a little to the right of the middle of the view, of which a considerable portion is still entire. This appears to have been a Vaishṇava temple with four columns in the maṇḍap. From the *pradakshina* a small door opens on the right or north side into a little room outside the enclosure wall; and at the back and south sides there are small openings or windows into similar apartments; these cells were probably for storing the clothing, jewels, and articles of value belonging to the idol. The roofs of the *pradakshina* and aisles in these temples have slanted downwards.

In the maṇḍap is a figure of Vishṇu, about 4½ feet high, broken across the neck, but otherwise scarcely damaged (plate XLVI. fig. 2). It would be worth removing to a local museum at Râjkoṭ, or even to Bombay. It was from these temples that Jacob removed the Trimurti figure of Brahma now in the Asiatic Society's Museum at Bombay.

These shrines, however, differ from most others in the way they are roofed; the *Śikhar* or spire being gradually contracted in dimensions inside, till it terminates in a square aperture of about a foot, covered by a single slab. In one of the larger temples, on the north side of this group, shown in the extreme right of the view, there appears to have been two floors and above the second, the area is gradually contracted in this way. The shrine is 10 feet 9 inches square inside, and the walls 3 feet 9 inches thick, with a *pradakshina* 6 feet wide, having four windows, one on each side and two behind.

At the east end of the Talâo is a temple with a pretty large *naus*, roofed over in a similar way, as is also its shrine. The walls of all are built of carefully squared stones laid on their beds, and most probably built without lime, though before they ceased to be used some of them, at least, seem to have been pointed and whitewashed.

Many carved stones, *pâliyâs*, images, &c. lie about.

The legend of the destruction of this place is thus told* by General Sir G. Le Grand Jacob:—"The Bhât's story of the cause why Bhumli fell," he says, "viz., the curse pronounced by Suän Kâsârîn, a coppersmith's daughter, as a punishment of the Râja for his attempts on her virtue, is founded on something less vague than the generality of such like legends; one of the temples on the hill is dedicated to her, and still bears her name. The following local tradition throws light on the manner of the times:—

"Son (or Suän) Kâsârîn, a celebrated beauty who flourished about A.D. 1113 (Samvat 1169) was demanded in marriage by a Bârwattia of Bâbriâwâḍ, named Rakhayit, as a reward for his valour against the Râṇâ's enemies; but on seeing her the Râṇâ was himself captivated by her charms, and sent secret notice to the Bâbriâwâḍ chief, of the excellent opportunity for removing his rebellious vassal which the marriage ceremonies would present; the event happened as wished for, and the Bâbriâ hero was slain by the troops which his own chief brought thither for the purpose. Suän Kâsârîn was inconsolable; she refused all the solicitations of royalty, and at length fled from his violence to the shelter of a Brahman's abode; here her cause was espoused by all the brotherhood as a point of honour, and no less than one hundred and twenty-five performed *trâga*† on themselves, to bar the Râṇâ from his victim; all this blood, however, did not

* *Journ. R. As. Soc.* vol. V. p. 78.

† Self-immolation.

quench the prince's ardour; the virgin bride uttered the fearful imprecation which ruined his capital, and then escaped to offer herself to the flames, a victim of tyranny, love, and superstition." Tod relates the tale without mention of the Bâbriâ chief. "Soon after," he adds, "came the invader from Sindh, when Ghumlî was invested, and defended for six months. All that was precious to the people, their families and children, were placed in Bhimkoṭ," on the summit of the hill, "whose defence was entrusted to the Mhêrs, whilst the prince, his chiefs, and auxiliary Râjputs defended the *talâiti*, or lower town. As the siege slackened at night, the defenders used to visit their families in Bhimkoṭ, of which the besiegers took advantage, entered Gumlî, and following up their success, scaled Bhimkoṭ. An indiscriminate massacre followed, in which Śivaji, the Tarquin of Gumli, his kindred and friends, were cut to pieces; their names are enumerated, and amongst them are many of the ancient tribe of Dâbi." The date of this catastrophe Tod gives as S. 1109, or A.D. 1053, that is, 60 years earlier than that given by Jacob. "The *Asuras*," he adds, "(as the Islamites are generally styled by the Râjput bard) are distinctly stated to have worn long beards; and it is added, that, 'having read the Koran in the temple,' they forthwith returned to Sindh."*

If Suän Kâsârîn, however, lived in the eleventh or twelfth century, and Ghumli was not destroyed till the fourteenth, it is difficult to see what connection the one had with the other. The truth seems to be, that some time during the fourteenth century, and probably in the first half of it, Jâm Unâḍ invaded Baraḍâ and besieged the Râṇâ in Ghumlî. After a long contest, Unâḍ, despairing of success, returned with his army to Kachh. Here, according to tradition, his son Bâmani,† ashamed of the disgraceful termination of his father's expedition, assumed the command of the army and conducted it back to Ghumli, which place he reduced after an obstinate siege of twelve months. The Sammâs destroyed the city, which the Jaiṭwâs, from superstition, did not attempt to rebuild, but removed their capital to Chaya near the sea coast. Purbandar, said to be on the site of Sadâmapura, mentioned in the *Bhagavat Purâṇa*, was at first the port of Chaya, but has since become the seat of government of the Jaiṭwâ chief.‡

Probably owing to the resistance made by the Baraḍâ Râṇâs, the Sammâs, after reducing Ghumli, returned to Kachh, without establishing their authority in the country. Jâm Unâḍ, however, is said to have given his territory in Sindh in charity to the Chârans before setting out to conquer another, and on Bâmani's arrival in Kachh on his way back he formed the design of establishing himself there, and succeeded in doing so.

From Mukhâna I made an excursion to Sakrojâ Talâo, about nine miles off, but fully a third of the way was through jungle among the Baraḍâ hills, where riding was impossible.

It is a small artificial lake in the bosom of the hills, and has four shrines at the cardinal points. That on the south, facing east, seems to have been the principal one, and is the only one still used. The small Manḍaps of all of them have fallen, and the

* Tod's *Travels in Western India*, p. 416.

† May this not have been Manâi mentioned in the Kachh annals? See below pp. 197, 198.

‡ Conf. *Bombay Selections*, XXXIX. (N.S.) pp. 166, 207.

Vimânas or shrine towers measure about 7 feet 2 inches square outside. I found no inscription here.

Between three and four miles south of Mukhânâ is the Vethiyâ Wâv (plates XLIX., L., and LXIX. fig 1), which, with the *Chhatra* in front of it is 208¾ feet in length. The Chhatra or Maṇḍap at the east end is supported by twelve pillars, and measures 18 feet 6 inches square. From this the steps descend to the *Wâv*, which is 14 feet 10 inches wide, bridged over at intervals, about 40 feet apart, by three canopies, at one end of each of which narrow stairs descend into the *Wâv*, landing on the platforms below. The circular well at the west end is 18 feet 8 inches in diameter, but the whole is filled up with earth to about the level of the first platform below the surface, about 12 feet down, and large Banyan trees have taken root on the sides which have been faced with 2 feet 7 inches of stone in front of the rock out of which the whole has been hewn. The style of the pillars, &c. is in keeping with that of the Navalâkhâ temple : the same whimsical variety in the bracket figures is also very noticeable, and there can be little hesitation in referring it to the same age.

At Pâsthar, a little to the south, is an old temple to the sun-god Sûrya. It is of the same plan as those at Son Kâṅsârî, but roofed with long slabs of stone. The *pradakshina* has had a slanting roof, and two small windows at the back. One pillar of the Maṇḍap alone remains standing, with four-armed figures on the brackets. Gaṇeśa is carved on the lintel of the door, and Sûrya inside is represented much as Vishṇu usually is, but with only two hands, and holding up a flower in each, with a nimbus behind the head, ringlets descending from behind the ears, and wearing a sort of mural crown. (See plate LXV. fig. 1.) Beside him are three smaller figures, now somewhat defaced: one of them has been a well-carved female with a mace (?) in her right hand, and her hair dressed in the style prevalent in the great Śaiva temple at Paṭṭadkal.*

A small temple in front of this has been entirely seized upon by the roots of a *Vaḍ* or Banyan tree, which twine round the stones of the roof and walls and about the images—ten in number, and each about 2½ feet high, among whom are Gaṇapati and several female figures, one a horse-headed Kinnara, all in a sitting posture, but much worn by time. The Sûrya Wâv on the east side of this is also overgrown by a Banyan tree.

---

* See *First Season's Report*, p. 30.

OLD TEMPLE AT GOP.

PLATE LII.

1. PLAN

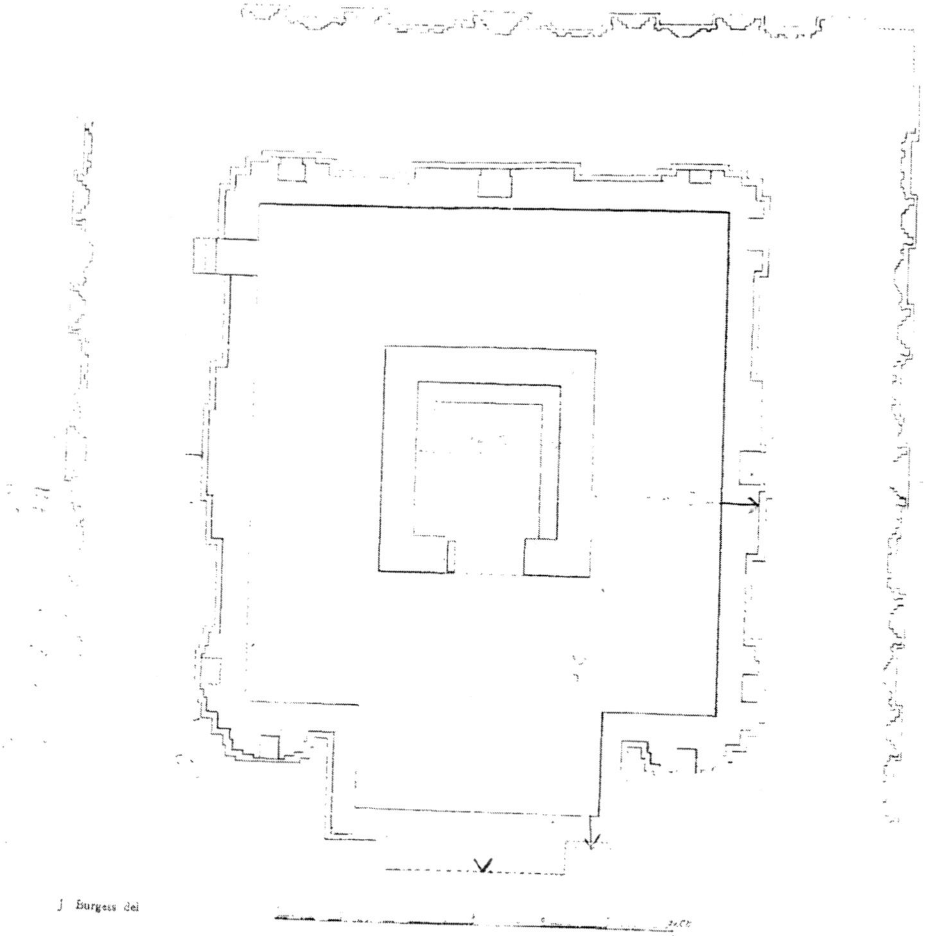

J Burgess del

3. LOWER BASE.

2. SKETCH OF THE ROOF - NORTH SIDE.

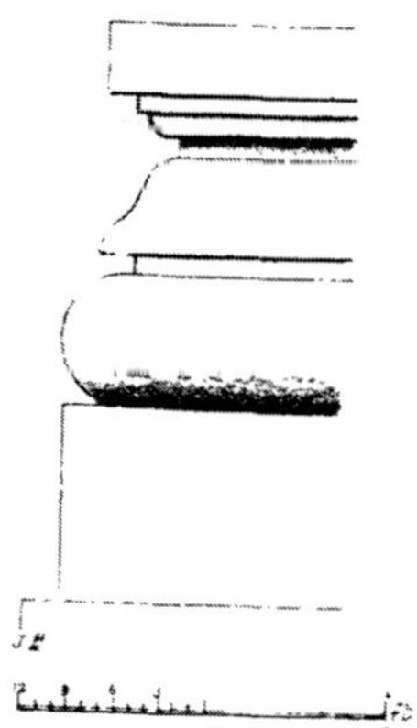

W Griggs phot-lith

XIII. GOP.

A march northwards from Bhumli brings the traveller to the village of Gop, a little to the south-west of the isolated Gop Hill. To the east of this, at Nânâ Gop or Junâ Gop, is a large cavern that has been occupied by ascetics, and on visiting it, I discovered in the village the shrine of an old temple,—perhaps the only fragment now standing of the old city, which appears to have covered a considerable area round the present village. This shrine seems to have been last used as one of the corner towers of a small fort, the east and south curtain walls of which have been built of the stones of the temple that once surrounded the shrine; for in this ancient type of temple the shrine occupied almost the centre of the building, and was surrounded by a double court, the outer one a few feet lower than the inner one and shrine. (See plates LI., LII., and LIII.)

The shrine itself is 10 feet 9 inches square inside, and about 23 feet high, with walls 2 feet 6 inches thick, built of coursed ashlar, each course about 8 inches deep and carefully jointed, but built without cement of any kind. At 11 feet from the floor are four holes in the back and front walls, each 14 inches high, as if for joists; and over them, in the side walls, are six smaller ones, as if for rafters.

For 6½ feet above this the walls are perpendicular; then the area contracts as in the temples of Son Kânsârî at Ghumli, six or seven courses having bevelled edges, but those above them square faces, until the apex is covered by a single slab.

Part of the front wall over the door has some time or other fallen, and been rebuilt, but with the inner sides of the stones turned out, showing the sockets of the clamps with which the stones had been secured. On the left jamb of the door is carved the line—

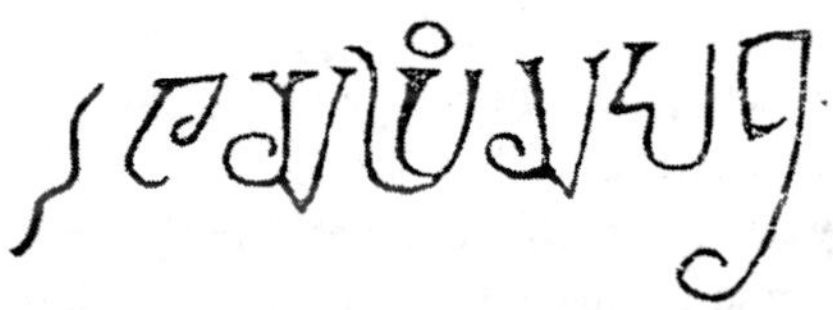

It is not easy to say what may be the age of these letters; but I feel inclined to regard the building as the oldest structure of the kind in Kâṭhiâwâḍ, and probably not later than the sixth century; how much older I am not at present prepared to say.

Inside are two figures in yellow stone to which the villagers give the names of Râma and Lakshmaṇa :—Râma with a high square *Mukuta* or headdress, and Lakshmaṇa with a low crown, long ear-rings, ringlets, and holding a spear in his right hand.

On the fragments of the basement that remain are many curious dwarf figures like the *gaṇa* we find on the caves of Bâdâmî, and on the old Vaishṇava temple at Aihoḷe; but the stone is very much weather-worn.

The roof is quite peculiar, being a hipped one,—pierced with two chaitya-windows, or dormer arches on each side (plate LII. fig. 2), which have all originally contained figures. Gaṇapati is still in one on the west side, and another *Deva* occupies one on the north. About 2½ feet below the string-course on the wall-head are a series of holes as if for the ends of beams—doubtless those that once supported the roof of the surrounding temple, or inner court, which has been 35 feet 2 inches square, with a bay on the east side 18 feet 4 inches by 7 feet 3 inches. The outer court, possibly open above, or at least laterally, must have been about 9½ feet wide.

XIV. JÂMNAGAR OR NAUÂNAGAR.

The town of Jâmnagar the capital of the Jâḍejâ Jâms or chiefs of the province of Hâlar is quite of recent origin, having been founded by Jâm Râval as his capital, when he was driven out of Kachh by Râo Khangâr in Samvat 1596 (A.D. 1539). Its founder called it Navânagar, a name by which it is still as well known as by the alternative one of Jâmnagar. Being a comparatively new city there is not much of antiquarian interest about it. Indeed the most important buildings belong to the present century, the city having been largely built by the Jâm Raṇmalji about forty years ago, though some of the large Jaina temples may possibly be somewhat older. At the village of Nâgnâ close by, are many monumental Pâliyas and some old temples, but in no way noteworthy.

The front of the Palace (plate LIV.), the Dehli gate (plate LV.), and a small corner fort of the town,—built by the Jâm Raṇmalji, the sixteenth chief in succession, who came to the *gadi* in A.D. 1814,—are fair specimens of modern Hindu architecture. In the first example will be recognized at once the same style as in the Maqbârâ at Junâgaḍh (plates XXXVII. and XXXIX.), only here applied to a dwelling instead of a tomb. The perforated stonework is confined to the arches over the windows on both floors. The balconies to the windows in the upper stories are much in the style of those in Jain temples of an earlier date, but the wider portions of the balcony are here opposite to the piers between the windows, and the details of carving, though even more minute than in older works, are by so much the less artistically effective. The upper cornice, carved more elaborately than any piece of upholstery, is, however, in strange contrast with the plain red tiled roof that surmounts it; and the whole effect is spoiled by the repeated coatings of whitewash it is thought proper to bestow upon it regularly.

The gateway was *intended* to be a fine one, and the inner one, partly seen through the doorway, is really fine so far as it was finished, but Jâm Raṇmal died before it was completed, and a new Jâm arose who cared for no such things, so the scaffolding was pulled down and even the holes in which it was supported were left unfilled up, and so it stands as when its projector died.

A new temple of Vishṇu or Dwârkânâthji in the modern style, is in course of erection by the old Diwân—"the Dives" of the town, and which, curiously enough, was mentioned in the last report of the district as 'a Dharmaśâlâ—a work of general public utility'! A set of six images of black marble—Vishṇu or Kṛishṇa, his vâhana or carrier—Garuḍa, and his wives—Satyabhâmâ, the daughter of Satrâjit, Lakshmaṇâ, Jâmbavatî, the daughter of Jâmbavân king of the bears, and Râdhâ—are ready for installation as soon as the temple is completed.

XV. KACHH.

The tongue of land forming the province of Kachh lies between 22° 46′ N., the latitude of Navanâr Point, and the parallel of 24°, and between 68° 22′ and 71° 3′ of East longitude, having an extreme length of 168 miles, and a breadth varying from 48 miles in the west to scarcely 30 in the east, and at one place between Dudhî and Bachâu, of only 13 miles. It is bounded by the Raṇ on the north, east, and south-east; by the Korî or Lakpat river on the north-west, by the Arabian Sea on the west, and by the Gulf of Kachh, separating it from Kâṭhiâwâḍ on the south. The great salt desert marsh or Raṇ to the north contains the Islands of Khaḍiar and Pachham, with some smaller ones, and the grass tract called Banni. The principal sub-divisions of the main-land are—1. Pâvar—said to be the original seat of the Kâthîs,—about 50 miles in length by 20 in breadth along the southern margin of the Raṇ, and bounded on the south by the Charwaḍ range of hills; its capital is Bhuj, founded by Khangâr in Samvat 1605 or A.D. 1548; 2. Gardâ Pathak, between Pâvar and the Korî river; 3. Abḍâsâ, so named from Jâm Abḍâ, the fourth in descent from Jâm Lâkhâ who gave the name of Jâdejâ to the tribe,* between the Chârwaḍ range and the Arabian Sea; 4. Kuṇḍa Pargaṇa, a small district in the extreme west; 5. Kâṇṭhâ or Kâṇṭhi along the south coast; 6. Mîyâṇi, east of Pâvar, taking its name from the Mîyâṇâ tribe which resides chiefly in it;† and 7. Vâgaḍ, occupying the peninsula in the east.

Of these, Kâṇṭhi evidently gave origin to the name of Κάνθι κόλπος applied by Ptolemy to the gulf that washes its southern shore, but which the author of the *Periplus of the Erythrean Sea* calls the gulf of Barakē. Ptolemy, however, also places an island hereabouts (long. 111°, lat. 18°) which he calls Barakē, indicating perhaps the Bêt or island of Śankhodâr, or perhaps more probably Okhamaṇḍal, which may have been then an island, as it is almost still so at high water; the Greek ΒΑΡΑΚΗ here representing the vernacular Dvârakâ (in Magadhî—Baravavâe).

The Raṇ ‡ is also mentioned in the *Periplus* as "another gulf beyond the Indus, of which the northern coast is unexplored and called Eirinon," the Sanskṛit Iriṇa; "and consists," the author continues, "of two parts, of which one is called the Greater and the other the Lesser; but both these seas are full of shoals and of eddies that are rapid and close to one another, and stretch far out from the shore, so that frequently when the mainland has been lost sight of vessels run into them, and being carried forward into the inner circles of the vortex, are destroyed. Now a promontory stands out above this gulf which, after running east and south, trends from Eirinon towards the west, encompassing the gulf called Barakē, which contains seven islands. Those escape who falling back a little round the entrance to this and make their way into the open sea, while those who are once fairly locked into the hollow of Barakē are destroyed, for great and exceeding heavy is the surf, and the sea is boisterous and muddy, and

* Jâm Abḍâ ruled over this district, and his descendants are still known as Abḍâs,—*Ind. Ant.* vol. V. p. 167.

† See *Ind. Ant.* vol. V. p 172.

‡ On the Raṇ conf. Pottinger in *Journ. Roy. As. Soc.*, vol. I. pp. 206 ff.; Burnes, *Trans. Roy. As. Soc.*, vol. III. pp. 569 ff.

has eddies and rapid currents. The bottom in some places is broken, and in others rocky and sharp, so as to cut the cables that lie upon it, sometimes snapping them at once, and at others fraying them away on the bottom. And the indications of these places to those coming from the sea are enormously large black snakes meeting them; for in the parts beyond these and about Barugaza, the snakes they meet are smaller and of pale-green or golden colour. Immediately beyond Barakē is the gulf of Barugaza and the mainland portion of Ariakē (or Larikē), the principal state of the kingdom of Mambarus and of all India. Of this realm, the inland portion which borders on Skythia is called Abēria, while the portion along the coast is called Surastrēnē."*

Professer Lassen locates the Audumbari of Sanskrit writers—the Odœmbaræ of the Greeks—in Kachh. The Kori mouth of the Indus also, which separates this province from Sindh, is identified as the Sanskrit Lonivarî, known to the Greek geographers as the Lonibarē, as being the outlet of the Lonî or Lunî river which falls into the Ran at its north-eastern extremity.†

Capt. Wilford ‡ says the conquest of Kachh "by Menander is well attested, for unquestionable vestiges of it remained in the second century, such as temples, altars, fortified camps, and very large wells of masonry, with many coins of Menander and Apollodotos." This is founded on the statement of Strabo already referred to (p. 13).

The early history of Kachh has been but little, if at all, investigated and is involved in the greatest obscurity. The only scrap of information we have from published sources is the notice by Hiwan Thsang (cir. 640) in his *Si-yu-ki*, which runs thus:—"Ce royaume (de *K'ie-ch'a*) a environ trois mille *li* de tour; la circonférence de la capitale est d'une vingtaine de *li*. Sa population est très-nombreuse, et toutes les familles vivent dans l'opulence. Il n'y a point de prince (*indigène*). Ce pays est sous la dépendance du royaume de *Ma-la-p'o* (Mâlvâ) auquel il ressemble par la nature du climat, les produits du sol et les mœurs des habitants. Il y a une dizaine de couvents,

---

* *Perip. Maris Erythræi*, § 40, 41:—40 Μετὰ δὲ Σίνθον ποταμὸν ἕτερός ἐστι κόλπος ἀθεώρητος παρὰ τὸν βόρεαν. νομάζεται δὲ Εἰρινὸν, ἐπιλέγεται δὲ ὁ μὲν μικρὸν ὁ δὲ μέγα· πελάγη δέ ἐστιν ἀμφότερα τεναγώδη καὶ δίνας ἐλαφρὰς ἔχοντα καὶ συνεχεῖς καὶ μακρὰς ἀπὸ τῆς γῆς, ὡς πολλάκις, τῆς ἠπείρου μηδὲ βλεπομένης, ἐποκέλλειν τὰ πλοῖα, ἐνδοτέρω δὲ προληφθέντα καὶ ἀπόλλυσθαι. Τούτου δὲ ὑπερέχει τοῦ κόλπου ἀκρωτήριον, ἐπικαμπὲς ἀπὸ τοῦ Εἰρίνου μετὰ τὴν ἀνατολὴν καὶ τὸν νότον ὡς εἰς τὴν δύσιν, εμπεριλαμβάνον αὐτὸν τὸν κόλπον λεγόμενον Βαράκην, νήσους ἑπτὰ ἐμπεριειλημμένον, οὗ περὶ μὲν τὰς ἀρχὰς οἱ περιπεσόντες ὀλίγον ὀπίσω καὶ εἰς τὸ πέλαγος ἀναδραμόντες ἐκφεύγουσιν, οἱ δὲ εἰς αὐτὴν κατακλεισθέντες τὴν τοῦ Βαράκου κοιλίαν ἀπόλλυνται· τὸ μὲν γὰρ κῦμα μέγα καὶ βαρὺ λίαν, ἡ δὲ θάλασσα ταραχώδης καὶ θολερὰ καὶ δίνας ἔχουσα καὶ ῥοώδεις εἰλίγγους. Ὁ δὲ βυθὸς ἐν τισὶ μὲν απόκοπος ἔν τισι δὲ πετρώδης καὶ ἀπόξυρος, ὥστε τέμνεσθαι τὰς παρακειμένας ἀγκύρας διὰ ταχέων ἀποκοπτομένας, ἃς δὲ καὶ συντριβομένας ἐν τῷ βυθῷ. Σημεῖον δ' αὐτῶν τοῖς ἀπὸ πελάγους ἐρχομένοις οἱ προαπαντῶντες ὄφεις ὑπερμεγέθεις καὶ μέλανες· ἐν γὰρ τοῖς μετὰ ταῦτα τόποις καὶ τοῖς περὶ Βαρύγαζα μικρότεροι καὶ τῷ χρώματι χλωροὶ καὶ χρυσίζοντες ὑπαντῶσιν.

41. Μετὰ δὲ τὴν Βαράκην εὐθύς ἐστιν ὁ Βαρυγάζων κόλπος καὶ ἡ ἤπειρος τῆς 'Αριακῆς χώρας, τῆς Μαμβάρου βασιλείας ἀρχὴ καὶ τῆς ὅλης 'Ινδικῆς οὖσα. Ταύτης τὰ μὲν μεσόγεια τῇ Σκυθίᾳ συνορίζοντα 'Αβηρία καλεῖται, τὰ δὲ παραθαλάσσια Συραστρηνή.

For 'Αριακῆς, the MS. reads 'Αραβικῆς, and some editors have proposed Λαρικῆς, others 'Αριακης. Müller's *Geog. Græc. Min.*, I. 288, 289; and conf. Lassen, *De Pentapotamia Indica*, p. 26.

† *Bârâ* is a "roadstead," or "to the seaward," connected with *bâr*, Sank. *vâri*, "water."

‡ *Asiat. Res.*, vol. IX. p. 231. "Tradition," he adds, "says that the ancient city of Teja in Kachh," at a remote period the metropolis of Surâshṭra, "was founded by an ancient king called Teja, or Teja-Karṇa There were three brothers descended from Ikshwaku,—Puru, Buj, or Boj, and Teja; the two first are noticed in the *Purâṇas*, in the prophetic chapters, where Puru is generally called Puru-Kachha, and the other Buja Kachha."

qui renferment environ mille religieux, et où l'on étudie en même temps le *grand* et le *petit Véhicule*. On compte plusieurs dizaines de temples des dieux; il y a beaucoup d'hérétiques."*

The provincial language, Dr. Wilson says, "is nearly identical with the Sindhî spoken on the lower banks of the Indus, from which the immigration of population into Kachh seems principally to have taken place. The Kachhî is now but little used in any literature or business." Gujarâtî and Hindustânî are spoken by great numbers of the people; understood by all except those in the north, who follow a pastoral life and speak Kachhî. Gujarâtî is principally used in business correspondence and taught in the schools.

The Kâṭhis are probably the earliest race we can now identify as occupants of Kachh, where they were a powerful, if not the ruling, race till the arrival of the Sammâs: their stronghold was Pâvargaḍh, but they probably held the southern coast also. They seem to have been originally, as to some extent they yet are, a fair race, among whom, even still, blue eyes are not uncommon. From their physiognomy and name they have been supposed by Tod and others to be of Skythian descent. It can scarcely be questioned that like many later immigrants they entered Kachh from Sindh. They were doubtless pressed upon by the Châvaḍâs from Panchâsar and northern Gujarât, and by the Vâghelâs from Sardhâr and Munjpur before the invasion of the Sammâs. They were driven out of Kachh in the fifteenth century by Jâm Abḍa into Panchâl Deśa in the Surâshṭran peninsula, where probably offshoots from the tribe had previously settled, and to the whole of which province they have since given the name it is now best known by,—while in Kachh there is not now probably a single native Kâṭhî family.

With the the Kâṭhîs in early times were doubtless also settled the Abhirs or Âhirs† still pretty numerous in different parts, and who probably came across the Ran from Pârkar. They are worshippers of the goddess Mâtâ, and of Vâcharâ—a Râjpût saint. They are divided into five sub-tribes:—(1) Machhua, living about Dhori, Kunariâ, &c.; (2) Prânthaliâ, in the district of Prânthal, in Kachh; (3) Borichâ, in Kâṇṭhi; (4) Soraṭhiâ, who came from Soraṭh and are scattered over Vâgaḍ; and (5) Chorâḍâ, from Chorâd, living about Âdesar, Palânśwâ, Sanwâ, Umiyu, Jâtâwâḍâ, Belâ, &c. They have long since spread into Kâṭhiawâḍ.

With the Âhîrs we naturally associate the Rebârîs—also called Bhopâs from their being priests of Mâtâ—the Hindu Cybele—almost universally a favourite divinity of the aboriginal tribes. They are a pastoral tribe, tending flocks of sheep, goats, and camels. Their women make woollen yarn, from which they get their blankets and *suḍis* woven by the Ḍheḍs. They are from Mârwâḍ, but most of them have the peculiar Persian physiognomy. They are tall and robust, and have an oval face and aquiline nose. They live for days almost solely on the milk of camels.

---

* Stan. Julien, *Mémoires sur les Contrées Occident.* t. II. pp. 161, 162; and conf. p. 403, and *Vie de Hiouen Thsang*, pp. 205, 206. M. Vivien de Saint Martin supposes that the *A-ch'a-li* which Hiwan Thsang visited before *Kha-ch a* may have been the Thal or Thar on the north of the Ran. It was only 300 *li.* or 59 miles distant.

† *Trans. Bom. Lit. Soc.* vol. I. p. 287; vol. II. p. 232; Tod's *Rajasthan*, vol. II. p. 443; *Travels in Western India*, pp. 353, 421; Lassen, *Ind. Alt.* (1st. ed.) I. 539, or (2nd ed.) 652; *Ind. Ant.*, vol. II. p. 214; vol. III. pp. 86, 227; Elliot's *Races of N. W. P.* vol. I. pp. 2, 102, 136, 180, 388, 396.

Another pastoral tribe are the Jats,* well known on the banks of the Indus, and found in the north and west of Kachh. They have been supposed to be Skythians or Getæ, but in the country they are said to have come from Aleppo in Turkey, and at one time ruled over part of Kachh, but were driven by the Jâḍejâs into Warâi and Bajânâ.

The Kolîs are an aboriginal race scattered over Gujarât and Kachh, where they are found chiefly in Vâgaḍ and Anjâr Chovisi. They used, 'in the good old times,' to live by robbery, but that having now failed to be a paying profession they have betaken themselves to cultivation. They are of many clans, and probably the Bâbriâ Kolîs, driven out of Thân by the Parmârs before the Kâṭhîs arrived there, had come from Kachh. They are now found in Bâbriâwâḍ to which they give name, and have been conjectured to be the Barbaras of Sanskrit writers,† who are said to have expelled the Brahma Kshatris from Sindh,‡ when they came into Kachh, where they are still numerous.

The Mîyâṇâs, another half civilised tribe,§ reside chiefly in the district of Mîyâṇî, which receives its name from them. They serve as Sipahis, and also, till but recently, lived by robbery. They are of the following family and sub-tribal names, some of which indicate their Râjpût origin, though they came originally from Sindh, and have long been Muhammadans:—Bânthâ, Bâphan, Bâpû, Bhaloṭa, Bhâmdâ, Bhukerâ, Chalângâ, Châniâ, Châvaḍâ, Chhuchhiâ, Dândhi, Dhusâ, Gagadâ, Hoḍâ, Jâm, Jesâ, Jesar, Jhâbai, Kakal, Kandechâ, Katia, Kechâ, Kevar, Khârâ, Khirâ, Khod, Lâḍak, Lûniâ, Makwâṇâ, Malak, Maṇkâ, Mathadâ, Mayântrâ, Mayâtrâ, Meḍ, Mendhâ, Mokhâ, Nângiâ, Notiyâr, Pâḍâ, Padehâr, Parit, Patrâ, Pehâ, Râjâ, Râyamâ, Rochâ, Sâd or Sâl, Sândhâni, Sannâ, Sayechâ, Sedôt, Siâriâ, Sîrâchâ, Sisodiâ, Śodhâ, Trâyiâ, Trilângâ, Vârâ.

The Châvaḍâs crossing into Vâgaḍ may have been supported by the Gujarât kings of the ninth and tenth centuries: indeed, tradition seems to point to some of the earlier of these sovereigns as having held at least the eastern portions of Kachh, while Kanak Châvaḍâ and his successors Akaḍ and Bhuvaḍ ruled the country just before the Solankis became supreme in Gujarat. "After the accession of Mularâja Solaṅki to the throne of Paṭṭan, and the subsequent expulsion of the Châvaḍâs, in about A.D. 942," writes Major J. W. Watson, "one of the queens of Samantsiñha Châvaḍâ, by tribe a Bhâtiâni, fled to her father's house at Jesalmer with her infant son, then a child of a year old. This boy was named Ahipat, and when he grew to man's estate he became a formidable outlaw, and used to ravage the Paṭṭan dominions. He conquered nine hundred villages in Kachh, and built Morgaḍh, which he made the seat of his government, and here, consolidating his rule, he reigned for many years. He was succeeded by his son Vikramsî, whose son was Vibhurâja. Vibhurâja was succeeded by his son Tâkulji, whose son and successor was Śeshkaranji. Śeshkaranji was succeeded by his son Vâghji, who was succeeded by his son Akherâja, and Akherâja by his son

* Conf. *Ind. Ant.* vol. III. p. 227; Tieffenthaler's *Desc. de l'Inde*, II. 206; Elliot's *Races*, vol. I. pp. 130, 179, 299 ff., *Hist.* vol. I. pp. 104, 119, 151, 190; Tod's *Rajasthan*, vol. I. p. 106; vol. II. pp. 370, 431; Cunningham's *Arch. Rep.* vol. II. pp. 50, 54 ff.; *Râs Mâlâ*, vol. I. p. 364.

† *Ind. Ant.* vol. III. p. 228; vol. IV. p. 193; *Râs Mâlâ*, vol. I. pp. 103, 185, 316, 320; and conf. *Harivaṅśa*, c. 108,—where they are mentioned with the Savaras and Pulindas, as wild tribes.

‡ *Ind. Ant.* vol. V. p. 171.

§ Burnes's *Narrative*, p. 236; Postans's *Cutch*, p. 135; Wilson's *Infanticide*, p. 349; *Trans. Bom. Lit. Soc.* vol. II. p. 230.

Tejasî, Tejasî by Karamsiñha, Karamsiñha by Tâkhansiñha, Tâkhansiñha by Âskaranji, Âskaranji by Mokamsiñha, and Mokamsiñha by Punjâji. Punjâji lived in the reign of Sulṭân 'Alâ-ud-dîn Khilji" (A.D. 1295–1315). "When the Jâḍejâs extended their sway in Kachh, they drove out Punjâji Châvaḍâ." From this it may be inferred that the Jâḍejâs had only lately come into the country, and were scarcely masters of it in the end of the thirteenth century. By the Solankis the earlier of these Châvaḍâs were probably driven westwards, for Mularâja Solanki occupied Kanṭhkoṭ when pressed by the Châlukyas of Kalyâṇ (cir. A.D. 982), and it was at Pâtgaḍh in Gardâ that one of their chiefs Wâgam Châvaḍa was slain by the fratricide Moḍ and the Sammâ refugees from Sindh. We find traces of their rule here and there in small townships till the end of the thirteenth century. There is a temple of Mahâdeva at Bhuvaḍ which bears an inscription, dated Saṁvat 1346 (A.D. 1289), containing the name of a Ṭhâkur Vaṇarâma, who is supposed to have been a Châvaḍâ. At present the Châvaḍâs have degenerated into Khavâsas, or Muhammadan sipahis, and a family of pure Râjpût descent can scarcely be found in Kachh.

Other tribes of Râjput origin are numerous: among them the Śodhâs, a branch of the Pramâra race, remarkable for the beauty of their females, came from Umarkoṭ and the borders of the Raṇ between Kachh and Sindh.* They are both Hindus and Muhammadans; some are landholders, and others cultivators and sipahis. The Siṅdhal Śodhâs, now in Kâṇṭhî, formerly possessed Pachham. The Râmdepotrâs are another branch residing in Khâvaḍâ.

The Vâghelâ Râjputs were once powerful in the east of Kachh, where they ruled till overthrown by the Sammâs. They still hold some towns of importance in Vâgaḍ and Prânthal, such as Geḍi, Belâ, Jatâvâḍâ, Lodrani, Bhimâsar, Palâsvâ, &c., and are tributary to the Bhuj Darbâr. When the Vâghelâs came into Kachh the Gujar Râjpûts accompanied them, and it was chiefly through their assistance that they became masters of that part of the country, as a reward for which they obtained the right of tilling the land. They subsequently defended the Vâghelâs from invasions from without. They are found chiefly in the Vâghelâ towns, where they live by cultivating lands. They are of the following races:—Makvâṇâ, Chanesar, Khoḍa, Châvaḍâ, Chahuvân, Gohel, Umat, Ḍuḍîâ, Dâbhi, Pâdariâ, Chând, Parmâr, Tank (Tuar), &c. They do not object to the remarriage of their widows, or to their females appearing in public.

The Bhansâlîs, also called Vegus, were originally Râjpûts of the Solanki race, but have long ago ceased to have any intercourse with them. They put on the sacred thread and consider themselves Kshatriyas. Most of them cultivate lands, and are said to have come with the Jâḍejâs and become their first râyats. Some of them are merchants. They are to be found in the southern and western parts of Kachh.

The Lohâṇâs or Lavâṇâs,† said to derive their name from Lohogaḍh, were originally Râjputs of the Râṭhoḍ race, who were driven from Kanauj into Sindh, whence they migrated into Kachh about the thirteenth century. At present they wear the sacred thread like the Bhansâlis, and call themselves Kshatriyas. They are to be

---

* Conf. *Râs Mâlâ*, vol. I. p. 294; Tod's *Râjasthan*, vol. I. p. 93; Elliot's *Hist. of Ind.*, vol. I. p. 217; Postans's *Cutch*, p. 136; *Tr. Bom. Lit. Soc.*, vol. II. pp. 238 ff.

† Conf. *Journ. R. As. Soc.* vol. I. pp. 239, 247 ff.; *Trans. R. As. Soc.* vol. III. p. 564; *Trans. Bom. Lit. Soc.* vol. II. p. 232; Elliot's *Hist.* vol. I. pp. 145, 151, 192.

found in every part of Kachh. Once they took a leading part in the affairs of Kachh, and were its most able kârbhâris and generals. They take up any profession that suits them. They are porters, menial servants, shop-keepers, cultivators, clerks, and kârbhâris. Some of them are as handsome as the Râjpûts of the purest blood.

The Saṅghârs were one of the tribes that accompanied the Sammâs from Sindh. They were subdivided into four castes when they entered Kachh. Other tribes of Râjpûts, such as Châvaḍas, Châhuvâns, &c., joined them, and there are at present seventy-two family *nukhs.* Some are Muhammadans and others Hindus, but all worship the Yakshas, which are supposed to be some foreign race that saved them from the oppressions of Jâm Puvarâ by killing him. The Hindu Sanghârs, of whom the Bhamḍâs in Vâgaḍ are a branch, are chiefly found in Kâṇṭhî; the Muhammadans, said to be of Arab descent, are settled in Abḍâsâ, Moḍâsâ, and Mâk.

The Bhâṭiâs, originally Bhâṭi Râjputs from Bhaṭṭiner on the north of Mewâḍ, like the Jâḍejâs, claim to be Yâdavas. After their migration to Sindh they degenerated, it is said, into fishermen, but the Mahârâja of the Valabhâchâryas gained them over to wear the sacred thread, and to follow the rules of his sect with much strictness.* They have of late greatly risen in the social scale, and are among the most enterprising merchants, trading with Bombay, Arabia, the coast of Africa, &c.

The Khojâhs or Khavajâhs, now Shiah Muhammadans, were originally mostly Hindus of this Bhâṭiâ caste. Now they have a separate religion of their own, consisting of the *Das Avatâras* of the Hindus grafted on the Shiah tenets of the Muhammadans. Their high priest is His Highness Agâ Khân of Bombay, to whom they pay extraordinary reverence. They do not go to the masjid, but have a separate place of worship called the *Khânâ.* There are some reformers of late among them who, rejecting the mixed creed, have become Sunnis. They are chiefly cultivators in Kachh. The Pals are also Muhammadan converts from Bhâṭi Râjputs.

Among the other tribes of Râjput descent may be named the Bâraḍs, Bhambhîyâs, Chhugars, Dals, Jhâlâs,† Kâṇḍâgarâs, Mâyaḍâs, Kanaḍes and Pasâyâs, Pehâs, Mokalsîs and Mokâs, Relaḍîyâs, Varamsîs, Verârs, &c.‡

But the most numerous are the different divisions of the Sammâ tribe of Râjputs, to which the Jâḍejâs, or ruling class, and their kindred families belong. These divisions or families have assumed different names from their various ancestors. From Jâm Sammâ, the son of Narpat, the ancestor of the race, we have the Sammâs and Samejâs, who came into Kachh at an early date in the history of their tribe and settled in Pachham, where they are still to be found as Muhammadan girâsiâs and herdsmen. The Kers are descendants of Manâi, one of the first chiefs who came into

---

* *Hist. of the Sect of Mahârâjas*, pp. 44, &c.; Briggs, *Cities of Gujarashtra*, pp. 237, 238; *Tr. Lit. S. Bom.*, vol. II. pp. 230, 231.

† "We first hear of the Jhâlâs," says K. Forbes, "under the name of Makvânâs, at Kerantîgaḍh, or Kerokoṭ; at which place Vehiyâs ruled in succession to numerous ancestors, when the Vâghelâs were the sovereigns of Gujarat." He supposes Kerantîgaḍh to be the same as Kaṇṭhkot. May it not be the modern Kheḍâ?—*Râs Mâlâ*, vol. I. p. 297; conf. Wilson's *Infanticide*, p. 159.

‡ For further information respecting these and the other castes, see a paper in the *Indian Antiquary* (vol. V. pp. 167–174), drawn up at my request, and on the basis of a list of my own, by Mr. Dalpatrâm Prâṇjivan Khakhar, Inspector of Schools at Bhuj. As no list previously existed, it supplies an important want, and has been made to a very large extent the basis of the notes here given. It was prepared, however, too hurriedly to be complete, though it may form an excellent basis for more extended research in the province.

Kachh. The fourth in descent from Unâḍ, the brother of Manâi, was Jâm Lâkhâ, the son of Jâḍâ, from whom his descendants derive the common name of Jâḍeja.* It is to this Lâkhâ that the introduction of female infanticide is attributed. The descendants of Rata Râyadhaṇ, the son of Jâm Lâkhâ, pass by the general name of Dhaṅg, who have either become poor peasants on account of their lands having been sold, or divided among the fraternity, or encroached upon by their powerful brethren of more recent descent from Râo Khangârji, the founder of Bhuj. The following are among the principal Dhang tribes:—Abḍâ, Âmar, Bârâch, Bhojde, Bûṭṭâ, Dedâ, Gâhâ, Gajan, Hothî, Jâḍâ, Jesar, Kâyâ, Koret, Moḍ, Paër, &c.

Hâlâ, the second son of Gajan and grandson of Rata Râyadhaṇ, subdued all the villages in the south and west of Kachh, and founded the Hâlâ tribe, the chief of which, Jâm Râval, in the sixteenth century, usurped the Government of the whole country, but was finally driven out by Râo Khangâr. He went to Kâṭhiâwâḍ, of which he conquered the western part from the Jaiṭwâs, and gave it the name of Hâlâr, where he founded the town of Navânager and made it his capital. The Jâm of Navânagar is descended from him. Those who remained in Kachh hold some villages as their *girâs* in the districts of Kâṇṭhi and Hâlâchovisi.

These are all, properly speaking, Jâḍejâs, but the name Jâḍejâ or Jhâḍejâ is specially applied at present, in the province at least, to the descendants of Jâm Hamirji (cir. A.D. 1530), who are of the Sâheb, Râyab, and Khangâr branches.

Many of the Jâḍejâ clans have adopted the Muhammadan religion, but still retain their *nukhs* or family names.

The other tribes who belong to the same faith are,—the Mehmaṇs, who are Sunni converts from the Lohâṇâs and came from Sindh; Bohorâs, Shiah converts from the Brahmans, having their Mullâ at Surat; Âgarîyâs, originally Râthoḍs, from Âgrâ; Âgâs, Bhanḍârîs, Bhaṭṭis, Dârâḍs, Maṅgâriâs, Oṭârs, Pâḍyârs, Phuls, Râjaḍs, Râyamâs—converts from Mokalsî Râjputs, Seḍâts, Vehans, &c.; and of Sindhî Muhammadans—Hâlepotrâs, Nâraṅgpotrâs, Noḍes, Hiṅgorâs and Hiṅgorjâs, Ners, Poärs, &c.

Among the Brahman castes are,—Audich, Saraswat, Pokharṇâ, Nâgar, Sâchorâ, Śrîmâlî, Girnârâ, Moḍh, and Râjgur Brahmans.

Of Vâṇiâs, there are Śrâvaks of the Oswâl, Śrîmâli, Bhojak, and Lokâ gachhas; and Vaishṇavas of the Mesri, Kandoi, Soni, Soraṭhiâ, Muḍh, Vâiḍâ, and perhaps other divisions.

There are three divisions of the Châraṇs:—1, Kâchhelâs (Kachhis); 2, Mâruvâs (from Mârwâḍ); and 3, Tûmbels (from Sindh). The last two are the family bards of the Jâḍejâs, and enjoy several villages as *girâs* given by Jâm Râval and the Darbârs of Kachh. The Mâruvâs and Kâchhelâs reside in Mâk, and the Tûmbels in Kâṇṭhi. The Kâchhelâs are money-lenders, and trade by caravans of bullocks. The difference

* The origin of the name is thus given by a late Râo of Kach, in a *yad* furnished to the Political Agent in 1850:—"At first Jâm Jâḍo had no son; and at that time the Rani of his younger brother Virji, named Rupajibai Chahuvan, bore twin sons, the eldest, Lâkhâji, and the youngest Lâkhiarji. A twin in the Sindhi language is called a *jâḍâ* birth. Jâda Jâm adopted the elder Lâkhâji, from which time Lâkhâ was called the son of Jâḍa Jâm. In the Gujarâti language he is called Phulano Putra (such a one's son), and in the Sindhian language Jâḍâ Junya (a twin). From that the name of Lâkhâ Jâḍejâ or Jâḍâ Jâm has been derived, and the descendants of Lâkhâ Jâm have been called Jâḍejas."—*Bombay Selections*, XV. p. 205.

between a Bhâṭ and a Châraṇ lies chiefly in the latter being a simple reciter of a Râjpût's praise in short, rude, poetical pieces, while the former is a regular genealogist, and sometimes the historian of the family.

The Kuṅbîs or Kulaṁbîs of Kachh are chiefly of the Ânjanâ and Levâ divisions; few, if any, Kaḍavâs are found.

The Ḍheḍs, the lowest caste among the Hindus, are found in every town and village. From their *nukhs*, or family names, many of them appear to have been originally of Râjpût descent. For instance, we find among them Solankis, Châvaḍâs, Jhâlâs, Vâghelâs, &c. The Hindus consider themselves polluted by their touch. Their profession is that of weavers, cobblers, wood-splitters, and tanners. They also take the hides and entrails from the carcasses of dead animals. Those who serve as guides to government officers are also called Meghvâls.

XVI. JÂDEJÂ HISTORY.

The Jâḍejâ or Jhâḍejâ princes of Kachh, who claim to be descended from Kṛishṇa and the Yâdavas, trace their descent through a mythical line of eighty sovereigns of Sonitapura and Misr—the latter Egypt, the former (otherwise called Devikoṭa) the capital of Bânâsura, a legendary king in Southern India, whose story is told in the *Vishṇu Purâṇa*.* We come to something more like a real personage in Jâm Narpat, though he is said to have fled with three brothers from Misr, 'embarking from the port of Urmârâ' and to have gone to Ośam hill in Soraṭh, where his eldest brother, Ugrasena, became a Muhammadan and took the name of Aspat, while a younger brother, Gajapat, is the traditional ancestor of the Chuḍâsamâs of Soraṭh. Narpat is then said to have taken Gazni,† killing Firuz Shâh. He was succeeded by his son Sammâ, the ancestor of the Sammâs, who was driven from Gazni 'by Sultân Shâh the son of Firuz Shâh,' and went to live at Kijarânand; by his wife Kalubâ, a Makwaṇî, he had a son Jêha or Têjêkar, married to a Parmâr, by whom he had a son and successor Jâm Neta. Neta was married to a Rathoḍ, and had a son Jâm Notiyâr, who, by one of his wives, a Châvaḍî, had a son Jâm Udharbad. One of his wives was a Śodhî, and bore Jâm Udhâ, who was married to a Gohil, by whom he had Jâm Rân, or Râhu, the father of Udhâr by a Śodhî. Jâm Udhâr's son was Jâm Abḍâ, who married a Châvaḍî and became the father of Jâm Lâkhiyâr, who finally established himself at Nagar Samai in Sindh. He in turn is said to have married a Śodhî, and by her

* Wilson's *Vishṇu Purâṇa*, bk. V. ch. 32, 33, pp. 591–96 (4to. edit.); and conf. *Hindu Theatre*, vol. II. pp. 396–99; *Harivaṅśa*, caps. 55, 171, and 172; and my *Elephanta*, § 18, and note 26; Fr. Buchanan places Sonitapura in Bengal, H. H. Wilson in Southern India, and Wilford identifies it with Munjapaṭṭana,—*Asiat. Res.* vol. IX. p. 199.

† Gazni is also an old name of Khâmbat or Cambay.

had Jâm Lâkhâ Ghurârâ or Dhoḍâra. These seem all to have been petty chiefs of the Sammâ tribe in Sindh, probably before the middle of the thirteenth century. Lâkhâ Ghurârâ was succeeded by his son Unaḍ, who was murdered by his brothers Moḍa and Manâi. Moḍa and three of his brothers were then obliged to flee into Kachh, where their relative Wâgam Châvaḍâ was reigning; here also they killed Wâgam Châvaḍâ, reduced the seven Vâghelâ tribes, and obtained possession of the province. After five reigns the line became extinct with Puvarâ.

The only name that figures prominently among these five is Lâkhâ Phulâni's,—the fourth on the list,—but, though probably belonging to the fourteenth century, it is a matter of no small difficulty to fix his date. The Bardic chronicles differ widely respecting it, some placing his death as early as Samvat 901, *i.e.* A.D. 844, and others in S. 1201, or A.D. 1144. Unless, as is most probable, there were other Lâkhâs with whom the son of Phula has been confounded, both these dates are too early, even the latter by, perhaps, about 200 years. Different attempts have been made to rectify this. Capt. Raikes, taking the traditional date about S. 900, says: "Lâkha is supposed to have come to Kachh about A.D. 843." And Dr. Wilson, starting from this *converted* date, says: "'About A.D. 843' should be 'about A.H. 843,' the equivalent of which, Samvat 1521, is given as the year of the ascent of the *gadî*" (at Vinjan) "by Râyadhaṇ the son of Lâkhâ Jâḍanî."* Now the Hijirah year 843 really corresponds with S. 1496; but if there were an error at all of the sort supposed by Dr. Wilson, it would be in the *Samvat* year itself, not in its *converted* form, and to read A.H. 900, or *Samvat* 1551, manifestly gives too late a date; for we have nine princes between this and Samvat 1605, and therefore can scarcely assume Râta Râyadhaṇ's accession to have occurred later than S. 1450, nor perhaps earlier than S. 1400, while his father Lâkhâ Jâm, the son of Virji, and adopted son of Jâm Jâḍâ of Ṭhaṭhâ may have come into Kachh about S. 1407, or A.D. 1350.

Lâkhâ Phulâni's Pâliya at Adkoṭ in Kâṭhiâwâḍ is variously reported to be dated S. 901, S. 1101 (in the time of Bhîma of Gujarat), and in S. 1201 (in the time of Kumârapâla). If the Pâliyâ is genuine and the inscription legible, it is to be regretted that we have no copy of it for the settlement of this point. Lâkhâ is said to have been killed in a war with Mularâja of Gujarat; but Mularâja Solanki flourished S. 998 to 1053, which is much too early. Major J. W. Watson therefore argues † that it was with Muluji Vâghela, aided by Siñhoji Râthoḍ, that Lâkhâ contended at Âdkoṭ, and an inscription on a well near Morwâḍâ, of Râṇa Vîsal Dê, the fifth in descent from Muluji, is dated S. 1516; hence Muluji must have lived about Sam. 1400–1420,—in perfect accordance with the date assumed above.

Previous to this, Singhâr, the fourth of the Sûmrâ princes of Sindh, about the beginning of the twelfth century (A.D. 1092–1107), "directed his efforts against the country of Kachh, and extended his sway as far as Mânikbai."‡

In Mr. Malet's translation of *Târîkhu-s Sind*, the following passage occurs: "After the death of Khafîf,§ the people, the men of weight under government, and those out of

* See *Bombay Selections*, No. XV. p. 9; and *Indian Antiquary*, vol. III. p. 228.

† *Indian Antiquary*, vol. II. pp. 316, 317; vol. III. p. 42 ff.

‡ *Bombay Selections*, No. XIII. p. 41, has "Nanik Nai," Elliot's *Hist. of India*, vol. I. p. 216.

§ About A.H. 536 or A.D. 1142.

employ, agreeing that it was proper, raised Dûdâ, the son of 'Umar, and grandson of Pitthû, to the throne of the Salṭanat in his place. When all the affairs of the state were firm in his hands, Singhâr, a zamîndâr, came to pay his yearly taxes. He became acquainted with Dûdâ. This had lasted some time, when one day he spoke of Kachh in the following terms, in his presence, saying that he had heard that the Sammâ tribe had determined to come to Ṭhâṭhâ to take it, and that he should be prepared for this. On hearing this, Dûdâ, collecting forces out of number, marched to Kachh, and he severely twisted the ears of those people. Then a man of the Sammâ tribe named Lâkhâ came as ambassador, bringing presents and a Kachh horse, making offering of these, and asking pardon for their sins. Dûdâ with great kindness, gave him presents in money, a horse and a *khil'at*, allowing him then to depart." * This must have been about the middle of the twelfth century.

In the end of the thirteenth century or early in the fourteenth, the throne of the Sumrâs was usurped apparently by Armîl,† a tyrannical oppressor. "Previous to this," says Mír Muḥammad M'asûm, "some men of the Sammâ tribe had come from Kachh and had settled in Sindh, where they formed alliances with the people of the country. In this tribe there was a man named Unaṛ distinguished for intelligence. The chief men of the country brought him secretly into the city, and in the morning a party of them entered into the house of Armil, slew him, and placed his head over the gate of the city. The people then placed Unaṛ on the throne." This event probably took place not later than A.D. 1351,‡ and it is to be remarked that the Sammâs are almost invariably spoken of as a Kachhi tribe. After a short reign Unaṛ was slain by his own subjects, and was succeeded by Jâm Jûnâ, another Sammâ, and Jûnâ by Tamâchi, who at least in one MS. of the *Taríkhi M'asúmí* is called "the son of Jâm Unaṛ."§ Tamâchi was succeeded by his son Malik Khairud-dîn, who was invaded by Muhammad bin Tughlak, A.D. 1361. He was succeeded by his son Jâm Babaniya, and he by his brother Jâm Tamâchi II. (A.D. 1367 ‖). Jâm Salâhu-d dîn (A.D. 1380–1391) followed Tamâchi, and "his first act was a rectification of the frontier, which had been encroached upon by refractory subjects. He accordingly sent a force to punish them, and after inflicting salutary chastisement he marched against Kachh. Some obstinate fighting ensued, but in every battle the breeze of victory struck the standards of the Jâm, and he returned home in triumph with the spoils."¶

The next mention of Kachh in the Sindh annals is that "on the 6th of Jumâd al awwal in the year 858 A.H. (May, 1454 A.D.) Jâm Râyadhaṇ came forth. During the reign of Jâm Tughlak (1425–1452 A.D.) he had lived in Kachh, and had formed con-

* *Bombay Selections*, No. XIII. pp. 41, 42; Sir H. M. Elliot's *Hist. of India*, vol. I. pp. 217, 218.

† The *Muntukhabu-t Tawârîkh* calls him Hamîr Sumrâ; Elliot's *Hist. Ind.* I. 345.

‡ The *Tuhfatu-l-Kirâm* places this in 1351 (A.H. 752). The *Beg Lâr Nâmâ* seems to indicate that it was in A.D. 1334 (A.H. 734).—Elliot's *Hist.* vol. I. p. 494. If this is the Unaṛ who invaded Kâṭhiâwâḍ and besieged Ghumli (*ante*, p. 185), both these dates are rather late,—that is if the traditional date of the destruction of Ghumli can be depended on as correct, which, however, is doubtful to the extent of a few years.

§ *Bombay Selections*, No. XIII. 48.

‖ This date was correctly given by Prinsep in his *Tables*, p. 149, but the corresponding Hijirah date was misprinted 782. In Mr. Thomas's edition of the *Tables*, A.H. 782, is allowed to stand, and its equivalent A.D. 1380, inserted with it.

¶ *Bombay Selections*, No. XIII., 49–50; Elliot, *Hist. of India*, vol. I. p. 227 ff.

nexions with the people of that country. He had maintained a considerable body of tried men, to whom he paid great attention, and to whom he used to give fine horses and other suitable presents. These men looked upon him as a wise and superior man, and devoted themselves to him with great sincerity. When he heard of the death of Jâm Sikandar he proceeded with his entire force to Ṭhâṭha, and there assembling the people, he addressed them to the effect, that he had not come to take the kingdom, but that he wanted to secure the property of the Musalmâns, and to accomplish their wishes. He did not consider himself worthy of the throne, but they should raise some fitting person to that dignity, when he would be the first to give him support. As they could find no one among them who had ability for the high office, they unanimously chose him and raised him to the throne. In the course of one year-and-a-half he brought the whole of Sindh under his rule from the sea to Kâjarîki and Kandharak,* which are on the boundaries of Mâthîla and Ubâwar. When he had reigned eight years and-a-half, the idea of sovereignty entered the head of Jâm Sanjar, one of his attendants." Eight years is then assigned to Jâm Sanjar who died in A.D. 1461, only seven years and nine months from the death of Jâm Sikandar! There is evidently some error here; but what is of more importance is to observe that Râta Râyadhaṇ of Kachh cannot, as Dr. Wilson suggested, be the same as the Jâm Râyadhaṇ here mentioned, who must be placed 80 or 90 years later; but in the Kachh family there is another Jâm Râyadhaṇ Hâlâ, the great-grandson of Râta Râyadhaṇ, who might be the contemporary of, if not identical with, this Râyadhaṇ who entered Sindh in 1454; the name, however, seems to have been of not unfrequent occurrence. Possibly inquiry in Kachh might clear up this.

And now, assuming the approximate dates adduced above, the Chronology will stand thus:—

About A.D. 1250 (S. 1307). Lâkhâ Ghurârâ, Guḍârâ, or Dhoḍârâ of the Sammâ tribe was Jâm of Nagar Ṭhâṭha in Sindh. He had eight sons.

Jâm Unaḍ or 'Umar, his eldest son, succeeded him,† but was put to death by his brothers Moḍa or Muḍa and Manâi, who then with Sândha and Phula fled to Kachh, where they defeated the Châvaḍâs of Pâṭgaḍh, and the Vaghelâs of Kanthkoṭ, and established themselves as rulers.

About A.D. 1270. Jâm Muḍa slew his maternal uncle Wâgam Châvaḍâ and established himself at Gunthari: he was succeeded by

About A.D. 1290, Sara the son of Muḍa.

„ 1305, Phula the son of Sâra.

About 1320 (S. 1376). Lâkhâ Phulâni ruled at Kheḍakoṭ, subdued the Kâṭhîs, and conquered part of Kâṭhiâwâḍ, according to some reports, he was slain at Adkoṭ in Kâṭhiâwâḍ, others say he was murdered by his son-in-law.

About 1344 (S. 1401), Purâ or Puvarâ Gahâni, his nephew, after a short reign, was killed by the Yakshas; he left a widow Râjî, who invited Lâkhâ Jâm to Kachh.

About 1350 (S. 1406). Lâkha Jâm, the son of Virji and adopted son of Jâm Jâḍâ of Ṭhâṭhâ; Jâḍâ, who gives name to the Jâḍejâs, was the son of Sandha, a son or descendant of Ṭamâchi Sammâ the son of Jâm Unaḍ, the elder brother of Muḍa.

* One MS. has only Kajar; Mr. Malet gives "Kajar, Malli, and Khundí."

† Can this be the same Unaḍ who succeeded Armil in Sindh, and was put to death 'by his subjects'? See above, p. 198.

About A.D. 1365 (S. 1421). Rata Râyadhaṇ, son of Lâkhâ succeeded; he had four sons, of whom the third Gajan, ruled at Bârâ near Therâ in the west of Kachh; his son Hâlâ gave to his son Râyadhaṇ (cir. A.D. 1450) and descendants the name of Hâlâ. With the Jâm of Navanagar they now possess Hâlar in Kâṭhiâwâḍ. Râyadhaṇ's eldest son Dedâ or Dâdar ruled at Kanṭhkoṭ.

About A.D. 1385, Athoji, the second son of Rata Râyadhaṇ, ruled at Ajâpur to the north of Bhuj.

About A.D. 1405, Gâhoji or Goḍaji, son of Atho.

„ 1430, Vehanji, son of Gâho.

„ 1450, Mulvaji, or Maḍvaji, son of Vehan.

„ 1470, Kânyoji, son of Mulva.

„ 1490, Âmarji, the son of Kânyoji.

„ 1510, Bhîmji, the son of Âmarji.

„ 1525, Jâm Hamirji, son of Bhîmji, murdered in 1537 by Jâm Râval Hâlâ, who was afterwards driven out of Kachh, and founded Navânagar or Jâmnagar in Kâṭhiâwâḍ (A.D. 1539).

In A.D. 1548 (S. 1605). Râo Śrî Khangâr, son of Hamir, who had fled to Ahmadâbâd, was aided by Maḥmûd Shâh in regaining his dominions, and distinguished by the title of Râo. He founded Bhuj as his capital. From this date the chronology is well ascertained.

A.D. 1585 (S. 1642). Râo Bhârmalji, son of Khangâr.

1631 (S. 1688). Râo Bhojarâja, son of Bhârmal.

1644 (S. 1702). Râo Khangâr II., nephew and adopted son of Bhoja.

1654 (S. 1711). Tamâchi, brother of Khângâr, son of Meghaji.

1662 (S. 1722). Râyadhaṇ II., son of Tamâchi.

1697 (S. 1754). Mahârâo Śrî Prâgmalji, after murdering his brother Revaji, placed Kahânji, Reva's son in command at Morbi, which his descendants have held ever since. In his time Jâm Tamâchi, the sixth in descent from Hâla, was driven out of Hâlâr and came to Prâgmalji, who sent his son Ghoḍaji with an army and restored Tamâchi. Hâlarji, the son of Prâgmalji's brother Nâgalji founded the towns of Kotârâ, Koṭri, Nangarchi, Godrâ, &c., and was the ancestor of the Halâni branch of Jâḍejâs in Âbḍâsâ.

1715 (S. 1772). Mahârâo Śrî Ghoḍaji, son of Prâgmalji.

1718 (S. 1775). Mahârâo Śrî Desalji, son of Ghoḍa, imprisoned by his son and died A.D. 1751.

1741 (S. 1798). Mahârâjadhîrâja Mirza Mahârâo Śrî Lakhpatji, or Lâkhâ, son of Desalji, obtained from Ahmad Shâh, Pâdishah of Dehli, the title of Mahârâo Śrî and the "Mai Moratab."

1760 (S. 1817). Mahârâjadhîrâja Mirza Mahârâo Śrî Ghoḍaji II., son of Lakhpatji. In his time Kachh was four times invaded from Sindh.

1778 (S. 1835). Mahârâjadhirâja M. M. Śri Râyadhaṇ III., son of Ghoḍaji.

1813 (S. 1870). Mahârâjadhirâja M. M. Śri Bhârmalji II. (Mânsiñgh), son of Râyadhaṇ, by a concubine, dethroned.

1819. (S. 1876). Mahârâjadhirâja M. M. Śri Desalji II., son of Bhârmalji.

The genealogy of the Jâdejâs may be represented thus :—

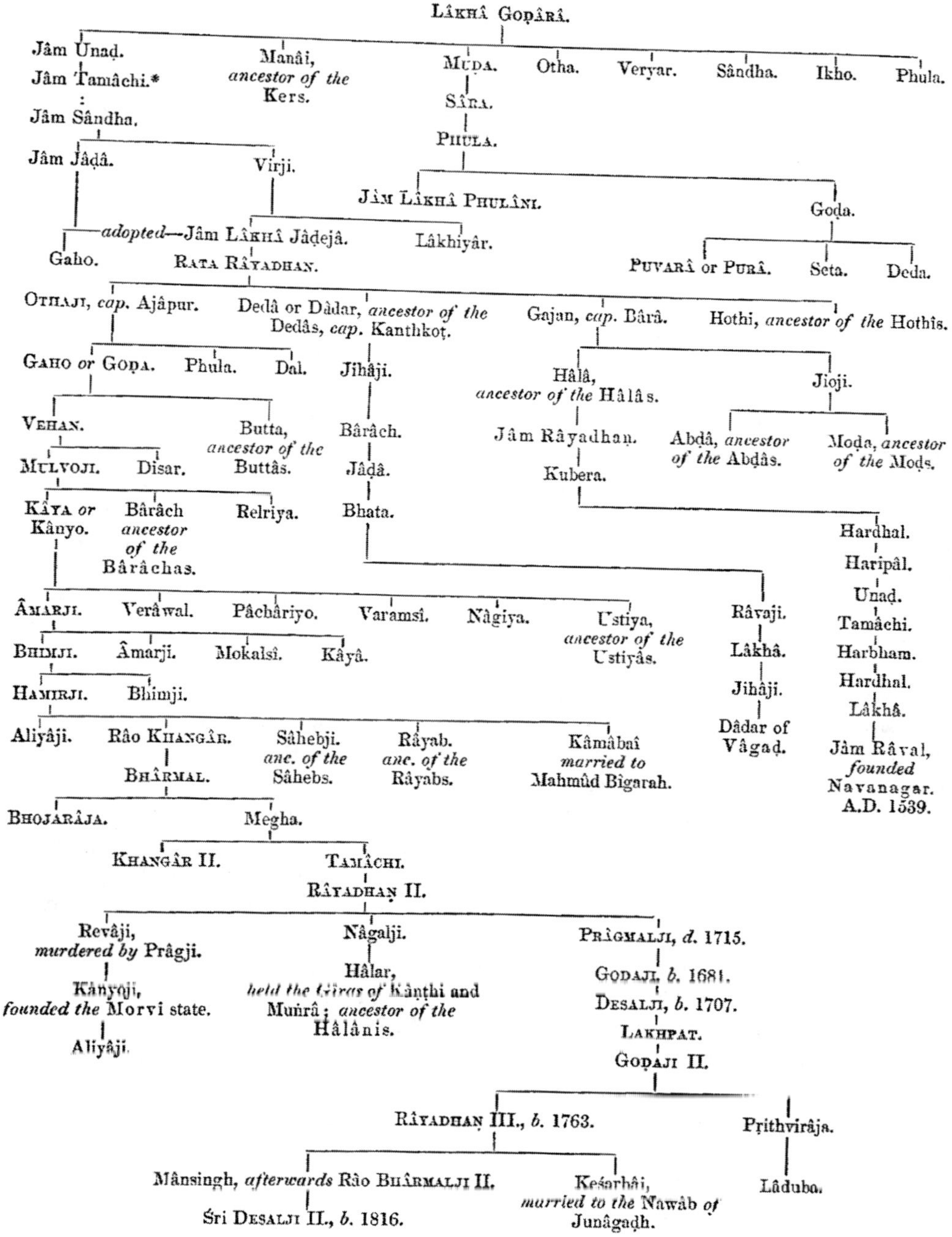

* Instead of Tamâchi, some genealogies insert Sama, Kâku, Râyadhan, and Pratâp or Pali, between Unaḍ and Sândha or Sândhobad.

The history of the princes from Khangâr has been succinctly told by Dr. Burnes in his *Sketch* of the *History of Cutch*,* and by Lieut. Raikes, in his *Memoir*,† and need not be further noticed here. Neither of these accounts, however, mentions the invasion of Kachh by Mirza Shâh Husain Arghun (1522–1544).‡

The narrative of Mir Muḥammad M'asum runs thus:—"When Shâh Husain had returned from the capture of Multan to Bhakkar, a petition came from the Amirs of Ṭhaṭha saying that Khangâr was preparing to come against him."§ Shâh Husain immediately went in that direction with expedition. On arriving near it, ambassadors came to him from Khangâr, saying: 'My relation Amîr Amravî was formerly slain in your quarrels. My people collected to take their revenge, but you had gone to take Multan,‖ and I preserved your reputation in not coming upon your families at that time. Now it is necessary for you to make peace, and to give me a portion of Sindh; if not I will make war with you.' Mirza Shâh Husain replied: 'There is no other language for me except war. The plain which I coloured with the blood of Amîr Amravî still retains the mark of the blood of him, and before your arrival, I am coming there." Shâh Husain, leaving some troops at Ṭhâṭhâ to protect the families, marched against Khangâr. Having passed the intermediate space, he came near Kachh, where the failure of grain came upon his army, from which his people became much distressed. Shâh Husain and all his chiefs agreed that it was advisable for them to attack Khangâr from four directions, and that whoever by chance first felt him, those who were near should come to his assistance. The first of these bodies directed upon the enemy was that of Sulṭân Muḥammad Khân Bakri; the second was that of Mir Furukhi; in the centre was Shâh Husain himself; and with the fourth were Mirza Isa, and Mîr Abik. Khangâr only received news of Shâh Husain alone coming with a weak force, so he marched with 10,000 men, horse and foot, in his direction. By chance, marching along, the noise of the beating of Nagarahs reached the ears of Sulṭan Muḥammad, who said to his men: 'the noise of the Nagarah comes to my ears.' All expressed their wonder at such being heard in the jungle. He then again heard the noise, and sent some people to the top of a hill to look about and bring the news. These brought word that Khangâr was moving with a large force towards Shâh Husain. The Mirza having heard of the approach of the enemy towards him, marched quickly with his troops to meet him. In the meantime Sulṭan Muḥammad, having come across, arrived in front of Khangâr. He then sent a stirrup-holder to Shâh Husain, saying, 'Do not advance from where you are; God willing, I will not allow him to come upon you.' He also sent a Kassid to Mir Furukh, to come up quick. When Khangâr's forces came in sight of their foes, they dismounted from their horses, forming lines, and taking their shields and spears in their hands, tied themselves to each other by the ends of their waist-cloths. Sulṭân Muḥammad directed the brave men with him to take nothing in their hands but their bows and arrows. In

---

* Appended to his *Narrative of a Visit to the Court of Sinde*, pp. 147–221 (Edin. 1831).

† *Bombay Government Selections*, No. XV. pp. 11–44, 96–133.

‡ This passage, like too many others, is also omitted from Elliot and Dowson's translations from the Muhammadan Historians. It is greatly to be regretted that where passages are omitted in this otherwise valuable work, clear résumes of their contents are not given. From this serious defect the work is frequently misleading. The want of Indexes, too, renders it troublesome to consult.

§ Conf. Wilson's *Suppression of Infanticide*, p. 59; *Bombay Selections*, No. XVI. pp. 93, 94.

‖ This was in A.H. 932, or 1526 A.D.

this manner there was good fighting for two or three hours. Khangâr's two leading lines became food for the eagles of the brave men of Sulṭân Muḥammad like pigeons: the remainder of his troops placed their faces in the direction of flight, and those, running away, came upon Mir Furukh, who made grass of them with his sabres. The troops remained there that night; the next morning the whole went forth to plunder the villagers and country, making many prisoners, and numbers of horses, cattle of all sorts, and property of various kinds fell into the hands of sipahis, Shâh Husain, returning with victory, arrived at Ṭhâṭhâ."

In the reign of Râo Goḍaji or Gorji, Kachh was invaded by the Sindhians with 80,000 men, under Mir Ghulâm Shâh Kalorâ, in 1762. A most sanguinary battle was fought at Jârâ, about 18 miles from Lakhpat, immediately after which Ghulâm Ṣhâh retired, and, at the village of Mora, on the north side of the Raṇ, threw a *band* or dam across the Pharan branch of the Indus, causing the stream to flow into other branches of the river. The flow of fresh water into and from the Raṇ being thus stopped, and no resistance offered to the sea, a large area which had formerly been a fertile plain, yielding from rice cultivation an annual revenue of 20,000*l*. to the Kachh Darbâr, was converted into a dreary barren salt marsh.* This, as may easily be supposed, has considerably modified the physical aspect and conditions of the west of Kachh.

Of more importance, however, in connection with the architectural remains of the province, was the great earthquake of 16th June 1819, which extended from Nepâl in the north to Pondicherry in the south, and from Mekran in the west to Calcutta in the east, but the force of which most violently affected Kachh and the tracts immediately to the north of it. The shock probably did not last more than two minutes, but the waving of the surface of the earth was perfectly visible, and so strongly undulatory that it was no easy matter to keep on one's feet, and in attempting to walk the motion was aptly compared by an eye witness to "that felt when walking quickly on a long plank supported at both ends:—when one foot was elevated, the earth either rose and met it, or sunk away from it in its descent." At Anjâr, the tower, "after rolling and heaving in a most awful degree, gave way at the bottom, on the western face, and crumbling down, buried guns and carriages in the rubbish: a moment after the towers and curtains of the fort wall, and upwards of fifteen hundred houses were reduced to ruins," and about a similar number rendered uninhabitable: all excepting four were cut as it were in two, one half crumbling into ruins; and a hundred and sixty-five lives were lost, besides a number who afterwards died of their bruises. In Bhuj "nearly seven thousand houses, great and small, were overturned, and eleven hundred and forty or fifty people buried in the ruins, and of those stone buildings which escaped ruin, about one third were much shattered. The north-eastern face of the town wall, a strong modern building, on an average four and a half and five feet thick, and upwards of twenty feet high, was laid level nearly to the foundation."

The fortifications of Therâ, among the best in the province, "had scarcely a stone unturned." Koṭhêri, five or six miles from Therâ, was reduced to a heap of rubbish, only about fifty or sixty gable ends of ruins left standing. Mothorâ suffered equally in

* *Bombay Selections*, No. XVI. pp. 99, 100; Burnes's *Narrative*, &c., pp. 153, 154; *Trans. R. As. Soc.* vol. III. pp. 551, 584; *Journ. R. As. Soc.* vol. I. p. 200.

houses and ramparts, and seventy-three lives. Naliyâ, Kothârî, Viñjan, Rohâ, and many others suffered similarly, whilst Mandair, Muṅdrâ, Sandhau, Punri, Bachâu and Addhovî escaped with comparatively little damage.*

In Kâṭhiâwâḍ—Purbandar,† Morbi, and Âmran suffered considerably. At Khambay the largest and loftiest dome of the Mosque, built in A.D. 1325, and under which the remains of the founder Sher Muhammad Naubahâri were entombed, was thrown down.‡ At Ahmadâbâd the shaking minarets of the great mosque fell,§ and at Siddhpur a portion of the ruins of the Rudra Mâla are said to have been shaken down.||

This convulsion must have totally ruined many of the oldest buildings in Kachh. At Khêḍâ, as will be noticed again, a very fine old temple attributed, as most old buildings in Kachh are, to Lâkhâ Phulani, but probably of much older date, was partly thrown down.

But probably the country was never very rich in remains; and they have certainly been less investigated than those of almost any other similar area in the Bombay Presidency. It was only in May 1872 that Captain Goodfellow, acting Political Agent at Bhuj, at my request, drew up a list of the old buildings, principally from native information, to which a supplement was afterwards added. But these dry lists were anything but a satisfactory guide, and are still incomplete: the interesting old temples at Kotâi on the borders of the Raṇ; the ruins of Wâgam Châvaḍâ-ka-gaḍh, an early capital, of which the walls—about two thousand yards in circumference—are still to be traced; and the deserted city of Guntrî in Chitrâno, the oldest seat of the Sâthsand Râjputs, with walls two thousand two hundred and fifty yards in circumference, are entirely omitted; and Puvar-no-gaḍh, the capital of Puvarâ, the nephew, or son-in-law of Lâkhâ Phulâni, is mentioned in terms that rather dispel than excite interest, though forty or fifty years ago Dr. Burnes said it contained "a two-storied palace within its walls, which was a great curiosity, and in very good repair."¶

The season, however, was too advanced before I reached Kachh to permit of a tour through the western portions of it, where, probably, the oldest remains are. It seemed advisable, therefore, on leaving Bhadreśvar, to confine the survey to the eastern part, so as to visit Râdhanpur, Sankeśvar, and Jhinjuwâḍâ on the return journey.

---

* Capt. McMurdo's account in *Trans. Lit. Soc. Bom.* vol. III. pp. 90–107.

† Capt. Elwood's account in *Ibid*, pp. 113, 115.

‡ *Statistical Report of Cambay, Bom. Gov. Selec.*, No. IV. p. 21.

§ Briggs's *Cities of Gujarashtra*, p. 203.

|| Tod's *Travels in Western India*, p. 141.

¶ Burnes, in *Trans. R. As. Soc.*, vol. III. pp. 586, 587. Mrs. Postans's *Cutch*, pp. 152 ff.

XVII. MUNRÂ, BHADREŚVAR, AND ANJÂR.

The town of Munrâ or Mundra has been largely built of the stones of the old city of Bhadreśvar, about twelve miles north-east from it. It contains little of note except a dome or *chhatra* over the *pâdukâ*, or footprints of a Jaina high priest of the Achalagachha,* 13½ feet square inside, with a small *śikhara* over the *pâdukâ*. (Plate LVI. and XLIV. fig. 3.) Round them is an inscription. The interior of the dome is neatly carved with standing musicians at intervals, as is usual in Jaina domes.

The substructure, screen wall, pillars, and interior of the dome are all executed in a style that would suggest that it probably belongs to the fourteenth century, and as the inscription round the *pâdukâ* inside is dated as of A.D. 1744, we must suppose that it was an old building, perhaps the Maṇḍap of a temple appropriated as a mausoleum and repaired, if not modified. The outside of the dome is certainly modern. The photograph (plate LVI.) shows the sculptured details of the two pillars of the porch and of the screen wall sufficiently to indicate the prevailing characteristics of the Jaina style in their temples of the thirteenth to the fifteenth century; and the sketch (plate XLIV. fig. 3) exhibits the front of the *Śikhara* over the marble slab bearing the footprints of the Guru, "Harshaji the disciple of the Guru Râdhaji, the disciple of the Guru Jîvaji," surrounded by an inscription, which states that he "went to the gods in S. 1797 (A.D. 1740) in Mârgaśîrsha badi 10th day."

Near it is a Pâliyâ, with a ship carved on it, indicating that the person to whose memory it is erected was a seafarer.

At Barâi, about a mile from Mundrâ, is a temple of Nîlakaṇṭha Mahâdeva, or Śiva of the blue-neck, enclosed in a small court. And at the right side of the shrine door is an inscription dated in Samvat 1724, A.D. 1667. The *linga*, which is over-shadowed by a large seven-headed brass snake, is said to have been brought from the temple of Dudâ at Bhadreśvar, and enshrined here.

Bhadreśvar.

The site of the ancient city of Bhadreśvar or Bhadravatî, extends to a very considerable distance east of the present village, but most of the area has been dug over for building stone, and we may legitimately infer that before this trenching up of the foundations was begun many buildings above ground had been carried off. What now remains are—the Jaina temple, the pillars and part of the dome of the Śaiva temple of Dudâ, the Wâv or well close by it, two Masjids—one near the shore almost buried, the Dargah of Pir Lâl Shobah, and a fragment of the temple of Âśâpurî.

The Dudâ Wâv has been a large and substantial well, without much architectural ornamentation about it. Over it is a lintel 17 feet 7 inches long by 2 feet 1 inch square. Many of the stones, however, have been carried off for building purposes.

---

* The four gachhas of the Jains about Munrâ are the Achala, Tapâ, Lokâ, and Khartaragachha.

The dome of the Dudâ temple that still stands near the Wâv is 15 feet 8½ inches over all; the pillars are 1 foot 4 inches square.

The old Vasâi temple or temple of Jagadevaśâh, as the Jaina shrine is called, is the work of several ages; it has been restored and altered no one knows how often. (Plates LVII. to LXI.) The lower part of the shrine is perhaps the oldest of all; the spire is a comparatively recent erection, or has more probably been carefully repaired; the temple itself and the corridors may be the work of Jagadeva-Śâh about Sam. 1232 (A.D. 1175); the two outer wings can hardly be very old; the arches put in to support broken lintels in the corridors, &c. are perhaps of the same age; and the outside porch in front is quite recent.

Connected with its history there are a series of traditions, collected early in the present century by a Jaina Guru Khantavijaya, who seems to have used every endeavour to recover the old *inâms* or royal gifts of land to the temple.*

The temple, it is said, was first founded by Siddhasena of the race of Hari, whose capital was Bhadrâvati, in the twenty-first year of the Vairat era, and dedicated to Vasâi. Siddhasena's successors were—his son Mahâsena; his grandson Nârasena; and great-grandson Bhojarâja, the contemporary of Sampriti of Mârwâḍ, the great patron of the Jains, and who also installed an image, and placed a figure of an elephant in the Bhadravati temple. Bhoja was succeeded by his brother's son Vanarâja, who repaired the temple; Vanarâja's son was Sarangdeva; Sârangdeva's was Virasena; and his Harisena, a devoted Jaina, who left the kingdom to his widow Lîlâvatî, the contemporary of Gandharva Sena of Mâlvâ, the father of Bhartṛiharihara and Vikrama,† the latter of whom established his own era when 450 (*or* 470) years of the Vairat had expired. Kirtidhara, the nephew of Harisena, succeeded Lîlavatî; and his successors were his son Dharnipâla, and grandson Devadatta; then followed Danjirâja, in whose time many chiefs plundered the country.

Vanarâja Vâghelâ of Munjpur then seized on the country (S. 213): he was a Jain, and was succeeded by his son Yogarâja.‡ He was succeeded by his son Ratnadatta or Sivâditya, and he by Vijayarâo or Vaisiddha, when the kingdom was shattered by the inroads of neighbouring tribes, and the Kâṭhis from Pâvargaḍh made themselves masters of Bhadrâvati, and held it for 147 years. Kanak Châvaḍa of Paṭṭan then subjugated the country (in Samvat 618), rebuilt the temple and installed an image in it in S. 622. His successor Akaḍ Châvaḍâ, was a Śaiva, and was invaded by Sayyid Lâl-Shâh and the Mughuls. His son was Bhûvaḍ.

The Solanki Râjputs of Bhângaḍh next conquered the country and changed

* Unfortunately the Guru has apparently tried to square his materials with his chronology, and he has assigned reigns of 32 years and *upwards* to all the earlier kings whose names he supplies, making sixteen reigns cover a space of upwards of 900 years. How this has been accomplished it is difficult to see, unless he has assigned to each the whole length of his *life* as that of his *reign*.

† Here the story is interrupted by the legends of Bhartṛihari and Anangasenâ (*Ind. Ant.* vol. IV. p. 2; vol. V. p. 1), and of Vikrama, and the division of the earth among the various races, among which we find the Dhâbi in Kapaḍvanj; Khopra in Gajni; Wâlâ in Chotilâ; Vâghelâ in Munjpur; Kâṭhi in Pâvargaḍh; Jeṭvâ in Ghumli; Jâḍejâ in Kachh; Jhâlâ in Pâtri; Châvaḍâ in Paṭṭan, &c.

‡ Vanarâja Châvaḍâ of Aṇhilvâḍâ (A.D. 745–806) was succeeded by his son Yogarâja (A.D. 806–841), and it is possible these may be the same as those named in the text. This Vâghelâ rule, at least, could scarcely have commenced much before the middle of the seventh century A.D.

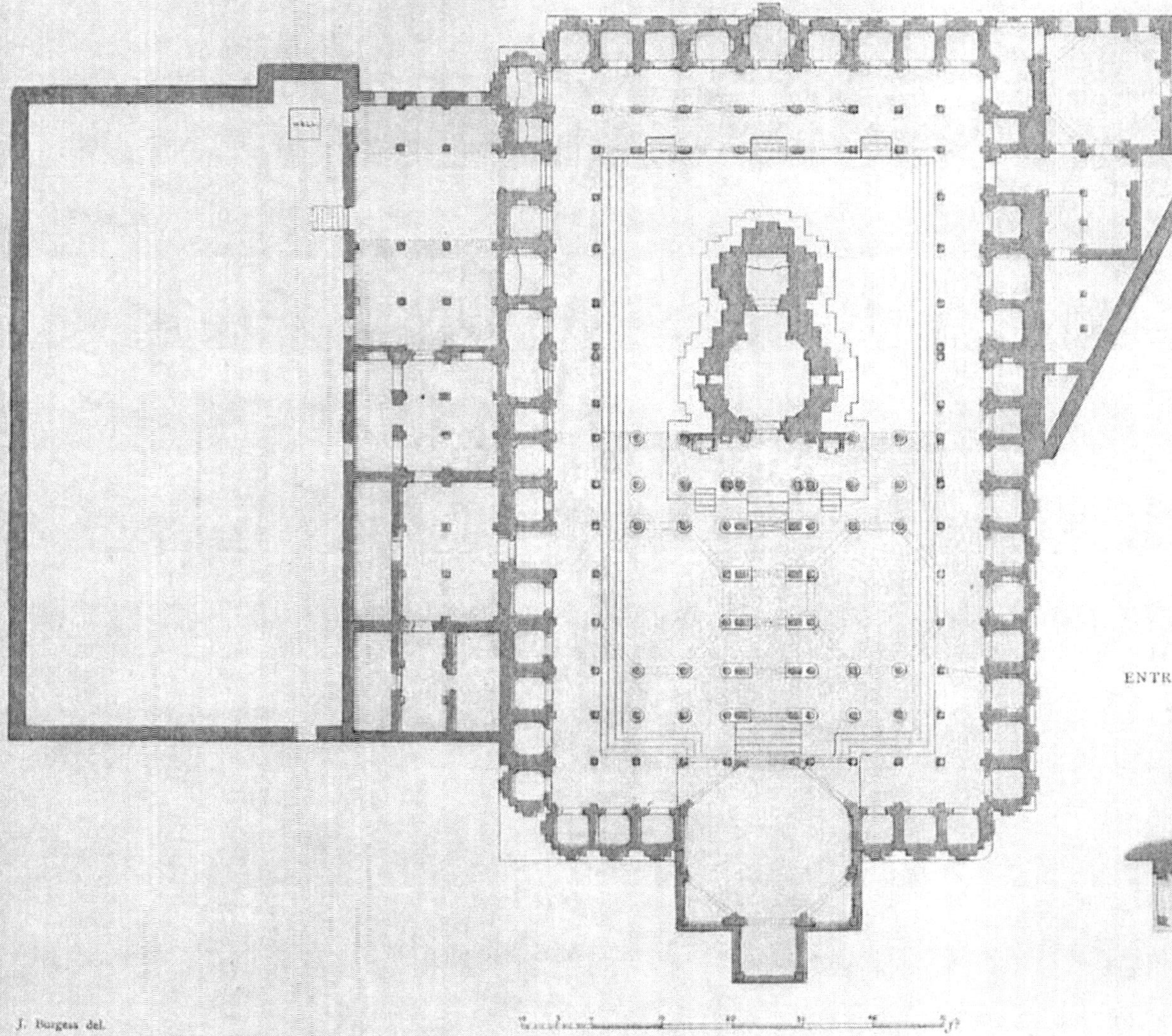

ENTRANCE PORCH BELOW.

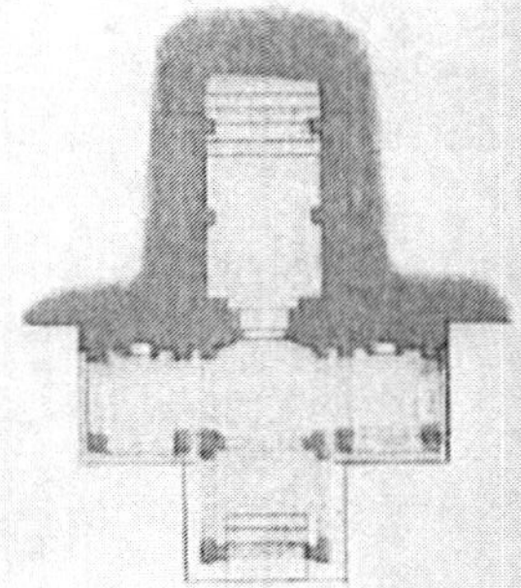

J. Burgess del.

W. Griggs photo-lith.

the name of the city to Bhadreśvar (S. 798). The Solanki was also a Jain, and ruled for four years.* This dynasty held sway till S. 1189 (A.D. 1132), Naughan the son of Bhimrâo† being the last of them. During his time the kingdom was split into fragments and infested by robbers and plunderers, and the Râja gave Bhadreśvar in *girâs* to a Vâniâ who aided him with the means of raising supplies for his army (S. 1149).

In S. 1182 (A.D. 1125) one Jagadeva-śâh‡ a wealthy merchant received a grant of Bhadreśvar in absolute right for ever, and caused the Vasâi temple to be repaired on an extensive scale, "thereby removing all traces of antiquity." He died without heirs in S. 1238. To this man is probably due the present plan of the temple and most of the building as it now stands. On several of the pillars of the corridors are inscriptions dated S. 1223 and 1235, but generally so obliterated that little can be made out, except that the pillars bearing them were votive offerings by individuals, made, doubtless, while the temple was being rebuilt. One in the back corridor, of more than usual length, appears to be dated 'Samvat 1134, Vaiśâkha, bright fortnight, 15th day,' and to be a record of repairs and perhaps of a grant to the temple by a Jaina of the Śrîmâli gachha.

Jagadeva-śâh's affairs fell into the hands of Naughana Vâghelâ and his *vakîls* Ajjaramal Sântidâs and Nagandâs Tejapâl, the latter of whom visited Anhilavâḍâ Paṭṭan, and returned, in S. 1286, with a *sangh* or pilgrimage to Bhadreśvar, led by the great Dosâ Srîmâli Vâniâ brothers Vastupâla and Tejahpâla. These were so well entertained by Vâghelâ Naughan that, on returning home, the Kârbhari or Prime Minister Vastupâla managed to get a daughter of Viridhawala the Vâghelâ sovereign of Gujarât (A.D. 1214–1243) married to Sârangdeva, the grandson of Naughan Vâghelâ. The Bhadreśvar temple seems to have been much visited in the twelfth and thirteenth centuries, and to that age accordingly belong the buildings which enclose it on both sides behind the *bâmti* or range of shrines, and those which surrounded it outside,—for there is mention of numerous other temples erected by *sanghvis* or leaders of pilgrimages. After this, however, troubles arose.

Still later Jâm Hâlâ the son of Gajan, tried to get hold of Bhadreśvar, but failing, retired to Viñjan; Harbham founded Pâvaḍyâla in the neighbourhood; and his descendant Jam Râval seized Bhadreśvar fort in S. 1592 as a defence against Khangâr, and it is said was advised by the high priest Ânand Vimal Sûriśvara to betake himself to Kâṭhiâwâḍ. Hâlâ Dungarji, a relation of Râo Bhârmalji's seized the temple-lands, and the Râo had to visit the place in S. 1659 to arrange matters between the Śrâvaks and him. After this it was plundered by a Muhammadan force under Mohsum Beg (A.D. 1603), and many of the images broken, from which

---

* Vide *ante*, p. 192. The Guru's chronicle here introduces Solanki Mularâja in Sam. 802,—the date of Vanarâja's accession to the throne of Anhilvâḍâ, whereas Mularâja Solanki succeeded to the throne either in Sam. 998 or 1018. To fill the space from 802 to 1124 he brings in the Solanki dynasty of Gujarat, but, curiously enough, omitting Kumârapâla, giving Vallabha a reign of 69 years, instead of six months, and altering the lengths of other reigns. If we assume the Solanki conquest in S. 998, we may place Kanak Châvaḍâ in S. 918.

† Bhimrâja Solanki reigned S. 1078 to 1130; Bhimdeva S. 1235–1243.

‡ In his time a Jaina Guru arrived named Deva Suri, who warned him of an approaching famine at the beginning of the new century, which was to last for twelve years. Jagadeva-śâh accordingly collected vast stores of grain, and when the predicted fam ine began in S. 1204, he had abundance which lasted till 1215 (A.D 1158), the last year of dearth. Even kings are said to have sent to him for grain. Conf. the story of Bhadra Bahu and the twelve years' famine.—*Ind. Ant.* vol. III. p. 155.

period it seems to have been neglected. In 1763 the walls of the old fort began to be pulled down, and the stones used for building, and about 1810 even the old temples were razed to supply stones to build the new seaport town of Muṅra or Muṅdra.

The general plan of the Bhadreśvar temple is similar to that of the Jaina temples at Delvâḍâ on Mount Abu. It stands in a court about 48 feet wide by 85 feet in length, round which runs a corridor in front of the cells or small shrines, about forty-four in number, nine of them in the back end where the corridor has a double row of pillars. The temple is placed towards the back of this area, and from the line of the front of the temple the court is covered by three domes, supported by pillars. It is entered by a flight of steps ascending from the outer door to the covered area in front of the sanctuary. Over the porch is another large dome covering an area separated by a low screen wall from the area of the Maṇḍap between it and the front of the temple itself. Behind the cells on the left side is a row of chambers, and at the south-west corner are others, some of which at least have been used as places for the concealment of images, &c. There are other chambers below them, entered by lifting up flagstones in the floor. On occasions of danger from Muhammadans or others, the idols were hurriedly deposited in these vaults, and sand thrown in after them to the level of the floor. On the east side of the temple is a large enclosed court with a well in it, perhaps for open air caste feasts, or for dispensing charity when the Sadavrit for that purpose existed in connection with the temple.

The temple faces the north—an unusual position for a Jaina shrine—and the view in plate LVII. is taken from the north-east, showing the backs and spires of four of the small cells at that corner with the entrance-porch on the extreme right, leading into a small verandah, extending across the front the length of the area covered by the large dome above. All this portion, with its scolloped arches, is quite modern, and the balcony wall or front in the upper storey,—which is a good specimen of work of the kind,—may be compared with the screen walls of the *Chhatra* at Munrâ or of the Navalâkha temple at Ghumli to show the differences of detail in work of the kind.

In the shrine are three images of white marble, the central one, not at all large, is Ajithanâtha, the second of the Tîrthankaras, and has carved upon it the figures ६२२ probably for S. 1622 = (A.D. 1565).* On his right is Parśvanâtha with the snake hood, marked S. 1232, and on his left Sântinâtha, the 16th Tîrthankara also marked S. 1232 or A.D. 1175—the date of the restoration by Jagadevaśâh. On the back wall, round the central figure, are *Kausagiyas*, indicative from their position that the shrine was once occupied by a larger image. On the extreme right is an image of the black or Sâmlâ Parśvanâtha. On the belt of sculpture which is immediately above the base, having a Devi on each principal face, there are, on each side the Devi, and on all the smaller faces a pair of small figures, mostly in obscene attitudes; this is not at all usual in Jaina temples.

The pillars on the raised platform immediately in front of the temple itself, and their corresponding pilasters, are more elaborately carved, somewhat in the style of those in the porch of the Munrâ *Chhatra* but the pillars of the two domes are of the

* In the account of the temple already given from a Jaina MS. it is said that Kanak Châvaḍâ, in the fourth year of his reign (Sam. 622) rebuilt the temple and 'installed the image of the holy Jina in it.' It may, however, be suspected that as the account is not an old one, in this instance at least, the date was made to suit the figures on the image.

PLATE LX.

KACHH.

1. PILLAR IN THE TEMPLE
AT BHADRESVAR.

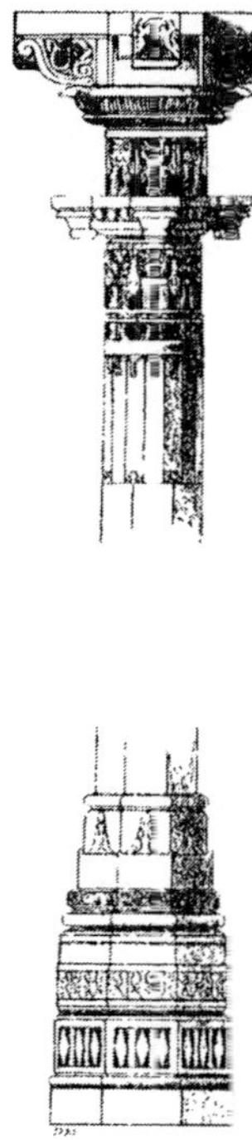

2. BASE OF A PILASTER
IN THE TEMPLE AT BHADREŚVAR.

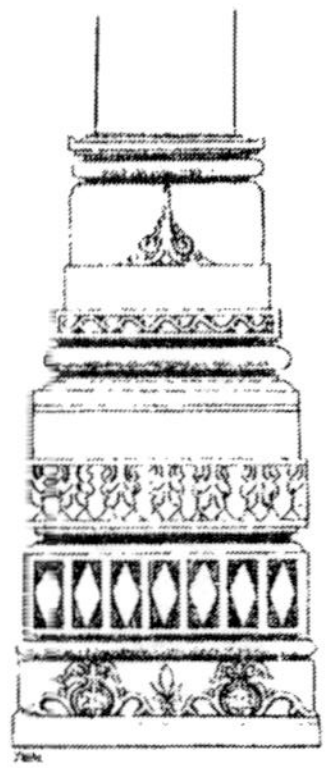

3. PILLAR IN AN OLD MOSQUE
AT BHADREŚVAR.

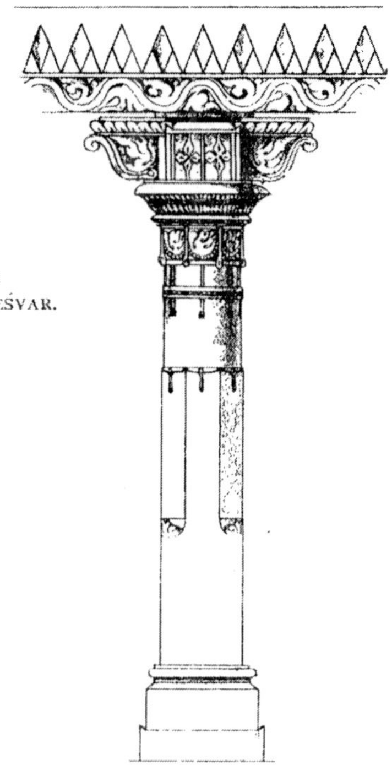

4. OLD TEMPLE
AT KOTAI.

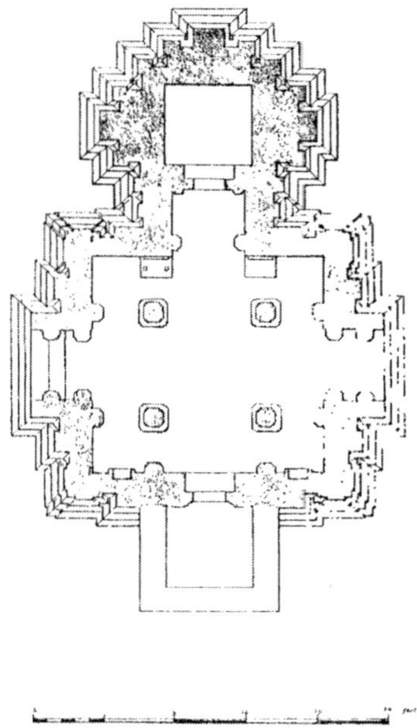

J. Burgess, delt.

W. Griggs, photo-lith.

style represented in plate LX. fig. 1, while to five pillars on each side the central aisle leading from the landing up to the front of the temple strong pilasters have been added of which the base is represented in fig. 2.

The doors of the small shrines are mostly surrounded by neat mouldings, none of them very elaborate in detail, and many of them alike. One, which may be regarded as a fair type of them, is represented in plate LXI. fig. 1.

Plate LIX. represents the back of the building as seen from the south, from which we should suppose that when the temple was built the level of the surface on this side was higher than it is now. It will also be observed that a wall has been raised between the *śikharas* of the shrines in the back corridor, doubtless as a defence work in the lawless times of the seventeenth and eighteenth centuries.

South from this temple are the remains of a large Mosque nearly buried in the sand. It has been built of large blocks of stone, with pillars, square at the base, octagon in the middle, and circular above, having bracket capitals, and supporting massive lintels of 9 feet long. In front of the *Mehrab* are two rows of columns undisturbed; of the next two rows but little remains; then there has been a wall, and outside it, other four lines of columns, and beyond them again are some others, probably belonging to the porch.

Pir Lâl Shobah's place has a round dome on eight pillars set against the walls; outside however this dome is a square pyramid and contracts upwards by steps. The roof of the porch is flat and divided into 9 × 3 small squares, each with a lotus flower inside. Round the architrave, above the vine-ornamented wall-head course, is a deep line of Arabic inscription in large square Kufic characters; and on the right-end wall there are two lines of inscription. The *Mehrab* is a plain semi-circular recess without any sculpture about it. The building stands in a small enclosure formed by a rough ruble wall built on the more solid foundation of the original court wall. In this court are some graves with inscriptions, also in the square Kufic character.

South-west from this last is another mosque; now entered from the north side, but the original entrance is on the east side, within which is built a small chamber, apparently never finished. The porch is raised on eight pillars, with pilasters against the walls. At the back is a *Mehrab*, a plain semi-circular recess, and two neat doors leading into an inner apartment, possibly a second place of prayer for a select number. It has four doors, two at each end. This mosque is built of pretty large stones, most accurately jointed, and all the roofs are of flat slabs. The doors have drips over them, and the two into the front apartment have semi-circular arches, the others lintels. The architraves are carved with neat *veli* or creeper patterns and with large flowers below, where the Jains employ human forms. On Plate LX. fig. 3 is shown one of the columns of this masjid, which are much the same in style as those of the Jaina temple, only not quite so slender.

At Bhuvaḍ, the temple of Bhuvaneśvara Mahâdeva is much ruined; the roof of the shrine having entirely fallen in. The *Mandap* measures 31¾ feet by 39¼ inside, and is supported by 34 pillars and four pilasters, 18 on the screen wall and 12 of them round the dome, which covers 22 feet 9 inches square inside the columns. The pillars are square to about one third their height, then octagon, and lastly round. The shrine has been a large one, fully 23 feet square, domed on 12 pilasters, 18 inches by 12 inches, with four-armed figures on the brackets. The brackets of the columns of the Maṇḍap are plain, but a plinth of 9 or 10 inches deep above the bracket is carved with a raised geometrical pattern. The front of the brackets are also carved as in those of the Bhadreśvar temple. The temple has been built of stones the whole thickness of the walls. Over the shrine door is a Devî—probably Bhavânî.

There is an inscription on the pilaster to the right of the shrine door, dated S. 1346 A.D. 1289–90; but of the 20 lines of which it consisted, only the names of Ṭhâkur Vaṇarâma and a few other Ṭhâkurs, probably his ancestors, with a few letters here and there, can now be read.

Anjâr.

In the large town of Anjâr the temple of Mâdhavrâo is a Vaishṇava shrine with a domed Maṇḍap, the floor laid with black and white marble. The image is of black marble decked out in petticoats like a child's doll, and placed on a table overlaid with silver, under which is the image of Garuḍa. The shrine doors are also plated with silver, and bear an inscription by the donor dated in 1869 A.D. On some of the eight pilasters that support the dome are carved mermaids * and Nâgâ figures. There is also a fountain in the middle of the floor, but the pipe is out of order.

Mohanrâi's temple is smaller and plainer, with a neatly carved wooden door. It is also a Vaishṇava shrine, the idols being Kṛishṇa, with Râdhâ on his left and Chatturbhuj—the four-armed Vishṇu—on his right, small paltry images that would not pass as good dolls. This temple was rebuilt some fifty or sixty years ago.

Ambâ Mâtâ's temple and the adjoining *maṭh* or monastery are built of fragments of older temples. To a room over the enclosure gateway is a door of hard reddish stone, carved all round, which, from the repetition of Devî on the jambs and lintels may have belonged to a Vaishṇava Śâkta temple (plate LXI. fig. 2); sculptured slabs also lie about, and are built into walls. The adjoining Maṭh belongs to the Atîts† of Ajaipâla.

Ajaipâla's place is outside the walls, and is a small modern domed room, with images of Ajaipâla on horseback, and of Gaṇapati—both well smeared with red paint. At the door are two inscriptions dated in A.D. 1842; but the Atits, who wear pagḍîs of brick-red colour and have a good revenue from the State, could not give much information respecting their patron saint, whom they worship, except that he was a Chauhân

* See plate LXIII. fig. 4.

† Atits.—"These people are known under many appellatives in Kachh. Some marry, and others do not, whence they are called *Gharbâris* (family men) and *Maṭhḍhâris* (ascetics or monks). These are, again, divided into ten tribes:—1, Gir; 2, Parvat; 3, Sàgar; 4, Puri; 5, Bhârthi; 6, Van; 7, Araṇ; 8, Sarasvati; 9, Tirth; 10, Ashram. The Atit of any one of these sects attaches to his name the name of his sect as a termination, to make up his full name, as Karan-*gar*, Hirâ-*pûri*, Chanchal-*bhârthi*, &c. By this he is distinguished as a member of a particular sect. A member of any of these sects may be a Gharbâri or Maṭhḍhâri, who, again, may hold intercourse with each other. Most of them are professional beggars, but they take up any profession. They are found as ordinary sipâhis, bankers, or merchants, and also taking a prominent part in the affairs of state at native courts. Bâwâ Rewâgar Kuvargar is one of the greatest bankers of Kachh, and his firm is held in great repute throughout Hindustân for its credit; and Bâwâ Savâigar was much trusted by the late Ṭhâkur of Bhâunagar. There are three heads of the Atits, who are called Pirs; one is the Pîr of Kâlyâṇeśvar, another that of Ajaipâl, and the third of Koteśvar."—*Ind. Ant.* vol. V. p. 168. Conf.; *Journ. R. As. Soc.* vol. V. p. 268; Mrs. Postans's *Cutch*, p. 120: *Trans. R. As. Soc.* vol. III. pp. 570, 579, 587; H. H. Wilson's *Rel. Sects*, Works, vol. I. pp. 18, 206, 213, 216 ff.

DOOR OF A SMALL SHRINE AT BHADRESVAR.

DOOR OF A SHRINE AT ANJAR.

J. Burgess.

King of Ajmer, who abdicated his throne, became an ascetic, and ended his days as a Samâdi by a voluntary death. They are a Śaiva sect, and the Nandi or sacred bull, with brass horns, occupies a prominent point on the platform facing the door of the shrine. Their pîrs or gurus are buried around, and the *chhatras* or small cells over their remains are marked by the linga.

Jaisal was a Jâḍejâ Râjput of Kedânâ, near Tuṇâ, who, with his wife Turî Kaṭhiânâ, it is said, gave themselves up to a voluntary death about four hundred years ago, and like Ajaiâpâla, they now enjoy divine honours. Their shrine is a small tile-roofed room with tombs of Muhammadan pattern in it of Jaisal, Turî, and a Vâniâ devotee. Round the place are a number of small Chhatras over Pâliyâs. This shrine has also an allowance from the Darbâr. It would be of interest if some one who has opportunity would investigate the history, traditions, and peculiarities of these Atits of Ajaipâla and Jaisal.

Klaneśvara Mâtâ's temple is also outside the walls, and is comparatively modern, with a dancing Yoginî as its goddess. In front of the Nandi is a tortoise.

Wankal Mâtâ's, on the north-east of the town, is also dedicated to a form of Bhavânî.

Baḍeśvara is at some distance to the south-east of the town. The shrine and śikhar are probably old, but it has been repaired, and the Maṇḍap rebuilt in recent times. On the withdrawn faces round the shrine is carved the lion-bodied figure, or *śardula*, remarked elsewhere, but here with a considerable diversity of heads—in this differing from those on Muni Bawâ's (p. 92, and see plate LXIII. fig. 5).

On the west of the town a new temple is being built to Dwârkanâth, and close to it is an unfinished one to Bahucherâji, with three shrines on as many sides of the intended Maṇḍap. Bahucherâ is the "looking-glass" goddess, before whom the votary worships his own image in a piece of silvered glass. This is practical Hinduism, groping in childish superstition in spite of the beautiful moral maxims that are to be found in its Sanskṛit literature. The other two shrines are dedicated to Bhavânî and the Linga.

XVIII. BHUJ, KHÊḌÂ, KOTAI, &c.

Bhuja was made his capital by Râo Khangâr in S. 1605 (A.D. 1548) when he recovered his kingdom from Jâm Râval Hâlâ, and became the first Jâḍejâ ruler of the whole of Kachh. Though previously dedicated to the snake divinity Bhujâṅga or Bhujiya,* it does not seem to have been a place of any historical importance, and consequently there are no remains about it of earlier date than the time of Râo Khangâr.

The Mosque inside the gate of the city is remarkable for the thickness and closeness of the piers, of which there are four lines each 3 feet 10 inches thick, by 5 feet 5 inches to 5 feet 11 inches in length, separating aisles only 1 foot 10 inches wide, except the central one, which is 3 feet 2 inches wide. The bays are 9 feet 3 inches wide by 46 feet 4 inches, the whole length of the building inside. The consequence of this arrangement is that but few of the worshippers can ever be within sight of others.

The five *Mehrâbs* are merely semicircular niches in the backwall. Inside it measures 61 feet 6 inches from front to back, and 46 feet 4 inches from end to end, with five doors, the width of the aisles in front, and three in each end, 1 foot 11 inches wide each. The building is lofty and very heavy with round turrets at the corners, and an outside stone *mimbar* or pulpit from which public addresses can be delivered to an assembly in the enclosed court,—the building inside being quite unsuitable for such a purpose.

Beyond the Residency are the Mausolea of the Râos of Kachh. The older ones are Chhatras, but most of them were more or less damaged by the earthquake in 1819, and no attempt seems to be ever made to repair any tomb that is falling to ruin. Râo Lâkhaji's is the largest and finest. It was built about 1770, but like the older one behind it, it is fast going to ruin, the south porch having fallen. The central dome covers an apartment surrounded by a wall with a door on the east. Across the floor of this is a line of Sati Stones, Râo Lâkhâ being represented on horseback in the centre with seven *Satîs* on the left and eight on the right of him. On the twelve pillars of this dome are dancing females, and on one a mermaid (plate LXIII. fig. 4), all about 5 feet high, while at the entrance are two Chobdârs. On the capitals are smaller figures, musicians, &c., about 3 feet high including their supports, but some of these latter are damaged. Since *Satî*, or the cremation of widows with their deceased lords, was given up, the Râos are denied the honour of a chhatra on their tombs.

There are a number of shrines and Muhammadan Dargahs, &c., about Bhuj, but nothing of great age or specially deserving of notice.

KHEḌA.

At Kheḍâ, the Kheḍâkot of Kachhi tradition, about 13 miles south of Bhuj, is an old Śaiva temple of, perhaps, the end of the tenth century, thrown down by the

---

* Tieffenthaler says, "Bhoudj (ou Bhodj) est la capitale du district de Catsch ; elle est grande et munie de deux forteresses ; située dans un terrein sablonneux sur le golf de la mer de Soreth, on bat monnoie ici sous l'autorité et au nom du Rajah. Cet endroit a reeu son nom d'un serpent ; car beaucoup de personnes assurent : le fait est même tres certaine, que l'on revére ici un Serpent, et que tous les jours on ui sert du lait et du ris. Il a le nom de *Bhoudj-bávan, i.e.,* que signific : le serpent long de cinquante-deux aunes."—*Description de l'Inde,* t. I. p. 396. Bhujâṅga, it will be remembered, is one of the five-snake brethren mentioned in connection with Thân,—*ante*, p. 92.

FROM KHEḌÂ TEMPLE

FROM KHEḌÂ

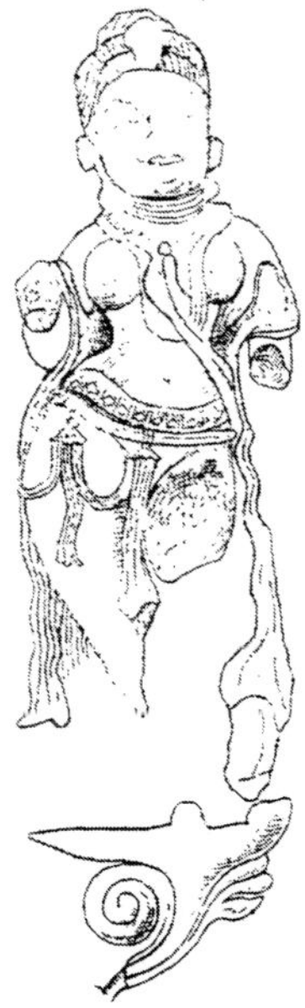

FROM KHEḌÂ

FROM BHUJ

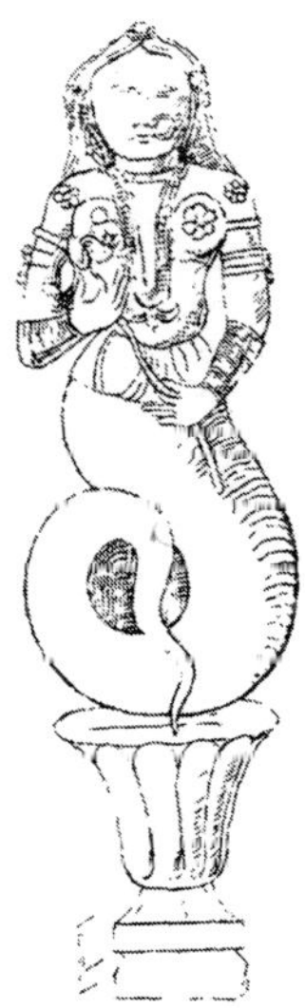

GRÁSḌÂ FROM KOTAI

Dinkar Moreshwar delt.

earthquake (plate LXII.). The shrine still stands, and measures 8 feet 6 inches square inside, with walls 2 feet 7 inches thick, surrounded by a *pradakshina*, or path for circumambulation, 2 feet 6 inches wide,—the *vimana* measuring 24 feet over all. This temple has been built partly of red and partly of a yellowish stone, very hard, and standing exposure very well. Of the Maṇḍap, which was 18 feet 9 inches wide, only a part of the north wall with one window in it is left; all the rest is a heap of ruins, and the Amla Śila of the Śikhar lies outside, a block about 6 feet in diameter. The sculptures on the walls are not numerous, but have been superior to the usual run of such work (plate LXIII. figs. 1, 2, 3), and the elaborate ornamental work on the faces of the spire has been largely undercut; it represents the outlines of a Chaitya window, repeated over a triangular face, with human figures between. Of these triangles of sculpture there are eight on each side, gradually diminishing in size as they rise higher and higher, one behind another, like so many gable ends. In the photograph (plate LXII.), those on the back of the spire are seen directly, while those on the left side are viewed edgeways, showing how one recedes behind another as they ascend. The corners of the shrine are surmounted by miniature spires, reaching not quite half the height of this sculpture, and above them are other four similar, but set further inwards; above these and the sculpture rises the massive outline of the great central spire or *Śikhara*, all beautifully carved. To light the *pradakshina*, there is a window of perforated stone on each side.

To the south-east of Kheḍâ is a small village on a rising ground, above which is the place of Pîr Ghulâm 'Ali. It is surrounded by trees, and there are few prettier places than this, perhaps, in Kachh. The principal buildings within the enclosure are—1st. The Dargah, facing the east, with one large dome, and in front of it three smaller ones. Inside is the tomb under a canopy supported by twelve small columns of the usual Muhammadan style. Against the pall lies the photograph of a Mughal pir, a water-colour portrait of 'Ali with a nimbus round his head, and below him Hasan and Husain, also with aureoles, and in a third frame Muhammad in a blue chogah, but the face left blank, a curious compromise between the prohibition in the Qoran (*Sura* V. 92) and the desire for a palpable representation of the objects of reverence. Looking-glasses, glass balls of all colours, cloth-parrots that look like purses, &c., &c., are hung up as votive offerings. The verandah or vestibule is 28 feet long inside, and the doors of copper bronze. 2nd. A canopy or chhatra stands in the middle of the quadrangle in front of the dargah, with a flat roof and balconies on each side. And, 3rd. Dadi 'Ali Shâh's dargah or cenotaph has lantern minarets, and is a neat, plain building with three doors in front and two in the east end. The roof is supported by two arches the whole width of the building. It contains no tomb, the body having been buried in Iran. The doors of both the dargahs have the projecting shield between floral ornamentation found at Maijî Sâhiba's tomb at Junâgaḍh, and on the palace, &c. at Jâmnagar. The windows are of pierced stone, the patterns being very simple ones, and all well whitewashed.

These buildings were erected about eighty years ago, Ghulam Ali Shâh having died at Karâchi about 1792. He was a Persian, and the estate attached to this establishment is said to yield 50,000 koris, or between 18,000 and 19,000 rupees which is distributed in charity, &c.

KOTAI, &c.

From Kheḍâ I had to return by Bhuj from which, marching northwards to the shores of the Raṇ, I came to Kotai, where are the remains of an old city with several ruined temples of perhaps the earlier part of the tenth century. It was at this place that the coins described on page 77 were found. The Sun temple (plates LXIV. and LX. fig. 4), known as Râ Lâkhâ's, ascribed to Lakhâ Phulâni who is said to have had his capital here for a time, is built of the yellowish and red stone used also at Kheḍâ, and is roofed in a peculiar way. The aisles are covered by a sort of groins, like the side aisles in some Chaitya caves; the nave is roofed the same way as at the Amarnâth temple,—the central area being covered with massive slabs hollowed out in the centre, in which a pendentive has been inserted. Outside it has a slanting roof divided into four sections of slightly different heights,—that next to the spire being the highest, and the remote end the lowest; each section is terminated by a neatly carved gable end. The whole has been built without any cement, and most of the stones are hollowed out on the under or inner side as if for the purpose of making them lighter.

The porch has long since fallen away. The door of the temple has been neatly carved with the nine *graha* or patrons of the planets over the lintel; the jambs are also carefully sculptured. In the Maṇḍap, which is 16 feet 4 inches square, are four pillars, measuring 9 feet 4 inches to the top of the bracket, and with a square block sculptured below the bracket, and six pilasters apparently inserted for the sake of uniformity only, for they are not of any structural use. The shafts, 5 feet 11 inches high, support a plinth 10 inches high, on which stands a block carved with colonnettes at the corners, and crowned with an *amlaśila*-shaped member, the faces of the block being sculptured with figures of men and elephants. The total height is 8 feet 5 inches. Among the four-armed figures on the brackets of the columns one is a female, and one has a face on the abdomen as at Aihoḷe. In the window recesses are also pilasters with four-armed figures on the bracket capitals. The pillars and pilasters are all of the Hindu broken-square form. The shrine door is elaborately carved with two rows of figures on the frieze, Gaṇapati, on the lintel, and the jambs richly ornamented.

The area behind the central one is roofed with large slabs carved with sixteen female figures linked in one another's arms in a circle, with the legs crossed and turned towards the centre. Each holds a rod or bar in either hand, the left hand being bent down and the right up, and so interlaced with the arms of the figures on either side. The roofs of the three aisles, at the sides and in front of the central area, are very prettily carved with flowered ribs, and three horizontal bands inclusive of that from which they spring.

In two neat *gokhles* or niches advanced from the front wall of the shrine, and with two colonnettes in front of each there have been standing images in *alto rilievo* neatly canopied by a lotus flower and buds growing over the *muguts* or head-dresses. Enormously elongated *Munis* or Bringis seem to have been the supporters.

This temple faces the west. Of the three small temples to the west of it, two face the east and one the north. The last has been a very small Vaishṇava temple, but only a fragment of the shrine remains. Of the middle one also only the shrine remains standing; on the walls are carved a figure of Sûrya on the west face, and *sardulas* in the recesses, Varâha has fallen off from the south wall, and there is a figure of Gaṇapati on the lintel, which seems to have been used in Kâṭhiâwâḍ, on Sun Temples as well as

PLATE LXV.

1. SÛRYA FROM KANTHKOT

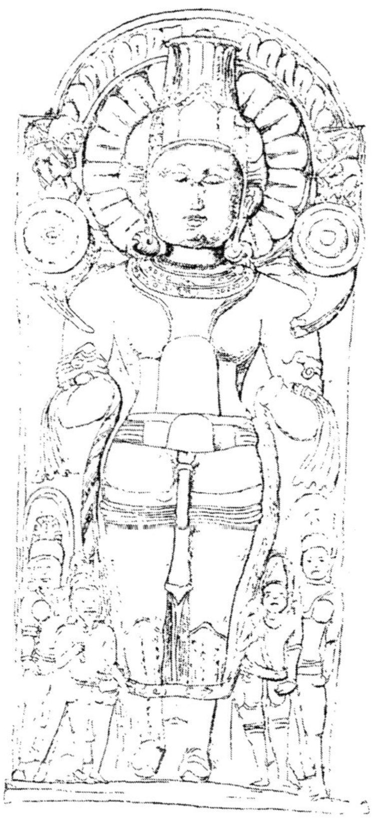

2. SÛRYA FROM ARASAVALLI

From a Native drawing

3. SÛRYA FROM A METAL FIGURE

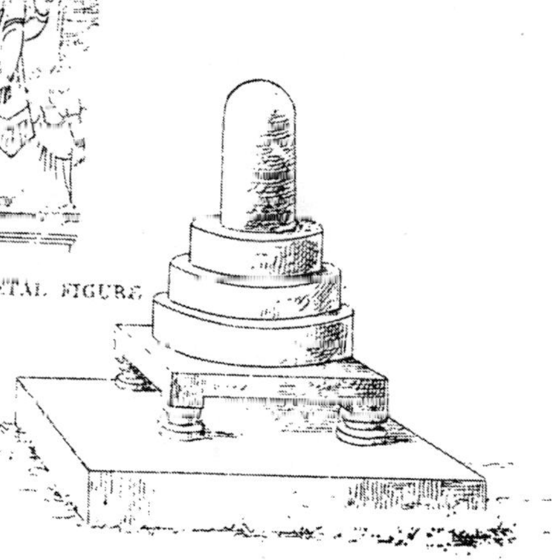

4. TOMBS OF ATITS AT KANTHKOT

those of Śiva. Of the third temple a portion of the porch as well as the shrine remains. Over the head of the shrine door are carved the nine *graha*. On the north wall outside is Nṛisiñha, and on the west Vishṇu, both much time-worn.

Across a ravine to the north-east from this group are fragments of two others facing west. Of the first, and higher up of the two, only plain square pillars of the Maṇḍap and the lower part of the Vimâna are standing. The door is surrounded by an architrave of three members, two fasciæ carved with *veli* or creeper pattern, and a cyma recta with leaves. On the lintel is a Gaṇapati, and outside two figures much weather-worn. The general style is the same as that of the other temples, but much plainer. The stones are cut away below as at the first temple.

The lower of the two is also only a fragment of the shrine of a Sûrya temple, with Gaṇapati on the lintel, and the nine *graha* on the frieze. There are no figures outside.

Foundations still remain on this part of the hill, showing that whole edifices must have been carted away for building purposes elsewhere.

We had now a long march along the borders of the Raṇ, first to Jhuran, and thence to Dudhâi, near which it was reported there was a temple of Mâtâ Bhavânî excavated in a hill. This turned out to be a wretchedly small natural cavern at a considerable distance from the village, which had been appropriated as a cell for the Mâtâ, and where some Bairâgis stay.

At Dhamarkâ was reported a Jaina temple of Pârśvanâtha built about 250 years ago. There is indeed a Jaina temple, such as is to be met with in almost any village where there are Śrâvaks, but of no interest either for size or decoration, and probably not more than 80 years old.

From this I went on to Bandrî, and thence to Kaṇthkoṭ, an old fortress on the top of an isolated rocky hill, the steep scarp of which has been crowned by a wall built of massive blocks, but it has in later times suffered severely, and been repaired or largely replaced with one of much smaller stones. It was the stronghold to which Mularâja Solanki of Gujarat betook himself when hard pressed by Tailapa of Kalyân about A.D. 982,* and afterwards it was the capital of the Vâghelâs in the middle ages, and of the Dedâ branch of the Jâḍejâs in the fifteenth century.

There is a portion of an old Jaina temple in this fort which has had a double *Maṇḍap*, but it is much ruined, some of the lintels having been used a century or two ago for Satî stones at the old burning ground close by. The temple has doubtless been a fine one, and on some of the pillars are inscriptions only very partially legible, one of which dated Samvat 133+, (*i.e.*) about 1280 A.D., whence we may infer that it was built under the Vâghelâ rule. It is so situated that it would be difficult to get a photograph of it except from a considerable distance, and the details are too weather-worn to be clearly made out.

There is an old temple close by of Sûrya,—the sun-god, the favourite object of worship with the early Kâṭhîs,—on which is an inscription in small characters, from position and present condition not suitable either for taking a rubbing or an impression of, but which might have been copied had I only had a qualified śâstri or paṇḍit with me. The temple still contains the image, figured on plate LXV. fig. 1. On the same plate are given two other representations of the same divinity from the south

* Tod's *Râjasthan*, vol. II. p. 446 (or Madras ed. p. 411); Forbes's *Râs Mâlâ*, vol. I. p. 51; and *ante* p. 193.

of India (figs. 2 and 3), in all which the general resemblance to the figures of Vishṇu is evident, indeed the third could scarcely be distinguished from an image of Vishṇu. In all the older images Sûrya is represented with a nimbus or aureole. In the Kaṇṭhkoṭ one, he is represented with a male and female attendant on each side, the female being the farther from him, is represented as the taller, perhaps simply to show her head and shoulders the better over the male's. In all the figures he is represented with full or fat breasts, and holding his symbol—the lotus flower—in each hand. In that from Arasavalli he is represented, as he is also sometimes in Kâthiâwâḍ, (in the temple of Bhimanâth, for example,) as described in the mythology—

"Seven lucid mares his chariot bear,
Self-yoked, athwart the fields of air,
Bright Sûrya, god with flaming hair."*

Near a more modern shrine on the wall are a number of graves of Śaiva Atits, some of which present somewhat novel forms, usually a *linga* mounted on a series of plinths, superimposed one over another,—either round or square (see plate LXV. fig. 4).

At Kokrâ or Kakrâ, about a mile south of Kaṇṭhkoṭ, are two ruined temples, quite in the jungle, both of them Śaiva. In the most easterly one there is a fine door to the shrine, which, had time admitted, I would have made a drawing of. It is evidently old, of hard, compact stone, and has a Chaitya-window ornament over each jamb and the different compartments of the lintel. On the lintel Śiva is carved in the centre, Brahma on the left, and Vishṇu on the right, in a very spirited style, with Kirtimukhs between. Some well sculptured pillars also lie about.

Had time permitted I should now have proceeded to Rav and Geḍi in the north east of Vâgaḍ; but the season was advancing and getting very sultry, and water was scarce and bad; besides my information had hitherto proved very unsatisfactory, and much time was lost in making long excursions to find that the remains reported were of but very little interest, and at Shahpur, I decided on moving towards Râdhanpur.

---

* Muir, *Sanskrit Texts*, vol. V. p. 161.

XIX. GUJARÂT.

a. Śankheśvar, &c.

From Shâhpur the route led by Bhimeśvar to Âdesâr, whence I crossed the Raṇ to Sânthalpur, and marched first to Wârai, and next to Râdhanpur, where I hoped to have been able to trace some copper-plates found about a year before, and said to be in excellent preservation. This I quite failed to do, but it is to be hoped careful inquiry will yet be made for them, and accurate facsimiles of them obtained.

Śankheśvar, though traditionally a place of great antiquity, being mentioned by Merutunga Achârya as Śankhpur, contains but little of note now. To the north of the village is an old inscription much weather-worn, of which the date is doubtfully read S. 1322, AD. 1265. It is on an upright stone standing by itself. Over the inscription are the sun and moon, and under them a cow and calf, and a pig, in sing of a joint agreement between Hindu and Muhammadan.

A little way from this, on the site of an old fort or town, are two carved stones, one of them a circular slab with three figures on it: the central a male figure with four hands holding a rod and a chhatri or umbrella; on his left is a female *chauri*-bearer, and on his right another female holding a cup and some other object. The sculpture is 2 feet 3 inches in diameter, and the legs stand inwards to accommodate the circle. The other stone, about 3 feet 8 inches long, is a representation of Vishṇu on Śesha, with three figures between Brahma and Lakshmî. The males have all square-topped *mukuts* or caps as at Bâdâmi, while the females have chignons.

In the village is a pretty large temple of Pârśwanâtha, the lower part of it mostly of marble, and with a *bâmti* or surrounding corridor of small shrines. It was built in 1811, and is no ways remarkable, either in general style or execution of details, and the Pardeśi keeper was obstructive and annoying, as his class usually are in such places.

In the town are the remains of an old brick Jaina temple of S. 1652, AD. 1596, much ruined. Outside is a neat Chhatra to a Śripuja or high priest, with a memorial inscription.

b. Jhinjuwâḍâ.

Jhinjuwâḍâ, said to derive its name from a Rebâri of the name of Jhinjû, was probably a border fortress of the Balhara kings of Aṇhilvâḍâ Paṭṭan in the twelfth century, towards Saurâshṭra, as was Dabhoi on their south-east frontier. The original walls formed a square of nearly half a mile on each side. In the middle of each was a gate; the Dhâmâ gate on the north, the Nâgavâḍâ on the east, the Madâpoḷa on the west, and the Râkshasapoḷa on the south,—the latter now built up. At the south-west corner is the only tower of the original four left standing. These towers were square in general plan, but broken in the peculiar way so frequent in the plans of shrines. Between each corner tower and the central gateway there were four rectangular bastions. But much of the old wall and enclosed town has long disappeared, and a much smaller square has been re-enclosed by one of the Ahmadâbâd kings by a wall with circular bastions and an arched gateway, and is now held by a petty Koli chief. Between the east and north gates is the old multilateral tank, about 300 yards in length and not much less in breadth, originally surrounded by a neat platform with steps and inclined planes at intervals; but one side of it has entirely disappeared, and the other has been much ruined since Mr. K. Forbes described it, little more than twenty years ago.*

The gateways are much in the style and of the dimensions of the Râmapoḷa at Bhumli and those at Dabhoi, but have never been so elaborately carved. (Plates LXVI. and LXVII.) Like these, and all Hindu gates, the roof is supported by brackets projected beyond each other until they approach within about 4 feet at the top, where they support massive lintels often the whole width of the gate. There are six pilasters supporting these brackets on each side of the gateway, grouped in threes, with a wider space in the middle to allow the leaves of the doors to open back to the walls. All the pilasters and brackets are richly carved on both sides, the brackets with musicians, dancing figures, men on horseback, *Śardulas*, &c. Below, both outside and in, on the faces of the jambs were niches containing images of the favourite gods—Gaṇeśa, Bhavânî, Mahâdeva, &c. Above, on each side, was a chamber with two projecting balconies or windows, one towards the town, the other looking outwards. Of these, however, there are now but small remains at Jhinjuwâḍâ. The walls were throughout ornamented by six sculptured bands, repeated at intervals, as shown in the photographs, and surmounted by *kângras* or crenellations, such as may still be seen at Dabhoi, behind which was a platform path or terre-plein for sentinels, and, in case of siege, for the soldiery. Two of these paths connecting the gates with the corner bastion are still traceable and in some places tolerably perfect. Again and again on the stones are carved the letters† :—

महं श्रीउदल—*Mahaṁ Śrí Udal.*

This, Mr. Kinloch Forbes says, is "supposed to indicate that Udâyan Mantrî‡ was the minister employed in the direction of the work." I cannot see the grounds for such a supposition: Udal and Udâyan are quite distinct names, and Udal is still a common name among the Chârans in this part of Gujarat.

The country to the east and north-east of Jhinjuwâḍâ would probably well repay a visit, but it must be undertaken at an earlier season of the year. The Nâgwâdâ-wâv—said to be about 8 miles east of Jhinjuwâdâ—is reported to be a fine one. Mudherâ had one of the finest temples in Gujarat, standing only six years ago,§ and possibly it may have still escaped the Vandalism of the Gaikwâḍ's people. And there are other places round the ancient capital Anhilvâḍa Paṭṭan that ought at least to be inquired about.

c. Dabhoi.

Dabhoi is an ancient walled town in the south of Gujarât, in the Gaikwâḍ's territory, about twenty miles south-east from Barodâ, and is now reached by the narrow

* *Râs Mâlâ*, vol. I. p. 251.

† It may be read three times on the left jamb in plate LXVII.

‡ Udâyan Mantrî was a Vâniâ minister under Siddharâja Jayasiñha, and the protector of Kumârapâla when in hiding.—*Râs Mâlâ*, vol. I. pp. 181 ff., 196.

§ See *Notes of a Visit to Gujarat* in Dec. 1869, pp. 103 ff.

gauge railway from the Miyâgâṁ station on the Bombay and Barodâ line. In the times of the Solanki kings of Gujarât, Dabhoi and Jhinjuwâḍâ were probably sister fortresses, very similar in construction, as well as in form and extent. Dabhoi, however, was the less regular, "two of its sides meeting in a sharp angle, and exceeding the others in length." The shorter sides extend about 800 and the longer about 1,000 yards.* The walls are somewhat lower than those of Jhinjuwâḍâ, and its four gates have, in most instances, suffered so severely as to destroy the magnificence of their original appearance, having been repaired by the insertion of Muhammadan arches. That which perhaps has been least injured is the Baroda gate, of which a view is given in plate LXVIII.

The city of Dabhoi is mentioned under its Sanskṛit name of Dharbhavati in inscriptions of the twelfth and thirteenth centuries,† if not earlier. It is said to have been built and fortified during the glorious reign of Siddharâja Jayasiñha (A.D. 1093–1142) as a frontier fortress, and the style of building both here and at Jhinjawâḍâ, as well as the elaborate richness of the sculpture, fully bear out the tradition that it was raised in the same age as the temple at Mudherâ and the Rudra Mâla at Siddhapur.

Forbes, in his *Oriental Memoirs*,‡ gives the following tradition respecting the place:—

"I may observe that the Bhâts and Chârans, the only historians of Gujarât, account for their expensive and sumptuous portal and the other magnificent structures in the city by the following story; which is probably founded on fact, though blended with fable. Their traditions relate that, many centuries ago, a Hindu Râja, named Siddharâo Jaya Siñha, the 'Lion of Victory,' reigned in Paṭṭan, the *Paithana*, or *Pattana*, of the ancient Greeks; § a city built on the banks of the river *Godavari*, at a great distance from Dabhoi.

"According to the privileged custom of oriental monarchs, this râja had seven wives, and many concubines; the first in rank, and his greatest favourite, was called Rattanâlî, the 'Lustre of Jewels,' an additional name conferred upon her, expressive of transcendent worth and superior beauty; in which and every elegant accomplishment, she excelled all the ladies in the haram. She thus preserved an ascendency over the râja, notwithstanding she had no child, and several of the rest had presented him with princes. The intrigues and jealousies among the secluded females in the eastern harams are well known; they prevailed powerfully at Paṭṭan, where the ladies were all jealous of Rattanâlî, and used every means to alienate the râja's affection from his favourite; but when they found that she also was in a state of pregnancy, their hatred knew no bounds. According to the superstitious customs of the Hindus, they employed charms and talismans to prevent the birth of the child; and the beloved sultana, superstitious and credulous as themselves, imagined their spell had taken effect, and that while she remained in the palace her infant would never see the light.

"Impressed with these ideas, she departed with a splendid retinue to sacrifice at a

* K. Forbes, *Râs Mâlâ*, vol. I. p. 252.

† *Ante*, p. 171.

‡ J. Forbes, *Oriental Memoirs*, 4to. ed., vol. II. pp. 335–337, or 8vo. ed., 1834, vol. I. pp. 543–545. I have, however, taken the liberty of modernizing his odd spellings of proper names, such as "Sihng" for "Singh" or "Siñha."

§ Here Forbes is all wrong: the capital of the Gujarat kings was at Aṇhilvâḍâ Paṭṭan on the Sarasvati,—the Neherwalah of the Arabic geographers, in northern Gujarât.

celebrated temple on the banks of the Narbadâ, and after a long journey arrived late in the evening at a sacred grove and lake, about ten miles from the river, on the very spot where Dabhoi now stands; there the princess pitched her tents, intending to conclude the journey the next morning. In this grove dwelt a Gosain, who had renounced the world, and passed his life in religious retirement. On hearing of Rattanâlî's arrival, he requested to be admitted into her presence, a request which is seldom refused to those holy men: he desired her not to proceed any further, as that grove was sacred, and there in a few days she would be delivered of a son. The princess followed his advice and continued in her encampment until the birth of her child, who, at the Gosain's desire, was named Visaldeva, or 'the child of twenty months.'

"This pleasing news was soon conveyed to the râja, who declared young Visaldeva heir to the throne; and finding his mother delighted with the spot where she had obtained the blessing, and fearful of returning among the ladies of the haram, he ordered the lake to be enlarged, the groves extended, and a city erected, surrounded by a strong fortification, and beautified with every costly decoration. The most eminent artists were engaged to build this famous city, and over them was placed a man of superior abilities, who lived to complete the immense work, thirty-two years after its commencement. At that time Visaldeva had succeeded his father on the throne of Paṭṭan, but generally resided at the place of his nativity, where, on dismissing the several artists, he made them suitable presents; but desirous of more amply gratifying the man to whose superior taste it was indebted for such extraordinary beauty, he desired him to name a reward for his services. The architect respectfully replied, that being happy in the prince's favour, he wanted neither money nor jewels; but as the place had not yet received any particular name, he entreated it might be called after his own, Dabhove, which was immediately granted, and with a slight alteration is the name it still retains."

Whatever may be the value of this legend, founded doubtless on facts, it makes a sad jumble of the history of them, in bringing together as father and son two kings who lived at a distance of fully a century apart. Jayasiñha never was blest with a son, and it may have been to this very fact that is in part due the magnificence of the gates of Dabhoi. He wanted to escape oblivion, and he strewed "with a liberal hand over Soraṭh and Gujarâshṭra the sumptuous edifices and reservoirs whose ruins, still remaining, excite the wonder of the rustic and the admiration of the student of ancient history."* Visaldeva Vâghelâ, the successor of Viradhavala, ruled from A.D. 1243 to 1261, and, as the tradition relates, may have been born here and made it temporarily his residence, as being less liable to attack by the restless and ruthless Muhammadans from the north than Aṇhilvâḍa Pâṭhan, the old capital, and he or his father doubtless repaired its defences and those of Visalnagar, and perhaps beautified the city, or even endowed some of its temples.

With the rest of Gujarat, however, Dabhoi early fell before the Muhammadans† and remained in the possession of the Ahmadâbâd kings, and afterwards of the Dihli

* Forbes's *Râs Mâla*, vol. I. p. 178.

† Forbes gives the following legend of its first invasion by the Muhammadans:—

"Dabhoi for a long time was inhabited only by Hindus, no Musalman being permitted to reside within the walls, nor under any pretence to bathe or wash in the tank; but a young Muhammadan stranger, named Sayyid

emperors, until the decline of the Mughul power in Western India, early in the last century, when the Marâṭhâs took it and repaired the walls in the present patchwork way, with brick and rubble, building into them many pieces of old sculpture, especially near the gates. During the campaign of 1775 it submitted to Raghobâ, who at once levied a contribution of three lâkhs of rupees from the inhabitants. It was then made the winter quarters of a portion of the Bombay army. In the beginning of 1780, on General Goddard's appearing before it, the paṇḍit who held it evacuated the city with his Marâṭhâ troops without attempting any resistance. General Goddard left a small garrison in it, and Mr. James Forbes to collect the revenue. Not many weeks after, however, it was surrounded by a Marâṭhâ army in great force, but was speedily relieved by the approach of Goddard, when the Marâṭhâs at once broke up and retreated towards Puṇâ. After this Mr. Forbes says he "put the fortifications and public buildings at Dabhoi in the best possible repair."* With its dependent Parganas it was again restored to the Marâṭhâs in 1783, much to the regret of its inhabitants. Its population was then estimated at 40,000, of whom a large proportion were Brahmans, and about 300 Muhammadan families; it is now probably very much less, and the city seems to be gradually falling into decay. Much of the area within the walls is regularly cultivated.

The gate that has suffered most is the Hirâ gate on the east, beside a temple of Kâlkâ Mâtâ, remarkable for its profuse sculpture: the most entire are the Nândoḍ gate on the south and the Baroda gate on the west. Original portions, however, of the four still remain,—they have only been repaired or partially rebuilt, and Muhammadan arches substituted for the old Rajput mode of spanning the aperture by corbelling inwards by means of a series of carved brackets supporting long stone lintels above. The gates are about 16 feet wide by 30 deep, with six arches in the depth, the pilasters to which contract the clear way to little over 13 feet. The space between the middle pair of arches is about 8½ feet, and to the outer of these two the gate was hung. Inside there is one small room on each side, about 6½ feet by 9, for the *darwân* or guard;

Balâh, on a pilgrimage with his mother Mamah Dukhri, on their way to Mecca, alighted at a caravanserai, without the gates of Dabhoi; and Sayyid Balâh, having heard much of its magnificence, walked in to gratify his curiosity. After viewing the curious gates and temples on the borders of the tank, and ignorant of any prohibition to the contrary, he rashly ventured to bathe in the sacred lake: the Brahmans, deeming the water polluted, prevailed on the râja to punish the delinquent by cutting off his hands, to deter others from following his example: he was then turned out of the city with disgrace; and thus covered with shame, and weak with loss of blood, he could but reach his mother at the caravanserai, and there expired.

"These strangers were Muhammadans of distinction then on their way to Surat to embark for the Red Sea, from the interior parts of Hindustan. Mâmâ Dukhri, after the first paroxism of grief, laid aside her pilgrimage, and vowed revenge. She immediately returned to her own country, and sued to her sovereign to redress this disgrace and cruelty to her family. He immediately ordered a large army to march, under the command of his vazir, against Dabhoi. The siege continued for several years; at length famine raging in the city, the garrison having no hopes of foreign assistance, made a sally, and fought with enthusiasm. A dreadful slaughter ensued; but the besiegers were at length victorious; the principal Hindus fled to a distant country, and the Muhammadans entered the city. On viewing the strength of the works, the vazir determined to destroy them: the three sides of the fortress were immediately razed to the ground. The beauty and elegance of the west face, and the magnificence of the four double gates, preserved them from his fury. They remain to this day splendid monuments of the architectural taste of the ancient Hindus.

"After the destruction of Dabhoi, the Muhammadans returned to their own country, and the city remained for many years in a state of desolation. Mâmâ Dukhri, the lady on whose account the expedition had been undertaken, came with the army against Dabhoi, and dying during the siege, was revered as a saint, and buried in a grove near the 'Gate of Diamonds,' where her tomb still remains. . . The monument of Sayyid Balâh is near that of his mother."—*Oriental Memoirs*, original ed., vol. II. pp. 337 ffg.; 8vo. ed. vol. I. pp. 545 ffg.

* *Orient. Memoirs*, 8vo. ed., vol. I. p. 516.

otherwise the lower portion on each side of the entrance is a solid mass of masonry 30 feet by 12.

The brackets, lintels, and upper portions of the side walls have all been elaborately carved with mythological figures and architectural ornament; and over the top of the inner façade of the Nândoḍ gate, on the south, there are remains of a line of statues. Most of the larger figures on all the gates, however, have been damaged by the Muhammadans. The Hirâ gate, on the east, is often called the "Gate of Diamonds,"* but is said to derive its name from the mason or master-builder under whose superintendence the gate and the temple beside it were built. This gate, as well as the Mori gate on the north, have suffered so much that they have been almost entirely rebuilt, with plain pointed arches, inserted in place of the richly sculptured Hindu bracketing. There are fragments of two inscriptions on the Hirâ gate, but so situated and so much injured that I could get neither rubbing nor impression of them. Had I only had a paṇḍit with me, copies might, with some care, have been obtained, as also of a much more perfect one on a marble slab on the base of Kâlkâ's temple and of another in Persian and Sanskṛit near the large talâo or tank, in the town.

The gates are all double, the inner being at right angles to the line of entrance of the outer, with an area between them; and it is only the inner gateways that seem to have been been so elaborately sculptured, though the outer ones were probably also carefully finished. They have been so ruined, however, and repaired in such a way that we cannot speak of them with certainty. The curtain walls had six square towers or bastions between the central gates and the corner towers, which were generally round in plan with re-entrant angles, or with a series of faces and angles lying in a circle, and crowned by a cavalier bastion, with Hindu *Kângrâs* along the top of the walls. One of these corner towers, between the Morî and Barodâ gates, is so singular in plan that the author of the *Râs Mâla* has made a drawing of it to show "that the walls of the tower slope inwards." The plate LXXII. taken direct from a photograph will, however, indicate that Mr. K. Forbes had probably been mislead by an inaccurate sketch or his memory had on this occasion failed him, for the walls of this tower, as those of all the others, are perpendicular.

The walls were originally constructed of large blocks of hewn stone built up as shown in the views of the Barodâ gate (plate LXVIII.) and the corner tower (plate LXXII.). They are much ruined in many places, but on the west, where they have been least injured, there are still considerable remains of the covered piazza or colonnade that extended along the inside of the walls and supported the terreplein. This colonnade, generally over 9 feet in width, but portions of it 16 feet 4 inches deep, was at the same time not only highly ornamental but also most useful, as it almost certainly formed the barracks of the Hindu garrison, sheltering them from sun and rain, and affording the sort of accommodation they would most prefer for cooking and rest. But little of it now remains however; one of the most entire specimens is to the right on entering the Barodâ gate, and is shown on the plan (plate LXIX. fig. 2).

* J. Forbes says, "Whether this portal was dignified with the appellation of the Gate of Diamonds from the brilliant eyes of the deity," in Kâlkâ's temple beside it—said to have been diamonds,—"or from its costly architecture, I cannot say."—*Orient. Mem.*, 8vo. ed., vol. I. p. 540.

APPENDIX.

TRANSLATIONS OF INSCRIPTIONS FROM BEḶGAUM AND KÂLADGI DISTRICTS.

FROM THE FIRST SEASON'S REPORT OF THE ARCHÆOLOGICAL SURVEY,

BY J. F. FLEET, ESQ., BO.C.S.

1. CANARESE INSCRIPTION of the RAṬṬAS from SAUNDAṬṬI (Plate LXXIII.).

See First Report, page 11.

Reverence to Śambhu, who is made beautiful by a *chowri*, which is the moon that lightly rests upon his lofty head, and who is the foundation-pillar for the erection of the city of the three worlds! May this Lord* of the Mountain-born, who has in his love commanded his eight excellent forms of Earth, Sky, Moon, Sun, Fire, Air, Water, and Spirit to proceed into the world,—he, Sadâśiva, who is resplendent on the sacred hill† with mental joy, (being one with) this same lord Mallikârjuna, —confer endless happiness upon those who betake themselves to him!

In the land of Bharata, to the south of the Golden Mountain‡ which is in the centre of the world encircled by the ocean, shines that country that bears the name of Kuntaḷa; lovely is that country, and in it is the district of Kûṇḍî. The supreme lord of that district, king Lakshmaṇa, was resplendent; to Kârtavîrya, who was his son, Mâdêvi herself became wife,§ and to them was born Lakshmidêva, who, if we describe him, was the delight of the wise people born in the world, the torment of all hostile kings, valorous as that (famous) Râma and other lords of the earth, endowed with all virtues. If you reflect upon it, Lakshmidêva was verily born to that virtuous woman,— possessed of a comely form, the preserver of the whole circle of the earth, the son of the king Śrî-Kârtavîrya, born in the family of the Raṭṭas, worthy to be honoured amongst kings; if you regard him, verily this Lakshmidêva excels in might, manifesting his glory in the race of the sun.|| This fruitful offspring of the Râshṭrakûṭa race, Lakshmidêva, of unequalled might, became famous, rivalling and surpassing Kandarpa¶ in beauty, and the sun in splendour, the son of the wind** in valour, and

* Śiva, the husband of Himâlaya's daughter, Pârvatî.

† The mountain Śrîśaila, in the Karnul country, on which is a temple famed for its sanctity.

‡ The mountain Mêru.

§ But in line 15 of the Kalhoḷi inscription—No. V. of the Raṭṭa Inscriptions, *Journ. Bom. Br. R. As. Soc.*, vol. X., p. 220, the name of the wife of Kârtavîrya is Êchaladêvî. Possibly the translation here should be "to Kârtavîrya, who was his son, she who was a most chaste wife" (compare one of the epithets applied to Êchaladêvî in the Kalhoḷi inscription, line 15) "became queen;" but Mâdêvî seems to be used here as a proper name, and, though the word '*mâdêvi*' or in its full form '*mahâdêvi*' has the sense of *queen, empress*, it is usual to add it in that sense to a proper name, *e.g.*, Êchalamahâdêvi, and not to use it in that sense as an independent word.

|| The Raṭṭakula is a subordinate branch of the Sûryavaṁśa.

¶ Kâmadêva.

** The Pâṇḍava prince Bhîma, who was the son of Kunti, the wife of Pâṇḍu, by the god Vâyu, the wind.

the Lord* of Rôhiṇî in being the delight of all mankind, the Lord† of the beautiful woman that is the Eastern Region in fortune, and Karṇa‡ in generosity.

Having with joy extended the Raṭṭa rule, Munichandra, the royal spiritual preceptor of the Raṭṭas, the lord of the woman Fortune, was considered the firm sustainer of the kingdom of the Raṭṭas. A very moon of a sage in that he was the delight of the lotuses§ (that were his friends), a very moon of a sage on account of his lustre which dealt destruction to the lotuses‖ which were the faces of the hostile kings, a very moon of a sage through his might which, traversing the ocean of the Raṭṭa kingdom, extended so as to touch the borders of the regions,—such was Munichandra, possessed of the name of "Moon." Through his mystic knowledge he became the spiritual preceptor of king Kârtavîrya; through his close acquaintance with the treatises on the use of the weapons he became the instructor of Lakshmidêva; through subduing many kingdoms he became the anointer of other kings;—thus, listen thou, did the title of "Spiritual Preceptor" become applicable to him; and truly (the name of) "Spiritual Guide" did belong to the excellent Munichandra. While this same Lakshmidêva, who was the son of Kârtavîrya the chief of kings, was firmly enduring, Śrî-Munichandradêva made the earth all of one standard of morality through his administration, and, decorated with arrows, pursued with the excellent might of his arm the hostile kings, being a very lion to the elephants that were his enemies. Worthy of respect, most able amongst ministers, the establisher of the Raṭṭa kings, Munichandra surpassed all others in capacity for administration and in generosity. The counsellors of that same Munichandradêva, who were praised in the earth, were Śântinâtha, best of clerks, the son of Kâmarâja, the granter of all the desires of his friends,—the glorious Nâga of Kûṇḍi, of great valour,—and Mallikârjuna who enjoyed happiness resulting from the greatness of his excellent and brilliant good fortune.

If you ask what was the unrivalled lineage of the thus-glorious Mallikârjuna:—The seven sages¶ are worthy of worship in the assembly of the Fourfaced,** and among them the sage Atri is the best and greatest. Anasûye, the chief wife of that sage, true to her lord, accomplished for her husband every thing that is pleasing and useful and supreme prosperity, and Hari†† and Hara‡‡ and the Lotus-born§§ became the sons of that lovely woman; from the eye of Atri was born the moon, and thus that race (became known) in the earth as the Indukula. In the race of Atri, which became diffused over the earth as the Induvaṁśa, were born many Brâhmaṇs,‖‖ versed in the best sciences, and among them was Rudrabhaṭṭa, the king of poets. He acquired from Sarasvati excellence of speech, and from king Kanna the supremacy over eighteen villages; who may be compared in the excellence of his poetry and the greatness of his power with that same lord Rudrabhaṭṭa, the members of whose race used to become excellent poets in six months (after commencing their studies)? Through

---

* The Moon. Rôhiṇî is the ninth lunar asterism, and the favourite wife of the Moon.

† Indra.

‡ A Purâṇic prince celebrated for his liberality; he was the son of Kunti, before her marriage with Pâṇḍu by the Sun.

§ '*Kumuda;*' *i.e.,* the blue lotus which flowers in the evening.

‖ Here the original has '*abja,*' *i.e.,* the white lotus, which opens its flowers at sunrise and closes them in the evening.

¶ Marichi, Atri, Aṅgiras, Pulastya, Pulaha, Kratu, and Vaśishṭha; or, Marichi, Atri, Aṅgiras, Pulastya, Vaśishṭha, Daksha, and Bhṛigu; there are other variations in the list.

** Brahmâ.

†† Vishṇu.

‡‡ Siva.

§§ Brahmâ.

‖‖ In the original, '*iḷâmarar,*' ='*bhûdêvar,*' *gods upon earth,* a common name for Brâhmaṇs.

W. Griggs Photo-lith.

that excellent poet Rudrabhaṭṭa, the family of Atri, known as the Sômakula, acquired the name of Sâmâsigakula,* and in that good family occurred a spotless achievement. For Rudrabhaṭṭa, having pledged a letter of his name as security for (a loan of) a thousand (pieces of) gold, received from people the appellation of "Rudraṭa" only, as a substitute (for his full) name, until the day when he redeemed the pledge. In the celebrated Sâmâsigavaṁśa were born many of matchless strength, and amongst them Kalidêva, praised in the earth, rose to an eminence of power through his spotless fame. His offspring Śrîdhara was resplendent with the supremacy over eighteen (villages) of which the town of Banihaṭṭi was the chief; to him was born Mahadêva, the abode of increasing happiness; his fair son was Śrîdhara, brave and proud, and to him was born Mahadêva, who enjoyed happiness as long as he lived. Enmity having arisen between that same Siripati† and the people of the city of Gaganasarôvara, Siripati was slain‡ at Hōlavĕre in the front ranks of battle by the inhabitants of that city. His father having become a butt for the arrows of his enemies, he (Mahadêva), having heard it, straightway arose and went to other lands, and, having during twelve years§ amassed wealth in the island, he brought and gave it to the king; and thus Mâyidêva, the most excellent one, destroyed his foe with the vehemence of his anger and with his infuriated elephants. As formerly Jamadagni-Râma, like a foul mist, twenty-one times destroyed the lords of the earth,‖ so Mahadêvanâyaka, the native lord of Banihaṭṭi, destroyed with his elephants the race of his enemies, and performed for his father the customary rites of the gift of water. Mahadêva, raising his hand against the Mâtaṅgar¶ who are thieves and who were scorched by his enmity, valorously afforded protection, while all mankind honoured him as being ever the protector of those that took refuge with him. Having afforded protection to those that fled to him for refuge, having overcome the might of his enemies, and having done honour to those that deserved to be honoured, Mahadêvanâyaka shone in the earth, diffusing abroad a majesty because he was verily like one of the elephants of the quarters. The sons of the thus-described Mahadêvanâyaka were three, Śrîdhara, and Mallikârjuna, and Chandra; amongst them Mallikârjuna shone gloriously as the sun of the white lotuses of his family, becoming the advancer of his race and the increaser of its pure fame. A very ocean of good qualities, a mass of glory, the granter of the desires of learned men, of men of culture, and of his friends, the chief of the Sâmâsigakula,—thus was the lord Mallikârjuna resplendent. The pure wife of the thus-majestic Malidêva was the lovely woman Gaurî eager in offering worship to deceased ancestors, to Brâhmaṇs, and to gods, devoted to her husband; let me describe the lineage of that lovely woman.

Amongst the seven sages, Vaśishṭha, chief of sages, was esteemed the greatest; and, becoming manifest in the lineage of that sage, Mâdirâja, the lord of the city of Kolâra,** shone in the earth. The son of Mâdirâja was the famous Bhûtanâtha of spotless deeds, and to this prince were born five children, resplendent with fame, worthy

---

* *i.e.*, as explained to me, a family in which the direct lineal descent has never been interrupted.

† *i.e.*, the second Śrîdhara mentioned above.

‡ Lit., "went to the city of Yama."

§ Lit., "during years counted by the number of the sun;" the forms of the sun are twelve, and any word meaning sun may, therefore, be used to represent the number twelve.

‖ This refers to the legendary extermination of the whole race of Kshatriyas by Paraśurâma, son of Jamadagni.

¶ The Mâtaṅgar are Chaṇḍâlas; the goddess of the caste is Mâtangi, hence they are also called Mâtaṅgî-makkaḷu, "children of Mâtaṅgi."

** This is either the town of Kolhâr on the banks of the Kṛishṇâ about twenty miles to the north-east of Kalâdgi; or, perhaps, the more well-known Kôlâr, which also is, I understand, pronounced Kolhâr, about forty miles to the east by north of Beṅgalûr in Maisûr.

of praise in the world; and amongst these five Mâdirâja became most celebrated, who acquired a name through the excess of his glory, so that people praised him as "a fish-hook to the throats of his enemies, most high in majesty." Being himself a very cage of thunderbolts in respect of protecting those that fled to him for refuge, the lord Ḍoṅkara*-Mâdirâja acquired for himself the title of "an outer shell of a cocoa-nut to (excoriate) those that opposed him." He, while living at Kôlâra, having well protected the sons of the lords that were of equal rank with himself when they sought refuge with him distressed in mind because they had been deprived of their estates, entered with his younger brothers into war, and there acquired victory but also met his death, and then amidst the sounds of all the drums of the gods took his departure for the skies, followed by the acclamations of mankind. The elder sister of that same Mâdirâja, Bijjiyavve, praised in the earth, in the same fashion continued excellently well the magnificence of her younger brothers and that supremacy (of Kôlâra). That supremacy shone in Kôlâra, and Bijjiyavve, having become, as it were, herself the broad creeper of sovereignty, joyfully gave in marriage† to the lord Mallikârjuna, amidst the sound of auspicious musical instruments, Gaurî, the charming daughter of Mâdirâja, together with that lordship, in his name,‡ and thus obtained mental happiness. In that the lovely woman Gaurî, born in a most famous race that had acquired greatness by its glory, such (as has been described above,) was his wife, Mallikârjuna equalled in majesty the Eternal one.§

Whilst they, husband and wife, were living happily together:—To Śrî-Gauri and to the lord Mallapa,—(to whom belonged) the eighteen villages which were considered his own lordship, a heritage received from his father, and, because he had become daughter's-son‖ to Mâdirâja,—the single lordship of Kôlâra,—was born a son, Kêsirâja, of brilliant achievements, a Chakôra, as it were, fluttering in the rays of the moon that is the nails of the feet of the lord of the daughter¶ of the sacred mountain. Having attained tranquillity through his excellent liberality, through his discrimination in recognizing the Supreme Lord in this same Lord of the Mountain-born, and through his firm belief and devotion towards him when he knew him, the lord Kêśavarâja was beautiful in the earth on account of his bravery which was (innate in him and) not dependent upon (the sensations of) joy, pride, or despair. Destroying not the wealth of others, and having no longing for their wives, how perfect in all his deeds was Kêsirâja, through having his thoughts intently fixed upon the feet of Hara! The wife of the thus-glorious Kêsirâja, Mâḷaladêvi, born in the celebrated lineage of Agastya, obedient to her husband, became renowned in the earth for her pious deeds. Her pleasing deeds were only such as were agreeable to her husband, her mind was devoted to him, and her only speech was in praise of him,—thus the title of true wife was confirmed in her; and so Mâḷaladêvi, the lovely wife of Kêsirâja, renowned for her descent, was resplendent in the earth with a plentiful offspring of excellent children and grandchildren. How could other women, who hoard up their riches for themselves, denying the existence of that which they have in their houses, be compared in merit with Mâḷaladêvi, the ocean of affability? Can women who, concealing what is in

---

* This must be his surname.

† Lit., "brought near, united."

‡ *i.e.*, acting as the representative of her deceased brother.

§ Gaurî is one of the names of Pârvatî the wife of Śiva; hence the point of the comparison between Mallikârjuna and Śiva.

‖ It should be "granddaughter's-son;" for the meaning evidently is that as Bijjiyavve, after the death of her brother, the younger Mâdirâja, became a mother to his daughter Gaurî, Mallikârjuna, in wedding Gaurî, became the son of Bijjiyavve, and, therefore, granddaughter's son of the elder Mâdirâja.

¶ Pârvatî.

their houses, refuse even so much as an oil-seed to their husbands or their children, be considered family-women (good housewives)?; (no; but) the wife of **Kêsirâja**, devoted to her husband, full of pleasing virtues, was indeed a good housewife in the earth. How can women, who, if any one comes to their houses, run inside and hide themselves, or, if any one comes before them, say "Who are you? (I know you not)," be compared to **Mâḷiyavve**? Cross, of bad conduct, contemptible, ugly, unfortunate, of bad character, vixenish, depraved, deceitful, of evil disposition, thoroughly wicked, bad, sinful, vexatious, — such are women, full of dissimulation; and can any of them be compared in merit to even the great toe of **Mâḷiyavve**?: if you ask whether any other women in this world (may be so compared, the answer is 'None'). Women who think it a great thing to despise their husbands and who attract other men with wanton behaviour,—say now, how may they be compared with **Mâḷiyavve**?; they are contemned. Can women who look at* their neighbours' houses, the yards in front of their own houses, or their front doors, and who mix with low people under pretext of going to . . . . †, or to visit other women that are pregnant, or to perform a vow, or of going to shops, or to the vegetable-market, or to present offerings to a goddess,—(can they) be termed "family-women"?; if you consider it, there are no others but **Mâḷaladêvi**, resplendent as being so full of devotion towards her husband, (to whom that name may be given). The multitude of sins, (that a man is considered to have committed in) having looked at wicked and shrewish women who put their husbands to shame by their improper behaviour is destroyed by enumerating the virtues of **Mâḷaladêvi**. What manner of family-women are those who in their deceit use poisonous herbs in order to bring their husbands under their control, and thus cause their husbands to waste away with consumption, jaundice, leprosy, or spleen disease?; but **Mâḷiyavve**, true to her husband, is indeed a family-woman in the world which is encircled by the ocean. The most virtuous wife **Mâḷaladêvi**, devoted to her husband, the fair mother of **Malidêva**, famous because to her belonged preëminently the virtues of a true wife of the **Kṛitayuga**, was pleasing. In simply looking at that most virtuous woman **Mâḷaladêvi**, who is praised by mankind and who is possessed of unrivalled good qualities, one obtains the reward of worshipping the river of the gods;‡ how shall it be described? **Anasûye**, the wife of **Atri** the chief of sages, through her devotion to her husband, bore, amidst the praises of the three worlds, **Viriñchi**,§ **Achyuta**,‖ and **Triṇêtra**,¶ so that they were called her sons; and **Mâḷaladêvi** was resplendent, in that through her deeds devotion to a husband existed (again) in this fair age in the lineage of **Atri**. Through the deeds of **Mâḷaladêvi** the saying that "offspring and integrity of conduct become firmly established in the character of a family-woman through the quality of devotion towards her husband" became well known in the earth.

His mother was **Gauri**, a most devoted wife, born in the family of **Vasishṭha**,—his father was **Mallikârjuna**, a bee at the lotuses which are the feet of the Unborn,—his elder brother was **Mahadêva**, profound as the ocean, and his younger brother was that (famous) lord **Mâdirâja**,—his wife was the celebrated **Mâḷale**; thus the lord **Kêśavarâja** was pleasing.

Enjoying the choice pleasures of love with those good women, **Mallikârjuna** and **Mâdirâja**** begat sons, and, doing obeisance as counsellors to the fortunate royal

* *i.e.*, frequent through curiosity.

† "*Îṛilu*;" meaning not known.

‡ The heavenly Ganges.

§ Brahmâ.

‖ Vishṇu.

¶ Śiva.

** This must be a mistake on the part of the composer of the inscription or of the engraver of the tablet for Kêsirâja.

spiritual preceptor Munichandradêva, who was the consecrator of the Raṭṭa rule and a very Javarâja* to the hostile Maṇḍaḷikas decorated with badges of honour, were governing in accordance with his directions the Sugandhavarti Twelve, which was an administrative circle of villages near to (? included in†) the Kûṇḍi Three-thousand and was the locality of the administration of the fortunate royal spiritual preceptor Munichandradêva; and if you ask "of what nature are the delights of the city Sugandhavarti the chief town of that *kampaṇa;*"—Sugandhavarti is conspicuous in the fair plain of Kûṇḍi, abounding in the most perfect pleasures resulting from the grove of mango-trees that is outside the city, from its assemblage of hills, from its fruits, from its dense grove of cocoanut-trees, from its pleasant plantation of Aśôka-trees, from its temple of Śiva, and from its beauteous shrine of Jinêndra. Twelve headmen, in whom abode all the qualities of the majesty of a noble disposition, celebrated for their achievements, of great fame, without rivals, were the governors of that locality.

In that locality:—Kêsirâja, the lord of Kôlâra, of spotless deeds, joyfully worshipped the Unborn, whose feet, which are like lotuses, are praised by demons, by snakes, by birds, by gods, and by Indra. When Kêsirâja went with joy to behold the feet of the famous lord of the sacred hill, there he vowed "If ever hereafter disease or other (troubles) shall manifest themselves among those whom I protect, I will come no more;" and so the Unborn, being propitiated, ordained that his sons and his wealth should endure in safety,—a most marvellous thing in the earth. And at that same journey to the sacred shrine:—"Let‡ death not come straightway, even when their appointed time has arrived, to those who assemble together (for me), not coming to me at my village with the intention of refusing to do my service with joy,"—uttering this urgent vow Kêśava was prosperous in the earth, the god Mallikârjunadêva being favourable to him. Having, with such fierce vows as these and others too, three times visited the god Mallikârjunadêva of Śrî-Śaiḷa, and having through affection for him brought a *liṅga* (made of the stone) of the hill, and having in the name of his father Mallikârjuna

---

* Yama, the god of death.

† The meaning of "*baḷiya bâḍaṁ*" is to a certain extent doubtful. "*Bâḍa,*" though not in the dictionaries and not known to Paṇḍits, is evidently a Tadbhava corruption of the Sanskṛit "*vâṭa,*" *enclosure, road, mud wall, or hedge surrounding a town, site of a building, house,* and as used in the inscriptions it means, according to the context, either *a town* or *a circle of towns formed into an administrative post.* "*Âḷkevâḍaṁ*" in the present passage, and again in line 61 of this inscription, corresponds exactly to "*vaḷitada sthaḷam,*" *locality of administration,* of line 46 of the Nêsargi inscription, (see *Journ. Bom. Br. R. As. Soc.,* vol. X., page 240). Again "*Kûṇḍimûṟusâsirada baḷiya bâḍaṁ . . . Sugandhavartihanneraḍu (emba) kampaṇada modala bâḍaṁ Sugandhavarti*" in the present passage and "*Kûṇḍimûṟusâsirada baḷiya kampaṇaṁ Sugandhavartihanneraḍaṇa modala bâḍaṁ . . . paṭṭanam Sugandhavarti*" in lines 60–1 below, correspond exactly with the Sanskṛit, "*Palâśikâdêśamadhyavartinô Dêgâṁvêkampaṇasya prathamavâṭaṁ . . . . Dêgâṁvêgrâmaṁ,*" *the village of Dêgâṁve, which was the chief town of the kampaṇa of Dêgâṁve, which was included in the district of Palâśikâ,* in line 34–5 of the Dêgâṁve inscription No. I. (see *Journ. Bom. Br. R. As. Soc.,* vol. IX., page 269). These two Canarese passages illustrate both the meanings of "*bâḍa,*" and show that in the second meaning that I have allotted to it above it is convertible with "*kampaṇa.*" And a comparison of the Sanskrit with the Canarese passages shows that "*baḷiya*" is of the same purport as "*madhyavartin*"; but "*baḷiya,*" means *near to, in the vicinity of,* and, though this meaning is not a suitable one here, for the Sugandhavarti Twelve was not *near to* but was *actually included in* the Kûṇḍi Three-thousand, I hesitate as yet to translate it actually by *included in,* which evidently is the meaning intended. We have however, in the Old Canarese "*oḷayiṅke*" = "*oḷage,*" *within, inside,* which actually occurs as "*oḷayiṅge*" in line 40 of the present inscription, a trace, I think, of an older form of "*oḷa,*" *inner, internal,* ending in "*i*" or "*e,*" and "*baḷiya*" may, therefore, be a secondary form of "*oḷiya*" or "*oḷeya*"="*oḷagaṇa,*" *internal, included in,* through a form *vaḷiya;* but here, again, the phrase now commented on being of frequent occurrence, "*baḷiya*" is sometimes written in other inscriptions with the older form of the "*l,*" thus, "*baḻiya,*" and I have not as yet found any instance of "*oḷa,*" with its derivatives "*oḷage,*" "*oḷagaṇa,*" &c., being written with the old "*ḻ.*" We have traces of "*bâḍa*" in Bastwâḍ, Arjunwâḍ, and other modern names of villages, and in Bâsigavâḍa in line 83 below.

‡ The first part of this verse is very obscure.

set up a shrine of the god Śrî-Mallinâthadêva at the tank of Nâgarakeṟe outside the city of Sugandhavarti which was the locality of the administration of the fortunate royal spiritual preceptor Munichandradêva and the chief town of the Sugandhavarti Twelve, a *kampaṇa* near to (? included in) the Kûṇḍi Three-thousand:—

Hail! In the Śaka year 1151, being the Sarvadhâri *saṁvatsara*, on Monday the day of the new-moon of Âshâḍha, on a very auspicious lunar day as being the occasion of a total eclipse of the sun, while the fortunate Mahâmaṇḍaḷêśvara king Lakshmidêva, possessed of all the glory of the titles commencing with "The great chieftain who has attained the five *Mahâśabdas** the supreme lord of Lattanûrpura, he who is sung to with the musical instrument called Trivaḷî, the ornament of the Raṭṭakuḷa, he who has the mark of vermilion, he whose fame is as pure as (the rays of) the moon, the owner of the banner of the golden Garuḍa, he who is a very Kâmadêva to wanton and amatory maidens, he who is a very Vṛikôdara to the forces of his foes, he who behaves as a brother towards the wives of other men, he who strikes the cheeks of Maṇḍaḷikas and curbs the pride of his mighty enemies, he who is most impetuous, Boppanasiṅga," was ruling at his capital of Vêṇugrâma amidst the delights of listening to pleasing stories;—in compliance with the order which the fortunate royal spiritual preceptor Munichandradêva had given to the cultivators, the twelve headmen of that same Sugandhavarti gave, as a grant to be respected by all, for the purposes of the *aṅgabhôga* and *raṅgabhôga* of that same god Mallinâthadêva, and for the repair and renewal of what might become broken or torn or worn out, six hundred *kambas* of cultivated land in a field to the west of the village measured out in the circle of Kaḍimaṉ to the south of the black-soil field of the *mânya*-lands† of (the measure of) twelve *mattars* (which are part) of the black-soil fields of Muḷugundavaḷḷi, and to the north of the road to Hasuḍi; and (with this land) they gave a house, five cubits broad and twenty-one cubits long in the royal cubits, in a street to the west of the king's highway to the west of the gate called Sirivâgilu. And all the people, headed by the same twelve headmen, gave one *koḷaga* on each post in the corn-treading floors as a perpetual gift to the god as long as the moon and sun should endure.

Also, in the presence of an assemblage composed of the same twelve headmen together with Mâdigâvuṇḍa of Kaudi and the ascetics of the five *Maṭhas* and the *Eṇṭuhiṭṭu*,‡ Nâgagâvuṇḍa of Kaḍale gave two hundred *mattars* of cultivated land, as a grant to be respected by all, measured in the circle of those rent-free lands of headmen in Kaḍaleyavaḷana-Haraḷahasuge, which were his rent-free service-lands, being included in the rent-free service-lands of Modalûr.

Also;—Hail! The entire guilds of the *Nakhara*§ and the *Mummuri*§ of the locality,

---

* In Prof. Monier Williams' *Sanskṛit Dictionary*, "*Mahaśabda*" is given as meaning *any official title commencing with the word "maha" (great)* "*pañchamahaśabda*," therefore, would mean five titles of honour, such as Mahâmaṇḍalêśvara, Mahârâja, &c. This seems a more reasonable explanation than that previously suggested to me.—See *Journ. B. B. R. As. Soc.*, vol. IX, No. xxvii., p. 307, note †. [See *Ind. Ant.* vol. V. p. 111, note *.—J. B.]

† "*Mânya*," lands either subjected to only a nominal quit-rent or altogether rent-free.

‡ "*Eṇṭuhiṭṭu*;" *hiṭṭu*—"flour, meal," has also the sense of *alms, gratuitously supplying food*, and *gratuitously performing services*, but the force of *eṇṭu*, "eight," prefixed to it here, is not apparent. Possibly *eṇṭuhiṭṭu* may mean "eight guilds" of some kind or another.

§ The guilds of the *Nakhara* and the *Mummuri* are mentioned also in lines 71–2 of No. VI. of the Raṭṭa inscriptions, *Journ. Bom. Br. R. As. Soc.*, vol. X., page 240, and in line 42 of the Gulhaḷḷi inscription (see *Bombay Society's Journal*, vol. IX., No. xxvii., page 298) we have "the guilds of the *Mummuri* of many places" and "the guilds of the *Mummuri*" again in line 54 of the same. Certain guilds of merchants are evidently intended, but I cannot at present offer any further explanation of these terms. In line 16 of a photographic copy of an inscription at Baḷḷigâve,—the modern Baḷagâṁve in Maisûr,—of the time of the Châlukya

—headed by the twelve headmen of Sugandhavarti, who were the protectors of the laws of the Vîrabaṇañju-guild,* which is the very embodiment of truth, pure conduct, brilliant achievements, morality, modesty, and learning, adorned with innumerable good qualities acquired by five hundred strict edicts celebrated through the whole world,—forming themselves into a great assembly on market-day, came to an agreement among themselves and set apart for that same god Mallinâthadêva the following taxes. They gave one hundred betel-leaves on each load of a beast of burden of betel-leaves, and fifty betel-leaves on each load of the same carried on the head. Inside the village and in the market-place the people of that place gave a spoonful on each kind of grain that was sold, and on each paddy-shop. They gave two betel-nuts on each shop. With respect to green ginger, jaggory, turmeric, and other miscellaneous articles, they gave one spoonful of each on each shop. Of cotton they gave on each shop as much as a man can hold in his hand. Also fifty cultivators gave a ladleful of oil on each oil-mill for the perpetual lamp of the same god. Also of oil that comes from Bĕrûru for sale they gave an *addu*† of oil on each *hâḍaru.* The potters‡ of that place gave on each kiln a vessel for the water of the god. Also five hundred (dealers in vegetables) gave two bundles on each cart-load of vegetables put up for sale and four vegetables on each load (of a beast of burden). The Bôvakkaḷ§ gave a small tax such as a gift in alms on the vegetables that they brought for sale.

Also the twelve headmen of Eḷarâve gave to that same god, as a grant to be respected by all, four *mattars* of cultivated land, measured in the circle of Navilgund to the east of the high road to Sirivûṟ and to the north of the watercourse of Kaddigura, within the boundaries of their own field (in the lands) of Savandhavatti and in the lands to the south of their own village, and they gave also a house five cubits broad by twelve cubits long.

Also the worthy Sindaramaileyanâyaka of Beṭṭasura, and the six headmen of that place, gave, as a grant to be respected by all, four *mattars* of cultivated land, measured in the circle of Navilgund to the south of the watercourse of Kaddigura, within the lands to the south of their village, and they gave also a house six cubits broad by twelve cubits long.

Also, to the same god, all the members of that sect of which Śubhachandrasiddhântidêva, who shared the same rites with Prabhâchandrasiddhântidêva, the priest of the Jain temple of Mâṇikyatîrtha of Hûli, and Indrakîrttidêva and Śrîdharadêva, the disciples of that same Prabhâchandrasiddhântidêva, were the heads, at Hiriyakummi which was the locality of that same Jain temple of Mâṇikyatîrtha, together with the six headmen of that place, gave, as a grant to be

---

king Vikramâditya II. (see No. 39 of a collection of photographic copies of inscriptions published for the Government of Maisûr by Major Dixon in 1865), we have, after the mention of the names of certain merchants, "the entire guild of the *Nagara* and the *Mummmuri* thus composed;" we have, therefore, here "*Nagara*" as a convertible term with "*Nakhara.*" As to "*Mummuri,*" it is given under No. 21, at page 402, of Mr. Kittel's edition of the *Śabdamaṇidarpana* of Kêśirâja, as meaning *heated sand;* I have not met with the word as yet in any other printed book or glossary.

* "*Baṇañju*" is the modern "*baṇajiga, baṇañjiga,* or *baṇijiga,*" which, though given in Sanderson's dictionary as a pure Canarese word, must be the original of or a Tadbhava corruption of the Sanskrit "*bâṇija bâṇijika,*" *merchant, trader.* The Vîrabaṇañju-guild is a division of the class of Lingâyat merchants.

† "*Yaddu*" is a provincialism for "*ettu*" ("*yettu*"), *an ox,* and "*addu*" in the text or "*yaddu,*" according as we regard the "*y*" as an initial letter, or as inserted for the sake of euphony, probably means some measure determined by the load of an ox.

‡ "*Aysâvantar*" or "*âyasâvantaru*" is equivalent to "*âyagâṟu,*" those who enjoy the "*âya,*" "*âyasâya,*" or "*âyasvâmya,*" *i.e.,* the hereditary village servants collectively, the "*bârâ-balutêdâr*" of the Marâṭhâs. Here the word seems to be used to denote particularly the potters.

§ "*Bôvakkaḷ*" or "*bôvakkaḷu*" is evidently the same as "*bôyi-makkaḷu*" for "*bhôyi-makkaḷu,*" *i.e.,* "*bhôyiyaru,*" *fishermen, the bearers of palanquins,* &c.

respected by all, a house six cubits broad by twelve cubits long, together with four *mattars* of cultivated land, measured in the circle of Navilgund, to the south of that same village, to the south of the cultivated land belonging to Nêmaṇa in the rent-free service lands* of Nelliya-Chaṭṭagauḍa, and to the east of the boundaries of the field of Ûrugōḷana.

Also, to the same god, two hundred merchants and the twelve headmen of Hasuḍi, the great *Agrahâra*† of the holy Anâdi,‡ gave three hundred *kambas* of cultivated land, as a grant to be respected by all, measured in the circle of Digîśvaradêva of Sōgala within the locality of Hebbasuge, which is to the west of their own Bâsigavâḍa, to the south of the tank of Ghaissagere which is to the south of their village, and to the west of the black-soil field of Savaṇubela of Savandhavatti.

Also Munichandradêva, at the request of . . . . . . ,§ gave through‖ those who received the contributions on the oil-mills a *sollage* of oil each Monday.

And that same Kêsirâja of Kôlâra, having obtained all this as a portion for the god Mallinâthadêva of the tank called Nâgarakere of Sugandhavarti, built up that tank and planted a grove round it and gave the place, with libations of water, to Liṅgayya, the priest of the original local temple of Beḷḷiṭage, who also bore the name of Vâmaśakti, the disciple of his own spiritual preceptor who practised the pure Śaiva rites which were the method of his own worship; and the account of his lineage is this :—"How is he, the descendant of the sage Durvâsa, overwhelmed with trouble!" thus saying, that same Vâmaśakti, the best of devotees, having taken an oath and having become victorious, became celebrated in the earth and acquired a name. His son, Dêvaśiva, of great fame, versed in all the sacred writings, of good conduct, owning great possessions acquired by the might of his arm, was resplendent in the earth. His offspring, Liṅgaśiva, acquainted with the Śaiva doctrines, the abode of an inestimable number of good qualities, of good and spotless deeds, worshipped devoutly the Unborn of Śrî-Saiḷa. Perceiving that this Liṅga, when worshipping the *liṅga*, shone like a bee at the lotuses which are the feet of Śrî-Mallinâtha, Kêsirâja gave to him this (grant above described).

May he, who preserves this land, which has become the subject of a praiseworthy edict, ever possess an increasing eminence of power; but may he, who, not willing to protect it, destroys (this grant), sink into misery! If a man destroy this, his sin is as great as if he were pitilessly to slay cows, or his own family, or Brâhmaṇs, at the sacred shrines of Gaye, Vâraṇâsi, or Kurubhûmi. He is born for the duration of sixty thousand years as a worm in ordure, who confiscates land that has been given, whether by himself or by another. That man who, not honouring piety, destroys (a grant of) land, whether it has been given by himself or by members of another family, shall afterwards become a worm and descend to hell. Those future rulers of the earth, whether born in my lineage, or in the lineage of other kings, who, with minds free from sin, preserve this my act of piety in its integrity,—them I now salute, joining my hands

* "*Baḷa*" is the old form of the Canarese "*baṇa*," *a party*,—either *a faction* or *a branch of a family of hereditary officials*, especially *of village headmen*; and it means secondarily in inscriptions, as in the present instance, but not in the current language of the present day, *the portion of the hereditary service-lands allotted to such a branch of a family of hereditary officials or to any member of such a branch*. In its secondary meaning it is equivalent to "*gauḍuvâṇya*" which we have had in several places above.

† "*Agrahâra*" means a village granted to a temple or to Brâhmaṇs for purposes of religion, education, and charity.

‡ "He who has no beginning."

§ "*Âyada chaṭṭimaragara*,"—meaning not apparent.

‖ *i.e.*, caused them to give.

together on my forehead. Whether it be the kings of the royal race which I myself serve, or other kings, if they do no injury to this deed of piety, to them I now join my hands (in respectful salutation). This is the saying of that same Kêsirâja.

Acquiring the benefit of good deeds performed in a former state of existence, Mâdirâja, esteemed the son of the lord Kêsirâja, has in accordance with the wishes of that lord composed and written this brilliant edict. The twelve headmen of Sugandhavarti shall protect this act of piety!

Remarks.

The following is the genealogy of the Raṭṭa Great Chieftains of Saundaṭṭi and Belgaum,* as derived from this and other inscriptions of the dynasty :—

Mĕṛaḍa.
- Pṛithvîrâma,† *about Śaka* 800.
  - Piṭṭaga, *married to* Nîjikabbe *or* Nîjiyabbe.
    - Śânta *or* Śântivarmâ,‡ *married to* Chandikabbe, *Śaka* 903.
      - (broken line) Nanna.
        - Kârtavîrya I., *or* Katta I.,§ *about* Ś. 960.
          - Dâvari *or* Ḍâyima.
          - Kannakaira I. *or* Kanna I.
            - Eṛega *or* Eṛaga.
              - Sêna I. *or* Kâḷasêna I., *married to* Maiḷalâdêvî.
                - Kannakaira II. *or* Kanna II. *Śaka* 1009.
                - Kârtavîrya II. *or* Katta II.,‖ *md. to* Bhâgaladêvî, Ś. 1010.
                  - Sêna II. *or* Kâḷasêna II.,¶ *about* Ś. 1050, *married to* Lakshmîdêvî.
                    - Kârtavîrya III. *or* Kattama, Ś. 1086,** *married to* Padmaladêvî *or* Padmâvatî.
                      - Lakshmaṇa *or* Lakshmidêva I., *married to* Chandaladêvî *or* Chandrikadêvî.
                        - Kârtavîrya IV. Ś. 1124, 1127, and 1141, *married to* Êchaladêvî *and* (?) Mâdevi.
                          - Lakshmidevâ II., Śaka 1151.
                        - Mallikârjuna, Śaka 1124 and 1127.
            - Âṅka,§ Ś. 971.

* From *Ind. Ant.* vol. IV. p. 280.—J. B.

† Subordinate to the Râshṭrakûṭa Kṛishṇarâja who was ruling in Śaka 798 and 825.—*Journ. Bom. Br. R. As. Soc.* vol. X. p. 187.

‡ Subordinate to the Châlukya Tailapadêva II., Ś. 895 to 919.

§ Subordinate to Sômêśvaradeva I., Ś. 962 ? to 991 ?

‖ Subordinate to the Châlukyas Sômêśvaradeva II., Ś. 991 ? to 998, and Vikramâditya II., Ś. 998 to 1049.

¶ At first, under Jayakarṇa, son of Vikramâditya II.; afterwards he was independent, as were his successors.

** Inscription at Bail Hoṅgal.—*Ind. Ant.*, vol. IV. p. 116.

J. Burgess surv.

W. Griggs photo-lith.

2. An Old Canarese Inscription on a Stone Tablet at the Temple of Panchalingadeva, Manôḷi, in the Parasgaḍ Taluka of the Belgaum District.

Plate LXXIV.* and *First Report*, page 15.

Reverence to Śambhu,† who is made beautiful by a *chauri*, which is the moon that lightly rests upon his lofty head, and who is the foundation pillar for the erection of the city of the three worlds!

In Jambûdvîpa,‡ the most excellent region to the south of Mêru, which is worthy of great worship in this earth encircled by the ocean, is Bharatakshêtra, which is equally resplendent and beautiful. In Kuntaḷa, which like a beautiful braid of hair adorns the land of Bharata, is the broad district of Toragale; the very pleasant city of Munipura is esteemed the chief beauty of that district. So that you may say that it is like the city of the gods resplendent in the universe, Munipura is more glorious than a crore of other sacred places of pilgrimage from (its being the favourite residence of the sages) Vêda-vyâsa, Kutsa, Jamadagni, Vaśishṭha, Bharadvâja, Attri, and Viśvâmitra, who confessed that it was the birth place of Pañchaliṅga § and the abode of the goddess of fortune, and that, being possessed of the waters of the Râmagaṅgâ,‖ it was worthy to be worshipped both in this world and in the next. To describe the pleasure garden of that city:—Munivaḷḷi has always been considered to be the birth-place of the goddess of fortune on account of its black bees and its cocoanuts, and arecanuts, and rose-apples, and the fruits of the Mâdhu; on account of its jack-trees, and mango-trees, and lime-trees, and orange-trees, and clove trees, and betel-plants, and Surahonne trees, and Supâṭaḷi trees, and Pârijâta trees, and Punnâga trees, and Aśoka trees; and on account of the betel creepers that cause a dense gloom. This same Munipura was the abode of the sages Sanaka, Sanandana, Jamadagni, Vibhâṇḍuka, and others; he who with joy protects it, daily delighting in the perpetual beauties of the pleasure garden of that city, is Pañchaliṅga; its high prosperity shall outshine riches and gold as long as the earth and Mêru and the moon shall last.

Hail! While the valorious universal emperor, the glorious King Siṅghaṇadêva,—the favourite of the world, the supreme king of great kings, the supreme lord, the most venerable, the sun of the white lotuses of the family of the glorius Jaitugidêva,¶ the best among the Yâdavas,—was ruling at his capital of Dêvagiri with the recreation of pleasing conversations:—King Siṅghaṇa, the sovereign of the Yâdavas,—having invaded and acquired with the edge of the sword which was his arm the territory of the hostile kings, and having charmingly become the sole ruler of the world,—by means of his mighty rule made the whole earth (*which rests*) upon the tusks of the elephants

* Mr. Fleet's transliteration being into modern Canarese, I find it impracticable to reproduce it.—J. B.

† Siva, who bears a digit of the moon on his tiara.

‡ Jambûdvîpa is the central division of the world. The golden mountain Mêru is the centre of Jambûdvîpa Bharatakshêtra, "the land of Bharata," is India.

§ Siva, who is the ultimate object of the *linga* worship, is called Pañchaliṅga, "he who has five *liṅgas*," probably from the chief places at which he is worshipped under that emblem being five in number, viz.:—1, Conjevaram, where there is the "*prithivi-liṅga*," or *liṅga* made of earth; 2, Jambukêsvara, where there is the "*ab-liṅga*," or *liṅga* from which water is said to exude perpetually; 3, Tirunamale, where there is the "*têjô-liṅga*," or *liṅga* which sparkles with light; 4, Kâlahasti, where there is the "*vâyu-liṅga*" or *liṅga*, the lamp of which is said to be kept in constant vibration by the wind; and 5, Chidambara, where there is the "*âkâśa-liṅga*," or aerial or sham *liṅga*, *i.e.* where the *liṅga* is worshipped without any material form of it being kept in the temple.

‖ This would seem to be another name for the Malaprahârî. Many rivers are called Gaṅgâ because the waters of the real Ganges are supposed to flow into them periodically.

¶ Jaitugi was the name of the father, as well as of the son, of Siṅghaṇadêva.

(*that stand*) at the points of the compass, his prey. While the kings of Mâḷava and Chêra and Chôḷa and Magadha, and the lords of the countries of Gûrjara, Pâṇḍya, Lâḷa, Nêpâḷa, Turushka, Barbariga, Kêraḷa, Pallava, Aṅga, Veṅgi, Pâñchâla, Kaḷiṅga, and Sindhu were reigning,—Siṅghaṇa, the king of men, governing the earth in happiness, was glorious like the king of the gods. The world has become his his prey; and, saying "Let him rule the earth with justice," King Siṅghaṇa gave the government of the earth to Jagadaḷa Purushôttama. On a religious occasion King Siṅghaṇa, who was pre-eminent in respect of his renown, saying "Let him build the city of Śivapura," gave the celebration of the rites of Purushôttama * to Jôgadêva. Best among a hundred millions is the family of Purushôttama, who is a very Mêru in respect of his firm dignity and the lustre of his excellent fame, and who, through the influence of his star, is a very asylum of mankind, a very jewel of a man. And the lineage of that same Jôgadêva is this:—Pañchaliṅga, the lord of the daughter † of the mountain, is the propitious lord of his family; his *gôtra* ‡ is that of Kauṇḍinya with (the *pravara* § of) Vasishṭha and Maitrâvaruṇa; Râmadêva, firm in truth, is adorned with the qualities of a father (*towards him*); the honoured Lôkâmbike is his mother; Gaurbhâyi is his charming wife; Sômanâtha, the bridegroom of the goddess of fortune, is the son of him, the husband of the goddess of fortune;—how fortunate, then is Jôgadêva!

And, that same Jôgadêva having exercised authority over many countries and having ruled happily;—Hail!—On the holy occasion of an eclipse of the moon on Monday, the day of the full-moon of the bright fortnight of the month Kârttika of the Chitrabhânu *saṁvatsara*,‖ which was the year of the glorious Śaka era 1145, at the command of the Daṇḍaṇâyaka Purushôttama, ¶ who was the manager of all the affairs of the glorious Singhaṇadêva, Jôgadêva gave with gifts of gold and libations of water (*the village of*) Kaḷḷavoḷe, as a grant to be respected by all, to the god Śrî-Pañchaliṅgadêva, the self-existent one, for the purposes of his temple with beautiful pinnacles, for the purpose of repairing anything that might become broken or torn or worn out, for the purposes of the perpetual offering, for the purposes of the *aṅgabhôga*** and the *raṅgabhôga*,** and for the purposes of a charitable dining-hall. Jôgadêva, the excellent husband of the goddess of fortune, being gracious, in his affection respectfully gave to (*the god*) Śrî-Pañchaliṅga (*the village of*) Kaḷḷavoḷe, as a firm grant to be respected by all, for the purposes of Chaitrapavitra,†† of repairing anything that might become torn or worn out, and of a charitable dining-hall; the lords of the earth shall preserve this grant as long as the ocean and the moon and the sun may last. Śrî-Jôgadêva, the Daṇḍâḍhîśa, the good man, the younger brother of Purushôttama, gave as a firm grant the city of Śivapura to Brâhmaṇs, for as long as the earth and

---

* Vishṇu, "the supreme spirit."

† Pârvatî, the wife of Śiva and daughter of the mountain Himâlaya.

‡ "*Gôtra*,"—*family* or *kindred*.

§ "*Pravara*," means the invocation of those ancestors whose names are to be coupled with that of Agni, the god of fire, when the latter is invited to be present at the consecration of the sacrificial fire.

‖ According to the table in Brown's *Carnatic Chronology*, the Chitrabhânu *saṁvatsara* is Śaka 1144, and Śaka 1145 is the Subhânu or Svabhânu *saṁvatsara*.

¶ "Daṇḍanâyaka," "Daṇḍâdhipa," "Daṇḍâdhîśa," or "Chamûpa," as used in inscriptions, appears to denote a military officer with administrative charge.

** I have not been able to obtain any satisfactory explanation of these terms as used in connexion with the worship of idols.

†† Perhaps "the purificatory rites of (the month) Chaitra." In other passages the words are separate,—"*chaitrakke pavitrakke*;" *e.g.* in line 75 of the Nêsargi inscription, *Jo. Bo. Br. R. A. S.*, vol. X., No. xxix., pp. 240 *et seqq.*

Mêru and the moon may endure. Jôgadêva, the Chamûpa, joyfully gave sixteen allotments, each of two hundred *kammas** (of land), to the excellent Brâhmaṇs of Śivapura, in four out of the ancient villages. And if you ask in what villages respectively:—In Munipura, in Sindavige, in Âganûr, and in Nâgarapura. Jôgadêva, who followed the precepts of Manu, with affection and modesty gave sixteen allotments to Brâhmaṇs. In order that it might be esteemed pre-eminent in the world, Jôgadêva the Daṇḍâdhîśa, the younger brother of Jagadaḷa-Purushôttama, declared that Śivapura surpasses the charming land of enjoyment.†

And on the same occasion:—The gardeners of the jewel-mine Munipura, who were the receptacles of great liberality, acquired renown through the strength and the power and the eminence of their wealth, their truth, their firm determination, their perseverance, and their heroism. The gardeners, who had obtained the excellent favour of the lotuses which are the feet of (*the god*) Pañchaliṅga, who is resplendent throughout the world, gave perpetually year by year for the purposes of the *raṅgabhôga* a *kaṇḍage*‡ on the (*total produce of*) dried fruits, grain, &c.§

Honourable, worthy to be accounted foremost among the brave, possessed of a most excellent reputation by reason of the strength and the eminence and the greatness of their firm determination, the preservers of all religious rites, worthy to be worshipped, more glorious than any others, abounding in holy deeds, possessed of a profound firmness that comprised a number of various good qualities, firm in truth, the granters of all requests,—such are the Ugura Three-hundred,‖ who are worthy to be worshipped in this world. Even the Unborn cannot describe the greatness of the Five-hundred-and-four, who occupied themselves in all the rites of religion, which greatness, resulting from their protecting might, their generosity, the powerful attraction of their truth, and the eminence of their energy, was such that you might say that one who asked them for protection or begged of them a freedom from old age and death was certain to attain his desired object; who, then, may describe it? And whenever those same Three-hundred and the Five-hundred-and-four asked with importunity (?),¶ they gave one coin such as is given on marriage occasions.

And the boundaries of the three hundred *kammas* of cultivated land, (*which were given as a grant*) to be respected, to the god Śrî-Pañchaliṅgadêva, are:—on the east, the high-road that goes to the valley; on the south, a rivulet; on the west, the cultivated land called Akkasâligeyi; and on the north, the cultivated land called Hebbaḷḷahara-

---

* "*Kamma*" or "*kamba*"—an ancient land-measure, the value of which is not now known.

† Svarga, or paradise, where people enjoy the reward of their works.

‡ "*Kaṇḍage*" is the modern "*khaṇḍaga*," or "*khaṇḍuga*," equivalent to about three bushels.

§ "*Tâṟinge*";—but the meaning to be given to "*tâṟu*," of which we have the dative case here and the genitive case, "*tâṟina*," in line 48 below, is not certain. In Sanderson's *Canarese Dictionary* "*târu*" is given as meaning as a noun *an omen, the bar of a door, a particular tree*, and as a verb *to become thin, exhausted with fatigue, dried up*. As he gives also a form "*tâṟu*" in the meaning of *a door-bar*, and *the tree so called*, "*tâṟu*" may be assumed to be also the old form of the root in its verbal significations. And it would seem to me that the word as used in this inscription is connected with the root in its verbal signification *to become dried up*, and means *dried produce generally*.

‖ It is not apparent who are the "Ugura Three-hundred," and the "Five-hundred-and-four." Some large religious establishment appears to be alluded to, and perhaps it is the establishment of the priests of the temple of Ellammâ or Rênukâ at Ugargoḷ, which is close to Saundatti in the Parasgaḍ Tâlukâ of the Beḷgaum district. The temple is one of great note, it has a large establishment of priests, and great numbers of people go on pilgrimages to it at stated times; but, though the shrine has every appearance of being of some antiquity, I have met with no allusions to it in inscriptions, unless the present is one. The "Ugura Five-hundred" and the "Eḷeya-Bôjagaru Five-hundred-and-four," are mentioned also in lines 28–9 of No. IV. of my Sindavaṁśa inscriptions in the *Jo. Bo. Br. R. A. S.*, vol. XI., No. xxxi., p. 254.

¶ "*Chaṭṭurâsigeṟidalli*;" but the meaning is not at all certain. In analysing it as "*chaṭṭurâsige eṟidalli*." I would connect "*chaṭṭurâsige*" with "*châṭṟâyisu*" *to be obstinate, hardened.*

ḷakeyi. And the boundaries of one *mattar** (*of land, which also was given to the god, are*) :—On the east, (*the temple of*) the goddess **Kâḷikâdêvi**; on the south, the tank called **Haṇitegeṟe**; on the west, (*the village of*) **Kaṟuveṭṭa**; and on the north, the high-road (*to the village*) of **Hûvinakal**. Also the fixed contribution that was allotted, free from all opposing claims, on the betel plantations measuring five hundred *kuḷis*,† which was to the south of (*the temple of*) the god, to the west of the rivulet called **Yaṅgarattihaḷḷa**, to the north of the (*river*) **Śri-Râmagaṅge** and to the east of of a stone set upright in the ground, was the impost of the *Harikekuḷi*;‡ and the contribution on the profits was the impost of a bundle of betel-leaves levied on the road; and (*there was allotted*) to that same god one *vîsa*§ on each load of a beast of burden of betel-leaves. Two *solasages*‖ of oil (*were given*) on (*each*) oil-mill, to provide for the ceremony of averting the effects of the evil eye which was held on Mondays at **Siṅgavaṭṭi** of that locality. And one oil-mill was set apart for the god. Sixty cultivators gave a *kaṇḍage* of dried fruits, grain, &c. And the reapers of the betel-plants will give (*a contribution*) when they reap, and the consumers of betel-leaves will willingly give (*a contribution*). The ministers of the king shall recognise these imposts. And the sellers of betel-leaves and arecanuts inside the village will give (*a contribution*) when they realise in cash the prices that they obtain.

The east and south boundary of a flower-garden, (*which was given to the same god,*) is the river **Śrî-Râmagaṅge**; the west boundary is the garden of the **Basadi**;¶ and the north boundary is a plantation of betel-plants.

And the boundaries of a garden on the river containing five hundred betel-plants are :—On the east, the river **Śrî-Râmagaṅge**; on the south and west and north, stones set upright in the ground. (*Also there were given*) three flower-gardens in the waste land called Suruganahâḷ.

Having established the shrine of the god **Śrî-Mâdhavanârâyaṇa** and having given as a grant to be respected by all, with gifts of gold and libations of water, (*the village of*) **Sattiyakere** for the purposes of the *aṅgabhôga* and *raṅgabhôga* of that same god, (*there was given*) a betel-plantation of five hundred *kuḷis* to the east of **Munivaḷḷi**, to the south of a rivulet, to the west of the river **Śrî-Râmagaṅge**, and to the north of a stone set upright in the ground.

And on the same occasion there were given to the Brâhmaṇs of **Brahmapuri**, with libations of water, two allotments at (*the village of*) **Kaḍakuḷa**, two at **Baḷḷigeṟe**, two at **Hulukund**, two at . . ṭṭase, two at **Kuruḷanûr**, two at **Bannivûr**, two at **Dâḍeyabâvi**, two at **Goravanûr**, two at **Jaṅgavâdanaṟuvanûr**, and four at **Haḷevûr**.

And, while that same **Jôgadêvanâyaka** was cherishing the practices of religion, sixty cultivators** acquired and gave to the **Ugura** Three-hundred and the Five-hundred-

---

* "*Mattar*"—an ancient land-measure the value of which is not now known.

† "*Kuḷi*," a pit, hole. The meaning of the text is probably "a betel-plantation capable of holding five hundred plants."

‡ Meaning not known. "*Harike*" is a *vow*; and "*kuḷi*," in addition to the meaning given in the preceding note, means, as a verb, *to dig a hole, to protect, to journey*.

§ Explained to me as being the same as "*duḍḍu*," *the fourth part of an anna*. In Sanderson's *Dictionary* "*visa*" is giving as meaning *one-sixteenth, a share, portion*; and we have also "*vîse*" *five seers*.

‖ "*Solasage*" is perhaps a mistake for "*sollige, solige, solage*, or *solege*," *the sixty-fourth part of a* "*koḷaga*," which is equivalent to about three twentieths of a bushel.

¶ "*Basadi*,"—modern "*Basti*,"—*a Jain temple*.

** This seems to be a technical expression; we meet with it again in line 44 of the Gulhaḷḷi inscription in the *Journ. B. B. R. As. Soc.*, vol. IX. No. xxvii., at pp. 296 *et seqq.*; in line 38 of the Kittûr inscription at pp. 304 *et seqq.* of the same; in line 2 of No. III. of the Raṭṭa inscriptions, vol. X. No. xxix. at pp. 204 *et seqq.* of the same; and in line 78 of No. VI. of the Raṭṭa inscriptions at pp. 240 *et seqq.* of the same; and I have found the same expression in other inscriptions not yet published.

and-four, with gifts of gold and libations of water, at Śivapura, as a token of union, certain land of which the boundaries are :—To the north-east there is a row of tamarind trees arranged in the form of a festoon of flowers hung over a doorway. To the south of the row of tamarind trees, arranged in the form of a festoon of flowers hung over a doorway, there is the garden of Bâ . . rakkura, which is to the south of the ornamented gateway of the temple of (*the goddess*) Kâraṇikemasaṇikabbe which stands together with the land of Jinêndra, the foe of passion. From the boundary of that garden towards the west there is the garden of the merchant Kimbharakâḷiseṭṭi; from the north-west of this garden towards the south there are the gardens of Harûmbabâvi-Brahmaya, Âlahiṭṭaya, and Banavaya; thence towards the west there are the road that goes to Kallavoḷe and the sacred shrine on the (*river*) Malaprahârî called Rudratîrtha; thence to the north (*we come to the village of*) Kāṛuguppe, from the centre of which (*we come to the village of*) Kuppe, below which is the road to Modalûr; thence (*we come to*) the row of tamarind trees, arranged like a festoon of flowers hung over a doorway, and commencing from a tamarind tree which stands at the junction of the cultivated land called Koḍagadikeyi and the field called Kâḷikaveyola and the stream. Such is the course of the boundaries.

Since . . . . all belongs equally to the god Śrî-Pañchaliṅgadeva, the regents of the four principal points of the compass, and kings, and the Five-hundred who are perfect in respect of their religion, and the One-thousand, and the (*inhabitants of the*) four cities, and the people of (*the locality called*) the "Seven-and-a-half,"* and of (*the locality called*) the "Eleven-and-a-half"* and of many districts on both sides, shall preserve this religious grant of rent-free service-land as long as the earth and the water and the moon and sun and stars may last, avoiding the commission of the ten faults.

He is born for the duration of sixty thousand years as a worm in ordure who confiscates land that has been given whether by himself or by another.

3. Inscription from Cave III., at Bâdâmi.

First Report, Plate XXXII., and pages 22 *ff.*

Transcription.

स्वस्ति ॥ श्रीस्वामिपादानुद्ध्यता(ध्या)तानाम्मानव्यसगोत्राणाङ्हारितीपुत्राणाम्
अग्निष्टोमाग्निचयनवाजपेयपौण्डरीकबहुसुवर्णाश्वमेधाव-

* *Êḷuvaresthaḷa* and *Hanneraḍuvaresthaḷa* are technical names and mean literally *the place* (*or locality*) *that is* (*called*) *the* "*Seven-and-a-half,*" and *the place* (*or locality*) *that is* (*called*) *the* "*Twelve-and-a-half.*" In No. V. of the Raṭṭa inscriptions (*Journ. B. B. R. As. Soc.* vol. X. p. 227), line 63, we have *the place* (*or locality*) *that is* (*called*) *the* "*Eleven-and-a-half.*" These terms probably originated in some local custom of which no traces now remain, but the clue to the explanation of them may perhaps be found in a custom formerly observed at Baṅkâpûr in the Dhârwâḍ district; the Shâhâbâzâr of that town was taken as a kind of limit dividing not the town only, but the neighbouring country also, into two parts; and the inhabitants of the two divisions thus constituted used, at the festival of the Hôḷi-Huṇṇuve, to meet in opposition to each other and engage in a contest called *kalla-kâḷaga*, literally "the war of stones." If the number of villages on each side of the line-division was not specified, the contending parties would be "the people of many countries on both sides," as the expression is in the text of Inscription No. VI. (*Journ. B. B. R. As. Soc.* vol. X. p. 240 *et seqq.*); if the two divisions contained, the one seven villages and the other twelve, then, including in each division half the town of Baṅkâpûr itself, the contending parties would be "the people of the locality called 'Seven-and-a-half,' and the people of the locality called 'Twelve-and-a-half.'" Technical and traditional Canarese names often contain, for reasons which are not now known, numerical components; thus at Râyara-Hubbaḷḷi (the king's Hubbaḷḷi) in the Dhârwâḍ district there is a *maṭha* that is always spoken of as Hanneraḍu-Maṭha, literally "the Twelve-*maṭha*," and there is at the same place an *Ayya* or priest whose title is *Mûrusâviradayya*, literally "the Three-thousand-*Ayya*?" This *Ayya's* title may have originated in his ancestors being the high-priests of the Kûṇḍi Three-thousand. As another instance of a name with a numerical component we have in No. V., line 60 (*Journ. B. B. R. As. Soc.* vol. X. p. 226), the Jain temple called *Pañcharasadi*, that is, "the Five-*Basadi*."

म्हृयस्वानपविचीकृतशिरसां चल्क्यानां वंशे संभूतः शक्तिचयसं-
पन्नः चल्क्यवंशाम्बरपूर्णचन्द्रः अनेकगुणगणालंकृतशरीरस्स-
र्वशास्त्रार्थतत्वनिविष्टबुद्धिरतिबलपराक्रमोत्साहसंपन्नः श्रीमङ्गलीश्वररणवि-,
क्रान्तः प्रवर्द्धमानराज्यसंवत्सरे द्वादशे शकनृपतिराज्याभिषेकसंवत्सरे-
ष्वतिक्रान्तेषु पञ्चसु शतेषु निजभुजावलम्बितखड्गधारानमितनृपतिशिरोम-
कुटमणिप्रभारञ्जितपादयुगलस्चतुस्सागरपर्य्यन्तावनिविजयमङ्गलिका-
गारः परमभागवतो लयनो(नं) महाविष्णुगृहमतिदैवंमानुष्यकमत्यद्भुतक-
र्मविरचित(तं) भूमिभागोपभागोपरिपर्य्यन्तातिशयदर्शनीयतमं कृत्वा
तस्मिन् महाकार्त्तिकपौर्णमास्यां ब्राह्मणेभ्यो महाप्रदानन्दत्वा भगवतः प्रल-
योदित(ता)र्कमण्डल(ला)कारचक्रचपितामरारिपचस्य विष्णोः प्रतिमाप्रतिष्ठाप-
नाभ्युदये(य)निमित्त(त्तं) लञ्जीश्वरन्नाम† ग्रामन्नारायणबल्युपहारार्त्थं षोडशसंख्येभ्यो
ब्राह्मणेभ्यश्च सत्रनिबन्धम्प्रतिदिनमनुविधानकृत्वा शेषं च परिव्राजकभो-
ज्यन्दत्तवान् सकलजगन्मण्डल(ला)वनसमर्त्थाय रथहस्त्यश्वपदातसंकुला-
नेकयुद्धलब्धजयपताकावलम्बितचतुस्समुद्रोर्म्मिनिवारितयशःप्रता-
नोपशोभिताय देवद्विजगुरुपूजिताय ज्येष्ठायास्सद्भ्राते कीर्त्तिवर्म्मणे
पराक्रमेश्वराय तत्पुण्योपचयफलमादित्याग्निमहाजनसमच-
मुदकपूर्वं(र्वं) विश्राणितमस्मद्भ्रातृशुश्रू[षि]णि यत्फलन्तन्मह्यं स्यादिति [॥]त(न) कैश्चि[त्]
परिहापयितव्यः ॥ बहुभिर्वसुधा दत्ता बहुभिश्चानुपालिता यस्य
यस्य यदा भूमिः तस्य तस्य तदा फलम् [॥] स्वदत्तां परदतां वा ये(य)-
त्नाद्रच युधिष्ठिर महीम्महीचितां श्रेष्ठं दानाच्छ्रेयो नुपालनं [॥]
स्वदत्तां परदत्तां वा यो हरेत वसुन्धरां श्वविष्ठायां
कृमिर्भूत्वा पितृभिस्सह मज्जति [॥] व्यासगीताः श्लोकाः ॥

Translation.

Hail! In the twelfth year of his prosperous reign, five hundred of the years of the royal installation of the Śaka king having expired, Śrî-Maṅgalîśvara, who is valorous in war,—whose two feet are tinted with the lustre of the jewels in the diadems of kings who have been caused to bow down before him by the edge of the sword which is wielded by his arm,—who is the auspicious abode of victory over the (*whole*) earth as far as the four oceans,‡—who is a most excellent worshipper of (*Vishṇu as*) the Holy One,§—who is born in the lineage of the Chalkyas who meditate on the feet of Śrî-Svâmî,‖ who are of the kindred of Mânavya, who are the offspring of Haritî, and whose

---

* In the original this letter is inserted below the line, having been at first omitted.

† In the original the ज् and the ई are clear, but the first consonant of the compound letter has been effaced; judging from the space left and the position of the ज्, the missing letter is probably ञ्, but it might of course be ग्, ज्, or ब्.

‡ *i.e.*, the northern, southern, eastern, and western oceans.

§ "*Parama-bhâgavata*," a most excellent worshipper of Bhagavân or Vishṇu.

‖ A name of Kârttikêya or Mahâsêna, the god of war. This and the following two titles belong also to the kings of the older Kâdamba dynasty of Palâśikâ, (see Nos. 2, 6, and 7 of the inscriptions published by me in the *Journ. Bomb. Br. R. As. Soc.*, vol. IX., No. xxvii. page 235 *et seq.*), and probably to the kings of other old dynasties also.

heads are purified by ablutions performed after the celebration of the Agnishṭoma, Agnichayana, Vâjapêya, Pauṇḍarîka sacrifices, and horse-sacrifices which cost much gold,—who is endowed with the three constituents of regal power,*—who is the full moon of the sky which is the race of the Chalkyas,—who is possessed of a body which is adorned with a multitude of many good qualities,—who has an intellect which is intent upon the true essence of the meaning of all the sacred writings,—who is possessed of extreme strength and prowess and energy,—having erected a temple, an abode of the great Vishṇu, surpassing everything which is celestial or human, fashioned with most curious workmanship, most worthy to be looked at on the surface of any primary or secondary division of the earth,† and having given rich gifts to Brâhmaṇs in it on the holy full-moon of the month Kârttika, granted, on the occasion of the installation of the image of the holy Vishṇu, who destroyed the army of the enemies of the gods with his discus the shape of which is like that of the sun risen (*again*) after the destruction of the universe, the village called Lañjîśvara,‡ having made a daily observance the bestowal of food and alms upoṅ sixteen Brâhmaṇs for the purpose of offering the oblation to Nârâyaṇa and (*having set apart*) the remainder for the sustenance of wandering religious mendicants,—saying "In the presence of the Sun, Fire, and the (*guild of*) merchants,§ the reward of this accumulation of religious merit has been made over with oblations of water to my elder brother Kîrttivarmâ, the lord of valour, who was sufficiently powerful to protect the whole circle of the earth, who was adorned with a canopy consisting of his fame which was propped up by standards of victory acquired in many battles in which there were mêlées of chariots and elephants and horses and footmen, and which was bounded (*only*) by the waves of the four oceans,‖ and who was worshipped by gods and Brâhmaṇs and spiritual preceptors; let whatever reward belongs to (*me who am*) possessed of a desire to obey my brother accrue to me." (*And this grant*) is not to be diminished by any one; (*for*) :—"Land has been given by many and has been continued in grant by many; he, who for the time being possesses land, enjoys the benefit of it. Carefully continue, O Yudhishṭhira, land that has been given whether by thyself or by another; continuing a grant is the best (*act*) of kings and is more excellent than giving. He, who confiscates land that has been given whether by himself or by another, becomes a worm in the excrement of a dog and sinks (*into hell*) with his ancestors:"—(*these are*) the verses sung by Vyâsa.

Remarks.

The Inscription records the erection of a Vaishṇava temple and the allotment of grants on behalf of it by the Châlukya king Maṅgalîśvara or Maṅgalîśa in the Śaka year 501 (A.D. 579–80).

This is the first instance that I have met with of the name of the dynasty being spelt as "Chalkya"; the usual form is Chalukya or Châlukya, and it is, I think, also occasionally written Challkya.

* *Sc.*, majesty, the power of good counsel, and the force of energy.

† The meaning of the compound "*bhûmibhâgôpa*, &c." is obscure, and my interpretation of it may perhaps not be correct.

‡ See note † to the transcription.

§ The merchants, or probably the chief men among them, constituted a village jury and investigated disputes, pronounced the results of trials by ordeal (see the Kâdamba inscription of Kittûr at page 304 *et seq.* of the above-mentioned number of the *Journ. Bom. Br. R. As. Soc.*), witnessed grants with a view to subsequently proving them if required, &c.

‖ *i.e.*, which spread over and enveloped the whole inhabited earth.

The early Châlukya kings appear to have been very tolerant in matters of religion. In an inscription at Aihoḷe* in the Kalâdgi district, not far from Bâdâmi, we find Pulikêśî II., the nephew and successor of Mangalîśa, erecting and making grants to a Jain temple in the Śaka year 507, and Liṅga or Śaiva temples were erected and endowed by others of them.

The present inscription fixes the Śaka year 490 as the commencement of the reign of Maṅgalîśa. Śaka 488 is the date obtained by Sir W. Elliot for his predecessor Kîrttivarmâ I. This inscription also determines, with a precision not hitherto, I think, attained, the commencement of the Śâka era. The era has been considered to date "from the *birth* of Śâlivâhana, a mythological prince of the Dekhan, who opposed Vikramâditya, the Râjâ of Ujjayinî."† It is here said distinctly to "date from the *royal installation* or *coronation* of the Śaka king."

4. Bâdâmi.—Cave III. Inscription No. 10.

On one of the columns of the great Cave Temple. See *First Report*, page 23, and Plate XXXIV., No. 10.

Translation.‡

May prosperity attend the bastion, which was built, at the order of the great king Koṇḍarâja, on the fifteenth day of the bright fortnight of (*the month*) Âshâḍha, of the Sôbhakṛit *saṁvatsara* !§ Śrî !

5. Bâdâmi.—Inscription No. 19.

On an old temple in the hill fort to the north of Bâdâmi. See *First Report*, page 27, and Plate XXXV., No. 19.

Translation.

May prosperity attend the bastion, which was built, at the order of the Nâyaka Akrushappaṇa . . . . ‖ of the King Sadâśivarâya,¶ on the fifteenth day of the bright fortnight of (the month) Âshâḍha of the Śôbhakṛit *saṁvatsara* !** Śrî ! The superintendent of the administration of the king Koṇḍarâja! Śrî !

6. Paṭṭadakal. Great Temple.—Inscription No. 20.

In the Gupta character, from the south side of the east porch, near the door. See *First Report*, Plate XLI., No. 20, and page 31.

---

* An impression has been taken of this inscription and will appear in the *Indian Antiquary*, where a translation of it has been published : vol. V. pp. 67 ff.

† Prinsep's *Useful Tables*, page 154, in Thomas' edition of *Ind. Antiquities*, vol. II.

‡ Mr. Fleet having transliterated the 1st, 2nd, 4th, 5th, and 6th of these inscriptions into Canarese characters, I regret that I am unable to reproduce them satisfactorily in this country. J. B.

§ Probably the Śaka year 1465 (A.D. 1543–4).

‖ The meaning of *Haḍapadaḷa* is not apparent.

¶ Probably Sadâśivadêvamahârâya of Vidyânagari or Vijayanagara, whose dates, as known to me from other inscriptions, are Śaka 1474, 1476 or 1477, and 1483. [See Inscription No. 8 on plate XXXIII. of the *First Report*.—J. B]

** Probably the Śaka year 1465 (A.D. 1543–4).

Translation.

Hail. (*Glorious are**) the customs of former times, which were established . . . . † by Śrî-Vijayâditya,‡ in whom truth was inherent,§ the favourite of the world, the supreme king of great kings, the supreme lord, the venerable! Śrî-Vikramâditya,‖ the venerable, is the preserver of (*the rites of the goddess*) Lôkamahâdevi¶ . . . . ** He, who destroys this, is on a par with people who destroy a thousand tawny-coloured cows, or a thousand Brâhmaṇs at Bâraṇâsi! By the fort of Eṟeyadi-Śrîguppa . . . ††

7. Inscription No. 23.—On a Pillar in the E. Porch of the Great Temple at Paṭṭadkal.

First Report, Plate XLII. and page 31.

Transcription.

भरतनुतवचनरचनाविरचितनटसेव्य-
सिंघ(ह)नादेन पर‡‡नटमदान्धहस्ती परिहीनमदो
भवत्येव ॥ नटसेव्यभरतमतयुतपटुत-
रवचनाशनिप्रपातेन कुटिलोन्नतनटशैल (लः)
सु(स्फु)टितानतमस्तकः फ(प)तति ॥

Translation.

As an elephant, blinded by rut, is deprived of his frenzy by the roaring of a lion, so other actors are deprived of their presumption by the rules which are to be adhered to by actors and which are comprised in the arrangement of the celebrated precepts of Bharata.§§ As a curved and lofty mountain falls, having its summit torn open and thrown down by the fall of a thunderbolt, so disingenuous and arrogant actors fall, having their heads cleft open and bowed down by a very clever composition in accordance with the opinions of Bharata, which are to be adhered to by actors.

---

* The construction being the nominative case plural of "*maryâde*," preceded by the relative participle, some such phrase as this is needed to complete the sentence.

† The meaning of "*Gândharvvante*" is not apparent.

‡ Either the first of this name in Sir W. Elliot's Châlukya genealogy, about Śaka 617 (A. D. 695–6); or the second of the same name in the same genealogy, about Śaka 890 (A.D. 968–9).

§ "*Saytâśraya*," a family name of the Châlukya kings.

‖ Either the first of this name in Sir W. Elliot's genealogy, about Śaka 655 (A.D. 733–4); or the second of the same name, also called Taila or Tailapadêva, about Śaka 900 (A.D. 978–9). In either case Vikramâditya was the son and successor of Vijayâditya. [From the character of the letters, and as the temple seems to belong archæologically to about the beginning of the eighth century, I incline to adopt the earlier of these princes as being meant.—J. B.]

¶ Perhaps Lôkshmi, who is called Lôkamâtâ, "the mother of the world."

** Again the meaning of "*Gândharvvante*" is not apparent.

†† The meaning of the rest of this sentence, beginning with "*durgamâra*," is not apparent.

‡‡ This letter,—न,—was at first omitted in the original and then inserted below the line.

§§ The author of a collection of rules on the subject of dramatic composition and theatrical exhibition.

8. INSCRIPTION No. 33.—ON AN OLD VAISHṆAVA TEMPLE AT AIHOḶE.

First Report, Plate LV., No. 33, and page 40.

Transcription.

स्वस्ति [॥] जम्बुद्वीपान्तरे कश्चित्
वास्तुप्रासादतद्भृतः [।]
नरसोब्बसमो विद्वान्
न भूतो न भविष्यति ॥*

Translation.

Hail! There has not been and there shall not be in Jambudvipa any wise man, proficient in (*the art of building*) houses and temples, equal to Narasobba.

* The initial letters of the lines in these transcriptions correspond to the initial letters of the lines of the originals. In the originals the lines are for the most part all of the same length; in this respect, however, it is not possible to imitate the originals in the transcriptions.

The following extra Photographs illustrative of this Report are not published, but the negatives are deposited at the India Office :—

1. Old Gate of the Uparkoṭ Junâgaḍh.
2. Mihrab in the Jâmi' Masjid, Junâgaḍh.
3. Caves at Sânâ.
4. Southern Portion of the Group of Temples on Mount Girnar.
5. Northern Portion of Ditto.
6. Interior of the Central Manḍap in Vastupâla's Temple, Girnâr.
7. Tombs of the Nawâbs at Junâgaḍh.
8. North-west Corner of Navalâkhâ Temple at Ghumli, showing the Sculpture.
9. Sculpture on the North Side of Ghumli Temple.
10. Sculpture on the West Side of Ditto.
11. Jethânî Wâv at Ghumli.
12. Loose sculptured Stones at Suvan Kânsârî Talao, Ghumli.
13. The Vethiya Wâv near Mukhana.
14. Râma and Lakshmana from the old Temple at Gop.
15. Tank and Corner Tower at Jâmnagar.
16. Vaishṇava Images for a new Temple at Navânagar.
17. Temple at Bhadreśvar from the North-west.
18. Bhadreśvar—Sculpture on Shrine Walls. (small.)
19. „ Sculpture over the Front of the Corridors. „
20. „ Pillar at the Shrine Door. „
21. Dudâ's Temple, Bhadreśvar. „
22. The Mosque at Bhuj.
23. The Mahâsatî or Royal Tombs at Bhuj.
24. Door of the Ruined Temple at Kheḍâ.
25. Nandod Gate at Dabhoi.
26. Baroda Gate at Dabhoi, from Inside.
27. Hîrâ Gate at Dabhoi, from Inside.
28. Temple of Kâlî, from Outside the Hîrâ Gate.
29. Temple at the Hîrâ Gate, from Outside.

With some alternatives and duplicates.